Cybernetic Principles of Learning and Educational Design

Cybernetic Principles of Learning and Educational Design

Karl U. Smith
University of Wisconsin

Margaret Foltz Smith

Holt, Rinehart and Winston, Inc.

New York · Chicago · San Francisco · Toronto · London

TO P. J.

Preface

This book represents an effort to establish a new scientific approach to human learning phenomena—one that will be as meaningful in educational practice as in laboratory research. Such an approach has long been needed to bridge the gap between the experimental psychology of learning and the practical needs of teaching and training. We believe that the existence of this gap is due not to any lack of diligence on the part of learning psychologists or educational researchers but rather to the fact that conventional learning psychology is largely inappropriate in the educational arena. General theories of learning, based as they are on animal research, make no allowance for the highly specialized nature of human behavior organization, as manifested particularly in instrumental and symbolic skills. Even research on human learning has so often dealt with meaningless behavior in such restrictive ways that the results have little relevance to problems of educational design.

The broad outlines of a new scientific approach to human learning became apparent more than twenty years ago when the research efforts of wartime training psychologists laid the foundations for the discipline known as human engineering. The central idea that emerged was that performance and learning must be analyzed in terms of the control relationships between a human operator and an instrumental situation. That is, learning was understood to be determined by the nature of the behaving individual as well as by the design of the learning situation—an understanding that structured the human factors approach to training research. Further, human engineering analyses called attention to the concept of the behaving individual as a closed-loop or cybernetic system utilizing the processes of sensory feedback in the continuous control of behavior. These ideas are central to the area of theory and research known as behavioral cybernetics.

The central thesis of this book is that the cybernetic interpretation of behavior represents not a specialized field of interest but a general theory of behavior organization which challenges much psychological thinking including the conventional theories of learning. Cybernetic theory views the individual as a feedback system which generates its own activities in order to detect and control specific

vii

stimulus characteristics of the environment. In keeping with this point of view, cybernetic research analyzes the intrinsic mechanisms by means of which control is established and maintained—that is, the closed-loop sensory-feedback mechanisms that define the interactions between the individual and his environment. In contrast, conventional learning research conducts open-loop analyses of the relationships between extrinsic events—stimuli and reinforcements—and observed responses.

The difference between closed-loop and open-loop analyses represents more than a difference in research strategy: it reflects a fundamental difference of opinion concerning the regulating factors in behavior and learning. Whereas conventional learning psychology proposes that learning is defined by the occurrence of external events in appropriate temporal relationships, cybernetic theory proposes that learning as well as other aspects of behavior organization are determined primarily by the nature of the feedback-control processes available to the behaving individual. Thus, if we are to structure the course of learning, we must design the learning situation to fit the control capabilities of the learner.

The various implications of this cybernetic view have determined the content of this book. A primary idea is that principles of human learning are clarified by an evolutionary and historical approach. Thus, we launch our argument by describing the distinctive features of evolutionary development of human learning. Modern man is partly a product of his own educational design, for his ability to exercise control over the physical and social environment and the particular behavior patterns which he uses in such control are defined by feedback interactions with tools, instruments, machines, symbol systems, and institutions of human design. Biosocial evolution has involved feedback interactions between human characteristics and the accumulated structures and symbolism of the man-made environment. As a result, the cybernetic control patterns in human behavior and learning differ markedly from those of subhuman animals; studies of animal learning have but limited relevance to problems of educational design. For this reason, we make only passing reference to animal learning research and set the stage for research on human learning by an evolutionary rather than a phylogenetic analysis.

The central portion of the book deals with research on human learning in meaningful educational settings; we believe that restrictive, nonmeaningful settings, such as are used in many laboratory experiments, do not reveal the distinctive processes involved in instrumental and symbolic control. The cybernetic view that human factors and educational design factors interact to define learned changes in behavior indicates that the determining factors in education are related to the particular instrumental and symbolic features that characterize the learning situation. Accordingly, we survey the important techniques used in teaching and training and summarize research findings concerning their effectiveness. In one section, the implications of the feedback concept of learning are considered in relation to the design and use of audiovisual media in the classroom. In another section, we describe the origins of the human factors approach to learning in training research and contrast cybernetic principles of training design with those based on reinforcement learning theory. In a third, we describe the techniques of teaching machines and self-instructional programs and review the evaluative research on programed learning.

This latter area is of particular interest because it represents the first major foray of animal learning psychology into the educational arena. We explore the design factors in self-instruction from a cybernetic point of view, skeptical of the claims that programed learning follows the principles of operant conditioning or reinforcement learning.

The last part of the book presents an overview of behavioral cybernetics, describes its experimental foundations, and discusses its meaning in relation to human behavior specializations. Cybernetic or feedback research constitutes a new type of experimental science of behavior and learning which has been developing for some twenty years since the first studies of feedback delay in military machine operations. Since that time, electronic, optical, acoustic, television, and computer techniques have been developed to vary spatial, temporal, and kinetic properties of the sensory feedback of dynamic response patterns. Although the major techniques are fairly new, they are related to a long experimental tradition introduced by Stratton: studying the organization of visually controlled behavior by displacing the visual field with lenses, prisms, or mirrors.

One of the aims of this book is to introduce the concepts and methods of the closed-loop hybrid analog-digital computer system as a generalized laboratory instrument in cybernetic research. The senior author has been concerned for some time with designing a laboratory system in which a high-speed digital computer is used not for data processing but as a scientific instrument to control experimental feedback variables. In this book we explain how such an operation is set up for systematic research on the effects of delayed, space-displaced, and perturbed sensory feedback on performance and learning of many different kinds of response patterns. Feedback research is especially relevant to education for much of it is directly concerned with the control and learning of educational skills—speech, reading, writing, and other instrumental and cognitive skills. These areas of research are described in some detail.

An important implication of the cybernetic view is that studies of development complement studies of learning in furthering our understanding of organization and change in behavior. In the last part of the book, we define the role of continuous dynamic activity and its space- and object-related feedback processes in the development and elaboration of motor coordinations, verbal and instrumental skills, and cognitive behavior. Both maturation and learning are thought of as involving interrelated feedback mechanisms by means of which responses are integrated, differentiated, and changed. By emphasizing the significance of somatic behavior in regulating development and learning as well as psychophysiological function, cybernetic theory provides a new approach to all aspects of teaching, training, and rehabilitative science.

The underlying theme of this book is that behavior must be conceptualized as space-organized rather than time-organized as implied by associationism, S-R learning models, and the synaptic concept of neural integration. Feedback research has accumulated a considerable body of evidence showing that somatic response is controlled by detection of spatial differences in stimulus patterns and that temporal organization in behavior is derived from its continuous spatial patterning. We believe that the human individual at the outset—in early childhood or in prehistory —has no real sense of time but lives in a space-ordered world. The most important aspect of cognitive development in the human species as well as in the human individual is the process of capturing numerous different modes of sensing, conceiving, and predicting time relationships. Over all, education is a behavioral, an institutional, and a social process for preserving the record of and extending the adventures of Homo sapiens into the fourth dimension.

The feedback research described in this book has been carried out in collaboration with many students. Particular credit should be given to Dr. John D. Gould, Sherman D. Ansell, and Terence J. Schuh, who collaborated in several research projects and helped to develop laboratory resources.

Special credit is due Gerald Servos and Harold Washington, whose technical expertness was a major aid in designing and developing the computer laboratory system.

The senior author has received major financial support from the National Science Foundation and the National Institutes of Health. Regular grants from these sources have made possible the development of a computer-controlled laboratory of experimental behavioral cybernetics and have supported the research described in this book.

A major part of the artwork in the book was finished by James Hett.

We express our appreciation to Mrs. Marion Masse who typed the manuscript.

The patterns of thinking developed in this book owe much to some of the authors' early training experiences in psychology. We wish to acknowledge particularly the influences of the late Professor E. B. Delabarre of Brown University and the late Professor R. H. Stetson of Oberlin College, whose interests in the motor aspect of response and in the multidimensionality of motion have served as continuing stimulating guides in our search for meaningful concepts of human behavior.

KARL U. SMITH
MARGARET F. SMITH

Madison, Wisconsin
November 1965

Contents

CHAPTER

1

Human Factors
in Learning Science

This is a book about human learning and how it is determined by human design and the design of the learning situation. The emphasis on human design implies that man differs from other animals in his behavior organization to such an extent that a science of human learning cannot be founded primarily on animal research. The emphasis on situational design extends our analysis from the laboratory to the educational arena, where individuals learn the meaningful skills and patterns of symbolic knowledge that fulfill their human potential. This means that we shall deal from time to time with many applied educational problems, but we do so with an orientation that is primarily scientific and experimental. We are attempting to discover the nature of human learning not by paring away the trappings of behavior until the "essence" of the learning process is revealed, but by studying meaningful learning in terms of the

events of behavior organization that determine its course and rate.

Factors of human design long have been ignored in experimental learning psychology. It has been believed that learning could be studied as a general process—that its manifestations in rats and monkeys could be applied directly to human problems. We take issue with this point of view, believing instead that the behavioral design of the learner, which develops to a significant extent independently of specific learning change, determines what he can learn, at what rate, and under what conditions. Learning is not just a function of extrinsic stimuli and reinforcements in certain temporal relationships as implied by generally accepted theoretical models, but also a function of the intrinsic stimulus-response organization of the behaving individual. We propose to base our study of learning on an analysis of the sensory-feedback organization of behavior in relation to both intrinsic and extrinsic variables. This we describe as a *cybernetic* approach, utilizing a term that implies self-regulation of activity.

Concepts of the behaving individual as a feedback-control system have developed since the years of World War II, when it was realized that a human operator guiding the actions of a machine according to perceptual-feedback information is analogous to a mechanical self-governing system or servomechanism. One important difference between the human feedback-control or cybernetic system and the servomechanism is that the former can learn; the human individual can improve his control or change the nature of that control by learning. It appears to us, then, that a valid description of learning change must encompass this feature of control. Learning is more than the forming of new associations between stimuli and responses and the strengthening of existing associations. It is a process of reorganization of sensory-feedback patterning which shifts the learner's level of control over his own behavior in relation to the objects and events of the environment.

Human design changes as the individual develops from infancy through childhood and adolescence to maturity and then old age, so that our understanding of behavior patterning and learning potential is incomplete without reference to the developmental context. Consequently, our analyses and interpretations either explicitly or implicitly acknowledge the importance of the developmental variable.

Human design has changed as well in the evolutionary development of the human race, and we believe that important insights about the nature of behavior organization in contemporary man can be gained by investigating man's evolving abilities and learned skills in history and prehistory. We shall attempt, in the first part of the book, to understand man's psychological nature in other ages and other cultures by studying his tools, instruments, and utensils; his markings, drawings, and writings; the design of his buildings, villages, and cities. These artifacts not only reveal much about patterns of behavior and patterns of living, but they also reveal much about what man learned by showing how he learned—that is, by revealing the design of his significant learning situations. Human skills and knowledge are as much a function of the specialized tools, instruments, and symbol systems of the culture as they are of the behaving system.

In our age as in other ages, human learning is understood best with reference to the meaningful situations in which it occurs, especially in schools, training classes, and rehabilitation centers for people of all ages. In order to explore the reciprocal relationships between the learner and the educational context, we shall devote the central section of the book to an analysis of current educational techniques and devices.

The last part of the book will deal primarily with our efforts to define a new experimental approach to the study of learning in man—a systematic endeavor that goes beyond the specific problems of learning to a consideration of the general determinants of behavior organization. Our sensory-feedback methods of analysis investigate the intrinsic stimulus-response relationships of patterned behavior and attempt to define their role in determining the course, rate, and level of learning. Studies of the phenomena of space-displaced and delayed sensory feedback contribute materially to our understanding of the feedback control of basic educational skills and disclose how learning is related to the pattern of control.

TECHNOLOGICAL EXPLOSION IN EDUCATION

Throughout the history of education, many tools have been developed to help the teacher in his task. Foremost among these are the instruments by means of which verbal knowledge has been communicated and stored—stylus, pen and pencil, parchment scroll, and printed book. In contrast to these generally useful instruments, the tools for skill training usually are specific to the skill. The novice learns to plow by using a plow and learns to shoot by being trained with a gun. Yet, whether it is a matter of teaching general knowledge or of training skills, the teacher always has depended on the tools of his trade.

In recent years, educational methods and instrumentation have been changing at a pace commensurate with the rapid technological advances in other phases of our society. Each month brings its new ideas and new devices—automated teaching machines, television teaching from airplanes, audiovisumatic systems, computers adapted to self-instruction, telemation, and so on. This onslaught of technology in the classroom has been greeted with varying degrees of enthusiasm. Some think that the new techniques and devices enhance the educational process and others fear that they pervert it. Although we shall make some evaluative judgments of these various techniques and devices throughout the book, such an evaluation is subordinate to our main interest in the relation of educational design to the organization of human learning.

Inasmuch as studies of teaching techniques and devices contribute to our scientific understanding of human learning, we look on the teaching machines, skill trainers, and other educational innovations as research tools which hold the promise of an exciting new era of learning research. In this section, we shall illustrate some of the types of instrumentation that have been adapted to educational purposes during the last few years, emphasizing particularly how the devices and procedures can be used for basic research.

Television Recording

Television's specialized usefulness in education is due very largely to the television tape recorder, as shown in Figure 1.1. As the combined photographs show, a video-tape recorder can be used to record a televised lecture or series of lessons and demonstrations on tape which can be played back to different classrooms throughout a state or region. It can be broadcast over a licensed video channel or distributed by means of a recording truck to closed-circuit systems within particular schools or districts. Video recording can be adapted to many special teaching techniques heretofore impossible. For example, the performance of a specialized skill, such as a dance sequence or a pilot's activity in landing an aircraft, can be televised, recorded, and then played back to the dancer or pilot so

Figure 1.1.   The Ampex Videotape Recorder used as a teaching tool. The two-inch magnetic tape recorder makes possible a permanent audiovisual record of instructional procedures and subject matter, which can be presented to individuals or groups at any desired time. (Courtesy of WHA-TV, University of Wisconsin.)

that the exact pattern of behavior can be analyzed and evaluated.

The television tape recorder has additional significance as a new type of laboratory instrument for learning research. When it is properly arranged to control the time between visual recording and playback of performance, it can be used to vary the time relations between performance of a motion and the visual feedback that a person receives of that motion. Investigations of *delayed visual feedback* carried out in this way will be described later, along with studies of *displaced visual feedback*. Such sensory-feedback analyses of behavior have direct implications for our understanding of the determinants of learning.

Computer Programing

Other machines which can be used to collect, store, and program information for teaching purposes are computers, such as the one shown in the computer teaching-machine facility in Figure 1.2. There is much current interest in adapting computer systems to the special purposes of educational research as well as to teaching. The objective of some of this research is to investigate the *programing* of material, or the arrangement of subject matter and questions for efficient instruction. The varying concepts of programing that have been proposed constitute one of the most controversial areas in educational theory.

A further use of computer systems in behavior research is in analyzing the feedback control of many kinds of behavior and physiological activity. A computer system is tied directly into the feedback-control loop of a behaving individual in order to measure the effects of varying or distorting different properties of the feedback. Such techniques show considerable promise for the experimental analysis of behavior organization and learning.

Skill Training

Many complex trainers have been developed for training operators in the specialized skills required in modern military and industrial installations. The photographs in Figure 1.3 show a system that can be used to train air-traffic controllers for large airports. Figure 1.3*a* shows a radarscope on which appear simulated targets very much like those seen by a controller in an air-traffic control center. Figure 1.3*b* pictures the numerous operators behind the scenes whose task is to generate the radar targets seen on the scope and to control their speed, direction, and aspect of movement. This elaborate instrumental system can be used for research as well as for training purposes.

Designing trainers and programing

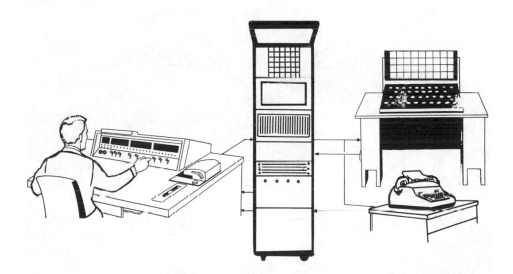

Figure 1.2.   A computer system used as a teaching machine research facility. The desk-type computer can program and present either visual or auditory material and questions. The student indicates his answers either on the electric typewriter or on a special electronic teaching control device.

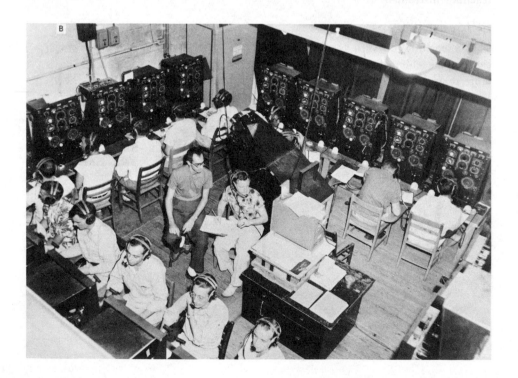

Figure 1.3.   An air-traffic control simulation trainer and research facility. *a*. Radar target display simulating aircraft targets as they might appear in the air-traffic control center of a large urban or military airport. *b*. Operators generating and controlling the simulated targets seen in *a*. Up to thirty target courses can be generated simultaneously by this system. (Courtesy of Dr. Paul M. Fitts.)

tasks and lessons for instrumental systems represent major research problems in both engineering and psychology. Although some psychological studies along these lines were done as early as the 1920s, there were no major systematic analyses of trainer devices until World War II. The ideas developed during the war years about trainers and programing of training material laid the foundation for the present human factors approach to understanding learning and teaching instrumentation in general.

Self-instruction in the Classroom

The teaching devices known specifically as teaching machines originated more than thirty-five years ago but only recently have aroused widespread interest leading to their use in the classroom.

Figure 1.4 shows students working with one of the commercially developed machines. Instructional material and questions are presented, and the student is required to write an answer in the space provided. After he writes an answer, he pushes the mimeographed sheet up to bring the correct answer to the question into view.

Figure 1.4.   Self-instruction devices in use in a classroom. This teaching machine is designed to present instructional material and questions mimeographed on standard-size paper. The student answers each question by writing in the answer slot and then advances the paper to bring the correct answer and the next unit of material into view. Thus he has immediate knowledge of the correctness or incorrectness of his answers. (Courtesy of Teaching Machines, Inc.)

Marked differences of opinion exist among teaching machine proponents relative to the design of the machines, the type of programing used, and as to whether programed instruction can be relied on to teach entire courses effectively. One of our objectives is to inquire into some of these questions about self-instruction. This inquiry leads us into the general problem of the organization of specialized knowledge—the relation of verbal and nonverbal symbolism, the many dimensions of meaning, and the relative specificity and generality of different kinds of learned reactions.

SIGNIFICANT FEATURES OF THE EDUCATIONAL PROCESS

In their function as tools for teaching, the devices that we have just discussed are a far cry from the pencil, slate, and McGuffey reader of the little red schoolhouse, yet the complex new instruments have this in common with the simpler ones of the past—they promote the learning of symbolic knowledge and educational skills. There are certain salient features of the teaching-learning process that are found in all educational contexts but which are specialized in particular situations by the instruments, devices, and techniques being used.

Communication

One feature common to all of human education is the communicative interchange between teachers and learners. Whereas the most primitive men relied almost entirely on face-to-face communication to transmit knowledge and skills from one generation to the next, the pattern has shifted gradually to greater and greater dependence on remote communication techniques. The first men who drew pictures in caves or marked their tools with symbolic patterns started the trend toward the use of stored information to structure human learning.

The normal communicative interchange between the teacher and the taught always has been an audiovisual process, and it always has involved both verbal and nonverbal elements. Although the term *audiovisual* may suggest modern technology, the audiovisual, verbal-nonverbal communicative process is as old as man himself and has helped to mold him in his present form. Thus the significance of modern audiovisual techniques must be assessed in this larger behavioral context.

Many psychologists and educators tend to regard the audiovisual techniques as "aids" to education, rather than as an integral part of the learning process. Our own belief that human learning is understood best relative to man's own operational adaptations in society convinces us that the problems of audiovisual communication are basic to learning science and cannot be dismissed as of secondary importance. Studies of rats or pigeons in a feeding box tell us little or nothing about how the human student integrates visual and auditory information, communicated by both verbal and nonverbal symbolism, to build up his general understanding of the world and human affairs. Learning studies restricted to discrete stimulus-response pairs give us no pointers on how to illustrate a textbook most effectively or how to integrate lectures, discussions, and illustrative materials to promote the most efficient learning. Descriptions of learning in animals, of necessity, include no account of the role of symbolic communication in determining the rate of learning and the nature of what is learned, but this deficiency in animal behavior should not blind us to the significance of symbolism in human learning.

Control

The specialized devices and techniques used in teaching and training not only extend and enrich the sensory and symbolic aspects of the learning environment but also enhance the student's control over his own responses in relation to the environment. The human individual exercises varying levels of feedback control which develop progressively through his educational lifetime. The simplest form is direct, *unaided* control. A more complex process, *instrumental* control, involves the use of tools or instruments to effect environmental change. The patterns of verbal and nonverbal symbolism are used to develop *symbolic* control, which deals originally with concrete events and concepts but in time encompasses abstract concepts and relationships as well. At this level, the individual develops *abstract* control—that is, he learns to control complex physical and social interrelationships that have no concrete reality except in some symbolic representation.

Human education is concerned almost entirely with the development of instrumental and symbolic control—both concrete and abstract. Thus it is almost completely dependent on tools and instruments on the one hand and devices to transmit symbols on the other. The growth of science and technology in our modern era constitutes greatly enhanced human control over the environment. In order to teach the new skills and knowl-edge, we have many specialized instrumental and symbolic techniques to enable students to keep abreast of advancing human abilities.

The element of control has been recognized explicitly in educational design only in recent years with the development of self-instructional training devices, teaching machines, and teaching programs. The principal value of self-instruction to the student is that it puts him in more complete control of the learning situation than is possible with standard group teaching procedures. His responses provide immediate feedback information about their correctness or effectiveness so that necessary changes and corrections can be made.

Meaning

A self-evident feature of the educational process is that it deals with meaningful behavior; educational skills and symbolic knowledge are transmitted from generation to generation because they have some adaptive meaning in human life. This is not necessarily true of the learning that goes on in psychological laboratories, where human subjects often learn responses quite unrelated to adaptive behavior. From such experiments we are supposed to derive some understanding of human learning, even though the learned responses have no meaning to the subject beyond the restricted conditions of the experiment, are never confirmed in another setting, and provide him no control over human or physical events outside the laboratory.

In contrast to this approach to learning psychology, the central problem of educational psychology is to understand the nature and conditions of meaningful learning—that is, the acquisition of systematized patterns of knowledge or skill which can be used in diverse adaptive situations. The meaning of a response for the individual depends on the specific situations in which it is used. Thus we try to broaden the meaning of educational skills by varying the contexts in which they are taught and practiced. In other psychological terms, this means that we try to assure the generality of learning by setting up conditions favorable to transfer. In still other terms, this is a matter of extending feedback control of behavior from specific sensorimotor patterns to many related but different patterns.

It should be recognized that some teaching techniques and devices impose arbitrary restrictions on the learning context and thus teach more specific meanings than may be desirable. Self-instructional programs in particular may have limited generality. However, when the knowledge or skill to be taught is by nature very specific, as a particular machine skill, then it is taught best by standardized procedures. Teaching and training needs vary widely and require different types of learning situations that cannot be specified by research on non-meaningful learning.

Motivation

It has become almost axiomatic in psychology to say that behavior is motivated, in the sense that the energizing of activity is described as a motivating process. Most psychologists also hold the position that learning results from motivation in a more specific sense, that is, that a drive state must be reduced or a motive satisfied by reinforcement in order for learning to occur. This specific position still is a controversial one in psychology and its resolution is of utmost significance to the educator, whose efforts in assembling the personnel and materials for teaching would be wasted on students who were not motivated to perform and to learn. Fortunately for our educational system, it is a rare individual who is completely indifferent to the learning situation. Most students do, in fact, learn, but their sources of motivation or energization are subject to more than one interpretation.

The most prevalent psychological interpretation is that motivation is derived from basic physiological drives which activate the individual to seek goal objects or situations and to avoid punishments. The Freudian variation of this theme makes the sex drive primary but is similar in attributing the energizing force in behavior to conditions extrinsic to the behavior patterns themselves. To explain the fact that most behavior seems to bear little relation to physiological needs, psychological theory has postulated derived or secondary drives, learned motives, generalization of learned motives, and so on. It is assumed that classroom learning is motivated almost entirely by secondary or derived drives. Further, reinforcement learning theory postulates that all learning is dependent on specific reinforcements. The reinforcements in classroom learning may be obscure, but if the learning theorist fails to identify any elements that appear to be positive rewards, he always can fall back on the concept of negative reinforcement or punishment. In fact, at least one learning theorist has condemned traditional classroom methods for relying almost exclusively on negative reinforcements (Skinner, 1954).

It appears significant to us that reinforcement theories of learning have been derived for the most part from research on animals. It is true that if an experimenter is to get the cooperation of an animal in a learning experiment, he must arrange the situation so that the animal at least does something—preferably the thing that is expected. The most reliable way to get the animal moving in the right direction—either literally or figuratively—is to make sure that it is motivated and then provided with a reward when it makes the response that the experimenter is waiting for. The cooperation of human subjects is secured much more directly, simply by telling them what to do. In the earliest psychological experiments on human learning and memory, no one worried about identifying either the drive or the reinforcers. These factors invaded learning theory when the animals entered the laboratory and very nearly swept the field. Reinforcement has been put forward as a theoretical necessity in the learning process although it may be just a practical necessity in learning research.

It appears to us that motivation, like other aspects of behavior, has become highly specialized during the course of human evolution and has significant components quite unrelated to physiological drives or tissue needs. The most significant patterns of human behavior involve the use of tools and machines to control the environment and the use of symbolic and communicative responses which grew out of the tool-using function. We believe that human manipulative and communicative skills are in themselves a potent source of motivation; that is, these typically human activities are energized intrinsically rather than extrinsically by some learned association with a physiological need. In human education, the student's motivation to perform cannot be divorced from the books, the tools, the work situations, and the audiovisual patterns of the classroom. The primary problem of educational motivation is to design the perceptual, instrumental, and symbolic features of the learning environment so that the learner can increase his control over patterns of response that have adaptive utility in society.

Evolution
of Human Learning

The comparative study of learning in subhuman animals contributes to our understanding of human learning insofar as the progressive changes in phylogeny provide insights into how human patterns have developed. However, this type of analysis is hampered by the great gap that exists between the learning abilities of animals and man. The instrumental and symbolic skills that define human learning are found in man alone, with no more than a hint of their origins in the behavior of subhuman primates. The only way to bridge this gap in comparative learning science is to attempt to analyze the development of human patterns of behavior and learning in prehistoric and ancient man.

Human evolution has involved changes in behavior as well as changes in body form, but the psychological changes are due to more than genetic modifications. Since early man became a tool user and a symbol user, he has developed a society and a technology that are cumulative in their impact on succeeding generations. Thus the behavior of man has been modified progressively by social as well as by genetic factors—a process we refer to as biosocial evolution. All human activities, including those involved in learning, have become specialized through these evolutionary changes. The most significant factors in this specialization of behavior are the use and design of tools, and the use of meaningful symbolism.

The use of tools, machines, symbol systems, and organized institutions by human social groups has built certain features of design into the educational process so that human learning in any culture reflects the evolutionary level of that culture. All of the significant features of human education that we have described here—communication, control, meaning, and motivation—are structured by technological and symbolic design and change progressively as these design features change in the biosocial evolutionary process. The way man's tools are constructed, the way his symbols are formed, the way his languages are organized, and the way his society integrates its institutions for learning—all of these features of the human social order define the educational context and thus leave their mark on the developing human design of the individual learner.

Let us consider again the communicative aspects of education. The patterns of communication used to transmit educational skills and knowledge are a direct function of the instruments, techniques, and symbol systems that are used for communicative purposes. Man has progressed from cave drawings and smoke signals to the age of computers not by any supernatural enhancement of his abilities but by the hard labor of performing, revising, redesigning, and adding to his educational and communicative skills. Where once he pegged clay tablets for hours to record a simple transaction or spent years learning how to make artistic hieroglyphics, the individual today can manipulate millions of items of information within a few minutes time.

Consider a second feature, that of behavioral control. The level of feedback control that can be achieved by a learner depends on the tools, instruments, machines, and symbolic representations that he uses to extend and transform his direct, unaided behavioral abilities in space and in time. It is unnecessary to point out that man's control of the environment depends on his level of science and technology, but it should be stated explicitly that the design of knowledge and technology defines how an individual enhances his control through learning. To learn how to use electronics or higher mathematics to control people and events requires complex integrations of response that never occurred in ancient man.

The meaning of learned behavior is also directly dependent on the design of the educational and cultural context. The influence of cultural and social meanings on the learning patterns of individuals sometimes is strikingly revealed when different cultural patterns clash. Individuals who reach adulthood in one culture may never gain control over the meaningful response patterns of another culture. It has been related that an early European sea captain who sought to entertain a group of Polynesians with his violin found that his skill was greatly admired—that is, his digital skill (Greenway, 1964). But the natives regretted that such dreadful noises accompanied a demonstration that was meaningful to them only as a display of manual dexterity. Their culture had not developed the instruments or the musical symbolism that would have enabled them to understand the music.

Finally, patterns of human motivation evolve and alter with changes in the instrumental-symbolic context of education. People are motivated to learn those patterns of behavior that fit their culture or their social group. Individual goals and aspirations are defined by the patterns of work, recreation, religion, family living, artistic and cultural pursuits of their society; these patterns in turn are defined by symbolic, technological, and institutional design. The educational system that is out of step with general social progress may be trying to teach knowledge and skills that are losing their meaning and thus are not highly motivating to the learner.

An analysis of the evolutionary context of human learning does not automatically solve the problems related to the design of teaching methods and machines. However, it does provide a base from which to launch our analysis of the human factors involved in learning and education. A study of human history shows that patterns of communication and learning are cumulative as well as being subject to continual evolutionary change. The learning that goes on in a modern classroom is defined in part by the modern devices used; but it is also structured by patterns of verbal and nonverbal communication, by the social structure of a class, by the design of symbol systems, and by the instruments used to record and transmit symbolic knowledge—all of which trace their origins to the dawn of history and beyond. An evolutionary analysis of educational design tells us more about the nature of human learning than a learning theory derived from animal research.

SECTORS OF LEARNING SCIENCE

Our aim in writing this book is not so much to spell out a theory of the learning process as it is to define a science of learning, in particular a science of human learning. In doing this we make no real distinction between a basic science and an applied science of learning, for we believe that such a division is arbitrary and serves no useful purpose. The unhappy fact is that theories of learning developed and tested in psychological research laboratories have had but limited applicability to the practical problems of learning encountered in human education and training. Our belief is that research carried out on meaningful learning in its human educational context *is* basic and is necessary if we are to develop valid learning theory.

The Psychology of Learning

In Chapter 2, we shall survey the conventional approaches to learning research that have been developed in laboratory psychology and the theories that have grown out of the research. Originally, this laboratory science of learning had little direct contact with the problems of educational design, but recent interest in trainers and teaching machines has stimulated the learning theorist to apply concepts and generalizations formulated in the laboratory to the practical problems and needs of the classroom. For the most part, this effort has not met with notable success. Standard theories of learning based on such concepts as association, conditioning, and reinforcement are alike in several respects that limit their relevancy to educational design.

In the first place, learning psychology has tried to deal with the phenomena of learning in the simplest possible terms —in terms of units categorized as stimuli, responses, and reinforcements. These units then are manipulated in experimental designs, juggled statistically, and assumed to be the proper events for learning research at all levels. Although this type of analysis may seem useful in the psychological laboratory where the significant variables can be restricted arbitrarily and controlled with some degree of success, it is almost meaningless when applied to the normal adaptive behavior involved in human education.

In the second place, standard learning theory describes learning in terms of patterns of response units which are chained together in time by the effects of temporal contiguity or specific reinforcements. Little or no attention is given to the spatial organization of behavior. In our opinion, the spatial patterning is of primary importance, for in all significant perceptual-motor skills, the pattern of motion conforms to and is controlled by spatial patterns of the stimulus environment. For example, a child learns to read and write by conforming with his motion systems to the spatial patterns of letters and words. The temporal organization of behavior is derived from the primary spatial patterning and its regulatory mechanisms. We shall have more to say about these ideas later.

In the third place, prevailing learning theory implies that all kinds of learned changes in behavior, both in animals and in man, are essentially equivalent. The great effort of learning research has been to isolate the "learning process" in its stark biological simplicity. The practical problems of teaching and education then must be reduced to the prescribed formula, whether it was derived from rats, cats, or pigeons. In our view, this approach to learning science is both inadequate and invalid. The problems and challenges of education arise from the fact that human individuals are able to perform educationally significant skills and to acquire almost unlimited symbolic knowledge. To explain these human patterns of behavior in terms of an animal's reactions in a feeding box is to miss the entire significance of human evolution.

Educational Research

A sector of learning science directly concerned with human problems is the area of educational research, much of it devoted to evaluations of specific classroom techniques, especially educational technology. For several decades the main focus of educational research was on the audiovisual communicative techniques—AV education. Chapters 5 and 6 will be devoted to a survey of this area, with the emphasis on an evaluation of television teaching. In order to set the stage for our discussion of these modern classroom methods, we shall use Chapters 3 and 4 to trace the evolution of nonverbal and verbal communication as used in the educational process. Contemporary audiovisual techniques serve the same function in education as the nonverbal and verbal communicative skills and devices of earlier man.

During the past decade, a great amount of research activity has centered on the use of automated teaching machines and self-instructional teaching programs in the classroom. This is the one major educational development that has been championed by learning theorists as a direct contribution of "basic" psychological research to education. However, the main ideas behind teaching machines were developed first by an educational psychologist and then were elaborated by psychologists engaged in training research during and after World War II. For that reason we shall introduce our discussion of teaching machines and programed learning in Chapters 10, 11, and 12 with an account of training psychology in Chapters 7, 8, and 9.

Training Research

In our opinion, the most significant research contributions of learning science have grown out of the training psychology of World War II and its lineal descendant, human engineering. The human engineering approach to training problems explicitly recognized —almost for the first time—the importance of human design factors in defining the course of learning. As a scientific discipline, human engineering goes beyond specific learning or training

problems to deal with more general aspects of behavior organization in machine operations. It is concerned with how the human individual organizes his control movements in relation to the perceptual information provided him.

In the human engineering context, the study of learning assumes a subordinate role, for the primary features of human design that define the patterning of perceptual-motor behavior are independent of learning. These primary characteristics of human motion systems in relation to the design of the operational situation determine how efficiently an individual can perform and to what level he can improve his performance by practice and training. Thus the training psychology of the war years and after focused attention on the intrinsic determinants of learning in contrast to extrinsic determinants such as temporal contiguity and specific reinforcements that continued to hold the attention of academic learning psychologists.

The human factors approach to learning science is as applicable to problems of general educational design as it is to human engineering or training design, for it deals with the factors determining human behavior organization in performance and meaningful learning. In applying this point of view to education, we view both the individual and the educational pattern as changing adaptive systems. As the tools and systems of education have become more complex and refined, the instrumentation of the educational process has come to present the same kind of problems that are met in designing machines for human work. Not only must the machine be planned for optimal human use, but its design must be conceived in terms of the specialized operations to be instrumented and the specific functions to be served.

The most significant feature of the human factors approach to educational design is the effort to deal with meaningful learning in terms of the organizational features characteristic of human behavior. Our human factors analysis of learning proceeds from this basic postulate: The primary factors governing meaningful learning—and thus the efficiency of our educational system—are defined by the intrinsic regulatory mechanisms of patterned human behavior. That is, the features of the human system that determine how an individual responds to his perceptual (and thus his social and symbolic) environment also define what he can learn, his learning efficiency, and the meaning of his learned responses. We look for the most critical determinants of meaningful learning within the human response mechanisms themselves and not in some chance contiguity of external stimuli or the presence or absence of some extrinsic reward.

Feedback Research

Experience in systems analysis and study of behavior factors in machine design have taught that questions about human behavior organization can be approached on different levels—for example, at the level of a general theoretical understanding of how a response system is organized, or at the level of understanding the behavioral properties of specific instrumental situations. In this book as in our own research, we deal with the problems of human learning and educational design at both of these levels. After chapters dealing with

the design and research evaluation of audiovisual systems, training techniques, teaching machines and programs, and textbooks, we shall turn to a description of our research analyses of behavior patterns and their feedback control.

In order to establish a theoretical foundation for studying problems of human learning, we have turned our attention to the spatial organization of behavior. One of our principal experimental methods of studying spatial organization is an extension of a classical psychological technique—that of inverting and otherwise displacing vision. Since Stratton's (1896, 1897, 1899) original studies, this type of experiment usually has been carried out by having subjects wear experimental spectacles or other optical devices. We have relied more extensively on the use of closed-circuit television systems to displace the visual field of performance and to measure the effects on performance and learning (Smith and Smith, 1962).

Figure 1.5 indicates how closed-circuit television can be used experimentally to displace the visual feedback of performance. The subject is required to write or to perform other tasks while viewing his movements in a television monitor. Direct vision of his hand is prevented by a screen, but he can see a televised image of his own performance transmitted to the monitor by means of a closed-circuit camera system. By controlling the position of the camera and its lenses and by electronic control, we can invert, reverse, or otherwise displace the televised visual feedback that he receives of his own behavior.

Television methodology also can be used to study the fundamental time rela-

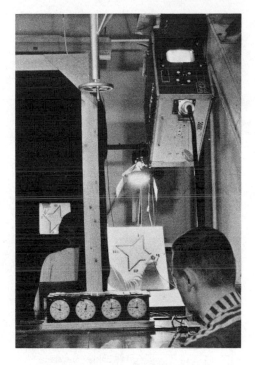

Figure 1.5.   Using closed-circuit television to invert the visual feedback of performance.

Figure 1.6.   Using video-tape recorders in a closed-circuit television system to delay the visual feedback of manual performance. The televised image of the subject's movements is recorded on magnetic tape and played back to his monitor after a specified delay interval.

tions between motions and their governing stimuli. As shown in Figure 1.6, these time relationships can be varied by introducing a video-tape recorder into the closed circuit between the camera and the monitor. Now the televised image of performance is recorded on the magnetic tape and stored for a controlled interval of time before being played back to the subject's monitor as a delayed visual-feedback pattern. Studies of feedback delay indicate that even minor variations in the time interval between movements and their feedback stimuli disrupt the organization of the ongoing motion pattern and jeopardize the learning process (K. U. Smith, 1962).

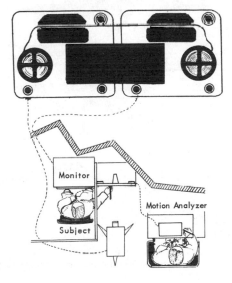

As mentioned earlier, a closed-loop computer system also can be used to analyze the feedback control of speech, handwriting, drawing, and other perceptual-motor skills. Figure 1.7 illustrates the appearance of a laboratory designed around a computer for many kinds of studies of human performance and learning. The general purpose computer can be programed to delay, displace, or distort either visual or auditory feedback signals in many ways. In studies of handwriting, the subject writes on the electronic writing board shown on the small desk. Electronic recorders transduce the handwriting pattern into two electrical signals representing the horizontal and vertical components of the movements. These signals are converted to digital form and fed into the computer, which then is used to delay or distort them in various ways. The two signals then are reconverted to visual form and displayed on a type of oscilloscope that holds an image for a period of time. If a delay has been introduced, the subject sees the image of his writing only after that delay interval. A spatial displacement results in a displaced feedback image. For example, a

Figure 1.7.   A feedback analysis laboratory designed around a computer, which is used to delay, distort, or otherwise vary different properties of sensory feedback.

normal *a* written by the subject might appear inverted or flattened out. The purpose of such an experimental system is to study the time and space factors in the stimulus-response process itself and to see how variations in these intrinsic relationships affect the course of learning.

After describing our basic research and outlining the theoretical concepts which have grown out of it, in Chapters 14 and 15, we shall go on to transfer of training in Chapter 16 and cognitive behavior in Chapter 17. In both cases, we shall apply feedback concepts to an analysis of these special areas of learning science. In Chapter 18 we shall describe some of the high points of developmental psychology, showing how human behavior organization changes progressively during the educational period of life because of maturation as well as learning. Learning science is not complete without an understanding of the maturation-learning interaction, for one of the primary problems of educational design is to adjust the techniques and instrumentation of teaching and training to the level of the development of the learner.

SUMMARY

1. This book examines the phenomena of human learning as they are determined by human design and the design of the learning situation, especially the techniques and instruments of education.

2. The individual, looked on as a feedback-control system, is seen to improve his control of behavior in relation to the environment by learning.

3. Recently developed devices being used for educational purposes include video-tape recorders for storing televised teaching for later presentation, computers for programing the materials for self-instruction, complicated simulation trainers for specialized machine skills, and many types of teaching machines for both classroom and individual use. All of these devices are important research tools for learning science as well as being educational instruments.

4. An important feature of human education is that it involves communication both auditory and visual, and nonverbal and verbal. Audiovisual and other communicative techniques in the classroom are an integral part of the educational process.

5. The techniques of human education are useful insofar as they extend the learner's control of his behavior and the environment. Because educational learning is concerned almost entirely with instrumental and symbolic behavior, it is dependent on tools and devices which mediate instrumental and symbolic control.

6. Educational learning is meaningful learning. We broaden meanings and enhance the learner's general knowledge by varying the learning context. Specific skills can be taught by more restrictive procedures and devices.

7. The conventional interpretation of human motivation is that it is derived from physiological drives extrinsic to the behavior mechanisms themselves. Presented here is an alternative view that human manipulative and communicative skills are energized intrinsically and thus can be learned without recourse to external rewards or reinforcements.

8. In the course of human evolution, cumulative patterns of instrumental, symbolic, communicative, and educational behavior have generated an organized context which helps to determine the course of subsequent learning. All of the significant features of human learning have become specialized by bio-social evolutionary development.

9. Conventional learning theories are limited in their relevance to human learning because they treat learning phenomena in the simplest possible terms; they emphasize temporal association of responses and ignore spatial patterning; they imply that there is a basic biological learning process unaffected by human specializations.

10. The area of educational research has dealt mainly with evaluations of specific classroom techniques and devices such as audiovisual techniques.

11. The most significant research contributions to learning science have come from training psychology and human engineering studies made during and since World War II. The human factors approach emphasizes intrinsic determinants of performance and learning in relation to the perceptual and instrumental design of the performance situation.

12. The human factors approach has generated a type of learning research based on analyses of the intrinsic stimulus-response organization of behavior as a feedback-control process. Techniques of displacing, delaying, and otherwise varying different properties of sensory feedback are used to study the spatial and temporal patterning of behavior and to show how these intrinsic relationships determine the course of learning.

CHAPTER
2

A Century of Learning Psychology

The study of learning had no place in formal science until just a century ago when Helmholtz (1856–1866) launched what came to be known as the empirical doctrine of space perception, a theory as notable in its day as Darwin's theory of evolution. Helmholtz was dealing with both specific and general questions about human behavior. The specific question was whether space perception is learned or is innate. The general question is as pertinent today as it was a century ago and as controversial: To what extent can we attribute the organization of behavior to learning? Helmholtz recognized, as we do, that there are great flexibility and variability in both human and animal behavior in responding to particular conditions of stimulation, and that experience affects the way in which situations are perceived and how behavior is organized. The importance of the development of individual flexibility and specialization of behavior through experience has kept the consideration of learning at the forefront of psychological theory and research. Any contributions toward an understanding of the basic mechanisms of the learning process or of the role and significance of learning in general patterns of behavior represent major advances in behavior science.

MILESTONES IN LEARNING METHODOLOGY

In learning science perhaps more than in most scientific areas, theories have been defined to an important degree by experimental methods. Each significant technique for studying learning has produced its own special type of learning data, and often a specialized set of data has been used as the basis of a distinct theory of learning. We begin our survey of learning science with a description of the most important laboratory techniques that have given learning theories their special flavor.

Studying Memory with Nonsense Syllables

Ebbinghaus (1913) set the stage for an important area of research on human learning by his use of nonsense syllables in developing experimental methods for the study of memory and forgetting. Although his hope that unfamiliar combinations of letters would constitute units of equal difficulty and thus permit exact comparison of different experimental conditions was not entirely justified, nonsense syllables have been and still are being used widely in learning research. The memory drum, which presents words or syllables at regular intervals in a small window, has played an important role in this type of experiment on human learning and memory. Nonsense-syllable studies have yielded many kinds of data, including some which define a general curve of retention, as shown in Figure 2.1.

Ebbinghaus's work was important not only as the first systematic laboratory research on learning, but also because it defined a methodology for analyzing the conditions of efficient human learning. His unit of measurement of memory was the frequency of repetition needed to master a sequence. This same unit was used to measure retention or forgetting by means of the method of savings, that is, determining the percentage of trials saved in relearning a sequence after a period of time had elapsed. Ebbinghaus found that practice was beneficial beyond the point of mastery (in overlearning) and that spaced practice in general improved retention more than massed practice. He also devised a method to show that practice formed associations between noncontiguous items in a sequence and that these associations were stronger for items close together than for those further apart. He defined a standard curve of retention which has been substantiated by later research. When he discovered that this curve was roughly logarithmic in form, he fitted a

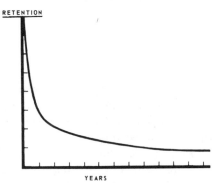

Figure 2.1.   The memory drum, similar to an instrument developed and patented in the United States almost a century ago as a rotating speller for classroom use. As a laboratory tool for experiments on learning, the memory drum has played a role in defining the general curve of retention (or forgetting) and other functions of serial learning.

logarithmic equation to it and became the first learning psychologist to express his empirical data as a mathematical function.

Trial-and-Error Learning

The growing interest, during the latter half of the nineteenth century, in Darwin's theory of evolution gave impetus to the psychological study of animal intelligence. Experimental expression of this interest was found in the first experiments on animal learning, for it was judged that learning ability was a valid criterion of intelligence. Thorndike (1898) was one of the first to instrument these ideas, carrying out experimental observations on chickens, cats, and monkeys.

Thorndike's best-known experiments on animal intelligence are those dealing with cats in problem-solving situations, such as the box illustrated in Figure 2.2. The technique was to enclose the cat in a box which could be opened by manipulating a latch mechanism in some way, for example, by pulling a string. The time required for the animal to give the correct response leading to escape and food was recorded in successive trials and could be plotted as a learning curve. Thorndike observed that the animals displayed a good bit of random activity in such situations before the appropriate response finally appeared. Lloyd Morgan's (1900) description of this variable behavior as *trial-and-error* learning introduced a new phrase into comparative learning psychology which

is still used frequently to describe problem-solving behavior and has been thought by some to express a general truth about the nature of learning. Although many psychologists today believe that responses are not emitted randomly, that errors are not a necessary component of learning behavior, and that *exploratory* behavior is a better term, Thorndike's puzzled cats have left a permanent mark upon the terminology of the learning field.

Thorndike's (1932) more significant contribution to learning theory was his reformulation of one of the old laws of idea association as the *law of effect*: reactions followed by satisfying consequences are selected through learning, while reactions followed by annoying consequences do not produce this positive change. Thus motivation was brought into a description of learning, and the concept of effect or goal achievement was added to Ebbinghaus's repetition as a determinant of learning.

Thorndike extended his animal-based principles to more generalized analyses of human verbal learning. On the basis of such studies and other sources of scientific information, he prepared one of the first experimentally oriented treatises on educational psychology (Thorndike, 1913–1914), which has influenced the programs of teacher training throughout the modern period of American education.

Maze Learning

Whereas most of the important innovations in learning methodology are associated with well-known names in behavior science, the maze was introduced by a psychologist who is remembered currently for no other con-

Figure 2.2.   The cat in the puzzle box—E. L. Thorndike's (1898) original technique of analyzing animal learning. The door of the box can be opened by pulling a string inside the box.

tribution. Working with rats in the early period of animal psychology, Small (1900) adopted the maze because its labyrinthine nature suggested to him the natural habitat of rats. For several decades, mazes of various designs and degrees of complexity were standard equipment in many laboratories and contributed significantly to the heyday of "rat" psychology. Several patterns are shown in Figure 2.3, including Small's original Hampton Court maze.

Small's idea of studying animal learning in a situation comparable to the habitat to which the species is adapted was a good one, and it called attention

Figure 2.3.   Maze patterns used to study learning in rats and men. *a*. The Hampton Court maze. *b*. A semilinear U-maze. *c*. A linear maze with alternating right-left choices. (*a* based on W. S. Small. An experimental study of the mental processes of the rat. *Amer. J. Psychol.*, 1900, 11, 133–165; *b* based on C. J. Warden. The relative economy of various modes of attack in the mystery of a stylus maze. *J. exp. Psychol.*, 1924, 7, 243–275; *c* based on J. Buel. The linear maze. I. "Choice-point expectancy," "correctness," and the goal gradient. *J. comp. Psychol.*, 1934, 17, 185–199.)

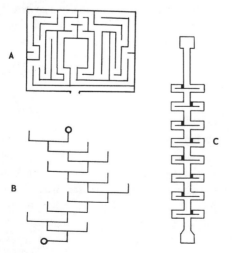

A

B

C

to the spatial organization of behavior as few other techniques have. Complicated mazes such as the one Small used offer few problems to rats. They learn their way about readily even when not motivated by a specific drive such as hunger or thirst. They are not dependent on any one kind of sensory information; rats deprived of sight, hearing, touch, or smell can learn as well as normal animals. Rats that have learned to run through a maze are able to wade or to swim through it, and if crippled by neurological surgery they can drag themselves to the goal. Few laboratory learning patterns have been so difficult to deal with in terms of conventional stimulus and response concepts.

Eventually, however, psychologists found a way to beat the rats at their own game. They simplified the mazes in order to standardize the responses required and thus to secure more reliable learning scores. Figure 2.3*b* and *c* are examples of such standardized patterns. The second of these is linear from entrance to goal with a simple alternation required at the choice points—left, right, left, right, and so on. Although human subjects with their symbolizing abilities find such a maze extremely simple to master—especially in comparison with a complicated spatial pattern like the Hampton Court maze—it presents a fairly difficult problem to a rat. In effect, the rat has been promoted from a spatial problem that it can solve easily to a temporal problem that is foreign to its natural behavior patterning.

Some of the early research workers who ran rats in simple mazes observed that the animals showed a tendency to vary their responses in successive trials. In T-shaped or Y-shaped mazes, spontaneous alternation behavior was very marked whether or not there were specific rewards at the end of the runways. Since about 1950, many studies have shown that animals tend to explore novel situations even when they are not motivated by a physiological drive and when no external reinforcement is provided (Glanzer, 1958). Furthermore, they will learn specific responses in order to gain access to novel or changing situations. The maze technique more than any other learning method used with animals under the primate level has emphasized the importance of exploratory or diverting behavior in animals—behavior which is analogous to perceptual and intellectual curiosity in human individuals.

Many prominent psychologists have used the maze as a technique for learning research, but only one—Tolman (1932)—based a general theory of learning on data derived mainly from maze experiments. Tolman's cognitive theory has had limited impact on learning science—perhaps unfortunately, inasmuch as he attempted to account for the fundamental space patterning of behavior. He never came to grips with some of the questions raised by maze performance in rats and men. Why is it that rats can perform so well in a complicated maze and do so poorly when the pattern is simplified? If learning is essentially similar in animals and men, why do rats find a complicated spatial maze easier to learn than a linear alternation maze while just the reverse is true of human subjects? If learning is a temporal linking of responses, as assumed in all conventional S-R theories, why do rats find a simple temporal sequence so difficult? And by what means has the human species gained

mastery over temporal patterns? These questions never have been answered in learning psychology. Indeed, they have scarcely been asked.

Our own approach to these questions is based on the assumption that behavior is feedback controlled according to spatial characteristics of the stimulus environment, and that human individuals manipulate temporal sequences by symbolic representations that are themselves spatially organized. Inasmuch as such symbolic skills—as well as related instrumental skills—are developed only at the human level, men behave and learn differently from other animals. These ideas will be presented more fully in the next chapter and later.

Discrimination Learning

Early comparative psychologists were interested not just in learning but in all aspects of the animal mind, and special techniques were devised to study sensory capacities. Out of this effort was developed the discrimination experiment in which an animal was trained to respond positively to one of two stimulus cues so that its ability to discriminate differences could be tested. At first, the learning phase of the experiment was merely a tedious preliminary to the main testing phase, but in time the technique was accepted as one way of studying the learning process.

Early in the twentieth century, Yerkes (1907) described a discrimination box that he had devised to test the visual capacities of mice. It was a simplified maze with one choice point; the mouse could go either to the right or to the left as it entered the box. The correct choice was indicated by a pair of visual cues. For example, the positive cue might be a light square and the negative cue, a dark square. Once the animal had learned to turn toward the brighter of the two cues, the brightness difference between them could be reduced gradually until the brightness discrimination threshold was reached and the animal no longer could make a consistently correct choice.

In a box such as this, rats and mice learn a discrimination habit very slowly, for at first they seem not to be paying attention to the cues. A more efficient technique for studying discrimination learning in rats was devised by Lashley (1930). As shown in Figure 2.4, rats were trained to leap from a platform toward one of two discrimination cards.

Figure 2.4.   Lashley's (1930) technique of studying visual discrimination learning in the rat. *a*. The rat facing two choices. *b*. The correct door falling inward, permitting a safe landing.

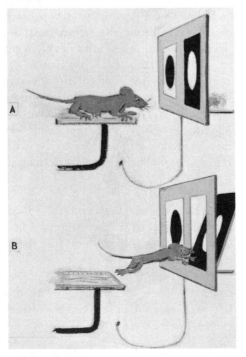

One of the cards—the correct choice—fell back when hit to permit the animal a safe landing on a feeding platform. The other card was locked in place, so that a rat leaping against it fell into a net below. With this technique, rats quickly learned to discriminate visual patterns, relative brightness, or relative size.

Using both the discrimination and the maze techniques, Lashley (1929, 1934, 1944) carried out an extensive series of experiments designed to analyze the role of the cerebral cortex in mediating learned responses. After rats had learned specific habits, they were subjected to various types of experimental injuries to the brain. Over all, Lashley's findings were in direct conflict with established views that learning involves discrete stimulus-response units that are linked by specific neural pathways. He found instead that restricted lesions did not produce specific losses in learned habits but resulted rather in a general retardation of learning ability. The larger the lesion, the greater the retardation observed. The ability to discriminate visual patterns was not destroyed by partial lesions of the visual cortex but only by complete lesions. Any part of the visual projection areas enabled the rats to discriminate visual detail and form. Further, Lashley found that he could cut entirely through the cortical association areas without seriously disturbing learned patterns. His results suggested that the cerebral cortex is organized on a general basis to mediate learned responses—an interpretation that conforms more to gestalt concepts of organized wholes than to conventional learning concepts of specific response units.

Still another phase of discrimination learning research—known as the transposition experiment—has challenged the specificity of stimulus cues utilized in learning. Animals are trained to discriminate between two stimuli and then are tested on a new pair to determine which of the new pair is *equivalent* to the learned positive choice of the original pair. Frequently they respond to the new situation on a relative rather than an absolute basis. Klüver (1933) showed that monkeys trained to choose the heavier or larger of a pair almost always chose the heavier or larger of a new pair, even when the original positive choice was used as the negative choice in the transposition test. Lashley's (1938) studies of form discrimination in rats also emphasized relational factors. Rats trained to discriminate between geometrical forms—triangles, squares, diamonds, and so on—in various orientations and figure-ground relationships apparently based their choices on certain relational properties of the figures rather than on absolute stimulus properties.

Lashley's work was objective and carefully controlled and might have had great impact on American learning psychology, but he never crystallized his experimental findings into a strong theoretical position. The implications of his research—that organized behavior should be conceptualized in terms of relational or differential processes rather than as a chain of specific stimuli and responses linked by discrete neural pathways—were more or less ignored by those at the forefront of learning psychology. Trial-and-error learning, maze learning, and discrimination learn-

ing were interesting but became peripheral, for other techniques and sets of learning data were in vogue.

Conditioned Reflexes

When the problem box, the maze, and the discrimination box were introduced into psychological laboratories, comparative psychology was in its infancy and was almost as mentalistic in its terminology and implications as its parent—the study of the human mind. Such a science had not yet provided a basic substantive demonstration of learning as a biological or physiological process. The technique that was to do this and the learning data that were to define a new course for objective learning theory originated in the laboratory of a Russian physiologist, Pavlov (1927). Now that the conditioned reflex is almost a household word, it is difficult to realize the significance of the first demonstration that overt behavior patterns, including vital reflexes of the organism, can be modified by means of experimentally presented combinations of stimuli.

The first experiments on stimulus conditioning were reported in Russia in 1903 but apparently were unknown in America until 1909 or later (Boring, 1929). They were carried out somewhat as indicated in Figure 2.5. Dogs were used as research subjects and the salivary reflex was chosen as the unit of behavior to be studied. The dog was placed in a stock and presented with a selected stimulus, such as a bell sound, that originally elicited no specific observable response. Food then was presented after a short interval of time and the resulting salivary fluid was collected

Figure 2.5.   Pavlov's (1927) method of sa-livary conditioning. The salivary gland of the animal is inverted so that its secretions can be accumulated externally and measured. The animal is presented with an external stimulus, which causes no measurable salivation; then the sight of food, which produces salivation. After a number of paired presentations, the animal learns to salivate to the first or *con-ditioned* stimulus.

and measured. Following a number of trials of this sort in which the sound always was followed by food, the sound alone became effective in bringing about the salivary response.

The course of this conditioning proc-ess is diagramed in Figure 2.6, which indicates the sound or conditioned stimulus (CS), the food or uncondi-tioned stimulus (UCS), and the con-ditioned response (CR). Before condi-tioning, at the time of the first trial, salivary response to the bell is either nonexistent or variable, and the animal gives the *unconditioned* salivary re-sponse when food is displayed (we have omitted the UCR from the diagram).

Figure 2.6.   The process of classical conditioning. The bell or conditioned stim-ulus (CS) is followed by food, the unconditioned stimulus (UCS), after an interval of 0.2 to 0.5 second. Successive lines represent different trials in a series of twenty-five. At first the bell elicits no salivation, but after successive pairings of CS and UCS, CS gradually becomes effective in inducing salivation. The strength of this conditioned response (CR) builds up gradually, as indicated by the size of the droplets representing salivation.

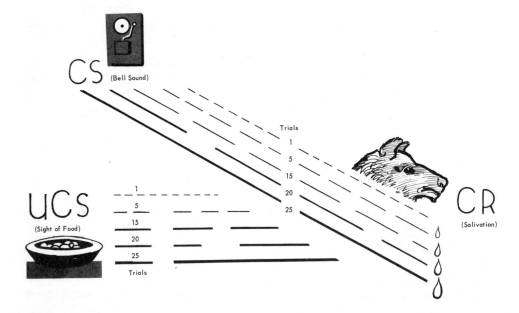

With repeated presentations of the paired stimuli, the conditioned response of salivation to the bell appears and gradually increases in strength. While both UCR and CR are designated as salivation, careful analysis shows that they differ somewhat—perhaps in magnitude or in temporal patterning.

Pavlov carried out many experiments to identify conditions that would affect the formation of a conditioned response or alter such a response after it was formed. He showed how learned reactions of this nature, once set up, would disappear if the conditioned stimulus were presented repeatedly without being followed by the unconditioned stimulus. He called this process experimental extinction. He demonstrated further how other stimulus effects would inhibit learned reactions and how variation in the time relations between CS and UCS would alter the nature of the learning. He found that an interval of 0.2 to 0.5 second between stimuli was optimal for effective conditioning.

The animal conditioning experiments, more than any other single innovation in research methodology, stimulated the shift of modern psychology from a mentalistic to a behavioral orientation. From the 1920s on, many attempts have been made to apply these methods to the analysis of learned behavior in man. Although psychologists describe their experiments on conditioning of somatic responses, such as the knee jerk and the eyelid reflex, as studies in classical Pavlovian conditioning, their findings never have duplicated those of the original studies of salivary conditioning in the dog. Conditioned reactions in man often are variable and unstable, and some subjects may not condition at all.

Those who do acquire the CR likely will do so erratically and will not show a gradual acquisition curve such as Pavlov described. Furthermore, some of the special phenomena of conditioning cannot be demonstrated as clearly or as consistently in human subjects as in dogs.

Pavlov and some of his associates seized upon the conditioning process as a general explanatory concept for behavior organization, and their enthusiasm was shared in this country by many psychologists of *behaviorist* persuasion. Watson (1924), in particular, attempted to interpret all of human behavior in conditioning terms, describing the whole process of early development as a series of conditioning operations imposed upon the infant's limited repertoire of innate reflexes. Some years later Hull (1943) incorporated certain features of conditioning into a general *drive-reduction* theory of learning, based on the assumption that a response is reinforced or strengthened to the extent that it reduces a drive state.

Hull's elaborate system and its implications preoccupied a considerable segment of learning psychology for more than two decades, but is far less influential today than when it was being developed. In fact, it was Hull's own integrity as a scientist that in the end revealed the weaknesses of his system. In attempting to test and to quantify his basic postulates by direct experimentation, he established a number of particular facts about conditioning but made no breakthrough in relating these facts to his sweeping generalizations about human adaptive behavior.

In judging all such systematic attempts to interpret human behavior in conditioning terms, we must not lose sight of the fact that the somatic behavior of man does not condition in the classical sense. Attempts to find evidence that conditioning processes account for the acquisition of skilled motions and language behavior have been entirely unconvincing—if not downright failures. Hull's inferences for a time were logically inviting, but they produced no useful specifications for regulating educationally significant skills in adaptive human situations.

Operant Conditioning

The animal learning technique that has been adopted the most widely and that has had the most influence on general learning theory during the past three decades was invented by Skinner (1938) and became the basis of a systematic theory of behavior and learning. Skinner's original apparatus, which is known generally as a *Skinner box*, was essentially an automated food dispenser for rats. It consisted of little more than an enclosed box with a lever or bar at one end which, when pressed by the rat, automatically released a pellet of food into a food tray. Later Skinner (1948) extended the method to work with pigeons. Both of his arrangements are illustrated in Figure 2.7. In Figure 2.7a, the rat presses a bar to get food, and in Figure 2.7b, the pigeon pecks a disk to get a piece of grain.

A novel feature of Skinner's rat box when it was introduced was the method of recording and measuring behavior. Each press of the lever raised a marking pen one notch on a slowly moving record, so that a cumulative record of responses as a function of time was obtained automatically. For graduate

Figure 2.7.   Skinner's (1938, 1948) techniques of studying operant conditioning. *a.* The *Skinner box* in which a rat presses a lever to get a pellet of food. The apparatus schedules certain times or rates at which responses will deliver the reinforcement. *b.* Pigeon facing the disk that it pecks to get reinforcing bits of grain.

students and young experimentalists accustomed to running rats, cats, or dogs for hundreds or thousands of trials to get their data, this was a great idea. The rat could be put in the box to record its own behavior while the experimenter went about his business. One wonders whether the widespread adoption of Skinner's methods and the promulgation of his views was due in part to the ease with which the data were collected. Possibly learning theory might have taken a different course had someone come up with a different kind of automated technique!

Be that as it may, Skinner's main interest was in the type of behavior that his box permitted. By pressing the lever, the animal secured a desirable effect which reinforced or strengthened the lever-pressing response. Although this situation was arranged quite differently from a classical conditioning experiment, Skinner borrowed some of Pavlov's terminology and described his rats' behavior as *operant* conditioning as distinct from the *respondent* conditioning studied by Pavlov.

The reason for these terms lies in the arrangement and control of stimuli and reinforcement. In classical conditioning, the experimenter controls the presentation of both conditioned and unconditioned stimuli and in the early learning trials presents the second or *reinforcing* stimulus before the animal has given the desired response. In operant conditioning, the response is not elicited by the experimenter directly but is *emitted* by the animal in the course of its behavior. The effective stimulus or pattern of stimuli for the first response is not identified. This situation is very much like Thorndike's trial-and-error learning, although ideally the Skinnerian experimental arrangement is such that the animal stumbles upon the correct response without wasting much time. The important thing is that the response

is instrumental in producing the food reward—that is, the reinforcement is directly contingent upon the bar-pressing response. Inasmuch as this response is not elicited by any known stimulus, Skinner calls it an *operant*, in the sense that the animal is operating on its environment. A response elicited by a known stimulus, as in classical conditioning, is called a *respondent*. An operant is strengthened by positive reinforcement, which might be the attainment of a desirable effect, such as food, or the avoidance of an undesirable effect, such as shock. Elimination of the operant by withholding the reinforcement is known as extinction, as in classical conditioning.

Although experimenters who use this methodology have adopted the terminology of Pavlov, they specify that operant conditioning, in which the animal operates on the environment, is a different kind of learning from classical conditioning, in which the environment, via the experimenter, operates on the animal. One difference sometimes noted is that classic conditioning is *passive* learning, in which the animal stands quietly while the experimenter's stimulus arrangements modify its behavior, while operant conditioning is *active* learning, requiring the animal to make some overt operation that in itself leads to the reward. After drawing the distinction between the two kinds of conditioning, Skinner himself admitted that respondent conditioning probably cannot be demonstrated in "pure" form and, in fact, may not exist. At any rate, the behavior he was interested in and built his theory upon was the kind in which the reinforcement is directly related to the response.

The experimental methodology of operant conditioning has been used extensively to analyze the temporal patterns of unit responses in relation to motivational state and certain other variables. In particular, this method has been used to study the effects of reinforcing only some of the animal's responses in specified patterns or schedules. For example, the animal might receive food after every response, regularly at certain temporal intervals, after one response in ten, or at random intervals. The apparatus in Figure 2.7a is designed for automatic presentation of *partial* reinforcement schedules, known variously as fixed-interval, fixed-ratio, and aperiodic reinforcement. Many studies have been carried out to analyze how different reinforcement patterns affect the strength of the operant—that is, the rate of responding. In general, an animal learns more slowly with partial reinforcement than with 100 percent reinforcement, but the response learned with partial reinforcement is more resistant to extinction. This same general result has been noted for a number of kinds of learned behavior in animals and man, including human gambling, and is assumed to have considerable significance for educational behavior and human behavior in general.

Skinner (1953, 1961b) and some of his colleagues in the operant conditioning research field apply their results on rats and pigeons almost without qualification to human learning, education, and general behavioral adaptation. They say that behavior is molded or organized in sequential patterns of unit responses by the consequences, or reinforcements, following the responses. Some efforts have been made to apply operant procedures of learning to young children and mental patients and, as we shall see in Chapter 10, operant methodology has been construed as theoretical justification for automated teaching-machine instruction. However, it appears to us that analyzing temporal sequences of animal lever-pressings throws little light on the organization of human instrumental and symbolic skills. In fact, we question whether the operant conditioning experiment offers a valid interpretation even of animal behavior. There are no tools in the animal's natural adaptive environment, and its natural reinforcements or incentives rarely are doled out in temporally separated units. Animals, like men, normally organize their behavior according to spatial patterns, and they must find the temporal series of discrete responses in a Skinner box as foreign to their nature as we do.

GENERAL THEORIES OF LEARNING

The experimental methods that we have described, save that of Ebbinghaus, were developed originally for animal research, but they derive their principal significance not from what they reveal about animal behavior but from the fact that they have structured most of the general theories of learning. By a general theory, we mean one that attempts to account for all learning phenomena in both animals and man within one logical, parsimonious system.

In order for stimuli and responses to be organized within one behavior pattern, they must come together in space and in time—that is, they must have some degree of spatial and temporal contiguity. The fact of temporal contiguity has been the starting point of most stimulus-response theories of learning, but they differ as to whether it should be accepted as a causal principle for learning change or should be thought of as just a mechanical arrangement that permits other factors to operate. If one accepts temporal contiguity as causal, one must determine whether any other organizing principle is necessary to explain learning. If one does not accept contiguity as causal, then of course the main effort is to identify the factor or factors that do cause learning to occur. The factor other than contiguity that has been proposed most often is some statement of *effect* or *reinforcement*. Thus a simplified classification of stimulus-response learning theories includes three categories: contiguity-alone theory; reinforcement-alone theory; and contiguity-plus-reinforcement theory, or two-factor theory. The distinction between the second and third types of theory is not always clear inasmuch as some theorists emphasize reinforcement seemingly without making a final decision whether or not to espouse contiguity.

An unfortunate aspect of learning psychology is that stimulus-response theorists almost always have ignored the facts of spatial contiguity or spatial organization in learning change. Those psychologists usually grouped together as *cognitive* theorists have recognized the importance of spatial patterning in structuring learning, but their ideas never have been expressed objectively in stimulus-response terms and thus resist scientific analysis and evaluation. The general theoretical aim of this book is show that it is possible to account for the spatial patterning of behavior

and learning in terms of objectively identifiable stimulus-response mechanisms—the sensory-feedback mechanisms of patterned behavior. However, our ideas about learning do not constitute a parsimonious logical system and are not strictly comparable to the general theories to be discussed here. Our position is more nearly allied with that broad psychological point of view known loosely as *functionalism*, although the self-styled functionalists of today embrace quite a different set of concepts from our own.

Contiguity Theory

Modern contiguity theory is associated closely with the name of Guthrie (1952), who more than any other psychologist was responsible for translating the associationism of the English empiricists into a plausible stimulus-response theory of learning. Whereas the empiricists dealt with the association of ideas, Guthrie gave a strictly behavioristic interpretation of the association of stimuli and responses. His basic law of learning was that a pattern of stimuli that accompanies a movement will on recurrence tend to be followed by that movement. His other main principle was that a learned association between stimuli and response gains its full strength on its first occurrence. If learning occurs at all, it occurs at maximal strength.

Guthrie showed great ingenuity in interpreting all kinds of learning phenomena in terms of his basic assumption of automatic association of contiguous stimuli and responses. To explain the obvious fact that many performances continue to improve with practice, Guthrie distinguished between complete acts which are made up of many movements and the unit responses or movements to which his all-or-none learning principle was meant to apply. To learn an act or skill, each movement in it must be associated with the appropriate stimuli or cues. If the act must be performed under varying conditions, each movement in it must be associated with a number of stimulus patterns. Thus for the total act we see improvement with practice, but each individual association involved in the activity, according to Guthrie, is learned fully in one trial.

Guthrie's theory denies that either drive state or reinforcement is necessary to learning. The function of a reinforcing stimulus or reward following the learned association is to change the stimulus complex and thus to permit the association to be preserved. For example, an animal escaping from a puzzle box preserves the last learned association that it made in the box because the escape changes the situation and permits no further associations to be formed to the effective stimuli. When put in the box again, the animal tends to repeat the *last* response that led to the escape because no more recent associations are interfering with the effective one. Performance is not perfect after one trial only because the cues are complex and the animal's movements are variable, and more than one stimulus-movement association must be learned. The only function of the drive state in learning is to cause the animal or individual to perform certain kinds of movements which then become associated with whatever stimulus patterns occur at the same time.

Experiments on sensory conditioning, or sensory preconditioning, sometimes are cited as evidence that learning does occur according to the contiguity principle without the need for reinforcement. In Brogden's (1939) original experiment, a bell and a light first were presented simultaneously to dogs many times and then one of these stimuli was conditioned to elicit forelimb flexion by being paired with shock. After this training, the other one of the original stimuli also elicited flexion in test trials although it never had been paired with shock. Although it appears that some kind of learned association occurred here without benefit of reinforcement, a determined reinforcement theorist is never at a loss to find some kind of reinforcer at work. Spence (1951), for example, after discussing the implications of the sensory preconditioning experiments concluded, "there remains the possibility that one or the other of the two stimuli is sufficiently intense to produce a mild drive state, and hence for its cessation to produce a reinforcing state of affairs." (This is not necessarily Spence's own interpretation.) The beauty of reinforcement theory is that it is next to impossible to disprove.

Reinforcement Theory

Reinforcement theory in some form or another has been very much in the center of the stage in learning psychology ever since Thorndike (1898) first formulated the law of effect. Thorndike himself was not a rigorous systematist but always placed his main emphasis on the strengthening or weakening of responses according to their effects. His early position was that learning took place in accordance with three laws: readiness, exercise, and effect (Thorndike, 1913–1914). Subordinate to these were five additional principles which seemed to Thorndike important: multiple response (variability of reaction), set or attitude, prepotency of elements, response by analogy, and associative shifting. These various laws or principles came and went in Thorndike's writings, but he gradually developed what was essentially a two-factor theory recognizing learning by selecting and connecting, governed by the effect; and learning by associative shifting, governed by contiguity (Thorndike, 1932).

Skinner (1938) also proposed what amounted originally to a two-factor theory by recognizing respondent and operant conditioning. He speculated that pure classical conditioning dependent on contiguity might be limited to autonomic responses while skeletal behavior follows the laws of instrumental or operant conditioning. Inasmuch as his entire interest has been centered on this latter kind of learning—in which the strength of an operant is increased by the occurrence of a reinforcing stimulus directly contingent upon the operant—his position appears to be equivalent to reinforcement-alone theory.

Hull (1943) and his adherents maintained persistently that learning requires the occurrence of reinforcement, and that temporal contiguity in and of itself is not enough to produce learning. There have been a number of efforts to devise critical experiments to prove or disprove this position, so far to no avail. As we indicated above in connection with the sensory preconditioning experiments, it seems impossible to disprove the action of reinforcement, at least to the satisfaction of a reinforcement theorist. Hull postulated an elaborate system of secondary reinforcers which derive their

original potency from their association with primary drives and primary reinforcers. In time, secondary reinforcers may become divorced from the primary drive so that they can strengthen responses without actually reducing drives. This position is flexible enough to allow the reinforcement interpretation in almost any kind of behavior.

Another out for reinforcement theorists is to assert that such events as perception, exploration, curiosity, and the like are motivated by specific drives that are satisfied by the behavior. Thus a rat in a maze may be reinforced by its own exploratory activity. A monkey in a cage may learn to open a peephole because it is reinforced by being able to look out. Woodworth (1947) even postulated that perceptual learning is motivated by "a direct, inherent, motive which might be called the will to perceive," so that the individual or animal is reinforced by attaining a clear perception. If this kind of flexibility of interpretation is permitted, reinforcement theory probably never can be put to a critical experimental test. The question is whether such a poorly defined concept as reinforcement can be taken seriously as a rigorous scientific principle or whether it must remain at the descriptive level.

One of the early proponents of Hull's reinforcement-alone theory revised his views to include contiguity conditioning as a second type of learning. Mowrer (1951) felt that much emotional learning, such as conditioned fear, is a result of simple contiguity conditioning without necessarily involving reinforcement through drive-reduction. Later Mowrer (1960) revised his theory still further and proposed that the consequences of instrumental acts affect future responses because they evoke such positive affective states as hope or such negative states as fear. In his revised theory, Mowrer stated that all learning is sign learning —or conditioning by contiguity—and instrumental learning is just a special case. The *two-factor* designation was retained to indicate that there are two kinds of reinforcement, drive decrement (reward) and drive increment (punishment).

Mowrer's writings exemplify an important trend in learning theorizing in the past quarter century. Caught in the upsurge of abnormalistic-clinical psychology, especially in the years since World War II, many learning theorists have been more concerned with interpreting emotional learning—the development of anxieties, neuroses, psychoses, and other forms of disordered behavior—than in analyzing how individuals learn their characteristically human verbal, symbolic, and perceptual-motor skills.

Cognitive Theory

The great weakness of S-R learning theories, either the contiguity, reinforcement, or two-factor variety, is that they have little to say about how an individual acquires his perceptual knowledge of the world about him and is able to conform with his movements to the patterns that he perceives. Temporal contiguity and reinforcement would seem to be at best very haphazard arrangements for teaching a person all the myriad details about how the world with its objects and events is structured, and yet people acquire just such detailed knowledge. Furthermore, most perceptual knowledge is reasonably accurate, for it enables the individual to exercise precise control over his own movements in relation to the environment and over objects, events, and other people in that environment. The notion that this accurate, usable perceptual-motor knowledge is acquired as a temporal series of associations—either as a result of chance contiguity or of the effects of discrete reinforcements—strains one's credulity.

Many S-R learning theorists recognize that perception is a problem that cannot be ignored. Hilgard (1956), for example, stated, "The problem of perceptual discrimination is a central one for learning theory." However, he offered no other approach to analyzing the problem than to cast it in the familiar drive-motivation-reinforcement mold of conventional S-R learning theory. Describing the perceptual factor in such terms as the *goals* of perceptual stability and definiteness, and the *motive* of curiosity, Hilgard drew the analogy that seems to follows inevitably on this line of thinking: "The organism seeks a perceptually stable environment in a fashion somewhat parallel to that in which it seeks an internally stable environment. There is a kind of environmental homeostasis parallel to physiological homeostasis."

If the motivation of behavior is thought of as conforming to the principle of homeostasis, then it follows that adaptation is a matter of reducing drives or satisfying motives. This principle, which is accepted almost universally by psychologists (for a note of caution, see Davis, 1958), implies that the organism is always seeking equilibrium. In our opinion, the homeostatic principle exactly reverses the true state of affairs in behavior, for the living organism or individual is constructed to be active, not to achieve equilibrium. One of the basic movement mechanisms of the body, the tremor caused by reciprocal innervation of opposing muscle groups, has as one of its functions the continuous activation of the sense organs. A receptor such as the eye when it is artificially fixated on a stimulus pattern quickly adapts to the unchanging pattern and in effect becomes nonfunctional (Riggs *et al.*, 1953). Normal tremor activity plus periodic *flick* movements are enough to keep the eyes functional even though there are no gross movements of the body or of the visual environment. Maintaining activity might be called the basic form of behavior motivation, but it is not a drive that can be reduced toward a steady state, for the activity goes on.

The dynamic quality of perceptual-motor behavior was recognized first by gestalt psychologists, although their emphasis was on perception, not motion. Köhler (1929), Koffka (1935), and other gestalt theorists rejected associationism in both perceptual and learning theory. They maintained and planned experiments to demonstrate that perception is not made up of a bundle of discrete sensations, nor is learning a process of linking together discrete associations. Learning is a dynamic restructuring of the individual's perceptions of a problem situation leading to understanding and insightful solutions. Gestalt learning theory is in direct opposition to the blind, automatic associationism that is implied in most S-R learning theory. It emphasizes cognitive understanding of relationships in the field of the observer—awareness of how means lead to consequences.

Tolman's (1932) cognitive theory of learning had much in common with classical gestalt theory, although he called himself a behaviorist and based his analyses on the overt behavior of animals—principally of rats in mazes. Tolman thought of learning not as the linking of movements to stimuli, but as the acquiring of cognitive knowledge of relationships in the behavior field. He thought that rats in a maze learned their way about in it by learning "what leads to what," not by acquiring a fixed sequence of movements from start to goal. He felt that this learning could occur without any specific motivation or reinforcement but just as a result of experience in the maze.

Cognitive theories of learning have served the very useful purpose of emphasizing many characteristics of behavior that are handled poorly by S-R theorists. They emphasize the importance of the perceptual component of behavior, and the fact that perceptual patterns are organized into meaningful wholes. They emphasize the spatial patterning of the individual's interactions with his environment. They emphasize learning situations in which meaningful organization of the subject matter enables the individual to take insightful short-cuts to the solution, thus elevating the learning process above the level of blind associationism. Their weakness is that they have not defined their perceptions, cognitions, and organizational processes in objective terms and thus are not able to say how the perceptual or cognitive patterns influence subsequent behavior.

DIMENSIONAL ANALYSES
OF HUMAN LEARNING

Although a large segment of learning science has focused its efforts on the definition and evaluation of general theories of learning, another important segment has been less concerned with identifying the basic nature of the learning process than in analyzing how specific kinds of learning are affected by specific variables. This is essentially the dimensional approach to learning research and is representative of the functionalist point of view in psychology. A part of the functionalist tradition is that our understanding of behavior is still so incomplete that rigid explanatory systems are suspect. Thus research on specific problems is preferred to any involvement in general theoretical issues. This approach has been responsible for much of our detailed knowledge about how learning varies as a function of many different environmental, behavioral, and individual variables.

The vast amount of research literature that falls within the general *dimensional analyses of learning* category is difficult to classify and even more difficult to summarize. For our present purposes, we shall review some of the main research trends that are relevant to our discussion.

Principles of Learning Economy

Many factors have been shown experimentally to affect the rate of learning. Some of these are individual factors —age, sex, intelligence, level of motivation, intent of the learner, set, and so on. Some factors have to do with the type of material to be learned—whether it is meaningful or nonmeaningful, verbal or motor skill, serial items or paired associates, composed of similar or dissimilar items. A third group, situational factors, have to do with the general arrangements for practicing the material to be learned. These often are discussed as general rules of learning economy.

One of the rules that dates from Ebbinghaus (1913) is that a series of short practice sessions is more efficient than the same amount of practice in one continuous session. This rule apparently is valid for the sort of rote verbal learning used in laboratory experiments and for simple motor skills, although the optimal interval between practice sessions has varied from one experiment to another. However, there are some situations that definitely favor massed practice over short-session practice. When a warm-up is required for a learner to perform a task efficiently, distributed practice may be less efficient because it wastes time in repeated adjustment periods (Hovland, 1951). Ericksen (1942) has stressed the value of a massed attack in a problem situation where a variable approach leads to a more rapid solution. Distributed practice tends to produce stereotyped behavior. Most importantly, when the task to be learned is complex or composed of several differing parts, there is no general rule about the most efficient practice schedule. A series of studies reviewed by Lumsdaine (1961) attempted to determine optimal teaching sequences for technical skills but found contradictory and ambiguous results.

The experiments just mentioned also

are relevant to another practice factor— that of whole versus part learning. The earliest studies comparing the learning of whole sequences with the learning of parts that later were combined into wholes seemed to favor wholes, but it was not long before other studies produced contradictory results. The relative advantage depends on the type of material being learned, its complexity, its intrinsic organization, and other factors. In complex tasks, it sometimes is advantageous to practice parts first and then to progress to practicing the whole. There are no universal rules for the sequencing and organization of practice.

A principle that appears to be definitely established is that active participation of the learner in the task facilitates learning. The earliest experiments in this area established the advantages of reciting a lesson before mastery instead of just rereading it. In learning verbal sequences, it is advantageous for the learner to try to anticipate the next item. We shall analyze the participation variable in more detail later in relation to research on actual teaching and training techniques. Since the introduction of teaching machines and teaching programs, there has been a great deal of interest in the relative advantages of overt and covert participation by the learner. Here again there is no universal rule, for covert responses often are just as effective as overt and sometimes are more efficient.

Related to the participation variable is that of learner *set*. Since the early day of this century, functionalist psychology has recognized that the set or intention of the individual can affect his line of thought, his performance, and his course of learning. Set has several implications as it is ordinarily used in psychology. It implies the readiness of the individual to perform, and it also implies directional orientation; that is, the individual is set to perform in a certain way. Sometimes the term is given motivational overtones which add nothing to the clarity of the concept.

The learner's set facilitates learning when it prepares him to respond in the appropriate way. It is disadvantageous when it is not oriented adequately toward the learning task. For example, if the learner does not understand the task or misinterprets the instructions, he may be prepared to respond in the wrong way. Or if he is oriented toward the clock on the wall or toward what he is going to do after class, his set is not facilitating the learning. Thus we think of set as one level of participation. The learner may be going through the motions of the task—he may be doing sums, writing words, or reading his lesson—but he is not participating fully unless all of his motion systems are being used in an integrated manner for the most efficient performance.

Full participation and an efficiently integrated performance cannot always be assured by simply instructing the learner or by motivating him to "do his best." In complex tasks, especially in complicated machine skills, the learner may not understand the nature of the integrated movements he is to perform. Sometimes even the teacher or experimenter does not understand initially and must use the procedures of *task analysis* and apply other human engineering principles to structure efficient performance in the learner.

Knowledge of Results

One principle of learning economy that is accepted without question is that learning is facilitated by *knowledge of results*. The interpretation of the nature of this factor is open to some difference of opinion, although most writers describe it as a motivational factor.

The interpretation of Woodworth and Schlosberg (1954) exemplifies the conventional treatment of knowledge of results while also revealing some of the ambiguities of the motivational approach. These authors started by suggesting that sensory feedback from one's own movements provides information that serves a *directive* or *corrective* function. However, they placed more emphasis on the *incentive* value of such knowledge of results and described a number of experiments where signals used to indicate Right or Wrong or some other measure of success improved performance and learning. Even if a disagreeable or punishing signal such as shock is used to indicate Right, learning proceeds just as efficiently as if a neutral signal or simply the word Right is used. The knowledge that one is performing correctly is assumed to reinforce the response even though punishment accompanies the knowledge.

In our opinion, the interpretation of such experiments would be less difficult (except for a reinforcement theorist!) if one deemphasized the *incentive* function of knowledge of results and emphasized instead the directive and corrective function of sensory feedback. Here again, the usual interpretation of a learning variable in relation to simple tasks breaks down when it is applied to more complicated forms of learning than

are used ordinarily in laboratory experiments. In learning complicated machine skills, the *knowledge of results* that is needed by a learner is not just a signal for Right or Wrong but immediate sensory feedback by means of which he can judge the effect of his movements. We shall consider the relationship between sensory feedback and knowledge of results in Chapter 8.

Transfer and Interference

Some of the most significant problems of learning behavior are those related to the interaction effects between different learning tasks. Practice on one task not only can affect the learning of a new task, it also can affect the degree of retention of a prior learned task. We speak of positive or negative transfer when we measure the influence of prior learning on new learning. Possibly the first formal learning experiment in America was a transfer experiment carried out by William James (1890). When we measure the influence of new learning on the retention of prior learning, the effect is known as reproduction facilitation or reproductive interference (retroactive interference). We shall consider some of the problems related to transfer and interference in Chapter 16.

Serial Verbal Learning

Learning research in the Ebbinghaus tradition usually is concerned with the learning of a series of discrete verbal responses. This type of experiment has revealed a special learning phenomenon known as the *serial position effect*, which refers to the fact that items in a series are not mastered at the same speed. Items toward the beginning and end of the list are learned first, followed by the middle items. Hull *et al.* (1940) tried to explain this effect in terms of excitatory and inhibitory tendencies—concepts drawn from Pavlov—but their theory of rote learning has had very little effect on subsequent learning research (Irion, 1959).

In our opinion, the serial learning effect is related to the primary spatial organization of behavior. We believe that a temporal series of discrete responses is remembered or internalized by the learner by being represented in spatial terms. When a serial list of nonsense syllables is thought of as a spatial instead of as a temporal pattern, one can assume that the syllables at the beginning and end stand out more sharply because of contour or boundary effects, whereas the ones in the middle are less sharply differentiated and thus are more difficult to learn. This interpretation sounds very much like gestalt psychology, but it also is similar to a discussion by Woodworth and Schlosberg (1954). These authors suggested that the serial position curve could be predicted by assuming that a learner does not learn *sequences* of items, but rather learns each item according to its *position* in the whole pattern.

Perceptual-Motor Skills

Research on motor skill learning often deals with behavior similar to or identical with the skills used in human work, education, and recreation. The pioneering work of Bryan and Harter (1899) was on the learning of telegraphy, and other studies have been made of typewriting, digit-symbol substitution, simple industrial skills, and such athletic skills as ball tossing, dart throwing, and archery. During and since

World War II, the applied study of motor skills has expanded enormously to include many kinds of machine operations.

The period from the late 1920s to the early 1940s might be called the pursuit-rotor era of the study of motor skill. A target-following task could be made from a phonograph turntable, as shown in Figure 2.8a. The subject tried to maintain contact with a target on the rotating disk while his total contact time was recorded. In time, the pursuit rotor was elaborated to provide a bimanual tracking task, as shown in Figure 2.8b, and all of the learning functions that had been studied with the one-handed

Figure 2.8.   The pursuit rotor used to study perceptual-motor skill learning. *a*. One-handed pursuit rotor. *b*. Bimanual pursuit rotor.

pursuit rotor could be repeated with the two-handed apparatus.

Research on motor skills has had little or no impact on the theoretical formulations of learning psychologists, but it has pointed up weaknesses in conventional theory by calling attention to the effects of behavior organization on the course of learning. Bryan and Harter's original learning curves were characterized by a *plateau*, a temporary lag in improvement which was followed by a spurt in improvement. Although some later workers failed to find plateaus, these effects have occurred often enough in learning experiments to be accepted as valid. Bryan and Harter suggested that the plateau occurred when the learner was making a transition to a higher order of habits. Others have interpreted the effect as motivational. Davis's (1935) observation that plateaus occur more frequently in complex skills than in simple tasks lends support to the idea that a shift in movement organization or integration may permit the learner to go on to a higher level of performance efficiency. At any rate, most motor skills cannot be characterized as temporal sequences of discrete responses; rather they are multidimensional behavior patterns which are not well conceptualized by conventional learning models.

Prior to World War II, few psychologists had studied the basic organization and regulation of perceptual-motor behavior, and most studies of skills were designed to analyze the effects of conventional learning variables. The inadequacies of this approach quickly became apparent when psychologists were called upon to design trainers and training programs for the complicated machine skills needed in military operations. Faced with human engineering problems beyond the scope of their tradition, these workers developed new concepts and methods of analysis. However, conventional learning theory was abandoned by only a few and survives in military research programs as well as in academic laboratories. A statement made by Nissen (1954) many years after the war, which would have been appropriate any time during the present century, testifies to the reluctance of learning psychology to shift its grounds. Said Nissen, "before investing all our time and effort in problems of learning or behavior modification, we should determine carefully what the behavior is before it is modified."

COGNITIVE LEARNING

Psychology has made little headway in analyzing the kind of learning behavior that is most distinctively human —that known as cognitive behavior and thought. Here even more than in other areas of learning research we are dealing with processes that are hidden from view, the nature of which is undetermined. At one time there was considerable interest in devising experimental tests of the motor theory of thinking, to determine whether thinking does in fact consist of minimal muscular responses. Jacobsen's (1932) recordings of electrical activity in the appropriate muscles of subjects who were thinking about specific activities and Max's (1935, 1937) recordings showing that deaf-mutes who use their hands for "speaking" also use them implicitly during thinking far more than hearing subjects —these studies and others demonstrated that implicit responses are correlated with thinking at least part of the time, and there the matter rests.

Although Mach (1905) established the objective point of view about cognition and described thought as an *experiment*, the first objective studies of the thought processes can be compared to Thorndike's first attempts to analyze animal learning—as studies in problem solving. As a matter of fact, the term *trial and error* had been used by Bain (1879) to describe creative or inventive thinking many years before it was applied to animal behavior.

Problem Solving

Experiments on cognitive problem solving have been designed to analyze the course of behavior in reasoning, transfer and blocking between different types of problems, habits and individual differences in thinking, and the motives and goals of thinking. In Ruger's (1910) early study, subjects were given mechanical puzzles and asked to try to solve them without overt manipulation. They found this very difficult, and even after they thought they had discovered the effective principle, they often encountered difficulties in trying to carry it out. Their implicit trial and error usually needed checking and support from overt trial and error, or manipulation.

The value of exploratory trials has been noted in more abstract or symbolic problem situations as well. Often the subject is unaware of the processes by which a solution is obtained or at least cannot explain verbally his course of action. Heidbreder (1924) asked subjects to discover general rules for marking geometrical figures. When completely at a loss, they would resort to

seemingly random responses and somehow arrive at the solutions. Gestalt psychologists tend to deplore the use of trial and error as blind, inefficient behavior, but even Wertheimer (1945), the founder of the gestalt school, described such exploratory procedures as examining parts of the whole, shifting the point of view, and investigating false leads. All analyses of problem solving indicate the importance of a flexible approach (Luchins, 1942) and an open mind to novel solutions, which may entail a novel use for familiar objects and materials (Adamson, 1952; Maier, 1931).

The problem-solving experiment has been extended by social psychologists to explore the effects of group factors and social pressure on thinking and decision making. Some of these studies have developed special communicative procedures to restrict the flow of information among members of a group in order to simulate organizational channels of communication and their effects on decisions.

Another important development is the use of electronic computers to study the rational manipulations performed by man with symbolic systems. Various aspects of human thinking, decision making, and problem solving are explored by simulating the symbolic processes involved with computer programs.

Developmental Analysis of Thought

There has been a great deal of interest throughout the history of comparative psychology in determining the extent to which animals use symbolic behavior or can be said to think. This area is interesting and important in its own right but throws little light on the organization of human cognitive processes because of the vast gap that lies between the cognitive abilities of man and those of his closest primate relatives. Symbolism apparently originates phylogenetically in such behaviors as postural sets and orienting responses, and subhuman animals seem unable to "escape" from their immediate spatial environment by the use of symbolism.

Studies of the ontogenetic development of thought provide far more insight than does animal research into the nature of symbolic and cognitive behavior. This type of study originated with the work of Piaget (1928), who was interested in tracing the development of human thought processes during the early years of life. Using observational methods, Piaget described the emergence of successive stages or levels of thought proceeding from ego-centered thinking in the young child to the logical thinking and formal patterns of thought in mature individuals. Piaget (1957) has described the development in very young children of such concepts as the reality of objects, space, causality, and velocity. He found that infants have a certain built-in knowledge of spatial relationships centered on their own bodies and only gradually respond to other objects as having independent existence.

According to Vinacke (1951), who observed the appearance of different types of thought concepts in children, development of thinking follows the general course pictured in Figure 2.9. He observed that concrete concepts of form develop before the age of four, those of magnitude and time, somewhat later, and those of cause and effect and interaction typically between the ages

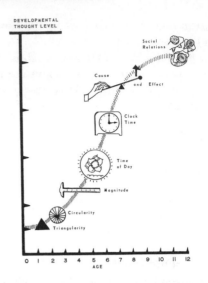

Figure 2.9.   The development of concepts in children according to Vinacke (1951). (Based on Smith and Smith. *The behavior of man: introduction to psychology.* New York: Holt, Rinehart and Winston, 1958.)

of nine and twelve. Both Vinacke's and Piaget's work emphasizes the contribution of maturational processes to the organization of cognitive behavior.

Studies (Chard and Schwartz, 1947; Heidbreder, 1946) of concept formation in adults have revealed that the development of concepts in experimental situations is similar in some respects to the ontogenetic process outlined by Vinacke. When subjects are required to abstract the common characteristic of varying patterns, object concepts are evolved first, spatial concepts next, and numerical concepts last.

One of our interests in analyzing the evolutionary development of learning behavior in prehistoric and ancient man is in searching for clues that reveal the gradual development of various levels of human thought. There are reasons to believe that prehistoric man thought in spatial terms and had only the dimmest awareness of historical time and temporal causality. Only with the development of written language did he gain adequate tools to handle temporal events and relationships.

LEARNING PSYCHOLOGY AND EDUCATION

In the century since Helmholtz focused the attention of the infant science of psychology on learning as a principle of behavior organization, there have been many thousands of learning experiments and theoretical discussions of the learning process published in the psychological literature. Yet all of this interest and activity on the part of psychologists has produced singularly little that is relevant to the applied problems of human education and training. Less than a decade ago, Bugelski (1956) observed in a masterpiece of understatement, "Learning psychologists have not been very active in applying their theoretical principles to practical problems." Even when a sustained effort was made to analyze the implications of learning research and learning theory for education, the results were disappointing. In a book published during the 1950s, Thorpe and Schmuller (1954) analyzed nine theoretical approaches to learning and tried to derive the implications of each for education. In the end, in Bugelski's (1956) words, they "managed to salvage or discover in current learning theory" the following five practical principles of learning:

1. "Learning proceeds most effectively and tends to be most permanent when the learner is motivated, that is, when he has a stake, as it were, in the activity being undertaken."

2. ". . . learning proceeds most rapidly and tends to be most permanent when the activity involved is geared to the learner's physical and intellectual ability to perform that activity."

3. "Learning proceeds most effectively and tends to be most permanent when the learner is provided with the opportunity of perceiving meaningful relationships among the elements of the goal toward which he is working."

4. "Learning goes forward with relatively greater effectiveness when the learner is provided with some criterion for indicating specifically what progress he is making."

5. "Learning is facilitated when it goes forward under conditions in which the learner also experiences satisfactory personality adjustment and social growth."

There are two things to be noted about this list of principles. The first is only too obvious, that they are of little immediate practical value to the teacher or educator in designing classroom procedures and techniques. The second is that these so-called principles of learning, except for one or possibly two, are concerned not with the learning process as studied by conventional learning psychologists but with other aspects of behavior organization. The first principle acknowledges the necessity of motivation. It might be construed to mean that learning requires reinforcement, but it does not say so specifically. The second principle recognizes that whatever learning occurs can only be superimposed, as it were, on the individual's normal developmental patterns of behavior. The third and fifth principles state the importance of organized patterns of perceptual-motor and symbolic behavior in the operational and social environments. Only gestalt psychology has stressed such organizational patterns as determinants of learning. The fourth can be said to deal with learning as studied by conventional learning psychologists. As the principle of knowledge of results, it has been known by both psychologists and educators for many years.

Since these principles were formulated, there has been a flurry of interdisciplinary activity involving academic psychologists in the applied problems of education. In the first major foray of learning psychology into the educational arena, a group of reinforcement theorists of Skinnerian persuasion introduced the teaching machine and programed learning into American classrooms. This was a little bit like carrying coals to Newcastle, inasmuch as the first automated teaching devices had been devised and tested some years before by an educational psychologist, Pressey (1926, 1927, 1932), but was heralded widely as a significant contribution of basic learning science to the applied learning field.

The final effects of the programed learning movement cannot yet be assessed, but it appears that enough opposition to the Skinnerian approach has been aroused to stimulate a countermovement among both psychologists and educators. A number of psychologists who find Skinner's (1953, 1961b) point of view about the learning process inadequate are emphasizing the reinforcing power of exploratory activity which serves the functions of conveying information or simply of diverting the organism or individual. Berlyne (1960) has developed ideas such as these at great length. It seems clear that the concept of external reinforcement will have to be revised to make allowance for the many perceptual and intellectual activities that appear to be intrinsically motivated. Among educators, opposition to the rigid, authoritarian regime imposed by teaching programs is stimulating investigations into alternate techniques that will encourage inquiry and self-discovery among students rather than passive acceptance of a programer's statements (Kersh, 1962; Suchman, 1961).

The surprising thing about the Skinnerian approach to automated learning is not that it has suffered major setbacks but that it enjoyed widespread approval and apparent success for as long as it did. Skinner's principles about reinforcement-regulated learning were derived from a very limited type of research on rats and pigeons. He himself made no effort to adjust his theory to fit other types of learning data, for example, from maze learning or discrimination learning research, but ignored inconsistencies and contradictions that have troubled other theorists such as Thorndike and Hull. Yet he showed no hesitancy in trying to apply his operant conditioning concepts to the whole complicated area of human education. Even Lloyd Morgan could not have anticipated such parsimony!

The disturbing thing about all S-R learning theories is that each fits some kinds of learning data but not all kinds. The only theorist who made a sustained effort to encompass all kinds of experimental data into one systematic theory was Hull, and he bogged down in trivialities. In our opinion, we never will have more than a superficial understanding of learning until we shift the emphasis of learning research to the design of the behaving system.

SUMMARY

1. Modern learning theory of behavior organization originated with Helmholtz's empirical theory of perception. This attempt to account for the flexibility of behavior established learning as the central area of psychological research.

2. Ebbinghaus launched the experimental study of learning by conceiving of the idea of using nonsense syllables in some of his studies of the many phenomena of serial learning and retention. His methods still are used in studies of rote learning.

3. Thorndike's research on trial-and-error learning introduced the concept of reinforcement into learning theory in the form of the law of effect.

4. Small used mazes to study rat behavior because they suggested the rat's natural habitat. Maze studies emphasize the spatial organization of behavior and call attention to exploratory behavior with or without specific rewards. Tolman's cognitive theory is based principally on learning data from maze studies.

5. Animal discrimination studies show that animals often respond on the basis of relational factors rather than according to absolute stimulus dimensions. Lashley's neural studies also indicated that learning does not involve specific neural connections, for if limited specific pathways or areas in the cortex are destroyed, other areas take over their functions.

6. Pavlov's studies of conditioned responses in dogs represented the beginnings of systematic objective S-R theory of learning. Later studies showed that somatic conditioning in human subjects is not comparable to that demonstrated by Pavlov in dogs, but the conditioning model still is used by some psychologists to describe human learning. Hull combined conditioning and reinforcement concepts in his drive-reduction theory of learning.

7. The concept of reinforcement as a basic determinant of learning is indicated both by Thorndike's law of effect and Hull's drive-reduction theory, but was emphasized more explicitly by Skinner's studies of operant conditioning. The instrumental learning situation in which responses produce specific reinforcements has been widely used to analyze the effects of different schedules of reinforcements and other variables on rate of response, rate of learning, and rate of extinction. The results have been extended to interpretations of all human learning, and serve as a theoretical basis for automated teaching-machine instruction.

8. General S-R theories of learning can be classified roughly as contiguity-alone, reinforcement-alone, and two-factor theories. Only the cognitive theorists emphasize spatial organization of behavior.

9. Guthrie is the main exponent of contiguity theory. He assumed that learning occurs automatically when stimuli and movements occur simultaneously, and that the association attains its full strength on first occurrence.

10. The theoretical postulate that re-

inforcement is necessary for learning is very difficult to test experimentally because reinforcement theorists always can find some effect that they assume is reinforcing. For example, reduction in intensity of stimuli, exploration, curiosity, and so forth, are said to be reinforcing.

11. Mowrer's revised two-factor theory assumes that all learning is sign learning that occurs by contiguous conditioning but that there are two kinds of reinforcement—drive decrement and drive increment. In this theory, effects are mediated by negative or positive affective states—fear and hope.

12. Cognitive theory emphasizes the dynamic quality of behavior and thus offers a way out of the homeostatic concepts that are used by S-R theorists. Gestalt theorists and Tolman postulated that learning occurs as a result of perceptual and cognitive understanding of significant relationships in the behavior field. However, their concepts were not stated in objective terms.

13. Dimensional analyses of learning have in general ignored general theory to concentrate on analyzing the effects of many different variables on learning and memory.

14. Principles of learning economy, including short practice sessions as opposed to massed practice and whole over part learning, are valid in some situations but do not always hold, especially in complex tasks.

15. Active participation by the learner, including an advantageous learning set, facilitates learning.

16. Knowledge of results is accepted universally as a positive aid in learning. It is usually interpreted as a motiva-

tional factor but is a more generally valid principle if it is understood as directive and corrective feedback.

17. Transfer and interference effects indicate interactions between different learning tasks.

18. The serial position effect has been interpreted by Hull et al. as a function of excitatory and inhibitory tendencies set up between units in a series. The differential rates at which serial units are learned also can be interpreted as due to their relative positions in a total pattern. Those units near the outer boundaries are learned first.

19. Studies of perceptual-motor skills have called attention to the multidimensional nature of patterned behavior and the dependence of behavior control on maturational development. In World War II, training research focused interest on design factors in behavior organization.

20. Objective studies of cognitive problem solving emphasize the value of exploratory trials and a flexible approach.

21. Children develop concepts of form first, then magnitude, time, cause and effect, and interaction. Experimental concept formation in adults follows roughly the same course, and there are indications that a similar developmental course occurred in human evolution.

22. Learning theorists offered little to the applied fields of education until Skinner promoted teaching machines as an educational application of basic reinforcement theory. Considerable opposition to Skinnerian principles has developed among psychologists and educators.

CHAPTER
3

Evolution of Human Learning: Nonverbal Communication

In the previous chapter, we indicated how each of the methods used to study learning has produced a different kind of learning data. Each method, in effect, has structured a specialized kind of learning which can be related to the other kinds in only the most general terms. In contrast to this diversity in learning data, however, we see sustained efforts on the part of most learning theorists to reduce all learning to a single systematic model. Although these efforts have occupied some of the most analytic minds in psychology throughout the present century, there has been no apparent progress toward unification of the divergent views.

We do not venture to predict whether or not learning theory ever will achieve its Holy Grail, but we do feel, in common with a number of other behavior scientists, that the search has led a large segment of psychology into a kind of never-never land of precisely defined variables that never seem to occur in pure form outside the laboratory.

Meanwhile we are inclined to accept the evidence from learning research at face value as indicating that there are different kinds of learning, at least in the operational sense, and that they are structured by the learning situation. It follows that we understand very little about meaningful human learning from analyzing animal research, inasmuch as human situations incorporate significant features that play little or no role in animal learning. The two most significant features of human learning are these: that it involves skill in the use of tools, instruments, and machines for environmental control, and that it involves facility in symbolic forms of behavior that evolved originally for communicative purposes.

EVOLUTION OF SYMBOLIC CONTROL

The differences between animal and human behavior organization and learning are due to changes that have been occurring progressively during the past half million or so years. Although the significant stages are not subject to experimental investigation, there is a growing body of evidence from anthropological and archaeological analyses that supports us in some definite psychological conclusions. We look upon the individual learner as a control system and interpret the progressive changes in human learning as an elaboration of man's abilities to exercise symbolic control over himself and over other people and environmental events. The changes in nonverbal and verbal communication during the course of man's existence represent systematic expansion of symbolic control of different aspects of the physical and social environment. In developing and refining expressive movements, expressive vocalization, spoken language, writing, economic and quantitative communication, machine communication, and electronic communication, man has achieved specialized forms of control over different levels of organization of his man-made environment.

Concepts of Behavior Organization

Our analysis of the forms and levels of learned symbolic control is based on a number of postulates about behavior organization. Ours is essentially a motor theory of behavior: we believe that all psychological phenomena, including perception and thought, involve complete stimulus-response circuits. Our theoretical position thus can be classed as stimulus-response psychology, but we make the further assumption that the basic principle of behavior organization is a feedback principle. We assume that behavior involves continuous feedback processes by means of which the individual maintains control of his movements in relation to the environment.

A functioning organism always is behaving—that is, it always is responding and thereby is stimulating itself by means of feedback. Even during periods such as sleep, when exteroceptive responsiveness is at a low level, postural positions are maintained by feedback loops involving kinesthetic and tactual receptors. During active states, behavior is organized to a greater extent by feedback from the distance receptors, particularly visual feedback. As we have said earlier, one of the basic functions of the movement systems is to keep the receptors sensitive by continuously changing their pattern of stimulation. A general implication of the feedback principle of behavior organization is that specific external changes in the stimulation pattern or discrete external stimuli should not be thought of as initiating responses but simply as modifying the nature, directional characteristics, or other organizational features of the continuous behavior-in-progress that is being maintained by sensory feedback.

An important feature of our general theory of behavior organization is that responses are multidimensional. They consist of several different kinds of movement components which are controlled differentially even though they also are integrated in normal behavior patterning. There are *postural* movements that support and position the body in space; *transport* movements that propel the body, limbs, or extremities from one point in space to another (or, in the case of the speech musculature, propel the syllable pulses); and *manipulative* or articulative movements by means of which the hands, feet, eyes, and speech apparatus make the fine adjustments that are superimposed upon the larger postural and transport movements.

It is impossible to understand or

analyze the organization of highly complicated human skills, including symbolic skills, except in the context of multidimensionality. Human behavior has changed most significantly in its manipulative or articulative components, but these finer skilled movements cannot be performed except as they are supported by the larger movement components which maintain orientation and attention and establish the over-all response pattern within which the skill is executed. We believe this to be no less true of the implicit responses known as thinking than of overt psychomotor skills.

Basic to our entire theory is the assumption that behavior is primarily space-organized—that responses are structured according to spatial patterns of stimulation. By means of his continuous feedback information, the individual adjusts his movements to conform to spatial patterns. The significance of this concept with respect to learning theory is that we reject the idea of sequentially linked stimulus-response chains—that is, of time-coded behavior —that is postulated or implied by conventional stimulus-response theories. To be sure, responses follow each other in time, but we believe that a temporal pattern is mediated in all cases by movement-produced changes in the spatial patterning of stimulation on the sensory surfaces. That is, we do not believe that one response in a learned habit automatically triggers the next but that at each moment the individual reacts to the stimulus patterns as they have been defined by his own previous responses to the environment.

It always has been difficult to conceptualize the learning of a complicated response pattern in terms of conventional notions of response sequences linked in time. One problem is that there are different kinds of responses going on simultaneously in a multidimensional motion pattern. Another problem is that a so-called learned response may consist of quite different movements at different times. (As an example, consider the rat that can walk, run, swim, or limp to the goal box in a maze.) Our theory of space-organized behavior assumes that the individual's highly refined abilities to adjust his movements to environmental patterns develop independently of specific learning. Through the processes of maturation, he acquires feedback-control mechanisms by means of which he can make integrated postural, transport, and manipulative adjustments to spatial features of the environment. As a result of practice and learning, these species-defined abilities are refined and modified by directional orientation habits and by tendencies to make specific responses to specific environmental events, but the underlying organization of behavior continues to be spatial and characterized by feedback control.

We shall consider these ideas at greater length and in relation to specific research findings in several chapters toward the end of the book. Meanwhile, what are their general implications for a theory of developing symbolic control in the human species? The main point we are trying to make is this: that man is basically a spatially organized control system, as are lower animals, and that his cognitive understanding of time, of history, and of scientific causation is an artificial achievement that he has accomplished through the use of symbol systems. Man did not gain a real understanding of time and an ability to control events in time until he transformed temporal sequences by means of symbols into spatial patterns that possessed behavioral reality.

The symbolic skills that have extended and elaborated human control of the environment developed gradually in relation to progressive changes in tool-using behavior and correlated changes in social organizations and institutions. Human abilities have been extended in part by evolutionary changes in genetic make-up, in part by the accumulation of human technology, symbolic knowledge, and social institutions that structure the learning of each new generation.

It is fruitless to speculate on the genetic capabilities of human children divorced from their cultural heritage, for genetic and environmental factors interact in determining the course of development. However, it is important to realize that a maturing child manifests some of the same changes in behavior organization that must have occurred in the history of the species. From making only direct responses to the environment, the child shifts more and more to symbolic responses. From patterns of orientative control, he shifts toward manipulative control and then more and more to symbolic control. In time he escapes from the immediate spatial patterns of his environment to an awareness of time sequences, causation, and abstract interrelationships. In mastering these human skills, he is learning to extend his control from the people, objects, and events in his immediate sensory environment to control of people, events, and systems in distant locations or in the future. He also learns to use his symbolic and abstract responses to achieve some measure of self-control, thus becoming not only a cognitive but a moral creature.

Coordinate Development of Human Systems

Some of the main stages in the development of human social, technological, and symbol systems are suggested in Table 3.1. Seven main stages of symbolic communication or symbolic control are differentiated, including expressive movements, expressive vocalization, oral language and graphic design, written language, numerical and economic (money) communication, printing and machine communication, and remote electronic communication and computer language. We assume that each of these forms of communication has had its origins within a distinctive pattern of feedback control of the human environment in which tools and communication have been brought together to integrate social behavior and the man-made social system.

Each type of symbolic communication that has developed represents an extension of the individual's ability to influence and regulate his own actions, the behavior of others, and the course of environmental events. Expressive movements and vocalizations represent an advance over direct pushing, pulling, striking, manipulating, or otherwise acting on the environment inasmuch as visual and auditory communicative patterns exert control at a distance beyond the range of direct action. In living primates, such expressive activities are used in conjunction with basic emotional or motivational states such as aggression or sexual activity, but when early man became a tool user, he refined his movements and vocalizations to convey more

TABLE 3.1. COORDINATE STAGES IN BIOSOCIAL EVOLUTION

Communication Patterns	Social Design	Technology	Symbolic Control Functions
Expressive movements (*Homo erectus*) (1,000,000 years ago)	Natural environment	Eoliths; stick and bone tools	Familial grouping; training of young
Expressive vocalization (*Homo erectus*) (250,000 years ago)	Cave environment	Hand ax; flake tools	Tribal kin grouping; hunting; training in tool making
Speech; graphic design (*Homo sapiens*) (100,000 years ago)	Temporary and permanent caves and villages	Handicraft tools; body cover; food processing	Tribal councils; magic; training rituals; time and space marking
Written language (4000 B.C.)	Temple system; regional village and city systems	Simple engines; metal tools; stone structures	Time and history concepts; administrative gov't; work supervision; law
Numerical and economic communication (2000 B.C.)	Mercantile towns and cities	Ships; land carriers; metal; glass; cloth; diversified bldg	Literature; concepts of historical causation; wages; money standards; accounts; recording contracts; professions
Printing and machine communication (1500 A.D.)	Mercantile and industrial cities	Factories; compound machines; powered carriers	Standardization of money; popular gov'ts; formal education
Electronic communication; computer language	Industrial systems	Universal machines; electronic control; automatic control	Remote communication and control; integration of verbal, numerical, and nonverbal control

precise information about processes of work and systems of social organization. Thus he extended his possibilities of control from his own activities and the objects and events he could respond to directly to the activities of others in his social grouping. As tool-using behaviors became more elaborate, communicative patterns also became more complex, more refined, and more abstract. These changes in behavior organization in the individual accompanied basic changes in the social and work structure of human society. One cannot say that one type of change caused the other, for technological, communicative, and social design have influenced each other reciprocally as man has extended his sphere of control and thus the range of his learning ability.

In Table 3.1, we indicate successive stages in social design and technological organization in relation to developing modes of symbolic communication and their functions in environmental and social control. The general course of technological and social change is well documented, and the indicated interrelationships in the historical period can be established. The correlations that we have indicated between technological-cultural and behavioral development in prehistory represent our own interpretation of how man evolved in these interrelated processes.

As the table indicates, we believe that expressive movements evolved in the natural environment in conjunction with the use of eolithic tools. Expressive vocalizations must have been used for some hundreds of thousands of years before refined articulative movements of the speech mechanism and associated refined manipulative movements of the hands established a systematic oral language with organized symbolic meanings. Oral language is judged to be associated with the emergence of *Homo sapiens* and with the formation of the first organized tribal groups living in villages, either on temporary or permanent sites. Writing first appeared in the urban temple systems of society about 6000 years ago. Economic and numerical communication, which we consider distinctive nonverbal forms,

arose in ancient mercantile cities about 4000 years ago. Printing and machine communication date from the fifteenth and sixteenth centuries and electronic and computer communication from the first half of the twentieth century. The next step is molecular control of electronic communication and interstellar transmission of information.

Different patterns of communication emerged in conjunction with distinct types of tools and technologies which were used to devise and control particular environmental and social organizations. For example, we believe that the development of oral languages was associated with use of handicraft tools and graphic forms of communication, and that written language was made possible by metal tools used in pottery and stone industries.

The level and sphere of symbolic control exercised by man at different stages of his development are related directly to the patterns of communication in use at the time. Expressive movements and vocalization were used by early man to maintain social contact in the natural environment and in cave living. Oral speech functioned as a tribal device in hunting, in educating the young, and in magic and burial rituals. The first functions of graphic design and of writing were to mark events and objects in space and in time. Using their accumulated visual symbolic records in this way, the Sumerians and Egyptians created space-ordered concepts of history which gradually gave way in subsequent systems to concepts of time and of temporal causation. Numerical and economic communication standardized values of objects and work in ancient city-states and led eventually to economic concepts of

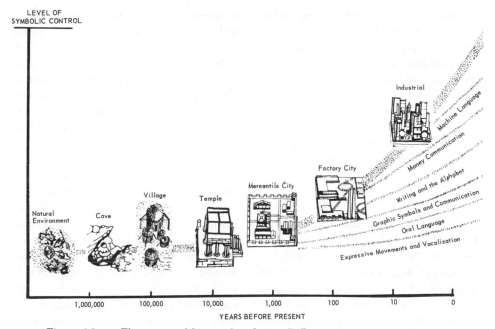

LEVEL OF
SYMBOLIC CONTROL

YEARS BEFORE PRESENT

Figure 3.1.   The course of biosocial evolution. Different forms of symbolic communication have developed at different stages in man's evolutionary progress and
then have followed their own developmental course. At any given time, all available
forms of symbolic communication are integrated to achieve the level and sphere of
environmental control that is demanded by that particular developmental stage.

social control in seventeenth- and eighteenth-century Europe. Such concepts
probably were prevalent in ancient
Phoenicia as well, but never were written down by the Phoenicians. Machine
communication established uniformity
of symbolic control in all avenues of life
and provided the means of disseminat-
ing scientific and social-political concepts. Modern electronic and computer
communication not only makes possible
high-speed numerical processing but also
provides the means of integrating numerical, verbal, and nonverbal symbolic
control of all aspects and levels of the
human social system.

We speak of the gradual but continuous development of man as a control
system as a process of biosocial evolu-

tion, for it has been defined by both biological and accumulating social changes.
The over-all pattern of this evolutionary
progression is suggested in graphic
form in Figure 3.1, where the gradual
evolution of symbolic control is plotted
as a function of time. On the main curve
of human social progress, represented by
the heavy black line, appear the different
levels of village, temple, urban, and industrial organization. The dotted lines
emerging at different levels and following their own evolutionary course represent the distinctive forms of symbolic
control generated at different levels of
biosocial organization. We believe that
the selective evolutionary factors that
defined progressive changes in expressive movements, language, writing, and

the more advanced forms of symbolization were related in all cases to features
of technological and social design. That
is, patterns of communication have
changed with the changing demands of
symbolic control of different levels of
human organization.

The composite curve in the figure
implies that the evolution of symbolic
control and communication is continuous but that new patterns appear which
reflect human organization at the particular time. Once a new level of symbolic control is generated, it continues
to develop and change at a rate dependent upon the level of environmental organization with which it is associated.
Thus we believe that expressive movements and oral speech are relatively
more resistant to change than written
language and economic communication.

At any given time, all forms of symbolic communication that have evolved
are integrated to achieve systematic control over the functions of work, education, and other human systems. As a
result of this functional integration,
newer forms of communication tend to
influence the development of older
forms. Thus writing has altered the patterns of oral speech, and machine communication encompassed and altered
patterns of both writing and speech.

Learning as a Function
of Human Organization

It often is noted that because of technological and scientific progress, the
human student in school has ever more
to learn. In our opinion, succeeding generations of students not only have more
to learn but also must learn in different
ways. That is, they must achieve different types of feedback transformation at

different stages of human progress in
order to establish patterns of control
that are currently meaningful and useful.

In our present state of knowledge, we
have very little objective information
about how direct reactions to the environment are transformed to indirect
symbolic and abstract reactions which
then can be internalized to short-cut and
extend the learning process. Our opinion
is that these transformations involve
shifts in feedback-control patterns from
those that are structured directly by the
natural environment to symbolic patterns that represent natural objects and
events. We believe that this continues on
to general symbols and abstract symbols
until the individual is dealing with
events and interrelationships that do not
exist in the sensory environment except
in their symbolic representation. In several later chapters of the book, we shall
describe how we analyze the feedback
control of speech, reading, writing, and
other symbolic behaviors by varying or
perturbing the spatial and temporal
properties of the feedback patterns.

For our present purposes, we wish to
point out that human learning is structured by the formal educational context,
and that this context is a function of the
level of biosocial evolution that has been
achieved. Man has not always been as
intelligent or as rapid a learner as he is
now because he has not had the facile
and high-speed symbolic tools which
permit him to realize his present potentialities. Man's intelligence and learning ability depend on special features of
his symbolic systems and their integration as well as on the genetically determined sensory-feedback mechanisms
that make the use of such symbolic systems possible.

NONVERBAL MEDIATION
OF HUMAN THOUGHT

To carry on his symbolic learning and thinking, man has had available for tens of thousands of years the formal symbol systems of spoken language, but formal systems of written language were not developed until about 6000 years ago. Before this time, prehistoric man was greatly dependent on many forms of nonverbal symbolism to mediate his learning processes and to give them some permanence in the accumulated knowledge of his culture. Patterns of nonverbal communication are important today, but to prehistoric man they were indispensable in defining his concepts and in giving meaning to his life activities.

Evolution of Concepts

By studying the evidence about the nature of prehistoric and ancient cultures and of analogous groups that persist in modern times, we can estimate the developmental course of the appearance of organized concepts in human thought. We guess that the concept of survival developed very early, for the first manlike creature who not only used tools but kept them with him for future use must have had some dim awareness of their survival value for him and his family. Only later did concepts of action, events, locations, objects, and so on emerge. Concepts of specific objects must have accompanied the use of specialized tools for hunting, drawing, fishing, and other tasks, and thus can be judged to be at least 80,000 years old and perhaps much older. Cave drawings, which can be traced back nearly 50,000 years, are evidence for concepts of symbolic representation of objects. Specific symbolic concepts of form, however, probably did not develop until nearly the dawn of civilization. These reached a high degree of perfection roughly 4000 years ago in Egyptian geometry. By this time, formal systems of writing also were being developed.

Ancient people had the behavioral capacity to form and to regulate concrete space and its structures, but they had no true understanding of how to represent three-dimensional space on a two-dimensional surface. This skill was developed initially by the Greeks and Arabs at about the beginning of the Christian era but was not perfected in graphic art until the Renaissance. The concept of the spatial structure of the world was related to this type of knowledge.

We believe that prehistoric and ancient man had no real sense of the sequence of events in time. His world was a spatial one, symbolized in spatial terms and regulated by spatially organized activities. Before history was written, early peoples used graphic design and other spatially organized symbols to plan and to tell about their world and the events in it. Even as late as the era of the great temple cities of Sumer and its neighboring regions, the course of history was conceived of in terms of the spatial growth and expansion of the temple of the king-god and the subordinate structures around it. The Sumerians and others like them in the thousands of temple cities lived and learned and worked in their limited space-structured universe and organized their lives according to its spatial plan. These cities were to disappear, to be rediscovered only in the modern period of archaeol-

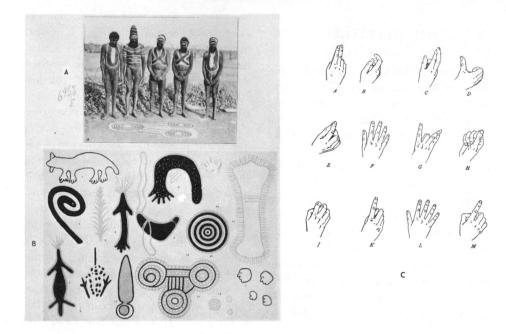

Figure 3.2.   Three basic types of nonverbal communication in Australian aboriginal society. *a.* Body adornment and totemic ground-drawings of the Warramunga tribe. *b.* Rock drawings of animals, human heads, tools, animals, plants, and totemic symbols. *c.* Gesture symbols, used by individuals under a ban of silence. A and B represent small kangaroos; C, kangaroo rat; D, opossum; E, dog or dingo; F, camel; G and H, emu; J, eagle hawk; K, small lizard with long tail; L, very large lizard called Parenthie; M, large lizard, but smaller than Parenthie. (From Spencer and Gillen. *Across Australia.* London: Macmillan, 1912, 2 vols.)

ogy. No one knows, for sure, why the temple cities were doomed, but we can speculate that they engineered their own destruction by one of the most important advances ever made by man—the development of writing. For with writing and the recording of events, man came to recognize the temporal course of history. The old spatial worlds lost their unity and meaning, and new patterns of social organization emerged.

Throughout the long course of human development, each advance in instrumentation or in manipulative or communicative skill not only added to man's repertoire of specific performance patterns but raised the level of his understanding and learning capabilities. When Stone-Age man developed the skill of drawing pictures on the walls of caves, he very likely expanded greatly the scope of his understanding of himself, the animals whose pictures he drew, and the interrelations among them. When man's drawings became graphic symbols, his capacity for symbolic thought increased. Modern man continues to multiply his abilities to learn and to think creatively by means of specialized machines and refined scientific techniques. Thus, we say that human learning is structured by the learning situation. The available devices and skills not only determine what is learned, they also determine how it is learned, and set upper limits of learning and creativity within the lifetime of an individual.

Stone-Age Symbolism

We begin to appreciate the richness of nonverbal communicative patterns in prehistoric peoples when we study the customs of Stone-Age cultures that persist in modern times. The photographs and drawings in Figure 3.2 illustrate nonverbal communication among the Australian aborigines, the most primitive people still surviving on earth. We see in Figure 3.2a and b examples of their use of elaborate totemic designs for body adornment, ground designs, and rock drawings. Such designs are used in special rituals and magic rites, for teaching the young, and on occasions of death, birth, mating, and conflict. The body designs identify both the persons and their roles. The manual signs in Figure 3.2c are very expressive and are comparable to the hand signs used by the deaf in our own culture.

From the point of view of our contemporary understanding, the symbolic activities of primitive man are characterized by two important limitations: they express no real sense of historical sequence of events or of causation. Lacking these concepts, primitive man tended to locate causes of events in the objects that participated in the event. Thus each perceived object and animal came to represent a whole series of events. When the events concerned a person or a family, the graphic representation of the animal or object became a totemic sign for the person or family. Great and powerful animals became signs of king-gods and their fertility and prowess. For example, totemic

signs of the lion, the great snake, and the hawk symbolized king-gods in the religion and civilization of ancient Egypt, from which culture much of our own art, science, and language derives.

One important function of totemic signs and other nonverbal symbols was to identify persons and families and to delineate personality. In prehistoric times, as now, people were differentiated in terms of the work roles they performed and their skills and special abilities in their tasks. Some were hunters, some gathered food, some were good warriors, and so on. A person and his tools were marked with an appropriate sign—for example, an animal or plant sign—to define his personality and social role, and this system of identification could be extended to a family line. In some cases, fine tools as such, without any special sign, might mark a man or his family. In New Zealand, fine greenstone hand axes were used to mark a warrior or chieftain, and might be carried over from generation to generation to represent a family line. Thus a limited sense of time and history was partially compensated for by means of a relatively permanent sign or tool that represented the deeds and achievements of dimly defined ancestors.

Another function of totemic signs was their use in primitive magic as a means of regulating natural forces. Because of his limited understanding of causation, early man tried to control natural events by manipulating the objects in which the "causes" resided. Thus the elaborate rituals involving tools and symbols were essentially attempts to control the environment—to ward off evil and bring about good. Every major event in life was prepared for by particular kinds of ceremonies held in particular places. In

Figure 3.3. Totemic markings used to motivate the young in difficult tasks and to aid in learning and growing. *a*. Totemic body markings on young men who are about to go forth to kill an enemy in a neighboring tribe. *b*. Totemic animal and plant markings on wooden slabs for a ritual ceremonializing the growth of young men and women and to make them grow strong and healthy. (From Spencer and Gillen. *Across Australia*. London: Macmillan, 1912, 2 vols.)

Figure 3.3*a* we see totemic markings on the bodies of young aborigine warriors who are getting ready to go out and kill an enemy of an adjacent tribe. Figure 3.3*b* shows how slabs of wood were designed in a yam totem of the Tjingilli tribe of Australia for a ceremony that was conducted to make the boys grow up strong and the girls grow up plump. In general, totemic designs such as these served to identify the conditions of the use of an object or tool at the particular place where the action was to be carried out. By such combined place and object marking, Stone-Age peoples attempted

to control the important events of their lives. When a man died his tools often were buried with him, and his burial container was marked with his totem. These precautions, along with the other practices associated with death and burial, were to insure the well-being of the dead man's spirit as well as the safety of the living.

Evolution of Graphic Design

Of all patterns of nonverbal communication, those of graphic design and pictorial representation are the most adaptable to various purposes and thus have been the most significant in the evolution of human behavior and learning. Some of the earliest graphic designs that can be dated are primitive drawings of bison on the walls of caves in France. These drawings of Aurignacian man and others of Magdalenian man are estimated to be around 40,000 years old or even older (Kühn, 1955). More recent cave drawings found in France, Spain,

Figure 3.4. Rock drawings from the Sahara Desert dating from about 6000 B.C. to a period contemporary with early Egyptian civilization (3000 to 1200 B.C.). (Redrawn from Lhote. Saharan rock art. *Nat. Hist.*, 1960, 44(6), 28–43.)

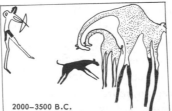

and northern Africa show a gradual course of development of concepts related to work. The oldest drawings were mainly of an object character, featuring the outline of animals that were hunted. Later drawings represented instrumental relationships, including designs of hunting tools with animals that were hunted. In time the tools were shown in operational use by the hunter. Finally, human figures appeared without tools, but in some ritual relationship with each other. These later phases of graphic representation are illustrated by the drawings in Figure 3.4 which were executed in northern Africa from about 6000 B.C. to a time corresponding to the Old Kingdom of Egypt. Egyptian and Libyan cultures interacted during this later period, as is suggested by the Egyptian style of the drawings.

Progress in graphic art can be considered one phase of man's increasingly complex organization of behavior to structure the environment for human adaptive purposes. Tools and body cover were devised prior to the first efforts to produce graphic designs, and the first designs probably represented efforts to control the tool-using operations in hunting. Man and beast were joined in a totemic concept which did not differentiate the activities and symbols of hunting from the animal that was hunted. Later, as weaving, pottery making, sculpture, architecture, and other media of design appeared, the processes of tool using and pictorial symbolic representation interacted to advance creative planning and thinking in both tool design and the construction of the first villages.

Nonverbal communicative patterns in the first villages and cities not only extended the methods of graphic represensation, sculpturing of figures, pottery marking, body adornment, and so on that were developed in earlier periods but also introduced some significant new techniques. One of these was time marking—the use of systematized graphic designs to keep track of time. Another was the use of a sequential series of pictures to tell a story. Thus a series of designs put on a knife handle or a plaque might tell a story about the exploits of some great chieftain or king-god. These early pictographs represented to the people who developed them their concepts of behavior organization and life plan.

The designs shown in Figure 3.5 are from ancient Egypt, one of the first civilized societies. Designs such as these were used on headdresses, clothes, tools, and buildings. They were used to decorate jewelry, mummy cases, sphinxes, temples, and almost all objects of Egyptian life. These graphic symbols helped define all aspects of culture and thought —at the verbal, social, artistic, architectural, and industrial levels—and helped to bridge the gap between ancient and modern understanding of temporal patterns of causation and the sequence of historical events.

For education and the teaching profession in general, the development of the temple cities marked a turning point, for it was here that the graphic storytelling symbols or pictographs were adapted to represent verbal speech. The Egyptian hieroglyphics and the Sumerian cuneiform symbols were the precursors of alphabetic writing in the Western world and thus formed the basis for the organization of our knowledge in writing and books.

Several examples of early Egyptian pictorial symbolization that immediately anteceded hieroglyphic writing are shown in Figure 3.6. One of these pic-

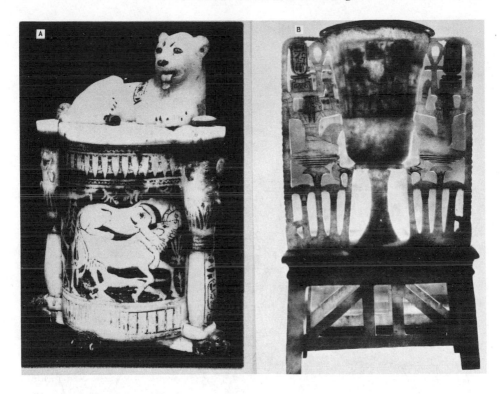

Figure 3.5.   Ancient Egyptian symbolic representation. *a*. Time-marking symbols and symbolism depicting action, from the Old Kingdom. *b*. Translucent chair combining pictorial and hieroglyphic event-telling. (Courtesy of the Cairo Museum.)

ture stories is inscribed on the handle of a stone knife. The others are inscribed on plaques and tell of the exploits of a king of the Old Kingdom of Egypt around 3000 B.C. The first uses of actual writing were to keep records and to memorialize the king's places and achievements. A real verbal literature was not to develop for centuries.

The development of writing was a significant milestone in the long evolutionary process of human adaptation in tool using and social communication. In this process, the fundamental behavior and physiological bases of learning were modified. Human learning shifted more and more toward the systematic types of learning that we know today, wherein knowledge of organized relationships and skill in performing organized instrumental operations dominate the learning process.

After the development of writing, graphic representation was no longer as indispensable a medium of human thought as in the prehistoric era. Consequently, graphic design followed a more specialized course of development, which is classified usually as a phase of the history of art. Although the evolution of design rarely has attracted the interest or attention of scientists, it probably is as crucial for understanding the history of science as it is for the understanding of art. What we know as science today did not originate specifically

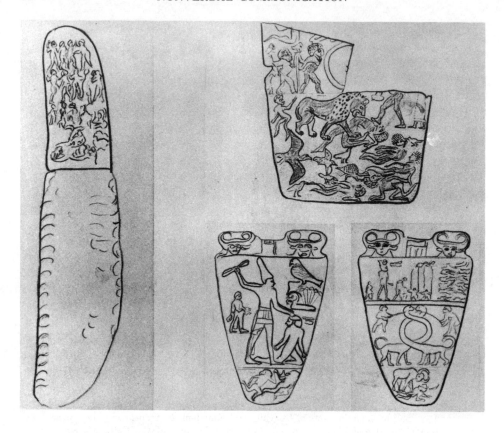

Figure 3.6.   The process of differentiation and transformation of nonverbal ar-
tistic designs and symbols to hieroglyphic writing in the Old Kingdom and First
Dynasty (2769 B.C.) and in ancient Egypt. (Redrawn from Wolf. *Die Welt der
Ägypter.* Stuttgart: Kilpper, 1954.)

within the tradition of verbal symbolism
and literature but can be traced to much
more primitive origins in human activities related to design of tools, architecture, geometric displays, and graphic
forms. Ancient scientific achievement
grew out of explorations in primitive
magic, basic tool-using processes, artistic
design, and geometric design. Creative
thinking in the sciences always has had
significant nonverbal components. This
is no less true today than in prehistoric
times.

SPECIALIZATION OF NONVERBAL COMMUNICATION

Just as verbal symbols have been specialized to deal with many areas of literary, professional, commercial, and
scientific knowledge, nonverbal symbolism has become diversified and has
helped to regulate organized learning in
various areas. Two important applications of nonverbal techniques are in
book illustrating and advertising.

Book Illustration

Since ancient times, a widely applicable use of pictorial design is in book illustration. One of the oldest books known, the *Book of the Dead* of ancient Thebes, contains pictorial illustrations. In one of these, shown in Figure 3.7, a boat, containing a boatman, a hawk-headed figure denoting the king-god, and a mandrill holding a service, crosses the river of the dead toward three dismal figures who sit on the other side.

Greek and Roman books apparently were not illustrated except for geometry books, which utilized newly developed abstract line drawings. Our line graphs, bar graphs, and related quantitative functions used in book illustrations have this ancient origin. The drawing instruments used both for the preparation of plans and for preparing illustrations were developed by the pyramid builders. The Greeks improved metal drawing devices and used them in illustrating geometric principles. Their instruments were similar to many still in use.

The oldest dated European book illustrations were printed from wood blocks in 868 (Poortenaar, 1935). Examples of book illustrations from the fifteenth to the eighteenth century shown in Figure 3.8 include an illuminated manuscript page from the fifteenth century, woodcuts from the fifteenth and sixteenth centuries, and an engraving from the eighteenth century. The first collaboration of author and artist in the production of a book in which specific text references to the illustrations occur is said to be one in which woodcuts of Wolgemuth were used (Fig. 3.8b). The book was a series of meditations on the life and sufferings of Christ and is attributed to a friar, Stefan Fridolin. Albrecht Dürer's woodcut in Figure 3.8c is taken from the first work on perspective on a mathematical basis which also included descriptions of several drawing instruments invented by Dürer. In a subsequent work, Dürer proposed, possibly for the first time, the principle that human physique and character could be described in terms of measurements of geometric proportions.

The development of photography has greatly modified techniques of book illustration, and books have been changed in format to accommodate lavish use of photographs. This advance in pictorial technique has provided greater flexibility of the nonverbal components of books with consequent improvement in the over-all communicative pattern. An interesting point in the history of photography is that the first venture into

Figure 3.7. One of the first illustrated books known—*The Book of the Dead* of ancient Thebes. (Courtesy of the Cairo Museum.)

Figure 3.8.   Early European book illustrations. *a.* Illustrations and page from an illuminated manuscript of the fifteenth century. *b.* Late fifteenth-century woodcut of Wolgemuth. *c.* Sixteenth century woodcut from Albrecht Dürer's work on the theory and practice of art. *d.* Eighteenth-century engraving from a French work on arts and crafts.

the domain of motion-picture making not only produced a successful demonstration, but also culminated in one of the greatest books of all time. The collection of human and animal photographs made by Muybridge (1887) stands as a unique artistic achievement, approaching in the field of graphic illustration the works of Leonardo da Vinci, Agricola, and Audubon.

Muybridge's photographs, one series of which is shown in Figure 3.9, were made between 1872 and 1884, when photography was young and motion pictures were unknown. He turned an agile mind to making a portfolio of "motion pictures" with a series of 24 still cameras placed in a row parallel to a running track about 50 feet away. As animals or human individuals walked or ran along the track, the cameras were triggered to take sequential pictures of the movement. These photographs, especially some of the naked human body in motion, have influenced techniques of artistic design throughout the western

world. They have changed the course of teaching and level of execution of both objective and abstract design and have influenced especially the drawing of human and animal figures to depict motion.

We are so accustomed to having our books illustrated by drawings and photographs that the significance of these printed graphic records in the development of human knowledge is likely to escape us. According to Ivins (1953), modern science and technology are directly dependent on the invention of techniques to print graphic designs. Since the development of writing, man had been able to repeat verbal statements by copying them and in this way verbal knowledge was recorded and disseminated. However, a nonverbal drawing could not be repeated exactly until the invention of prints in the late fourteenth century, and the cost was not reduced to a reasonable level until the development of photographic reproduction in the nineteenth century. Inas-

Figure 3.9.   Some of the first "motion pictures" ever made, from a portfolio of over 500 plates made by the photographer Muybridge. (From Muybridge. *Animal locomotion*. Philadelphia: Lippincott, 1887.)

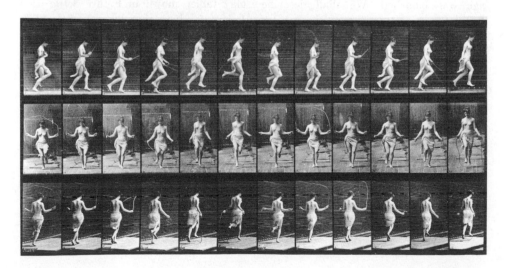

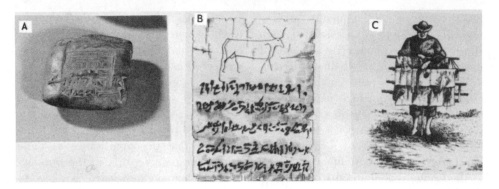

Figure 3.10.   Ancient forms of advertising. *a.* Clay tablet showing seal of the scribe. *b.* An Egyptian notice about cattle written in hieratic script. *c.* Ancient Chinese textile display. (*a* courtesy of Prof. Menahem Mansoor; *b* and *c* from Butterworth (ed.) *The growth of industrial art.* Washington, D.C.: U.S. Government Printing Office, 1892.)

much as science and technology are greatly dependent on exact graphic representations, their progress prior to the age of prints was very limited. When careful drawings of plants, animals, anatomy, technical devices, and so on could be copied exactly in large numbers by means of printing processes, scientific and technological observations, discoveries, and inventions could be preserved in both their verbal and nonverbal aspects and the modern scientific age was launched. We shall describe Ivins' convincing argument in greater detail in Chapter 13.

Advertising Techniques

Advertising is another area of specialization of nonverbal communication which has educational significance. The oldest relic of advertising in the English language is said to be the name *Smith*, from the display of a metalworker craftsman. Signs of this sort which identified a type of work or merchandise are very ancient in origin and have used both verbal and nonverbal components.

Trade displays can be traced to the trade fairs of ancient Phoenicia, where city bazaars were used as a systematic method of commerce. Other ancient forms of advertising were the use of seals on clay tablets and notices of estates, fairs, sales, and slave auctions. The latter described some of the main features of the slaves.

Examples of early forms of advertising are shown in Figure 3.10. If we can consider the seal of the scribe on the clay tablet shown in Figure 3.10*a* as a form of advertising by a lawyer, then this little object may be one of the oldest advertisements known to man, for it is over 4200 years old. The other two displays shown in the figure are an Egyptian notice about cattle written in hieratic script and an ancient Chinese textile display.

In the nineteenth century, various ingenious methods of visual advertising became common, such as the use of flamboyant tombstones to keep the family name prominently displayed, billboards, balloons, banners, animated displays, door plates, railroad posters, wagon posters, clock devices, rotating signs, reflectors, luminous displays, and newspaper and magazine displays. The visual factor always has been emphasized in advertising because well designed visual displays attract almost universal attention and can be understood immediately. Motion pictures, radio, and television have necessitated a reorganization of existing nonverbal techniques for these media as well as the development of new methods. The advent of television has altered most existing procedures because of its nearly unlimited scope in integrating all of the older graphic and photographic techniques with immediate long-distance audiovisual communication.

With the development of radio and television, the dividing lines between conventional education, advertising, and technological communication have become less distinct. The immediacy and efficiency of these newer methods of expressive communication have had the effect of identifying commercial products with the company organization and the plant that produces them and of elevating the public's technical knowledge of both product and company. Thus, marketing and advertising programs tend more and more to incorporate technical information about company organization and engineering and to utilize the audiovisual techniques of education in their displays.

NONVERBAL TEACHING TECHNIQUES

At all levels of evolution, the human child has had much to learn to take his place as a contributing member of adult society. From prehistoric to modern times, much teaching and learning have gone on in the normal home environment, and additional teaching and learning have occurred on the job, where the individual learns the knowledge and skills of his work role. But from time immemorial, human children also have been given formalized instruction by people who have acted as full-time or part-time teachers. Specialization of the teaching role was affected by many factors, but perhaps the most decisive among these was the development of the tools and the work of graphic representation. For the symbolic representation of work activities alienated the processes of instruction from the actual labor and skill that were represented, thus laying the groundwork for a separate teaching profession.

Formal instruction always has involved an integration of verbal and nonverbal communication with interdependent effects on learning. However, we shall confine our discussion here as far as possible to some of the nonverbal tools and techniques that have been used for educational purposes through the ages.

Prehistoric Teaching Tools

As far as we can tell from analyzing evidence of the behavior of prehistoric peoples, the education and training of their young included roughly four types of activities: the use of folklore, myth, and song; instruction and supervised practice in the use of specific tools; instruction in the making of totem symbols and designs; and using certain symbols and instruments of magic to teach the fundamentals of tribal taboo and action. Instruction in verbal story and song had the disadvantage of being transitory, whereas the tools, devices, and visual symbols were more or less permanent aids to learning. Inasmuch as primitive man apparently lacked a sense of causation between events separated in time except as he could bring these events together spatially, the totemic signs and symbols that could be carried about on a tool or on his body served to remind him continually of what he was about, just as written rules and directions guide the modern novice.

Tools evolved in prehistoric cultures for the express purposes of nonverbal communication included marking sticks and stones for making cave and rock drawings; weaving devices and pottery marking styluses, sometimes made of metal; and the props and devices of the sorcerer or witch doctor, which were used to beat the ground in animal ritu-als, mark bodies, stab and cut in mutilation rituals, cure disease, and kill enemies at a distance. (Pointing sticks were among the tools used to kill at a distance.) The tools of the sorcerer were true teaching devices, for they were used to teach and control the young warriors, make them respect their elders, toe the line with respect to their sexual responsibilities, and strive to succeed in battle.

The tribal sorcerer created the symbolic totem markings in tribal ceremony and devised the headdresses and body markings which served to represent the magic forces over which only he had control. The photograph in Figure 3.11 illustrates the use of magic symbolic markings, including ground designs, body display, and ceremonial equipment, by Australian aborigines. The picture shows the removal of helmets following a ceremony of the snake totem. The symbolic markings are the tools

Figure 3.11.   Body display, helmets, and symbolic ground drawings used in ceremonials of the Warramunga tribe of Australia. This ritual involved the Wollunqua totem—the great snake. (From Spencer and Gillen. *Across Australia*. London: Macmillan, 1912, 2 vols.)

used by the tribal sorcerer to control the hidden forces in nature and to educate and impress the members of the tribe with his powers to protect them from the great snake. The purposes of the rites are to make the snake happy and put him to rest for a year and to educate the young in how to achieve this great feat.

The developing pattern of education in prehistory was affected by the dual function served by the witch doctor in relation to ordinary tribal members. The grotesque masquerades and body cover assumed by sorcerers or witch doctors identified them not only as individuals with special powers but as protectors of the other people. The sorcerer protected the tribe from the terrible dangers and powers of the spirit figures that he could address with his sticks, mumbo-jumbo, and other props and techniques. This dual role of controller of spirit power and protector was carried over in the fundamental pattern of education to the later urban cultures, where the temple priest represented the power and authority of a dynastic king as well as the authoritarian knowledge of how the people could be protected from the terrible powers of the king. Both prehistoric and ancient historic education involved the use of various devices and props to achieve this dual symbolic activity of the sorcerer or priest.

When tribal societies became stabilized in village and urban patterns, there were sometimes special buildings for teaching the young in the ceremonials of their culture. For example, the Mesa Verde Indians of ancient North America, who lived in cliff cities like the one pictured in Figure 3.12 almost a thousand years ago, had special rooms known as kivas for education and ceremonials. The kivas were cellar rooms built in a precise octagonal design which had directional significance.

In addition to their instruction in rituals and symbolism, prehistoric tribal youngsters were trained with the real tools and techniques of work and survival, in learning to fight and hunt and in learning the domestic work of animal care, plant control, and harvesting. Dyson-Hudson (1960) has given a detailed account of how children of the Karamojong of Uganda, Africa, work and use simulated weapons to practice battle combat. A young man of the Karamojong receives a calf as an instrument of education, for when he becomes a man, his cattle provide his livelihood and define his status and wealth.

Instruments for Plotting Space and Time

An important factor in the process of becoming civilized was man's development of techniques for orienting himself spatially and temporally in the world and universe. This involved making observations of geography, astronomy, and meteorology, developing tools for accurate measurements, devising recording devices for keeping track of space and time, and developing mathematical systems for handling all these facts. Even Stone-Age men were adept at finding their way about in the world. For example, the ancient Polynesians were expert navigators and made accurate astronomical and meteorological observations. They used the constellations as guides and also observed the direction of the ocean swell. Many Stone-Age

Figure 3.12.   Mesa Verde's Cliff Palace. This prehistoric cave city lies high up
in the canyon wall just below the plateau. The circular rooms at the front are
kivas, ceremonial and ritual rooms that can be considered prehistoric school rooms.

tribes recorded lunar months and designated them according to the natural
changes of the seasons. Solar calendars
were used by more advanced groups,
such as the Mayas and other early civilizations of Central America.

Globes and ancient maps for teaching
the movements of the stars were among
the first formal educational devices. One
of the first known references to a specific
educational device, other than instruments used for writing, concerns a globe
that was supposed to have been carried
from Egypt to Greece by the legions of
Alexander the Great. The globe was said
to have been made by the men who constructed the pyramid of Cheops in the

Fourth Dynasty, that is, sometime prior
to 2560 B.C. (Butterworth, 1892).

A very complicated device that most
certainly was used by the Greeks for
teaching purposes is an ancient computer mechanism which was picked up
from the sea in 1901 and only recently
recognized as a computer (de Solla
Price, 1959). According to various careful estimates, it dates from about 82 B.C.
Its apparent purpose was to give quantitative information about the movements
of the sun and the planets. It contains
the first scientifically graduated numerical dials known and has an extraordi-
narily complex gear mechanism, proving
that the Hellenic world knew the prin-

ciples of building epicyclical gear systems.

Beckmann (1846) long ago gave an account of an ancient Roman device that apparently functioned as a planetary computer. In describing the history of clocks, Beckmann referred to papers dealing with the acts of St. Sebastian the Martyr, in which appears the following account. Chromatius, a governor of Rome in the third century, when about to be cured by St. Sebastian tells the Saint, "I have a glass chamber in which the whole learning and science of the stars is constructed mechanically, in making which my father Tarquinius is known to have expended more than two hundred pounds of gold." St. Sebastian then tells him that if he has chosen to keep this machine whole, he will have destroyed himself. Chromatius asks, "How so?" and goes on to question why such a machine differed from almanacs wherein courses of the months are distinguished numerically for every hour, and the full new moon is, by means of certain calculations, forecast by a motion of the fingers. Beckmann deduced from additional information that the mechanism under discussion was not a clock but a device to point out the sun's course through the twelve signs of the zodiac, the motion of the other planets, and their relative situation in every month or at any period of the year. In any case, the Saint apparently destroyed it, but we have no reason to doubt the authenticity of Beckmann's story about learning in antiquity.

Another Roman instrument for teaching nonverbal information in ancient times, which was preserved in the ruins of Pompeii, is shown in Figure 3.13.

Figure 3.13.   Cubicle calendar found at Pompeii. (From Knight (ed.) *The arts and industry of all nations.* London: Dutton, 1860, 2 vols.)

This is a cubicle calendar that apparently was used to teach the signs of the months of the year, along with other information. The abacus is one of the few ancient computing and teaching devices for nonverbal learning that has persisted in modern times in nearly its original form. Its survival is probably due to the fact that it is a fine instrument for teaching number combinations visually in terms of space-object relationships as well as a highly efficient calculating device.

One of the first known applications of teaching devices in Europe after the fall of Rome was the use of a globe for teaching geography in a school in Rheims, France, about 1000 A.D. This globe had been brought from the Moorish school at Cordova, Spain, substantiating the fact that the Arabs were teaching geography with celestial globes at a time when most Europeans taught that the world was flat. Columbus may have got his notion of a new route to the Indies from such Moorish globes (Butterworth, 1892).

Some examples of European devices and maps for teaching that existed prior to the nineteenth century are shown in

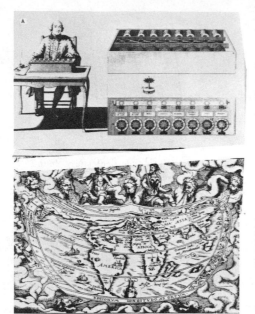

Figure 3.14.   Teaching aids used prior to 1800. *a*. Pascal's arithmetic machine. *b*. Sixteenth-century map of the world. *c*. A planetary machine made in England in the 1780s.

Figure 3.14. These include Pascal's arithmetic machine, a world map of the sixteenth century, and a planetary machine dated between 1781 and 1786. This planetary device mechanizes the relative movements of the planets and gives directions and information about these movements in relation to the signs of the Zodiac. It is significant that the Greeks and the Romans, centuries before, had devised similar maps and calculating and planetary machines for undoubtedly the same educational purposes.

Laboratory Demonstration and Experimentation

The use of laboratory demonstrations and experiments as a combined nonverbal and verbal technique of organized learning has a long history. One of its origins is in museum displays or collections of natural curiosities. Another is

the use of automata, mechanical demonstrations, and acts of ritual, sorcery, and juggling, either to amuse or to train others to accept some belief.

As we have seen, ritual demonstrations for healing and training the young are prehistoric in origin. Such methods were carried over into the ritual of ancient religions, athletics, and public amusement. Juggling, fire breathing, fire walking, demonstrations of great strength, sleight of hand with ropes, cards, rods, peas and cups were all practiced in antiquity and carried on thereafter as forms of entertainment. Comparable manipulations are still used by some teachers to maintain and direct attention of students and to illustrate natural phenomena.

The concept of automata is closely allied to the ancient use of ritual objects, for in primitive times movable figures representing objects and people were used to symbolize the real thing. The scalps and shrunken heads collected by some primitive tribes possibly are related in function to automated figures. The importance of automata for organized learning is indicated by the fact that Descartes' concepts of stimulus and response and of the reflex are said to have been based on observations of automated figures in the gardens of Paris. These figures moved when persons nearby stepped on hidden plates, and Descartes found this stimulus-released movement analogous to reflex behavior.

According to Beckmann (1846), the building of efficient automata was coincident with the devising of clocks in the seventeenth century. Some of the first effective automated figures built in Germany operated in conjunction with tower clocks. The technique of providing statues with voices was a favorite eighteenth-century amusement and was accomplished by having hidden persons speak into tubes. Another eighteenth-century technique was to produce mobile animal figures by moving jointed pasteboard cutouts behind an illuminated screen and using hidden pegs attached to the cutouts to hold and activate the parts.

Museum displays constitute another significant antecedent of modern educational procedures and instruments, for they have been used consistently to instruct in the record of history or in the properties and classification of objects in nature. According to Beckmann, the first museums of educational materials were Greek medical collections that Hippocrates himself was supposed to have used for self education. The Greeks brought rare animals and unusual natural objects to the temples and consecrated them to the gods. It is said that Alexander gave orders to all herdsmen, birdcatchers, and fishermen to send whatever animals they might find to Aristotle. The Roman Apuleius also formed a collection of natural objects, especially zoological specimens.

During the Middle Ages, there were bird and fish displays in the ruling palaces of the Arabs and collections of curiosities in the treasures of the emperors, kings, and princes of Europe. Live menageries also were established in the courts. Private collections appeared for the first time in the sixteenth century, and catalogues of such collections were made as early as 1565. One of the oldest museums, the Ashmolean Museum at Oxford University, was launched by the gift of the private collection of Ashmole, who had purchased it from others. The British Museum was started in 1753 from a private collection of medals, metallic ores, and precious stones purchased from the estate of Hans Sloane, the Harleian collection of manuscripts, and certain other items. Since then, museums of art, history, natural objects, antiquities, and biological material, and menageries of many sorts have been set up as general educational facilities in almost every major city in the world.

Although rarely discussed in such terms, the training laboratory with its special devices represents a significant means for communicating nonverbal experience and knowledge to the student. Laboratory procedures not only train the individual to use his eyes and ears in observation but also provide practice in the motor skills that may be used later in science and in the professions. These nonverbal communicative aspects of the laboratory have ancient origins in the use of demonstrations of animated and automated devices and in the museum collections of curiosities.

The early science laboratory was an offshoot of sixteenth-century metallurgical testing procedures that were described by Agricola (1912) and of the museum displays. The work of such a laboratory included both exploration and teaching—that is, search by the scientist and re-search by assistants and students. Public demonstrations often were given for the benefit of important people. The physical science laboratory developed in Europe at approximately the time of the American revolutionary war. Figure 3.15a illustrates a large English chemical laboratory in 1763. The museum nature of the place is immediately apparent, and its origins in metallurgical procedures are indicated by some of the tools and by the picture on the back wall showing a view of a preindustrial glass furnace. This drawing was taken from Agricola. Various furnace devices and tools for metallurgical study are evident, and balances appear in glass cases at the right. A picture of some sort of heating and blasting system is seen on the wall to the left.

Some idea about the division of activity in the chemical laboratory of Lavoisier in France is given in Figure 3.15b. Here we see a museum display of jars and an early study of respiratory gases in process. Notice that the recording is done by a secretary using quill pens. The experiment represents a phase of Lavoisier's work that laid the foundations of the physiological chemistry of respiration. Lavoisier's research generally is considered the beginning of modern experimental chemistry.

Up until fairly recently, the actual na-

Figure 3.15.   The early scientific laboratory as a combined scientific and teaching facility. a. A view of a large chemical laboratory in England in 1763, which discloses the connection between the evolution of the physical science laboratory, the early mining and metal testing techniques of Agricola, and museums of the eighteenth century. b. Lavoisier's laboratory around 1790. (From Partington. Evolution of the chemical laboratory. Endeavour, 1942, 1, 145–150.)

ture of research laboratories changed very little from those shown in Figure 3.15. The most important change involved the introduction of new machines and devices for observation, experiment, and demonstration. The organization of work was in the German or English tradition; a major teacher or professor headed the laboratory and was aided by research associates and assistants in both teaching and study. However, in the last few decades more specialized training laboratories have been established to train students in the special techniques needed in medicine, engineering, industry, agriculture, and other fields. Thus we have laboratory-trained specialists at many levels, some of whom got their training in vocational schools or worker training programs. An interesting historical phase of this development is the establishment of laboratories and courses for training women technicians. Figure 3.16 illustrates one of the first of these courses—a training course for girl wireless operators at Hunter College in New York in 1917. At first the Navy objected to this program but later certified the female operators.

The training and research laboratory is itself a source wherein are generated new devices for teaching as well as knowledge leading toward technical change. The tools and procedures in the basic laboratories are being altered continually to meet new needs. New laboratory ideas eventually lead to changes in industrial and professional methods, which in turn are adopted in the technical and training laboratories for teaching and further research. This reciprocal feedback system defines the interaction between basic science, science training, and technological development in modern scientific teaching.

Classroom Instrumentation

Until relatively recent times, classroom instrumentation in the ordinary school was meager indeed. The main instruments were a blackboard and chalk and the writing material on the desks. In this respect, however, American pupils of the nineteenth and early twentieth centuries were somewhat better off than their predecessors in antiquity. Egyptian students, for example, sat on the stone floors of the temples, and the students of Socrates sat in the open under the trees. After free schools were established generally in America in the 1830s and 1840s, numerous patents were granted for blackboards, maps, slates, and cumbersome desks, but these innovations made little change in the rather dismal appearance of the school environment.

Since about 1920, marked improvements have been made in the design of

Figure 3.16.   An early vocational training laboratory in the United States. The girls were taking a wireless operator's training course at Hunter College in 1917. (Courtesy of the Wisconsin State Historical Society.)

schoolrooms and in the methods of instruction available to the teacher. The differences between the old and the new classrooms are more than just differences in the kinds of visual and auditory communication used in instruction. In the more modern classroom, the student gets far more feedback from his own various learning activities, and much of this feedback is nonverbal. By such means, he is made aware of the comparative level of many of his scholastic and social activities.

During the past century, many mechanical devices and instruments were developed for nonverbal and verbal instruction, although some of them apparently saw limited use in actual class-rooms. Examples of devices for which patents were granted before 1900 are shown in Figure 3.17. Such instruments were the teaching machines of the nine-teenth century. Some of them persist to-day, not so much as schoolroom aids but as educational toys for children. One of them, the rotating speller, was the pre-cursor of one of the most widely used scientific instruments of learning psy-chology, the memory drum.

Of all the developments in classroom instrumentation in the last century, modern methods of reproducing visual and auditory material have had the

Figure 3.17.　　　Nineteenth century "teaching machines" for which patents were granted. *a.* Spelling board. *b.* Blackboard with adjustable numbers. *c.* Folding paper device for illustrating evolution and involution. *d.* Grid device for teaching geography. *e.* Device for illustrating aeration. *f.* Rolled maps. *g.* A moving-block speller. *h.* A mechanical aid for teaching handwriting. *i.* A rotating speller. (From Butterworth (ed.) *The growth of industrial art.* Washington, D.C.: U.S. Government Printing Office, 1892.)

greatest impact on teaching techniques. Until the 1850s, pictorial displays could be reproduced only by hand reproduction, printing, or drawing apparatus. The latter included pantographs for copying designs, profile drawing devices, and geared drawing devices for making ellipses and compound curves. Printing had not had the same far-reaching effects on nonverbal communication as on verbal communication, for the techniques of printing designs and pictures were slower, more expensive, and more skilled than setting type for printed verbal material. Photography provided a quick and efficient method of reproducing pictorial displays, and, in addition, techniques of printing both line drawings and photographs have been improved to the point where the expense is no longer prohibitive. Consequently, modern textbooks and classrooms present a wealth of pictorial material to the eyes of the learner.

The real story of the development of modern audiovisual techniques we shall reserve for a later chapter. Edison paved the way with his invention of the kinetoscope, a device for projecting motion pictures and the phonograph, which played back recorded sound. The other important advance was the perfection of methods of remote transmission of sound and pictures, leading up to radio and television. One of the original inventions in this area also can be attributed to Edison. He devised a *word transmitter*, in which holes punched in a paper tape generated signals that were transmitted over a multichannel wire and reproduced as a pattern of dots on a receiving cylinder. At about the same time that Bell devised a successful telephone for oral speech, devices were developed for transmitting handwriting by wire. One of these, Cassell's Autographic Telegraph, utilized an electrochemical method which was the precursor of television.

SUMMARY

1. The evolution of communicative behavior patterns represents a systematic expansion of man's abilities to exercise symbolic control over himself and his social and physical environment.

2. The individual is considered a feedback-control system which possesses genetically defined mechanisms enabling it to adjust to spatial features of the environment. In human evolution as well as in individual development, we see a progressive shift from direct control to symbolic control, which in time permits a shift from primary spatial patterning of behavior to symbolic conceptualization of time, history, and causation.

3. Successive stages in the evolution of communicative patterns and techniques were correlated with technological changes in behavior organization and progressive changes in social and institutional organization. The parallel developments reflect expansion of the level and sphere of human symbolic control.

4. The scope of human learning and intelligence is defined by the level of biosocial evolution that has been achieved.

5. The type of concepts developed by man have been limited by his patterns of work, communication, and symbolism. In prehistory there was a limited understanding of temporal causation and historical sequence. Thought based on spatial concepts became enriched by an understanding of temporal organization only after the development of writing.

6. Stone-Age peoples developed totemic symbols which to them represented causative relationships between objects and the events with which the objects were associated. Rituals and magic were attempts to control the environment by symbolic means.

7. Prehistoric drawings represented first objects, then instrumental relationships, operational functions, and social interactions. This development was correlated with the level of human thought.

8. Patterns of nonverbal communication in the ancient cities, in graphic design, architecture, and so forth influenced all aspects of culture and learning. Pictorial symbols developed into formal writing.

9. After the development of writing, graphic design became more specialized but still was an important determinant of creative learning and thinking.

10. Nonverbal communicative techniques have been specialized for use in a number of areas, including book illustration and advertising.

11. Verbal writing has been illustrated by nonverbal displays ever since the early days of writing. In the development of book illustrations, new tools and techniques were all important. Modern books have been revolutionized by photographic techniques, and all methods of printing pictures have been highly significant for the development of science and technology.

12. Advertising displays can be traced back to the dawn of history and have always combined verbal with nonverbal patterns. Modern radio and television have obscured the dividing lines between advertising and other aspects of communication and education.

13. The earliest educational instruments were the tools used for nonverbal communication and the ritualistic devices used by sorcerers and priests. From the earliest times, educational tradition involved a dual role for the protector of the people. Prehistoric and ancient education also included training with actual tools and work processes in very young children.

14. Accurate astronomical, geographical, and meteorological observations were made by prehistoric man. Tools for plotting space and time and mathematical manipulations date from ancient times. These include calendars, maps, globes, planetary computers, and the abacus.

15. Laboratory demonstrations and experiments, important nonverbal educational techniques, have origins in rituals, demonstrations for public amusement, the use of automata, and museum displays. The earliest science laboratories grew out of metallurgical testing procedures, and developed into modern training and research laboratories which are an important source of new ideas. One modern development in laboratory training is the establishment of training courses for women technicians.

16. Many tools and devices have been developed for classroom use since free schools were established more than a century ago, but technological developments became more significant in recent years with the adoption of modern audiovisual techniques.

CHAPTER

4

Evolution of Human Learning: Verbal Communication

The individual achievements of thinking man are closely interrelated with the achievements of the human species in accumulating knowledge and transmitting the results of creative learning from one generation to the next. Lower animals benefit only to the most limited extent from the learning of their elders. Man has achieved his preeminence not only because of progressive evolutionary changes in biological make-up but because of the advancing level of technological and communicative skills that serve as an ever higher intellectual springboard for succeeding generations.

Of all the developments that have facilitated the accumulation of human knowledge, the most significant is that of writing—the application of tool using to verbal communication. This achievement, in some ways the greatest instrumental invention of all time, is inseparably related to the appearance of urban cultures, the beginning of recorded history, and the development of what modern man knows as rational thought. The development of writing

occurred in the continuous evolution of human communication and tool using, but by combining the flexibility and the abstract symbolism of oral speech with the visual permanence of graphic design, writing crystallized the human potential.

ORAL SPEECH

At the dawn of history, man had available a wealth of communicative patterns, both verbal and nonverbal. He could represent people, places, things, and events pictorially and symbolize them totemically. Further, he had developed methods of counting and recording the numbers of things, including the days, months, seasons, and years that marked off his activities. In some cultures, including the ancient Chinese, the Chaldeans, and the Peruvians, knotted cords were used to keep records and mark off the passage of time. Other peoples used stylized graphic time markings on rocks, pottery, or other objects. All early cultures used a multitude of pictures, signs, and symbols for keeping records, for outlining rules and regulations, for memorializing events and the achievements of their king-gods, and for magic control of the environment.

The basic trouble with the visual communicative patterns lay not in paucity but in abundance. To learn all the forms and to learn how to use them was a matter of a long, specialized education which few children were given. The matter of standardized meanings was a problem also for there was no basic reference system against which the symbols could be checked from one person to another, from one place to another, and, especially, from one time to another.

In contrast to nonverbal graphic communication, oral speech was relatively standardized in a culture, was learned from infancy by all individuals, and was flexible enough to symbolize all the things, places, numbers, events, actions, and ideas of which a people was cognizant. Yet this limitless number of ideas could be expressed by using a very limited number of movements of the speech mechanisms. Certain closures or partial closures of the air passages—the lips pressed together, the tongue against the teeth or the roof of the mouth, the nasal passage closed or open, and so on —defined what we know now as consonants. Certain shapes of the resonating cavities defined what we know as vowels. In any one language, prehistoric or modern, the number of consonants and vowels in standardized use is relatively small, yet these few movements combine to produce the infinitely variable patterns of speech.

The real discovery in the evolution of writing was not to tell stories in pictures, but to develop a limited number of graphic designs—an alphabet—to represent in permanent visual form the limited number of speech movements that produce only a transitory pattern of sound. Some symbol systems known as writing never did achieve this breakthrough. For example, Chinese characters never became a phonetic alphabet. They remained difficult and cumbersome and never lent themselves to universal education or the great strides forward in creative science and technology that have characterized Western cultures. The advantages of alphabetic writing lie in its basic simplicity, its efficiency, and its close correspondence with the components of oral speech.

We would like to preface our discussion of some of the early forms of writing with an account of the preceding evolution in the patterns of speech but, unlike some of the nonverbal forms of communication, oral speech left no permanent record of its course of development. To understand something of what this development must have been and the relation between oral and written verbal behavior, we shall analyze speech as a form of behavior and try to assess its significance among other adaptive behavior patterns.

The Behavioral Nature of Speech

The patterns of speech have been described and analyzed on many levels— for example, as a series of psychic events occurring within the mind or brain, as a system of linguistic forms, and as a pattern of sound that can be recorded and analyzed acoustically. But speech is primarily a form of behavior, and it can be described most meaningfully in terms of its movement patterns and their integration. All vocal activity, including whistling, humming, singing, as well as verbal speech, is patterned motion made up of postural, transport, and fine articulative movement components. It is misleading to think that the organization of speech is as complex as the word structure of a given language, for the movement structure is far more parsimonious. All the diverse sounds of spoken language are produced by means of integrated movements of a few muscle groups.

The movement patterns of speech have been described by Stetson (1951), who was the first to appreciate fully the significance of such a motion analysis. Figure 4.1 illustrates Stetson's general ideas of how different muscular systems of the body are integrated to produce speech. The postural control movements of the trunk and diaphragm maintain a steady pressure on the respiratory cavities, making possible the syllabic air pulses that are released by dynamic movements of the small muscles between the ribs—the intercostals. Superimposed upon the series of pulses are the articulations and vocalizations produced by movements of the neck, jaw, mouth, lips, and tongue. All of the systematized sounds of a spoken language are produced by relatively few of these movement patterns.

According to Stetson, the muscles of the abdomen and diaphragm execute the movements that maintain the pressure level and mark off the breath-groups of speech. Movements of the intercostal muscles force into the upper vocal canal distinct pulses of air which constitute the syllable units of oral speech. Syllable pulses can be released or arrested or both by partial or complete closures of the throat, nose, or mouth. It is these articulations that we know as con-

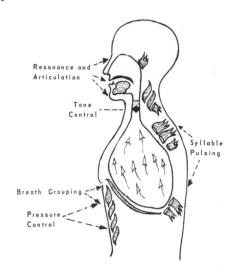

Figure 4.1.   The speech mechanism as described by Stetson (1951). Oral speech is an integrated process of postural (air-pressure generating and modulating), dynamic ballistic (syllable pulsing), and articulation movements. All of the phonetic variations in speech are made with a relatively few articulatory modulations of the syllable pulse. The basic movement patterns of alphabetic writing correspond closely to the movements that articulate the syllabic structure of speech. Accordingly, combinations of letters are related to patterns of speech movements as well as to the cognitive or ideational structure of a language.

sonants. The characteristic vowel sound of a syllable is determined by the size and shape of the resonating cavities of the throat and mouth. Vocal tone is added at the larynx but does not modify the basic movement pattern of speech.

In Stetson's analysis, syllables are the primary units of speech, for all speech is made up of one or more syllables. The so-called phonemes, the distinctive *sounds* of speech, are produced by the specialized articulatory movements but cannot be uttered except as an integrated part of a syllable pulse. However, while the consonant and vowel articulations do not occur as independent speech units, they supply the definitive characteristics that differentiate one syllable unit from another.

In alphabetic writing, the letters and letter combinations represent the articulated movements that produce consonants and vowels. The correspondence is neither perfect nor complete, but as a form of subsyllabic notation, the alphabet is used to symbolize most of the definitive sounds of a language. Learning to write, then, involves learning a limited set of manipulative movement patterns to represent the limited number of articulatory patterns used to define the syllables of oral speech.

Oral speech also is characterized by rhythmic patterning and phrasing of groups of syllables, features that depend on the postural movements of the trunk and diaphragm and the syllable-forming movements of the rib cage. In writing, these temporal patterns are suggested to a limited extent by marks of punctuation.

Origins of Speech

The development of speech as a pattern of human behavior is a fascinating subject for conjecture but for the most part remains cloaked in mystery. No known ethnic group lacks a spoken language, and we assume that a developing speech was one of the most primitive traits of the human species. If the use of words as systematic symbols developed originally along with the sustained use of tools within a group, then language may be as much as a half-million years old. Peking Man, for example, lived in groups in caves about 360,000 years ago and probably knew

how to use fire. Anthropologists assume generally that speech originated at least as early as the late Pleistocene period—about 80,000 years ago—in conjunction with the appearance of Neanderthal man and other early forms in Europe and Africa (Critchley, 1960).

The general evolutionary approach to the problem of language has prevailed for some time. It was noted by contemporaries of Darwin that a theory of evolution can be applied to languages themselves. Like some species, certain languages evolve and then die out. If one dies, it never reappears. Darwin (1871) himself attributed the genesis of language to the achievement by some early hominoid form of mental powers that raised it above the level of the apes. He believed that the use of speech reacted on this primitive mind, increasing the psychic capacity of man and making him capable of pursuing long trains of thought. Neo-Darwinians have discussed language as an aid to tool using in determining the survival of early human forms. In this context, language has been referred to as parasitic (Critchley, 1960).

Because of the gross similarities between the neuromuscular systems of apes and man, it is sometimes assumed that speech is mental or learned in human individuals and has no specific genetic basis. Thus the ape's inability to learn speech is attributed to a generally lower capacity for learning rather than to specific inadequacies in the vocal mechanism. This type of thinking tends to obscure the fact that very real genetic factors differentiate between the behavior of man and apes. The hand of a gorilla looks very much like the hand of a man, yet the gorilla is absolutely incapable of the complicated manipulative skills commonplace among men. The difference lies not so much in the musculature as in the sensori-neuromotor mechanisms for its control. The ape is probably just as incapable of the fine articulatory patterning of human speech as it is of the symbolic manipulations of human thought. In addition, the ape lacks the highly mobile and expressive face, the gestural and constructive capabilities of the hands, and other nonverbal communicative patterns by means of which man clarifies, reinforces, and possibly originally generated his verbal speech patterns. We feel sure that the appearance of speech in the human species was related to genetic changes as well as to distinctive changes in behavior organization.

Theories of Language Development

Theories of how language developed have been proposed since ancient times. In early Hebrew thinking, language was revealed by God. The different languages of man were caused by divine intervention when the descendants of Noah were so presumptuous as to try to build the tower of Babel to heaven. The Greeks thought that objects have a natural meaning and make their names known directly. In the nineteenth century, Max Müller ranged himself against Darwin and restated this mystic harmony concept of language in the form of the *ding-dong* theory (Noiré, 1917). His idea was that language is a result of harmonious verbal mimicking of sounds and events in nature.

Other and more recent theories vary this idea of the harmony of language and nature. The onomatopoetic or *bow-wow* theory traces words to direct echo-ing of sounds in nature. Roback (1954) modified the echo idea by attempting to relate certain words to the mimicking of natural sensory properties of softness and hardness.

Another type of theory stresses the importance of emotion and motivational states in originating vocal expressions. The *pooh-pooh* or interjection theory attributes sounds and words to emotional ejaculations of fear, surprise, and so on. This was a theory supported by Darwin. Jespersen (1922) thought speech originated in the apes, with the songs and sounds of sexual mating, love, and jealousy. To Révész (1956), language represented the need for contact.

Still another approach recognizes the role of gestures in the development of communication. This type of theory holds that the sounds of language originally were by-products of movement which became learned associations of these movements in social interplay. Paget (1930) proposed a gesture theory which attributes the origins of language to mouth gestures and contortions that were associated with hand gestures and sign language. In this view, oral speech came into more general use because of its greater efficiency.

Several theories of language have related it to work activities and the cries used in cooperative behavior. The *yo-heave-ho* theory of Noiré (1917) stated that the ejaculations accompanying intense effort came to be associated with work patterns and later evolved into language. According to an early theory, words originated with a few basic sounds used in tool manufacture. De Laguna (1927) attributed language to the needs of social cooperation in work, and Diamond (1959) restated the work interjection theory, with the additional idea that language growth depended on requests for assistance. Such requests originated the verb forms of language, and from these verbs, nouns were differentiated. Diamond presented evidence to show that in the evolution of language from early agricultural societies, there has been a reduction in verb forms and a great increase in nouns and adjectives.

All of these theories of language development are hampered by what amounts to a single-factor approach. Early man very likely uttered sounds in relation to many types of activities and environmental events and developed language to symbolize all of them. The activities of tool using and social work probably contributed most significantly to the evolution of language, but any activity or event of importance to survival would have generated communicative behavior.

In our view, the development of oral speech is one of three major advances in the biosocial evolutionary process that defined the nature of modern man. The first of these was the initial use of eolithic tools to control the environment, a phase that established the original human species, *Homo erectus*. This first primitive man evolved into *Homo sapiens* in conjunction with the expansion of tool using and the tool-making tradition into diversified handicraft, and with the systematization of oral speech to transmit knowledge and skills from parent to offspring and from one member of a group to another. The diversified activities of multitooled handicraft in hunting and prehistoric agriculture were instrumental in producing the thousands of words found in primitive languages. The third main phase of man's evolutionary process was the creation of writing in the ancient temple-building cultures.

Sounds that functioned as words undoubtedly were used by *Homo erectus*, but, in our view, systematic languages evolved along with the work diversification of tribal handicraft as *erect man* became *thinking man*. Finally, the development of writing launched the epoch of recorded history and set the stage for the civilized nature of modern man.

ORIGINS OF WRITING

One of the fascinating aspects of human development is the apparent fact that writing was developed independently during the same general period by the Sumerians, Egyptians, East Indians, and Chinese. All of these cultures had achieved a high level of pictorial representation and organization of work at the time that systematized forms of writing appeared. But of these original innovators, only the Egyptians developed a system of writing phonetic letters within their own tradition. We do not know the reasons for this superior achievement by the Egyptians. It may have been related to a higher level of work organization, a more advanced level of development of oral speech, or other factors. It is possible that there was a greater movement of foreigners in and out of the Egyptian cities at the time their writing was being developed, leading to efforts to provide a phonetic notation in writing for those unfamiliar with the symbolic tradition.

Chinese Ideograms

In contrast to Egyptian and Near Eastern forms of writing, which either incorporated or lost out to phonetic letter notations thousands of years ago, Chinese writing continued to use signs for words from its beginnings to the present day. Thus, instead of reducing the number of different symbols needed for writing, as happened with alphabetic forms, the Chinese continued to develop new word-signs through the centuries to keep pace with their developing ideas.

The first written language in China dates from almost 5000 years ago, when a system of graphic signs was developed which represented some elements of oral speech. This system utilized sets of horizontal bars in different arrangements, and is said to survive still in the graphic notations of the soothsayers (Cohen, 1958). Classic Chinese writing was based originally on pictographs, and is dated traditionally from about 2500 B.C. Up until about 200 B.C., the realistic features of the characters gradually disappeared, and classic Chinese writing, much as it exists today, was evolved in the era of the Han, from 200 B.C. to 200 A.D. By the eighth century, the Chinese were engraving whole pages of characters on blocks of wood and printing them, anticipating the introduction of printing in Europe by hundreds of years. In the eleventh century, a Chinese developed the technique of using movable type, but the process did not spread directly to Western countries.

The individual characters of Chinese writing are each inscribed in an ideal square of constant size and are arranged in vertical columns which are read from top to bottom, proceeding from the right column on a page toward the left. All words are composed of a single syllable, and each character represents a specific word. Some characters are simple ideograms, representing specific objects or things, other ideas connected to the original object or thing, or abstract ideas or qualities derived from a character that symbolizes the idea. Certain other ideas, principally abstractions, are represented by combining two simple ideograms; for example, the characters signifying *work* and *action* when combined in a single character would signify *to get to work* or *to attack*. Then in some cases a simple ideogram is used to represent a word that sounds the same as the original thing represented by the character. Thus a type of phonetic representation was introduced into Chinese writing, and this phonetic classification of words is one important principle for constructing Chinese characters. However, most characters also are identified ideologically as well as phonogrammatically. According to Cohen (1958), fully ninety percent of Chinese characters are sign-complexes made up of a phonogram, indicating roughly the pronunciation of the word, plus an ideogram which indicates the category of meaning to which the word belongs. There are of the order of 214 of these *keys* indicating categories of meaning. Either the phonograms or the key ideograms can be used independently to indicate specific words.

Since Chinese characters represent words, a new sign had to be developed to represent every word in the written language. Accordingly, the proliferation of the Chinese written vocabulary more than any other form of writing tells us something about the elaboration of ideas in a developing complex society. According to Cohen, a Chinese dictionary composed in the year 100 A.D. had 9353 distinct signs and another in the sixth century, 24,000 signs. An official dictionary in 1716 listed some 50,000 explained signs, but historical and scholarly works include as many as 80,000 signs. Thus there has been perhaps a tenfold increase in the number of Chinese sign-ideas during the course of about 2000 years. Current usage by an average person necessitates knowledge of 6000 to 8000 distinct characters. Learning to read and write his classical language is an immeasurably more tedious process for a Chinese child than for a Western child who can begin to construct meaningful verbal writing with a few different letter symbols.

Although China has a great scholarly tradition, its written language remained cumbersome and inefficient. In the modern period there have been some efforts to introduce alphabetic symbols, not to displace the traditional characters, however, but to aid in identifying them. It is interesting to speculate why this old culture never developed a phonetic alphabet of its own. Our guess is that the evolution of writing in all cultures has been intimately tied in with the evolution of work processes and social organization so that developments in one area feed back to stimulate developments in another. In Egypt and the Near East, highly complicated urban societies with diversified work patterns were associated with the development of efficient written languages. In China, the organization of work remained essentially at the village level almost to the present day, and the impetus for modern change came not from within the culture but from without. Writing in China was used principally for religious, scholarly, and artistic pursuits. It served to set the religious or moral or cultural tone of the society but for the most part was not

needed by ordinary people to carry on their day-to-day affairs. Thus the lag in social and work evolution in China was reflected in the relative inefficiency of their writing techniques.

Cuneiform Writing

Although we can trace some of the most important stages in the development of our modern alphabetic writing system, the full story of human efforts and achievements in this area never will be known. The clearest ancient records presently available for examination are from Sumer and Egypt, whose symbolic notations and their progressive modifications have been known for many years. As long ago as 4000 to 3000 B.C., the temple cities of Sumer were using a system of writing that developed into what is called cuneiform, named for the wedge-shaped characters that were made with specific pointed reed imprinting tools. A typical Sumerian written record was a tablet or brick made of clay, imprinted with the cuneiform characters, and then hardened in the sun or baked in a kiln. This form of writing was modified and used by the Babylonians, Assyrians, and other Middle Eastern cultures for several thousand years. Bricks and tablets have been found that are imprinted with a variety of information, including allusions to astronomical phenomena and other information that might have been records of tides and floods.

The small clay cone shown in Figure 4.2 is imprinted with Babylonian cuneiform writing and dates from about 2300 B.C. It is suspected to be a training tablet because it contains writing also found on larger tablets. Tablets of this sort have been found in many forms—

some round, some square, some rectangular.

In the beginning, cuneiform writing may have been based on pictographs, but the method of pegging clay to form the triangular and linear symbols greatly modified the form processes involved so that it eventually appeared as a series of wedge-shaped triangles interlaced with lines. Originally, each cuneiform symbol represented an idea or its equivalent word. Several of these symbols with their meanings are shown in Figure 4.3.

It is also possible that the nonpictorial quality of cuneiform symbols was due to graphic origins that were nonpictorial in character—for example, simplified abstract markings used for the purpose of record-keeping, time and event marking, and so on. There was much building in the temple cities, and much business and trade. It is very likely that non-pictorial records were kept in all of these activities for a variety of purposes. Consequently, the cuneiform symbols may not have been entirely pictographic in origin. In any event, this system of writing eventually died out, to be replaced by the more efficient alphabetic forms.

Although there was no continuous development based on this ancient Sumerian technique that has extended to the present day, cuneiform writing may have had some influence on other forms that were evolving. As cuneiform writing developed in various cultures, some of the signs represented syllables and thus had a phonetic quality, although they were not used to represent individual consonants. There is also some indication that late cuneiform systems contained signs related to the vowel sounds. If so, this type of notation might have influenced the development of vowel-consonant alphabets in the Near East.

Figure 4.2. An ancient teaching instrument —a clay cone with Babylonian cuneiform writing. (Courtesy of Prof. Menahem Mansoor.)

Figure 4.3. Cuneiform symbols with their approximate English equivalents. Cuneiform writing is thought to be of pictographic origin, although it may have been derived in part from abstract symbols used for counting, time and event marking, and so forth.

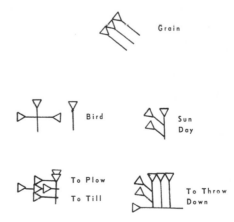

Egyptian Hieroglyphics

While the Sumerians and Babylonians were keeping their records and memorializing their great events with cuneiform symbols, the ancient Egyptians were evolving a form of writing that was to have great significance for the entire civilized world. The name that we generally apply to Egyptian symbols reveals something about their original function as well as the original technique of producing them. Hieroglyph means literally a sacred carving, and the original hieroglyphic inscriptions were beautifully engraved on tombs, temples, monuments, tools, and so on to record the sacred activities of the king-gods and related notable events.

The first hieroglyphic symbols were recognizable pictures which represented people, objects, actions and events. Wolf (1954) notes that the ancient Egyptians' first dim awareness of the course of history was occasioned by the marking of tools or plaques with semipictorial representations of notable events. Gradually the pictures became more abstract and were assigned general symbolic rather than literal meanings. The uses of hieroglyphic writing were extended from monumental purposes to the day-to-day needs of the people, both religious and secular. Egypt's formal educational tradition indicates the usefulness of their developing written language and their over-all progress in science and arts. Figure 4.4 pictures a scribe writing on a tablet with a stylus while the man to the right is using a balance to measure weights. The symbols above the two are hieroglyphs of the Fifth Dynasty, or about 2300 B.C.

Figure 4.4.   Egyptian writing from the fifth Dynasty, about 2300 B.C. (Courtesy of the Cairo Museum.)

In the course of Egypt's history, hieroglyphic writing was simplified to two other forms, known as hieratic writing, and demotic writing. Hieratic writing was used for religious matters, while demotic writing, literally the writing of the people, was used for ordinary affairs of the professions, business, and trade. Examples of the three forms of Egyptian writing are shown in Figure 4.5.

Almost from the beginning, Egyptian writing was both ideographic and phonetic in character—that is, its signs represented both ideas and the sounds of speech. A hieroglyph representing a definite object might stand also for something else similar in meaning or quite a different object that was pronounced the same. For example, the English words *sun* and *son* might be represented

Figure 4.5.   Forms of ancient Egyptian writing. *a.* Hieroglyphic. *b.* Hieratic. *c.* Demotic.

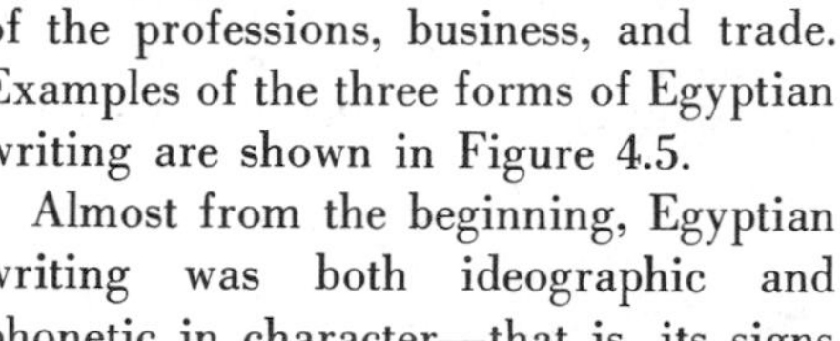

hieroglyphically by the same symbol, but the symbol for *sun* might also represent *day*. Such a method of writing, where symbols were transferred both according to meaning and according to sound, would have been very confusing had not the Egyptians adopted certain complementary symbols. Alongside their hieroglyphs they inserted extra signs to indicate categories of meaning, analogous to the Chinese keys, and—more importantly—other signs to specify pronunciation. At different times in Egyptian history, up to about thirty of these phonetic signs were used to indicate one or more consonants. Although the Egyptians never learned to indicate vowels, their phonetic system of writing was reasonably accurate and used only some hundreds of signs in contrast to the thousands that make up the Chinese written language.

The Egyptians also introduced an important technological improvement into writing—the development of papyrus as a writing material. Papyrus is a tall grass-like plant that grew in marshy areas near the Nile. By slicing the marrow of the papyrus shoot into thin strips, criss-crossing the strips and then beating them into a sheet, the Egyptians made a splendid ivory-colored paper. Papyrus was by far the most efficient writing material yet discovered. It could be marked with a brush or reed pen with pigment or ink. Sheets of papyrus were stuck together and rolled into the first scroll books. But more importantly, writing on papyrus changed the whole organization of writing motions, making them simpler and more efficient. A cursive script style of writing was developed that has been refined and improved to the present day. Writing on papyrus

with pen or brush probably did much to develop the simplified hieratic and demotic styles of writing that were to replace the hieroglyphic pictures in ordinary usage.

PHONETIC WRITING

Although the Egyptians wrote letters, they did not abandon the use of ideographs and thus did not develop a true alphabetic system. Alphabetic writing involves only phonetic representation, with no ideographic signs at all. This development occurred in Asia Minor and later in Greece. An intermediate phase was the use of syllabic writing in some cultures of the eastern Mediterranean region. Our discussion of these developments is based principally on Cohen (1958).

Syllabic Writing

The use of signs to represent syllables, usually a consonant-vowel combination, is of very ancient origin and evolved originally in an ideographic context. Cuneiform writing used some syllabic notations, and the phonograms in Chinese writing roughly approximate syllables. However, there were some systems of writing in the eastern Mediterranean and Near East which relinquished all use of ideograms and used signs that represented only phonetic syllables.

One culture that certainly used syllabic notation to some extent was ancient Crete. There are several types of writing that have been discovered in Crete, corresponding to periods of Cretan history from about 3000 to 1200 B.C. Although the earlier inscriptions have not been deciphered satisfactorily, it appears that there was a progressive evolution from hieroglyphic writing to syllabic writing. The most recent type of Cretan writing is known as linear, a cursive form that includes the so-called linear *A* (around 1800 to 1400 B.C.) and linear *B* (1450 to 1200 B.C.). Linear *A* includes some 130 signs, of which perhaps a third are believed to be ideograms and the rest syllabic phonograms. Linear *B* is further simplified, including only about 80 signs.

The linear script in Crete undoubtedly was influenced by Semitic and Egyptian writing, for this island in the eastern Mediterranean had trade relations with all the early seafaring peoples. Linear *B* was used after Greece had invaded Crete, and its current interpreters read this script in the Greek language.

A syllabic writing that is thought to be related to Cretan writing has been found on the island of Cyprus. This is an entirely phonetic system that utilized a syllabary (analogous to alphabet) of fifty-five signs. Most of these represent a consonant followed by a vowel. Thus there are signs for va, ve, vi, vo, ra, re, ri, ro, ru, and so on. A syllabary of this order of complexity—that is, fifty-five signs—can represent many phonetic combinations, but still is not as efficient as an alphabet. For twenty-five to thirty alphabetic characters can combine to represent far more than fifty-five syllables.

Consonant Alphabets

The first phonetic alphabets were originated by Semitic peoples of Asia Minor sometime between 2000 and 1000 B.C. The oldest inscriptions that have been found in alphabetic writing clearly show the influence of Egyptian hieroglyphs, and some show some relation to

cuneiform writing. But a real break had been made with these more ancient traditions by constructing a limited set of signs which corresponded to the consonants of oral speech. There are some who believe that this development was a deliberate invention by seafaring traders who needed an efficient system of writing with which to deal with peoples who used a number of different spoken languages.

Traditionally, the consonantal alphabet that spread to the West is attributed to the Phoenicians, whose language is also called Canaanean. However, there are inscriptions dating from before 1000 B.C., including Paleosinaitic and Ugaritic, which are in somewhat different alphabetic form although they show many similarities to Phoenician writing. It is not known for certain whether a consonantal alphabet was developed just once in Asia Minor and was modified into various forms, or whether several alphabets, showing interrelationships, were constructed at about the same time in history.

Phoenician or Canaanean writing was used not only by the Phoenicians in the centuries just prior to the Christian era but also by the Hebrews, Moabites, and Samaritans to write their own languages. In each tradition, the numbers and forms of the letters were subject to progressive modification, until the various alphabets became very different in superficial appearance. However, the Hebrew alphabet and our own can be traced back to a common source. Various forms of writing used by the Arabian peoples and by East Indians also stem from the ancient consonantal alphabets of Asia Minor.

Although our designation *alphabet*

comes from *alpha* and *beta,* the first two characters of the Greek alphabet, the names of the letters go back to Hebrew and Aramaic and undoubtedly came to them from the Phoenicians. Most of the names of the letters can be traced to words in the various Semitic languages.

Vocalic Alphabet

The eventual development of the vocalic (consonant-vowel) alphabet is attributed to the Greeks, who might have appeared to be an unlikely source for this significant advance. The Greeks were an Indo-European people who came to the lower Balkan Peninsula and the islands of the Aegean Sea more than a thousand years before the Christian era. They brought no writing system of their own, but some time around 1000 B.C. they borrowed the Phoenician Semitic form of consonant writing, added vowel characters to it, and thus completed the alphabet.

The interchange between Greeks and Phoenicians probably was due to Phoenician navigators who aided or exploited the Greeks in trade. The main focus of their interchange may very well have been the island of Crete, which had one of the most brilliantly advanced civilizations of the era. The various forms of Cretan writing show both Egyptian and Semitic influences, and the Greeks who invaded this island undoubtedly came into contact with all of the languages and forms of writing of the Near East. Lacking a pictographic or graphic tradition of their own, the Greeks used both the syllabic writing of the Cretans and the alphabetic writing of the Semites and finally adopted the latter as the more efficient and flexibile for use in keeping records and accounts in their cosmopoli-

tan centers. Their introduction of vowel signs to the alphabet probably was a matter of necessity. Having developed no pictorial methods of conceptualization, the Greeks were hampered in using a system of writing until they made it conform more closely to the sounds of speech than was possible with consonants alone. The peoples who had developed writing originally drew upon their nonverbal graphic traditions to add meaning to their symbols; when the Greeks borrowed writing, they gave it meaning by relating it closely to the patterns of oral speech.

The Greek form of writing, which was to determine subsequent systems in the entire Western world, evolved gradually and cannot be dated precisely, but its dependence on Semitic alphabetic writing cannot be doubted. Greek inscriptions dating from the eighth century B.C. show separately outlined characters that resemble Phoenician letters very closely. Some of the Greek names for letters resemble Semitic names for letters, and the order of the letters in the alphabet approximates that used in the Hebrew tradition. Early Greek writing was from right to left, as in Semitic writing, although examples have been found that alternate directions back and forth in the style called *boustrophedon* ("on return of ox," as in plowing a field). Later the Greeks changed the direction of their writing to the left-to-right style that we use today. At first Greek writing ran all the letters together, as in the inscription shown in Figure 4.6, but later Greek writing separated words and adopted some marks of punctuation.

By the time the Greeks learned to write, the Egyptian technical processes

Figure 4.6.   A Greek inscription from the fifth century B.C., read from left to right. The words are not separated. (From Cohen. *La grande invention de l'écriture et son évolution.* Paris: Imprimerie Nationale, 1958.)

of using ink had spread throughout the Mediterranean world. Hellenic scribes wrote with ink on shells and other surfaces and with stillettos on waxed surfaces. They wrote on leather and apparently on papyrus, but the climate of this part of the world, unlike the dry lands of Egypt, did not preserve these precious early records. From the avalanching nature of the expansion of Greek thought, we would judge that there was a far more extensive practice of writing in this culture than in any prior civilization.

In the evolution of what may be mankind's greatest invention—writing—the Greeks occupy an anomalous position. They entered late upon the scene, borrowed an efficient alphabet which had originated quite outside their own tradition, and then supplied what might seem to be minor additions—the signs for vowels. But by this contribution, the Greeks were to make possible the brilliant potentialities of the written word, not only in keeping records but also in stimulating creative expressive literature and scientific thought. For just as we owe our style of writing to the Greeks, we trace to them our cultural and intellectual heritage.

The evolution of the alphabet and its reciprocal relationships with human progress make a fascinating account of human motives and adaptive processes. Our own interpretation of the development of the Semitic and the Greek alphabets stresses several factors. First, we recognize the fact that this general advance in writing technique accompanied major changes in social and cultural organization. It was a period when the ancient temple civilizations were being transformed from building cultures into competing mercantile systems. The first machines of civilization were being adapted to work. Codes of laws were being refined, and the professions were being differentiated. For the first time in the long stretch of human evolution, teachers, lawyers, scribes, and business men required a formal education to serve their own needs. The very existence of a civilization such as this depended on educating many individuals rapidly and efficiently. This task required a style of writing in which the written symbols automatically represented the movements of oral speech, so that the problems of daily living could be approached with equivalent behavior patterns of speaking, writing, and processes of thought.

Another factor that influenced the Semites toward the development of a phonetic alphabet was their traditional rejection of the use of idols and graphic representation. Yet they were concerned with their origins, with the historical process, and with law and order. To write, they had to borrow—from the Egyptians and perhaps from others—but instead of borrowing picture symbols they adapted or evolved abstract signs and notations which could be related to oral speech.

A third factor that influenced the development of the alphabet was the nature of teaching in the various ancient cultures. Where the priests controlled education, the original sacred forms of writing persisted. But the Phoenicians used writing more to promote their trades and professions. In the interests of efficiency and communication with other peoples, they perfected the techniques of phonetic notation. The introduction of the vowel signs by the Greeks very likely was motivated by the same needs in trading with and teaching others. As Cohen points out, the advanced Near Eastern cultures must have recognized the differences between alphabetic notation and the older more cumbersome

styles and deliberately developed the more efficient style.

Alphabetic writing apparently was used for hundreds of years in trade and mercantile record keeping before a real literature and poetry were developed. It is our opinion that expressive literature was made possible by the Greeks' vocalic alphabet. The incomplete consonantal alphabet was adequate for record keeping and the needs of the marketplace, where the context reinforced the meaning of the symbols, but the addition of vowels provided writing with the flexibility and thus the creativity of oral speech. Thenceforth the written word provided as unrestricted a mode of communication as the spoken word. Thus the Greek alphabet provided more than a technique of preserving the words of creative men; it stimulated the development of entirely new verbal talents.

HUMAN FACTORS ANALYSIS OF WRITING

The evolution of the written languages of the world—their style, efficiency, and adaptability to human needs has been inextricably tied in with the development of writing instruments and materials. As we already have indicated, it was probaby more than a coincidence that the first really efficient written language developed concurrently in Egypt with the development of the first good writing material—paper. Today our pens, pencils, and paper are so commonplace that we tend not to realize how much the tools structure the writing behavior, and, conversely, how much the human factors of behavior organization have influenced the success and failure of the different techniques and styles of writing.

Writing Techniques

During the long course of history, man has written with many tools and on many different surfaces. The Sumerians used cut reeds to mark clay. The ancient Egyptians used chisels and knives to carve rock and wood. Stone, metal, ivory, wax tablets, and bamboo have been marked or engraved. Pigments, lacquers, and soot-and-water inks have been applied with sticks, brushes, and stiff reed pens to bark and palm leaves, to sheep and goat skins, to silk and linen, and to papyrus and other forms of paper. Some of these techniques are shown in Figure 4.7.

When the symbols of writing were executed individually, by cutting, imprinting, or stroking with a brush, the direction in which they were to be read varied considerably. In different kinds of writing, the symbols proceeded from left to right, right to left, back and forth, top to bottom, bottom to top, or even in a spiral. Hebrew symbols, for example, are read from right to left; Chinese symbols usually go up and down, as did some early Egyptian inscriptions. But eventually the Greeks developed an easy, cursive, paper-and-ink style of writing, proceeding in a line from left to right— the easiest writing movement pattern to execute with the right hand and the easiest to check visually, as the hand moves along.

The style of writing developed by the Semites and modified by the Greeks spread throughout the civilized areas of the Near East and western Europe before 500 B.C. Important documents, or at least most of the documents that have survived, were written on parchment or

Figure 4.7.   Some early writing techniques. *a.* and *b.* Egyptians writing with reed. *c.* Japanese using brush and ink. *d.* Chinese method of using brush and ink. Lamp black molded into a stick with gum or gluten is rubbed in water on an ink stone. (*a* from Knight (ed.) *The arts and industry of all nations.* London: Dutton, 1860, 2 vols.; *b* and *c* from Butterworth (ed.) *The growth of industrial art.* Washington, D.C.: U.S. Government Printing Office, 1892; *d* from Carter. *The invention of printing in China and its spread westward.* (Rev. ed.) New York: Columbia University Press, 1931.)

the finer-grained vellum, but papyrus was used widely for many kinds of records and scroll books. Stiff reed pens and brushes were used as writing instruments, and split pen points similar to our own may have been used in the Near East. The different designs of writing implements in different localities probably helped to determine the great variations in writing style that emerged among the numerous cultures of the Near East and ancient Europe.

The next important advance in the development of writing tools with related changes in the movement coordinations of writing came centuries after the decline of Greece and Rome, with the introduction of the quill pen. Beckmann (1846) dates the development of the goose-quill pen in the seventh century and cites two references for its use at this time. The first picture showing goose-quill pens in use dates from the ninth century. The modern split-point metal pen was developed toward the end of the eighteenth century, and within a few years many millions of steel pen points were being produced annually in England (Beckmann, 1846). No further important changes were made in ink-writing pen points until the introduction of ballpoints in the 1940s.

Our most common writing instrument, the so-called lead pencil, was developed early in the seventeenth century after the first deposit of graphite was discovered accidentally in Elizabethan England. Graphite was known as *black lead* and was considered so valuable at first that the mine owners instituted methods of guarding and examining workers not unlike those used in gold mines. Miners changed clothes going in and out of the mine, and those who sorted the graphite were guarded carefully. For over two centuries, this original mine was worked only about once in seven years to obtain a supply of black lead for pencils. In the nineteenth century, it was worked several weeks each year to produce enough graphite to meet market demands.

Fully as important as a good instrument to the art of writing was a good writing surface, not too cumbersome and not too expensive. In the Western world, parchment and papyrus were used throughout most of the Middle Ages, although a far cheaper and more efficient material had been invented in China early in the Christian era. In 105 A.D., a method of making paper of tree bark, hemp, fish nets, and rags—a method which is basically similar to modern paper making of cellulose fibers—was reported to the Chinese emperor. The use of paper spread rapidly throughout China, and the method was taught to Arabians at Samarkand by Chinese captives in 751. Throughout the next several centuries, the use and manufacture of paper spread throughout the Moslem world and displaced papyrus even in the country of its origin, Egypt, by about the end of the tenth century.

Although Arabian papers were imported into Europe from the Middle East, the secret of manufacture traveled to Europe indirectly, from Egypt to Morocco and thence to Spain, where the Arabs were manufacturing paper in the twelfth century. The first recorded paper mill in Christian Europe was set up in 1189 at Hérault, France. Other early paper-making factories were established in Italy in 1276, in Germany in 1391, in England in 1494, and in Philadelphia in 1690. Paper achieved its full significance in Europe only with the invention of printing, but when Europeans adopted paper for their printed books, they also adopted it for writing by hand.

Pencils, pens, and paper have become so inexpensive that we forget their intrinsic value, but this was not always so. Writers in the Middle Ages, when good tools were hard to come by, valued a good pen and writing materials as extraordinary possessions, to be guarded and kept throughout their lifetime.

Mechanization of the Scribe

It is only too obvious that our present accumulation of written verbal knowledge and its wide distribution would never have been achieved by scribes writing by hand, however efficient their pens and pencils. The European development of printing with movable type in the fifteenth century revolutionized not only the art of bookmaking but our entire Western culture. The Phoenicians and Greeks invented alphabetic writing, but the Europeans mechanized it.

For centuries after books were printed, however, private writing still was carried out by hand. Young men of professional ability sometimes spent years acting as secretaries, writing out letters and records in a carefully executed longhand script in which they took great pride. The invention of the typewriter in the nineteenth century almost abolished the work role of professional scribes and, along with systems of shorthand, dictating machines, and so forth, increased the output of a secretary many times over.

The educational significance of these and related technological developments is quite apparent, for the Western dream of universal education has hinged on our ability to reproduce written material quickly and in large quantities. It is less well recognized, however, that mechanized writing has been successful in the Western world only because our style of alphabetic writing lends itself to efficient duplication. The Chinese invented a printing process many centuries ago, and even printed from movable types more than three centuries before this process was used in Europe, but it did not have the same impact in China that it was to have on the Western world. The apparent explanation is that the many characters in Chinese writing make typesetting far more difficult than an alphabet of twenty-six or so letters. And a typewriter, as we know it, would be out of the question. In writing as well as in other areas of human achievement, an efficient instrumental process stimulated further technological advances, whereas an inefficient process was relatively nonproductive.

Writing for the Blind

We begin to appreciate the interactions between human factors and instrumental processes when we come across a case in which the two are incompatible. For example, consider the factors involved in teaching the blind to read and write. Up until fairly recent times, attempts to educate the blind were hampered by the inappropriateness of writing and printing developed by and for seeing individuals for use by persons without sight.

In schools for the blind in the nineteenth century, especially those in Paris and Edinburgh, two different approaches were used to train blind children in alphabetic reading and writing. One approach was to keep the same letter forms that make up our visual alphabet but to present them in such a way that they could be discriminated tactually. Movable letter blocks were used, and letters printed in relief. Another technique was to stick pins into large pin cushions to outline the letter forms in a kind of corrugated texture. None of these methods had notable success.

The other approach was to break away from the forms of the visual alphabet and devise a tactual alphabet that the blind children could learn efficiently. In the Edinburgh Blind Asylum, an alphabet was devised of angular symbols, some of which duplicated standard letters and some of which differed considerably. Two teachers at Edinburgh also developed a string alphabet, in which knots of different kinds arranged in different patterns on a string represented numbers and letters. These alphabets are illustrated in Figure 4.8. The most successful method, which is in common use today, was developed by Louis Braille in Paris from about 1840 to 1852. Braille devised an alphabet and number system in which each letter and number is represented by a specific pattern of dots printed in relief on stiff paper or plastic.

READING, BOOKS, AND LEARNING

The primary instrument guiding organization of learning in reading is the book. Books are so well known to us that we forget that they are teaching devices based on principles of technical,

Figure 4.8.   Tactual alphabets developed at Edinburgh Blind Asylum in the nineteenth century. (From Knight (ed.) *The arts and industry of all nations*. London: Dutton, 1860, 2 vols.)

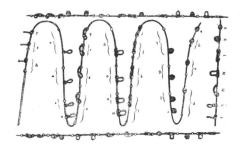

artistic, and behavioral design, which have evolved to their present form from very different origins. The first books were clay, wood, and stone tablets, such as the cuneiform tablet in Figure 4.9a. The Egyptians established a literature of a sort and professional scientific works written in scroll book form. Other types of books were developed in ancient times in other parts of the world. The Chinese bound sheaves of bamboo strips by perforating them at one end and stringing them on cords or thongs, and the Indians bound palm leaves into books. Several types of Chinese books are shown in Figure 4.9b. Books as we know them are not over seven or eight hundred years old.

Recently discovered Hebrew religious tracts, long hidden in caves on the edge of the Judean desert, give us a clear idea of the nature of scroll books just prior to the Christian era. The *Book of Isaiah* in Figure 4.10 shows letters of a square design which later were adapted for the first printed Hebrew Bibles. At a later time, the Hebrews made bound wooden books with thongs or rings through which rods were passed. Similar bound books made of flat wooden boards, such as *Runic Almanacs*, were made in northern Europe and the British Isles. The Greeks and Romans collected sheaves of parchment and tied them into books. Both scroll and bound tablet types of books were found in the excavated ruins of Pompeii.

Written books were not produced in northern Europe to any significant extent until the seventh and eighth centuries, when monastic scribes began to reproduce, in their finest scripts, the ancient and comparatively crude manu-

Figure 4.9.   Precursors of modern books. *a.* Cuneiform stone tablets from about 2300 B.C. *b.* Evolution of the book in China, showing a silk roll (lower right), a paper roll (lower left), a folded paper book, and a stitched book bound in boards. (*a* courtesy of Prof. Menahem Mansoor; *b* from Carter. *The invention of printing in China and its spread westward.* (Rev. ed.) New York: Columbia University Press, 1931.)

scripts that they possessed. European monastic writing from the tenth to the fourteenth century led to a standardized writing style which later was to define the format and type used in printing. Books written laboriously by hand were the distinctive products of individual scribes who devoted months and even years to single volumes. After the scribe had finished, decorative capital letters, borders, and illustrations (rubrication and illumination) were added by other artists. The old books were colorful and frequently glowed with pure gold within and without. Leather bindings frequently were tooled and inlaid with precious metals and jewels, and each volume became a jealously guarded addition to the library of a monastery, church, or castle stronghold.

In the thirteenth and fourteenth centuries, the work of most European scribes centered on the writing of Bibles, especially pocket-sized volumes in the tiniest possible handwriting. Psalters for use in churches also were produced in relatively large numbers. Only after the introduction of printing in the fifteenth century were secular manuscripts produced in quantity. Some of the first printed books besides the Bible were Latin and Greek classics and the poetical and oratorical exercises of the Italian humanists.

Development of Printing

Although the invention of printing with movable type is attributed popularly to the German Gutenberg, he by no means was the first to use the process. In Europe, the Dutchman Coster is said to have introduced typography some years before Gutenberg, but the process

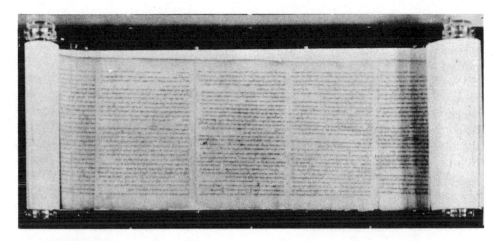

Figure 4.10. An opened Dead Sea scroll. (Courtesy of Prof. Menahem Mansoor, obtained from the Israel Office of Information.)

was developed first in China as one of a long series of innovations in printing techniques (Carter, 1931). The art of printing had its first Chinese origins perhaps three centuries prior to the Christian era in the use of seals made of stone, metal, wood, ivory, and rhinoceros horn. Seal impressions were stamped in soft clay to authenticate documents, much as men of the Western world have stamped impressions in sealing wax. Around the fifth century A.D., seals were inked in red ink and used to print inscriptions. From this practice, it was but a short step to printing pages of pictures or text from engraved blocks of wood.

Another forerunner of block printing in China was the practice of taking inked rubbings on paper from stone inscriptions, possibly as early as the second century A.D. Classic writings were inscribed in stone, after which a dampened tough paper was brushed carefully into all the depressions and crevices of the inscription. When dry, the paper was brushed with an ink pad to produce an inked background for white characters that conformed to the inscription.

True block printing from blocks of wood on which the characters were engraved in relief and reversed from their normal orientation was developed in Buddhist monasteries in China during the first half of the eighth century. The engraved block was laid with the characters up and inked with a brush. Then a sheet of thin paper was laid on the block and brushed on the back with a dry brush to transfer a clear impression. A man working alone could make as many as a thousand copies a day. Block printing was developed into a high art in China, Japan, and Korea and persisted to modern times.

About the middle of the eleventh century, four centuries before Gutenberg, a Chinese printer devised movable type of earthenware which he fitted into a metal or earthenware form for the first printing from type. Type made of tin also was devised, but neither this nor the earthenware type was used widely. In the thirteenth and fourteenth centuries, wooden type was cut, which proved more satisfactory to use with the ordinary Chinese ink of soot and water. In 1390, the king of Korea ordered bronze type cast in a foundry, and books were printed in Korea from the metal type in the early years of the fifteenth century. Thus all the basic processes of typographical printing were developed in China and Korea. The strange thing is that they made little impact on Chinese culture and education, whereas Gutenberg's equivalent invention was a major factor in propelling Europe out of the Dark Ages into the enlightenment of the Renaissance. The difference between Chinese and European printing is not so much in the printing process itself as in the styles of writing that were reproduced. The thousands of characters of Chinese writing required thousands of separate type, which made the storage problem cumbersome and the work of typesetting laborious and time-consuming. Printing from type was not a commercial success in Korea, China, or Japan, and by the nineteenth century, it had almost lost out to the older block printing (Carter, 1931).

In Europe the first block printing was fairly crude and made from illustrative woodcuts, dating from about 1380. Later a brief text was also cut into the wood to accompany the picture, to produce block-books. These were printed in folio form, on one side of a sheet of paper only, and were available between about 1430 and 1460. Block-books dealt almost exclusively with religious themes, and the printed letters faithfully copied the written letters of the scribes, even to the extent of copying the errors and irregular abbreviations that had appeared in handwritten manuscripts. Block printing in Europe never achieved the high degree of perfection that was seen in China, for it was displaced very quickly in Europe by printing with movable type.

The introduction into medieval Europe of printing with movable metal type led to wide dispersal of standardized skills in reading and writing and was instrumental in launching the intellectual Renaissance of the Western world. Printed books were to make possible the introduction of organized learning and education to masses of people, instead of to a limited few.

Books as Educational Instruments

The first extensive literature of knowledge, or wisdom, was established in ancient Egypt, where a body of medical knowledge was accumulated and recorded in writing from before 2400 B.C. Papyri from around 1600 B.C. contain detailed accounts of impressive Egyptian medical knowledge, including the idea of the functional dependence of the body on the brain (Wolf, 1954).

The Greeks made great strides forward in the use of books, founding an expressive literature, writing history, and establishing extensive libraries for the use of students and scholars. The Greek tradition of an extensive general literature and learning from books was carried on by the Romans, only to dim in Europe after the fall of Rome. For centuries, reading and writing in Europe were restricted almost entirely to the Bible and religious tracts prepared by monks. General education based on books was for a time almost unknown, and certainly there was no thought of educating the masses. In time, schooling was neglected even among the priests and monks.

The eventual expansion of literacy and reading skill among the people of the Western world depended upon two major features lacking in ancient writing— standardization of writing form and of the terminology of writing. The first steps toward standardization were provided in the Middle Ages by the developing art of book making and by the compilation of dictionaries by the Arabs in Spain. The Arab culture in Spain around the ninth and tenth centuries constituted a spur to European education not only because of their dictionaries but because of their general interest in books and schools at all levels. The Arabs founded great universities in the Spanish cities of Cordova, Granada, and elsewhere which greatly influenced European and our own university traditions (Draper, 1860). These were the first universities in Europe and were attended by students from all over the continent. In addition, libraries were founded in all major Spanish towns and public schools were attached to every mosque. The Arabs originated the first complete Western dictionaries, as well as lexicons of Greek, Latin, and Hebrew and encyclopedias of science. They established professional schools in such areas as medicine. Northern Europeans who were educated in Spanish Universities were instrumental in spreading learning and bookmaking arts to the northern seacoast and as far as Ireland.

The enlightened Arabian culture in Persia, Africa, and Spain stood in marked contrast to the rest of Europe, although the development of reading and book learning among the transal-pine peoples of Europe was promoted by Charlemagne, during the early years of the ninth century (Lawrence, 1871). Unlike most feudal rulers of medieval Europe, Charlemagne had learned from his teacher Alcuin to admire learning, and as emperor he established free schools throughout the region that is now France and Germany. However, after his death in 814 his schools disappeared and learning again declined. As the centuries wore on, however, learning and literacy gradually became more widespread in Europe. In the twelfth century, the activities of eminent teachers led to the establishment of the University of Paris, and other universities were established at Bologna and elsewhere. By the fifteenth century, it has been said that there were 25,000 students congregated at the University of Paris (Lawrence, 1871), and the English universities at Oxford and Cambridge were flourishing institutions, rivaling their European counterparts. During the Reformation, free schools again were established in Europe and constituted a model for the rest of the world.

Development of Textbooks

After the invention of printing, the Latin Vulgate Bible, based on some of the oldest available manuscripts, quickly became the most important and widely printed book. As the first generally available book, the Bible assumed an importance for education far beyond its religious significance and later was translated into the various spoken languages of Europe. It was used as the basis of most of the teaching in some of the newly established schools and, for a person taught at home by parents or tutors, may have represented the only textbook. Only at the great universities were large libraries available.

By the sixteenth century, there began to appear in Europe printed books prepared especially for general educational purposes, including scientific and technical works. Some of these were reproductions of the old classical manuscripts, but another source was the writings of the intellectual giants of the early Renaissance years. One of the most versatile of these was Leonardo da Vinci, who lived during the latter part of the fifteenth century and the early sixteenth. Leonardo's works were as influential scientifically and technically as they were artistically. Besides defining the foundations for modern anatomical and biological sciences and a new scientific era in the teaching of artistic design, they contained what amounted to the blueprints of the industrial revolution—endless designs for gear systems, for massive power-driven machines, for mobile vehicles, for cranes and lifts, for irrigation and water power systems, and many others. Leonardo's manuscripts, as Figure 4.11 shows, were lavishly illustrated by his own hand and written left-handed in a mirror script.

One of the first printed books to achieve eminence as a scientific text was *De Re Metallica*, written by Georg Agricola and printed in Latin in 1556. A copy of this book is shown in Figure 4.12. It deals with mining and its methods, materials, and management during the Middle Ages. It was important as a scientific text and also valuable in defining the pattern of work in the periods that it covers.

Some understanding of the development of printed textbooks in Europe can be gained by tracing the history of books

Figure 4.11. Example from Leonardo's manuscripts, which profoundly influenced the teaching of art and science in Europe and established a systematic foundation for engineering mechanics. (From *Leonardo da Vinci*. New York: Reynal, 1956, by permission of Reynal and Co.)

on mathematics. Mathematics was the earliest developed science and, in contrast to many branches of knowledge, remained in active use both scientifically and practically throughout the Middle Ages. In actual fact, the scholars of the Renaissance inherited four different types of mathematics, each of which was indicative of different social, financial, and educational strata (Karpinski, 1925).

The first type of mathematics text was the *theoretical* book, based largely upon the manuscripts of fifth and sixth century Latin writers who, in turn, had

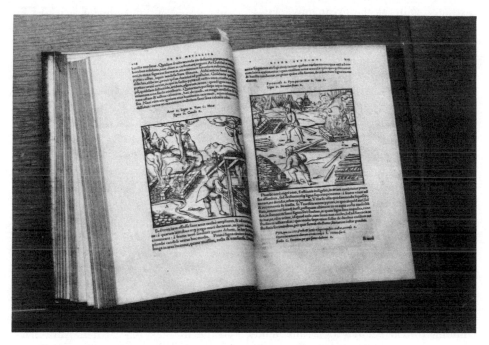

Figure 4.12.   *De Re Metallica*, one of the first books on physics and engineering, showing the method of illustration. This book was translated from the original Latin of Agricola (1912) by Herbert Hoover and his wife Lou Henry Hoover, who considered it one of the most important scientific books of all times. (Courtesy of Rare Books Department, University of Wisconsin Memorial Library.)

followed the Greek models of Nichomachus and Euclid. The second type were the *algorisms*, more practical arithmetics written to supply sufficient mathematical knowledge for business computation. These were based on the Arabic number system of nine numerals plus zero, a system which had been used without the zero in Hindu India as early as the third century B.C. Gradually perfected by Arab scholars in the eighth and ninth centuries A.D., the algorisms provided a basic arithmetic for business, trade, and finance. The third type of book, the *abacus arithmetics*, also was commercial but used Roman numerals which had to be computed with *calculi* (Latin: pebbles used in reckoning),

jetons (French: things thrown or cast), or counters. From these systems were derived some of the earliest teaching and demonstration devices, with a strictly utilitarian purpose. The English language expression "to cast accounts" can be traced to this arithmetical source. The fourth type of arithmetic book, written by astronomers and poets as well as arithmeticians (note the odd classificatory grouping), were the *computi*, treatises upon the church calendars that also included simple directions for computing the movable dates of Easter and the other important religious holidays.

The first arithmetic books written specifically for teaching the young were prepared by teachers of the early Latin schools of Padua and Venice. These were based upon arithmetic as it had been studied and developed in the monasteries of Europe and Africa. They supplemented the basic arithmetic of the Arabs and were extended to include problems of barter, partnership, and practical matters connected with the coinage of money in the days when this was not controlled by great central governments. In 1499, Martianus Mineus Felix Capella combined and edited an encyclopedia of the arts and sciences of the past thousand years that was used widely as a comprehensive scientific and arithmetic text. A medley of prose and verse, it contained an account of geometry and the Greek theory of arithmetic.

At the dawn of the Renaissance, there still was general disagreement in Europe as to whether the algorisms or the abacus systems were more efficient for practical purposes. Italian merchants had been the first to abandon abacus arithmetics, long before this was done in other countries. The Venetian traders, through their contacts with the East, were instrumental in distributing knowledge of Arabian arithmetic throughout the trading world. According to Beckmann (1846), Lucas de Burgo published in Venice in 1494 the first algebra by a European author. This friar was a great mathematician of the fifteenth century, and one of the first Europeans to learn algebra from the Arabs. During the sixteenth century, knowledge of Italian arithmetic and double-entry bookkeeping spread throughout Europe. The oldest German textbook of double-entry bookkeeping was written by Frederick Peypus in 1531, and some of the oldest English bookkeeping texts were dated 1543, 1588, and 1589. These books not only prepared students for a trade, but in time defined the organized symbolic structure of commerce and thereby left their mark on the organization of governments. These few historical facts about the development of textbooks in mathematics point up the close relationship that exists between educational instrumentation and the general organization of work and social interchange in a culture. At all stages of human development, educational techniques have influenced and have been influenced by other phases of organized social activity. As types of social organization and fields of knowledge have been expanded and diversified, the types of educational tools, including books, also have been diversified.

It seems significant that from its earliest beginnings the written word never has been completely divorced from graphic and pictorial illustration. Just as nonverbal gestures and expressive movements add meaning to the spoken word, so do pictures and other illustrations bring meaning to the written or printed word. However, the relative significance of nonverbal material in books for different educational purposes and the design and arrangement of verbal-illustrative material are open questions. Inasmuch as these problems of book design never have been resolved by objective study, decisions concerning the make-up of our most universally used teaching tool are made by publishers and commercial artists rather than by psychologists and educators. It is to be hoped that current interest in teaching techniques and educational design will be extended to include a long overdue examination of the standard textbook.

As we have surveyed human communicative patterns, we have tried to emphasize the cumulative nature of the educational context as well as its progressive development. The student of today starts his education in his pre-reading nursery school or kindergarten days in a way not too different from the training of children in primitive societies. In a relatively small group regulated by an adult, using simple instruments, devices, toys, and pictorial materials, he learns something about the organization of his home and family and the work and social structure of his culture. The older child learning the *three R's* does so in a social and instrumental context that is similar in some ways to the schools of ancient systems. The college student goes to a center of learning, for, ever since the Middle Ages in western Europe and even earlier in certain other cultures, advanced learning has taken place where great libraries, museums, and finally laboratories have supported the teaching efforts of learned men. The advancing course of biosocial evolution, thus, is reflected not only in the technological, social, institutional, and educational design of society but also in the pattern of learning and symbolic control that develops in the individual.

As we go on in the next chapters to a consideration of the educational devices and techniques of our contemporary society, we think of them not as revolutionary innovations but as refinements and extensions of earlier devices and techniques. The functions served by the new teaching tools are the same general functions served by teaching tools and methods in the past. Their over-all effectiveness depends on how well they promote the significant features of human learning which we described in Chapter 1—how well they serve to communicate with the student; how well they enhance his control of new knowledge and skill; how well they establish the significant human meanings of the material learned; how well they motivate the student to stick with his educational task; and how well they represent developing patterns of symbolic control that have current utility in society.

SUMMARY

1. By facilitating the accumulation and transmission of knowledge, writing made possible human civilization.

2. Verbal communication utilizes relatively few movement patterns to express a limitless number of ideas. Alphabetic writing is efficient because its limited number of manipulative patterns correspond closely to the articulatory movements of oral speech.

3. The unit movements of speech are syllable pulses, released by intercostal muscles, sustained in temporal groupings by movements of the trunk and diaphragm, and given phonetic character by articulatory movements of the neck, mouth, and tongue. Letters of the alphabet represent the phonetic articulations.

4. Speech probably evolved in prehistoric man along with the sustained use of tools within a group. Communicative oral sounds may have been used originally in many different contexts— to mimic sounds of nature, to express emotions, to facilitate social activities, especially of work, and so on. Organized languages probably evolved coordinately with the diversification of tool using and tool making into tribal handicraft.

5. Systems of writing were developed independently four to six thousand years

ago in Sumer, Egypt, India, and China. The Egyptians' use of phonetic notations contributed to the later development of alphabets.

6. Chinese writing uses ideograms, one character for each different word. This difficult system probably hampered the intellectual and technical progress of the Chinese.

7. The Sumerians apparently originated cuneiform writing, a system of wedge-shaped characters usually imprinted in clay, which was used widely in Asia Minor. Although it may have influenced later Semitic alphabetic writing, cuneiform writing as such died out.

8. Egyptian hieroglyphs were a relatively efficient writing system which from the start incorporated phonetic notations into the ideographic symbols. These ancient phonetic *letters* were precursors of the consonants of our alphabet.

9. Hieroglyphic writing gradually was simplified into hieratic and demotic writing, used respectively for religious and secular purposes. This simplification probably was related to technical improvements introduced by the Egyptians. They learned how to make a type of paper of the papyrus reed and wrote a cursive script with ink.

10. An intermediate phase in the development of writing was syllabic writing, in which a relatively limited number of characters stood for consonant-vowel combinations or syllables.

11. Consonant alphabets were developed first by the Phoenicians and other Semitic peoples of Asia Minor. This advance probably was spurred on by the practical needs of the seafaring traders.

12. The Greeks, who had developed no writing of their own, borrowed the Phoenician alphabet and introduced the symbols for vowels, thus completing the vocalic alphabet. This perfection of a flexible mode of writing closely allied with oral speech probably was instrumental in the development of a creative, expressive literature.

13. Styles of writing are interrelated with the instruments of writing. The eventual development of an easy, cursive paper-and-ink style, proceeding from left to right shows a trend toward efficiency in a human instrumental movement pattern.

14. Technical improvements in writing were confined for thousands of years to changes in handwriting implements and writing surfaces. Paper was introduced to Europe by the Arabs who learned paper-making from the Chinese. The invention of printing, typewriters, and so forth revolutionized processes of reproducing verbal materials.

15. Problems encountered in teaching the blind to read and write illustrate the dependence of instrumental skills on human factors. Writing developed by seeing individuals is not appropriate for the nonseeing.

16. The original books were various types of plaques, tablets, and later scrolls of paper or parchment. Their present form was developed during the Middle Ages.

17. Printing and typography were invented in China but were not as important there as Gutenberg's introduction of printing was in Europe.

18. The Egyptians had the first large libraries of recorded knowledge, and the Greeks and Romans extended this literary and educational tradition. In Medieval Europe, however, reading and writ-

ing became less common and were confined principally to religious materials.

19. The rebirth of literacy and learning from books was facilitated by Arabian advances in book preparation and compilation of dictionaries but was hastened most of all by the invention of printing.

20. The history of textbook writing demonstrates the interactions between educational processes and the practical needs of the working world.

21. We need objective study of problems of book design for various purposes, including questions of the relative significance of verbal and graphic material and their most efficient arrangement.

22. Teaching tools and techniques must be evaluated not only according to their success in communicating, in promoting control, in establishing human meanings, and in motivating the learner but also according to how well they incorporate current developing patterns of symbolic communication and control.

Modern Audiovisual Techniques

In this chapter and the next, we shall survey the use of audiovisual techniques, their research evaluation, and various theoretical interpretations of their significance. As an introduction, we shall describe in this chapter some of the history and techniques of educational broadcasting, particularly the use of educational television. The main problems and challenges of audiovisual education today revolve around the use of television, which not only constitutes a new and important technique in its own right but also serves as a means of utilizing and integrating all other forms of audiovisual instruction.

REMOTE TRANSMISSION TECHNIQUES

Phonographic recording and motion picture photography were developed by Edison and others late in the nineteenth century and have been used to some extent for educational purposes almost from their inception. Educational radio and sound motion pictures were perfected in the 1920s, and educational television was introduced during the next two decades. Although motion pictures have had a great impact on education, their effect is by no means as great as that of remote transmission by means of radio and television. Radio and television have made possible a certain universality and standardization of educational procedures and have broken down some of the barriers between the classroom and the outside world of experience and action.

Educational Radio

The first radio station in the nation was not a commercial system but an educational unit developed at the University of Wisconsin, which began a regular broadcast service in 1921. Figure 5.1 shows the original studio of WHA, the "oldest station in the nation," which early boasted a great number of listeners. This mural shows among others Professor E. M. Terry, who developed the first educational radio station, and Professor W. H. Lighty, his colleague who directed and did much of the work

Figure 5.1.   Mural depicting activities of the first educational radio station, WHA, University of Wisconsin. (Courtesy of Station WHA, University of Wisconsin.)

of the station. From its start, educational radio effected significant changes in the whole pattern of communication between the university and the public. It served as an important medium for extending the activities of the university to persons off the campus and gave reality to a proud university slogan that "the boundaries of the campus are the boundaries of the state." Important early services were statewide weather broadcasts, college sports, and musical programs.

The enthusiasm generated in educators by the broadcasting medium is attested to by the fact that during the fifteen years from 1921 to 1936, 202 broadcast licenses were issued to educational institutions, seven-eighths of them issued before 1925 (Skornia, 1962). However, 164 of these licenses were revoked or allowed to expire during the same fifteen-year period, so that only thirty-eight licensed educational stations remained in 1937.

The first enthusiastic opinions that radio would revolutionize education were modified gradually as commercial broadcasting burgeoned and provided many of the program services of the first educational stations. In time, however, educational radio established itself in several important roles in addition to its continuing but limited "School of the Air" activities: that is, as an adjunct to extension education for farmers; as an instrument of town and gown interaction in public and economic affairs; and as a medium for bringing to the public fine recorded music and, to a lesser extent, literature and literary criticism. The great hope of a nationwide FM network was kept alive mainly by educational radio and was fulfilled in part by the development of regional educational FM systems. In fact, we owe the current advances in frequency modulation broadcasting mainly to the foresight of a few exponents of radio education.

The greatest educational impact of radio has been in expanding the audience of university extension teaching rather than in influencing the style of conventional classroom teaching to any great extent. In emphasizing the verbalistic approach to education at the expense of visual and audiovisual techniques, educational radio has had quite a different effect from educational television (ETV). In integrating sight and sound, ETV from the start has served as a stimulus to promote change in conventional classroom techniques.

Educational Television

Experimental television was a product of the 1930s, and the first educational programs were broadcast to a limited audience at the State University of Iowa between 1932 and 1939 (Hull, 1962). The development of commercial television and home reception was delayed until the end of World War II. Although the educational significance of television was recognized from its inception, the costs involved delayed its application to educational purposes. In the late 1940s, a few steps were taken by some large universities and technical schools to install television facilities, but no major effort was made until 1952, when the Federal Communications Commission allocated 242 channels in the broadcast spectrum to educational television. With this impetus and with the

financial help of foundations, university and public-school ETV was launched in many parts of the country.

One of the early educational television broadcasting facilities was set up at the University of Wisconsin in conjunction with their radio station and, like WHA, is operated by the University through the guiding support of a state Radio Council. Like many other educational television facilities, WHA-TV was started with the help of the Ford Foundation. The station broadcasts a schedule of general-interest programs in addition to offering various courses of study at all educational levels, largely by means of conventional lecture, demonstration, and conference methods of teaching.

In assessing the progress of ETV, it should be borne in mind that the high-frequency transmission equipment, large camera installations, and special lighting facilities are not only cumbersome but very expensive and thus impose general

Figure 5.2.   Controlling the design and quality of a television program. The production director controls the program make-up by switching from one camera to another. (Courtesy of Station WHA-TV, University of Wisconsin.)

limitations on the adaptability of the medium. Further, the characteristics of television cameras themselves help define the primary instructional dimensions and design of educational programs. The television camera brings an image to focus on a special photoelectronic tube that is scanned by a moving cathode-ray beam at rates of 200 to 600 lines per second. The resulting signal, which varies in intensity according to the brilliance of the various areas of the picture, is transmitted as a video wave, picked up by a microwave receiver, and reconverted to a picture on a cathode-ray tube. The definition of the picture depends on the scanning frequency as well as on the precision of the optics and electronics of the camera system. Television production requires constant control of camera action by a production director and by electronic technicians. As shown in Figure 5.2, a director monitors the program and controls its make up by watching the televised images from the various operating cameras.

Educational television makes use of two types of transmission, broadcast or open-circuit and closed-circuit. Standard broadcast television uses a tower antenna to spread a signal by electromagnetic waves over a limited area some thirty to fifty miles in diameter. However, one ETV facility has expanded its effective broadcast area by transmitting from a roving airplane. In time, global television transmission will be possible through the use of satellite relay stations.

Closed-circuit television utilizes camera-monitor chains that are linked by cables. These may be located within the same building, in different buildings, or even in different localities, but in any case the video signals are transmitted by wire. Closed-circuit television is simpler and less expensive than broadcast television, for by transmitting the signal from the camera to the monitor by wire, it avoids several complicated and costly steps involved in broadcasting. A relatively simple camera can be used and sound can be conveyed by an intercom or public-address system. Most closed-circuit instruction makes use of small cameras like the vidicon cameras in Figure 5.3. These can be set up for close observation of slides or other materials for effective classroom demonstrations.

Two special developments in television

Figure 5.3. Closed-circuit transmission by means of small cameras. *a.* Televising microscopic slides. *b.* Demonstrating dental techniques. (Courtesy of General Electric Company.)

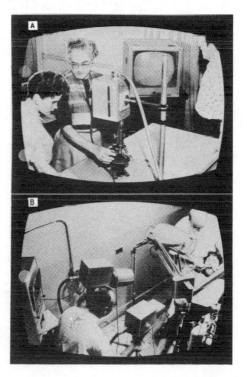

technology which are used to a limited extent in educational television are color and stereoscopic transmission. Colored television pictures are produced by transmitting on three separate scanning circuits, each of which presents a different primary color on the monitor. Superimposing the red, blue, and green images gives a color display which is marked by very poor resolution because each color circuit scans the tube face with only about one-third the frequency of the ordinary black-white scanning circuit. The educational use of color television is limited largely to displays in which color differentiation is important, as in medicine or dentistry.

In a number of special applications of ETV, it is desirable to have stereoscopic or three-dimensional vision. It is possible to obtain a stereoscopic television image in several different ways. Figure 5.4a illustrates a *color separation* system which is based on the same principle as 3-D motion pictures. Two cameras located in positions corresponding to the right and left eyes of an observer provide two separate images, one red and one blue, for the monitor screen. The observer must view the slightly displaced images while wearing spectacles fitted with red and blue filters, a different color for each eye. In this way the two eyes receive the disparate images that have been transmitted by the two cameras, and the observer perceives a picture with depth.

A stereoscopic television image also can be achieved with prisms, as shown in Figure 5.4b. In this case, the two camera images are split in the monitor projection, so that a right eye picture is seen on the right side of the monitor and a left-eye picture on the left. These two pictures are fused by wearing prism spectacles that superimpose the separate images. Again the perceived effect is of one picture with depth. Stereoscopic television also can be obtained by means of a method using polaroid spectacles and another utilizing flicker techniques.

Recording Techniques

The remote transmission techniques have in themselves one basic disadvantage—their transitory character. Whereas pictures, slides, motion picture films, and phonograph records are relatively permanent and can be used as often as desired and at any desired time, radio and television signals leave no permanent trace. In order to realize the full potential of educational radio and television, we need to capture their patterns of sound and sight for later use.

An efficient method of recording radio programs was made possible with the commercial development of magnetic recording of sound after World War II. First magnetized wire was used, but since the late 1940s, wire recording has been displaced by magnetic tape recording. Magnetic reproduction is relatively inexpensive inasmuch as the tapes can be erased and reused.

Recording television images has presented a more difficult problem than recording sound. The first method used to obtain permanent records of television programs was to photograph the monitor image on moving picture film, using a special picture tube called a Kinescope. The resulting film can be televised or shown by means of an ordinary 16mm projector. Motion picture film recording has the disadvantage of requiring some time for processing, so that recorded television material cannot be projected

Figure 5.4   Stereoscopic television systems. *a.* Diagram of color-separation system being used for remote handling of nuclear materials. *b.* Prism-separation system, also being used for remote handling. (*a* from Mengle. 3 dimensional TV system. *Radio TV News*, 1958, **60**(4), 45; 128; *b* based on photograph, courtesy of Du Mont Manufacturing Company.)

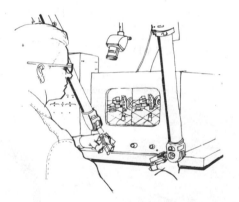

immediately after recording. However, methods of developing film recently have been improved so that nearly instantaneous processing now is possible.

A somewhat more satisfactory method of recording television programs became available in the 1950s with the development of magnetic recording for television, known as video-tape recording. This technique had the initial disadvantage of cost, for the original video-tape recorders were very expensive items of equipment for the relatively limited budgets of ETV facilities. On the other hand, video-tapes can be used immediately without further processing, and like audio-tapes can be erased and reused.

An Ampex Videotape recording system was shown in Figure 1.1. This recorder uses a two-inch magnetic tape, as seen in Figure 5.5. Whereas audiotape is imprinted longitudinally, this video-tape is imprinted transversely in a repetitive track by a rotating head that is carried diagonally across the face of the tape. The same head is used for playback, in much the same way as with an audio-tape recorder. By throwing a switch to change the circuits, the recording head is converted immediately to a playback head.

A somewhat less costly type of television tape recorder is diagramed in Figure 5.6. In this Helical Scan Recorder, the tape travels diagonally across the outer surface of a large rotating cylinder which carries a magnetic recording head. The cylinder can be seen at the center of the console in Figure 5.6a, located between the two reels that carry the recording tape. Figure 5.6b shows the arrangement of the tape as it

Figure 5.5.   Close-up of Ampex Videotape Recorder (VR–1000) control panel, recording head, and tape. (Courtesy of Station WHA-TV, University of Wisconsin.)

Figure 5.6.   Helical Scan Videotape Recorder (Ampex VR–8000). a. Appearance of recording head and control panel. b. The helical scanning technique. (Based on photograph, courtesy of the Ampex Corporation.)

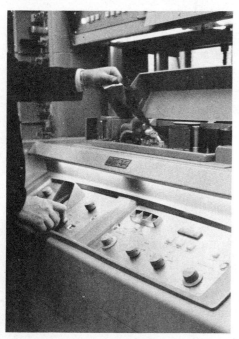

is passed around the cylinder and also indicates the recording head that is mounted on the cylinder. This instrument and other even smaller recorders are much less costly than the original Videotape machines and bring television recording within the means of many educational and business institutions.

An entirely new technique of visual

recording developed at General Electric Research Laboratories (1960) opens up new possibilities for television recording and playback. Known as thermoplastic recording, this method uses special plastic materials which record a visual image in the form of a ripple pattern by means of a charging and heating process. The special advantages of this technique are its speed and its recording density. Theoretically, all twenty-four volumes of the *Encyclopædia Britannica* could be recorded at the rate of one volume per minute on a reel of tape that could be held in the palm of one hand.

The photograph in Figure 5.7*a* compares the size of a thermoplastic record with that of an ordinary straight pin. A very acceptable visual image was recorded on a strip of tape just a tenth of an inch wide, and recent improvements in the technique give even better results. The diagram in Figure 5.7*b* shows a checkerboard pattern recorded on a piece of tape approximately 0.003 inch wide. If such a pattern were used to represent the binary digit system for computers, with the light squares representing 0 and the dark squares 1, forty million bits of information could be recorded on one square inch of thermoplastic tape. This recording density is hundreds of times better than with magnetic tape.

Thermoplastic recording uses film with a thin conducting coating and a thermoplastic surface. The film is scanned by an electron beam to charge it electrically in a pattern corresponding to the input pattern. When the film is heated by inducing a current in the conducting coating, the melted plastic coating is pulled into microscopic in-

Figure 5.7.   Thermoplastic recording. *a.* A thermoplastic record compared in size with a straight pin. *b.* A checkerboard pattern on a piece of thermoplastic tape approximately 0.003 inch wide. (From General Electric Research Laboratory. *Thermoplastic recording.* Schenectady, N.Y.: General Electric Research Information Services, 1960.)

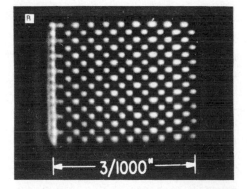

dentations by the attraction between the charges and the current-carrying conductive film beneath. As the film cools, this ripple pattern "freezes" into place as a permanent image. The image can be erased by reheating the film, allowing the charges to leak away so that the plastic returns to its original smooth state.

A thermoplastic image can be seen with the naked eye if light strikes it at an angle. In order to project the image on a screen, a special projector is needed that uses line light sources and a set of bars in front of the projection lens. These bars permit light to pass through only where a ripple on the film scatters the light.

The importance of efficient methods of recording televised information as well as other forms of visual and auditory information is obvious but cannot be overemphasized. The cost of educational television would be prohibitive if each presentation were a one-shot live program. Further, the quality of the presentations would suffer. Prerecorded programs can be assessed, edited, recorded again if necessary, and then distributed to different stations and used as often as desired. The National Educational Television and Radio Center (NETRC), which was organized in 1953, serves as a central production and distribution agency for its affiliated stations (fifty-three in 1961) and thus makes possible countrywide exchange of recorded programs. Other sources of recorded instruction are state departments of education, commercial enterprises, and all of the schools and universities engaged in ETV production. There is a current trend toward more extensive exchange of information concerning the availability of recorded programs.

Besides the general advantages of televised recording, there are several special educational advantages. Recording makes possible storing observations of such events as surgical operations for widespread instructional uses. This is especially important for demonstrating unusual and infrequent procedures. Also the television eye provides a close-up view never achieved by observers in a surgical amphitheater.

Television recordings that can be played back immediately are highly useful in training for high-speed, complicated, or dangerous operations in such areas as missile guidance, aircraft carrier landing operations, skilled machine operations, and athletic performance. A televised record of a performance pattern can be played back immediately to the performer to point out his errors or weaknesses in control. Immediate visual knowledge feedback of this sort is inestimably more valuable than any amount of delayed verbal analysis and instruction.

ETV Distribution Systems

The overwhelming advantage of the remote transmission techniques for education is that they can be used to distribute a single carefully designed instructional program over a wide area, that is, to many localities, classrooms, or groups simultaneously. Several basic patterns of distribution are in use, utilizing both closed-circuit and broadcast television (*Teaching by Television*, 1959).

Some universities and public school systems install closed-circuit television equipment in order to originate their own programs and distribute them to various classrooms. Such closed-circuit ETV often originates in a laboratory-classroom, such as the one diagramed in Figure 5.8. This figure illustrates what might be called the minimum arrange-

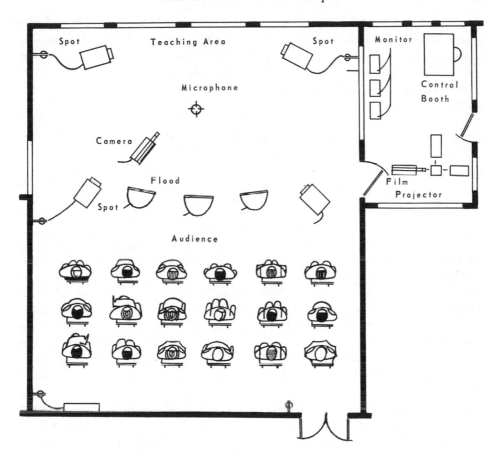

Figure 5.8. The general arrangements for closed-circuit school programs originating within a classroom.

ments for a laboratory-classroom and control room for closed-circuit operations within a school. The staging area is equipped with controlled lighting that should be mounted on overhead supports. An overhead camera boom may be needed along with a conventional tripod and dolly mount. The control room contains a director's booth, monitors, and the equipment for kinescope recording and film and slide projection. Projected material can be used to supplement a program with titles and background information, or, at times, to

provide the main part of the program. If video-tapes are to be used, a video-tape recorder will add another major expense item to the installation.

The room-to-room hook-up within a school can vary considerably, depending on the scope of operations. The simplest possible arrangement would consist of a single input to provide one program at a time to the classrooms that are linked to the chain. In more ambitious set-ups, a number of different studios and classrooms are equipped to originate programs, and many classrooms can receive them. Several control rooms permit a flexible distribution arrangement to the receiving classrooms. Installations of this sort are used in various public schools and teachers' colleges throughout the country.

An ETV broadcasting facility is of necessity a more complex and costly system than a closed-circuit system, but where one is established, small schools within the broadcast area can receive televised instruction simply by installing a receiver in a classroom. A schematic ETV studio broadcasting facility characteristic of any one of several in large state universities is illustrated in Figure 5.9. This diagram is meant to indicate all of the various activities that go on in program preparation by showing the rooms needed for preparation, rehearsal, programing, control, and so on. Studios such as this not only originate instruction, but also serve as laboratories to provide training for students interested in television broadcast production.

An unusual plan has been put into

Figure 5.9.   Generalized design of an ETV facility used for broadcast television.

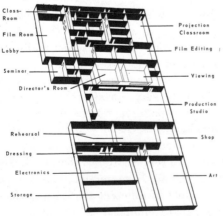

effect to extend the geographical limits of ETV broadcasting. The Midwest Airborne Television Program uses a roving heavy airplane based at Purdue University to extend the range of ETV broadcasting from a radius of twenty-five to fifty miles to over 150 miles (*Teaching by Television,* 1959). By circling a small area over Indiana, a plane equipped with television broadcasting facilities can reach schools in most of Indiana and Ohio and parts of Illinois, Kentucky, Michigan, and Wisconsin. The potential audience has been estimated at five million students in 13,000 schools and colleges (Kilbourn, 1961).

The broadcasting problems encountered in this regional project are enormous. Weather, technical difficulties, costs, and aircraft maintenance all are serious considerations. Even if the cost problem were solved with major continuing Ford Foundation support, there would seem to be no respite from natural and technical difficulties. In time, however, this type of operation may be no longer needed. A communications satellite or a lunar television facility may make possible nationwide or even hemispherewide broadcasting of both commercial and educational programs.

TRAINING TELEVISION

In addition to its general educational uses, television is being used more and more as a training medium for many types of business and industrial purposes. The uses of training television or TTV range from the conference-type informational program to skill training for complicated and dangerous operations. For these specific training needs, closed-circuit transmission is used by means of either long-distance wire-service hookups or permanent camera-monitor chains within an institution.

Commercial Meetings

For more than a decade, large businesses and industries have been turning to closed-circuit television as a communication medium for business conferences, demonstration meetings, and the like. Closed-circuit installations provide for effective intercommunication within large plants and long-distance hookups can be used to communicate simultaneously with salesmen and other representatives in several cities. The purpose of such a television conference might be to demonstrate new products and to outline plans for merchandising. As a rule, companies do not own their own equipment but rent it as needed and hire a TTV producing service to arrange the program and get it on the coaxial cables.

An industry that decides to use TTV for its marketing and sales personnel has an effective and time-saving medium for demonstrating new products. Instead of scheduling the customary series of regional meetings over a period of time, which top executives rarely attend, the manufacturer can assemble his salesmen and dealers in his major marketing areas at one time to hear and see the story behind the new line straight from the company's top executives, engineers, salesmen, and advertising men. In this way the manufacturer concentrates his efforts and expenditures and uses his best speakers and instructors for an equivalent presentation to all his representatives in the field.

In an unpublished survey, the senior author obtained evaluative reactions to televised intercity commercial meetings from a number of companies. Upjohn Company said TTV is murderously expensive, extremely difficult to do well, but worth the investment and will be continued in this company on a limited scale indefinitely. Ford Motor Company considered TTV superior to written communication as a means of getting important information from company executives to all distant plants and divisions simultaneously. They liked the personal touch provided by television and found that attendance at meetings was always high. Sun Oil Company reported that using TTV to introduce new products resulted in large savings.

Observation Training

Many types of human relations situations in business and industry can be televised for the purpose of training apprentices or students either as individuals or as a class. Some of these are indicated in Figure 5.10. In these situations, the closed-circuit television chain provides a kind of one-way vision by means of which the student can observe methods and procedures without actually being present.

Research results show that television training can be carried on successfully in the situations shown in Figure 5.10, that is, in supervisory training, in labor-management operations, in counseling and executive procedures, in human-relations techniques including child-care, and in human engineering practices. The possibilities for giving students a little vicarious experience in actual problems of the business and industrial community are especially significant.

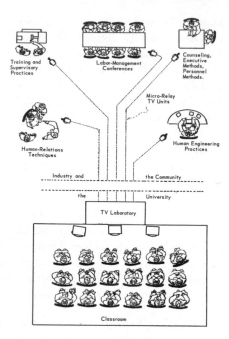

Figure 5.10.   Using television observation for human relations training.

Simulation Training

One of the most effective uses of TTV is in simulating visual displays to teach such important skills as driving and piloting operations. Figure 5.11 describes the equipment used for simulating the visual approach to airports for pilots in flight training. The basic procedure is to move a television camera over a simulated landing field. Early models of this type of simulator were of considerable size and had the television cameras mounted on moving gantries. The present simulator has been made much smaller, and, as shown in the figure, the television lens is smaller than the head of a wooden match. Dynamic simulation is achieved by attaching the camera to the controls of an aircraft

trainer-simulator so that every movement of the controls brings a corresponding change to the student's view of the landing field. In the apparatus diagramed, the student must perform visual landings after instrument flight rule approaches have been made.

This type of visual simulation is unique in the history of flight training and never before has been achieved in ground training operations. The student is given tasks that appear quite real. He must decide, as he would in the air, where the runway is, whether his plane is too high or too low, whether he is properly aligned and whether his aspect angle with the runway is correct at every moment. He makes these decisions by watching the screen in front of his trainer cockpit. As he operates his levers and controls, the camera position is shifted and the appearance of the airfield changes just as it would were he making an actual approach to the ground. A special optical system attached to the camera simulates the three-dimensional movement of the aircraft, in azimuth, elevation or pitch, and roll. Training in landing at particular cities can be given by using scale models of the appropriate landing field.

Remote Control Training

Television is used for many kinds of remote observation, from simple monitoring tasks to remote handling of dangerous materials. Some remote monitoring is of the nature of police spying, as in penal institutions, but there are other more palatable monitoring functions of closed-circuit systems, as in hospital patient care, banking operations, and in-

Figure 5.11.   Visual flight simulation achieved by moving a television camera over a model landing field display. The student, located in an aircraft trainer, adjusts the controls to bring the plane to the simulated ground pattern. (From Electronic Flight Visulator. *Mech. Engng*, 1959, 81(3), 82–83.)

dustrial processing. In any case, a closed-circuit installation within an establishment can be used as a training medium for new workers as well as an observational network.

There are many uses of closed-circuit systems for industrial monitoring. Television eyes are used to watch or inspect water level gauges, dangerous machining operations, steel processing, furnace view ports, explosive materials, unexposed film, boiler furnace interiors, position of heated parts and metals, hot glass, radiation processes and materials, jet engine performance, crane action, and yard operations. All of these situations can be used for visual training, but closed-circuit chains used to control complex visual interactions are particularly helpful in training. For example, a closed-circuit installation in a bank not only is of value for regular operations but also can be used to train new employees in the nature of the over-all operation of the bank. Camera systems located in the bookkeeping and savings departments provide information to tellers, drive-in tellers, new accounts and credit clerks, and savings tellers. In addition, reverse chains can provide for inspection of checks and other forms of exchange at tellers' windows.

TELEVISION INSTRUCTION PROCEDURES

To most professional educators in the immediate postwar years, the apparently unlimited possibilities of television as an educational medium offered an exciting prospect. It was said that this new medium would create educational opportunities richer than any in history, that it would resolve the teacher shortage by teaching the seemingly endless hordes of new students, that it would reduce juvenile delinquency, elevate the adult cultural level, and generate a new era of science-minded students who could challenge the products of Russian education.

In the past decade, ETV has penetrated almost every area of instruction and has been utilized by thousands of schools and universities throughout the country. Early in 1959, it was estimated that more than half a million school children and 100,000 college students were being instructed by television (*Teaching by Television*, 1959). By the spring of 1961, fifty-five ETV stations were on the air and an estimated 250 to 300 closed-circuit systems were in operation. Over a thousand televised courses were being broadcast over open-circuit TV in addition to hundreds transmitted to classrooms by means of closed-circuit operations (Meierhenry and McBride, 1962). Approximately one-third of all public school students were in schools using television.

In all this flurry of interest and activity, certain fundamental problems haunt the educational ETV studio and the teachers who have been called upon to instruct over the video waves. One problem has to do with the hierarchy of control in the ETV studio. The educator who ventures into what he thinks is an exciting new medium for mass education and mass communication may find that it is better characterized as a maze of wires, technicians, and aggressive program directors. The activities of the studio conform not so much to the theories and opinions of the educators as to the established views of speech specialists and theatrical producers. Amidst this pulling and hauling, there has been little systematic investigation of the various types of televised instruction and most of it follows fairly conventional procedures.

Studio Lectures

Many ETV programs follow the classic pattern of lecturing from a podium but originate within the television studio. In addition to his verbal presentation, the lecturer can use illustrative material in the form of charts, blackboard material, or other displays. He is fixed in a circumscribed position before the television camera, and is linked to the recording room by means of the wired microphone hung about his neck. His scope of action and modes of bodily expression are necessarily limited, for he must remember not to step on his microphone cable or to move too far from the myopic eye of the camera. Accordingly, he tends to assume the stilted appearance of a Daguerreotype rather

than following his natural flair for ges-
ticulating wildly, dancing about, or performing other acrobatics that may have
endeared him to his regular students.

Studio lectures are either recorded for
later transmission or transmitted live to
formal classes, to enrolled TV students
outside the school, or to the public at
large. The main advantages of using
televised lectures on the teacher's home
campus are that he can record them at
his own (and the studio's) convenience
and that several sections of the course
can be scheduled instead of one large
lecture section. In 1960–1961, there
were more live presentations of courses
over open-circuit ETV than recorded
(Meierhenry and McBride, 1962), but
the use of recorded programs is increasing.

The Television Classroom

Another method of televising lectures
is to go into the lecture room or amphitheater with the camera and lighting
equipment and record a lecture as it is
being given to a class. Figure 5.12 illustrates some aspects of a televised university course in sociology. The lecturer
must remain in a relatively restricted
area and confine his visual materials to
those that can be picked up by the television camera.

Classroom lectures can be transmitted
to remote classrooms in much the same
way as studio lectures. The photograph
in Figure 5.12d shows a regularly scheduled class being instructed by means of
a monitor propped up before them. Their
view of the televised image is inevitably
somewhat limited, inasmuch as a rather
low level of illumination is needed in

order to display the detailed movements
of the lecturer, particularly any writing
he may do on the blackboard.

Team Teaching

Public school systems that make use
of closed-circuit television have evolved
techniques of team teaching to use the
medium to best advantage. The studio
teacher typically is responsible for just
one presentation a day, which is transmitted to classrooms throughout the system. Classroom teachers are responsible
for eliciting student participation, for
leading discussions, answering questions, giving individual help, stimulating
outside activity in the subject area, giving assignments, and conducting tests.

Team teaching can be very effective
where the participants have mastered
the techniques. The studio teacher has
plenty of time to prepare the daily lessons, while the classroom teacher, relieved of much of the preparation, has
time to devote to the students. In periodic conferences of the studio and classroom teachers, the course can be evaluated and improvements made.

Specialized Demonstrations

One of the most effective uses of ETV
is as an audiovisual medium to give a
variety of specialized instructions and
demonstrations. These include laboratory demonstrations, do-it-yourself
courses, medical demonstrations, and, as
we have indicated in the section on
TTV, industrial training courses and
displays. Laboratory or therapeutic demonstrations can be given in the studio if
not too much apparatus is required, or
the television camera and lights can be

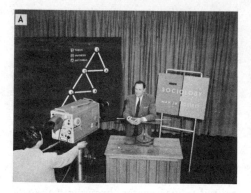

Figure 5.12.   Classroom-originated program. *a.* Lecturer before the camera. *b.* General arrangement of equipment and personnel. *c.* Students discussing the presentation with a quiz section instructor after class. *d.* Receiving classroom with monitor. (Courtesy of Station WHA-TV, University of Wisconsin.)

installed in the regular demonstration area.

One example of a specialized demonstration is given in Figure 5.13, which shows a post-mortem examination of the organs of tuberculous cattle televised for a farm audience. In this case, the university specialist can work in his own laboratory unhampered by observers, while the observers get a reasonably good view of the demonstration by means of monitors placed here and there around the auditorium. Special-purpose programs of this sort can be an effective contribution of ETV particularly on a state university campus where

many special meetings and institutes are scheduled. Certain types of difficult-to-observe procedures, for example, therapeutic procedures, lend themselves naturally to ETV demonstration.

Television is used for many types of medical demonstration. Figure 5.14 illustrates some of the techniques used to demonstrate surgical procedures. Typically, two cameras are used to record an operation, one mounted on a floor dolly and one on a movable boom to give superior close-up shots. Figure 5.14*a* shows how the floor camera gets a view of the operative field by means of a mirror mounted on a light. Small plastic

Figure 5.13. Special demonstration of cattle tuberculosis. *a.* Postmortem examination of tuberculous organs. *b.* Farm audience viewing the demonstration on closed-circuit monitors. (Courtesy of Station WHA-TV, University of Wisconsin.)

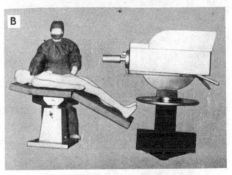

Figure 5.14. Techniques used to apply ETV to medical demonstration and instruction. *a.* Dolly-mounted camera viewing operation by means of a mirror. *b.* Models used to demonstrate operative approach. *c.* Integrating explanatory slides into the demonstration. (Courtesy of RCA Manufacturing Company.)

models can be used to explain the nature and approach of the operation and to indicate the location of the camera, and explanatory slides can be integrated into the demonstration. Tape-recorded surgical demonstrations of this sort, complete with related explanatory material, are highly effective when used to instruct medical students and others.

Improved television projection facilities have been developed for medical ETV, as shown in Figure 5.15. By means of a highly efficient Schmidt optical system, the light from the video tube is collected and projected onto a screen, so that the audience views a picture larger than the ordinary monitor image. Efficient screen projection of this nature

transforms the "21-inch classroom" into something more nearly approaching a motion-picture theater. However, the optical projection system is very expensive and hardly within the means of the ordinary ETV facility.

In addition to its value for close-up

Figure 5.15.   Projecting a television image to a larger screen. (Courtesy of RCA Manufacturing Company.)

demonstrations, the television eye is a very effective observer of interpersonal and group behavior for demonstration purposes. Some human relations situations in industry that lend themselves to television instruction were pictured in Figure 5.10. A comparable technique is to televise classroom procedures in a laboratory school for the benefit of student teachers. By this means, large classes of teacher trainees can observe simultaneously a skilled teacher in ac-

tion. The pupils under observation become accustomed to the television eye and find it less distracting than changing groups of observers.

Telemation

We have made the point earlier in the chapter that one of the most significant characteristics of television as an educational medium is that it can incorporate all other forms of audiovisual display. By this we meant simply that any type of visual or auditory material can be transmitted by means of television. The teaching system dubbed *telemation* that we shall describe here does indeed incorporate all audiovisual techniques but in a somewhat more elaborate fashion than provided by television alone. The main purpose of telemation is to provide four or five sources of audiovisual stimulation to the student automatically and, if desired, simultaneously. Depending on one's conception of educational design, the effect might be considered either a symphony or cacophony of sight and sound in the classroom.

The photograph in Figure 5.16 shows a specially equipped classroom where the teacher has available three viewing screens along with various sound sources. He can show motion pictures on the large screen, still projections on one of the small screens, and a television image on the other small screen. Further, all of these displays can be cued on and off automatically as the teacher reads his lecture. A teleprompter device contains the script, which is reflected in a glass plate before the speaker's eyes. As the lecture unrolls, small metal strips placed at appropriate points beside the words serve as keys to operate the various audiovisual devices. That is, the movies, slides, film strips, television image, and

Figure 5.16. A classroom equipped for telemation. (Courtesy of University of Wisconsin.)

recorded sound are switched on and off according to the occurrence of the electrodes alongside the printed script of the lecture.

Telemation has been referred to as an *automated classroom,* although on the surface the classroom appears little different from any other. All of the audiovisual paraphernalia—two slide projectors, a movie projector, a tape recorder, teleprompter units, an opaque projector, a four-speaker sound system, controlled lighting, a television projector, and the elaborate system of electronics to control all these—are out of sight of the student. The cost of modifying the classroom and installing the equipment was said to be in excess of $100,000 and the yearly operating costs at least $25,000.

In the development of this telemation system for general educational purposes as in some of the expensive training development programs that we shall describe in a later chapter, we wonder whether general enthusiasm for the latest wonders of technology has been substituted for a systematic evaluation of their worth. In our opinion, no educational advantage has been achieved with the telemated classroom that could not have been gained with simpler equipment at a fraction of the cost. For example, there is an audiovisumatic teaching machine to be described in Chapter 10 that can be keyed to present tape-recorded sound and visually projected material automatically in much the same way as the teleprompter unit does in telemation. This machine costs at most several hundred dollars. Add a standard television receiver and a movie projector and you have approximately the facilities of the telemated classroom. The advance preparation time required of the teacher would be no greater and the man hours needed for operation and maintenance might be considerably fewer.

Our point is that, as of now, we have difficulty judging how much money to invest in alternative techniques because we do not have enough facts to make a conclusive evaluation of their relative worth. Our confidence in audiovisual teaching may be entirely justified but before we go much further in designing new educational technologies we should acquire a better understanding of the ones we already have. One way to go about this is to analyze the research evaluations, as we shall do for the audiovisual procedures in the next chapter. Another way is to try to interpret the procedures in terms of theoretical concepts of learning. As we have said, our judgment is that attempts of this sort have not been very successful. We shall try to justify that opinion in the next section.

THEORETICAL INTERPRETATIONS OF AUDIOVISUAL LEARNING

Until recently, specialists in audiovisual education have expressed little or no concern with theory, while behavior and learning theorists, on the other hand, rarely have considered the problems of audiovisual learning. Consequently, certain recent efforts (Meierhenry, 1961; Miller *et al.*, 1957) to achieve some communication between the theorists and the practitioners seem a little forced and leave one with the feeling that the theorists would like to do their duty by AV education and then get back to the safety of their own laboratories. We shall summarize here some of these theoretical interpretations, paying particular attention to a series of papers published by the *Audiovisual Communication Review* in 1961 under the editorship of Meierhenry (1961). The papers were prepared by a number of prominent learning theorists at the request of a committee of AV specialists whose purpose was to promote more and better research in the audiovisual field by considering the relationship of learning theories to instructional materials.

Motivation Interpretation

Perhaps the easiest way for a psychologist to categorize audiovisual techniques is as motivational devices, or aids to the "real" learning process. This characteristic is given primary importance in McDonald's (1961) theoretical analysis of audiovisual materials. He did not deny that audiovisual devices might serve as specific instructional tools, but he attached more importance to their motivating value in arousing the interest of students and in directing attention to the relevant aspects of a task.

Inasmuch as audiovisual devices may be highly motivating without guaranteeing that the right kind of learning will take place, McDonald stressed the importance of using the devices properly to create *learning sets*, or to orient the individual in the right direction. However, the orienting effect may depend on the personality of the individual as well as the nature of the audiovisual material. For this reason, McDonald suggested that an area of audiovisual research should be concerned with the interaction between particular classroom procedures and individual variables. A further implication drawn by Deese (1961) was that it would be helpful if each film or instructional device were accompanied by normative information about its effects on different groups.

Stimulus-Response Learning Theory

Interpretations of audiovisual learning in terms of current stimulus-response-reinforcement theories of learning are disappointing, in that they fail to come to grips with the realities of the classroom. In a representative analysis, Kendler (1961) called attention to the important variables of learning as described by the stimulus-response model. In this language, learning means that a response become *connected* to a stimulus because of the occurrence of reinforcement. Kendler pointed out what has become all too obvious, that the tendency in "pure" learning research during the last few decades has been toward simpler and simpler experimental procedures. The opinion of S-R learning theorists is that this limiting of experimental variables has brought them closer and closer to the heart of the matter—to the real learning process which presumably is the same for all kinds and conditions of learning. Kendler's advice to AV researchers was to emulate this method of attack and to simplify AV research by developing a few "basic research procedures" with a limited number of variables. However, Kendler recognized that AV evaluative studies deal with materials containing a "conglomeration of variables" that defy isolation and analysis. How does the learning theorist handle this problem? The answer is that he doesn't. He passes the buck back to the educator. In Kendler's words, ". . . the evaluation of training films presents a different problem from that of under-standing the audiovisual learning proc-ess. As such, they demand two different kinds of solutions."

To our mind, this voluntary with-drawal of learning theorists from the real-life problems of meaningful learn-ing is a measure of their inadequacy in dealing with human behavior. But the thing that we deplore about current learning theory—the artificial simplicity of their model of behavior—is a source of pride to the theorists themselves. To quote Kendler, "Their (the S-R learning psychologists') productivity is in some measure due to the fruitful and cleansing effect that stimulus-response language has upon designing, reporting, and in-terpreting research." We agree with this statement to some extent; S-R learning research certainly has been cleansed of most of the difficult, troublesome, and yet fascinating aspects of man's day-to-day behavior. But in purifying their ap-proach, the learning theorists are in danger of losing contact with reality.

There is, however, one area of rapport between S-R learning theory and the ed-ucational arena, and that is the teaching machine or procedures of self-instruc-tion. Here S-R psychology comes into its own, for the Stimulus, the Response, and the Reinforcement can be identified, serialized, and manipulated. The re-searcher is relieved of the responsibility of guessing or trying to analyze what the student is doing while watching a film or television, or listening to a record or radio. For better or worse, his behavior (at least some of his behavior) is brought out into the open where it can be chopped up and accounted for. S-R learning theorists feel more comfortable

with teaching machines than with other audiovisual techniques, for they feel that the student's (overtly) active role with a self-instruction device is more condu-cive to learning than his (seemingly) passive role before audiovisual displays. Kendler concluded that the "best of all education worlds will result" from in-corporating audiovisual techniques with those of teaching machines or pro-gramed texts. Glaser's (1961) paper on "Learning and the Technology of In-struction" considered autoinstructional devices almost to the exclusion of all other techniques. Finally Deese (1961) threw the standard AV devices back into the motivation hopper by distinguishing between what he called "true audio-visual *aids*" and direct instructional techniques. We shall return to a theoreti-cal analysis of teaching-machine learn-ing in a later chapter.

Pragmatic Approach

A more practical approach to the problems of audiovisual learning was taken by Postman (1961), who confined his analysis largely to some of the em-pirical findings of learning research that have meaning for classroom education. He stressed the importance of requiring students to practice or recite the re-sponses to be learned. Such rehearsal not only makes the responses more available to the learner but probably serves to motivate him more highly than when only passive observation is required.

Other factors that influence learning are the associative contexts of stimuli and responses that have been built up prior to the immediate learning situa-tions. In other words, the meaningful-ness of material affects the speed of learning. However, the effect of prior associations on new ones involves the tricky problems of transfer of training, which may be either positive or negative. Postman gave these two general principles of transfer: (a) "the magnitude of the transfer effects increases as a function of the similarity of the stimuli"; and (b) "the degree to which the effects are positive or negative depends on the relationship between the responses required in successive tasks." The obvious implication for teaching and training is that procedures should be designed to maximize positive transfer from earlier habits and to new situations. Thus classroom tasks should be made very similar to later applications.

Postman concluded his paper with this statement: ". . . the analysis of the process of audiovisual education does not call for the formulation of special principles; it calls for the application and elaboration of the general laws of human learning." We have no particular quarrel with the "laws of learning" as far as they go, but would like to point out that their usefulness is as limited as the research designs that have defined them. Postman's generalizations have been drawn almost entirely from studies of verbal rote learning with some minor emphasis on simple motor-skill learning. As we suggested in Chapter 2, complicated perceptual-motor skills can be neither understood nor controlled in the traditional "laws of learning" framework, and we are sure that this is just as true of the complicated integrations of sight and sound and of verbal and nonverbal knowledge in the classroom. We believe that the analysis of audiovisual education *does* require special princi-

ples and special research designs, going beyond the type of study championed by Postman and S-R learning theorists in general.

Implications of a Gestalt Analysis

To our mind, the most interesting and in many ways the most meaningful paper of the series we have been reviewing is the one prepared by Luchins (1961). Following the gestalt tradition, Luchins did not make an explicit statement of a theory of learning, but his comments about the important features in learning situations appear to us more perceptive of the realities of behavior than the analyses couched in behavioristic terms.

One of Luchins' important contributions was to call attention to the weaknesses in current motivation doctrine. The complementary concepts of motivation and reinforcement in learning theory have led to some outstanding examples of circular reasoning from which it is difficult to escape. The idea that individuals are activated by drives or motives or wants is accepted in psychology almost as a truism. Thus motivated, an individual learns an act that is reinforced. In order for learning to occur, the learner must want something and must get something that he wants (Miller *et al.*, 1957). Reinforcement learning theorists sometimes ignore the motive, but they cannot ignore the reinforcement because their learning model is based upon it. When it is impossible to identify the reinforcement in a particular situation, one can always fall back on the definition that a reinforcer is any condition which increases the probability of a correct response (see Postman, 1961).

Luchins recalled the words of Wertheimer to express his impatience with this kind of reasoning: "Wertheimer is against the idea that the natural state of man is inactivity, and that theories of motivation are needed to account for his activity. . . . He suggests that the problem is to account for inactivity." We feel that this idea has great merit and wish that Luchins had pursued it further. We too believe that man's natural condition is one of activity, and that it can be accounted for without resorting to drives or motives as energizing forces. To us this is more than a philosophical question and involves an understanding of the mode of action of the response mechanism. Our idea is that the sensorineuromotor system is organized in such a way that the individual constantly reacts to differences in his stimulus environment—visual, auditory, tactual, and so on. In an audiovisual situation, the student's responses need not be motivated extrinsically, inasmuch as they are intrinsically energized.

Luchins made a further comment that bears repeating: "To understand behavior, it is *not* sufficient to focus on the needs or motives (actual or theoretical) of the person *qua* person. The situation, too, may have requirements." Luchins was referring, of course, to what are known in gestalt psychology as field forces. While our own language and interpretation differ somewhat, we make a very similar point when we say that behavior is organized in part according to the spatial and temporal requirements of a particular situation.

Luchins' main emphasis was that we should be concerned not just with the responses involved in learning but with the *processes* that lead to responses. It is better to understand what one is doing even if some errors are made than to perform correct responses blindly or mechanically. It is in this connection that audiovisual devices might achieve their greatest importance. By providing superior displays, audiovisual devices promote better understanding of system and organization than might be gained from a verbal description alone. We have made this point in different words by saying that nonverbal communication supports and enhances the meaning of verbal communication.

In our opinion, Luchins' analysis has the strengths and weaknesses of gestalt psychology in general. It recognizes some of the significant organizational features of human behavior but fails to extend its explanatory principles beyond the cognitive and perceptual level. Gestalt psychology emphasizes perceptual features at the expense of the complementary motor features of behavior and ignores the basic feedback mechanisms underlying behavior organization. Because of its special emphasis on perception and cognition, gestalt psychology has been incapable of generating critical objective behavioral studies that go much beyond rather general demonstrations.

Approaches to Audiovisual Research

The S-R theories of learning have two general features that have prevented their generating significant research in the field of audiovisual communication and learning. One is the idea that all kinds of behavior, including nonverbal audiovisual patterns, are acquired according to the animal-based formulas of reinforcement learning or the association principles of verbal rote learning. Little credence is given to the idea that learning in audiovisual situations should be analyzed in terms of the operations involved. Audiovisual research can borrow general learning principles from the psychological laboratories, but at some critical stage these theoretical ideas, if they are to be used at all, must be extended to fit the human operations of audiovisual communication. The fact that great difficulty is encountered in designing meaningful audiovisual research in a traditional learning context is in itself a good index of the limited significance of the conventional concepts.

A second limitation of conventional thinking is the belief that any particular audiovisual device or medium of non-verbal communication has relatively invariant properties as an aid to verbal learning which can be studied and assessed independently of the operational situation. Kendler (1961), for example, urged AV researchers to develop a few "basic research procedures" as a base from which to evaluate all the effects of audiovisual variables. This point of view does not recognize that audiovisual variables cannot be studied in the abstract but are a function of particular operational systems.

The audiovisual research field needs more emphasis on the human engineering point of view that has been found necessary for research on other types of machine learning and training situations. This approach does not consider general learning variables of primary importance in understanding the effectiveness of instrumental teaching and training but emphasizes instead the influence of such design factors as the nature of perceptual displays and the pattern of response control. In the next chapter, we shall see that some audiovisual research adopts the human factors approach and attempts to study learning as a function of design variables in the particular situation. Other studies take a more conventional approach. All too often, however, the intent of audiovisual research has been to make a direct overall comparison between some new method and established classroom teaching procedures without analyzing the critical variables in either.

SUMMARY

1. Audiovisual technology has far outdistanced theory. Each new technique has been accepted at face value with no theoretical rationale.

2. Radio broadcasting originated in an educational context and was used for instructional purposes from the start. Educational radio has extended university influence in several special areas but has not influenced classroom teaching techniques to any great extent.

3. Educational television was launched on a large scale in the early 1950s with foundation support after the FCC released 242 video channels for educational use. A television facility requires extensive instrumentation and a large technical staff.

4. Television programs are transmitted either by broadcasting or by means of closed-circuit camera-monitor chains linked by wire. The latter are less expensive and usually make use of smaller cameras.

5. Color television and stereoscopic television have limited use in ETV. Color sometimes is used for medical and

dental demonstrations, and stereoscopic displays are valuable in training remote control techniques.

6. Two standard methods of recording television programs for later use are by means of kinescopic photography (motion pictures) and magnetic recording on video-tape. A video-tape can be played back immediately and can be erased and reused.

7. Newly developed thermoplastic recording promises to be a valuable storage technique because of the recording density it provides.

8. Television recording makes possible storing unusual demonstrations for instructional use. Immediate playback of a televised record is valuable in training in complicated or dangerous skills.

9. Closed-circuit ETV in school systems typically includes one or more laboratory-classrooms where programs are originated. Systems of distribution to receiver classrooms vary in complexity and flexibility.

10. Ordinary broadcast ETV is limited in its reception area to a radius of twenty-five to fifty miles. However, the Midwest Airborne Television Program has extended its effective range to over 150 miles by broadcasting from a roving plane.

11. Closed-circuit television via a national wire service can be used for commercial meetings and business conferences. The method is expensive but favored by the companies that use it because it provides effective communication with field representatives.

12. Training in human relations procedures in industry and elsewhere can be given by means of television viewing of actual problems and operations.

13. Television techniques provide ef-

fective simulation training in such skills as driving and piloting.

14. Closed-circuit chains installed in industries, businesses, banks, hospitals, and so on for the purpose of remote observation and control also can be used as a training medium for new workers.

15. Much ETV teaching is conventional in nature, following established procedures of lecturing with coordinated visual displays. Lectures may be televised either in studios or in classrooms.

16. ETV in public schools uses team teaching to advantage.

17. ETV is a natural medium for many specialized demonstrations of laboratory, therapeutic, and medical procedures. Installed in a laboratory school, ETV can televise classroom techniques for the benefit of teacher trainees.

18. Telemation is a name applied to an *automated classroom*, which provides facilities for automatic presentation of all types of audiovisual materials along with a formal lecture. This very expensive installation may not be justified in view of the fact that almost the same advantages can be achieved by much cheaper means.

19. In a recent series of papers, learning theorists attempted to interpret audiovisual techniques in terms of their own concepts. The common motivational interpretation is that AV devices function as aids to learning by arousing interest and orienting the student in the right direction.

20. The S-R learning model which stresses the importance of reinforcement is too simplified to deal with ordinary audiovisual situations. S-R theorists prefer teaching machines to other audiovisual devices, because the stimulus, response, and reinforcement can be

brought out into the open and controlled.

21. A practical approach to AV research is to try to fit it into the *laws-of-learning* mold, dealing with recitation, meaningfulness of material, positive and negative transfer, and the like. Since these laws were derived mainly from rote verbal learning studies, they are too limited to deal with complicated audiovisual learning.

22. Gestalt psychology points out the weaknesses in conventional learning theory and emphasizes the organizational approach without basing its analyses firmly on objectively defined behavior mechanisms.

23. Conventional learning theories have not generated significant audiovisual research. This field needs greater emphasis on the human engineering or human factors approach which analyzes design variables in the audiovisual learning situation.

CHAPTER

6

Evaluating Audiovisual Learning

Early research on audiovisual learning had very little background within the experimental psychology of learning. Early studies on the relative effectiveness of different sensory modes or channels in promoting learning were applicable to this area but were too limited in design and results to be of any real help to educators interested specifically in the new teaching techniques. On the other hand, the specialized research activity that was generated by each new audiovisual technique usually had little significance for a general science of learning. Many of the earlier studies of films and radio, for example, seem to reflect more interest in classroom gadgetry as such than in the behavioral significance of audiovisual procedures and the influence of audiovisual design on the course of learning. Consequently we shall not attempt a detailed summary of early audiovisual research.

Since the late 1940s, stimulated by the extensive use of training films in World War II, there has been a new orientation in the audiovisual research field which brings it into much closer rapport with functional learning psychology. Efforts to study specific design variables in relation to learning efficiency have produced experiments on the optimal arrangement of demonstration and practice sequences in training films, on the role of student participation, on the use of organizing titles in films, on the relative effectiveness of black-and-white and color, and many others. Such analyses of audiovisual design have general import for learning science in addition to their practical implications for teachers and educators.

RESEARCH ON SPECIFIC TECHNIQUES

The first research on the effects of motion picture films as an instructional medium was carried out by two prominent psychologists who are remembered not for this collaborative effort but for their separate impact on general theoretical psychology. In the 1920s, Lashley and Watson (1922) reported a study of the effectiveness of films in a venereal disease campaign. Their results showed that films were effective in inducing persons infected with venereal disease to seek treatment. Since that time there have been numerous studies on the general effectiveness of films, graphics, and other techniques in promoting learning and in motivating individuals to action. Detailed summaries of these evaluative studies have been prepared by Hoban and Van Ormer (1950), May and Lumsdaine (1958), McClusky (1949), Stenius (1945), and Wendt and Butts (1962). For our present purposes, we shall attempt to describe some of the most important results of research in this field without getting involved in detail.

Motivational Effects

The motivational effects of films on behavior outside the audiovisual learning situation have been studied a number of times since Lashley's and Watson's initial study, with generally inconclusive results. Hovland *et al.* (1949) found that films enhance the amount of reading done by school children, but no such motivational effect was found with soldiers trained by films. May and Lumsdaine (1958) reported equivocal results with school children from experiments designed to test whether showing portions of story films (for example, *David Copperfield*) would increase spontaneous reading of the book. No conclusive results were found. These authors cited slight evidence to show that seeing films in class improves reading readiness of school children. A study by May and Jenkinson (1953) indicated that boys who read the novel *Kidnapped* after seeing a short film made up of a few interesting episodes read more care-

fully and remembered more than those who had seen the entire film before voluntarily reading the book.

Another study reported by May and Lumsdaine tried to measure changes in attitude toward *due process of law* after showings of films depicting mob action such as lynching, and so on. The experimenters found the interesting but perhaps not surprising result that following the films, attitudes changed in both directions, socially desirable and socially undesirable. The positive effects on *good* and *poor* citizens among the pupils, as designated by the teachers, were about the same, but the poor citizen group showed a greater tendency toward changing their attitudes in a socially undesirable direction. The over-all result was a mean net gain in attitude scores among the *good* group and a mean net loss among the *poor* group—a difference that was statistically significant.

The difficulty in predicting attitudinal shifts caused by films has been found in other studies as well. Merrill (1962) tried to measure the changes induced by a dramatic and suspenseful film on traffic safety and concluded that if a film is fearful enough, it arouses "defensive avoidance" that may prevent a shift in attitude. The implication is that the propaganda effect of films is not as clear-cut as some have believed. The use of films for such acceptable propaganda purposes as the attempt to change ethnic attitudes has had only the most limited success. On the other hand, films are no more useful for deliberate deception, for it appears to be more difficult to deceive people with simulation and outright misrepresentation in motion pictures than with words. Thus it is not always possible to predict whether deceptive film propaganda will be accepted or will boomerang.

A study by Hovland and Weiss (1951–1952) indicated that original opinions about the source of material influence the effectiveness of the presentation. If a source was believed to be *trustworthy*, opinions were changed significantly toward acceptance of the material, whereas material from a source believed to be *untrustworthy* was remembered as well but did not change opinions.

A number of studies have tried to determine whether there is a correlation between interest in instructional materials and the amount learned from them. Although one investigation of radio presentations found a high correlation between expressed interest and amount learned (Chall and Dial, 1948), later studies of visual presentations found no such relationship. Brandon (1955), Jorgenson (1955), Vander-Meer (1954), and Vernon (1953a) all reported insignificant or very low correlation values between expressed interest in film or television material and amount learned.

Studies of the relation between age and learning from films may be applicable here. The early research of Jones (1928) showed that the level of informational learning achieved by film instruction varies significantly with age. The curve for such learning rises to a peak in the mid twenties and then declines thereafter—a much earlier peaking effect than is found with ordinary studies of learning at different ages. The effect probably is due in part to motivational differences; that is, younger people are more interested in the film presentations and observe them more

attentively. However, there is no conclusive evidence that learning from visual material correlates significantly with expressed interest. Studies that have approached this problem by trying to relate learning to affiliative attitudes toward characters in a film and prestige attitudes have found minor and inconsistent differences in learning—results which do not change our generally negative conclusion.

General Learning Effects

A major conclusion of the earlier research is that all of the principal audiovisual techniques have proved valuable in promoting learning at all grade levels of schooling and for certain parts, at least, of a great many school subjects. In general, it has been concluded that graphic-verbal means of communication are better than verbal alone, and that in some cases an appropriate film is equivalent to an average teacher. However, this result has not been found universally, for many variables in the audiovisual materials, in the audience, and in the teaching-responding situation influence the learning that occurs.

Recently there has been considerable interest in measuring the relative effectiveness of presenting full courses of integrated films (Wendt and Butts, 1962). In one study, the use of a carefully designed set of films on world history was instrumental in accelerating a ninth grade course from the normal one-year period to one semester with no loss in learning. Other studies measuring the effectiveness of integrated films have not always confirmed this finding. In some cases the films were advantageous, in some cases they produced no significant differences, and occasionally they proved disadvantageous. Apparently a steady diet of film presentations over an entire course, even when combined with conventional teaching, was just too much for some students and some teachers. Interactions between instructional value of materials and motivational factors occur again and again in educational research and make interpretations difficult.

For some limited teaching purposes, recorded materials have been found as effective as live teaching. Dworkin and Holden (1959) used two matched groups of graduate engineering students to compare the teaching effectiveness of a regular classroom lecture with four fifteen-minute sound filmstrips prepared by the same teacher. No significant differences in learning were found in terms of the criteria used, but almost half of the film group reported that they would have liked to have been able to ask questions. Popham (1961, 1962) compared a conventional lecture-discussion procedure with an experimental procedure of presenting the lectures on tape followed by discussion periods either with the instructor or with a student discussion leader. No significant differences were found on the criterion test. Follettie (1961) also reported that he found live and taped lectures to be equally effective.

Films and graphics, if properly used, aid in the acquisition of many perceptual and motor skills as well as verbal knowledge. Complex skills appear to be aided more than simple skills. In order to be successful, however, the visual materials must be presented in effective ways and especially at optimal times during the course of learning. Thus we see that the organization of the instructional situa-

tion is as important as the materials used.

Carefully prepared film demonstrations and graphic displays have been shown to aid in forming scientific concepts. Young children are aided relatively more by such visual presentations than older children. This should not be interpreted as meaning that children of lower knowledge levels generally benefit more from films, for other studies have shown that students who initially were better prepared either because of ability or knowledge gained more from films than students who were more poorly prepared. In any case, the materials should be appropriate to the ability level of the intended audience for maximal effectiveness.

Single Versus Multiple Channels

Hartman (1961b) has reviewed an extensive group of experiments on the relative effectiveness of different communication channels, singly and in combination. Most of these studies date from the 1930s, when the use of radio in the school stimulated research comparisons of auditory and visual presentations of verbal material. The so-called *audio* and *print* channels also have been compared with *pictorial* presentations.

According to Hartman, Münsterberg and Bigham made one of the first contributions to this area of research in their study of memory published in 1894. They observed that simultaneous presentation of *unrelated* auditory and visual material reduced the amount of learning from both channels. Even in studies that have presented related materials, the interference effect sometimes is found.

Hartman's summary of research results indicates that audio is generally a more effective single channel than print for young children and illiterates and for literate people when the material presented is simple and easily understood. Print shows an increasing advantage for literate individuals as the difficulty of the material increases. The few studies comparing pictorial presentations with print or audio have been poorly controlled and thus no definite conclusions can be drawn.

Studies of multiple-channel combinations present a number of difficulties and have produced somewhat inconsistent results. In general, presentation of the same material by simultaneous audio and print channels produces more learning than either channel alone. When related pictorial material is presented along with verbal material, there usually is an increment in learning, although the audio-pictorial combination is less effective than print-pictorial. Hartman concluded that the evidence strongly indicates an advantage for combined channels over a single channel.

An experiment carried out by Hartman (1961a) illustrates some of the difficulties of multiple-channel comparisons. He paired twenty-five portraits with names and then presented them by single channels or in all combinations of multiple channels. Testing was by recognition among a longer series. Combined audio-print was better than either verbal channel alone, but when pictures were added, the number of items learned decreased. Hartman interpreted this as an interference effect, similar to that described by Münsterberg and Bigham, probably due to divided attention. His results also led to the conclusion that multiple channel presentations do not

increase learning over a single channel *unless the testing condition also contains the additional cues.*

This conclusion of Hartman's points up one of the greatest difficulties and weaknesses of audiovisual research. Implicit in many of the older research designs which tried to make direct comparisons between different techniques was the assumption that different types of instruction promoted the same type of learning—presumably the learning of verbal knowledge. These experimental comparisons usually were based on verbal criterion tests, for it was not realized that specialized audiovisual procedures might teach specialized nonverbal knowledge.

Verbal and Nonverbal Learning

Learning from films, graphics, and other audiovisual techniques is likely to be very specific to the materials used, and it is not completely valid to try to make direct comparisons with learning from conventional verbal teaching. However, most studies of audiovisual techniques have assessed their effectiveness on the basis of verbal tests and have made no attempt to measure acquisition of nonverbal knowledge and skill. One reason for this deficiency in research design is that we have as yet few tests of nonverbal performance and, accordingly, no entirely satisfactory measures of the effectiveness of audiovisual instruction in promoting learning, problem solving, and retention. When verbal achievement examinations are used to measure the effects of both live verbal instruction and instruction by means of the audiovisual techniques, they inevitably tend to favor the verbal medium over the nonverbal or audiovisual medium. Many kinds of nonverbal performance—for example, the kinds of learned skills needed by the artist, craftsman, actor, architect, designer, inventor, scientist, production engineer, or the expert river or aircraft pilot—may benefit from audiovisual instruction even though the verbal tests cannot measure their progress.

In our opinion, many seemingly well controlled comparisons of two teaching media have failed to turn up important differences in learning because the achievement criteria have been limited to verbal tests. An example is a study carried out by Westley and Barrow (1959) designed to measure the relative effectiveness of radio and television in presenting *background-of-the-news* programs to sixth graders in public schools. The scripts were prepared carefully for radio and then adapted for television. The same narrator and commentator presented both radio and television versions. An adequate number of subjects were used (228 in all) and the two groups were equated roughly according to their mean IQ's as measured by the California Test of Mental Maturity. Four programs were broadcast to both experimental groups. After each program, immediate recall of factual information was measured by a twenty-four-item multiple-choice test. Delayed recall was measured six weeks after the last program by means of a thirty-two-item test consisting of the eight items from each immediate recall test which proved by item analysis to be the best discriminators. The results of this study favored television over radio for immediate recall of information, but the difference, while statistically significant, was small. The mean score for the television group was 16.48, while that for the radio group was 15.27. After six weeks, the slight remaining difference between the groups was not statistically significant. Our point is that the verbal tests used as criteria of learning may not have been adequate to differentiate between the purely verbal and the audiovisual presentations.

Some research evidence can be found to support our belief that audiovisual instruction cannot be evaluated in terms of verbal performance criteria. A study by Radlow (1955), for example, showed that the effects of film instruction assessed by means of a nonverbal diagram test varied significantly from the effects as measured by a verbal test. Nelson and VanderMeer (1955) showed much the same thing by comparing performance on tests consisting of line diagrams and tests made up of verbal items after instruction by means of films. Lefkowith's (1955) study revealed even greater specificity of learning from graphic materials. The results favored line drawings when learning was tested with line drawings but favored still pictures when the tests utilized still pictures. In a study designed to test the effect of verbalization on retention of a set of stimulus objects presented in pictorial form, Kurtz and Hovland (1953) found that subjects who verbalized their responses during the original presentation remembered the stimuli more accurately than those who simply circled corresponding pictures on another paper. However, the verbalization group achieved their superiority by performing relatively better on a verbal retention test; the nonverbalization group did almost equally well on a visual test.

Irwin and Aronson (1958) attacked

the problem of verbal versus nonverbal learning by trying to devise nonverbal visual test procedures specifically to assess audiovisual learning. In order to compare the effects of conventional methods of teaching and highly visualized instruction, they designed a series of film tests which presented performances and activities either correctly or incorrectly depicting what had been taught. Students were required to judge the correctness and incorrectness of the nonverbal items presented on film and were also tested by verbal tests. The results of this research showed clearly that test performance is related to the method of instruction. Students who were taught visually by films were able to perform in a superior way on nonverbal tests, while those who were taught verbally performed more effectively on verbal tests. Results of this nature make us question the validity of some of the early studies that failed to find any significant effects of visual training, for in most cases these studies were not designed to detect the specialized learning effects that occurred. Evaluations are no better than the evaluative procedures used, and it seems clear that verbal and nonverbal performance cannot be measured by the same yardstick.

RESEARCH ON DESIGN VARIABLES

Most of the studies to be described in this section could be incorporated very easily into conventional learning psychology as investigations of the principles of learning economy. However, here we are dealing with those principles in relation to specific audiovisual techniques, more often than not motion picture films.

Instructional Sequencing

We indicated in Chapter 2 that there are no generally valid statements that can be made about the sequencing of practice, that is, about the relative effectiveness of distributed versus massed practice or of part versus whole learning. This statement is amply borne out by research on optimal sequencing procedures in instructional films. A series of studies reviewed by Lumsdaine (1961) leads to no definite conclusion except that each kind of training presents its own special problems.

In teaching a complex motor assembly sequence by means of a demonstration film, it was found to be more effective to intersperse practice periods after each *natural* demonstration unit. On the other hand, in teaching a geometric construction task by means of film, it was found that breaking into the film for practice after small demonstration segments gave good results during training but led to relatively poor test performance. Another study attempted to determine whether it was more advantageous to demonstrate and practice each unit of a serial assembly task twice before proceeding to the next unit or to demonstrate and practice each unit once and then repeat the entire sequence. In a task with three parts, the first method was better both in practice and in the final test, but in a task with four parts, the first method was superior in practice but not in the final test. Other studies have indicated that *massed* review at the end of the film may be better than *spaced* review interspersed throughout.

Lumsdaine's conclusion was that the sequencing of instructional materials with practice and review must depend on the inherent organizational features of the particular task. Similarly, Naylor and Briggs (1963) concluded that although whole training methods should be superior to part methods for highly integrated tasks at all levels of complexity, an increase in complexity for relatively unorganized tasks will result in part-task schedules becoming superior to whole methods.

Participation Effects

In the years during and since World War II, there have been many studies investigating the value of various student participation techniques during the showing of educational films. Much of this research has been carried out for the Armed Services wherein training films are used extensively.

The first important study of audience participation was by Hovland et al. (1949), who used films to teach the military phonetic alphabet (Able for A, Baker for B) to men in the Signal Corps. Two forms of the film were prepared, one with *passive* review sequences in which the letters were presented along with their equivalent names and another with *active* review in which the letters only were presented and the audience was instructed to try to call out the names. In a criterion test given at the end of the training, the passive group recalled forty-eight percent of the names and the active group, sixty-eight percent, a significant difference. Further, the performance of the active group could be improved to near-perfect by increasing the amount of repetition (May and Lumsdaine, 1958). However, the difference between the active and passive groups was reduced considerably simply by announcing prior to training that a

test would be given at the end of the film.

This original phonetic alphabet experiment posed some questions that have been put to many experimental tests since (Lumsdaine, 1961; May and Lumsdaine, 1958). Are the effects of active participation due entirely to practice or in part to a general increase in motivation brought about by the participation activity? If the effects are due to practice, is covert or implicit participation as effective as overt? Although the investigations that have attempted to separate out the roles of practice and motivation have had somewhat ambiguous results, they permit the general conclusion that active participation almost always increases learning, but that its beneficial effects usually are limited to those items specifically practiced.

Our own opinion is that the *motivation* of students in a learning situation can be understood only in terms of participative activity of some sort. Students who are highly motivated, who are alert and *paying attention*, are in fact responding perceptually in a more highly organized and consistent fashion than students who are disinterested or not paying attention. On the other hand, if student motivation is complicated by anxiety, achievement may decrease; in this case we assume that the emotional involvement interferes with maximal perceptual-motor participation.

That participation need not be overt has been demonstrated in a number of studies in which students instructed to respond covertly (to *think* their responses instead of speaking or writing them) have learned as effectively as overt responders. In some cases it appears to be enough to emphasize significant parts of the instructional material, that is, to prompt the students watching the film to make appropriate implicit responses.

A few instances in which overt participation procedures actually were detrimental to learning have been reported. In one study of learning the names of mechanical parts, overt participation was beneficial when the film was shown at a slow rate but detrimental at a fast rate (Lumsdaine, 1961). This result leads us to believe that certain other learning tasks, such as knot-tying, which have not been aided by overt participation, might have benefited if more time had been allowed in the film-training procedure. Kale *et al.* (1955) found that requiring pronunciation of Russian words during audiovisual training interfered with learning *as measured by written vocabulary tests*. This result indicates again the specificity of learning. For maximal participation benefits, the activity required of learners during instruction should be identical to the activity desired as criterion performance.

To summarize the participation issue, we can say that audiovisual materials like any training medium should provide opportunity for the learner to make the desired responses to relevant cues. Sometimes this is a matter of optimal timing. For example, it has been found that although slow-motion improves the effectiveness of complex demonstrations and slow rates of presentation are best for promoting understanding of many visual components, verbal information should be given at medium speeds (Ash and Jaspen, 1953; Jaspen, 1950a). Sometimes repetition helps. There is some evidence indicating that showing

an instructional film twice may be as effective as using interspersed practice periods or questions with knowledge feedback at intervals throughout the film (Allen, 1957). Two complete showings take more time, however, than one showing with practice and participation sequences and the extra showing undoubtedly would lose its effectiveness if the audience became inattentive (that is, failed to participate implicitly).

In the long run, the important thing is to promote practice in the desired responses by one means or another. The value of overt participation is in making sure that the proper responses are given, but films and other materials should be designed to maximize the effects of covert or implicit responses as well. The problem is to determine what design features are most effective. Will any factors that attract attention and hold the student's interest also enhance learning? Studies bearing on these problems will be reviewed in the next section.

Analyzing Graphic Design

The early proponents of audiovisual instruction were inclined to overemphasize the importance of "fancy" materials as opposed to simple. Thus it was assumed by many that color, movement, realism, and so forth in visual materials would increase their teaching effectiveness when compared with black-and-white, nonmoving, unrealistic portrayals. As a matter of fact, children usually prefer materials that are colored, contain action, and tell an organized story, but they do not necessarily learn more from them. Special features apparently aid learning only if they aid important discriminations, promote understanding, or increase the probability that the learners will make correct responses. Color improves the effectiveness of training films when color cues aid discrimination of significant parts or confusing materials, but otherwise a technically inferior black-and-white version may be just as effective in teaching factual knowledge and promoting understanding of the subject matter as a finished color version of a film (May and Lumsdaine, 1958; VanderMeer, 1954). A film prepared in dramatic form with live dialogue was no better than one in which the same material was described by off-stage narration (May and Lumsdaine, 1958). For recognition of detail, photographs and shaded drawings were poorer than cartoon-type drawings, although better than line drawings (Ryan and Schwartz, 1956). Adding embellishments (music and humorous drawings) to a film may actually decrease its teaching effectiveness (May and Lumsdaine, 1958).

The implication of studies such as these is that films and other materials should be designed for the specific purposes for which they are intended. Whereas elaborate or artistic presentations might serve to introduce and to stimulate interest and further study in a general subject, they are not appropriate for instructing in specific verbal and perceptual-motor skills.

An important conclusion that can be drawn from audiovisual research is that the teaching effectiveness of films depends on a careful integration of the verbal and the pictorial or graphic materials. In general, it is important to prepare a class for film showings with introductory comments and discussion

(Allen, 1955. It is good to simplify the verbal commentary in the film itself according to standard measures of readability, and to use verbal titles, questions, review sequences, instructions on what parts to watch carefully, and so on throughout the film. Well integrated verbal-nonverbal materials usually teach more effectively than either type alone. Also, we believe that integrated materials promote better transfer to related situations, although there is little research evidence on this point.

A number of studies have investigated the nature of effective cues and prompts in instructional and demonstrational films. The use of simple animation techniques such as pop-in labels or moving arrows to emphasize important points has proved effective. In certain military training films instructing in equipment use, depicting negative examples and common errors was more helpful than explanations (Jaspen, 1950a, 1950b), and animated slide sequences were more effective than static ones (Silverman, 1958). In the use of cues and prompts, however, it is important to remember that the items or sequences which are especially emphasized may be learned better at the expense of other items not so emphasized. Thus any special attention-focusing or participation technique should be tested empirically to see whether it interferes with learning other aspects of the entire task.

Special design problems arise in connection with graphical presentation of statistical material and mathematical functions. Studies of graph design have indicated that students of all ages, including college students, usually require special training in order to use graphs effectively. Most graphs used in text-books do not convey meaningful information to the ordinary student unless verbal explanations accompany them (Wendt and Butts, 1962). Graphs and other displays are understood better if they are labeled with titles, arrows, and the like. The effectiveness of a graph depends also upon how well it fits the data, for particular kinds of data are best represented by particular types of graphs. It is well established that graphs should be as simple as possible, for understanding decreases as the complexity of the display increases. The design of graphs should be adjusted to age. Children below ten or twelve years of age rarely understand graphical interactions, and above this age range, the effectiveness of graphs depends on both age and training.

RESEARCH ON EDUCATIONAL TELEVISION

All forms of audiovisual instruction and all of the problems connected with their use have been brought to a focus in educational television, for it can incorporate almost every medium of verbal and nonverbal communication. It should be recognized that the research evaluation of ETV involves more than a detached scientific probing into problems of human learning, for this area is the urgent concern of industries, endowed foundations, government agencies, teacher organizations, school systems and universities, as well as of scientific psychologists. A subject which touches so many lives, jobs, and vested interests is bound to be controversial, and one of our tasks will be to try to distinguish between research facts and evaluative opinions.

ETV in College Teaching

In 1954, the Fund for the Advancement of Education made a large grant to Pennsylvania State College to organize an extensive closed-circuit ETV program and to evaluate it experimentally (Carpenter et al., 1955, 1958; Greenhill, 1958; Teaching by Television, 1961). The program grew steadily, and by 1958, 3700 of Penn State's 14,000 students were taking one or more of the thirteen television courses offered. The first experimental evaluations were carried out during the spring semester of 1955 and the fall semester of 1956–1957. The same teachers were used to teach television classes and regular classes, and care was taken to keep teaching conditions as similar as possible for the randomly selected television and control groups. When the students were tested at the end of the courses, no significant differences were found in achievement. However, the teachers and students using television did not like it very well; although most teachers were willing to give it a try and most students preferred it over live instruction in very large classes.

While these results are not particularly surprising, they were a bitter blow to enthusiasts who thought that television instruction in and of itself would revolutionize education. As similar results accumulated from other colleges making experimental comparisons (by mid-1961, out of 100 comparisons in college courses, three favored television teaching, thirteen favored conventional teaching, and eighty-four showed no significant differences [Schramm, 1962]), it became apparent that more work and study were needed to understand tele-vision's potential value and to develop teaching programs that would maximize that potential (Grosslight, 1958; Zor-baugh, 1958). That is, we need to de-termine where the medium is most ap-propriate and how it can be made most effective.

Television teaching has perhaps its greatest success in extending the audi-ence of experienced and skillful instruc-tors far beyond the limits of ordinary classrooms. These audiences range from relatively small groups taught by closed-circuit transmission within a college campus to classes on several campuses linked by an interinstitutional network, to the thousands of students, teachers, professional men, housewives and others who have taken credit courses in science in the *Continental Classroom* broadcast over a nationwide commercial network. Introductory science courses combining lectures with demonstrations are par-ticularly appropriate to television teach-ing, although it has been found advis-able to supplement the televised classes with regular discussion-quiz sections where possible. For obvious reasons, no experimental comparisons have been made between television classes taught by excellent teachers and other classes taught face-to-face by more pedestrian instructors, but it is very possible that students can learn more and enjoy their work more in a topnotch television course than with a relatively poor teacher. Also in some cases the alterna-tives for the student are not a televised class taught by a superior teacher versus a regular class taught by a poor one, but a televised class versus none at all. Stu-dents who receive instruction in their home via broadcast ETV might receive

it in no other way. It is not surprising that home-based students generally are more favorable to and learn relatively more from television teaching than do students who receive television instruc-tion on college campuses.

ETV for Laboratory Demonstrations

Using television to demonstrate labo-ratory procedures and medical and surgical techniques usually is judged to be effective. However, the two evalua-tive studies of ETV in engineering and laboratory courses described below yielded results no more favorable to television than the Penn State studies.

Bobren and Siegel (1960) tested the value of ETV in a university engineer-ing course in which small groups of about twelve students met for weekly two-hour classes combining a lecture-demonstration, a short discussion, and a quiz. Five sections were taught by means of closed-circuit television and five by conventional methods. The tele-vision sections viewed the lecture and experiment together in a large classroom and then divided into their small sec-tions for discussions, quizzes, and ex-aminations. Examination grades showed no differences in achievement between the two groups. The television students tended to judge the course less favorably than the conventional on an attitude rating scale. According to their answers to a list of specific questions, the televi-sion group understood the course less clearly than the control group, judged the relation between theory and experi-ments to be less clear, and rated their course poorer in relation to other engi-neering courses. The authors felt that their findings revealed significantly negative attitudes toward ETV among engineering students.

Seibert and Honig (1960) compared the relative effectiveness of television and conventional instruction for teaching chemical laboratory procedures to students who had had no previous training in chemistry. Instructional presentations were based on the contents of two sound films, one on techniques of mass determination and various types of balances, and the other on apparatus and procedures for volumetric measurements. The five groups of twelve subjects each were comparable in ability on the basis of a vocabulary pretest. Two groups were instructed by television, two groups by conventional methods, while the fifth or control group received no instruction. All groups were divided in half randomly for testing. Half were tested within two hours of the instruction and half five weeks later.

Two criterion measures were used to judge learning achievement—an eighteen-item knowledge test based on the film material, and a laboratory performance test in which the subjects were asked to carry out a simple titration while evaluators watched and scored their performance. In this performance test, all four instructed groups did better than the uninstructed group, but there were no significant differences between the television and the conventional groups or between immediate and delayed testing. The knowledge test was found to be worthless as a criterion measure, for it did not discriminate between instructed and noninstructed subjects. This finding indicates that the simple criterion tests used in experimental comparisons sometimes have no

more than face validity and suggests one reason for the negative findings sometimes reported.

ETV for Teacher Training

In the fall of 1956, closed-circuit facilities were installed in two New York state teachers' colleges to aid in teacher training. Several television cameras were placed in the classrooms of the campus schools and left unattended. These provided a choice of monitor pictures which showed behavior patterns of the children, the procedures of the supervising teacher, and the performances of the student teachers themselves when they practice-taught. Kinescopic records of the televised pictures made it possible for practice teachers to see their own performance.

An evaluation of this program after one year was generally favorable (Almstead, 1957). The principal advantage claimed for the television medium was that it helped to relieve tensions and distractions to which children are subjected when being observed by adults in the classroom. The classroom situation was much more normal and could be viewed by many students simultaneously. Students sitting in front of receivers saw close-ups of teachers, materials, individuals, and small groups of children. Finally, students at the practice-teaching level saw themselves in action and understood more clearly some of their own weaknesses and problems.

The classroom recordings have potential uses in addition to their immediate use in the teacher colleges. Selections from them are combined and edited to be used as demonstration lessons and resource material for college teachers and students in several areas. One of the most important uses is to provide additional training to teachers already in service, especially potential supervisors.

In-service courses for teachers promise to be a particularly valuable application of ETV (*Teaching by Television*, 1961). The state department of education in Texas has offered broadcast television courses for prospective teachers as well as teachers and administrators already holding jobs. In New York City, the Board of Education instituted a series of televised lecture-demonstrations combined with workshops conducted at various centers throughout the city. In addition, the courses in physics, chemistry, and mathematics presented by *Continental Classroom* have enabled thousands of high school teachers all over the country to bring themselves up to date in their field.

ETV in Military Training

Educational television has a longer history in the Armed Forces than in our colleges and universities. Since 1951, closed-circuit installations have been used in a number of different military instruction centers, including Signal School, medical centers, Transportation School, and Air Defense School. Almost from the start, the television techniques and procedures have been subjected to sustained research evaluations in order to compare the effectiveness of television and conventional instruction, to explore the special advantages of television, to improve television instruction, and to assess relative costs.

In many ways these military research programs have been more productive than research evaluations carried on in the colleges, partly because of certain advantages inherent in the military situation. For example, military instruction centers have available a controlled supply of subjects for whom standardized measures of aptitude and intelligence have been obtained. Also, the pressing training problems of the Armed Forces and their interest in reducing costs, training time, and training personnel have stimulated sustained efforts to develop efficient methods of teaching. Although the military situation is not entirely comparable to the colleges, there are some important similarities, including the fact that military trainees are from approximately the same age group as college undergraduates. Consequently, military research on ETV has implications for ETV in colleges and universities.

The earliest reports of military ETV were enthusiastic (Cline *et al.*, 1956; Fritz, 1952; Kanner *et al.*, 1954; Newsom, 1954). They indicated that television instruction was at least as effective as conventional instruction and in some cases superior, especially for poor students. Later reports have tempered this initial enthusiasm somewhat, but are more valuable in providing analytic data bearing on questions of how best to use television techniques. The following summary is based principally on a series of papers by Kanner and his associates describing television research in the army (Desiderato *et al.*, 1956; Kanner, 1957, 1958; Kanner *et al.*, 1954, 1955, 1958a, 1958b, 1958c; Kanner and Marshall, 1963; Runyon *et al.*, 1955; Runyon and Kanner, 1956). The drawing in Figure 6.1 illustrates how a large

Figure 6.1.   Educational television classrooms used in military training. (Based on Runyon *et al*. Factors leading to effective television instruction. *Aud.-vis. Commun. Rev.*, 1955, 3, 264–273.)

theater or lecture room was divided into nine television classrooms, each equipped with a monitor to provide all students with a satisfactory view of the television screen.

The army's general finding concerning television lectures and lecture-demonstrations was that they are likely to be less effective than conventional instruction, but with careful preparation and utilizing its special advantages, television can be made more effective than conventional lectures. If an instructor is plucked from his classroom, put before a television camera, and asked to present his material as usual, his teaching effectiveness will be less than usual. Even an experienced and good teacher may find that his timing is off and that he misses the ordinary interchange with his students. And a

relatively poor presentation is even worse on television. As Kanner (1957) put it, "the television camera can function as a bore amplifier . . . when used merely as a transmission medium it can exaggerate, not improve, ineffective teaching."

A study was designed to explore methods of improving television instruction in order to obtain standardized lessons which would equal or exceed the effectiveness of conventional instruction. Television scripts were prepared carefully and presented with the aid of a prompting device. After each presentation, the students were given objective tests and their performance was analyzed item by item. On the basis of these analyses, the presentation was improved by rewriting the script, adding visual aids, changing the demonstration procedures, and so forth. In the interests of reducing teaching time, all extraneous material was omitted. The results of this study showed that it was possible to reduce the duration of a lesson as much as fifty percent while still enhancing its effectiveness over conventional instruction. In most cases, the effectiveness of a presentation could be maintained with a thirty percent reduction in time. It undoubtedly would have been possible to improve live teaching fully as much as television teaching if the same analytic procedures had been used. The advantage of working with televised lessons was that they could be controlled better, standardized, and then recorded for later use if desired.

Other studies determined the particular teaching situations where television is superior to conventional instruction. By using close-ups, television is superior for training in the use of small pieces of equipment and in understanding the relations among small moving parts. Television is superior for situations that require simple rote learning and may be superior in recognition training. Besides close-ups, the techniques that are valuable are superimposures, split-screen images, and animation. With television it is possible to present both right and wrong procedures and to relate names to parts. These special advantages of television should be applicable to technical and laboratory courses.

A recent study (Kanner and Marshall, 1963) tested the use of after-hours reviews and previews to enhance the effectiveness of army basic training. Experimental television groups were taught all of their lessons by television and then were exposed to after-hours presentations in their barracks. Review programs stressing key points and brief orientation previews of subsequent lessons were presented. These groups learned significantly more than conventionally taught groups in eleven out of twenty-five comparisons; the conventional groups were better in six. A more interesting finding was that *low* aptitude trainees taught by the television procedures learned approximately as much as *high* aptitude trainees taught conventionally. Only one comparison out of fourteen favored the high aptitude conventional group significantly.

Army studies have shown that it is possible to train an inexperienced instructor in a few hours to present complicated material via television just as effectively as experienced instructors. Of course the presentation itself must be prepared by an expert and then should be analyzed and improved. However, once effective standardized lessons have been prepared, they can be presented by very rapidly trained instructors.

One difficulty inherent in television teaching is the lack of opportunity for questions and answers. In army research, the questions asked in conventional classes were analyzed, and it was found that most of them did not contribute to learning or achievement of the class. When questions indicated weaknesses in the presentation, changes were made to improve it. Finally, certain questions and answers that seemed to strengthen a presentation were adopted into television scripts. The instructor would ask the question rhetorically, pause for a moment and then give the answer. While this technique helps solve the question-answer difficulty at some levels, the army researchers felt that television teaching is inappropriate for certain advanced courses and seminars. Another drawback in television teaching is the passive role of the student in front of the monitor. Various types of participative activities can be required of the class to alleviate this difficulty.

The Armed Forces must judge the usefulness of an educational technique according to whether it can save money, time, or instructional personnel while maintaining or improving the effectiveness of instruction. Although the series of papers we have been summarizing indicated that television achieved these objectives, some military instruction centers have concluded that ETV is too costly to be feasible (Carroll, 1957).

ETV in Public Schools

Full-scale programs set up to evaluate television teaching in public schools began in 1955 and 1956 with financial support from the Ford Foundation and Fund for the Advancement of Education (a Ford Foundation subsidiary). In the fall of 1955, the St. Louis public schools started teaching several television courses through the facilities of community-owned Station KETC-TV. Their primary purpose was to determine the feasibility of teaching large classes by means of television without supplementary teaching in the classroom (*Teaching by Television*, 1961).

The first experimental lessons in ninth-grade science and English composition and in second-grade spelling were taught to large groups of children who met either in music rooms or lunchrooms. Teachers were present during the lessons but did no teaching. The results indicated that the ninth-grade pupils did as well as conventionally taught pupils of equal ability. The younger pupils taking

spelling by means of television achieved somewhat less than their counterparts in conventional classrooms. In spite of the special effort put into the television presentations, most of the students found them less interesting than classroom lessons and missed the personal interchange with the teachers (Rose, 1957). It was concluded from the St. Louis experience that television teaching cannot replace classrooms, but should be used in a supplementary role.

The largest single experiment in the use of ETV in public schools was started in 1956 in Hagerstown, Maryland, with a 100,000 dollar grant from the Fund for the Advancement of Education (Hale, 1957; *Teaching by Television*, 1961). An extensive closed-circuit system was set up to transmit as many as six programs at a time to the schools of Washington County. It was hoped that the cables eventually would be extended to the entire county school system, a total of fifty schools. Starting in 1956, with ten courses transmitted to 4941 students in eight schools, the television center in Hagerstown, by 1960, was sending a wide selection of courses to 16,500 students from the first to the twelfth grades in thirty-six schools.

The Hagerstown project hoped to provide a richer education in its schools at a lower cost than would have been possible by conventional methods. Studio teachers worked with classroom teachers to plan the courses, and team teaching techniques were used from the start. After the first few years, school officials believed that teaching in Hagerstown had been improved in several ways and that student achievement was higher than before. Studio teachers specializing in art and music provided programs

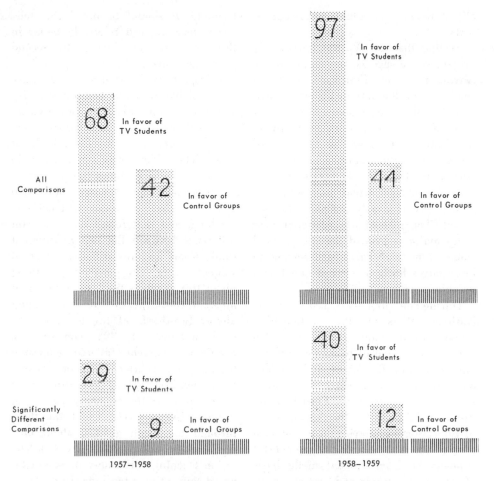

Figure 6.2.   The relative effectiveness of television and conventional teaching in the National Program in the Use of Television in the Public Schools. These results were all based on comparisons between ETV instruction and regular teaching in paired classes of students. The groups were matched in scholastic aptitude and pretest scores or were equated statistically. Total comparisons and significant differences are shown for two different school years. (Based on *Teaching by Television.* [2nd ed.] New York: Ford Foundation and Fund for the Advancement of Education, 1961.)

that classroom teachers could not equal. It also was believed that achievement in arithmetic had been boosted by television teaching, and a course in advanced mathematics was added to the High School curriculum. These appraisals were tentative, however. The interest

and activity aroused by the Hagerstown project might have brought about increased motivation and achievement on the part of the students and teachers irrespective of the techniques that were being tried out. Just knowing that they are taking part in a special activity usually stimulates individuals to greater efforts.

Feeling that the Washington County project was a success, the Fund for the Advancement of Education provided funds to launch a nationwide experiment in public school television (*Teaching by Television*, 1961). Known generally as the National Program in the Use of Television in the Public Schools, it included, by 1960, nearly 800 schools in fifteen municipal areas and eight regions, serving nearly 200,000 students in all. The schools are scattered over every major section of the country and range from small rural high schools to large city schools in Detroit and Philadelphia.

During the first two years of the National Program, the participating schools made many comparisons between achievement of television students and conventionally taught students. The data in Figure 6.2, which were taken from a 1961 report of the Ford Foundation and the Fund for the Advancement of Education, summarize those comparisons in which the television and control students had been equated on the basis of scholastic aptitude and pretest scores, or in which differences had been taken into account statistically so that legitimate comparisons could be made. Total number of comparisons favoring television and control classes and the number of statistically significant differences favoring each are given. In the second year of the experiment, the number of comparisons favoring television students was more than twice the number of comparisons favoring control groups, while the number of significant differences favoring television was more than three times the number favoring conventional

teaching. It should be noted that television teaching did relatively better in these comparisons during the second year than during the first.

A report by Schramm (1962) gave all available research comparisons between television and conventional teaching, both published and unpublished, that had been made to the middle of 1961. These data are summarized in Figure 6.3, which shows the percent of comparisons that favored television teaching, that favored conventional teaching, and that found no significant difference between the two at different grade levels and for different types of subject matter. The most obvious thing about this graph is the large number of *no significant difference* results, running almost two-thirds of the total. Of the total number of 393 comparisons, twenty-one percent favored television teaching and fourteen percent, conventional teaching. More interesting than these figures is the changing pattern at different grade levels. From the third through the ninth grades, about one-third of the comparisons favored television teaching while only one-tenth favored conventional teaching. In contrast, fewer than one-tenth of the senior-high-through-college comparisons favored television while more than twice as many were unfavorable. The difference between the results for the younger and older groups was highly significant, showing that television has been a more effective medium for younger students than for older.

When the comparisons were broken down according to subject matter, it was found that the humanities benefited significantly less from television teaching than did either science or social studies.

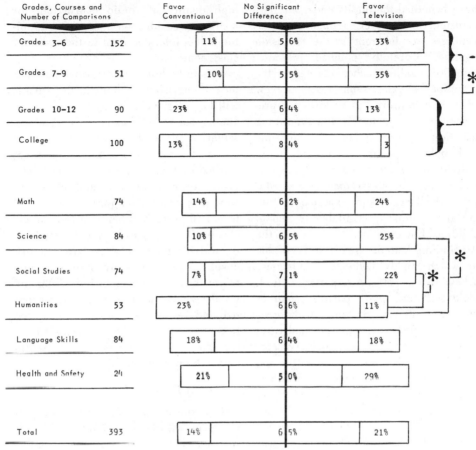

Figure 6.3.   Summary of research comparisons up to mid-1961 showing the relative effectiveness of television and conventional teaching at different grade levels and for different subjects. The relative ineffectiveness of television in teaching humanities is probably due to the fact that most of the comparisons in this area were reported from the high school and college levels, which were unfavorable to television over all. (Data from Schramm, 1962.)

However, this difference probably is related to the fact that no courses classified as Humanities appeared in the Grades three through six comparisons and only nine such courses in Grades seven through nine. In other words, this subject matter difference undoubtedly reflects the grade-level pattern.

The relative superiority of television classes in the lower grades probably was due to more than the particular characteristics of ETV. The planning that went into new television programs in the public schools resulted in a certain amount of reorganization of course material and curriculum changes that might have benefited the pupils under any circumstances. However, a number of advantages are inherent in the television medium. Carefully planned presentations of studio teachers bring to the attention of classroom teachers new ideas and improved procedures for presenting course material. Team teaching techniques permit a better use of time and make it possible to provide more individualized instruction. Television brings into the classrooms special educational displays and experiences that are not ordinarily available to school children. For example, art classes in the Austin-San Antonio area have been able to watch highly competent university artists throw pots on a potter's wheel, mold sculpture, paint portraits, and illustrate different drawing techniques (Schmid, 1963). Students in small rural schools are able to take courses not previously available and share in the excellent teaching of experts. Further, those schools using broadcast television reach audiences in schools and homes beyond their own classrooms. In the report of the National Program, it was said that ETV students made more extensive use of school libraries than other students and were not tardy or absent as often. However, these last benefits might accrue with any marked changes or improvements in teaching procedures.

The following problems were noted by the National Program: inadequate facilities for large television classes, difficulties in handling large classes, scheduling difficulties, problems of organizing and integrating the courses to take maximum advantage of television, and problems of adapting teaching to varying needs of individual students. Above all is the constant problem of maintaining high quality of studio instruction, for mediocre teaching on a television monitor is less tolerable than in the ordinary classroom.

It is to be hoped that further research on the television medium in the schools will be designed to investigate more advantageous ways of using ETV. A representative effort of this sort was carried out by Gropper and Lumsdaine, as described by Lumsdaine (1963). Two television lessons on heat and chemistry were prepared for the junior high school level and previewed before a few sample classes. The responses of these students on quizzes then were analyzed to discover which points were unclear and might benefit from revision. After revised versions were prepared, the original and revised lessons were presented to matched groups. Those groups receiving the revised lessons scored significantly higher on learning tests.

The Cost Factor

The constant nagging doubt that pervades all efforts at evaluating ETV is whether the game is worth the candle. In the past decade, millions of dollars have been poured into educational television. In 1961 it was estimated that more than forty million dollars already had been spent on capital outlay and another twenty million dollars was being spent annually for operating expenses (Nelson, 1962). This money comes from tax sources, private endowments, industrial sources, and, above all, from the large foundations, principally the Ford Foundation and its subsidiary Funds. Yet after all this investment of money, time, and some of the best minds of the educational profession and the television industry, the real finding of

ETV research is that the ordinary teacher operating in an ordinary classroom with no special aid or support often does as well as the best that television can offer.

The question that must be answered by the nation's public schools is whether television is an economical method of teaching the ever-increasing numbers of pupils. No final answer can be given to this question, for the pilot projects were highly subsidized, exploratory in nature, and of necessity superimposed television teaching on school systems designed for conventional teaching. One fact must be faced relative to broadcast television. One video channel can transmit only one lesson at a time, no matter how many classrooms and pupils are within receiving distance. On the other hand, the coaxial cable of a closed-circuit system can transmit a number of simultaneous programs, but the installation costs may be prohibitive. The Washington County project received the use of hundreds of thousands of dollars worth of equipment and cable from the television industry and the local telephone company in addition to large foundation grants by means of which they staffed their system and carried out evaluative research. Even with these original subsidies, it has not been certain whether operating costs would exceed the savings effected by the television method.

Representatives of the television industry have maintained that educational television is economically feasible for public school systems. For example, Chamberlain (1959) made an investigation of ETV feasibility for a region around Syracuse, New York, and recommended multichannel broadcast TV from a central point to cover a number of school districts. He suggested at least four stations served by four UHF transmitters housed in one building and utilizing the same tower for their antennas. These stations could broadcast four programs simultaneously to approximately ninety-two school districts located within thirty to forty miles of the central studios. With this system, television instruction would be available about one-third of the school day to every grade level from kindergarten through high school.

Since that time, the Federal Communications Commission has authorized private instructional television that would use low-power, low-cost, short-range equipment for transmission within a single school district (ETV channels going begging, 1962). In time it may be feasible to provide up to five channels for virtually every school district in the country.

Analyzing the costs of ETV at the college level is somewhat more difficult than for public schools, inasmuch as most university television stations offer a variety of public service features and serve training needs for students interested in television production in addition to teaching specific courses for credit. The Penn State project claimed some savings in TV teaching for large classes; their break-even point was reached when 200 students enrolled in a course. However, proposals to establish a *Junior College of the Air* to televise required freshman and sophomore courses have been rejected by some educators who feel that the value of ETV at the college level is not well enough established for such an ambitious program. Although a complete Junior College television curriculum was established in Chicago, the usual feeling is that voluntary participation in a few courses of proven effectiveness, either at home or on the campus, is safer than completely televised degree-granting institutions.

In the final analysis, the value of ETV may be too intangible for a dollars-and-cents appraisal. Research findings make it clear that it cannot be judged in terms of its use as a general pedagogical tool, but that its ultimate worth in education and training will depend on what it can do that cannot be done as well by any other technique. The ability to transmit an audiovisual display to a large audience spread out over a large area is an important advantage, but it is more important for some types of material than for others. The immediacy of television compared with motion pictures is advantageous but not always critically so. For scientific and technical demonstrations, for sharing in expert teaching and timely events, and for watching activities that would be disrupted by direct observation, television is superb. Finally, the possibilities for television storage and retrieval may in time establish video libraries of far greater educational significance than the film libraries now in existence.

MOTIVATIONAL EFFECTS OF TELEVISION

The impact of television is not confined to the classroom but starts in the home and often is extended to the place of work. The ordinary child entering school already has had several years of "instruction" in front of the television screen, and the influence of commercial television likely will continue throughout his formative years and into adulthood. The possible motivational effects of tele-

vision have aroused much interest and speculation. We would like to know whether television contributes to over-all positive motivation, to disturbances of motivation and behavior, to emotional reactions, and to general emotional attitudes in viewers of all ages and different walks of life. What is the action-potential of commercial and educational programs? To what extent does television lead to overt changes in behavior or to specific action?

These questons are difficult to approach experimentally and have scarcely been touched in objective studies. General evidence indicates that television displays do not influence human reactions as decisively as the large motion picture screen with its wonderful depth quality. People who scream or cry in a motion picture theater rarely react in the same way while watching movies on television. One of the authors has observed that educational motion pictures of animal brain operations which produce marked reactions in a student audience have little or no emotional effect when shown by means of television.

There is good reason to believe that the exaggerated violence and human distortions so often seen on commercial television have been developed intentionally or unintentionally to counteract the generally neutral motivational impact of the twenty-one-inch box. Television needs large overdoses of energy and action in order to make it look alive. The *empathy* with this box and its sundry assortment of exaggerated characters is relatively low for all people except young children and those adults whose activity outlets are not easily fulfilled. This situation is a problem for both commercial and educational television and may account for the relatively low acceptance value of ETV in the classroom.

One new motivational aspect of television is that it serves as a nearly universal *household eye*. The millions of television sets are like so many flexible telescopes and microscopes that can be used by household members to examine each new product, each new personality, and each new idea transmitted over the air. Television has not solved the problems of commercial advertising—if anything, it tends to exaggerate some of them—but it has speeded up the whole process. Successful advertising campaigns succeed in a hurry, and those that fail can be buried promptly.

Television advertising and even ETV put a premium on favorable personal images associated with certain products and programs. Thus television appears to humanize and personalize the physical articles of commerce as well as the components of educational programs that are conveyed over the video waves.

Psychological Effects on Children

The psychological effects of commercial television on children in the home have been the subject of countless questions, discussions, arguments, and harangues—but few objective investigations. One major study carried out by Schramm et al. (1961) was based on questionnaire and interview information from 5991 children, 1958 parents, and several hundred other adults in ten culturally varying communities, one of which had no television. The main conclusions confirm what is assumed generally, that the television programs watched by children are concerned predominately with excitement, violence, and crime, and that television plays an overpowering role in the lives of young children. Eight out of ten children at age five were watching television regularly and nine out of ten at age six. Children in the lower grades were found to spend an average of two hours each day before the home screen. This average increased to three to four hours for sixth to seventh graders and thereafter declined slowly. Similar results were found by Witty (1963) in surveys conducted annually from 1949 to 1962. The average child at sixteen has spent as much time before television as in school.

The effects of television on the education and activity of children were found to vary in relation to age, intelligence, and sex. The vocabulary of young children is increased somewhat by television —an effect that was confirmed for sixth graders by Witty—but this effect declines during adolescence. Television may actually depress the performance level of bright children on knowledge tests, and chronic viewers during the adolescent years may do less well in school than nonviewers. The "broadening" effect of television, if any, is spotty and is more concerned with superficial facts than with basic knowledge and educationally significant subjects.

The question as to whether television portrayals of crime and violence generate similar behavior in young viewers cannot be answered with assurance. The question involves more variables in the life of a child than television, including the nature of the child, his family, and his social life. Schramm et al. drew the conclusion that television may be a

contributory cause of violence and delinquency. They distinguished between
fantasy and *reality* experiences and went
on to show that it is overwhelmingly the
fantasy needs that are met by television.
Children having unsatisfactory social relations with their family or peers tend to
escape into television, where antisocial
behavior, aggression, and fantasy are
reinforced. This effect is more pronounced in middle-class than in lower-
class groups. Fears induced by television
are mainly by violence of a nonritualized
nature, stepping into traps or any kind
of body cutting. Standardized gunfights,
fistfights, and the like are accepted with
little emotion.

Television occasionally has a very direct neurophysiological effect on some
viewers that is not generally known. A
slow flicker of about ten to twenty flashes
per second sometimes has marked effects, such as nausea, on normal individuals and may induce attacks in epilep-
tics. In fact, some epileptic children induce seizures repeatedly by flicking their
fingers in front of their eyes while looking at a bright light or by fluttering
their eyelids (Robertson, 1954). It has
been noted a number of times in the
medical literature that the slow flicker
of the television image can induce *petit
mal* or *grand mal* epileptic attacks (Abbott Laboratories, 1961).

Content Preferences
in Television Viewing

Some research efforts have been made
to identify broad trends or preference
patterns in program watching and film
viewing in terms of a few broad motivational categories. Smythe (1954) assumed three types of content of significance in television viewing, identifying
them as *form, substance,* and *source.*
Entertainment of different types was
said to be related primarily to form, information and orientation programs to
substance, and certain orientation programs to source. Jones (1942) has
attempted to classify the motives in
viewing motion pictures in terms of
wants—for safety, for income, for defer-
ence, and for security.

A survey by Stanley *et al.* (1955)
measured the attitudes of 225 residents
of a small midwestern town toward
seventy-six possible types of television
programs. The results showed that the
most highly preferred programs were
those related to news reports, weather
information, news commentary, popular
music, travel information, religious music, religious services, and institutional
spot news. Soap operas, pseudo sports,
science-fiction drama, classical dance,
farm information, individual local political activities, puppets, and folklore
were among the low-preference programs. Some sex differences in program
preferences occurred, although the male
and female subjects were fairly consistent in their high- and low-preference
choices. Some differences were found for
young and old age groups and for
groups with high-level and low-level education. It is very likely that preferences
depend also on geographic, regional,
and cultural factors.

In an attempt to determine whether
reliable groupings of program preferences might be identified, Carter (1957)
did a factor analysis of the data obtained in the study just described. His
results indicated wide differences and

discrepancies in possible solutions to the factoring problem. He succeeded in identifying eight factors, but they were not well defined.

Interaction between Speaker and Audience

In the public speaking field, the concept of *eye-contact* refers to the idea that a speaker can hold the attention of his audience better if he keeps his eyes glued on them. It has been claimed that the speaker needs such eye-contact in order to portray his convictions and to get feedback from the audience which will help him adjust his delivery to the needs of the moment. These ideas concerning interaction between a speaker and his audience have been generalized to apply to motion pictures and television.

Westley and Mobius (1960) tested the assumption that the effectiveness of a television lecturer will depend on his eye orientation. An experienced television actor presented three short speeches, each with three degrees of eye-contact —low, medium, and high. The taped speeches then were presented to three groups of seventeen students. Each group heard the three lectures in the same order but with different orders of eye-contact treatments. The results were entirely negative. The variations in the speaker's orientation toward the camera had no effect on the attention of the listeners as measured by their eye-contact with the monitor, no effect on their interest ratings, no effect on their image of the speaker or the subject matter as measured by semantic differential ratings, and no effect on their learning as measured by achievement tests. We are not sure whether these results should be disconcerting or reassuring to the novice television teacher who feels uneasy before the impersonal eye of the camera. One thing seems certain. To give an effective television lecture, the speaker must do more than project himself into the classroom.

Television Motivation in Institutions

Many general observations testify to the motivational value of television viewing facilities in almost any type of institution where normal social and occupational activity is restricted. Many types of institutionalized persons will utilize ETV courses if given the opportunity, and convicts especially are attracted to television instruction (Lantos, 1957).

In mental hospitals, some inmates react to television almost in the manner of young children, and viewing privileges can be used as in incentive to maintain discipline. Some hospital authorities feel that the quieting effect of television is comparable to that of the tranquilizing drugs. In addition, television programs can have both supportive and stimulating effects on patients. A study by Martin and Over (1956) reported that special therapeutic programs presented to patients over closed-circuit lines were more advantageous than regular open-circuit programs. Their experimental group were able to see and hear panel discussion, selected motion pictures, music, art, psychodrama, and individual therapy with questions and answers. Within the period studied, thirty-eight of this group manifested improving changes, including discharges, transfers to open wards, longer leaves, and yard privileges. Only seven of the control group, who had open-circuit television to watch, showed such changes.

In view of the obvious benefits derived from television by institutionalized individuals, this area warrants further study and exploration by educational television programers and producers. It appears that television could be a potent influence in directing mental and convalescent patients in therapeutic and rehabilitative activities, possibly in more effective ways than are open to custodial personnel. But television's more general institutional function is to help fill the activity void. It alleviates the effects of sensory deprivation in the hospitals, homes, and prisons, and, in the absence of work activities, helps keep inmates behaviorally organized. Like radio, television provides a source of sensory enrichment in a dull, routine environment.

CONTRIBUTIONS TO LEARNING SCIENCE

With the broad objective in mind of defining a systematic approach toward the study of meaningful human learning, what are the most important contributions of the audiovisual field? Although the evaluative literature lacks a systematic theoretical base and often seems to have little relevance to general behavior theory, nevertheless the best of this research has advanced our scientific understanding of human learning. In addition, there is an increasing interest in describing audiovisual communication and learning in terms of systematic behavior concepts.

Theoretical Interpretations

Each major audiovisual technique that has been adopted for classroom use has generated a certain amount of opposition and disdain among professional educators and academic learning specialists who have judged the AV materials to be expensive distractions rather than an integral part of the instructional situation. Even among those who have accepted the new techniques willingly, the tendency has been to consider them as *aids* to education serving mainly a motivational purpose. Further, theoretical statements made by learning psychologists, such as those we reviewed in Chapter 5, show a limited appreciation of the true significance of audiovisual communication in structuring the learning process.

Although no strong theoretical position has been advanced to counteract these conventional ideas, there have been some efforts in recent years to analyze the communication process and, in particular, to conceptualize pictorial perception and its role in communication and learning. The *Audiovisual Communication Review* during the dozen years of its existence has published a number of these interpretations which hopefully reflect a maturing theoretical orientation toward audiovisual learning that will in time leave its mark on behavior science and general learning theory.

The general theme running through most of the analyses of pictorial perception and communication is that these are specialized forms of behavior that contribute to specialized kinds of knowledge and skill. The genesis of pictorial perception in early behavior was recognized by Hochberg (1962), who hypothesized that our ability to perceive forms and shapes in pictures probably arises as a consequence of normal experiences with spatial objects early in life. This interpretation corresponds very closely with our own idea that symbolic responses develop out of direct responses to objects and events. The idea that symbolic responses have more generalized meanings than direct responses was expressed by Arnheim (1962) when he said that a picture does not present the object itself but a set of propositions about the object. Furthermore these propositions are stated in *visual* language; in other words, they produce specialized kinds of nonverbal information or knowledge.

Other analyses have emphasized the role of visual materials in supporting and extending verbal meanings. Gropper (1963), in his article entitled "Why *Is* a Picture worth a Thousand Words?", made the point that the usefulness of nonverbal visual materials in helping students to acquire, retain, and transfer responses derives from their capacity to *cue* and to *reinforce* specified responses and to serve as *examples*. Gropper recognized that students should make explicit responses to visual materials for effective learning.

Communication theorists generally recognize that symbolic behavior and learning have special features that distinguish them from the simplest forms of stimulus-response learning. Fearing (1962) made this point very well when he described three important characteristics of communicative symbols. To paraphrase Fearing somewhat, we can

say that the effective stimuli in communicative behavior—that is, the symbols—are produced by human agents, they acquire their meanings through human use, and they are used in attempts to control human situations.

Audiovisual theory is weak in that it has not yet generated a systematic set of ideas about learning going beyond general psychological theories. In fact, there is a tendency to use principles drawn from the conventional learning theories to explain audiovisual situations. For example, Toch and MacLean (1962) offered the transactional position about perceptual behavior as appropriate to audiovisual problems. This position assumes that perception is a form of learning, and that what we learn depends on the effects of responses. Perception that is followed by successful conduct is reinforced and thus learned.

In our opinion, the most important ideas suggested here are that nonverbal symbolic behaviors are specialized forms of human adaptive responses that develop out of more direct responses to the spatial environment. Verbal behavior comprises another specialized system of responses, but learned knowledge incorporates both verbal and nonverbal meanings. Thus the real significance of the audiovisual techniques in education is that they are excellent media for providing nonverbal support to the more traditional verbal interchange of the classroom. The media that are used most extensively and most successfully are the visual ones which supply a rich nonverbal context—graphics, slides, films, and now television, which can encompass all the others. In contrast, educational radio, which is primarily verbal, has faded into the background except for its few specialized functions.

Principles of Efficient Learning

A number of general learning principles have been confirmed or clarified by audiovisual research. The most clear-cut principle has to do with active student participation. Every effort should be made to structure the audiovisual situation so as to promote specific responses to significant features. Other principles of design are subordinate to the principle of participation. Graphic composition, timing of presentations, special cues and devices to organize material and call attention to its significant parts —these factors and others have the function of securing active participation and of enabling the student to refine his responses, to make them progressively more accurate, and to integrate them into larger organized patterns of knowledge.

One thing made clear by audiovisual research is that effective instructional design depends on the kind of behavior being taught as well as on the nature of the learner. All media of nonverbal communication used in teaching probably can be refined for human educational purposes far beyond their present state, but only if they are analyzed systematically in relation to specialized educational needs.

A recurring observation in the audiovisual research literature is that learning is likely to be very specific to the materials used. In cases where specific skills are to be taught, the specificity of learning provides a guiding principle of educational design. For example, many training films are used to teach special-

ized psychomotor or verbal skills and consequently are designed to promote very specific responses on the part of the learner. In other words, when the criterion behavior is well defined, the instructional situation can be designed to prompt just that kind of behavior.

A different situation exists in relation to the general knowledge and general educational skills which make up an important part of school learning. If learning in school is too specific, we cannot expect it to transfer effectively to situations outside the school. What can be said about the role of audiovisual techniques in enhancing transfer? Although there is very little research evidence on this particular problem, we believe that learning which goes on in a rich verbal-nonverbal context such as is provided by extensive use of audiovisual materials will be more broadly meaningful, and it thus will transfer more effectively to different but related situations than learning which is structured by more limited materials. However, in addition to a rich verbal-nonverbal context, the learner needs a certain variability in approach if his learned responses are to be retained well and transferred to different situations. That is, the more invariable the learning context, the more specific the learning. In this sense, any recorded or predesigned instructional situation has a built-in disadvantage, for it typically does not vary the learning situation as much as would be done by a live teacher.

An experiment on television teaching will illustrate this point. Hayman and Johnson (1963) presented Spanish lessons over television and then tested the relative effectiveness of repeating the same television lesson and of teacher-directed classroom practice. They found that exact repetition of the lesson increased learning somewhat if no other practice were given, but it was not as effective as classroom practice directed by a teacher. We believe that this finding illustrates a principle that probably has general validity—that more stable learning occurs when the practice conditions are varied. It is very likely that the good showing made by live teachers as compared to carefully planned expensive television classes is due in part to the factor of flexibility. A live teacher is more sensitive to the needs of a class and also varies the design of the learning situation either intentionally or merely because he is alive.

Merchandisers and advertisers are convinced of the general effectiveness of audiovisual techniques, and in their business of influencing the buying activities of the public, the hucksters usually have been several steps ahead of the educators in their use of the latest media of mass communication. We may ignore or we may deplore *what* is taught by advertising, but *how* it is taught and how effectively it is taught should be as interesting to the learning psychologist and educator as it is to the advertiser and his client. It seems reasonable to assume that the communicative media which are effective for advertising purposes probably can be used just as effectively at other levels of instruction. The problem remains of integrating different modes of communication into an educational pattern of maximal efficiency.

SUMMARY

1. Audiovisual research had limited relevance to learning science when it involved direct comparisons between a new technique and conventional teaching. Since the late 1940s, however, it has become more closely aligned with functional learning psychology.

2. Studies of the motivational effects of films and graphics have had inconclusive results. There is no conclusive evidence that interest in instructional materials correlates highly with their teaching effectiveness.

3. Audiovisual techniques in common with other instructional methods have very specific learning effects. Films may be equal or superior to conventional methods for some areas of teaching, including training in perceptual-motor skills. Tape-recorded lectures may be as effective as live teaching for limited purposes.

4. The audio channel is more effective than print only for nonreaders and poor readers or when the material is easily understood. Evidence indicates an advantage for combined channels over a single channel, although the addition of pictorial material to verbal sometimes retards learning of the specific items used.

5. Evaluations of AV instruction are hampered by the fact that we have no adequate tests of nonverbal learning. Verbal tests favor verbal instruction and thus do not permit valid comparisons between verbal and nonverbal media.

6. There are no general rules for sequencing demonstration, practice, and review units. The optimal sequence appears to depend on the complexity and intrinsic organization of the particular task.

7. In general, active participation during film showings aids learning, but covert participation may be just as beneficial as overt. Audiovisual materials

should be designed to elicit the desired responses, either overtly or covertly.

8. Special embellishments of films and graphics do not increase learning unless they aid specifically in making important discriminations or in promoting understanding. Devices that call attention to important points aid learning of those specific points.

9. The first direct evaluative comparisons of college television teaching and conventional teaching at Penn State and elsewhere showed no significant differences. Television classes were not well liked either by students or teachers. The greatest value in college ETV is to extend the limits of the classroom beyond the campus.

10. Although ETV is judged to be an effective way of demonstrating laboratory and other procedures, some evaluative studies have turned up no significant differences between television and verbal laboratory instruction.

11. Closed-circuit installations in teachers' colleges permit observation of classrooms and teaching procedures without disturbing the children with groups of observers.

12. Military research on ETV has been more analytic than most college research. Army research has shown that ETV can be improved to the point where it is time-saving and more effective than conventional teaching. Televised reviews after hours enhance learning. Television techniques are especially effective for training in the use of small equipment and the relations between small moving parts, for simple rote learning, and for recognition training.

13. ETV cannot replace classrooms in public schools but has been used effectively with team teaching techniques.

After two years, the National Program found that television classes were more effective than paired conventional classes in more than two-thirds of the comparisons. An over-all summary in 1961 was somewhat less favorable, although it indicated that ETV had been far more effective in grade schools than in high schools or colleges.

14. Whether ETV is economically feasible has not yet been answered. One broadcast station can present just one program at a time, and the cost of multichannel closed-circuit systems is high. One suggested possibility is to use low-cost, short-range equipment to transmit to a limited area.

15. The final worth of ETV must be judged on the basis of what it can do better than other techniques. Its special features are remote transmission of audiovisual displays, immediacy, presenting demonstrations, expert teaching and timely events, and recording and retrieval possibilities.

16. The emotional impact and action-potential of television appear to be less than the effects of motion pictures.

17. Studies of the effects of commercial television on children indicate that the educational impact is low or nonexistent and that the motivational impact may be undesirable.

18. The slow flicker of television sometimes induces epileptic attacks and may have other psychophysiological effects.

19. Attitude surveys of program preferences of television viewers have turned up no very clear motivational pattern.

20. Eye-contact between television speaker and audience apparently does not affect the viewers' attention, interest, or learning.

21. The institutional benefits of television indicate that it should be explored as a positive motivational source for hospitals, homes, and prisons.

22. Contemporary audiovisual theory emphasizes the specialized nature of nonverbal and graphic perception and learning and their genesis in human behavior and social communication.

23. The learning principle emphasized most by audiovisual research is that of student participation. Design factors should enhance participation and aid the learner to refine and integrate his responses.

24. Integrated nonverbal-verbal materials probably promote broader understanding and greater transfer than limited materials. However, predesigned recorded lessons do not have the flexibility of a live teacher, and variable presentations probably increase the stability of learning.

CHAPTER
7

Military Origins of Training Science

Promoting skill learning is usually called training as distinct from the more formal classroom teaching. Until recent years, our scientific understanding of training techniques had progressed little from that of Stone-Age man, whose training methods were as direct and effective as those of a nineteenth-century industrial supervisor. Workers almost always have been trained in a skill by practicing that skill with the tools, instruments, or machines actually used on the job.

The study of training and the related development of training instruments took a sharp new turn during World War II when it became necessary to train men in skills useful for military purposes. The demands were immediate and pressing. Thousands of men had to be selected and trained to operate the ever more complicated machine systems designed for aircraft and naval gunnery, radar detection, submarine control, communication, and the other highly technical operations of modern war. The areas of research and the scientific points of view generated by these needs gave rise to the discipline now known as human engineering or engineering psychology. Within this discipline traditional laboratory concern with simplified nonmeaningful units such as reflexes and nonsense syllables gave way to a new emphasis on the organizational factors of patterned behavior.

The activities of training psychologists and human engineers during and since the war years not only have contributed much practical information about techniques and instrumentation in training situations but also have originated what amounts to a new science of human learning. The central thesis of this new approach is that skill training can be understood and controlled only in terms of a scientific analysis of the relations and interactions between man and machine—between the patterning of behavior and the pattern of operations of the device to be used.

THE CHALLENGE OF WARTIME TRAINING

The educators, psychologists, physiologists, and other scientists who were recruited to organize the crash training programs of World War II themselves received little or no specific training for the jobs they had to do. Their introduction to the problems of selection, training, and the development of trainer equipment usually was very simple. A research director was given an empty barracks building, a few research colleagues to help do the work, and a trip to see a few installations of equipment— often so new it was scarcely off the designing boards—and then he was left to his own ingenuity.

What resources could this transplanted scientist call upon to guide him in designing a training program for equipment he never before had seen? Presumably there were two broad areas of scientific psychology that should have contributed significantly to training efforts. One of these was the study of perceptual-motor performance and the other, the study of learning.

Analyzing Motor Skills

Some of the earliest efforts to analyze overt behavior patterning were motivated by the interest of industrialists in the efficiency of their workers. Time-and-motion study originated late in the nineteenth century with Taylor's (1911) stop-watch measurements of work movements and his first systematic studies of tool design. This type of skill analysis culminated in Gilbreth and Gilbreth's (1917) classification of the "elemental" motions of work, such as assemble, disassemble, grasp, and position. Although these ideas and certain revised procedures of time-and-motion study have been accepted and used widely in industry, they never have achieved scientific status in laboratory analyses of motor performance. Gilbreth's basic idea that human motion can be dissected into

independent elements which can be added, subtracted, and combined in various ways without interaction among them is reminiscent of the reflex-chain concepts of learning psychology but has not been validated in scientific motion analysis.

Another line of effort in motor skill analysis arose out of the growing interest in differential psychology early in the present century. The great advances in intelligence testing made by psychologists during World War I stimulated related efforts to devise tests of motor skills that would serve as a basis for personnel selection. These efforts were doomed to failure for the reason that different motor abilities and skills are almost completely unrelated to each other. No simple tests could be found that would have general predictive value for success in skilled performances.

The most promising line of research on skilled motion prior to World War II went almost unrecognized among psychologists. Early in this century, Dodge (1903) analyzed patterns of eye movements and identified three basic components—fixation, pursuit, and saccadic (fast jerk) movements. The general validity of this type of analysis was established by Stetson et al. (Stetson, 1951; Stetson and Bouman, 1933; Stetson and McDill, 1923) in a significant program of research extending over several decades. Unfortunately, some of this work never was published and some was published obscurely so that it had little impact on psychological thinking. Stetson devised new recording techniques to study many types of movements, including gait, manual skills, and speech (see pp. 83f). He recognized the multidimensionality of motion and the fact that different components must be integrated precisely in the production of organized patterns. That is, a patterned motion is not an agglomeration of elemental movements, such as Gilbreth's "therbligs," nor is it a temporal chain of linked reflexes; rather it is a highly integrated pattern in which the components are interdependent and can be analyzed and understood only in relation to the whole pattern. These concepts are basic to a human factors analysis of skilled performance.

Learning Psychology Applied to Training

As we suggested in Chapter 2, the laboratory study of learning prior to World War II had but limited applicability to the problems of military training. A complex perceptual-motor skill cannot be described or studied as a series of response units linked together by the effects of contiguity, reinforcement, or any other general learning factor.

Of little more use to the training scientist were the generally accepted psychological conditions of efficient learning drawn from a half century of learning research (Gagné, 1962a). He could assume that, as a general rule, whole learning was better than part learning and distributed practice more favorable than massed practice. He could assume that the training situation should be meaningful to the learner, that the learner should participate actively, and that he should have immediate knowledge of results. Yet these general rules did not specify the decisive features of particular training situations and some of them proved to be of limited validity. Experience quickly taught that traditional learning principles were inadequate in dealing with the problems of

psychomotor training, particularly in areas of complex instrumentation, and that new concepts and new research strategies were needed.

Genesis of Human Engineering

With an inadequate scientific understanding of perceptual-motor skills and only the most general principles of learning efficiency to guide them, wartime training psychologists faced many special problems posed by the military machines themselves, and it was in dealing with these man-machine problems that behavior scientists evolved into human engineers. Much of the hastily designed military equipment was quite unsuited to human requirements and psychomotor capacities. There were monstrous electronic transformers which intimidated the novice operator, visual equipment which induced hypnotic fatigue and near-coma, and complex electronic trainers which neither recorded the performance of the trainee nor bore any meaningful resemblance to actual task situations. There were complicated devices beyond the operative ability of all but the most skilled individuals, gun systems which could not be directed, and tracking instruments which overshot wildly with a carnival flare. Not only was it necessary to design training procedures for military skills, it also was just as important to specify the human factors requirements of the military machines.

The significant research developments in training and training instrumentation during World War II are all but lost in the routine reports of whole areas of psychological research (Cook, 1947; Dailey, 1947; Flanagan, 1948), yet there were significant advances of both applied and theoretical importance. The first attempts to conceptualize the behaving individual as a control system were generated in training research programs in flexible gunnery and radar tracking, where it was realized that the trainee's control activities and learning are influenced by the design of the machine or trainer being operated. The first major step in understanding what we now call sensory feedback was achieved by analytic studies of the dimensions of *knowledge of results* in training operations. Specifically, this era of military training science made it clear that the *knowledge* needed to control and learn a precise skill is immediate sensory feedback of performance rather than the incentive or reinforcing knowledge provided by the end effects of performance. This revised conception of knowledge of results accompanied an inevitable reorientation of learning research toward the understanding of sensorimotor control in human learned skills.

PRINCIPLES OF TRAINING RESEARCH

Out of their practical experience in coping with specialized problems related to operational skills, the training scientists of World War II gradually developed some new principles of training design and research which went beyond their psychological tradition. The concepts and procedures that proved useful in solving these operational problems also provided new understanding about the nature of sensorimotor interaction in performance and learning.

Dynamic Simulation of the Task

One of the most generally accepted training principles was that of operational simulation, and some human engineers have come to insist that effective simulation is the prime requisite of training design. However, it was realized very early that simulating the static appearance of a task situation is less important than reproducing the tempo and patterning of the movements involved—that is, the dynamic pattern of the task. Thus, a first step in training research was to analyze tasks in terms of the interrelated actions of stimuli, machines, and the human body so that the essential spatial and temporal features could be reproduced in trainers. In flexible gunnery training, simulation of the movement patterns was found to be of decisive importance, and the tempo of target presentation was found to be a critical feature of flash-reading trainers for radar operation.

It was recognized fully in the early phases of wartime training research that effective simulation necessitated continuous presentation or programing of simulated task action. To achieve adequately programed sequences in radar and gunnery trainers, they were designed to present controlled target course paths with different stimulus dimensions and characteristics. Stimulus action was compared automatically with operator performance in order to give the trainee an immediate display of error. Both visual and auditory signals were used to indicate sighting accuracy when the trainee "hit" a target or plane.

The desirability of controlling the difficulty of successive parts of planned courses also was realized and was dealt with in terms of specified complexity variables. Thus trainees could be advanced from simple to more difficult training sequences. In some cases, tasks were broken up into parts or segments which could be presented singly or in combination. It was found that the relative effectiveness of *part* and *whole* practice sequences depended on the particular task and its organization.

The need for dynamic simulation of a task in training situations confirmed prior ideas about motion specificity. Psychological research on psychomotor skills between World War I and World War II had made few positive contributions to theory, but one unmistakable conclusion was that such skills are very specific in their organization. They bear little relation to each other and therefore can be learned efficiently only with specific training in the desired skill patterns.

Because learned skills are very specific, however, some provision should be made in training procedures for unusual or stressful conditions that may be encountered on the job. One aspect of performance stress that was recognized first during the war years is one related to very restricted conditions of stimulation. For example, a night lookout on a ship or a radar observer in a confined space before a scope has little to do in the ordinary course of events and has minimal change in his stimulating conditions. His basic task is to observe—to pay attention to a stimulus that may or may not appear. It originally was thought that the performance of such observers would be defined principally by their psychophysical functions including visual acuity, sensitivity to dim visual stimuli, and so on. However, it was found that it is very difficult for an observer to maintain a satisfactory level of performance efficiency under restrictive stimulus conditions and that vigilance typically declines over a period of time.

The central problem of vigilance is the same as in other stress conditions—that of maintaining control of the task. Restricted stimulus conditions reduce the operator's feedback information so drastically that he loses control. His behavior patterns become disorganized in the absence of organizing feedback stimuli. A person in such a situation typically increases the variation in stimulation by moving around as much as possible or by engaging in incidental activities that do not interfere with his main task.

Multidimensionality of Motion

Following the first principle of adequately programed dynamic simulation, a second major requisite of training research was found to be multidimensional analysis of motion. Prior to the 1940s, systematic recording and analysis of the interrelated movements of performance had received little attention except by Stetson (Stetson and Bouman, 1933). During the war years, multiple recording techniques were developed to obtain simultaneous records of movement error in different dimensions and records of different movement components in a given task. For example, in training research in flexible gunnery, separate recordings were made of the gunner's discrete triggering movements, of his manipulative ranging movements, and of the larger adjustments of the gunsight which were carried out with arm and trunk movements. These methods made it possible to determine the relation between the occurrence of a certain movement pattern of the operator and the extent of tracking error in different dimensions.

The application of multidimensional recording techniques to training research is illustrated in Figure 7.1, which

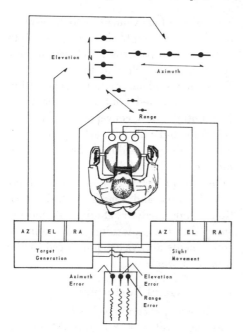

Figure 7.1. Recording movements in different dimensions from the operating pattern of a pedestal sight in the B-29 bomber.

shows how records were obtained of different dimensions of movement of a pedestal sight of the B-29 bomber. The polygraph recordings indicated the nature of the student gunner's coordinate movements in sighting. Careful analysis of such records early in the B-29 development program led to the conclusion that this particular gun-sight was poorly designed from a human engineering standpoint, for all but the simplest target courses posed nearly impossible problems of movement integration. A gunner was as likely to trigger his sight off target as near or on target.

Motion analyses of the performance of trainees over a period of time provided systematic data indicating that different movement components, although interrelated in a total task, vary independ-ently during training and show different learning functions. Different movement components and movements in different dimensions were learned at different rates during practice of the over-all motion pattern. These observations on the differential learning of movement components were confirmed in further studies carried out after the war (Johnson and Milton, 1947; Lincoln and Smith, 1952; Wehrkamp and Smith, 1952).

The procedures of multidimensional motion analysis developed for training research purposes contributed to the development of one of the major concepts about perceptual-motor behavior that we outlined in Chapter 3: namely, that all motion patterns are made up of independently regulated but interacting components of posture, body transport (rate control), and manipulation (contact or positioning movements) Smith and Smith, 1962). The principle of multidimensionality implies that different movement components have differential effects upon the operation of any device and are, in turn, affected differentially by practice and other variables related to the performance situation. For example, in tracking performance, positioning and rate control movements show quite different learning and transfer functions and are affected differently by certain situational and machine variables.

After the war, these general ideas about differential movement interaction in learning and performance were tested in a series of controlled experiments and were found to be applicable not only to tracking and sighting movements (Lincoln and Smith, 1952; Pearl *et al.*, 1955; Simon and Smith, 1956) but also to other types of patterned human motions (Smith and Bloom, 1956; Smith and Wehrkamp, 1951). Figure 7.2 illustrates the idea of the three basic movement components in a tracking operation. In systematic motion analyses of tracking and many other types of performance, we have shown that the different component movements in behavior vary independently in operational patterns and also in relation to different learning, perception, and motivation variables.

The concept of motion multidimensionality provides some insight into the nature of skill specificity. A particular motion or skill can be understood only as a pattern of independently variable but interrelated components. The skill derives its specific character not just from the types of components of which it is composed but also from the way in which these components are integrated into a spatial and temporal pattern. Thus

Figure 7.2.   Three basic movement components in tracking behavior—posture, transport, and manipulation.

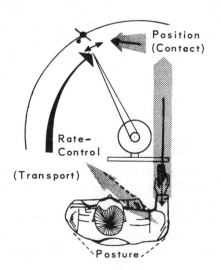

a number of movements which seem to be the same might be combined into different skill patterns which retain their specificity in relation to each other. These ideas about motion organization stand in marked contrast to the time-and-motion study concepts developed by Gilbreth and Gilbreth (1917) and still in use. Whereas Gilbreth proposed that motion can be subdivided into discrete, independent elements which retain their own identity and timing in task situations, our analytic studies of motion show that the patterning and timing of components always are influenced by the task as a whole.

Knowledge of Performance

All groups concerned with wartime training problems recognized the importance of giving the trainee a quick indication of the accuracy of his performance—that is, immediate knowledge of results. However, in training complicated perceptual-motor skills, it was found that general knowledge of success or failure was not always enough to promote efficient learning. It was necessary to inform the trainee more specifically about the nature of his movements and their error in relation to the action of the system or the perceptual display.

The problem of information feedback was particularly acute in designing trainers for sighting, steering, and tracking systems in which movement of the perceived target on the view screen depended on both the responses of the operator and movements of the actual target in space. If the operator's tracking instrument itself were located in a moving system, such as a ship or plane, still a third movement variable affected the relative movement of the target on the operator's view screen. In such a situation, what the individual saw depended on his own motion and on the motions of the two moving systems. His reference systems for judging the relative direction of movement and error were lost. For example, operators of night fighter radar equipment could not always tell from their own perceptual displays the nature of the maneuvers of an opponent's plane because they had to judge such movements relative to the action of their own craft in terms of the displacement of a single spot on a radarscope.

To train operators to operate these tracking systems with any degree of effectiveness, it was necessary to design trainers which provided more than one type of information to the trainee. Many of the training problems which never were solved satisfactorily during the war hinged on the difficulty of providing information about movements of both target and operator in relation to performance error.

The problems related to providing knowledge of results in complicated machine skills have significant implications for psychological theory. Learning theorists still usually interpret the *knowledge of results* factor as a type of reinforcement that defines what is learned. A response with successful results presumably is learned whereas an error response is not learned. However, most training psychologists recognize that there is more to knowledge of results than the general incentive value of success or failure. In complicated machine skills, it is not enough to provide the learner with reinforcing knowledge at some end point in a task. Rather, the learner needs continuous and immediate sensory feedback informing him of the effectiveness of his performance. Only with adequate feedback can he maintain effective control of his movements and show satisfactory learning improvement.

The term feedback has come into fairly general use and means different things to different people. By sensory feedback, we mean the pattern of afferent stimuli (visual, auditory, tactual, and so on) which result from a specific response pattern in a particular environmental situation. If the feedback is adequate for the task at hand—that is, if it is immediate, detailed, and accurate enough—the pattern of motion can be performed in a more integrated and effective way and can be improved more through practice than if the feedback is delayed, incomplete, misleading, or otherwise distorted.

Very often a complicated machine transforms, delays, or distorts feedback to the point of degrading the operator's performance. Thus an important part of human engineering and training research is to make careful analyses of the machines to be used in terms of the man-machine interrelationships. Can a machine of certain design be operated efficiently by a human individual, or does its technical design interfere with the normal patterning of human motion? In order to achieve optimal efficiency of operation, a machine system should be designed to permit optimal sensory control by the operator. That is, precise information about how his movements relate to the various reactions of the system in space and in time should be displayed perceptually to the operator as he carries out his task.

The years since the war have seen a

growing interest in sensory-feedback research but only the most limited appreciation, especially among learning psychologists, of the significance of feedback control in behavior organization, performance and learning. In our opinion, the principle of feedback control of performance has some very direct implications for all segments of training research and learning science. It means first of all designing performance situations to optimize control of the particular operations of the task. In training simulation, it means programing and adjusting different levels of control to meet the special needs of the learner. In educational design, it means arranging materials, communication processes, and programs to encompass variations and perturbations in control that may be encountered in real-life situations. In learning research, it means devising new methods of analyzing the dynamic processes of sensory-feedback control of behavior and devising new methods of measuring the effects of varying or perturbing different dimensions of such feedback control on performance and learning. We shall turn to a more detailed consideration of sensory-feedback research later in the book.

Minimizing Feedback Delay

One of the most troublesome behavioral problems that arose in military training research was that of delayed sensory feedback resulting when a delay was imposed between the action of an operator and the perceived effects of that action. In gunnery, a feedback delay is inherent in the nature of the task, for a gunner cannot know the effects of his performance until the bullets have traveled their course. Inasmuch as delayed

perception reduces accuracy, considerable effort was expended in Air Force gunnery training programs in attempts to simulate the temporal relationships of firing at remote targets while still giving the student gunners a fairly quick indication of their accuracy.

A persistent problem in human engineering research is to cope with feedback delays that are introduced into man-machine operations by the design of the machines themselves. Remote control systems used in gunnery, in tracking, and in steering of massive ships or planes involve many linkages in control and long-distance transmission of information which inevitably introduce feedback delays into the performance of an operator. Delays also are introduced into remote control systems by the computers that are used to integrate the many sources of information which must be combined to determine the course of action.

Automation techniques developed during the war to help operators control moving systems such as radar antennae, guns, direction finders, and aircraft generally involved supplying mechanical or electrical aid to a movement component or a dimension of movement in a control system. That these automated systems introduced problems as well as supplying aid soon became apparent, particularly in relation to tracking or steering systems. Basically, tracking is simply a following action, such as following a moving object with the eye, head, or hand, or bringing a gun to bear on a moving target. When the tracker executes the following action by his own movements without outside aid, the performance is known as *direct pursuit tracking*. However, heavy gun systems and other mobile military machines of great size and complexity can be positioned only if some mechanical or electrical aid is provided.

The first type of devices developed to supply aid to trackers, which were known as *velocity tracking* systems, provided automated control of the rate function. In velocity control, as diagramed in Figure 7.3*a*, the operator does not control his cursor (or gun or vehicle) directly but rather controls the direction and speed of rotation of a motor which in turn moves the cursor. Every movement of the operator's handwheel generates a rate of movement of the motor which varies according to the extent of the handwheel movement. Thus the operator adjusts the position as well as the speed of the cursor by adjusting the rate and direction of rotation of the motor.

Figure 7.3.   Automated tracking systems. *a.* Velocity control. *b.* Aided tracking or partially automated control.

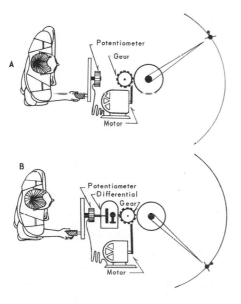

It was believed originally that this automation of the rate function would lead to more efficient tracking by relieving the operator of continuous control of the tracking movement. In actual practice, this proved not to be the case. It is extremely difficult to learn to control rate of movement of the cursor in velocity tracking with any degree of accuracy. In trying to pick up a target, the operator sets in a rate of movement and then must wait to see if this rate is correct. If he turns his handwheel rapidly, the cursor overshoots rapidly, and he must make a quick corrective movement which very likely will cause the cursor to lag behind. Each time he moves the handwheel he must wait to see the effect his movement has had on the cursor. With such a velocity system, steering or tracking in two dimensions—in azimuth and elevation—is almost impossible.

Notwithstanding the difficulties of velocity tracking, most of the engineers concerned with tracking systems were convinced that automated tracking was superior to directly linked control mechanisms. Accordingly, they tried to improve velocity control by giving the direct positioning function back to the operator, in what is known as *aided tracking*. As shown by the diagram in Figure 7.3*b*, the handwheel now is linked to a differential which positions the cursor directly, but it also causes the motor to generate a rate of movement in the same direction—a rate which still varies according to the extent of the handwheel movement. If the generated rate of pointer movement is the same as that of the target, there is no need of further action by the operator. Although rate-aided tracking was considered highly successful by most gunnery and radar engineers during the war, a systematic survey of Air Force gunnery systems by one of the authors convinced him that both velocity and aided tracking and steering devices were inferior to directly linked systems for all but the simplest target courses with minimal variation in speed of movement. This judgment subsequently was tested in the laboratory and confirmed (Lincoln and Smith, 1952).

The fundamental defect in both velocity and aided tracking systems is the inherent delay between the operator's movements and his perception of the effects of those movements. The magnitude of the delay varies according to the rate generated and sometimes is as long as a second or more. A delay factor of this magnitude seriously impairs accuracy. Even in aided tracking, where the operator can see immediately the *positioning* of the cursor, he must wait to see the *rate* he has generated. The detrimental effects of perceptual delays on precisely patterned motions have been recognized more generally in the past fifteen years since the introduction of controlled laboratory experiments on delayed sensory feedback, both auditory and visual (K. U. Smith, 1962). If wartime engineers and training psychologists had been fully aware of the significance of delayed feedback, costly errors in equipment design might have been avoided.

Analyzing Man-Machine Systems

One of the most general principles that emerged in wartime training research was that training problems related to complex machine operations cannot be considered apart from a comprehensive analysis of the entire operating system. If operators are to be trained to perform a task effectively, they must be provided with a machine that is designed according to valid human engineering principles—that is, a machine that *fits* the sensory and motor abilities and feedback controlled interactions of a human operator.

Our discussion of delayed feedback points up one general problem that must be taken into consideration in human engineering, but many others arise in the interactions of man and machine in operating systems. The design of some compound control systems is such that variation in one pattern of motion necessarily requires change in the pattern of a second movement if effective control of the device is to be maintained. That is, in some systems the controls interact in such a way that the nature of one movement pattern is contingent upon another pattern which is being executed simultaneously. Examples of such interacting control systems in wartime equipment included aircraft with turret gunsights in which movements of the turret modified sight controls, the B-29 gunsight which combined elevation tracking and ranging in compound variable ways, and vehicle systems in which movement of the vehicle changed gunsighting movements. Designing effective trainers and training procedures for such complex tasks hinged on an understanding of what the task involved behaviorally—on analyzing the nature of the sensorimotor control pattern that was demanded of the operator.

Under the pressure of military needs and demands, equipment design sometimes got completely out of step with human design. An example was one of the early applications of analog computers as control mechanisms in complex machines. A computer mechanism was used in the fire-control system of the B-29 bomber to integrate data concerning the position and rate of movement of the gun-sight with flight and ballistic data of the plane and gun mechanism in order to predict the path that a bullet should take to hit an incoming fighter. The guns were directed by the computer according to this prediction. According to original design, the computer was sensitive to every small variation in input from the gun-sight that was manipulated by the gunner. However, it soon was recognized that the gunner was providing input data other than the true position control and rate-control movements of the sight. His ordinary rapid tremor movements dominated the input system of the computer so that the guns acted more in accordance with the gunner's jitters than with his sighting motions. In an attempt to eliminate this unanticipated behavioral effect, the input gears of the complex servomechanism were slotted to filter out the effects of tremor. This modification introduced an appreciable delay into the computer operations. In fact, the computer's reaction time was so slow that the guns could not always be brought to bear on the target in a rapid attack by enemy fighters. The *slewing-on* time of the gun system sometimes was longer than the critical phase of the attack.

The main problems encountered in training gunners to use this fire-control system were related to the delay in computer reaction. The differential effects of different tracking movements made by the gunner had to be determined before a systematic training procedure could

be devised. The problems posed by this computer system arose from the fact that neither the original design nor the modified design made allowance for the behavioral design of the human operator.

Special training problems were imposed by many forms of automated and partially automated control systems developed during the war period. It has been shown that automated control systems usually are more difficult to learn than direct control systems. The reason for this is that the intermediate machine action introduces spatial or temporal transformations into the operator's feedback-control pattern. Some spatial transformations can be adapted to with little trouble, but even minor feedback delays are detrimental to performance accuracy.

Central to a human engineering analysis of a training situation are the space and time factors involved in the performance, the characteristics of movement specialization and integration, the pattern of control of the system, and the relation of sensory display and information to motor control. These factors can be analyzed most effectively in an over-all simulation of the operating system. Research on the system provides data that can be used both in designing effective training procedures and in checking and revising the design of the system itself.

POSTWAR MILITARY TRAINING

As suggested by more than one author dealing with military training programs, the art of training has far outdistanced theoretical formulations of the processes involved. This is nowhere more obvious than in the advanced training programs which have been developed to meet the operational needs of aircraft, aerospace, radar, electronics, and other military systems. A review of some aspects of recent military training design will serve to illustrate the technological advances that have been made since the war years while pointing up some of the problems that still must be faced by training scientists.

Complex Simulators and Simulation Training

From their relatively humble origins in simple simulation devices, gunnery and flight simulators have developed into highly complex training systems that combine automatic programing of task sequences and multidimensional recording and control of response with dynamic simulation of the task situation. For example, a recently developed flexible gunnery training system for the B-52 airplane presents target courses of attacking interceptor aircraft and missiles by means of film, radar, or television displays (Stave, 1960). Three characteristics of gunner performance are recorded—reaction time, range information, and integrated error of manual tracking in azimuth, elevation, and range. A graphic error record is obtained as well as a time-on-target record.

An even more elaborate and costly trainer is the multimillion dollar aircraft flight simulator shown in Figure 7.4. Complex aircraft simulators include controls and programing not only for the basic operations of the aircraft but also for variable conditions of weather, maneuvers, and coordination in operation. Recently there have been efforts to develop compound simulation trainers for multiple operations, such as the coordinated tasks of an entire aircrew

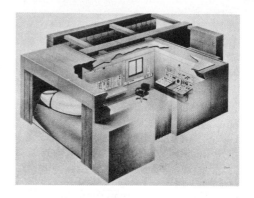

Figure 7.4. A complex aircraft flight simulator which can generate a flight environment and induce a pattern of movement of the plane which must be "flown" by the trainee pilot. Landing and take-off operations and varied weather conditions can be simulated by means of magnetic tape and computer components. (From Parker and Downs. *Selection of training media.* USAF Aeronaut. Sys. Div. tech. Rep. 61–473, 1961.)

(Hood *et al.*, 1960). All such efforts to achieve comprehensive simulation of flight operations have been exceedingly costly. One factor which has contributed heavily to the costs of simulator trainers has been the use of analog or digital computers to program the courses of action. This cost item may be reduced by standardizing computer components so that the same unit can be plugged into different training systems (Curtiss-Wright Corp., 1961).

Even if the costs of simulators could be disregarded, it would not be possible to simulate all features of the real thing. In view of the less than perfect realism of even the most complex simulation systems, it seems advisable to incorporate only those specific features which add significantly to their training effectiveness. However, there have been very few systematic attempts to differentiate between important and relatively unimportant simulation features. Newton (1959) has shown that a relatively simple simulator was just as effective in training for fast submarine operations as a highly realistic and complex simulator. Wilcoxon and Davy (1954) showed that the addition of rough air simulation in aircraft training did not improve later performance significantly. In some cases, deliberate alteration of task features in a simulator may be advisable, for it is possible that such systematic changes as increasing or decreasing the precision of the task, encouraging or discouraging the number of errors in training, and varying the sequence of part-practice to whole-practice may enhance learning (Gagné, 1962b).

In a general assessment of the usefulness of simulator trainers, Parker and Downs (1961) concluded that they are most effective for training in procedural sequences, understanding principles and relationships, decision-making, and skilled perceptual-motor acts. Simulators are relatively ineffective in perceptual discrimination training and too costly for identifications training. According to Gagné (1962b), the first stages of learning do not require simulators except in the case of motor skill learning, which apparently requires highly accurate simulation from the beginning. Procedures, identifications, and conceptual tasks can be taught initially by using verbal and pictorial materials such as check lists, charts, maps, and pictures. Initial training in team functions needs only a low degree of simulation. However, for more advanced training, for consolidation of many skills into operational proficiency, and for maintaining a high level of proficiency, simulators are highly useful.

Hazard and Stress Training

A special area of simulation training is concerned with preparing operators to cope with the emergency situations and hazards that are related to their jobs. Escaping from high speed aircraft by means of ejection devices is a hazardous but sometimes essential operation which requires extensive training. Demonstration films have been used with some success, but more effective training is provided by the ejection simulator illustrated in Figure 7.5. Nevertheless, pilots who have had experience with this ejection simulator, including experience in ejection from a tower, have reported that the actual shock of ejecting from a falling plane is far greater than they have been trained to expect (Beer et al., 1961). The seat trainers do not push as fast as real ejection seats and promote a certain complacency about ejection which should be countered by some revision in training techniques.

There has been very little systematic research in either military or industrial areas on the possibility of reducing accidents and hazards by specific training in accident avoidance and emergency procedures. The psychological literature on accident prevention, dating from the original work of Münsterberg (1913), deals mainly with psychometric attempts to predict individual differences in accident proneness and procedures for recording worker accidents (Thorndike, 1951; Vasilas et al., 1953). In general, these efforts have had little effect on accident rates, although Wilson (1962) has reported that an industry reduced

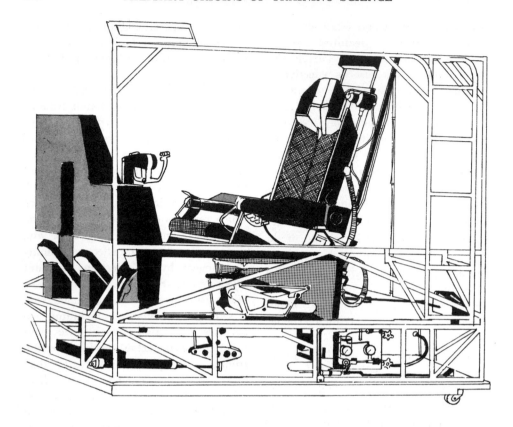

Figure 7.5.   The aircraft ejection trainer, an example of instrumentation for hazard training. It is essential for pilots to develop confidence and decision-making ability for emergencies necessitating ejection from jet planes when a mistake would lead to injury or death. (From Parker and Downs, 1961.)

accidents among its truck drivers by informing them whether they had scored high or low on an accident prediction test battery. The high scorers were told that with favorable aptitudes they should maintain a good driving record, and the low scorers were warned to be unusually careful. Obviously it should be more effective in the long run to determine whether there are factors in accident proneness that could be improved by systematic training.

Specific training can be given for hazards and emergencies only to the ex-tent that such situations can be predicted and also to the extent that certain aspects of the situations can be brought under the control of the operator. The pilot who ejects from a falling plane has lost control of his operational situation and is trained to escape from it with his life. In some cases, however, it is possible to predict emergencies in which the operator can maintain effective control of his task or his machine if he has been trained to make appropriate responses.

Training for specific hazards or emergencies related to jobs can be considered a special kind of stress training. In a more general usage, stress connotes some unusual or disturbing condition that may or may not be related to the job but which cannot be brought under the control of the operator or can be controlled only to a limited extent. (Whether stress should be defined as an external condition or as an internal state brought about by the stressful external condition will not concern us here.) Thus in military combat, operators must perform in the midst of noise, confusion, and danger that are beyond their scope of control.

It usually is assumed that stress is detrimental to performance, and some training specialists believe that stress should be introduced during training if it is to be expected during later performance. According to an analysis by Deese (1962), these assumptions are not necessarily valid. Deese assumed that stressful stimuli produce motor arousal and generalized tension, and that these general effects are associated with certain specific motor effects, including increase in the rate, amplitude, and variability of tremor; increase in the peak force applied by certain muscle groups; shorter latency of ballistic movements; increased variability of movement precision; and increased variability in corrective movements. If such relatively specific effects do occur as a result of stress, the implication is that different skilled movements would show differential effects. For example, Deese suggested that a tapping movement might be facilitated because of the shorter movement latency induced by stress, whereas a precision aiming movement would deteriorate because of the increased variability of movement precision. Thus the over-all effect of stress on an entire task would depend on the nature of the task's components.

In addition to these motor concomitants of stress, one must take into consideration the autonomic effects which probably interfere directly with the performance of skills. Deese's assumption was that autonomic arousal acts as a distraction to the performing individual. Our own opinion is that both somatic and autonomic effects of stress influence skilled performance by disturbing the sensory-feedback pattern of control. To anticipate our later discussion of feedback research, we have good evidence that increased tension and autonomic arousal produce both physiological and mechanical variations that are reflected in the pattern of sensory-feedback regulation. At all times, the breathing movements and heart pulse of the individual introduce rhythmic variations that both mechanically and by neural interaction perturb somatic control. Under proper experimental conditions, it is possible to see the effects of almost every breath and heart beat on a record of precise manual movement. If the subject's heart rate and breathing rate increase, the degree of perturbation is increased. Inasmuch as stress causes increases in heart rate and breathing, we expect direct effects on sensory-feedback control under such disturbing conditions. Part of the improvement that occurs during skill training undoubtedly is due to the reduction of physiological perturbation that results as the trainee becomes familiar with the task and the learning situation. If the skill is likely to be performed under stress, we believe that it is important to introduce deliber-

ately stressful conditions during training insofar as feasible. However, a
trainee's adaptation to the regular operations of a task and to training stress
should not be expected to eliminate the
physiological perturbation of feedback
control that can occur under unusual
conditions or hazardous emergencies.

There is some research evidence to
support the belief that the difference in
performance produced by two different
task designs, a *good* design and a *poor*
one, is enhanced under conditions of
stress (Murphy, 1959). If this were
generally true, the superiority of good
training design would show up far more
when performance is stressed than under
normal conditions. Fitts (1962) has suggested that this effect may be attributed
to the factor of overlearning, inasmuch
as a well designed task is overlearned
more than one of poor design. According to Fitts, extensive overlearning of a
skill makes it resistant to stress, fatigue,
and interference.

Radar Operation Training

Another important area of simulation
training is related to radar operations
and control. In Figure 1.3 of Chapter 1
we showed two photographs of a complex radar simulator for air-traffic control (Allen *et al.*, 1954). The spot targets which can be seen on the simulated
radarscope follow controlled patterns of
movement simulating movements of
planes. The system also simulates wind
effects, chatter and noise, and blip fading on the scope face. Producing this
radar simulation of aircraft movement
requires a whole roomful of workers and
instruments, as shown in Figure 1.3*b*.

This simulator was designed primarily for research on human factors in
air-traffic control and for the study of
specialized equipment and personnel
needs involved in radar approach control operations. The procedure used was
to relate behavioral variations in air-
traffic controllers to the type of information displayed on the radar system,
the patterns of communication used, the
nature of the targets tracked, the accuracy of the radar system, and other
variables. Although the system is a
highly realistic simulator, it does not
incorporate some of the features of a
standardized and controlled training
situation inasmuch as its primary use
is for research.

Radar operation is a type of performance that sometimes is called a perceptual skill, emphasizing the importance
of the perceptual display in organizing
the task. The motor output of a radar
operator appears to be relatively slight.
He remains seated and directs his en-
ergies toward keeping track of different
sources of information which must be
compared and differentiated. The operator's course of action depends on his
perceptual discriminations. However, the
relative prominence of the perceptual
aspects of a skill does not mean that the
motor aspect is less important, for all
skills are perceptual-motor control sequences that integrate perceptual information with motor output by means
of feedback processes. Perception always
represents some level of response control, although at times the activity may
be restricted to the receptor systems
working more or less independently of
the rest of the body.

When perceptual input and motor output are relatively slight, a perceptual or
observational skill always raises the
problem of vigilance—of maintaining

a high level of alertness and proficiency under the restricted conditions. Maintaining vigilance usually is treated as a perceptual problem, but we believe that a more fruitful approach is to recognize it as a problem of feedback control. The operator needs a certain amount of activity carried out in relation to the stimulating conditions in order to maintain his sensitivity and organized feedback-mediated control of the task. This is a problem in training and equipment design which has scarcely been considered.

Our own observations and theoretical concepts suggest that a very definite principle should be followed to enhance vigilance and thus to enhance the operator's control of a restrictive perceptual task. The task situation and equipment should be designed to maximize opportunities for activity, especially activity related to the task itself. First, the operator should be given room to move around and shift bodily position in order to maintain general bodily sensitivity and movement organization. Such gross movements also have the result of varying the spatial position of the eyes in relation to the visual field and thus of enhancing organizing visual feedback. Second, any specific control operations related to the task should require fairly large movements rather than minimal adjustments. This principle implies that a full-sized steering or positioning wheel is better than the small ones which actually are used on such devices as tracking systems.

Two different types of tracking performance will serve to illustrate how equipment design sometimes dictates gross differences in task activity. We already have described direct pursuit tracking as a following action. Another type of tracking is known as *compensatory* tracking, in which the operator makes compensatory adjustments on his control instruments to keep his entire mobile system *zeroed in* on a target. Compensatory tracking is compared with pursuit tracking in Figure 7.6. In the pursuit device, the operator makes his pointer follow the target by continual positioning and rate-control movements of his handwheel. In the compensatory system, an antenna pickup detects the presence of a target and transmits a signal to the view screen as a target spot. The task of the operator is to keep the spot centered either horizontally or vertically or both. That is, he compensates for movement of the target by recentering the system.

It can be seen that compensatory tracking involves quite a different mo-

Figure 7.6.   Two tracking tasks with different activity requirements. *a*. Direct pursuit tracking. *b*. Compensatory tracking.

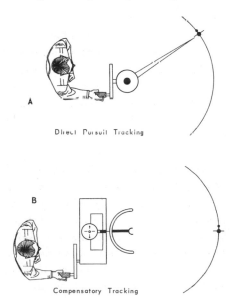

Direct Pursuit Tracking

Compensatory Tracking

tion pattern from that of direct pursuit tracking. Whereas pursuit tracking requires sweeping transport movements upon which are superimposed corrective positioning adjustments, compensatory tracking is made up almost entirely of small, discrete positioning movements which keep the target spot on center. Further, the compensatory tracker cannot see the movement of the target directly, but sees only the deviation of the target spot caused by the relative displacement between the moving target and the tracking system. It is known that compensatory tracking generally is more difficult and less precise than pursuit tracking. Our belief is that this difference is due to the different opportunities for sensory control in the two tasks. The restricted perceptual-motor activity of compensatory tracking does not provide enough variation in perceptual display and feedback patterns for the operator to maintain a high level of organized control.

Technical Knowledge Trainers

The principles of controlled knowledge of results, immediate perceptual feedback, and automated programing of training sequences, which were applied during the war years to combat trainers, have been extended since the war to the development of highly specialized military trainers to teach maintenance operations, electronic trouble-shooting, and other technical knowledge. Two types of such devices are those which provide practice in actual technical operations and those which train in the knowledge and principles of such operations. All of these trainers might be classified as teaching machines inasmuch as they in-

struct in technical knowledge more than in overt perceptual-motor skills.

The trainer shown in Figure 7.7 is a *malfunction and circuitry trainer*, commonly referred to as the MAC trainer (French and Martin, 1957; Hansen *et al.*, 1959). It is a self-instructional device for teaching trouble-shooting in a simulated electronic system. The student's task is to correct a malfunction in the system by replacing one of the small black boxes seen at the upper left on the front panel, by pressing one of the buttons on the top panel just above the black boxes, or by a combination of these operations. The student must learn to identify 200 possible malfunctions by taking measurements on the various dials and indicators. A buzzer sounds

Figure 7.7.   The malfunction and circuitry trainer (MAC). The student must identify malfunctions in the electronic circuits by using a sequence of steps of optimal efficiency. The device scores the time and number of correct and incorrect checks made. (Based on Kopstein and Shillestad. *A Survey of auto-instructional devices*. USAF Aeronaut. Sys. Div. Tech. Report No. 61–414, 1961.)

when he makes an incorrect response, and a recording system indicates his score in terms of the number of malfunctions correctly and incorrectly identified. It also indicates the measurements made to find the trouble.

We shall not extend our discussion of these military self-instructional trainers at this time because all of the questions related to self-instruction and programed lesson sequences have come to a focus in the more general educational arena. Starting with Chapter 10, we shall devote three chapters to developments in the teaching-machine and programed learning field.

SUMMARY

1. The training needs of World War II generated the discipline of human engineering, which not only has contributed much practical information about training instrumentation but also has originated a science of human learning.

2. Prior to the war years, research on motor skills had established few valid conclusions other than the general fact that skills are very specific and bear little relation to each other. Scientific motion-analysis techniques had been developed by Stetson.

3. Conventional learning theory and standard principles of efficient learning provided an inadequate base for wartime training programs.

4. A primary principle of training design is that of dynamic simulation of the man-machine operation, reproducing the spatial and temporal patterning of the task rather than its static appearance. Adequate programing of simulated action sequences, controlled variation in difficulty, and practice under stress conditions also are important.

5. Multidimensional recording and analysis of motion patterns led to the concept that motion is made up of basic posture, transport, and manipulation movement components which vary independently but also interact in patterned behavior. Different components show different learning and transfer functions.

6. In training complicated machine skills, it is not enough to give the trainee general information of success or failure. Effective knowledge of results entails information about the nature of the trainee's movements in relation to the action of the machine system and perceptual display. This sensory feedback is a normal means of motion integration and need not be interpreted as reinforcement.

7. Inasmuch as delayed sensory feedback is detrimental to performance, machine systems which introduce lags between the operator's action and the perceived effects of that action inevitably degrade the proficiency of the operator. An example is automated tracking.

8. Wartime experience demonstrated that trainer research should be combined with operations research in a comprehensive systems simulation which provides a means of analyzing the spatial and temporal organization of the task and the pattern of sensorimotor control.

9. Complex simulators have been developed since the war for many phases of military training. However there are few objective data to determine which simulation features are necessary and which are not. Simulation is most valuable for advanced training, for consolidating skills, and for maintaining proficiency.

10. Special training can be given for

emergency procedures only to the extent that hazards and emergencies can be predicted and can be brought under the operator's control. General stress training probably helps the operator to perform more effectively under stress conditions, although the perturbations introduced into feedback control by the somatic and autonomic effects of stress cannot be eliminated completely.

11. Perceptual skills such as radar observation and control should be recognized as involving special patterns of sensorimotor control. Restricted sensory input and minimal activity requirements cause a vigilance problem by reducing the operator's effective feedback and thus degrading his control patterns. Perceptual tasks should be designed to provide as much variation as possible in perceptual input and activity output.

12. Technical knowledge self-instruction machines, which have been developed to teach electronic trouble-shooting and other technical information, incorporate wartime training principles and have contributed to the development of teaching machines.

CHAPTER
8

Contributions
of Training Science

The military training experience of the war years has contributed to learning science and general behavior theory in several ways. A direct result is the realization that training design cannot be specified in terms of general learning principles but must be planned carefully for each new training situation according to the procedures of task analysis. A second effect is a renewed interest in the nature of psychomotor skills and sustained efforts to develop classificatory schemes to describe them and to identify their salient features. In a third line of development, military training contributed significantly to the experimental discipline known as cybernetics. The basic cybernetic concept of feedback has had direct repercussions on general learning theory. Most psychologists profess to make no distinction between feedback and knowledge of results or feedback and reinforcement, but there is accumulating research evidence that the reinforcement concept is incompatible with the experimentally determined characteristics of sensory feedback. Finally,

wartime innovations in training science have left their mark on all sectors of applied learning science, both in general education and in specific areas of industrial and rehabilitative training.

TASK ANALYSIS
AND TRAINING DESIGN

The design of every new training situation depends on a number of specific decisions concerning the requirements of this particular situation—decisions related to criterion requirements, perceptual displays, response categories, training media, practice sequencing, and so on. Recently there have been a number of attempts to systematize the steps that should be followed in reaching these decisions in order to expedite training design for new situations.

General Planning Procedures

Demaree (1961) proposed a set of ideas for developing training programs for specific military operations and systems. The procedure is based on establishing *training equipment planning in-*

formation, or TEPI. The essential steps of this phase of a training program, which are outlined in Figure 8.1, might serve as an initial guide to the administrative director of a training research project.

In one of a series of papers describing the use of task analysis to derive training requirements, Seale (1960) made the point that specifications for a piece of operational equipment tell what the parts and components must do, thus establishing criterion performance, but not necessarily how the operations are to be accomplished. Human engineers must develop operational procedures using relevant data from the engineers responsible for the equipment, from the psychological research literature, and from research on the system itself.

In a second paper in this group, Gustafson *et al.* (1960) said that the problem of converting task analysis into recommendations on training and training equipment is a formidable one, for virtually no laws of learning tell which combinations of training devices and teaching methods should be applied to particular problems. Further, the more complex the problem, the less applicable the rules of learning. These authors suggested that the following four categories of questions should be posed to help determine training requirements:

Figure 8.1.   Initial steps in establishing training equipment planning information (TEPI). (Based on Demaree. *Development of training equipment planning information.* USAF Aeronaut. Sys. Div. tech. Rep. 61–533, 1961.)

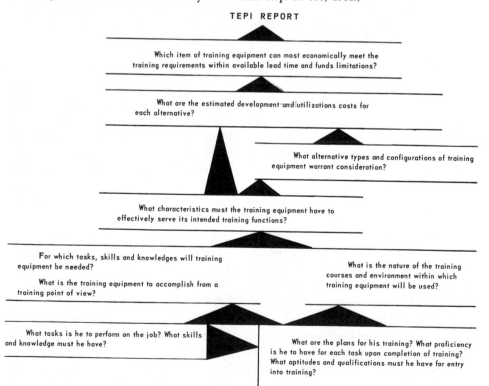

TEPI REPORT

Which item of training equipment can most economically meet the training requirements within available lead time and funds limitations?

What are the estimated development and utilizations costs for each alternative?

What alternative types and configurations of training equipment warrant consideration?

What characteristics must the training equipment have to effectively serve its intended training functions?

For which tasks, skills and knowledges will training equipment be needed?

What is the training equipment to accomplish from a training point of view?

What is the nature of the training courses and environment within which training equipment will be used?

What tasks is he to perform on the job? What skills and knowledge must he have?

What are the plans for his training? What proficiency is he to have for each task upon completion of training? What aptitudes and qualifications must he have for entry into training?

1. Is close attention required in the task?

2. Are hazards to the equipment inherent in the task?

3. Is the performance critical in an over-all mission or operation?

4. Is the performance dependent on the environment, on teamwork, or on other factors?

Answers to these questions help determine whether crew training is advisable, whether simulation of a systems type of environment is necessary, and whether the job environment is best for training.

Gustafson and Cahill (1960) described a generalized process of task analysis, diagramed in Figure 8.2, which is appropriate for training problems associated with system development. According to them, the main objectives of such an analysis are these: to recommend the number and types of courses required, to develop training equipment requirements, to specify applicable training methods such as lectures, demonstrations, and so on, and to indicate methods of assessing student achievement.

Classifying Task Functions

At the second level of analysis in Figure 8.2, the human performance requirements of an operational system must be identified. Gustafson and Cahill classified activities into system operation, including communication, supervision, monitorship, paperwork, decision making, discrimination among alternatives, and equipment control; and maintenance activities, including checkout, trouble-shooting, calibration, repair, supervision, and paperwork. From such

a list of tasks must be developed a list of skills and knowledge to be trained.

Parker and Downs (1961) classified the basic objectives of military training as follows: (a) learning identifications (identifying objects or locations by name or symbol); (b) learning perceptual discriminations (for example, of objects, highways, buildings); (c) understanding principles and relationships; (d) learning procedural sequences; (e) making decisions; and (f) performing skilled perceptual-motor acts.

In a classification similar in some ways to this one, Miller (1962) has attempted to identify the significant functions that are characteristic of nearly every training task. First is the ability to recognize the objects and symbols used in the task by appearance and name. A second task function is scanning, search, and detection of task relevant cues. This function is central in vigilance and inspection tasks. A third function is identifying cue patterns or interpreting cues that have been detected. Fourth, tasks require short-term recall or the temporary retention of information needed to complete a particular sequence. Fifth, tasks also require long-term recall of procedures and stimulus-response relationships. Miller's sixth task function is decision making and his seventh, motor response. This last category was included to emphasize the special features of motor activity that are involved in some tasks, such as the differentiation and coordination of body members and muscle groups.

Demaree (1961) classified training functions into four main categories, each of which includes a number of subordinate functions. *Learning of knowledge*

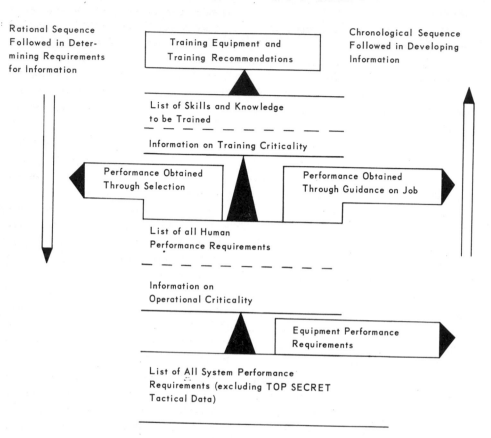

INFORMATION DEVELOPMENT PROCESS

Rational Sequence Followed in Determining Requirements for Information

Chronological Sequence Followed in Developing Information

Training Equipment and Training Recommendations

List of Skills and Knowledge to be Trained

Information on Training Criticality

Performance Obtained Through Selection

Performance Obtained Through Guidance on Job

List of all Human Performance Requirements

Information on Operational Criticality

Equipment Performance Requirements

List of All System Performance Requirements (excluding TOP SECRET Tactical Data)

Figure 8.2.   Suggested procedure for developing training and training equipment recommendations for a particular technical system. Data can be collected in terms of chronological sequence or in terms of a rational sequence. (Based on Gustafson and Cahill. The role of task analysis in deriving training and training equipment requirements for the AN/ULD–1 system. In *Uses of task analysis in deriving training equipment requirements.* USAF Wright Air Dev. Div. Tech. Report No. 60–593, 1960.)

comprises meaning of words and symbols, rules and principles, and relationships. *Learning of skills and task components* involves perceptual identification, naming and location, cue-attention habits, reading of technical materials, voice communication, written communication, numerical computation, practical judgment (decisions in face of information which is incomplete for prescribed courses of action), work planning, motor skills, and manual operations. *Learning whole-task performances* includes procedural, motor, perceptual and judgmental, tracking, complex decision-making, and communication. *Learning integrated task performances* includes performance of time-shared tasks, and crew performance and coordination.

These classifications of task functions represent efforts to develop a definitive scheme for describing and identifying the significant behavioral features of training situations. It can be seen that general agreement has not yet been reached, although there are some common features in the different schemes.

Selecting Training Media

The selection of training devices and procedures depends on the nature of the task to be trained. Glaser (1962) suggested that if we had a completely satisfactory method of specifying the different parts of a task, presumably we would also know the learning features characteristic of each part. In that case, we might also know the training design of optimal efficiency for each different type of behavior. Although our knowledge is not yet that complete, certain general rules about the use of training media can be given.

According to Parker and Downs (1961), training media should be selected which are appropriate to the task and which present an environment conducive to learning. To be conducive to learning, the training media plus other aspects of the situation should provide the following general features: trainee readiness, opportunity for correct response, guidance toward correct responses, reinforcement, and motivation. More specifically, training media themselves should have these characteristics: (a) appropriateness to initial performance level of the trainee (so that he will get some things right initially); (b) relation to the training objective; (c) repeated practice of difficult performances; (d) a sample of problems of graded difficulty; (e) similarity to operational tasks; and (f) a measurement of training performance. Training media were classified as:

a. *simulators,* which reproduce operational tasks without providing instrumental teaching controls

b. *training devices,* such as procedures trainers, which permit practice of parts of a complete task

c. *training aids,* such as charts and films

d. *teaching machines,* or automated training systems

e. *training parts,* items of operational equipment set aside for training purposes.

Each type then was evaluated in terms of how well it meets different training objectives.

Demaree's (1961) analysis of how to develop training equipment planning information (TEPI) indicated that each item of equipment can be evaluated on the basis of ten main characteristics, each of which was broken down into a number of descriptive subheadings. The main characteristics listed by Demaree were: equipment representation, task coverage, trainee responses, trainee orientation, performance aids, information feedback, programing, proficiency evaluation, effective use of time, and acceptability. Armed with this detailed description of equipment characteristics, the training director prepares the charts for each item of training equipment representing in what manner the item serves the various behavioral functions of training (Demaree's list of functions was given on p. 193f). Thus each item would be described by ten evaluative charts. This type of operational analysis of a learning situation gives some indication of the many features that are considered significant in training design and bears little resemblance to the formulations of learning psychology, where the principal theoretical argument over the past thirty-five years has been whether one factor or two factors are responsible for learning.

Predicting Trainability

An important factor in training design is that of individual differences—a factor which must be taken into consideration both in selecting trainees for particular jobs and in adjusting training procedures to individual abilities. The tool of differential psychology is the psychometric test, and any psychometric techniques that prove successful in differentiating among individuals and in predicting their trainability presumably should tell us something about the significant types of behavior making up various tasks.

The standard psychometric approach to training prediction, using standardized intelligence, personality, and psychomotor tests to indicate the probable success or failure of trainees, has had but limited success. The general validity of such forecasting procedures usually is so low that the tests can be used only for rough group screening purposes. It has been found that the validity of psychometric training forecasting varies with the type of task and particularly with the design of training programs. Verbal and general educational skills can be predicted with greater success than the more specific psychomotor skills. Thus if training procedures emphasize verbal and other general skills more than the actual task does, we may find a discrepancy between the validity of forecasts as judged by training performance and as judged by actual job performance. In general, as training design is structured more carefully and is made to simulate operational design more closely, training becomes more effective, but the predictive validity of the tests for trainability is decreased. Thus, for complex psychomotor skills, the better the training design the more poorly can we predict trainability.

The general limitations of psychometric prediction in training are not surprising when considered in relation to typical learning behavior in such situations. In some cases, initial learning scores for the particular task are no more efficient in predicting the final level of performance than are the scores from psychomotor tests. In other words, it is not usually possible to make a reliable prediction of final learning either from initial performance of a task or from extraneous samples of behavior. In the present state of our knowledge, we can sample individual differences in skill only by measuring performances that simulate very closely the skill in which we are interested.

ANALYZING MOTOR SKILLS

Task analysis and psychometric prediction suffer from one major limitation—the lack of a generally accepted scheme for describing and understanding the basic components of skilled performances. Several different approaches have been used in attempts to identify the significant components. In this section, we shall describe one major effort based on psychometric and statistical procedures and shall also present some conclusions drawn from observational and experimental analyses.

Factor Analysis of Skills

More than a decade ago, Fleishman (1955, 1962; Fleishman and Hempel, 1956) launched an extensive military research program that attempted to analyze the make-up of skilled performances by using the facts of individual differences. The general strategy was to score the performance of many individuals on a large variety of psychomotor tasks (more than 200 have been used) and then to identify common factors by the statistical procedures of factor analysis. These factors are assumed to represent relatively independent psychomotor abilities which contribute in varying degrees to different skilled performances.

The first phases of this research confirmed the belief that was by then prevalent among training psychologists that there is no general psychomotor skill or general physical proficiency. The relatively limited number of factors that were identified were described in fairly specific terms. Some of these factors were identified by the following names: control precision; multilimb coordination; response orientation, found in visual tasks involving rapid directional discrimination and movement orientation; reaction time; speed of arm movement; rate control, found in pursuit tasks; manual dexterity; finger dexterity; arm-hand steadiness; wrist-finger speed or tapping ability; and aiming. In addition, Hempel and Fleishman (1955) identified several areas of ability related to the more gross kinds of motor activity such as athletic skills. The general factors identified were named strength, flexibility, energy mobilization or "explosive ability," balance, gross body coordination, and endurance.

Although these early results were encouraging, further studies made little additional progress toward the goal of establishing a definite list of skill factors. Analyses of specific training tasks usually revealed that *within task* factors accounted for an important percentage of the variance, sometimes a major percentage. For example, in a complex tracking performance, no more than twenty-five percent of the variance could be accounted for by identified ability factors. To account for the remainder, we either must assume that there are important abilities that were not identified by Fleishman or that differences in performances are related not so much to the traits or abilities that the trainees bring to the task as to the habits and skills acquired during training.

Fleishman's studies also revealed that the pattern of skill factors making up a task changes progressively with practice. For example, when performance on a Discrimination Reaction Time Task was analyzed over a practice period, the main skill factor in the original trials, Spatial Relations, decreased in importance from a thirty-six percent contribution to variance to an eleven percent contribution in later trials. On the other hand, two factors—Reaction Time and Rate of Arm Movement—which contributed nothing originally were contributing in combination more than thirty percent of the variance in the final stages of practice. In some cases, the factor pattern of a task became less complex with practice, especially when a *within task* factor increased in importance. These progressive changes in the pattern of skill factors or abilities, often involving the emergence of specific task factors, indicate why psychometric prediction of trainability or job performance has had such limited success.

Survey Analysis of Skill

Fitts (1962) has reported two attempts to identify the significant factors in psychomotor skills by sampling the opinions of highly competent and experienced observers. One study involved an analysis of stenographic reports of the statements made by instructors relative to 1000 aviation cadets who were eliminated from pilot training during World War II. The second was a study of tape-recorded interviews with forty coaches and physical educational instructors at a large university.

According to Fitts, the pilot instructors and athletic instructors emphasized the same general aspects of skilled performances, although the skills with which they were concerned were very different. First to be emphasized were the *cognitive aspects* of skill learning. Instructors believe that an understanding of the task is important early in training and use demonstrations, movies, lectures, and so forth, to develop such an understanding. Later in training, such cognitive aspects as strategy, judgment, decision making, and planning were important. Secondly, emphasis was placed on *perceptual aspects* of skill learning, including identifications and discriminations, in particular the use of proprioceptive cues to discriminate forces and pressures. The third point of emphasis was *coordination*—that is, integration and timing of movements in a pattern—and the fourth point was the

tension-relaxation continuum, indicating that tension becomes less as skill develops.

On the basis of these reports and other observations, Fitts suggested that skill learning probably progresses through three roughly differentiated phases which he described as *cognition*, *fixation*, and *automation*. He recommended that emphasis be placed on cognitive understanding or *intellectualization* in the first phases of training to provide the trainee with appropriate sets or expectancies and an over-all knowledge of what the task involves. In the second or fixation phase, correct patterns of behavior should be fixated and errors eliminated by extensive practice. Fitts described the third or autonomous phase as being characterized by gradually increasing speed of performance and gradually increasing resistance to stress and to interference. He suggested that this phase involves a shift from exteroceptive to proprioceptive control and a shift of neural control from higher to lower brain centers.

A second general principle proposed by Fitts is that complex skill learning involves the acquisition of a number of semi-independent subroutines which can go on successively or concurrently. This point of view was offered as more appropriate than models based on specific S-R elements. The practical implication of this principle is that subroutines should be identified in a training task so that they can be practiced extensively.

Third, Fitts observed that skilled performances continue to improve with extended training over long periods of time. Professional skills and other complex performances may not reach a peak until after years of intensive practice.

Learning experiments rarely investigate such long-term changes but they are highly important in real life. This point along with the first emphasizes the importance of extended practice in a task so that performance will continue to improve and will become autonomous and resistant to interference.

Experimental Analysis of Skill

All analyses of behavior start with certain assumptions or hypotheses based in part on general observations, and all must survive experimental tests sooner or later if they are to be accepted as valid. However, some analyses are structured more specifically than others by experimental findings and emphasize hypotheses that can be tested directly by experimentation. Our own analysis of motion into three basic components, which we described briefly both in Chapter 3 and in Chapter 7, is in this category. Classifying movements into postural, transport, and manipulative components was suggested originally by observation and experience, but our theoretical concepts have been extended and refined by many years of experimental research.

Our present tridimensional analysis of motion is proposed not necessarily as the last word in skill taxonomy but as a scheme which has proved meaningful and useful and which has generated theoretical concepts about behavior organization as well as hypotheses that can be tested experimentally. We have found that all kinds of patterned motions can be described meaningfully in terms of the three primary movement components, and that the scheme has certain other advantages as well.

The first major advantage of our tri-dimensional analysis of motion, which to us is of greatest importance, is that it can be related directly to the over-all organization of the sensori-neuromotor system. It is known that posture, locomotion and other transport movements are regulated by neural structures lower in the brain than those which control fine manipulative movements. Posture is controlled by centers of the medulla, the cerebellum, and the midbrain, whereas locomotion and other large transport movements undoubtedly are controlled by bilaterally differentiated centers in the new cerebellum as well as higher centers. In contrast, fine manipulative movements are mediated by specialized centers in the cortex. Thus, it appears to be possible to establish a structural basis for the functional differentiation of motion into basic components.

In addition to postulating that the three types of movements are controlled by separate brain centers, we assume that each type is organized relative to specialized sources of sensory information. In general terms, we say that the movements of posture are regulated according to the position of the body with respect to gravity. Transport movements characteristically propel body members through free space or a fluid medium; and a main source of their control lies within the body itself, in the bilaterally differentiated mechanisms that regulate movements of the right and left limbs with respect to each other. For example, under ordinary circumstances the large transport movements of the legs in walking are patterned intrinsically by bilaterally organized feedback loops. Whereas transport movements are executed in free space, we say that manipulative movements typically are regulated by the contours, surfaces, and other object characteristics of *hard space*. Thus, the manipulative component is organized for the most part according to patterns of exteroceptive stimulation. The articulatory movements of speech represent a specialized kind of manipulation. These movements too can be thought of as patterned according to the spatial characteristics and surfaces of the throat, mouth, tongue, teeth, and lips.

Experimental analyses have revealed that the different movement components have specialized properties and are independently variable in performance and learning. We attribute their specialization and relative independence to their differential regulation by distinctive neural mechanisms. On the other hand, a primary characteristic of patterned motion is that the different components are integrated precisely with reference to each other. They are never completely independent but are defined in part by the nature of the over-all pattern and the components of which it is composed. Thus, we assume that there are specialized centers in the brain that integrate postural and transport movements and transport and manipulative movements. A major part of training is improving the precision and efficiency of these integrations.

A second advantage of our tridimensional analysis is that it can be related closely to the progressive differentiation of behavior in phylogeny and ontogeny. Gross postural adjustments are of major importance in the behavior organization of the lowest vertebrates, but transport movements assume an increasing importance with the differentiation of limbs. The significance of fine manipula-

tion in the behavior organization of man is widely recognized. These progressive phylogenetic changes in behavior patterning reflect progressive anatomical developments of the neural structures that regulate the different types of movements.

Of greater importance in the understanding of human learning, however, are the progressive changes in the behavior patterning of children during the first years of life. Here we see the progressive development of postural control, transport movement control, and finally manipulative control. A more detailed discussion of our interpretation of the development of behavior in human individuals will be given in the final chapter of the book.

A third advantage of our classification of movement components is that they lend themselves readily to experimental analysis and measurement. In many skills, transport and manipulative movements occur consecutively and thus can be timed separately with appropriate recording devices. Most of our dimensional analyses of motion were carried out by means of electronic motion analyzers, such as the one diagramed in Figure 8.3, which time different transport and manipulative movements separately. These analyzers are designed to take advantage of the fact that manipulative movements bring the individual into contact with objects whereas transport movements typically break that contact. Each time the subject makes manipulative contact in an experimental task, a relay in the analyzer generates a subthreshold electric current which passes through the manipulated task objects, the subject's body, and an electrode held by the subject or attached to him. The relay also closes a circuit which operates a precision time clock. When the subject breaks manipulative contact in order to transport his hand to the next manipulative position, a flip-flop circuit activates a second relay which starts a second clock. These two clocks summate the durations of successive contact and transport movements until the end of the task. With this general technique we have been able to analyze the differential effects of many variables on transport and manipulative components.

A fourth advantage of our motion analysis scheme is that it provides a meaningful framework within which to analyze the spatial patterning of motion. Inasmuch as bodily posture is regulated with respect to gravity, the mechanisms of postural control can be thought of as

Figure 8.3. The main components of an electronic motion analyzer which times different transport and manipulative movements separately and summates transport time and manipulation time on the two clocks.

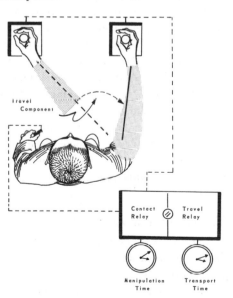

providing a vertically oriented or up-down reference system for patterned motion. The bilaterally organized transport mechanisms provide a horizontally oriented or right-left reference system. The orientation and directional characteristics of all movements can be described and analyzed with reference to these built-in axial systems. Our experiments on spatially displaced feedback, which will be described in later chapters, have been designed to analyze and compare displacements in the two *systematic* dimensions that are represented in the motion systems of the body as well as displacements in *nonsystematic* dimensions. In general, an individual can adapt to systematic visual displacements —that is, inversions or reversals of visual feedback—more readily than to extreme displacements in nonsystematic dimensions. Visual inversions, which disturb the most primitive motion systems—the postural up-down reference system—are more disturbing than visual reversals, which presumably are referenced by the bilateral transport movement system. Minor angular displacements of feedback usually cause no obvious disturbance of performance, but the extent of the displacement that can be tolerated depends on the complexity of the task and the movements involved.

Skilled motions vary in significant ways other than their component make-up. Some of the characteristics of stimulus-response-feedback sequences which can be specified quantitatively have been identified by Fitts (1962) as *coherence, continuity, frequency,* and *complexity.* We wish to call particular attention to the continuity factor, which Fitts described as a function of the duration of sequences of changing events, and the occurrence of pauses between sequences. Motion sequences at the extreme of this continuum are classified as *continuous* and *discrete*. Tasks like tracking or steering are continuous because they involve continuous feedback control with respect to a stimulus pattern. A discrete task involves one or a series of relatively isolated movements such as throwing a ball or typing.

Dodge's (1903) distinction between pursuit and saccadic eye movements and Stetson and McDill's (1923), between tense and ballistic movements recognize this difference in continuity. A tense or pursuit movement is controlled throughout its course by opposing muscle groups, whereas a ballistic or saccadic movement is controlled by the effective muscles only at its onset. Its direction, extent, and duration then can be modified by external surfaces or objects or by an arresting movement of the individual. In reality, most movements lie somewhere in between the two extremes, and a complex motion pattern typically involves both continuous and discrete movements. For example, a tracker imposes discrete positioning movements on his continuous rate-control movements, and a typist, whose task appears to be a series of discrete striking movements, supports the performance with a continuously controlled postural background.

Much of the behavior studied in conventional learning laboratories consists principally of discrete responses, such as specific conditioned responses to unitary stimuli, a series of bar-pressings, or serial verbal responses. The theories which describe behavior in terms of specific S-R elements can handle discrete responses reasonably well, but many training psychologists have found it impossible to conceptualize continuous skilled performances in conventional S-R terms. On the other hand, a feedback model of behavior which recognizes the multidimensionality of motion as well as emphasizing continuity of control can incorporate both discrete and continuous responses into its conceptual framework.

THE INDIVIDUAL AS A CONTROL SYSTEM

In our opinion, the most important conceptual development of postwar training science is the incorporation of the feedback idea into behavior theory. Although the feedback principle was recognized by training psychologists during the war years, its introduction as a formal behavioral concept usually is attributed to Wiener (1948), who published the first account of the discipline known as *Cybernetics.*

Cybernetics has been described as the comparative study of the human (or biological) control mechanism and electro-mechanical control systems such as computers. Wiener and other engineers and mathematicians were impressed with certain apparent similarities in living and nonliving control operations and developed the cybernetic idea as a formal analogy relating the two kinds of systems. Their hope was that such comparative study would provide new insights into the mechanisms of behavior.

The Cybernetic Analogy

The term cybernetics was derived from the Greek word, *Kybernetes,* meaning "steersman" and thus calls attention to the principle of feedback control. In general, the term feedback is used to describe a kind of reciprocal interaction between two or more events, in which one activity generates a secondary action which in turn redirects the primary action. Early mechanisms using the principle of feedback control were Watt's rotating governor on a steam engine and self-regulating temperature systems. Since World War II, the feedback principle has been identified especially with control systems known as servomechanisms such as are used to guide a ship or gunsight on a defined path in terms of a recorded error signal.

A feedback-control system incorporates three primary functions: it generates movement of the system toward a target or in a defined path; it compares the effects of this action with the true path and detects error; and it utilizes this error signal to redirect the system. Figure 8.4 illustrates three generalized components which carry out these functions—an action mechanism,

a feedback detection system, and a director or computer which translates the feedback signal into corrective action. Feedback control by means of servomechanisms is used in a wide variety of operations—to control temperature, to regulate speed of movement, to guide the action of cutting machines around a set pattern, to direct radar antennae, to sight guns, and so on. In the cybernetic analogy, the behaving individual is looked on as a control system which, like a servomechanism, generates a course of action and then redirects or corrects that action by means of feedback information. Other features of the cybernetic analogy as proposed by Wiener will be discussed in a later chapter.

Differentiation of the Feedback Concept

The feedback principle has found widespread acceptance among psychologists, partly because of its resemblance to the familiar *knowledge of results*

Figure 8.4.   Three functions of a feedback-control system: generation of movement toward a target or path, comparison of this action and the true position of the path, and redirection of the system in terms of the error signal.

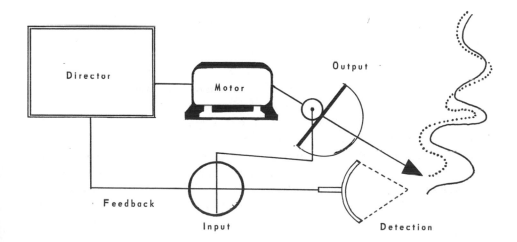

Director

Motor

Output

Feedback

Input

Detection

principle of learning efficiency. Many psychologists use the terms feedback and knowledge of results interchangeably, and since knowledge of results usually is thought to function as reward as well as information, many theorists have appropriated feedback as a form of reinforcement. Thus, in this cybernetic analogy of the human control system, the feedback signal may be interpreted as having reinforcing properties. Presumably this means that the smaller the magnitude of the error, the greater the reinforcement value of the signal. In other words, the response that minimizes error presumably is strengthened or learned. This type of interpretation is so widespread that feedback is indexed in the *Psychological Abstracts* as, "Feedback (See also Knowledge of results, Reinforcement)."

Although many training psychologists have tried to distinguish between different functions or roles of feedback, they have not tried to divorce the feedback concept from knowledge of results or from reinforcement. It is our purpose here to show that clear distinctions are possible and necessary. We shall use Ammons' (1956) review of the research literature on knowledge of performance as a starting point for analyzing some of the differences between dynamic sensory feedback and other kinds of knowledge of accuracy.

The experiments reviewed by Ammons all were concerned with the general problem of determining the effects of giving or withholding various kinds of information about performance during or for varying amounts of time after performance. The first experiment designed specifically to study this problem was carried out by Judd (1905–1906)

who asked his subject to make estimations of direction behind a screen which prevented visual knowledge of results. Other experiments have studied a wide variety of performances including two-hand coordination, lever positioning, knob turning, ball tossing, tracking, ranging, aiming guns, maze learning, code learning, estimating lengths or drawing lines of given lengths, writing, and school test performances. The results show generally that giving knowledge of results leads to more proficient performance and more effective learning than withholding or reducing knowledge, and that immediate knowledge is more effective than delayed knowledge. However, an analysis of the various results suggests many qualifying conclusions.

Providing knowledge of results does not automatically enhance the efficiency of performance and learning. The effects depend on the kind of task and the kind of knowledge provided. Ammons made the point that performers usually have hypotheses about what they are to do or about the workings of the apparatus so that when they are given inadequate knowledge of results, their performance depends partly on their preconceived ideas. In a complicated machine skill, extraneous stimuli may be interpreted by a performer as relevant cues to which he should attend. In such a situation, limited knowledge of success or failure does not provide the performer with enough information to discard his false hypotheses in favor of correct ones.

Another point made by Ammons was that a performer often needs information about the direction and amount of his error in order to improve performance. He proposed the following generalization: "The more specific the knowledge of performance, the more rapid the improvement and the higher the level of performance." However, he observed that there is an optimum specificity of knowledge beyond which additional knowledge will not improve performance or may even lead to its deterioration. Ammons' interpretation of this effect is that providing a complex display or complicated information may prove confusing to the performer. We add to this the comment that a performer may not be able to incorporate the complicated information into his pattern of control, and that his performance may deteriorate if, in trying to react to too many cues, he does not differentiate the critical pattern.

Another generalization proposed by Ammons is that there is always some knowledge of his performance available to the human performer. If knowledge of accuracy is withheld, a performer still has sensory feedback from his own movements. Although this feedback information may not permit the performer to react *correctly* according to the standards of the experimenter, it does provide a means of setting intrinsic standards in terms of which improvement can occur. For example, subjects who are asked to draw a line of a given length with no information about their accuracy gradually become more consistent in the lengths they draw although they may not be producing the length called for by the instructions. They show learning improvement when judged by their intrinsic standards although no improvement occurs when judged by the experimenter's standard.

All of these observations about different kinds of knowledge of results

suggest that one can make a valid distinction between the dynamic information provided by sensory feedback and static knowledge of success or failure given at the end of the task. Some tasks are arranged so that the dynamic feedback itself provides an indication of accuracy, whereas in other tasks, no dynamic feedback error signal is given. As a simple example, a performer who is asked to draw a line to match a sample line has a dynamic visual indication of accuracy, whereas a performer asked to draw a line "six inches long" has no dynamic error feedback although he may be given a verbal report of his accuracy at the end of his performance.

The general rule in training design is that dynamic feedback of performance is more effective than static knowledge of results at the end of a task or of a motion sequence. In complicated tasks, if the feedback available to the operator is inadequate, it sometimes can be augmented by specially devised visual or auditory signals which are tied in directly to the control operations. For example, it has been shown that trainees learned to use the B-29 gun-sight more effectively if the simulated target plane appeared red when they were on target. However, this augmented feedback was necessary only to improve ranging scores, presumably because the feedback available originally did not give sufficient information about ranging accuracy or it was difficult to discriminate. However, the original feedback was adequate for efficient tracking performance, so that tracking scores did not improve when the red filter was added.

The distinction between dynamic feedback and static knowledge of results becomes crucial when one attempts to study the efforts of introducing delay before providing the information. Ammons (1956) proposed the general rule that: "The longer the delay in giving knowledge of performance, the less effect the given information has." He then reviewed studies that tend to show a gradual drop in human learning efficiency when knowledge of accuracy is withheld for periods up to a quarter minute or so. Although Ammons' concluded that, "the learner may not be able to use information given more than fifteen or twenty seconds after the response," Bilodeau and Bilodeau (1961) question this interpretation and insist instead that the learning of relatively simple responses is not affected materially by delaying the knowledge of results if the periods between responses are free of interpolated responses.

This ambiguous situation with respect to delayed static knowledge of results contrasts markedly with the situation with respect to delayed dynamic feedback. As we indicated in Chapter 7, delaying the dynamic sensory feedback of performance by even a small fraction of a second seriously disrupts the patterning of motion and degrades its accuracy. This effect has been demonstrated many times by experimentally delaying the auditory feedback of speech and other sound-producing motions and has been substantiated by a more limited number of studies of delayed visual feedback (K. U. Smith, 1962). The marked disturbances caused by feedback delays of a few milliseconds are clearly different from the impairment that may or may not result when static knowledge of performance is delayed by some seconds. The difference indicates that we are dealing with two different classes of phenomena which should not be confused by lumping together feedback and knowledge of results in a single category.

Another attempt to differentiate between different kinds of knowledge of results contrasts *action* feedback with *learning* feedback (Annett and Kay, 1957), a distinction made in an experiment reported by Annett (1959). The task was to press a plunger to a specified pressure under several conditions of feedback or knowledge of results. All subjects were told that they were supposed to learn the *feel* of the plunger at the specified pressure condition. Two conditions of visual feedback were provided—one in which the performer could watch the indicator of a cathode-ray oscilloscope which informed him precisely how much pressure he was exerting, and another in which the oscilloscope was screened but a signal light came on when the indicator was within one degree of the target. In a third condition, no visual feedback was given but the experimenter reported the scale reading at the end of the subject's push. In the fourth condition, the oscilloscope was uncovered at the end of the push so that the subject could see the pressure achieved and could correct it.

Several specific results were noted. Both conditions of immediate visual feedback produced very accurate performances in which the subjects hit the target every time. However, removing this visual feedback during a test period caused a marked drop in accuracy. Obviously the visual group had not learned the correct *feel* of the plunger during their training trials. In contrast, the terminal knowledge group performed poorly at first but improved gradually during training. Annett suggested that the visual group was getting *action* feedback that did not produce learning but that terminal knowledge provided *learning* feedback to produce the desired improvement.

In our opinion, this distinction has little to recommend it. The two groups were not only receiving two kinds of feedback or knowledge, but they also were performing two different tasks—one a visually monitored task and one a proprioceptively monitored task. Instructing the visual group to learn the feel was not enough to cause a shift in their dominant control pattern to the proprioceptive cues. In a way, this was almost as unrealistic as telling individuals with normal eyesight to learn *facial vision,* that is, to learn to avoid objects as the blind do by a kind of echo-ranging system. An individual just does not establish this specialized type of feedback control unless he is forced to do so by the loss of his more efficient visual control mechanisms. In Annett's experiment, the proprioceptive task was far more difficult than the visual because the subjects had no intrinsic means of making a precise differential response. The static knowledge of accuracy given at the end of each trial promoted slow learning improvement by enabling the subjects to establish intrinsic standards by means of which to monitor their responses. However, the subjects who were provided dynamic visual feedback made little or no headway in establishing such intrinsic standards.

What Annett really demonstrated was that visual feedback did not teach these subjects proprioceptive control—a result that has certain implications for training design. Special perceptual guidance supplied during training, such as augmented feedback, sometimes helps training performance but does not help the trainee learn the type of control that will be needed in the actual task. For example, auditory clicks added during a difficult tracking or ranging task to indicate when the trainee is on target improve training scores, but performance sometimes deteriorates when the clicks are withdrawn. Such deterioration is only to be expected if the task situation does not supply a feedback pattern sufficiently precise and complete enough to structure a good performance. However, if an adequate feedback pattern is available both during training and during task performance, the addition of augmented feedback cues may on occasion enhance the learning process by enabling the trainee to differentiate critical cues that will be present during performance as well as during training. An experiment illustrating the differential effectiveness of auditory clicks when used with a *good* visual display and a *poor* one has been reported by Kinkade (1963).

The thing that seems to have been overlooked in making the action feedback-learning feedback distinction is that the same kind of dynamic sensory feedback that is used to control action also serves to define learning when improvement does occur. Pushing the pressure stick in Annett's experiment was such a simple task when monitored visually that no obvious learning occurred; the subjects were able to perform correctly from the first trial. More difficult visual tasks do show improvement with practice, and this learning is more efficient with dynamic feedback than with static terminal knowledge. We have tested this generalization experimentally a number of times with confirming results (for example, see "Dynamic versus Static Feedback" in Chapter 15).

Although we think it important to distinguish between dynamic sensory feedback and static knowledge of results, we also recognize valid similarities between the two types of knowledge. Either can serve to inform the individual about the accuracy of his movements. When a particular response provides no intrinsic feedback error signal, it often is critically important to give knowledge of accuracy in the form of an extrinsic signal at the end of the response. Verbal and symbolic learning often must be guided or defined in terms of static extrinsic knowledge until the individual has established intrinsic standards by means of which to monitor the learned responses. As the individual's body of symbolic knowledge grows and becomes better organized, he is able to monitor more and more of his own symbolic responses in terms of his intrinsic standards of accuracy, logic, and consistency. Thus, an extrinsic signal (such as, "That's right!" or "Correct!") may serve only to confirm a response that already has been monitored intrinsically. For example, an individual who is asked how many months Franklin D. Roosevelt served as president can give the answer with assurance, although it never has been learned specifically, if he knows that F.D.R. was inaugurated in March, 1933 and died in April, 1945. In such a case, extrinsically given knowledge of accuracy serves only to confirm the intrinsic feedback processes.

Inasmuch as the term *feedback* is used widely to refer to all kinds of knowledge of results, we see no reason not to conform to the practice, even though there is some possibility of confusion. In general, we shall speak of the immediate sensory processes resulting from responses as *dynamic sensory feedback* and terminal knowledge of results as *knowledge feedback*. It should be noted that some types of performance, such as tool using, produce several kinds of feedback effects, some of which are not easily classified in terms of the dynamic feedback-knowledge feedback categories. However, all feedback effects have this important characteristic in common— they are related systematically to the reference response. In this sense, feedback differs from reinforcement, which need bear no relationship to the response it reinforces. Rather, a reinforcement is related to the drive which it reduces or the motive which it satisfies.

CYBERNETIC CONTROL VERSUS REINFORCEMENT CONTROL

The various attempts to distinguish between *action* feedback and *learning* feedback exemplify the stranglehold that reinforcement learning theory has gained over psychological thinking. Almost all psychologists accept the proposition that reinforcement is central to learning. Thus any effect that can be shown to enhance learning is assumed without question to be a form of reinforcement. The upshot is that the advances in military training science that promised so much for a theoretical understanding of human behavior have been largely nullified by the dependence of training psychologists on the safe and familiar learning models.

Almost any general discussion of training provides evidence of the confused thinking that prevails about the nature of sensory feedback with relation to the nature of reinforcement. Wolfle's (1951) chapter on "Training" in the *Handbook of Experimental Psychology* proposed as the first important training principle the necessity for specific and immediate knowledge of results. Then, in evidence, he cited indiscriminately data from a rat study of delayed reinforcement and data from human studies of knowledge of results. The implication was that food reward in a rat experiment and any kind of knowledge of accuracy in human training serve identical functions. A recent book on training research and education written by acknowledged training specialists shows no progress in differentiating among these concepts. For example, Glanzer (1962) cited as a general principle, "Immediate Feedback or Reinforcement," and spoke later of "the effectiveness of reinforcement, or feedback," without making any attempt to differentiate between the two concepts. Similarly, Adams' (1964) chapter on "Motor Skills" in the *Annual Review of Psychology* indicated that feedback stimuli which enhance learning serve "a reinforcing function." Although Lumsdaine (1962a) noted that, "the role of reinforcement . . . has seldom been disentangled from other functions of response feedback," he made no mention of the specialized concept of dynamic sensory feedback.

In our opinion, this confusion of the experimentally demonstrated processes of sensory-feedback control with what the learning theorists call reinforcement has had a stultifying effect on training science as well as on other areas of behavior theory. It is impossible to clarify the meaning of cybernetic control of behavior in terms of fuzzy concepts about the law of effect, rewards and punish-

ments, or reinforcement. Real and important distinctions can be made between cybernetic control and the type of control that is achieved experimentally by manipulating extrinsic rewards, and fundamental differences exist between dynamic sensory-feedback stimuli and reinforcers. It is high time that psychologists started clarifying these differences instead of continuing to obscure them. The most important features that distinguish sensory-feedback control processes from reinforcement contingencies are discussed in the following sections of this chapter.

Objective Definition

One of the most obvious differences between the concepts of sensory feedback and reinforcement lies in the objectivity and precision with which they can be defined. Sensory feedback can be specified quantitatively and qualitatively in a number of ways. We recognize not only the different sensory modes of feedback—visual, auditory, tactual, and kinesthetic—but also the different spatial, temporal, and kinetic variations in feedback patterns. Many studies provide evidence that both the nature of performance and the course of learning are defined by measurable variations in the physical properties of feedback patterns in relation to the response patterns of the individual.

In contrast, the definition of reinforcement has become—if anything—somewhat less precise over the years. Thorndike's original law of effect seemed to bear some relationship to rewards and punishments, but even that broad meaning proved untenable. In contemporary psychological literature, the only definitions of reinforcement are tautological, for they are based on the very process that they are supposed to explain. That is, reinforcement can be defined only as an event or a condition which strengthens a response or increases the likelihood that it will reoccur. Thus, it is impossible to specify the nature of reinforcement except in the context of an empirical demonstration that something has influenced the statistical probability that a given stimulus will produce a given response.

Although many parameters of feedback control can be studied experimentally, experimental manipulations of reinforcements are limited to changes in timing of discrete rewards in relation to discrete responses or changes in the number of rewards given in relation to the number of reinforcements. Inasmuch as a reinforcement can be anything that an experimenter finds effective, no cross-comparisons can be made except in terms of these temporal and serial relationships of discrete events.

Generality of Meaning

Whereas reinforcements are extrinsic effects that have theoretical meaning only in relation to learning change, sensory-feedback processes are intrinsic organizing processes that serve to regulate behavior at all times throughout life. Standard learning theory has ignored the organization of behavior prior to learning and has confined its analyses to specific learning changes. In contrast, sensory-feedback theory is interested in behavior organization under all circumstances and in relation to any kind of change, temporary or permanent. Thus, learning is not considered the primary organizational principle of behavior but only one of the ways in which behavior

patterns can be modified. Other important irreversible changes in behavior patterning occur in development as a result of maturation, in aging, and in relation to physical or psychological disorders. Specialized changes which may be called learning occur in thinking or problem solving. All of these changes as well as temporary changes, such as those due to motivational-emotional state, fatigue, adaptation, and drugs, can be analyzed in terms of changes in the patterning of feedback control. In contrast, the reinforcement learning model can deal with only a very limited kind of behavior change.

The most general implication of these ideas is to diminish the importance of learning theory in relation to other areas of behavior science. In time, the theory and study of learning may properly assume a role subordinate to a more general theoretical understanding of the organization and control of behavior.

Specification of Stimulus-Response Interactions

Although learning psychologists have been using the concepts of stimulus, of response, and of the reflex for the best part of a century, they never have studied or defined the intrinsic interactions involved in behavior sequences. Their analyses have been concerned only with gross extrinsic relationships in which stimulus, response, and reinforcement events have been described in only the most general terms. Cybernetic analyses of feedback control provide a means of specifying in quantitative terms the events of stimulus-response interaction, and of clarifying the nature of the integrative action of the nervous system in performance and learning.

Inasmuch as most psychologists consider the basic phenomena of reflex action and neural integration to be within the realm of physiology, they have accepted physiological interpretations such as inline synaptic transmission, integration, and inhibition as valid and have hoped that further physiological clarification of behavior organization and learning would be forthcoming. In our opinion, the analytic methods of many neurophysiological investigations have overlooked the basic feedback organization of behavior. Separate analyses of sensory, neural, and motor events have tended to obscure the over-all features of sensorimotor control. It is the task of psychology itself as the science of behavior to clarify the nature of reflex action and the integrative features of sensory-feedback control.

Generation of Response

Concepts of sensory-feedback control imply that organized behavior is dependent on the intrinsic generation of activity by means of which the organism supplies itself with differential feedback patterns. Evidence has been accumulating that built-in mechanisms for such self-generation of control feedback do, in fact, exist. Riggs et al. (1953) first demonstrated that the rapid *flick* movements of the eyes prevent them from adapting completely to the pattern of visual stimulation. Reciprocal tremor movements of the head are known to be necessary for discriminating the directional characteristics of sound, and some degree of body movement or stimulus change is necessary to keep cutaneous and kinesthetic receptors from adapting.

These concepts about a self-governing feedback system which continuously generates its own feedback signals do not fit the homeostatic or drive-reduction assumptions of conventional learning theories. The organism usually is conceptualized as a system whose optimal state is one of equilibrium. When activated by a drive state, it responds until the drive is reduced by appropriate reinforcers and thus regains equilibrium. As an alternative to this idea of homeostatic regulation, we suggest that the organism might better be described as *homeokinetic*—that is, as a system whose optimal state is one of feedback-generating activity.

Spatial Organization of Response

The spatial organization of behavior is a feature that is fundamental to the theory of feedback control but cannot be conceptualized by the reinforcement learning model. The directional guidance and control provided by differential feedback signals is most obvious in spatially organized skills, but we believe that all organized behavior involves responses to spatial differences in stimulation. Inasmuch as controlling feedback stimuli are produced by movements, they always bear some definite relationship to the position of the organism and its movements. Thus, responses to the spatial patterns of the environment are guided within the reference framework provided by the motion systems of the body. Research on displaced visual feedback is designed to investigate the spatial characteristics of behavior control and to determine the individual's ability to adapt to unusual spatial relationships between motion and its feedback pattern.

Concepts of spatial patterning and control can be applied meaningfully to the multidimensional interpretation of behavior. The various components of a complex motion pattern are integrated precisely by feedback processes defined by the spatial relationships of the components. That is, we believe that movements are tied together in precisely integrated motion patterns by interconnecting feedback loops that detect spatial relationships among the components.

Conventional learning theories always have conceptualized behavior and learning in terms of temporally linked stimuli and responses. A time-coded model is inappropriate for describing continuously controlled behavior and multidimensional behavior. Consequently, learning theorists have confined their experimental attention almost entirely to series of discrete responses. Occasional attempts to interpret complex human skills (for example, verbal behavior [Skinner, 1957]) in terms of the time-coded models have added nothing to our understanding of how these skills are organized and controlled.

Delay Functions

The distinction we made above between the effects of delayed sensory feedback and delayed static knowledge of results applies as well to feedback and reinforcement. In animal studies, reinforcement gradually loses its effectiveness if it is not presented immediately after the critical response. Quantitative measures of declining response strength in rats as a function of reinforcement delay showed a rapid drop during the first minute and a subsequent slow decline throughout delay periods that lasted up to twenty minutes (Wolfe, 1934). These data indicated that an extrinsic reward following a response is most effective if presented immediately but retains some effectiveness even when presented minutes afterwards. In contrast, if we break into the feedback control loop of a behaving individual and delay the feedback signals, even for a small fraction of a second, behavior is seriously disrupted. Furthermore, there is no evidence that an individual can learn to regulate the same pattern of behavior with the delayed feedback signals. He can shift to another sensory mode of control or shift from continuous to discrete control, but the original control pattern cannot be restored while the delay is in effect.

Intermittency Functions

One of the principal experimental findings of the Skinnerian school of reinforcement learning theory is the effect of intermittent scheduling of reinforcements in patterns of fixed or variable intervals or of fixed or variable ratios. The general finding is that although continuous reinforcement produces faster learning, optimal schedules of intermittent reinforcement produce higher and more stable rates of responding.

The intermittency effect has been established in situations requiring repetition of the same response which is reinforced only part of the time. Strictly comparable schedules of intermittent feedback cannot be studied for at least two reasons. One is that the normal individual always has some feedback from his movements—proprioceptive if not exteroceptive. Another reason is that human behavior rarely consists of a repetitive series of discrete responses. However, in some skill situations, such as tracking, operators sometimes must perform with an intermittent feedback display. In such a situation there is no possibility of increasing the stability of response, as is done with intermittent reinforcement. The operator can tolerate some minor degree of intermittency but cutting out too much of the feedback pattern inevitably degrades his performance.

Extinction Functions

Experimental extinction of a learned response by withdrawing the reinforcement presumably is a well-defined phenomenon of reinforcement learning. Extinction of classical conditioned reflexes and of learned operants has been demonstrated quite clearly by many investigators. Comparable functions related to the withdrawal of sensory feedback cannot be demonstrated. If the controlling feedback pattern is withdrawn there is an immediate and abrupt deterioration of behavior control. Under some circumstances, subsequent behavior may show improvement as the individual establishes new patterns of control, but there is no gradual decline similar to the extinction function. Sensory feedback clearly cannot be considered equivalent to reinforcement if judged in terms of withdrawal effects.

It should be noted that the concept of extinction is scarcely applicable to human behavior, for a regular extinction function cannot be demonstrated in human subjects except in relation to such restricted learned behavior as conditioned galvanic skin responses over which the individual has minimal control. In studies of so-called satiation, subjects repeatedly drew a pair of lines or read a short poem over and over for hours without being reinforced (Karsten, 1928). In time, performance was marked by variability, decreased quality,

and in some cases, emotional reactions or nearly complete blocking of activity, but a new instruction by the experimenter initiated another spurt of well-organized activity. These satiation effects, which are similar to the type of response decrement observed in vigilance tasks, do not appear to be equivalent to experimental extinction produced by the withdrawal of reinforcement. Activities which are less restrictive or less monotonous can be continued for equally long periods of time with less noticeable decrement.

On the other hand, a human response made specifically to secure an extraneous reward is not likely to show a gradual decline in strength if the reward is not forthcoming. For example, a child accustomed to going to the cookie jar immediately after coming home from school would not show a gradual extinction function if the cookie jar were empty. He would more likely look for a snack elsewhere rather than indulge in a series of useless "operants" (openings of the cookie jar) at a declining rate.

In our opinion, decrements in human performance must be analyzed not in relation to the occurrence of reinforcement but in relation to the level of control which the individual can maintain over the situation. *Satiation* decrement is more marked in restrictive tasks where perceptual-motor control is degraded by the limited change in feedback patterns. More varied performances are slower to show such decrement. On the other hand, a human individual whose activity is directed toward a specific incentive is likely to vary his responses if the first one does not secure the reward. Only in situations where he has little or no control—where he does not understand the situation or has no alternative choices open to him—will he continue to repeat a useless response in gradually declining strength. It is significant that the most regular extinction curves are obtained from animals which are restricted in harnesses or enclosed in boxes where there is little else to do except to give the learned response. It also is significant that certain learned human responses, such as nervous tics or repetitive doodling, are performed day after day and year after year without reinforcement and without decrement. Such activities seem to be divorced almost completely from the individual's organized patterns of control.

Role of Motivation

In reinforcement learning, the reinforcement always bears some direct relationship to a drive or motivating state. In animal studies, the reinforcing value of food is assured by making the animal hungry, and the reinforcing value of water is assured by depriving the animal of an opportunity to drink for a period of time. Although most learning situations, especially in human behavior, do not involve such clear-cut deprivation conditions, the reinforcement model dictates the assumption of a motivating state. A drive or motive must be activating the organism if a specific reinforcement contingency is to prove reinforcing. Widespread acceptance of this view of learning has generated a remarkable proliferation of motives and drives—including exploratory and curiosity motives, perceptual motives, and many kinds of social motives—for the purpose of accounting for learning change in terms of reinforcement contingencies.

In cybernetic control, the sensory-feedback signals are related not to a postulated drive state but to the somatic behavior itself. Inasmuch as feedback occurs as an outcome of movement or response, the stimulus patterns in feedback control bear some appropriate or integrative relationship to the movements that produce them. The temporal relationship between movement and feedback is rigidly determined by the intrinsic processes involved, and there are well defined spatial, kinetic, and time-sampled relationships between the feedback stimuli and their generating movements.

The difference we are pointing out here is of utmost significance for our feedback theory of behavior organization. Reinforcement control of learning implies the primacy of physiological drives in behavior organization. If an exploratory or perceptual drive is postulated, it is assumed to represent a basic need of the organism (possibly a need of the brain! [Nissen, 1954]) that can be satisfied by an appropriate reinforcement. Secondary or learned drives are assumed to be derived from basic drives and thus of necessity are consistent with the concept of homeostatic control.

Our own theory rejects both the concept of homeostasis and the primacy of physiological drives as explanatory principles of human behavior organization. As we have said, we describe behavior as homeokinetic rather than as homeostatic because the individual is a self-generating feedback system whose normal state is activity, not equilibrium. Furthermore, we believe that the primary directional and orientational patterns which define the nature of human motivation are derived from the feedback regulated action systems as they develop through maturation and learning. The needs of the body impose certain modifications on perceptual-motor behavior, but they are not the primary generators of that activity. The response system is designed so as to activate itself, and thus the primary motivational or energizing source can be ascribed to the mechanisms of perceptual-motor control.

Role of Perception

Concepts of cybernetic control effectively integrate for the first time the areas of sensory psychophysiology, perception, and learning, which heretofore have gone their separate ways with little interchange. A learning science based on the law of effect or reinforcement derives little or no benefit from specialized knowledge about vision, hearing, and the other sensory modes, and ascribes no particular significance to these areas. In contrast, a learning science based on concepts of feedback control assigns paramount importance to the sensorimotor capabilities of the individual. Feedback research looks for the definitive conditions of learning change in the phenomena of sensory control of motion rather than in the poorly defined events of extrinsic reinforcement. Information about the functional properties of receptor systems as well as an understanding of the mechanisms of feedback regulation of motion are basic to cybernetic studies of learning.

In our opinion, feedback theory provides a more meaningful approach to the old problems of selectivity and attention than has been possible in reinforcement theory. Recent interest among learning psychologists in curiosity, exploration,

investigation, manipulation, and other spontaneous perceptual and intellectual activities has led to a number of efforts to account for them within the conventional learning framework. The phenomena to be accounted for are not restricted to human behavior but have been established in animal behavior as well. Organisms do not respond to every stimulus in the sensory environment but select or pay attention to specific configurations, particularly novel stimuli.

Berlyne (1960) has suggested that stimulus selection can be brought within a drive-reduction theory of learning. He assumed that the nervous system relates a novel stimulus to familiar stimulus categories by generalization, but conflict is induced because a novel stimulus arouses more than one response tendency. Exploratory or investigatory behavior provides the organism with more information about the novel stimulus and reduces conflict by enabling the selection of an appropriate response. Thus, although the organism appears to be seeking increased stimulation or arousal, it is doing so in order to obtain relief from arousal in reduced conflict. This interpretation is well within Hullian drive-reduction theory.

Glanzer (1958) proposed that new stimuli are sought out because organisms are information processing systems that require a certain amount of information per unit time. Differences in optimal requirements are related to the age of the individual and his past experiences. This analysis implies, as did Berlyne's, that exploration is due to an undifferentiated drive state. Glanzer also postulated that satiation with novel stimuli results when continued observation or attention builds up a quantity of stimulus satiation which reduces responsiveness but which dissipates in the absence of the stimuli.

This idea of stimulus satiation is very similar to concepts of neural inhibition which have been used both by psychologists and physiologists to explain various phenomena of differential sensitivity and response strength. Mechanisms of inhibition have been used to explain the dominance of one response over another and the blocking of one sensory source by another. Examples of differential sensitivity can be found in the recognition of one part of the body rather than another in coordinate activities. For example, when the fingers are placed on the nose, the common impression is that the fingers are feeling the nose—not that the nose is feeling the fingers. In walking, the impact of the foot with the substrate is felt on the foot but not usually in the ankles, knees, or hips. When one writes with a pencil, the visual trace pattern is observed while tactual and kinesthetic effects in the hand and arm go unnoticed. In playing a musical instrument, the musician tends to hear the music rather than attending to the contacts that his fingers are making with the instrument.

Can we discover any general principle that will apply both to these common examples of differential sensitivity and to the more complicated phenomena of exploration and investigation of novel stimuli? In all cases, we are dealing with a selective aspect of behavior in which the individual attends to a restricted number of stimulus patterns out of all possible stimuli impinging upon his sensory surfaces. Postulating a drive state that motivates investigatory responses does not explain why the fingers feel the nose instead of the nose feeling the fingers or why the musician hears the sounds of the instrument instead of feeling the keys. Selection, attention, and differential sensitivity involve more than an undifferentiated drive to reduce perceptual or intellectual conflict or to provide an optimal level of information.

If we think of the individual as a cybernetic control system, we get some new clues bearing on the significance of stimulus selection. A directionally guided compound control system, such as the human body, integrates sensory input from a number of sources in order to maintain precise multidimensional control of response in relation to the sensory environment. This pattern must involve a gradation of sensitivity, with the individual most sensitive to or most aware of the feedback stimuli from the focal application of control. Thus, we conceptualize a situation in which sensitivity to different stimulus sources and precision of different movements are graded from focal activities to supportive postural activities. Paying attention to one set of stimuli does not mean that other sensory channels are inhibited but that they are relatively less definitive in the particular control pattern in progress.

One implication of these ideas is that the individual typically *selects* or pays attention to those stimuli which are being used to control the most precise component of motion—as a rule the manipulative component. Thus, the fingers feel the nose because they can manipulate the nose, and not vice versa. The feet rather than the ankles feel the impact on the walking surface because the feet make the fine adjustments to that surface. The musician listens to the music rather than feeling the keys because he controls his

actions focally in terms of auditory effects. Of course, it is possible for him to
focus his attention on the feel of his
fingers on the instrument—what this
shift of attention involves neurophysio-
logically we cannot specify—but by
changing the focus of control, he may
introduce modifications into the resulting pattern of motion.

The investigation of novel stimuli also
can be described in terms of the establishment of control. A familiar situation
is responded to almost automatically, as
an overlearned skill can be performed
without close attention. A new situation
or a new skill can be understood or controlled only after a certain amount of
practice in which the new focal activities
are integrated with background reference movements, or in which the new
information is related to prior knowledge.

It appears likely that many of the
phenomena of graduated action and sensitivity in common learned performances
reflect an intrinsic differentiation of sensorimotor processes. The exteroceptor
systems with their extensive and refined
articulation of motor control generally
are more prominent in focal activities,
while the somewhat less precise tactual
and kinesthetic sources of feedback control are perceived as background effects.
Differences in refinement of sensorimotor interaction are reflected in the relative size of different sensory projection
areas of the cerebral cortex, which vary
in different animals not according to the
relative size of the receptors themselves
but according to the degree of dynamic
refined motor control associated with the
particular receptor systems. It is very
likely that the common phenomena related to differential sensitivity in patterned motion are determined largely by
such built-in differences in the sensory-
feedback mechanisms of the body.

Transformations of Control

Any theory of behavior organization
should be able to conceptualize the orderly progression from the relatively
simple overt response patterns seen in
animals and very young children to the
complicated skills, symbolic responses,
and abstract thought that develop in all
normal human individuals. In sensory-
feedback theory, these orderly processes
of human specialization can be analyzed
in terms of systematic transformations
of sensory-feedback patterns.

Unaided movements of the body generate feedback stimuli with spatial, temporal, and kinetic properties that are
more or less equivalent to those of the
generating movements. When a tool is
used, however, the pattern of stimuli
generated by a movement may have
quite different physical properties from
those of the movement itself, but they
still maintain a systematic geometric,
temporal, and kinetic relationship with
the movement pattern. When compound
machines are used, the transformation
between the actual control reactions of
the operator and the stimulus patterns
generated by action of the machine may
be extremely complex. However, the
feedback stimuli still bear an entirely
systematic relationship to the movements
that produced them. In some cases, the
solution of complicated design problems
in human engineering hinges on an understanding of the systematic principles
of feedback transformation that apply
to the machine operations in question.

The shift from direct behavior to symbolic behavior involves not only trans-

formation of feedback patterns but the substitution of one type of movement for another to effect control. The main function of human communication is to permit control of physical and social events by means of indirect symbolic responses substituted for direct action.

Some of the simpler forms of non-verbal symbolism involve movements that represent direct transformations of the more direct control movements in that they possess some physical relationship to the direct response. For example, many gestures abstract some features of the spatial-temporal pattern of a direct action and are used in communication to achieve somewhat the same effect that the direct action would have achieved. Also, graphic drawings are systematically related to real situations and can be used to extend behavioral control in time and in space. Consequently, in drawing pictures or in preparing maps or blueprints, the feedback-control patterns represent systematic transformations of the patterns that would be used in more direct reactions to the situations represented.

The essential characteristic of formal symbolism is that it involves the substitution of one kind of movement for others when the symbolic responses bear no systematic physical relationship to the direct responses that they represent. Thus, the words of oral and written speech and the symbols of oral and written mathematics represent motion systems which can be used to control objects, people, and events but which are related arbitrarily to the direct control motions that might be used equivalently. However, once these formal symbol systems are learned, the symbolic patterns themselves can be transformed in vari-

ous systematic ways to extend the possibilities of control far beyond the scope of direct action. Thus, once numbers are learned, they can be added or subtracted or transformed in other ways to describe and control many features of many situations. Spoken and written speech function in a similar way to permit individual or social control by means of systematic transformational reduction, elaboration, conversion, and translation of the feedback relationships between responses and the perceptual properties of environmental situations. Symbolic control patterns can be checked for accuracy in two ways: against the logical rules and relationships that govern the use of formal symbol systems; and in terms of their utility as applied in actual situations.

The unlimited capacity of human responses to generate systematic transformations of feedback control provides the objective basis for human specialization of behavior and learning. In contrast, reinforcement learning theory proposes that each individual in turn must acquire the complicated skills and the systematic knowledge that are characteristic of all members of his culture according to the effects of a series of more or less fortuitous reinforcement contingencies. It strains the credulity to be told that all learning depends not only on the action of specific reinforcements but on the activation of the individual by relatively undifferentiated drive states which will assure the reinforcing quality of the reinforcements. There is nothing in this theory that would assure the systematic nature of human skills and human knowledge as they actually are learned.

In view of this theoretical inadequacy,

it is no wonder that reinforcement theorists have tried to incorporate more systematic concepts from other areas of research into their overly parsimonious model. Knowledge of results or knowledge of accuracy is known to enhance learning, so it is labeled "reinforcement." Even the specialized phenomena of sensory feedback are called "reinforcement." But applying this label does not clarify the nature of the feedback process or advance our understanding of the determinants of learning change in feedback control patterns.

Categories of Learning

The general inadequacy of reinforcement theory, as of all conventional association theories, is revealed by the many efforts of learning psychologists to classify or categorize types of learning (Melton, 1964). The so-called general theories attempt to identify one or two factors which presumably account for all instances of learning, but in practice it is found necessary to go beyond such general determinants as temporal contiguity and reinforcement and to distinguish among various categories of learning—for example, classical conditioning, operant conditioning, instrumental conditioning, instrumental reward training, orientation learning, incidental learning, psychomotor learning, probability learning, verbal learning, concept formation, and problem solving. In contemporary learning psychology, the problem of classifying categories and of analyzing their differences is of more general interest than the contiguity-reinforcement issue itself.

The interesting thing about the recurring efforts of learning investigators to identify categories is that the concepts upon which such taxonomic exercises are based are not derived from the general theories. Associationism of whatever variety assumes the generality of one or two learning factors in all forms of animal and human learning and makes no provision for different types or categories. In order to identify and label distinctive types, investigators refer to differences in the way responses control stimuli or are subject to intrinsic control by stimuli. This appears to be an implicit denial of the general validity of association models and recognition of the importance of human design factors in determining learning change.

In the cybernetic approach to learning, the so-called different types or categories are thought to reflect differences in patterns of feedback control. This approach recognizes no distinctive categories except in a general descriptive sense, for learning is assumed to vary quantitatively as a function of the variable properties, the integrative pattern, and the modes of transformation of the controlling feedback processes. Verbal learning differs from instrumental learning because the systematic transformations of closed-loop regulation of behavior are different in these two sectors. Instrumental learning differs from unaided psychomotor learning because the use of tools and machines involves spatial, temporal, and kinetic transformations of feedback which change the pattern of control. Psychomotor learning is different from orientation learning because the former incorporates the feedback mechanisms of manipulative movements whereas the latter involves integrating the larger transport and postural movements of the body into a more general pattern of control. And orientation learning is different from so-called classical conditioning because the animal or human subject in the latter case is restrained and deprived of much of the varied sensory feedback utilized in normal adaptive response. In such a situation, normal orientation responses are of necessity minimized while the subject learns a limited reaction to the CS. However, it is known that the specific CRs are not independent entities, but are incidental to more generalized bodily reactions.

The real hope of cybernetic research on learning is to provide a framework for understanding and studying all varieties of learning change. The behaving system conforms to the same basic principles of cybernetic control in all its diverse modes of adaptation.

SUMMARY

1. Wartime training research generated procedures of task analysis, renewed interest in the nature of psychomotor skills, contributed to the development of cybernetic concepts, suggested important modifications for behavior theory, and influenced training practices in many areas.

2. There have been a number of attempts in military research programs to systematize the planning procedures in training and operational research. Some of these have classified training objectives or functions, characteristics of effective training media, and the training media themselves. These schemes for planning training programs and analyzing performances are hampered by the lack of a generally accepted means of specifying the critical features of behavior patterns.

3. The general validity of training prediction is low, for it is difficult to

sample skills that will determine final performance. Final proficiency cannot usually be predicted from initial training scores.

4. Fleishman's factor analysis of skills has revealed a number of fairly specific factors that contribute to individual differences and variability in skilled performances. Usually there is one or more within-task factor. The factor pattern of a skill typically changes with practice.

5. Using survey and other data, Fitts described skill learning as involving phases of cognition, fixation, and automation. He stressed the importance of identifying subroutines and of extended practice to make skills autonomous.

6. Experimental motion analysis has supported a tridimensional analysis of skills into three basic movement components: posture, transport, and manipulation. This scheme can be related meaningfully to the structural and functional differentiation of the nervous system and to the different sources of sensory control. It is useful in describing the development of behavior in phylogeny and ontogeny. Movement components can be timed separately by electronic motion analyzers and provide a meaningful framework for analyzing the spatial organization of motion.

7. Skilled motions also vary in coherence, continuity, frequency, and complexity. The continuity continuum from discrete to continuously controlled movements encompasses the distinction between pursuit and saccadic or between tense and ballistic movements.

8. Wiener's cybernetic analogy describes the individual as a closed-loop feedback-control system.

9. Dynamic sensory feedback refers to movement-generated stimuli that provide an intrinsic means of regulating

motion in relation to the environment. Knowledge of results given after a response is a static aftereffect which may give information about accuracy but does not provide dynamic regulating stimuli. Dynamic feedback indication of error is more effective in performance and learning than static knowledge of results.

10. Feedback and reinforcement differ in the objectivity with which they can be defined and in the generality of their meaning in behavior theory. Feedback can be defined and varied in precise physical terms and provides a regulatory mechanism for all patterned behavior. Reinforcement is defined only in terms of observed learning change and has meaning only for instances of reinforcement-controlled learning.

11. Feedback concepts permit clarification of the meaning of stimulus-response interactions in behavior. The concept of the individual as a feedback-generating system whose normal state is activity is contrary to the idea of homeostatic control assumed by reinforcement theory.

12. Feedback control operates on the basis of spatial detection of stimulus differences and thus implies a primary spatial organization of behavior. Reinforcement theory assumes that responses are linked in temporal series in learning.

13. Delaying reinforcement up to an interval of many minutes causes a gradual decline of response strength. Delaying sensory feedback by even a small fraction of a second causes severe disturbances in behavior organization with little or no recovery.

14. The intermittency functions and extinction functions demonstrated in reinforcement learning have no counterpart in feedback control. Intermittent feedback and withheld feedback cause immediate degradation of performance.

15. The efficacy of reinforcement is assumed to depend on an active need or drive state. Feedback theory assumes that the organism is built as an action system and thus energizes itself. Body needs are satisfied by behavior that is structured primarily according to perceptual-motor organizational mechanisms.

16. Feedback theory assigns primary status to research in sensory psychology and perception, whereas these areas are of peripheral interest in reinforcement theory. Selectivity of stimuli and responses can be conceptualized as involving graduated sensitivity and precision of response from the focal area of control to the background supportive movements. Graduated precision of action and sensitivity in the different sensorimotor systems of the body reflect an intrinsic differentiation in the neural centers.

17. The orderly progression of behavior patterning from relatively simple overt responses to complex overt and symbolic skills is accounted for in feedback theory by systematic transformations of sensory-feedback patterns effected by the use of tools, machines, and symbol systems. In contrast, reinforcement theory describes all learning as due to the effects of reinforcements that bear no systematic relation to the different kinds of behavior learned.

18. Whereas general association theories of learning do not adequately conceptualize the various categories described by learning psychologists, feedback theory proposes that all varieties of learning reflect differences in properties, patterns, and transformations of feedback control processes.

CHAPTER

9

Contemporary
Training Issues

The concepts of feedback control, which were discussed in the previous chapter, represent a positive approach to training problems in all areas of society. Our main premise that individuals are self-regulating control systems implies that training programs, training devices, and instructional techniques should be evaluated in terms of their effectiveness in enhancing organized patterns of control. This cybernetic approach emphasizes the *intrinsic* organizational factors that define the nature of performance and the course of learning, whereas the standard learning theory approach considers drive states and reinforcements— factors *extrinsic* to the behavior patterns being learned—of paramount importance.

Many areas of training, especially those concerned with rehabilitation of persons afflicted with physical or emotional behavior disorders, are dominated by the clinical techniques of psychotherapy. In spite of their diverse origins, this approach has come to be allied very closely with the reinforcement theories

of experimental psychology, for the main idea underlying psychotherapy is that rehabilitation or retraining involves reduction of such extrinsic emotional states as anxiety.

It is our belief that neither reinforcement theory nor clinical psychology deals adequately with training problems because they focus on relatively undifferentiated factors external to the behavior which is to be trained. What success psychologists have had in devising training techniques and training programs has come for the most part when they have dealt with the intrinsic organization of the behavior itself. It is our purpose in this chapter to show that successful training techniques can be interpreted in terms of the principles of cybernetic design.

INDUSTRIAL TRAINING

Industrial training has grown to be a giant enterprise involving millions of workers and billions of dollars annually. For example, a survey of New Jersey industries reported in 1962 disclosed that out of a work force of 728,531 in 37,546 companies, 11.3 percent were employed by 6099 companies that sponsored training (Basic Systems, Incorporated, 1962). Of these, 82,740 workers were participating in 15,873 separate training programs for an average of only five trainees per program.

Industrial training techniques always have emphasized the visual factor in the well-illustrated teaching manual, the training chart, demonstrations, displays, television, and so on. It has been estimated that 2.8 billion dollars are spent annually on manuals alone (Basic Systems, Incorporated, 1962). Hence, our previous comments about the value of integrating nonverbal and verbal processes in audiovisual instruction are supported implicitly by industrial training practices.

In all of industry's extensive training efforts, however, there is little recourse to objective research. Training methods continue to represent conglomerations of past conventions, new military and educational fads, managerial and economic propaganda, and some of the newer wrinkles of social-clinical psychology and its group pressure techniques. In view of the billions of dollars spent annually on industrial training, it is surprising that there is so little concern about validating its techniques and establishing their theoretical foundations.

In our opinion, the central problem of industrial training is that its techniques are geared almost invariably to the needs of the company rather than to the needs of the worker. It is assumed that satisfactory performances will be maintained if appropriate incentives are offered and if the proper attitudes and job satisfactions can be established. An alternative approach is to emphasize the feedback regulation of behavior as the central factor in learning and to design the training situation to enhance the worker's ability to control his own patterns of response. Rather than manipulating the worker, this approach helps him to become a manipulator of his own job situation. There are reasons to believe that such a shift in emphasis is not a utopian ideal but can be justified on sound utilitarian grounds.

Two Approaches to Worker Training

We are going to contrast the two approaches to industrial training by describing two experiments: one utilizing the traditional pressure and constraint approach that tries to improve performance by promising wage and efficiency rewards; and the other emphasizing the principles of self-regulation and feedback control in learning and performance.

A training research project that was awarded special recognition in Britain illustrates techniques of developing and evaluating a reward-oriented training program. The project was carried out by Yates (1959) in a factory where women workers were employed to hand-assemble high-grade cardboard boxes in an endless variety of styles. Because of the great variation in tasks, new workers learned their skills very slowly and the over-all work rates were very low.

The project described here attempted to develop training techniques which would speed up training and increase production. The most important techniques used in the shop were selected and arranged in order of difficulty for a course of graded training exercises. The most suitable work methods, as determined by motion study, were taught the trainees and speed of production was emphasized from the start. Trainees were to learn how to construct ten different boxes to meet the firm's quality standards. When the criterion was met on one box, the trainee was given a monetary prize and passed on to the next box. With these methods, the training period was reduced to less than twenty weeks, in which time the trainees reached a proficiency level that formerly had been achieved only after one and a half to two and a half years.

However, there were other sides to the story. Out of every four girls starting the course, only one completed it and transferred to productive work. Further, those trainees who were successful could not maintain their performance standards in the shop and dropped back to around fifty percent proficiency, which was lower than the shop average. The speed-up pressure and incentives used in training brought the successful trainees up to a high standard very rapidly, but their performance standards were not maintained in work. Similar results are fairly common when workers trained outside a shop are transferred into a regular work group.

In our opinion, the failures of this project can be attributed to the fact that the workers were not self-regulating systems either during training or during work. The pressures and imposed work standards of training could not be adapted to at all by most of the starters. Those who adjusted to this situation and attained a high level of proficiency in training found quite a different set of outside pressures in work—those im-

posed by the older workers. Over the years the workers had developed their own ideas about how long it took to learn box-making, and how high a level of performance could be maintained year in and year out. The speed-up imposed on the trainees did not survive the pressures of the work group itself.

An experiment in factory training described by King (1962) was designed according to cybernetic principles such as those described in this book. King described the conventional organization of a production department as a "split system," in which the workers perform as the activity component while the supervisor acts as the control component. Such a system is diagrammed in Figure 9.1a. When trainees who have learned some self-regulation of activity in their training program enter such a loosely organized split system, their production drops, particularly if the relationship between workers and supervisor is unsatisfactory so that the exchange of information is hampered. The alternative design diagrammed in Figure 9.1b permits the worker to control his own activity within agreed limits while the supervisor, freed from detailed control tasks, has time for long-range planning and control. In this set-up, both worker and supervisor are self-regulating systems which interact to achieve more efficient production than in the split-system design.

Evidence that this second design for production control actually is more efficient came from an experiment on work reorganization in sewing tasks in a textile plant. Operators were retrained according to cybernetic principles which aimed at increasing their control over their own activities. These six specific

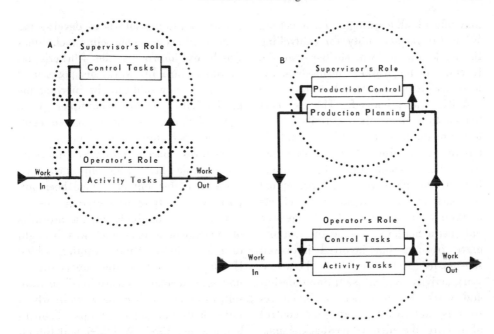

Figure 9.1.   Two organizational patterns in production shops. *a*. Conventional
organization showing the separation of *control* and *activity* functions between supervisor and operator. *b*. Cybernetically designed organization in which supervisor and
operator are interacting self-regulating systems. (Based on King. The operator
as a self-regulating system (A factory experiment). *Ergonomics*, 1962, **5**, 467–470.)

principles of training design were followed:

1. *built-in* instructions—that is, instructions implicit in the task

2. *built-in* feedback to permit correction of errors

3. considering the worker as a limited capacity system which should not
be overloaded at any level of learning

4. providing for choice of appropriate methods by the worker

5. regarding the instructor as a resource person who could be approached
for help and advice in a blame-free atmosphere

6. maintaining high performance
standards for periods of repetitive work

These principles were applied in a
training situation which was designed so

that the workers themselves participated
in reorganizing the work methods and in
establishing time and quality standards.
After the first six operators had completed their retraining, they were given
the opportunity to transfer their new
work organization and self-regulation of
activity to the shop. Agreements were
reached with management and the shop
foreman to permit these workers to design their own work layout and to agree
on fatigue and contingency allowances.
After an initial period of some confusion caused by the shift in decision-
making powers, new lines of control
became established and production increased.

This study illustrates how shifting the
pattern of control in training and work

may affect both learning and production. When the responsibility for controlling the work situation was shifted from the foreman to the workers themselves, the feedback regulation of the productive activity was changed. The workers tended to regulate their activity not in terms of the foreman's attitudes and behavior or in terms of the relation between the foreman and other workers but on the basis of direct perceptual feedback informing them of the effects of their own behavior. The change was not just a matter of giving the workers more freedom but involved improved sensory-feedback effects from the actual work activity. As long as training design and work design impose artificial restraints and direct supervisory control of activity, the effective feedback signals are displaced from the work activity itself to the actions of the supervisor. It is more satisfying as well as more efficient for the worker to regulate his productive activity directly.

Management Attitude Training

Industrial training at the executive level presents many different problems. Management personnel are expected not only to be well informed and up-to-date in technical matters but also to be well versed in company policies, to be able to make decisions, and to present the façade of a well adjusted personality.

The widely publicized Hawthorne experiments at the Western Electric Company in the 1930s established the fact that the attitudes and social relationships of workers in a plant may have more influence on their productivity than such factors as work schedules and environmental conditions (Roethlisberger and Dickson, 1939). This compelling idea

led to continuing efforts to develop human relations and counseling techniques which by improving the worker's attitudes toward his work, his peers, and his superiors would thereby increase his productivity. These techniques have been of particular importance to management personnel, for in many cases procedures based on psychotherapy, such as role playing, not only have been made available but also have been imposed willy-nilly on executive groups.

Interest in manipulating the attitudes of management personnel was brought to a focus in sensitivity training, which is supposed to help the supervisor or manager develop "sensitivities" to himself, to others, and to the ways in which individuals interact in groups (Tannenbaum et al., 1954; Weschler and Reisel, 1958). He is supposed to become aware of how he is influencing group effectiveness and whether he is a help or a hindrance.

In sensitivity training, the difficulties of the insecure executives are overcome by vertically structuring management groups in discussing emotional problems with the help of a clinical psychologist. This means that managers engage in a kind of open confessional of their attitudes toward others in a situation in which the management pecking order not only is retained but also is reinforced by the clinical technique. The clinical psychologist in attendance asks questions about group members' "liking-ness" of partners, and of their jobs and activities. The high-level executives taking part may be taught psychotherapeutic and nondirective counseling techniques which they can use thereafter to handle problems of their subordinates. Promotive literature claims that sensitivity training facilities "organizational harmony," "unblocking of communication," and "participant observation."

The techniques of sensitivity training are thought to conform to the reinforcement learning model. Four levels of reinforcement are thought to be possible. In order of significance, these are information or knowledge at the lowest level, then cognition or problem solving, attitudinal reinforcement, and organizational reinforcement at the highest level. It is believed that achieving the goals of proper attitude and organization are at higher levels than achieving knowledge or being able to apply knowledge in solving problems. A manager may show satisfactory progress in learning information and in solving problems but reach a plateau in learning proper attitudes and how to get along in the organization. Further progress to these allegedly higher levels of reinforcement may come about through sensitivity training or—if this fails—through psychotherapy.

Although there is no body of objective data by means of which to evaluate the attitude training techniques in industry, the rapidity with which the different fads have come into favor indicates that no one technique has had lasting success. The whole rationale of attitude training with respect to group performance has been questioned by Glanzer (1962) who suggested that the proficiency of a work team may determine its morale instead of the other way around. There is occasional evidence that participating in discussions about the nature of one's own behavior in groups may increase self-insight (Smith and Kight, 1959), and further, that self-insight in foremen is related to

the productivity of their departments (Nagle, 1954). However, there is no direct evidence that current techniques of attitude training are the most effective ways either to establish favorable attitudes or to develop understanding or to increase productivity.

Computerized Business Games

One of the most recent fads in management training is the use of computerized *business games* to give managers experience in making specific decisions about running a business. These simulation games are set up as a competitive exercise between two or more management teams and the computer, which has been given some undisclosed instructions about how to use accounting and cost figures to derive answers to business problems. The students are given a current financial report and then must decide how to spend funds for expansion, research, advertising, and so on. The decisions of each management team are then fed into the computer, which analyzes the economic end-effects of each decision and computes a score for the team.

Plattner and Herron (1962) described a "Top Management Decision Simulation" which simulates an entire business enterprise and places emphasis on decision making at the top executive level. The computer is programed in terms of an arbitrarily defined enterprise model, and the decision making of a given team is scored by being compared with the "true" or reference decisions of the computer which are based on cost and accounting considerations and do not deal with human, industrial relations, or social value issues. Each team's score is printed out as a financial statement. Another pattern of simulation, described as "Management Trial Exercise," incorporates community relations, manpower planning, and employee relations problems, such as leaves, terminations, and absences, into the games.

Plattner and Herron listed these advantages of computer games: they condense extensive decision-making experience into short periods of time; they give an integrative knowledge of overall business decision making; they emphasize the need of reaching decisions with the incomplete data at hand; they give role-playing experience; they make possible playback of training activities; and they induce feelings of participation. Other opinions are that they are rigid and artificial and promote over-simplified ways of thinking about complex problems.

There is no objective evidence that executive training based on rigid, conventional economic models does in fact improve a man's career potential. There are reasons for wondering whether such training might hurt more than it helps. In the absence of research validation of the computerized games, we feel that several questions are in order.

1. Assuming that the programing concepts are valid, do the business games deal with critical decisions, or are the executives being trained in routine problems that can be handled better by the computer itself?

2. Are meaningful value systems being used to program the games in the first place?

3. Do the games teach self-determined modes of decision making or do they force the trainees' thinking into conventional, pre-established economic patterns?

4. Does the computer simulation provide critical feedback effects of decision making which can be used by the trainee to regulate future performance?

To us, the last question is the most significant. We believe that these games provide only the most general knowledge of success or failure in the final score and no real differential feedback to the decision maker, inasmuch as those who plan the game do not disclose the detailed structure of their arbitrary value system. The computer score in itself does not provide enough information to assess the quality of a decision. These games do give executives some experience in computer technology and in conventional ways of handling problems, but they give no training in handling new problems or in handling old problems in new ways. If creative thinking is called for, the bases of the decisions cannot be programed. It seems ironical to use computers to train men in the routine type of decision making which inevitably will be automated.

RESEARCH ON GROUP PERFORMANCE AND LEARNING

The techniques of management training attempt to enhance the effectiveness of a group or team engaged in a common enterprise. Relevant to this effort are studies exploring the relationships between group organization and learning or training.

Leadership Structure and Performance

The early study of Lewin et al. (1939) and Lippitt and White (1952) compared the behavior and effectiveness of voluntary boys' clubs under varied types of leadership—authoritarian, democratic, and laissez-faire. Young men were trained in the three styles of leadership and then shifted from one to another as they rotated among the boys' clubs. It was found that the coercive procedures of the authoritarian clubs maintained a high level of production while the leader was present, but when he left, the boys stopped working. These boys were dissatisfied with their club; some of them became overly submissive and some became aggressive. Democratic leadership produced a happier atmosphere in which members worked even when the leader was gone. Laissez-faire groups were poorest both in production and in morale.

A variation of this study of leadership styles is to analyze how group participation in decision making affects morale and performance. The assumption is that group interaction in discussion followed by decision making is more effective in modifying attitudes and performance than authoritative or didactic techniques such as lectures. A study by Coch and French (1948) in an industrial setting provided supporting evidence. To initiate some changes in factory procedures, a control group of workers was taught the new methods. In the experimental groups, the workers or their representatives were permitted to discuss the changes and to participate in the decisions. Typical resistance to change was encountered in the control group but not among the participating groups. Furthermore, the participating groups increased their production after the changes while the control group did not. Lawrence and Smith (1955), however, questioned the interpretation that verbal discussion in itself caused the noted improvement. They designed an experiment which found that worker groups who jointly set production goals increased their production level significantly whereas groups who simply participated in discussions did not improve.

All of these studies and others indicate that in the long run it is advantageous for members of work groups to participate in planning the pattern of activity and control. However, this is not to say that all members of groups should have equivalent functions or that no leadership is necessary. On the contrary, effective group action depends on the differentiation of specialized roles, and such specialization develops readily even when it is not imposed on a group from without. For example, Bales (1955) showed how leadership and other roles emerge in discussion groups which are made up originally of equivalent members.

In free group situations, role differentiation depends primarily on the specialized abilities and personality features of individuals, but in more rigid situations, leadership may be imposed on a group or may develop as a result of certain organizational factors such as the access to information and channels of communication.

Communication Nets

One type of experiment on the relation of group organization to performance and learning studies the effects of different patterns of communication (Bavelas, 1948). The first studies described by Bavelas (1950) and Leavitt (1951) compared the problem-solving efficiency of five-member groups who could communicate with each other in different rigidly defined patterns. The subjects were isolated from each other by partitions, some of which contained slots which provided two-way communication channels. The four original patterns used were a circle, chain, wheel, and Y, as shown in Figure 9.2. Each of the five subjects was given specific information which would help solve a simple problem.

The original results showed a clear differentiation among the nets when judged for the speed with which they developed their organization and the satisfaction of the members. In decreasing order, the nets ranked wheel, Y, chain, and circle, that is, from the most centralized to the least centralized. They did not differ clearly in terms of speed of problem solving or learning rate, but the circle used more messages and made more errors. The centralized nets agreed that their leader was the central person who had to receive and transmit the most information.

The many studies of communication nets since those first reports have shown that the relationships are not as simple as they first appeared to be. In reviewing the literature, Glanzer and Glaser

Figure 9.2.   The communication nets or patterns used originally by Leavitt to study the effects of pattern on performance and learning: chain, wheel, Y, and circle. The circle used the most messages and the wheel used the fewest. (Based on Leavitt. Some effects of certain Communication patterns on group performance. *J. abnorm. soc. Psychol.*, 1951, **46**, 38–50.)

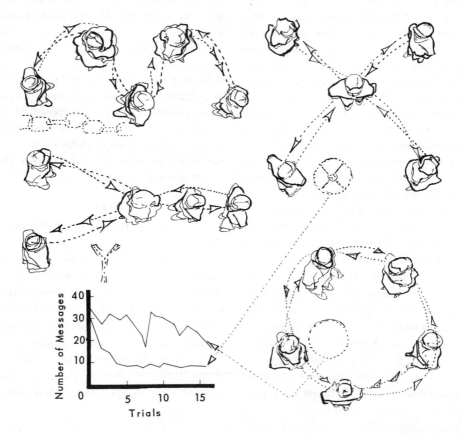

(1961) pointed out how introducing new variables or changing the original experimental design often changed the nature of the findings. The only general conclusion that can be drawn is that no one communication net is the best for all situations, for the relative efficiency depends on the characteristics of the task. Communication net research originally appeared to offer an objective technique for studying some of the complicated interactions in working groups, but the over-all results of analyzing these artificial nets are disappointing.

Research on Integrated Team Performance

The operations of work groups or teams require many different levels of organization and integration. To use athletic teams as examples, a swimming team represents essentially a collection of individual swimmers whereas a basketball team is a highly integrated group in which every member controls his actions according to the actions of the other members as well as those of the other team. An integrated team presents special training problems in that it must develop precise spatial and temporal patterns of action in order to function effectively. Recently there have been several attempts to lay the groundwork for training research on integrated teams.

On the basis of observations of several Navy teams in action, Glanzer (1962) noted that a team usually has indistinct boundaries, borderline members, overlapping membership with other teams, and relationships with larger patterns of organized control. A fairly large team may be made up of subsidiary functioning units, and its over-all structure may change markedly to meet the demands of different kinds of problems. It was difficult to summarize team interactions in any systematic manner, and the rate of interaction of a particular member was not related to his importance. In some cases, centralization of power was distinct from centralization of communication. The supervisor tended to stay aloof from the team's interactions until an error or difficulty occurred. However, a supervisor who could not see all of the team's activities might need a centralized communication pattern to keep track of everything. Glanzer suggested that the so-called democratic or decentralized structure is appropriate for an integrated team only when the entire system is visible to the responsible supervisor.

Glanzer found that team action even in busy teams usually reduced at any one time to the actions of about two individuals working in coordination. Thus he felt that most team training is unnecessary and that training time might better be spent training individuals to perform their specialized roles. However, he recognized the fact that there are cues for action in a team situation which may be impossible to identify and reproduce for individual training. Such cues might arise from specialized actions of other team members or from a series of events that prepares the individual for an eventual response.

In our opinion, the need for team training also depends on the degree of precision required in coordinate team actions. A symphony orchestra or an athletic team engaged in coordinate play needs continuous team training to perform effectively. Even when the pattern of activity is relatively simple and standardized, the required coordinate precision dictates the need for team training. The crew of a racing shell all perform the same standardized, repetitive movements, yet their effectiveness depends on training as a team.

What team training really amounts to—as Glanzer would agree—is training individuals to control their performances according to specialized feedback patterns, but in the case of integrated teams, some of the most significant controlling feedback effects are generated by the action of the team and cannot be reproduced in another setting. A recent experimental approach to the problems of team training is to analyze the effects of varying the kind of feedback provided to team members. Hall (1957) and Rosenberg and Hall (1958) required a number of two-man teams to perform simple tasks, such as turning a knob four turns. Each subject sat at a different desk with his own knob and received feedback regarding the number of turns. He might receive *direct* feedback from his own actions; he might receive *confounded* feedback, which was a function of his own and the other subject's responses; or he might receive only the feedback from the other's responses. As might be expected, direct feedback produced the best learning, but with confounded feedback, the two subjects were able to produce an accurate average score by learning a compensatory pattern in which one subject might turn his knob twice while the other turned his six times. No improvement occurred when they received only the other's feedback, but under this condition, the greatest role differentiation occurred. Without adequate feedback with which to control an effective performance, the subjects looked elsewhere

for guidance—to the interpersonal relationships that could be established.

Zajonc (1962) used a group reaction time apparatus to measure the success of groups and individuals under conditions of direct and confounded feedback. Ten seven-man groups were tested under each condition. He found that performance improved the most when the individuals received feedback concerning the performance of all members and of the group as a whole. Only slight improvement occurred with confounded feedback.

Cybernetic Approach to Group Training

Although much of the early work in group dynamics bore the imprint of Lewin's (1944) special orientation to psychological theory, the most prominent point of view in more recent research has been that of conventional reinforcement learning theory emphasizing social motives and the reinforcements available in group behavior. However, the high degree of specialization that can characterize group roles is extremely difficult to explain in terms of such relatively undifferentiated events as affiliation motives, anxiety reduction, and reinforcement.

It is more meaningful to think of the problems of group performance and learning in terms of feedback mechanisms. In this cybernetic approach, the group is conceptualized as an organized self-regulating system whose individual members represent specialized functions of feedback-controlled behavior. Group learning is viewed as being determined by the properties and conditions of organized feedback patterns which originate internally within the group activities or from sources external to the group. Such an approach to group behavior leads to more meaningful hypotheses and investigations than the conventional learning approach, for the significant variables in feedback control are highly articulated, can be defined objectively, and are subject to precise systematic control. In contrast, such variables as social motives, attitudes, likes and dislikes, and reinforcements are elusive concepts that can be identified and defined only in terms of events that already have occurred.

It appears to us curious and disturbing that those psychologists who are making the most original and promising attacks on group-learning phenomena investigate cybernetic variables but then turn around and identify themselves with the conventional reinforcement approach. Glanzer (1962), for example, equates feedback with reinforcement and assumes that any investigation of feedback control is within the area of reinforcement learning theory. As we pointed out in Chapter 8, feedback and reinforcement are incompatible concepts, and describing feedback control as a type of reinforcement learning only confuses the issue.

In our own cybernetic interpretation, the essential feature of group behavior is integrative interaction and coordination of individual response into more complex group behavior patterns that are controlled by internal and external feedback. Internal control is effected by verbal and nonverbal communication and by use of multimanned tools and machines. External feedback control relates the group to the social and physical evironment. Internal feedback regulates the internal organization of the group whereas external feedback regulates the group in relation to other groups and individuals and to the environment generally.

The cybernetic design of any given group depends on both the internal and external patterns of feedback control that define its operations. Some groups react almost completely in terms of internal feedback during particular operational sequences. A performing orchestra, for example, is sensitive to only unusual external events while playing. In industry, many subgroups at the production level operate for periods of time in terms of internal control, but management groups are oriented toward external feedback constantly. They must sell their product, maintain good relations with the union, project a good public image, and so on.

Internal and external feedback control of group activities is mediated by the specialized roles of different members, including leaders. One leadership function is to relate the critical instrumental or communicative activity of the group with the environment. The more diversified and complex the group's operations are, the greater the significance of this leadership function. In some highly specialized groups which exhibit precise internal feedback control, another leadership role is required. An orchestra, for example, needs a conductor, and a surgical team needs a head surgeon. This type of leader functions mainly to coordinate intergroup actions. Other specialization of action within a functioning group is defined by division of labor, by hierarchical structure of the different tasks, and by special instrumental and machine functions. The members of a work group or team vary not only in their specialized tasks, but also in their relative importance and responsibility to determine over-all group action. Training is needed to discover the potentialities of individuals at different levels of responsibility as well as to refine their specific activities. Training is needed also to establish coordinated patterns of action that enable the group to perform safely and to meet emergencies.

The dimensions of organization within a group—division of labor; stratification of roles and responsibility; verbal and nonverbal communication; integrative instrumental actions; and supervisory, headship, and leadership authority—are determined by the feedback parameters necessary to effect self-regulation both internally and externally. Patterns of group behavior are analogous to feedback regulation of behavior in the individual. Each specific role or task or operation achieves some phase of dynamic generation of directional action, some sensing and perceptual function, or some regulatory control of response in order to make the group operate as a unit. In complex groups, individual roles may represent limited aspects of over-all cybernetic control.

As in the case of individual behavior, the internal and external feedback effects that govern the behavior of a group may be delayed, spatially displayed, distorted, kinetically modulated, or transformed instrumentally or symbolically. In the course of group action, interaction, and information processing, many transformations of feedback control are inevitable. One function of group training is to identify feedback delays and distortions and to reduce perturbations of control to a minimum.

REHABILITATIVE TRAINING

There are many people in the world who for one reason or another never have learned or have lost the ability to exercise satisfactory control over their own behavior in relation to their physical or social milieu. These include individuals of all ages, of all levels of ability and education, and from all walks of life. They include the mental hospital patient, the retarded child, the child who cannot read, the neurologically injured, the delinquent, and the unemployed. These people represent many different problems and many different needs, but they have one thing in common—a failure in behavioral control so serious that it affects their whole life pattern.

The needs of handicapped individuals are very different, because their failures in control are at different levels of behavior organization. Whereas the spastic child's failure may be in basic movement coordinations, and the economically depressed worker's in the realm of complicated work skills, the neurotic individual's failure may be at the social level. On the other hand, an individual may be handicapped because his particular pattern of behavior skills does not fit his social or cultural context. Thus rehabilitative training to be effective should prepare the individual for a situation that really exists—for a job that actually is available, or a social context that is open to him.

In this section we shall consider some of the training techniques that have been used in different problem areas. We believe that some techniques conform more to conventional learning theory approaches, which consider extrinsic reinforcements and drive-reduction the prime requisites of training, while others focus on intrinsic feedback mechanisms of control. According to this latter cybernetic point of view, rehabilitative training should enable the individual to establish effective control at the level of his greatest need—at the level where he has failed.

Neuropsychological Handicaps

Many different kinds of neuropsychological disorders handicap individuals in making normal adjustments to social living. These include sensory, motor, and skill deficiencies arising either from disease or injury or from atypical or retarding conditions of development. Among the more severe limitations are those related to mental retardation and generalized neurological and neurohormonal diseases and injuries. More specific deficiencies include defects of vision and hearing and motor limitations from physical injury. Less precisely defined are developmental deficiencies in speech, reading, writing, and spelling.

Conventional learning concepts are applied to training in some of these areas—usually those in which the nature of the defect or injury cannot be identified precisely. In such specific deficiencies as blindness, deafness, and partial paralysis, concepts of learning by association, conditioning, or the effects of reinforcement are patently inappropriate. When an individual lacks normal sensorimotor mechanisms, one tries to find some means of providing him with differential feedback from his own responses by means of which he can learn to control them.

One of the best examples of establishing substitute feedback control can be found in training programs for the deaf. Completely deaf individuals can be taught to speak by using tactual and visual feedback. They feel the vibrations made by their own vocal cords, watch the speech movements of others, and can learn very precise vocal control by comparing visual records of their own speech sounds with records made by hearing individuals. Both in the use of visible speech by the deaf and tactual and sonic methods of control by the blind, the crucial factor involved is the establishment of feedback control. Similarly, a hemiplegic can be trained to walk in a fairly normal fashion if some substitute feedback signal is supplied to inform him of the action of his defective leg.

The situation is somewhat different with respect to such developmental problems as defective speech, reading, or writing. In cases where the source of the deficiency cannot be identified, training procedures usually have conformed to conventional learning theory as specialized along clinical-psychometric lines. The usual assumption is that the skill defect is due to some underlying emotional or anxiety factor which can be reduced by psychotherapy and tender loving care. Training programs of this sort have had limited success, and it is impossible to say whether their successes have been due to reinforcement controlled learning, the reduction of anxiety, or in fact to the establishment of effective patterns of control by systematic practice and drill.

Another approach to the treatment of such functional disorders in educational skills is to assume that they may involve gross deficiencies in perceptual-motor control that may have arisen earlier in development than the specific disorder being treated. There is evidence that inadequate control over postural coordinations, patterns of locomotion, limb transport movements, and bilateral coordination of bipedal and bimanual activities are important contributing factors—perhaps the most important—to serious deficiencies in speech, reading, and writing. Delacato (1963) has reported success in treating reading disorders by techniques that are designed to perfect basic body skills and to establish definite lateral dominance. These techniques are used as well to treat children with gross perceptual-motor disorders such as might result from birth injuries. The effect of such techniques is not only to repair developmental deficiencies in basic body movements and coordinations, but also to build the dynamic movement-generation resources of the individual for perceptual and movement control.

Our cybernetic view that perception is a dynamic space-structured activity dependent on intrinsic generation of both sensitizing and directional movements of receptor systems has certain definite implications for training. First, the individual must be developed, aided, and instructed as a self-governing sensory-feedback control system. Second, the capacity for control rests on dynamic generation of sensitizing and directionally integrated movements, which are governed by immediate feedback from both exteroceptive and proprioceptive sources. Third, organized control involves integration of posture and transport movements with articulated perceptual-motor activities. Fourth, the purpose of training is to establish or improve the coordinate space relationships between the sensory and motor systems for all levels of movement control and integration.

A final training principle is this: patterns of behavioral control are meaningful only insofar as they have social utility—insofar as they can be used to help the individual adjust to his particular social context. Retarded individuals, for example, not only need special training to help them master patterns of living and work skills within their range of abilities but also need to be located in a context where their limited behavior resources are appropriate and thus represent a measure of control.

Many mentally retarded persons can be trained to lead fairly normal lives and to support themselves at least in part in protected workshops or simple jobs. A program described by Patrick (1960) selects retardees who are eighteen to thirty-five years of age and have an IQ between fifty and seventy-five. They are trained in general work habits, such as punctuality, reliability, perseverance, speed, accuracy, and cooperative spirit, as well as in simple work skills. Special classes taught by volunteers deal with such subjects as time scheduling, handling money, and personal hygiene. After demonstrating some competence, trainees are placed, when possible, in an actual work situation in some department of the center to expose them to working with regular employees. They are paid for their work and after several months are able to work six or seven hours per day. The last phase of the program consists of group discussions regarding future employment. This program was said to be around fifty percent successful in placing trainees. Another twenty-five percent were placed in a sheltered setting and the remainder were returned home.

Psychotherapy and Behavior Disorders

One of the major challenges of psychology is to develop truly rehabilitative procedures for treating behavior disorders and mental illness. Up to now, the major effort of professional psychologists in this area has been psychotherapy—the verbal approach to behavior disorder. This is an extrinsic approach to training or reeducation, for it attempts to deal with hidden motivating conditions which are outside the disturbed behavior patterns themselves. It also is a learning theory approach, for the disordered behavior is assumed to be learned and—hopefully—unlearned according to the drive-drive reduction model.

The widespread belief that psychotherapy is a successful scientific technique for treating all varieties of behavior disorder has little basis in established fact. Methods used to assess different forms of psychotherapy or to analyze the changes in behavior produced by therapy include use of psychological personality tests, content analysis of speech (Mahl, 1956; Rogers, 1959), and recording of autonomic and somatic reactions during therapy (Sainsbury, 1955). Studies using the Minnesota Multiphasic Personality Test as a criterion measure reported limited effects of therapy (Welsh and Dahlstrom, 1956), but other psychometric appraisals have been generally inconclusive, as are the content analyses of speech. Data obtained from recording autonomic-psychophysiological reactions are difficult to interpret and of little value as criterion measures (Lacy, 1959).

One of the best evaluative studies was reported by Barron (1956), who studied thirty-three neurotic adults. About half of the patients were judged to have improved after six months of psychotherapy. This study indicated that the effects of therapy depended on the pattern of interpersonal relationships between the therapist and the patient.

Attempts to evaluate the use of psychotherapy with psychotic patients in mental hospitals indicate that it is relatively ineffective with psychotics except the very young, who sometimes recover without special treatment. Psychotherapy is especially limited in dealing with depressions or confused states and with elderly patients, who are inaccessible to the verbal approach. Group psychotherapy appears effective in the hospital setting inasmuch as it brings patients together and energizes them to do something about their problems.

It is becoming increasingly apparent that the processes of psychotherapy are not accessible to scientific analysis by means of controlled experiments. It appears to be impossible to design an experiment with double-blind controls such as are deemed necessary in evaluating drug treatment of behavior disorders. A recent authoritative summary of research findings relative to the treatment validity of psychotherapy offers no conclusive evidence that would contradict this opinion (Rubinstein and Parloff, 1959). Snyder's (1959) statement that the personality and actions of the therapist have more significance than the particular therapeutic technique is a fitting appraisal—possibly as good an appraisal as we are likely to get. Our opinion is that psychotherapy should be regarded as a private interpersonal reaction akin to other intimate human relationships. They cannot be defined objectively and thus should acquire no status as a scientific form of treatment.

Although psychotherapy does not seem to be accessible to direct scientific experimentation, it is subject to general analysis as a social process and a means of controlling the behavior of emotionally disturbed persons. It appears to enjoy its greatest success with educated and highly verbal people who welcome the opportunity to learn something about the type of psychological analysis and theoretical concepts that form the basis of the treatment. Many people find emotional relief in this kind of psychologizing about mental life and form strong attachments to their psychotherapist. Whether these bonds are always broken down by transference is not clear.

In some cases, there are specific positive feedback effects of psychotherapy. For example, giving verbal assurance to individuals suffering anxiety attacks often relieves the over-all psychophysiological symptoms. However, this function of psychotherapy is performed more quickly and economically by fast-acting tranquilizing drugs that can be prescribed by any physician.

In industrial and educational situations, psychotherapy and counseling are used for training, disciplinary, and custodial programs (Arbuckle and Gordon, 1949; McAtee, 1951; Weider, 1947). In these contexts, psychotherapy provides psychiatric restraint, informational training and some supportive service to the emotionally disturbed student or worker. The positive effects of such programs seem to depend almost entirely on the help given the individual in finding a career or in maintaining a satisfactory level of work. Even though failure to profit from counseling and psychotherapy in industry typically means loss of a job, these programs incorporate no meaningful concepts of work design or training design. The emphasis is on getting along with the supervisor or with other workers rather than in self-regulation of activity.

By and large, the positive effects of psychotherapy fall principally within the realm of information training wherein the psychotherapist gives information and suggestions about vocational interests and abilities, social skills, work responsibilities, and psychological concepts. Except for the excursion into psychological theory, these same services are given by vocational counselors. In summary, then, we would say that most of the positive functions of psychotherapy can be performed by other techniques—drugs and counseling, in particular. This conclusion in itself would not reflect on the status of psychotherapy as a mode of treatment, but there are serious limitations inherent in the psychotherapeutic procedure which do reflect on its status.

The most obvious limitations of psychotherapy are the cost and time involved. These restrict the technique largely to educated people in the upper income categories. Nondirective and brief therapy have been used to some extent in reform schools, minimum security prisons for adolescents and young adults, and certain other public institutions; but of the total population of emotionally disturbed people, only a few can tolerate the costs of psycho-therapy in any form.

A more serious limitation on the use of psychotherapy stems from its inac-cessibility to most individuals regardless of the cost problem. Davis (1938), Meyers and Shaffer (1945), and Holl-ingshead and Redlich (1958) have established in different decades and places that the application of psycho-therapy in public clinics and hospitals is discriminatory. These studies indi-cated that as a rule only educated and skilled persons can establish a relation-ship with a therapist conducive to treat-ment. Psychiatrists and therapists gen-erally express quite negative attitudes toward persons in the lower occupational classes (Hollingshead and Redlich, 1958).

Discriminatory use of the accepted treatment for behavior disorders has had generally negative implications for untreated individuals, for up until the discovery of the psychoactive drugs, the only alternative to successful treatment of serious disorders was custodial care in an institution. Individuals brought before courts often have been assigned to mental hospitals on the basis of a psychiatric interview of less than an hour's duration. In this time, an indi-vidual could be institutionalized in spite of the fact that psychologists and psy-chiatrists neither have reached an agree-ment on a definition of mental illness nor have been able to measure it objec-tively (Scott, 1958). Consequently, peo-ple are placed in legal custody by means of a process that has no objective stand-ards or scientifically defined concepts and is at best an interpersonal communi-cative interchange.

Custodial care in many cases has served only to intensify the behavioral disorganization that originated outside the institution. Few patients in public mental hospitals receive psychotherapy, for most of these patient are individuals who have not profited from or who are inaccessible to treatment. Most patients with functional disorders are relatively uneducated persons from the semiskilled and unskilled occupational groups (Pasamanick et al., 1959) who are rarely if ever treated by sustained psycho-therapy. Further, there is evidence (Greenblatt, 1959) that the severe symp-toms of mental illness—hallucinations, manias, catatonic postures, and regres-sive states—usually are hospital-induced effects of the extreme isolation of the patient from occupational, family, and community activity.

The isolation and extreme restriction of activity even in modern hospitals ap-pears to be the worst possible context within which to reorganize the behavior patterns of a disturbed individual. Yet the concepts of psychotherapy set no standards of human, educational, occu-pational, or social design. Emphasizing as they do internal mental states and conflicts, psychiatrists and clinical psy-chologists rarely have taken steps to provide such basic human resources as libraries, schools, training courses, or job opportunities for hospitalized pa-tients. Recently such facilities have been introduced into some of our mental hospitals, but the way was paved for their utilization not by psychotherapy but by the psychoactive drugs.

The psychoactive drugs do not cure the individual, but by alleviating some of the symptoms induced by the sensory deprivation, activity restriction, and custodial isolation of the hospital environment, they enable him to recover some of his resources and make him receptive to truly rehabilitative procedures. It is significant that if the individual can be gotten out of the hospital, the dosage level of drugs needed to sustain him usually can be reduced.

Our own over-all assessment of psychotherapy is that it is a current fad of the educated classes based more on faith and on beliefs than on objective facts, and that many of the beliefs are in the nature of misconceptions. One is that the technique is modern; rather, the technique of talking out guilt feelings is as old as religion. The belief that science has substantiated psychotherapy is unfounded; the percentage of people who benefit from the procedure is about the same as the number experiencing relief from placebos. The belief that psychotherapy can provide dramatic cures of personality disorders cannot be documented. The belief that the psychotherapist is benevolent and supportive in his attitudes is weakened by his failure to establish rapport with lower class individuals and by his administrative function of specifying institutional custody for those who do not benefit quickly from psychotherapy. Thus, the end result of relying on psychotherapy as the specific treatment for behavior disorders might be to induce more disturbances than are relieved. Finally, the belief that psychotherapy can establish a design for living is unrealistic, for clinical concepts and procedures have not been influenced in any way by advances in technology, art, human engineering, or any other developing phase of human culture. In general, the verbal procedures of psychotherapy are most meaningful when they are combined with more fundamental rehabilitative techniques designed to help the individual reestablish effective control of his behavior in a normal social context.

Rehabilitation for Behavior Disorders

A cybernetic approach to the behavior disorders emphasizes the importance of self-regulation of activity at all levels of behavior organization. For emotionally disturbed persons and other behavior disorders, the failure in control typically is in the family situation or at an occupational or social level. Such a person possesses skills and language resources but needs help in utilizing these skills in social situations. Inasmuch as the severe symptoms of behavior disorders may very likely be produced by institutional custody or the social isolation imposed on disturbed or limited individuals, initial efforts should be made to enlarge their scope of activity and to keep them out of custodial institutions. Such individuals need help in increasing their resources in self-regulation not only in finding and keeping a job, but in maintaining their social and emotional control.

Results of occupational rehabilitation programs provide supporting evidence for a cybernetic interpretation of behavior disorder. We interpret the practices in this field as being based in part on feedback concepts, for the effort is to increase the basic movement, skill, and social resources of the patient and to relieve his emotional problems by improving his capacity for self-regulation.

Occupational rehabilitation goes beyond the older concept of occupational therapy in that it strives to establish the individual in a gainful occupation rather than looking on the work activity merely as a form of therapy. Activities that sometimes are offered patients as occupational therapy may have no meaning beyond keeping them occupied within the custodial setting. This type of activity may help to relieve symptoms induced by the restricted environment, but does not reorganize their resources for life outside the institution. In contrast, true occupational rehabilitation is based on meaningful daily activity leading to regular paid jobs.

The effectiveness of work rehabilitation has been reported in a number of recent studies, some of which describe successful results in hospital work programs in spite of the fact that mental hospitals are poorly designed for such programs (Landy and Raulet, 1959). Chittick et al. (1961) used the following techniques in an extensive work-oriented hospital program for older, severely disturbed schizophrenics: (1) extensive use of psychoactive drugs; (2) relaxed ward care; (3) group therapy; (4) graded privileges adjusted to ability to accept responsibility; (5) occupational activity in assigned tasks in making clothes, preparing meals, making furniture, and so on; (6) industrial activity consisting of formal paid assignments in the hospital; (7) vocational counseling; and (8) establishing lines of communication between the hospital and community and generating community activity in the patients' interests. The results of this program as reflected in discharge figures for the first group of 275 patients are summarized in Figure 9.3. In two years, more than eighty percent of these patients were released from the hospital—a remarkable achievement for patients who were representative of

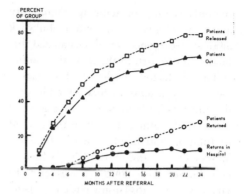

Figure 9.3.   The success of a hospital work program in rehabilitating elderly, severely disturbed schizophrenics. Eighty percent of the first 275 patients in the program were discharged within two years. (Data from Chittick et al. The Vermont story: rehabilitation of chronic schizophrenic patients. Burlington, Vt.: Queen City Printers, 1961.)

the most hopeless group in the hospital.

Wolfe (1961) employed procedures of occupational retraining oriented toward reestablishment of lost work skills with patients previously classed as chronic and nearly hopeless. Of eighty-nine who were rehabilitated successfully, eleven had been in the mental hospital more than ten years, twenty between five and ten years, and thirty-two between one and five years. Seventy-three of these eighty-nine patients were still successfully employed after two years, at weekly wages ranging between forty and one hundred dollars. Of the sixteen who were unsuccessful, seven were judged to have been unready for placement and five were placed unsuitably.

A survey of the employment status of patients released from mental hospitals reported by Olshansky et al. (1960) indicated that patients have less difficulty in work roles than in social and family roles. For many patients, work provides the only connection with the community and constitutes their main bulwark against recurrence of disorganized behavior and return to the mental hospital.

The protected workshop for mental patients or patients with chronic physical disability is built to operate like a small industry. Its aim is to return the patient to full-time independent work. In Altro Workshop of New York City, which is coordinated with state services and the city's welfare division, patients spend full days at work but alternate work with rest as their condition demands. Nonuniformed nurses monitor the health of patients, who work under specially trained and experienced supervision. Black (1959) has reported that Altro Services achieve eighty-seven percent rehabilitation, as judged by workshop graduates who maintain themselves with nothing more than medical supervision and occasional counseling and psychotherapy. Fifty-three percent get along without even this outpatient care. These are remarkable figures in view of the fact that the patients accepted in the program had been judged by experts to be in the bottom five percent of those likely to profit by occupational rehabilitation. Meyer and Borgatta (1959) studied a group of Altro patients who did not complete the program and concluded that even limited industrial retraining may prevent recommitment to a mental hospital by establishing regularized normal adult activities.

The main barrier to more complete success of occupational rehabilitation programs is the placement of the individual after training. Many individuals who have spent a major part of their lives in the mental hospital respond to the rehabilitative practices and could begin to live again if only jobs could be found to sustain them. According to Cohen (1963) and Olshansky (1959), the potential of occupational rehabilitation for controlling the blight of mental illness is limited mainly by the reluctance of employers to give jobs to former patients.

We thus meet in the occupational rehabilitation field the same problem that is encountered in training programs for the handicapped. Although daily work is an essential part of human design for living, it is not always an accessible part. Inasmuch as regular employment figures decisively in maintaining both physical and mental health, training design, educational design, and social design should incorporate that principle.

SUMMARY

1. Approaches to the many training problems of society emphasize either extrinsic factors, such as the motives and reinforcements of conventional learning theory and psychotherapy, or factors intrinsic to the behavior being trained, such as the feedback-control mechanisms of our cybernetic approach.

2. Industrial training emphasizes integrated visual-verbal techniques but without adequate validation of the procedures. Training programs usually are firm-oriented rather than worker-oriented.

3. A conventional training program reduced training time by using standardized lessons, speed-up, and incentives, but three-fourths of the trainees were dropped before finishing and the rest did not transfer their production rates to shop work.

4. In contrast, a training program which emphasized worker control of

activity achieved high production rates and maintained them without direct supervisory control of the work group.

5. Sensitivity training is supposed to make management personnel more sensitive to their own influence on group effectiveness and to promote harmony.

6. Computer games are programed on the basis of an arbitrary enterprise model to train management personnel to make decisions about running a business. Team scores are computed by testing their actions against the true decisions of the computer.

7. Computer games concentrate wide experience in executive decision making into a short training period but are likely to promote oversimplified ways of dealing with complex problems. They neither provide adequate differential feedback about how the computer evaluates decisions nor can they train creative thinking.

8. Studies have indicated that group morale and productivity are higher over all when the members can participate democratically in planning procedures and goals.

9. Studies of communication nets set up rigidly defined small group structures in which messages can be exchanged only along specified channels to solve simple problems. Although it was thought originally that centralized structures were more efficient, later studies showed that effectiveness depended on type of task.

10. Research on Navy teams indicated that they have indistinct boundaries and relatively decentralized control. Team training is needed to train members to respond to cues which are inherent in team situations, especially when precise coordination is required.

11. Studies of direct and confounded feedback indicate that individuals and teams perform and learn most efficiently if they get direct feedback from their own and others' performance.

12. Group behavior can be described more precisely and studied more objectively in cybernetic terms than in terms of drive-reinforcement learning concepts. The cybernetic approach considers the group an organized self-regulating system regulated by internal and external feedback.

13. One leadership function is to integrate the activity of the group with external environmental events and actions of other groups. The more complex the group's operations, the greater the importance of this leader role. Another leadership function is to coordinate group actions governed by internal feedback.

14. Specialization within a group is defined by differentiated member roles. Team training is needed to discover differential abilities as well as to enhance group efficiency.

15. Differentiated group roles in complex groups are analogous to different aspects of the feedback control of behavior in the individual. Training is needed to minimize perturbations of control.

16. Rehabilitative training is needed for individuals who cannot exercise satisfactory control over their behavior either at the level of basic perceptual-motor skills or at more complex levels of symbolic, social, or occupational control.

17. Successful techniques of training the handicapped establish intrinsic control of behavior by means of substitute feedback. Other rehabilitative training

can be based on cybernetic principles of self-regulation of activity.

18. The main problem of training the mentally retarded is to coordinate their work skills with a job that is available.

19. The psychotherapeutic process appears to be inaccessible to controlled experimental analysis and thus its scientific status is questionable. Evaluative studies indicate that the interpersonal relationship is more significant than the exact technique used.

20. Psychotherapy is most effective with educated verbal people. Some functions of psychotherapy often can be taken over by the psychoactive drugs and vocational counseling.

21. Lower class people neither can afford psychotherapy nor can they usually establish rapport with a therapist. In many cases the only alternative to successful therapy is legal custody.

22. The restriction and isolation imposed on patients of mental hospitals apparently intensify their symptoms. Psychoactive drugs relieve these symptoms and make it possible to use other forms of treatment and training.

23. Occupational rehabilitation programs have had outstanding success both inside and outside mental hospitals. The principal need is to establish the individual in a job where he can assume control over his own livelihood.

CHAPTER
10

Teaching Machines and Programed Books

Teaching machines were first developed in an educational context more than thirty-five years ago by Pressey (1926, 1927, 1932, 1950, 1959, 1960, 1963), but by one of the vagaries of science, they attracted little attention until they were popularized by Skinner (1954, 1958a, 1958b, 1961a, 1961b) in the past dozen years as an outgrowth of his research on rats and pigeons. The fact that teaching machines were developed in more than one context would not be particularly significant were it not true that the two sources represent different approaches to educational design—approaches which differ in their theoretical emphases as well as in their technical applications. These two diverse sources originated two lines of development in teaching machine technology and in teaching programs which have not yet been reconciled. In a sense, the teaching machine-programing effort has become a proving ground for the utility of Skinner's reinforcement learning theory in human educational situations. Because this issue is of paramount im-

portance both to psychology and to education, we shall describe developments in the field in some detail.

ORIGINS OF TEACHING MACHINES

More than three decades ago, Pressey's interest in objective self-scoring methods for standardized psychometric tests and achievement examinations gave rise to his development of mechanical devices for self-instruction. He discussed the extension of self-scoring of multiple-choice tests to the development of self-instruction devices as a revolutionary possibility in education (Pressey, 1932). After World War II, Pressey directed a Naval research project which was concerned with automatic self-instruction techniques, and one of his students from this period, Briggs (1956, 1958), subsequently helped to originate several sophisticated teaching machines for the Air Force.

Early in the 1950s, Skinner developed his automated teaching machines as a means of extending to human learning the operant conditioning principles that had been found useful with animals. Due perhaps to the authority granted reinforcement doctrine by many psychologists, Skinner's ideas attracted wide attention and the teaching machine movement caught fire.

Both Pressey's and Skinner's teaching machines provided for individual control of the materials of learning, insured active participation of the student, and provided immediate knowledge of accuracy. They permitted the student to work at his own rate and to know his progress in objective terms. All of these characteristics are recognized as good teaching principles.

Pressey's Self-instruction Devices

Pressey's first self-instruction machine presented typewritten questions in a little window and provided four keys to correspond to multiple-choice answers. The student answered each question by pressing the key which corresponded to what he thought was the correct answer. When used for testing, the machine scored the number of correct answers but gave no indication to the student of the correctness of each answer. The machine could be adjusted for self-instruction by repositioning a lever which locked the drive mechanism until the correct key was pressed. Now the student had to answer the displayed question correctly before a new question could be presented. Pressey first displayed this machine in 1924 and in a subsequent publication discussed its use as a teaching machine, noting that this use was "by all odds the most valuable and interesting" (Pressey, 1926).

Pressey (1927) designed his second teaching machine, shown in Figure 10.1,

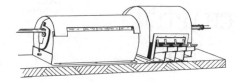

Figure 10.1.   A teaching machine designed by Pressey to control the sequence of questions according to the correctness of the student's responses. (Based on Kopstein and Shillestad. *A survey of auto-instructional devices.* USAF Aeronaut. Sys. Div. Tech. Report No. 61–414, 1961.)

to achieve what is called question dropout. This machine omitted a question as soon as the student answered it correctly a specified number of times on successive presentations. It could be adjusted to eliminate a question after one, two, three, or four successive correct answers. In his 1927 publication, Pressey raised a question which has not yet been resolved to every one's satisfaction— that of the efficiency of multiple-choice question-answer procedures as a teaching method. The theoretical objection to this method is that either the effects of temporal contiguity or reinforcement might lead to wrong as well as to right associations in the multiple-choice situation. Pressey was and still is of the opinion that if wrong alternatives represent errors that are made frequently by students, the multiple-choice format will help correct wrong associations rather than form them.

In a third machine development study, Pressey (1932) devised a punched-card scoring system which was a precursor to later electromechanical scoring machines. The student was given a thin cardboard strip on which were printed thirty rows of five small circles, representing multiple-choice answers to questions. He indicated his choice of answers by punching holes in the appropriate circles. The punched strip then was run through a mechanical scoring machine which automatically recorded and summed the correct answers.

Two simplified versions of Pressey's automatic self-checking devices, a chemically treated card and a punchboard, were developed and described by Peterson (1930). The Chemo Card provided a chemically treated multiple-choice answer sheet which was marked by the student with a special ink. When a correct choice was marked, the spot turned one color, while an incorrect spot turned another color. Peterson's punchboard consisted of an envelope enclosing several layers of cardboard with holes punched for answer choices. The student punched his choice with a pin, and if correct, the pin penetrated completely through the envelope. An improvement of this device was described by Pressey (1950).

Pressey's Drum Tutor, illustrated in Figure 10.2, is used with informational material and multiple-choice questions

Figure 10.2. One of the first teaching machines used for systematic research on meaningful learning, the Drum Tutor. This device was used by Stephens to study programing variables. (Based on Kopstein and Shillestad. *A survey of auto-instructional devices.* USAF Aeronaut. Sys. Div. Tech. Report No. 61–414, 1961.)

presented on mimeographed sheets, cards, or in booklets. The student indicates each answer by pressing one of the four buttons on the tutor and cannot progress until he has selected the correct answer. An item counter, seen at the left, indicates the number of the question which must be answered next, and an error counter, in the upper right hand corner, summates the number of errors made.

Research Evaluations of Pressey's Machines

The first research evaluation of Pressey's self-instruction concepts was a study reported by Peterson (1931). Matched groups of subjects were given an objective test three times, first as a pretest, then to be answered while studying a reading assigment, and finally as a posttest. The experimental group were given chemical scoring cards to use for self-checking while answering the questions during study, but the control group had no knowledge of accuracy. The use of the self-scorer increased final test scores significantly. In another comparison, the final test was not identical with the study questions but was reformulated and presented mainly as completion questions. Here again the self-checking study group scored higher on the final test.

Little (1934) carried out a carefully controlled experimental evaluation of Pressey's original machines. Four sections of Educational Psychology were run as a *test-machine group*, four as a *drill-machine group*, and the remaining six as a control group. As far as possible, sections were rotated among instructors and times of day, and data were used only from those students who could be paired fairly closely with students from the control group on the basis of course pretests and general intelligence test scores.

Twelve times during the course, all sections were given a thirty-item true-false test covering units of teaching material. The test-machine sections took these tests by punching answer cards which were run through Pressey's automatic scoring device immediately and returned to the student. The scores were tabulated on the board and a general class discussion emphasized the most frequently missed questions. All students making less than B were required to take an alternate form of the test the next day when the scores again were tabulated and discussed. The drill-machine sections took the same tests on Pressey's original testing-teaching machine. Their first scores were tabulated but then each student reset the machine and repeated the test until he could go through it without error. The control sections marked an answer slip which was graded after class and returned to the students the next day. Both experimental groups made significantly higher scores on examinations than did their paired controls, and this difference was more pronounced with poorer students. Those students who used the teaching machine drill to mastery moved further ahead of their paired controls than did the test-machine sections.

In the late 1940s, a series of experiments growing out of Pressey's work were conducted. Angell and Troyer (1948) and Jones and Sawyer (1949) found that using punchboard quizzes to give immediate knowledge feedback significantly enhanced learning in chemistry and citizenship courses. Briggs (1947) and Jensen (1949) found that superior students using self-study techniques with punchboards and other independent procedures could accelerate their course work, make good grades, become more capable of independent work, and have time left over for an additional course.

A summary by Pressey (1950) reported results indicating the efficacy of immediate knowledge feedback in promoting learning. Three types of verbal material were used, Russian vocabulary as rote matter, hard English vocabulary as meaningful material without any organization or structure, and the subject matter of psychology courses as material that was both meaningful and structured. Comparative studies showed that repeated practice tests given on punchboards promoted learning whether or not the order of test items remained the same or was changed. With more meaningful material, learning proceeded more rapidly and was less affected by changing the order of items. Students taking practice tests on punchboards during a course not only did better in examinations on the practiced items, but to some extent on items that had not appeared in the practice tests. Students who took the practice tests without punchboards and discovered their errors later made poorer scores on examinations than those who received immediate knowledge of accuracy.

In a later evaluative study, Stephens (1960) found that practice tests with the Drum Tutor enabled an experimental group to score higher on examinations than a control group in spite of the fact that the experimental students were inferior to the control group in general ability and over-all college achievement.

Using punchboards for practice tests, Stephens confirmed Pressey's findings that errors were eliminated more rapidly with meaningful material and found that students learned more efficiently when they could correct errors immediately.

Severin (1960), also working under Pressey, compared the regular punchboard practice test procedure with another in which students made no overt responses but studied the same practice test with the correct answers marked. For both Naval terminology and scientific material, no significant differences were found. Severin concluded that for short easy tasks, the automated response device was of little value. It was enough to point out the correct answers.

This summary of the work of Pressey and his students reveals an original and persistent attack on some of the problems of educational design. He was the first experimenter in the learning field to mechanize many of the significant aspects of knowledge instruction, which permit a controlled objective analysis of meaningful learning in the normal school situation. On the basis of his experimental analyses and many years of experience with various kinds of instructional techniques, Pressey (1959, 1960, 1963) recently has defined this point of view about self-instruction: that machine teaching of response-programed material is not sufficient unto itself but is a useful adjunct to other teaching techniques.

Military Knowledge Trainers

A second line of effort directed toward the development of automated self-instructional techniques has been carried out in military training research both during and since World War II. The Tab Item, which was designed primarily to test the proficiency of Air Force maintenance personnel in electronic troubleshooting, incorporates automatic knowledge of accuracy and thus has some value as a self-instructional technique (Glaser et al., 1954). The test consists of several pages containing the description of a malfunctioning symptom, a series of check procedures which might be employed to determine the cause of the malfunctioning, and a list of components which might, if defective, cause the trouble. Opposite each check is a perforated tab which can be lifted to reveal a description of the results which would be obtained if that check procedure were followed. Other tabs opposite the components conceal the words Yes or No, indicating that a component is or is not the source of the trouble. A person taking the test lifts the tabs opposite the procedures he would follow, attempting to use as few checks as possible. The sequence of steps taken is variable, for the actual response choices help to determine what material will be presented and in what order.

A technique similar to the Tab Item is provided by the Trainer-Tester, which was developed to teach troubleshooting in a Navy electronics school. In an experimental evaluation of the Trainer-Tester and a Punchboard-Tutor equivalent to Pressey's punchboard, Cantor and Brown (1956) found them both superior to equipment mock-ups for training Navy men in electronic troubleshooting. A large scale evaluation of Trainer-Testers for Air Force use by Dowell (1955) found that they were superior to actual equipment use for training troubleshooting but that the highest scores were achieved by men who received instruction on both Trainer-Testers and actual equipment.

Pressey's former student, Briggs, helped to develop the Subject-Matter Trainer, shown in Figure 10.3, to teach serial procedures, symbols, technical terminology, and limited problem-solving skills (Besnard *et al.*, 1955; Briggs, 1958). Questions appear one at a time in the window at the left of the sloping panel and are answered by selecting one of the twenty response choices displayed either verbally or pictorially on the panel. The student presses a button beside his selection and, if it is correct, a green light appears on the other side. An error activates a red light

Figure 10.3.   The Subject-Matter Trainer, a flexible teaching machine developed for the Air Force which permits several prompting, practice, and testing modes. (Based on Kopstein and Shillestad. *A survey of auto-instructional devices.* USAF Aeronaut. Sys. Div. Tech. Report No. 61–414, 1961.)

or buzzer. A new question is obtained by pressing a button at the lower left.

The Subject-Matter Trainer can be programed in five different teaching and testing modes. In the Coaching Mode, the student quizzes the machine and a green light indicates the correct answer. In the Single-Error Mode, the student selects an answer but, if he is in error, the green light comes on beside the correct answer and he must press that button before the next question will appear. In the standard Practice Mode, the student must try until he selects the correct answer by himself. He gets only one choice in the Single-Try Mode and in the Test Mode, one trial with no indication of correctness or incorrectness. Any of these five modes can be modified by Paced-Practice, in which the instructor controls the durations of each item presentation. In all modes, the total number of response attempts and the total number of errors are recorded automatically.

Experimental evaluations of the Subject-Matter Trainer found the coaching mode most effective for the early stages in learning with the single-error mode ranking second (Irion and Briggs, 1957). Use of these two modes followed by the practice mode also proved very effective. Students trained on this machine achieved significantly higher criterion scores than students trained conventionally. The most significant finding of this research was that prompting the student to give a correct response promotes learning more effectively than merely confirming correct responses after they have been made.

Briggs (1956) also developed the trainer known as the Multipurpose Instructional Problem Storage Device

(MIPS) to detect malfunctions in a complex electronic fire control system. The flexible sequencing technique that was a feature of the Tab Item was refined further in this MIPS trainer and later was recognized as the definitive feature of a specialized technique of self-instruction. Letting the student's responses dictate the order of items in an instructional program is known as *branching* programing in contrast to *linear* programing in which the sequence of items is fixed in advance and does not vary for different students.

Skinner's Teaching Machines

By the mid-1950s, the self-instructional devices and techniques already developed incorporated most of the significant features that are found in contemporary teaching machines and had been subjected to controlled experimental evaluations with generally favorable results. But the real impetus to machine teaching and programed learning came neither from Pressey's work nor from the military projects but from the work and writings of Skinner (1954, 1958a, 1958b, 1961a, 1961b) and his associates.

Skinner's principal innovation was to recast the whole idea of self-instruction in terms of reinforcement learning theory. He discounted Pressey's work as being concerned primarily with testing rather than learning and suggested that the important ideas about teaching machines and programed instruction were derived from his analyses of operant conditioning.

Skinner's (1954) first important paper on teaching machines began with a description of the techniques he and his colleagues had developed to control

behavior and learning in animals. Any response emitted by an animal can be reinforced, and a desired behavior pattern is taught by reinforcing first a response that resembles what is desired and then strengthening successive approximations to the desired pattern. Thus, the investigator is able to "shape" behavior almost at will. According to Skinner, his techniques were being adopted by animal trainers to shape the behavior of performing animals.

Skinner claimed that the species of animal made very little difference in the efficacy of his techniques. Comparable results were obtained on pigeons, rats, dogs, monkeys, human children, and even human psychotic patients, all of whom showed "amazingly similar properties of the learning process." To demonstrate such similarities and to achieve behavior control, however, reinforcement must be manipulated with considerable precision.

Figure 10.4 illustrates the reinforcement technique applied to human psychotic patients by Skinner and his collaborator Lindsley. The patient in this study is pulling the controls on a vending machine, one of which will deliver a reinforcement in the pay-off compartment at the base of the machine.

Skinner suggested that ordinary schoolroom practices are shockingly inadequate methods for controlling learning and that reinforcements in school are almost entirely aversive—that is, the child behaves for the most part so as to escape aversive consequences rather than to achieve positive rewards. Further, the child usually is not able to know whether his responses are correct for minutes, hours, or even days after he has made them, so that the effect

Figure 10.4.　　Skinner's method of controlling reinforcement in human subjects. The subject pulls knobs on a candy vending machine in order to get candy. (Courtesy of Dr. O. R. Lindsley.)

of that knowledge is greatly reduced. But the most serious weakness in classroom procedures, according to Skinner, is that the individual pupil cannot be reinforced after every response but only after blocks of responses have been made.

To remedy these inadequacies, Skinner proposed that mechanical devices be introduced into the classroom. His first teaching machine contained a roll of paper tape on which a series of arithmetical problems were printed, one of which could be seen through a small window. The child composed an answer to the problem by moving one or more sliders to make digits from zero to nine appear in square holes punched in the paper. If the answer was correct, a turn of a knob would ring a bell and bring the next problem into view. If an incorrect answer was given, the knob

would not turn and the child had to try again. A counter could be attached to this device to tally wrong answers. Similar models with letters appearing in the answer spaces were designed for spelling problems. The model shown in Figure 10.5 presents statements, words, or number patterns with words, letters, or numbers missing. The student moves sliders to fill in the missing symbols.

Skinner described the advantages of his devices in almost the same terms that Pressey had used. Knowledge of results was immediate and came after each response, the manipulative nature of the task was in itself reinforcing to most children, the student was kept active and could work at his own rate, and the teacher was relieved of routine drill. All of these features were provided by Pressey's machines. The only significant difference in Skinner's devices was the manner of answering the questions or problems. Pressey presented answers in

Figure 10.5.　　A slider teaching box for self-instruction in arithmetic, spelling, and reading. If the answer is correct, the crank can be turned for the next problem. (Based on Kopstein and Shillestad. *A survey of auto-instructional devices.* USAF Aeronaut. Sys. Div. Tech. Report No. 61–414, 1961.)

multiple-choice form and Skinner required the student to pull sliders to compose his answer.

Skinner insisted on "composed answers" or "constructed responses" because he thought of teaching machine learning as an operant conditioning procedure in which reinforcements are used to elicit the desired responses. He felt that multiple-choice questions are undesirable because they offer a chance for wrong responses. Because of this belief, Skinner attempted to design teaching boxes which could evaluate composed answers. Obviously this type of device has its limitations; it can score an answer as correct only if it is composed with the precise set of symbols decided upon by the programer. Since most of our verbal knowledge can be discussed and taught in many alternative combinations of words and phrases, many kinds of questions are beyond the scope of composed-answer scoring. Nevertheless, Skinner believed that the advantages of composed answers outweighed their disadvantages and designed his teaching machines accordingly.

In subsequent studies, Skinner (1958b) developed several new designs for teaching machines which would handle more informational material while still having the student compose his answer. Since mechanical scoring could not be used with more advanced verbal material, the student was required to score his own response as correct or incorrect. Printed verbal material was stored on tapes or disks and divided into frames that were visible one at a time. Figure 10.6 shows a model which takes a twelve-inch disk divided into thirty radial frames. All but one corner of the frame is visible through the window. The student writes

Figure 10.6.   A disk-type teaching box which provides for punch tabulating and question drop-out. (Based on Kopstein and Shillestad. *A survey of auto-instructional devices.* USAF Aeronaut. Sys. Div. Tech. Report No. 61–414, 1961.)

his answer to the question and then lifts a lever on the front of the machine which moves his written response under a transparent cover and also uncovers the correct answer on the corner of the frame. If the student scores his answer as correct, he moves the lever horizontally and a hole is punched in the paper opposite his response. This hole provides for the dropping out of the question on the next go-round. In any case, after a response with the lever has been made, the next question appears in the aperture.

Skinner's recent devices have the disadvantage that a wrong response cannot be corrected until the next time around the disk. Skinner sacrificed the feature of immediate correction of errors in order to keep the feature of composed answers. The rationale for this choice may not be immediately clear. If the discovery of a wrong response is aversive, then this consequence should not be permitted to stay in effect for a period of time. On the other hand, if turning the crank to get the next question is in itself rewarding, then the student who makes an error is reinforced positively for an incorrect response. In either case, Skinner appears to be ignoring his own principles. However, the inconsistency becomes less relevant in view of Skinner's position on error responses. Believing that wrong responses are out of place in an optimal learning sequence, he advocates arranging material in such a way that the student seldom if ever makes an error. Thus a Skinnerian program is designed to lead the student by short easy stages to the desired responses. In a virtually error-free situation it is not deemed necessary to make provision for immediate correction of errors.

Evaluations of Skinner's Machines

Skinner justified his teaching machines and programing principles from the start on *a priori* grounds derived from his animal-based reinforcement learning theory and made little effort to evaluate them experimentally. Both he and some of his collaborators have felt that it is enough to demonstrate what a self-instructional device or program can do—enough to demonstrate that it can, in fact, teach. They have been interested in exploring techniques for improving their programs, but they have made few controlled comparisons between their own techniques and more conventional teaching methods or other types of programs. Whereas Pressey was interested in determining how best to

integrate self-instruction into a total teaching situation, Skinner justified it on conceptual grounds and seemed to assume without question that complete courses could be taught most effectively by well-designed self-instructional programs.

Five years were to elapse after Skinner's 1954 article on teaching machines before a few research findings from his Harvard group began to appear in published form. The studies reported by Meyer (1959) and Holland (1959) were more in the nature of demonstrations; Meyer taught arithmetic to grade school children with the slider machine and Holland taught psychology to college students with the disk machine. Porter (1959) presented results showing that second and sixth graders progressed further in spelling achievement in less study time with machine teaching than with conventional methods.

One of the techniques used by Skinner and his colleagues was called "vanishing." Material was presented in almost complete form at first, but the amount of information was slowly reduced in successive frames until the student could supply the entire response without help. For example, to teach a poem, the lines were presented first with several unimportant letters missing, and in successive frames with different and more letters missing. That is, the text was gradually "vanished" until the poem could be emitted without a text. Skinner anticipated objections that material programed according to his principles will be too easy, but he asserted that there is too much emphasis on difficult material in traditional education and that his own easy methods of instruction are more effective.

DEVELOPMENT OF TEACHING MACHINES

In spite of the similarities between their teaching machines, Pressey and Skinner represented two diverse approaches to self-instruction which have generated different kinds of devices as well as different kinds of programed materials. Pressey regarded self-instructional techniques as an adjunct to other teaching procedures to be used for drill, review, and self-testing. He relied on multiple-choice questions and did not consider the order in which they appeared of particular importance inasmuch as the logical structure of the subject matter was presented by conventional teaching materials. In contrast, Skinner believed that the most important thing in self-instruction is to get the student to give a correct response so that it can be reinforced immediately. Errors are to be avoided by leading the student in slow, easy stages through an ordered sequence to mastery of the subject matter.

Composed-Answer Teaching Devices

A number of Skinner-type teaching machines have been designed specifically to teach arithmetic to children in the elementary grades, including the machine pictured in Figure 10.7. Twenty-four multiplication problems are shown on the face of the box, each below a hole. The student places a plug in the hole above the problem he selects and then sets the dials at the bottom to indicate the answer. A green light or buzzer indicates a correct answer when

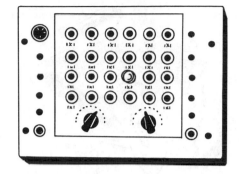

Figure 10.7.   Devereux Teaching Aid to teach arithmetic. (Based on Kopstein and Shillestad. *A survey of auto-instructional devices.* USAF Aeronaut. Sys. Div. Tech. Report No. 61–414, 1961.)

he presses the button at upper left. This device has no scoring feature.

In order for a teaching machine to be automated, the student's answer must trigger the device to advance to the next question. This is not an easy feature to achieve when composed answers are required, for some variability in verbal response usually must be permitted. One device designed to register a verbal response automatically is shown in Figure 10.8. The material to be learned and the questions are projected on the screen from microfilm, and the student composes an answer on the typewriter keyboard. Only one key can be depressed at a time, for all but the correct one are locked. After the correct answer has been typed, the next frame comes on to present the next question. No provision is made for recording errors. This device is used primarily to teach spelling but could be used for other verbal material when only one answer is correct.

A number of commercial teaching machines are based on the principle of the Skinner disk machine. They are rela-

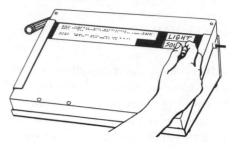

Figure 10.9.   Scroll-type teaching box which requires fill-in answers, the Foringer Teaching Machine, No. 2002. (Based on Kopstein and Shillestad. *A survey of auto-instructional devices.* USAF Aeronaut. Sys. Div. Tech. Report No. 60–414, 1961.)

Figure 10.8.   The Wyckoff Film Tutor. Composed answers typed on the typewriter keyboard advance the film to the next frame. (Based on Kopstein and Shillestad. *A survey of auto-instructional devices.* USAF Aeronaut. Sys. Div. Tech. Report No. 61–414, 1961.)

tively simple boxes which permit the controlled presentation of programed questions and provide a space for the student to write his answer. The correct answer to a question usually is presented along with the next question, whether or not the student has answered correctly. Most of these boxes have no automated features and differ mainly in their manner of presenting questions and informational material.

The device shown in Figure 10.9 contains a roll of paper upon which questions and answers are printed. Two questions can be seen at one time. The one toward the top already has been answered by the student, and the correct answer can be seen to the right of the question. The question below is being answered, and the correct printed answer still is hidden from the student. The paper roll is advanced by turning a crank. The principal disadvantage of using continuous rolls of paper to present questions is that the programs are difficult to reproduce in quantity. Several teaching boxes have simplified the problem of quantity reproduction by utilizing standard sheets of mimeograph paper or cards for the questions.

Where teaching devices are to be used regularly to present a variety of instructional programs, there are great advantages in using microfilm instead of paper or cards for economy of reproduction, ease of handling, and compactness in storing. The Wyckoff Film Tutor in Figure 10.8 uses film, and another film projection device is shown in Figure 10.10. Individual 35mm frames displaying textual material and drawings are projected on a small screen. Color film can be used if desired. This device is designed either for composed answers as shown or for multiple-choice answers with another attachment. Other devices have been constructed to present material either visually or aurally by audiotape. The student either writes his answer or speaks it into the tape recorder.

Programed Books

The trend in designing devices based on Skinner's composed-answer principle has been toward simpler and simpler

Figure 10.10.   A microfilm projection device that can be equipped for either composed answers or multiple choice. (Based on Kopstein and Shillestad. *A survey of auto-instructional devices.* USAF Aeronaut. Sys. Div. Tech. Report No. 60–414, 1961.)

procedures. Actually, no *machine* is needed for the essential characteristics of a Skinner teaching box, which are, according to Porter (1958): (a) to present a sequence of problem materials one at a time; (b) to provide some means by which a student can indicate or record his solution to each item; and (c) to indicate immediately the correctness or incorrectness of the response. These same features can be achieved if the questions and answers are presented not by device but in regular book form.

Programed books are books that present instructional material and questions and require that the reader supply answers before proceeding. This type of book has been around for a long time in the form of many kinds of workbooks, which may require either Pressey-type multiple-choice responses or Skinner-type composed answers in the form of fill-in or completion statements. How-

ever, workbooks as we have known them in the past pay no particular attention to the sequence of questions and usually give no immediate knowledge of accuracy.

A book programed according to Skinner's principles is shown in Figure 10.11. This particular book is divided into fourteen parts analogous to chapters, and each part is divided into from two to six *sets* of *frames*. A frame consists of a statement with one or more blanks which are to be filled in (on a separate sheet of paper) by the student. A set is made up of about thirty to sixty frames, each of which after the first includes the correct answer for the prior frame. In order that the student does not see the correct answer to the question he is answering, successive frames are placed only on right-hand pages and the frames on any one page are not consecutive but occur cyclically in a set of frames. The student reads the first frame at the top of the page, writes down his answer and then turns the page to see if the answer is correct. He then works the next frame and turns another page. When he reaches the frame on the last page of the cycle, he is directed to turn back to the first page for the check answer and the next frame. He must proceed through the cycle again and again until he has completed the frames at the bottom of the pages.

This book adopts a novel technique to avoid wasting all the left-hand pages. After the student has worked through the book from front to back he turns it upside down and works from back to front on the backs of the pages, which are now the right-hand pages. Thus if the book is opened at random, the

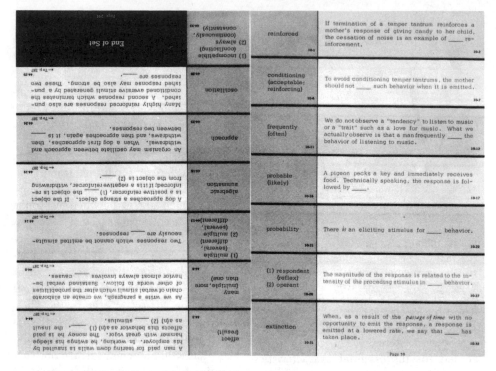

Figure 10.11.   Page design of a programed book arranged according to Skinner's principles of step-by-step programing. This is a textbook on *The Analysis of Behavior* by Holland and Skinner. (Copyright 1961, McGraw-Hill Book Company. Used by permission.)

reader sees upright material on the right and upside-down material on the left. Some programed books leave the backs of the pages blank instead of resorting to this coming-and-going technique.

The Holland and Skinner book we are describing is an example of linear programing, with frames that follow each other consecutively from first to last with no variability in order. It would be possible to use multiple-choice or true-false questions in such a program as well as completion questions. However, this type of program has come to be associated more with the Skinnerian principle of composed answers than with the Pressey multiple-choice technique. Later

we shall describe another type of programed book designed for branching programs.

Multiple-Choice Teaching Devices

Whereas Skinner's principle of the composed answer initiated a trend toward simpler and simpler teaching machines, Pressey's multiple-choice principle has been admirably suited to many types of devices incorporating automatic scoring and programing techniques. Multiple-choice teaching machines have been developed for a wide range of applications, from the teaching of simple discriminations to young children and handicapped individuals to instruction

Figure 10.12.   Devices for teaching young or retarded children. *a.* Simplified teacher-controlled teaching box developed at Devereux Schools. *b.* The Didak 101 preverbal machine. (Based on Kopstein and Shillestad. *A survey of auto-instructional devices.* USAF Aeronaut. Sys. Div. Tech. Report No. 60–414, 1961.)

the box. A child then is asked a question about the material displayed on the card —for example, "Which one is the largest?" or "Which one is the circle?"— and answers the question by pressing a button on the top of the box. A three-choice device for preverbal training is shown in Figure 10.12*b*. The problem displayed shows a comparison stimulus (a tree) over three letters from which the child chooses the one which appears in the word *tree*.

One of the authors has developed multiple-choice tactual discrimination teaching machines for use with blind children prior to their learning Braille. The child's task is to match a test form by selecting one of a series of forms outlined in metal or pressed in bas-relief on a plastic sheet. Correct choices can be made to activate a buzzer.

A teaching machine incorporating both multiple-choice and write-in features, shown in Figure 10.13, has been developed by one of the authors. This

Figure 10.13.   Duo-Mode teaching machine incorporating both multiple-choice and write-in features. The device is programed by slipping a punched plastic strip into position under the left-hand multiple-choice column. The operator is checking a true-false key.

in the most complicated areas of verbal and symbolic knowledge.

Two devices developed for young or retarded children are shown in Figure 10.12. A teacher using the one in Figure 10.12*a* programs the material item by item by depressing the correct one of three buttons located on the back of device contains a continuous roll of five-inch wide paper which stretches across the top and can be pulled out from a slit at the front. The plastic plate at the left contains sixty rows of small holes in groups of four and two. The student is given informational material including sixty questions and multiple-choice answers on separate sheets. For each question, he indicates first whether he is *certain* or *uncertain* of his choice by punching, with a stylus, through the appropriate one of the two holes toward the center, leaving a hole in the paper tape. Then he punches the one of four holes toward the left which corresponds to his selected answer, leaving another hole in the paper. If this choice is correct, a buzzer sounds. If the student makes an error, he tries again until he selects the correct answer and then writes it in the space to the right. If he has indicated that he is *certain* of an *incorrect* answer, he can be required to write the correct answer several times on a separate card or sheet. When he has finished the entire sixty items, he pulls out the portion of the paper tape which he has used and tears it off for a permanent record of his performance.

This device combines some of the principal advantages of both multiple-choice and composed-answer teaching machines. A student who understands the material and knows the correct answers can proceed rapidly through the series. Errors can be corrected immediately, not only by *selecting* the right answer but also by *writing* it, once or several times depending on the certainty of the original response.

Development of Branching Programs

It will be recalled that the technical knowledge trainers developed by Briggs (1956, 1958) for the Air Force incorporated two features new to self-instructional devices. The Subject-Matter Trainer was designed to permit several prompting, practice, or testing modes and the MIPS Trainer was designed for branching programing. Branching techniques have received considerable attention as an alternative to linear programing and usually are associated with Crowder (1959, 1960), who developed the MIPS Trainer further to produce the Autotutors shown in Figure 10.14. The circuits of these trainers are designed to make decisions about what item will be presented next according to the specific response of the student. Autotutor Mark I is an expensive instrument suited to instruction on electronic troubleshooting or any other task requiring sequential choices. Instructional material and questions are presented by means of short motion-picture sequences or still projection. Correct answers bring on the next unit of material but errors produce explanations. A hopelessly wrong answer produces a warning to pay closer attention. The machine records automatically the sequence of images viewed, the time spent on each image, and the total time. Autotutor Mark II has these same basic features but is less costly, is slower, has a more limited capacity, and cannot present motion-picture sequences.

Crowder's principles of branching programing led to what have been called

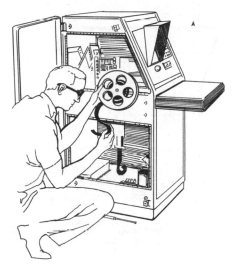

Figure 10.14.   Crowder's teaching machines designed for intrinsic programing. *a.* Autotutor Mark I. *b.* Autotutor Mark II. (Based on Kopstein and Shillestad. *A survey of auto-instructional devices.* USAF Aeronaut. Sys. Div. Tech. Report No. 60–414, 1961.)

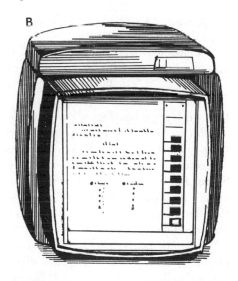

scrambled books, or TutorTexts, in which the sequence of items depends on the responses made by the student. While the items in a linearly programed book proceed from one page to the next in a cyclical fashion, the items in a scrambled book are distributed throughout with no apparent order. Each page contains one unit of material followed by a question, alternative answers, and a new page number beside each answer. The student selects an answer and turns to the designated page. If the answer is correct, it is confirmed and the next item is presented. If the answer is wrong, the student is given additional material and usually is directed to return to the question to correct his error. A sample page from a scrambled book written by Cram (1961) to explain teaching machines reads as follows:

4
(from page 8)

Right! The educational motion picture, as it is normally used, is not a "teaching machine."

1. Although the motion picture presents information, it does not require periodic responses from the student in the form of answers, selections, or motor responses.
2. Since it does not ask for responses, it does not indicate whether the responses are appropriate or not.
3. It does not allow the individual class member to adjust his rate of progress to his own needs and capabilities.

Imagine, however, an educational motion picture which requires that the students answer questions periodically on a printed answer form. Would this then constitute a "teaching machine"?

Page 2 Yes
Page 12 No

If the student selects the Yes answer, he turns to Page 2, reads an explanation of why his answer was wrong, and is told to go back to Page 4 and select the other answer. The No answer leads to Page 12, a confirming explanation, and a new unit. Self-instructional material arranged in this way is called a branching program because it provides sequences that branch off from the main line.

Audiovisual Teaching Machines

One of the problems in designing teaching machines is to achieve some flexibility in the mode of presenting the instructional material. Several ways of varying program sequences are made possible by branching techniques, but another approach is to apply audiovisual procedures to mechanized self-instruction, that is, to use both verbal and nonverbal material and to present it both aurally and visually.

Sound motion pictures can be used for audiovisual teaching machines if some means is provided for the student to control the presentation. Figure 10.15 shows a compact film viewer which can hold up to 200 feet of continuous sound film loop. This projector can be stopped on any desired frame. It was intended primarily to demonstrate step-by-step procedures to technical trainees, who could stop the projector while practicing

Figure 10.15.   Handy-Dandy Sound Film Viewer developed by Lumsdaine and Roshal. (Based on Kopstein and Shillestad. *A survey of auto-instructional devices.* USAF Aeronaut. Sys. Div. Tech. Report No. 61–414, 1961.)

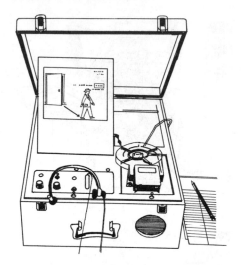

Figure 10.16.   An audiovisual machine used for instruction in foreign languages. (Based on photograph from the New York Center for Programed Instruction. In Katz. Some of Johnny's best teachers are machines. *Maclean's*, 1962, **75**(6), 9–11; 32–36.

the procedure that had just been demonstrated (Lumsdaine, 1959).

A number of teaching machines combine audio-tape recorded sound with visual displays, usually from microfilm. The first main use of such devices was to teach foreign languages. For example, the device in Figure 10.16 presents pictures to illustrate the meaning of phrases or sentences that are presented aurally. Some foreign language teaching machines provide a recording channel so that the student can record his responses and play them back.

There are many advantages to combining audio-tape recording and visual projection for purposes of self-instruction. Such combinations of aural and visual media can present almost any type of instructional material without excessive cost or complicated instrumentation. One of the authors has used tape

Figure 10.17.   A student using an audiovisumatic teaching machine for self-instruction. The answer stylus contains two sharp pointed electrodes which are punched through the circle next to the selected answer. If the answer is correct, the electrode points touch a conductive surface on the key sheet underneath and complete an electric circuit which reactivates the machine.

recorders and slide projectors as the basic components of what we call *audiovisumatic* teaching systems as in Figure 10.17 (Smith, 1960). An electronic control unit activates an audio-tape recorder and a standard slide or filmstrip projector. The instructional material includes a tape-recorded lecture complete with slides which are presented automatically at appropriate times. At the end of the presentation, a number of questions are asked either aurally or visually by means of slides. As each question is presented, the tape-recorder stops automatically and the student selects a multiple-choice answer from his answer sheet. With a stylus he punches opposite his selection and, if it is correct, the tape recorder proceeds with the next question.

The design of this audiovisumatic system is flexible enough so that it can be used in several different ways for self-instruction. Visual material can be used with the instruction and with the questions or omitted from one or both phases, as desired. Slides can be used as prompts during a question sequence and omitted from the same sequence later by turning off the slide projector.

The response mode also can be changed. The machine can direct the student to write a short essay answer to a question and then present a short summary of a correct answer when the student punches a key to turn on the machine for the next question. The system also can be used for classroom instruction. It can present an entire lecture automatically with slides introduced at appropriate times and, if desired, submit test questions for the students to answer with or without informational feedback. In this case, however, the presentation would not be under the control of an individual student but would be paced ahead of time by the recorder or during the presentation by an operator.

COMPUTER-CONTROLLED TEACHING MACHINES

The most sophisticated of all teaching machines are those that use digital computers as the central control component. Computer-controlled teaching systems can handle complicated branching programs automatically, but due to their complexity and cost, they have been used mainly for research purposes. The following features make them invaluable tools for analyzing learning and teaching procedures. First, computers can be programed to follow extremely complex schedules and thus can accommodate any kind of branching program. Second, they can store a tremendous amount of information, amounting to millions of numerical and verbal items, and draw upon it for immediate use. Finally, digital computers operate at such enormous speeds that they make possible the completion of validation research on programing variables that would be unfeasible by conventional procedures.

A computer can be used as a teaching machine if it has a student input station which accepts the student's responses and compares them with information stored in a program. The basic components of such a system are shown diagrammatically in Figure 10.18. The electric typewriter or flexowriter serves both as an output station to present questions and instructions to the student and as an input station that accepts the student's replies. The bulk of the instructional material is presented by means of an ordinary textbook. The computer gives specific reading assignments and then presents questions on the material. The nature of the answer typed out by the student controls subsequent instructions and questions. The computer evaluates an answer in terms of its stored information and chooses the appropriate next step.

The circuits of a digital computer can be connected to different types of devices to present instructional materials and questions and accept responses in various ways. For example, instructional material and questions can be presented by flexowriter, by means of 35mm slides, or aurally by means of magnetic tape, and responses can be either multiple-choice or composed-answer. Some set-ups have used closed-circuit television facilities.

Digital computers can be used to program self-instruction for more than one student at a time in different subject matters. The computer works so rapidly that it can handle data from a number of teaching stations—as many as 1000 have been proposed for large, fast computers (Herbert, 1963). The practical difficulties in multiplying the number of stations are the expense involved in each

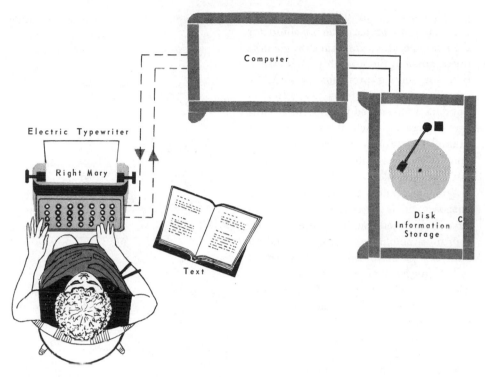

Figure 10.18.   Basic components of a computer-controlled teaching system with a textbook used to supply instructional material to the student.

station and its circuitry and the need for facilities to store and retrieve vast amounts of programed information.

Information Storage

The millions of bits of information used by digital computers are recorded in a very simple language. Instead of the ten numbers and twenty-six letters of our ordinary numerical-alphabetical language, computers use a *binary* system which has only two symbols or two basic operations. These may be the *off* and *on* position of a switch, the presence or absence of a hole in a card, a spot on a film, or a magnetized spot on a tape. All of the verbal and numerical information handled by computers must be rep-

resented in terms of this simple presence-absence, off-on, yes-no binary system.

Binary information is recorded and stored in a number of ways—on the familiar punched cards, iron crystal devices, magnetic core networks, cathode ray tubes, magnetic tapes, magnetic drums, and optic or photoscopic disks. Punched cards, magnetic tapes, films, disks, and the like provide portable long-term storage for computer information. However, in processing data, computers also make use of immediately accessible short-term memory units to keep track of an operation in progress. Devices such as magnetic cores are built into the computer itself for short-term storage, and after a particular operation is completed, the magnetic or electronic spots are erased to prepare the machine for the next operation. Internal storage units make possible the assembly of information for solving problems at fantastic speeds—millions of units per second—but data are retrieved from portable storage devices at much slower rates. For example, data can be retrieved from punched cards at rates of around 24,000 bits per second.

When computers are used for teaching purposes, it is necessary for them to have high-speed random access to an enormous amount of stored material so that any desired unit of information called for by the program can be retrieved quickly and put before the student. An IBM teaching-machine system uses magnetic disks which are not unlike phonograph records in appearance to provide bulk storage of programs, lessons, remedial material, and student records. For example, textbooks and dictionaries can be recorded on disks. The disks are filed in a stack that rotates continuously at 1200 rpm. Several access arms which are connected to separate teaching stations move up and down to any desired disk face to retrieve a unit of information after a delay no greater than 0.8 second.

Types of Programs

The course of a particular computer teaching program is diagramed as a *flow chart*, such as the example in Figure 10.19, which diagrams each item that can be presented by the computer and indicates when and if these items will be presented depending on the responses of the student. Errors may bring about repetition of previously presented items or presentation of new remedial

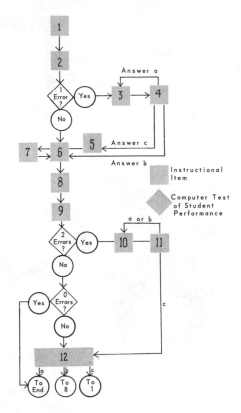

Figure 10.19.   A flow chart showing the types of decisions that a computer is programed to make in a particular lesson sequence. Item 12 is a self-evaluation item asking the student how well he feels he is doing. Answer *a* indicates that he thinks he is doing well and would like to finish now; he is directed to the end of the lesson. Answer *b* indicates that he thinks he is doing fine but would like some review; he is returned to item 8. Answer *c* indicates no understanding at all; he is returned to the beginning of the sequence. (Based on Coulson and Silberman. Automated teaching and individual differences. *Aud.-vis. Commun. Rev.*, 1961, 9, 5–15.)

material. The particular sequence diagramed in Figure 10.19 presents a self-evaluation item at the end. A student who is confident of his progress proceeds to the end of the lesson; one who is less

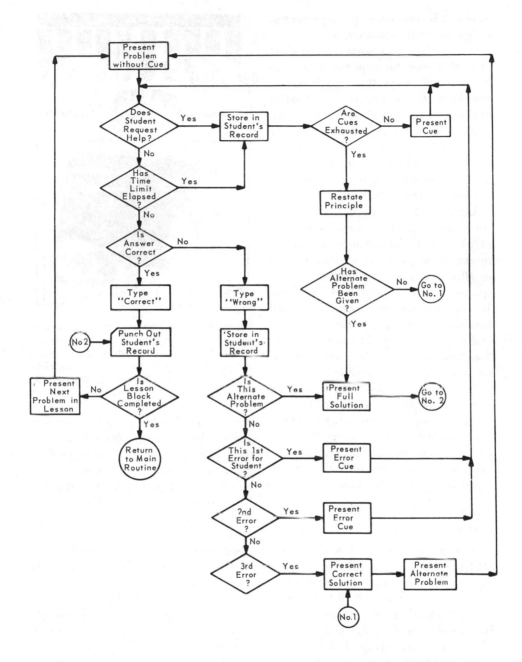

Figure 10.20.   A flow chart of decision logic used in a program prepared for teaching statistics. (From Grubb and Selfridge. *The computer tutoring of statistics: a preliminary report.* IBM Corp. Thomas J. Watson Res. Cent. res. Report RC–724, 1962.)

confident is returned to the beginning to repeat the entire sequence.

A flow chart represents a generalized plan of a program sequence which can be used with more than one lesson or subject matter. It indicates the type of decision made by the computer at each point in the program and the alternative subsequent steps depending on the nature of the decision. A chart indicating a number of different types of decisions is given in Figure 10.20.

Uttal (1961) described adaptation of computer teaching to a course in stenotypy, a shorthand system used in courts to obtain complete and accurate records of all conversation. Stenotypists use the special keyboard diagramed in Figure 10.21*a*. The keys are grouped into initial consonants, vowels, and final consonants, and a syllable is typed by pressing more than one key. In 10.21*b* are seen the student at the steno keyboard, the control panel which allows the student to communicate with the computer (to start and stop lessons, and so on), a set of cue lights indicating positions on the steno keyboard, and an electroluminescent display which gives the characters to be typed and other instructions.

Student Communication with the Computer

In computer-controlled teaching, the student communicates with the computer in a variety of ways. If a textbook is used to present the bulk of the instructional material, the console contains an instruction key that lights up to say, "Read your text." At the end of a numbered paragraph in the text, there is a code number which the student uses to elicit a specific problem from the ma-

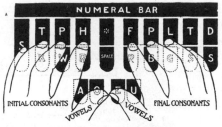

Figure 10.21.   Instrumentation for computer-controlled stenotype training. *a*. The stenotype keyboard. *b*. Visual display and student station. (From Uttal. *On conversational interaction*. IBM Corp. Thomas J. Watson Res. Cent. res. Rep. RC–532, 1961.)

terial stored in the computer memory system. When he decides on his answer, the student presses a button entitled, "I am ready," and the computer signals him to proceed (indicating that it is free to accept a message from this particular student). The student now types his answer and looks it over for errors. If he wishes to change it at this point, he can cancel it and retype. When satisfied, he presses a release key to send the message into the computer. Within a second or two, the computer either verifies the answer ("Right, John,") and directs him to a new problem or page of text or tells him he is wrong and branches to remedial material. A student can be addressed by name on the typewriter because he has entered his code number at the beginning of the lesson. Some communicator consoles include keys indicating readiness, a desire to stop the lesson, a request for the next problem, or a request for prompts. When a lesson has been completed the computer signals, "That is all for today."

Computer programs which follow simple branching and review sequences do not make full use of the computer's capabilities for flexible interaction with the student. Uttal (1962) suggested several further procedures that could be incorporated into computer programs. First, the computer's analytic capacity could be used to discover areas of difficulties to be improved and to generate solutions to the problems. Second, the computer could be used to analyze and classify errors so as to select related rather than identical problems for further practice. Third, reaction-time measurements might be used by the computer to anticipate difficulties and errors and to initiate corrective procedures before an error actually had been made.

Computer Simulation

The seemingly miraculous speed and complexity of the operations performed by computers lead many people to take an almost mystical view of their potentialities. Thus there have arisen the fanciful notions that computers can achieve logical solutions beyond human mental capabilities and that the brain itself can be understood as a form of computer. In assessing computers' contributions to modern science and technology, however, we must keep several facts in mind. First, the information that comes out of a computer is no more

valid than the facts and the program that were put into it. Second, computer operations never can duplicate behavior, for they proceed in terms of an artificial *machine language*. Finally, the workings of a computer never will reveal to us the organizational principles of human behavior and thought; to the contrary, full realization of the potentialities of computers for data processing and problem solving still hinge largely on our understanding of human thought processes and problem-solving procedures.

One special significance of computers in behavior science is that they make possible the simulation of many different patterns of symbolic behavior. Utilizing specialized instructions, they can divide and classify data into defined parts or sections and apply this information to the control or solution of problems. This classification of information simulates the human individual's ability to detect relations and similarities in terms of class properties.

Computers not only classify data but also examine its different classes and values in quite different ways. Different classes or variables can be correlated and the differences between classes can be analyzed simultaneously. Variables can be correlated over a period of time to plot a time function and their interactions can be measured. The factors determining correlations can be extracted, and trends and recurring features in the data can be measured. Computer operations can inspect complex interactions between functions and variables which would be almost impossible to discover by hand computation.

With computer technology, recorded events can be telescoped in time or expanded for special analysis. The relative time among events can be changed or displaced and correlations obtained among such time-displaced variables. The feedback that regulates events can be delayed to study the effects on the events or operations. Such time-freed analysis is of special value in simulating business, industrial, and economic operations in order to study events in these fields as short-term problems.

Computers simulate another fundamental operation in symbolic behavior and thinking by their ability to sample, reduce, and transform data in various ways. Continuous information, such as a graph of blood pressure, can be broken down by an analog converter into a series of discrete values and printed out as numbers. Data can be coded and numerically transformed to conform to different functions. Different sources of data can be brought together and the integrated value transformed for control purposes.

Computers can simulate aspects of teaching and social interaction at various levels of complexity. Among several basic types of simulation of vital importance for educational research, one is to program the machine to reproduce and control certain aspects of a response sequence. In this use, no symbolic knowledge as such is stored in the computer program; the machine is used simply to regulate the sequence of presentation by auxiliary devices in terms of student reactions. In this *sequence simulation*, the computer controls the presentation of questions, checks the correctness of coded answers, records errors, and regulates branching.

Computers also can be programed to simulate the manipulation of specialized symbol systems, such as numerical, verbal, or musical symbols, according to the principles and logic of special fields of knowledge. The computer is given comprehensive data covering a particular problem area and instructions regarding the basic variables involved in the operations. With these data and instructions, the machine can review various relationships among the data, solve problems, and test solutions. The problem-solving capacity of modern computers has made them an indispensable tool of research and operations in such specialized fields as business and industrial procedures, language translation, music and melody, medicine and diagnosis.

This *subject-matter simulation*, utilizing prescribed data, operations, and the theories and assumptions that define these operations, can be adapted to teaching or training purposes in the specialized fields. An example given in Chapter 9 was the use of computers to simulate business problems.

Inasmuch as computers can be used for dynamic cybernetic control of complex action systems, including those partly directed by man, they are potentially of great use in *systems simulation* and for training in machine operations and production systems. Analog computers were used in this way in wartime simulator-trainers, but the binary language of digital computers permits dynamic simulation and control by means of numerical and verbal instructions. Complex systems simulators are changing the patterns of work in business and industry and are providing the training media for understanding and carrying out dynamic man-machine operations.

Limitations of Computers
for Teaching

The exciting potentialities of computer simulation for educational purposes should not blind us to certain limiting factors involved in this application. First of all is the factor of cost. Computers themseves are extremely expensive machines and the cost of a single teaching station for student-computer intercommunication may be a thousand dollars or higher. Further, maintenance costs are high and the engineers, programers, and other specalists needed to install and run a computer system are highly paid personnel. Uttal (1962) suggested that computer teaching can be made less expensive than conventional lecture education on a per student course basis, but this estimate presumably applies to a situation where entire courses are programed through computers as an alternative to live teaching. If, when, and where this type of machine teaching proves desirable, computer costs may be justified. At present, the costs appear prohibitive for teaching machines used only to fill a subordinate role.

A second practical limitation on the use of computers is the highly skilled nature of programing. Only a limited number of trained specialists understand how to program a computer for different purposes, and surely very few of these trained programers are at the same time psychological or educational specialists with definite ideas about how to program subject matters for efficient learning. A school system or training center cannot utilize a computer-controlled teaching system without having available the specialized skills required to handle the problems of computer simulation.

A more serious difficulty is the restricted nature of the communicative interchange that is possible with computers. Effective teaching in a conventional school situation includes lectures, audiovisual displays and presentations, person-to-person exchanges between student and teacher, group discussions, and various types of adjunctive activities such as demonstrations, experiments, field trips, and so on. Out of this variety of verbal and nonverbal communicative patterns, computers can simulate only a few. The standard teaching station senses and presents visual-verbal and numerical information only. Other visual or auditory displays can be presented only with auxiliary devices that might be sequenced just as effectively by some other mechanism.

The main limitation of computers, as of all teaching machines, is that they function according to their own organizational principles and not according to the principles of human behavior. They can perform marvelously complicated operations at fantastically high speeds but only with information that some programer has been ingenious enough to convert into their own language. Basically all a digital computer can do is to answer Yes and No. It can *teach* only after some one has transposed some specialized subject matter into the rigidly prescribed computer code. Inasmuch as fields of knowledge and learning are all highly specialized, it takes ingenious and imaginative designers and programers to arrange a course of study for computer control without losing something of its special flavor and organization. In fact, there is always the danger that translating the fundamental concepts of a subject into the arbitrary logic and static classifications of computer language will distort the meaning of those concepts.

An aspect of human behavior and learning that is completely foreign to computer function is its spatial organization. Human perceptual-motor patterns are differentiated basically according to spatial patterns in the stimulus environment. Computer operations are time-differentiated, consisting of a temporal series of yes-no decisions. The almost unlimited geometric differentiation and integration that characterize behavior and define the course of learning cannot be simulated by a computer.

What we are saying, essentially, is that a digital computer is not a human teacher. The same could be said, of course, for any teaching machine, but we are emphasizing it here because the very real specialized advantages of computer systems tend to obscure their limitations. Within these limitations, the possibilities for computer automated teaching systems are great if the costs involved can be kept in line with the purposes served. Future computer systems very likely will incorporate visual sensing operations far superior to the verbal and numerical representations now in use. For example, visual displays might be sensed and reproduced from thousands of cells in mosaic form, or by integrating computer and television signals. Research in the area of computer simulation is in its infancy but already is making significant contributions to our understanding of behavior organization and performance.

SUMMARY

1. Devices called teaching machines, which present response-programed information by automatic means, were first developed by Pressey prior to 1930, but they attracted little attention until the last decade when they were popularized by Skinner as outgrowths of his operant learning research with animals.

2. Pressey's teaching machines were designed both for automatic scoring of multiple-choice tests and for teaching. Students answered multiple-choice questions by pressing one of four keys. The correct response triggered the next question. Chemo Cards and punchboards provided simpler feedback devices for self-instructional tests.

3. A series of experimental evaluations of Pressey's self-instruction devices confirmed their effectiveness in promoting learning when used in conventional and in accelerated classes. Self-instruction was relatively more effective for meaningful, structured material, and it promoted learning of material not specifically practiced as well as of practiced items. Immediate knowledge feedback appeared to be a significant factor. Overt responses were not always necessary.

4. Military research on self-instruction developed a number of devices in the 1950s which incorporated knowledge feedback. A significant new feature in some of these was branching programing, or variable sequences of items contingent upon student responses.

5. Research on the Subject-Matter Trainer indicated that prompting a correct response is more effective during

learning than simply confirming a correct response.

6. Skinner's teaching machines had these advantages also listed by Pressey: immediate reinforcement; reinforcement after each response; reinforcing nature of the task itself; assurance of active participation; adaptability to individual capabilities; and labor-saving features. The significant difference in Skinner's approach was that he rejected the multiple-choice technique in favor of composed answers.

7. In Skinner's first devices, students solved problems in arithmetic, spelling, or reading by positioning sliders. These boxes automatically evaluated correctness. Skinner's second type of device required the student to score his own answers as correct or incorrect, but he could not correct an error until the next time around.

8. Pressey's and Skinner's ideas generated two trends in teaching machine development. Skinnerian programs use composed answers and easy bit-by-bit sequences to teach entire courses. Pressey regards self-instruction as useful for drill and review and as adjunctive to other techniques.

9. Aside from special devices designed to teach arithmetic or spelling, most composed-answer teaching machines are simple boxes with no automatic features which present material and questions on paper rolls, mimeograph paper, cards, or film. The same type of program can be presented in programed books.

10. Skinner-type teaching machines and programed books use linear programs in which the sequence of questions is the same for all students.

11. Pressey-type teaching machines, employing the multiple-choice principle, are more versatile than the composed-answer boxes and can be used with young, retarded, and handicapped children as well as at higher educational levels.

12. Crowder's Autotutors were designed for branching programing in which the sequence of items depends on the response made by the student. Correct answers may lead to the dropping-out of certain items, or incorrect answers may bring on additional remedial material. Scrambled books are constructed to allow for branching programs.

13. Audiovisual teaching machines emphasize the integration of visual and aural, and verbal and nonverbal material to achieve flexibility in instructional presentations. Some audiovisual devices use slides and audio-tape for foreign language instruction.

14. An audiovisumatic system can combine lecture-demonstrations presented by tape, slides, and films with question-and-answer sequences controlled by the student's responses.

15. The most flexible teaching machines are those which utilize digital computers to control the program sequence. For such a use, a computer must be able to accept student responses and compare them with stored information in order to determine the appropriate next step. The computer must have high-speed random access to a large amount of programed information.

16. Computers can be used to teach a number of students in different subjects simultaneously. The practical limiting factors are the input stations and computer storage and retrieval facilities.

17. Computer programs are dia-

gramed as flow charts which indicate the types of items and the decision-making steps taken by the computer in controlling a branching program. Student communication with a computer can be made to simulate many features of a student-tutor interchange.

18. The most significant potentialities of computer techniques are to simulate many complex symbolic processes, communicative interactions, and problem-solving operations and to process data in complicated ways millions of times faster than would be possible by unaided human individuals.

19. Types of simulation useful for educational purposes are sequence simulation, subject-matter simulation, and systems simulation.

20. Using computers for teaching systems is limited by the costs involved, the special skills needed to install, maintain, and program computers, as well as the restricted nature of the computer language and therefore their simulation possibilities. These disadvantages must be weighed against the important advantages of speed, versatility, and flexibility.

CHAPTER

11

Programing for Self-instruction

In 1954, when Skinner published his first important paper on teaching machines, the devices then in existence, that were the direct antecedents of today's self-instructional techniques, included Pressey's experimental devices, one or more experimental devices at Harvard, and several trainers either being planned or under development in the Armed Forces. By 1960, there were an undetermined number being developed by industrialists, psychologists, educators, and training specialists, and the first few commercially available models appeared on the market. By early 1962, 104 different companies were engaged in planning, preparing, or producing either programs or devices or both for the school market—this in addition to the uncounted number of experimental and developmental projects gong on in noncommercial institutions (Finn and Perrin, 1962). The enthusiasm for programed self-instruction may have hit its peak in 1962, if one can judge by the number and the tenor of published books and articles in the field. As this book goes to press, it is not clear whether the apparent decline in active interest represents a natural leveling off of initial excitement or a general disenchantment with the utility of teaching machines and programs.

In the first years of development in self-instructional techniques, most of the interest centered on the devices rather than on the instructional materials themselves, but it soon was recognized that the devices were no better than the materials used in them (AERA-APA-DAVI Joint Committee, 1961, 1963). It was also discovered that programing was difficult, time-consuming, and had no generally accepted rules of procedure (Glaser, 1960). Nevertheless the number of programs available privately and commercially gradually increased to the point where a variety of self-instructional courses could be offered at all educational levels (Fry, 1961). A report to the U.S. Office of Education for the 1961–1962 school year listed 233 localities in forty-two states that were using programed materials (Hanson,

1963). A later summary reported that 400 programs would be available in September of 1963 (Filep, 1963).

Inasmuch as there still is no general agreement about the best way to construct a program or to use programed materials, we shall turn to a closer scrutiny of what programing involves. How are programs similar and how do they differ? Is one type of program better than another for all purposes? For some purposes? Is one type of response better than another, and why do we think so? Can a program be considered superior to a conventional textbook, inferior to it, or just different? There are many more questions to be raised in connection with programed self-instruction than there are confirmed answers.

VARIATIONS IN PROGRAMS

The term programing refers essentially to the arrangement of materials to be learned, and it goes without saying that good educational design demands an order of presentation that will be effective in promoting learning. This concept is not new. Teachers, textbook writers, and curriculum specialists always have tried to present material in effective ways—from easy material to more difficult, in logically ordered sequences, from general to specific and from specific to general and always with repetition and review of important points. But principles of this sort which have been implicit in effective teaching procedures suddenly took on an overweening importance in the self-instruction field, for most programs present arbitrarily restricted verbal sequences in which ambiguities may not become clear and errors of fact are intolerable.

In this section, we shall summarize the most important ways in which teaching programs can vary, most of which were mentioned in Chapter 10 in connection with the different kinds of devices. It should be noted that the design of a self-instructional program must be considered more carefully if it is intended to cover the entire subject matter of a course than if it simply is meant to be used as an adjunct to other teaching procedures. Thus, many of the points to be considered in this section are of small consequence to adjunctive programers.

Linear and Branching Programs

The main characteristics of linear programs constructed according to Skinner's principles are diagramed in Figure 11.1. The material is broken up into small units and presented in successive *frames*. After answering the first question (or filling in one or more blank spaces in a statement), the learner turns to the next frame where he gets a check answer and the next unit and question. This process is repeated to the end of the program. There is no provision for varying the sequence except to repeat a set of frames before proceeding to the next set. The characteristics stressed by Skinner are the step-by-step procedure, the active constructed response required of the learner, the prompt reinforcement of every response provided by the check answer, and the self-pacing permitted the learner.

Most linear programers believe that program steps should be gradual enough so that errors in response rarely occur. It has been suggested that the rate of errors should be below ten percent (Galanter, 1959), even below five per-

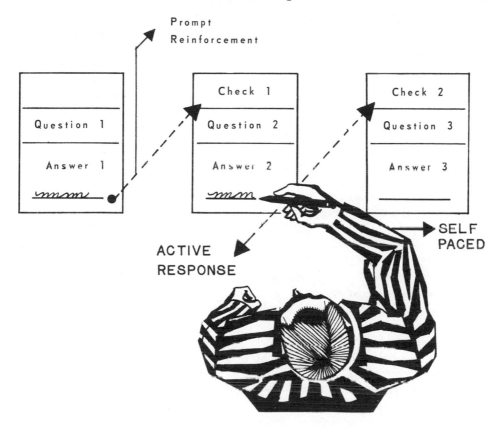

Figure 11.1.   The main characteristics of linear programs constructed according
to Skinner's principles.

cent (Holland, 1961). However, using
easy programs made up of very small
steps has revealed what Rigney and
Fry (1961) have called the *pall effect*—
the boredom induced by such material,
especially in bright students.

The term *branching* has been applied
to several different methods of varying
the presentation of items in a program.
Crowder's (1959, 1960) technique is to
introduce alternative sequences according to the response made by the learner.
An error leads to more information and
corrective procedures. Another type of
branching involves choice of alternative
subsets of items at key points in a program. For example, a set of questions
might be introduced to determine
whether or not the learner has attained
mastery of a principle. If he answers the
questions correctly, he is allowed to proceed to the next unit, but if he runs into
difficulty he is given more material dealing with the same principle. This type of
branching would require fairly complex
electronic circuits if handled automatically, but it could be achieved with simple
devices if the programs were packaged
in small units and given out to students
according to their previous performance.

The term branching also is applied to a technique that involves nothing more nor less than skipping over a number of items. If a learner answers a certain key item correctly, he is allowed to skip over a certain number of subsequent items.

Crowder (1960) described a number of different branching techniques as indicated by the diagrams in Figure 11.2. Most programers would prefer not to become involved in some of Crowder's more complicated sequences unless the superiority of such programs is established definitely.

Variations in Response Mode

The differences between multiple-choice and constructed responses have been the subject of many strongly worded statements but may be more factitious than real. Skinner and Holland (1960) stated baldly that they did not use multiple-choice "in order to avoid strengthening alternative wrong answers," although it never has been established that multiple-choice items do in fact strengthen wrong answers. On the other hand, Pressey, Crowder, and others feel that multiple choice is a valuable technique in self-instruction, both from the point of view of the teacher and from that of the student.

Since this controversy over response mode is not likely to be resolved to favor either type 100 percent of the time, a number of teaching devices have been designed to be used with either multiple-choice or constructed answers. Further there is some interest in combining both types of response in a single program. In Figure 10.13, we pictured our own technique of combining multiple-choice and constructed answers in the Duo-

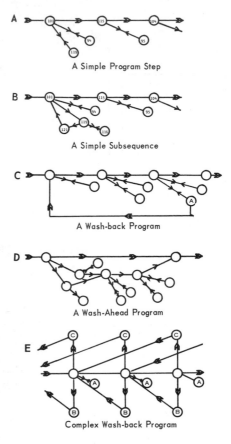

Figure 11.2.   Branching techniques described by Crowder. *a.* A simple program step with alternative frames to follow error responses. *b.* A simple subsequence providing further alternative frames following the first error alternative. *c.* A wash-back program. *d.* A wash-ahead program. *e.* A complex wash-back program. (From Crowder. Automatic tutoring by intrinsic programming. In A. A. Lumsdaine and R. Glaser (eds.), *Teaching machines and programmed learning: a source book.* Washington, D.C.: National Education Association, 1960, pp. 286–298.)

Mode device. The learner first selects an answer on a punchboard, but if an error is made, the correct answer must be written out one or more times. According to Carr (1959), Gilbert suggested a reverse procedure in which the learner first constructs an answer, then views a number of alternatives and chooses the one that best approximates his response. The teaching machine then provides feedback as to whether this choice was correct.

One of the disadvantages of using constructed responses is the time required to write out answers. A student who understands the material well often resents the slow pace imposed by this procedure. One way to speed up the process is to use a device such as the Auditutor, which presents instructional material aurally by means of Track No. 1 of audio-tape, and records the student's spoken response on Track No. 2. After each response, the Auditutor stops so that the student can choose whether to advance to the next unit, to review preceding questions and answers, or to re-record his previous answer. Vocal responses might be more advantageous than written responses in a number of circumstances.

Repetition and Drop-out

The repetition and review needed for effective learning and retention sometimes are built into a program and at other times are achieved by having learners repeat sets or programs until they have achieved mastery. Holland and Skinner's (1961) programed book used a lot of repetition of words, phrases, and principles in different frames and also provided review sets at intervals throughout the book. When a teaching device is used, a learner can be required to repeat a given set of items until he makes no errors. As we have seen, some devices are designed to drop out a question after it has been answered

correctly once, and some devices drop items after two or more correct responses. Since it is easier and more economical to construct a machine that drops an item after only one correct response, Rothkopf (1960) tried to determine whether there is any advantage to the more complicated procedure of dropping items after two correct responses. He compared the effectiveness of learning a set of items to mastery in these two ways: first, by eliminating an item from the practice series after one correct response and at the end repeating the entire procedure; and second, by eliminating each item after two correct responses. In both cases, each item was practiced to a criterion of two correct responses, and Rothkopf found that the two methods were about equally effective.

Prompts and Pacing

Most programers agree that learning in a self-instruction situation will be more effective if the learner does not make too many errors. In most linear programs, a low error rate is assured by designing the early frames with many cues and prompts. However, some of the more complicated teaching machines are designed to present and withdraw prompts automatically, so that the programs used in the machine need not be as lengthy. For example, the multiple-choice Subject-Matter Trainer (Figure 10.3) permits practice under several conditions, selected by turning a control knob (Briggs, 1958). In the coaching mode, the learner observes the item and then presses a switch which activates a green light beside the correct response. In another mode, the learner selects his own response but is allowed only one error per item. After each error the green light comes on next to the correct answer. The practice mode withdraws all prompts and requires the learner to make the correct responses on every item, the single-try mode allows only one attempt on each item, the paced-practice mode controls exposure time, and the testing mode provides no feedback but keeps score.

Although self-instruction usually is paced by the individual learner, it is desirable in some skill training to pace the learner automatically in order to increase his speed of response. For this reason, the Subject-Matter Trainer described above provides a paced-practice mode. The Solatron Automatic Keyboard Instructor (SAKI), which was designed to train card punching, automatically paces the student according to his demonstrated proficiency at the time (Pask, 1958). The SAKI trainer also employs an ingenious prompting mode. During the early part of training, a light comes on behind the key which is to be punched, but as the learner becomes more proficient, the prompting lights become dimmer and gradually disappear.

The gradual withdrawal of cue lights in SAKI is analogous to the technique known as vanishing or fading in verbal programs, which refers to the gradual withdrawal of prompts in a sequence of frames. Lumsdaine (1960) suggested the possibility of varying cue strength in verbal programs by physical changes rather than by semantic variations. Thus a stimulus cue might vary in brightness, duration, resolution or focus. If physical variations were used, the cue could be *faded in* during an item instead of being *faded out* over a sequence of items. The learner presumably would respond at successively lower cue strengths as learning progressed.

Feedback Schedules

A generally accepted requirement of programed self-instruction is immediate knowledge of results or confirmation of the correctness of the response. It also is considered desirable to provide opportunity for correction in case of error. In practice there are variations both in correction techniques and schedules of knowledge feedback.

The frequency of knowledge feedback is determined principally by step size and the size of the response segment that is confirmed by the program. Some teaching machines confirm one letter or digit at a time, as, for example, computers or the Wyckoff Film Tutor in Figure 10.8. In most cases, however, a longer answer must be chosen or one or more words filled into the blanks in a frame before knowledge of results is available.

Some work has been done with programs that delay definite confirmation until after more than one response has been made. Skinner (1961a) has described a two-stage response in which the student is given a question, constructs his answer, and then is given additional information. If his answer is wrong he may realize it from the new material and he has a chance to correct before uncovering the correct answer. In some of Crowder's branching sequences, a student who has erred may proceed for several frames of explanations and remedial material before being given the correction and told to return to the frame where the mistake was made.

CONSTRUCTING PROGRAMS

After the general design of a program has been established, the real work of writing and arranging material begins. In the first few years of activity in the self-instruction field, everyone who worked with programs freely shared his experiences, so that there were almost as many analyses of programing techniques as there were programers. Most of these analyses apply mainly to linear complete-course programing, including those summarized in the first part of this section. Relatively few suggestions have been made about how to construct branching programs or programs for adjunctive use.

Aspects of Program Planning

Meyer (1959) identified these three important questions that must be asked by the programer:

1. What relevant behavior is available at the start?
2. What behavior constitutes competence in the subject to be programed?
3. What is the best order of steps?

These points are broken down into greater detail by Quinn (1963), who prepared a description entitled, "How to Program (in 10 Difficult Lessons)," after spending three years at Fort Monmouth School programing courses and teaching others how to program. Quinn's first three steps have to do with Meyer's second point, identifying the final competence desired of the learner. First, according to Quinn, the programer writes out the Terminal Behavior Statement, specifying exactly what he is aiming for. Second, he defines the degree of competence required of the learner, specifying the relevant conditions under which the behavior is to be elicited, the accuracy and speed required, and so on. Third, it is a good idea to compose a final test of achievement at this early stage, to give the programer a clearer idea of his subject.

Quinn's fourth step is the identification of the student, which includes Meyer's first point. Before a program is written, the programer must identify the type of individual who will use it, especially the state of knowledge or previous education that can be assumed. Any other characteristics that are relevant should be stated—sex, age, visual acuity, and so on. Very often a pretest should be devised to accompany the program. Satisfactory performance on the pretest would indicate that an individual could proceed.

The remaining six steps in Quinn's analysis are related to Meyer's third point—determining the best order of steps. Briefly, Quinn's fifth step is to determine intermediate objectives or subgoals to be attained along the way to final competence. Then *prover frames* should be constructed to test the learner's mastery of each subordinate objective. A prover frame, as a test frame for a sequence, is *completely faded*, that is, without prompts of any kind. The overall sequence of the program then is determined by putting the prover frames in the most effective order. Finally, the *lead-up frames* are constructed for each prover frame. Each *achievement unit* is completed by applying specific techniques of cueing, redundancy, and fading. Quinn's last step is the Tryout and Revision, or the proof of the pudding. The program is tried out on subjects and each step is analyzed for imperfections. Quinn suggested that the actual number of frames be kept fairly low in the first writing, for it is much easier to add frames where they are needed than to delete frames from an overlong program. The main thing to watch for in the tryout is the error rate; any item or sequence which has an error rate of more than about ten percent may be ambiguous or too difficult. Corrective procedures are rewriting frames, adding new frames, and rearranging the sequence.

Klaus (1961a) suggested an evaluative procedure to be used prior to the tryout stage. His idea was to have the draft frames edited three times—first by another programer, second by a technical expert, and third by a skilled writer. Then after a tryout and revision, or more than one revision if necessary, the technical expert should be asked to review the frames again.

Writing Frames (Skinner and Holland)

According to Skinner's principles, the individual frames of a program should be written to lead the learner from ignorance to mastery of a subject matter with as few errors as possible. To do this, the programer breaks up the subject matter into very small bits or steps, arranges the steps in a meaningful sequence from easy to more difficult items, and uses many cues, prompts or ancillary information to insure correct answers. As the program progresses through a set of frames, the prompts are gradually withdrawn (vanished or faded) until the learner is emitting correct responses with no obvious props.

Holland (1959), who worked with Skinner in programing material on psy-chology, listed the following specific techniques for eliciting new or low strength responses with a minimum of error (examples are from Skinner and Holland [1960] and Holland and Skinner [1961]):

1. Give the student short passages of informational material, graphs, etc. to refer to while working on a particular set.

2. Use new words in a series of frames before requiring the student to use them. Example: In Holland and Skinner's (1961) programed book on *The Analysis of Behavior*, Part I, Set 1, the word "elicits" is required as a correct answer to Frame 8 ("A stimulus_____a response."). Prior to that, the word "elicit" had been used in Frame 4, "elicits," in Frames 5 and 7, "eliciting" and "elicitation" in Frame 8.

3. Move from definitions to examples within a single frame. Example: "A technical term for reward is reinforcement. To reward an organism with food is to_____it with food. (reinforce)"

4. "Lead-in" from assumed common knowledge. Example (Part I, Set 1, Frame 1 from Holland and Skinner): "A doctor taps your knee (patellar tendon) with a rubber hammer to test your_____. (reflexes or reflex)"

5. Indicate relevant categories to which the response term belongs. Example: "Reinforcement which consists of presenting stimuli (e.g., food or water) is called positive reinforcement; reinforcement which consists of terminating stimuli (e.g., loud noises or painful stimuli) is called_____reinforcement. (negative)"

6. Use high-association words or common phrases. Example: "A reward

simply makes it more_____that an animal will behave in the same way again. (probable, likely, or certain)"

7. Eliminate undesired alternative responses by careful phrasing of the frames. Example: "Coins are conditioned_____reinforcers. (generalized)" The item, "Coins are_____ reinforcers," will elicit the word "conditioned" in many cases; this is avoided by putting "conditioned" in the item.

Holland and Skinner also have used what they call *formal* prompts on occasion, for example, indicating the number of letters in the desired word, using the beginning or ending or other selected letters of the desired word, or presenting the item in rhyming form. The last is more suitable for young children.

Writing Frames (Smith)

D. E. P. Smith (1959) outlined the techniques of writing frames in somewhat the same way as Skinner and Holland, but in greater detail. According to Smith, frames are used to introduce concepts and to show the relationships between concepts and operations. Concepts can be introduced by definition, by example, by anticipation, or by prompts. If a definition is used first, it should be a common-sense statement rather than technical and should be followed in the same and later frames by examples. Contrast is used to refine the student's discrimination. If examples are used first, they should be followed by the general definition. Introduction by anticipation is Holland and Skinner's technique of using a word in a number of frames before requiring it as an answer.

Smith listed seven categories of verbal or mechanical prompts available to a programer. First, prompts can depend on *similarity* of ideas, of signals (for example, inserting a word or phrase to indicate the type of answer required), and of grammatical construction. Prompts also can depend on *contrast* of ideas or of signals. *Grammatical construction* sometimes limits the range of response, and *echoic behavior* may be used to elicit a word that has just been used in the frame. When a rule is stated in simple terms, the steps leading up to it can be elicited by a sense of *the whole*. *Hints* about previously learned material can be used if a problem requires use of that learning. Finally, there are *mechanical prompts* similar to those listed by Skinner and Holland.

Once the concepts are introduced into a program, "it is necessary to build a web of learning" to lead to true understanding of the subject matter. The principal techniques here are pure repetition, repetition by variation—by pointing out similarities and contrasts—and building developmental sequences. According to D. E. P. Smith, "if there are several ways to say the same thing, use them all. *Redundancy* is required." The purpose here according to generally accepted principles of linear programing is repetition not just to give practice but to elicit responses in many different contexts to insure transfer or generalization to future situations.

As a set of frames proceeds, vanishing or cue reduction should be used so that the learner becomes less and less dependent on the prompts and verbal structures in his responding. Finally, there should be a summation at the end of a sequence to integrate all the concepts and operations. Reviews should be inserted periodically throughout a program. D. E. P. Smith's last three points bear repeating as indicative of the linear programer's point of view:

> A. Don't expect much independent thought of the learner. Make the steps so small that he cannot err. . . .
> B. Stick to *one* element (concept or operation) at a time. Eliminate all irrelevancies except contrived "anticipators."
> C. Keep the amount of work (complexity of recall) very low per reinforcement.

The Ruleg System

In a paper presented first in 1959, Homme and Glaser (1960) tried to bring some precision into programing procedures. They started by analyzing hypothetical verbal interchanges between a tutor and a pupil, and they concluded that a large part of the tutor's verbal behavior could be classified as either principles or abstractions—that is, *rules* —or as instances or special cases—that is, *examples*. Proceeding from the premise that subject matter can be analyzed into rules and examples of different levels of complexity and abstractness, these authors evolved what they called a *ruleg* system of programing in which a rule is a *ru* and an example is an *eg*. As used in a frame, *rus* and *egs* are either complete or incomplete, that is, with one or more words omitted. There also can be false *rus* and false *egs*. Every frame in a program is composed of one or more of these units.

Working with this classificatory system, Homme and Glaser with their colleague Evans approached programing in a somewhat different way from Skinner. They felt that the important thing was to state the rule immediately in the first frame with an incomplete example. Once the concept is out in the open, it is refined by further examples and negative cases. Generalization of learning is achieved by using a wide range of *egs*, while discrimination between classes is dealt with by using false *egs*.

The differences between Skinner's original approach and the *ruleg* system can be illustrated by comparing a few frames from a program in High School Physics, which was described by Skinner (1958b), with a sequence of frames based on the same material rewritten by Homme and Glaser as *rus* and *egs*. From Skinner's program, we have selected Items 1, 2, 3, 12, 13, 14, 33, 34, and 35 to illustrate how the program progressed in difficulty:

> 1. The important parts of a flashlight are the battery and the bulb. When we "turn on" a flashlight, we close a switch which connects the battery with the_____. (bulb)
> 2. When we turn on a flashlight, an electric current flows through the fine wire in the_____and causes it to grow hot. (bulb)
> 3. When the hot wire glows brightly, we say that it gives off or sends out heat and_____ . . . (light)
> 12. Both the color and the amount of light depend on the_____of the emitting filament or bar. (temperature)
> 13. An object which emits light because it is hot is called "incandescent." A flashlight bulb is an incandescent source of_____. (light)
> 14. A neon tube emits light but remains cool. It is, therefore, not an incandescent_____of light . . . source)
> 33. Sunlight is_____by very hot gases near the surface of the sun. (emitted)
> 34. Complex changes similar to an atomic explosion generate the great heat which explains the_____of light by the sun. (emission)

35. Below about_____degrees Celsius an object is not an incandescent source of light. (800)

Now let us look at the first five items from Homme and Glaser's suggested program dealing with the same material, described in terms of *rus* and *egs:*

(*ru* + incomplete *eg*) 1. To "emit" light means to "send out" light. For example, the sun, a fluorescent tube, and a bonfire have in common that they all send out or_____light. (emit)

(incomplete *eg*) 2. A firefly and an electric light bulb are alike in that they both send out or_____light. (emit)

(*ru* + incomplete *eg*) 3. Any object which gives off light because it is hot is called an incandescent light source. Thus a candle flame and the sun are alike in that they both are_____ sources of light. (incandescent)

(incomplete *eg*) 4. When a blacksmith heats a bar of iron until it glows and emits light, the iron bar has become a(n)_____source of light. (incandescent)

(false *eg*) 5. A neon tube emits light but remains cool. Unlike the ordinary electric light bulb, then, it is not an _____ _____of light. (incandescent source)

The material that was dealt with in thirty-five frames by Skinner was completed in twenty-one frames in the *ruleg* program. Homme and Glaser reported that besides achieving some economy in programing, their vocabulary facilitated talking about programs and made instruction in programing techniques somewhat easier. More importantly, their approach facilitated the programing process itself. They felt that a programer who can state a rule and some examples is off to a good start. Further, this technique of stating the rule first meant that variables such as step size

and cue fading lost importance, for there was no need to work up to a concept gradually and prompts could be withdrawn almost at once. Such specific questions as these concern *ruleg* programers: How quickly should extensive variations in the *egs* occur? and, How many *egs* are sufficient? However, lest they might seem too sanguine about their system, Homme and Glaser reminded us that there are still important problems relative to the breaking of *rus* into sub*rus,* and the ordering and amount of strengthening of *rus* and *egs.*

A more complete exposition of the *ruleg* system by Evans *et al.* (1960) described a procedure for identifying the verbal relationships that ought to be established in a program. Their technique is to specify all the terms or *rus* that make up a subject matter of a program and to place them on both axes of a matrix. Each intersecting cell of this *ruleg* matrix identifies an intraverbal connection which might be useful in teaching the subject matter or providing prompts. From the total number of these connections displayed on the matrix, the programer selects some for inclusion in his program.

Evans *et al.* suggested that matrices be made up for every interrelationship that is to be developed among the *rus,* for example, one matrix for *relators* and one for *discriminators.* The cells of these matrices are filled in with appropriate examples which then are used for frames of the program.

The Pall Effect

The pall effect sometimes induced in learners by the products of linear programing is no more deadly than a similar reaction induced in readers by the many analyses of programing techniques. We could go on to recount Galanter's (1959) listing of programing problems, Beck's (1959) analysis of teaching rules and the teaching process, Gilbert's (1960a) classification of types of frames, Carr's (1959) bilevel description of programing as the curriculum specialist views it and as the psychologist views it, Klaus's (1961a) summary of twelve rules of programing, Jacobs' (1962) detailed comparison of program construction and test construction, and so on, not quite *ad infinitum*. However, we think we have given enough detail on the various programing techniques to demonstrate why the pall effect described by Rigney and Fry (1961) is a real and present danger.

Several characteristics of linear programs contribute to their implicit tedium, but the most obvious is the repetition that is deemed necessary to teach material in this fashion. All analyses of programing stress the importance of repetition. Smith (1959) said, "if there are several ways to say the same thing, use them all." Klaus said that when a particular response stops ringing in a programer's ears, it probably is time to review this response in the program. He claimed that monotony could be reduced by varying cues and contexts, but neither Klaus nor any other programer has found a sure way to eliminate monotony.

To give an example of the repetitious nature of linear programs, we have analyzed the first two sets of Holland and Skinner's (1961) *The Analysis of Behavior*, which, it should be noted, purports to present an introduction to psychology at the college level. Part I, the first of fourteen parts, is entitled *Reflex Behavior* and is divided into six sets. The first two sets deal with "Simple Reflexes" and "Conditioned Reflexes." The remaining four sets of Part I continue with conditioned reflexes, Pavlov's experiments, and the response mechanisms.

Set 1 of *The Analysis of Behavior* contains fifty-four frames which require seventy-six fill-in answers, almost always one-word responses. Out of this total, the following words are required most frequently:

Stimulus	14
Response (or responds)	9
Reflex	8
Elicit (elicits or elicited)	8
Latency	7
Threshold	7
	53 (out of 76)

Thus six words are used for seventy percent of the answers in the first set, and most of the other answers deal with such concepts as *magnitude, intensity, greater, smaller,* and so on. Set 2 contains thirty frames which require thirty-four answers. A few of these repeat the most frequent answers of the first set, but the majority deal with conditioning, as follows:

Conditioning (or conditioned)	9
Unconditioned (unconditioned reflex or unconditioned stimulus)	8
Extinguished (or extinction)	4
	21 (out of 34)

Again a few words are repeated for almost two-thirds of the answers.

Another characteristic of linear programs that makes them seem dull and lifeless is the deliberate simplicity of each frame. Programers proceed on the assumption that any portion of an item which is not necessary for the student to arrive at the correct answer probably is not taught by the item and therefore should be deleted. Smith (1959) said programers should "Eliminate all irrelevancies except contrived 'anticipators.'" Frames designed in this manner may lead the learner directly to the response desired by the programer, but they do little to stimulate the learner's interest in the larger aspects of the subject matter.

A third deadening feature of linear programs is the contrived artificiality of their structure. This is more serious in programs that deal with higher-level fields of verbal knowledge than in those that teach very specific systems of knowledge, such as spelling, mathematics, or foreign languages, and it is more serious for older learners than for younger. College students, for example, attempting to gain some understanding of a complex subject matter deserve more than the verbal and mechanical artifices of a typical linear program. The tiny bits of information doled out in discrete steps, the verbal and grammatical tricks, the mechanical prompts, the "turn to the next page," and "go back to page 10"—all this patronizing spoonfeeding is calculated more to frustrate them than to enlighten a student worthy of the name. Or consider a *ruleg* matrix. Why should it be supposed that relating terms to each other on a correlational grid will reveal the inherent organization of a subject matter? This technique, along with the other devices that structure a linear program, tends rather to obscure the meaningful interrelationships than to clarify them. It is a very

real danger that the student plodding through a linear program will not be able to see the forest for the trees.

Although to some of us it appears that linear programs are inevitably a dull and mechanical medium for the exchange of ideas, the programers themselves are always hopeful that this is not the case. Holland (1961) said that programing principles in themselves are no excuse for "dull, humorless, mechanical writing." And Quinn (1963) complained that programers get so involved with cueing, fading, and redundancy that their writing lacks the "divine fire" of the resourceful teacher. But then a resourceful teacher never learned his communicative skills in an animal laboratory.

Branching Programing

Crowder (1959, 1960) has not been as explicit as have the linear programers in describing his techniques for constructing branching programs. One reason for this is that branching programs usually are written in the familiar expository style of textbooks and oral lectures without the restrictions imposed by Skinner's principles of step-by-step progression. Another reason is that branching programers are not as concerned about the error rate as linear programers inasmuch as the technique is devised to provide remedial material after errors are made. An error indicates that the communication process has been faulty, so another approach is tried.

According to Crowder, if a student does make an error the problem is not solved simply by revealing the correct answer, as is done in linear programs, for the failure in communication occurred before the response was made.

What is needed following an error is an attempt to repeat or revise the communication process, as is provided by the alternative material in a branching program. There is some casual evidence to support this point of view. For example, Keislar (1959) reported a remark made by a fifth-grade pupil who had completed a program on understanding the areas of rectangles: "It's hard to know why you get something wrong. When I got it right, I knew it. When I got it wrong, I didn't know why."

Branching programs can be used effectively in areas where the alternatives are not clearly right or wrong. For example, branching programs have been written to play bridge with the reader. Complex choices which involve degrees of rightness or wrongness could not be handled effectively by linear programs.

As of now, the techniques used in constructing branching programs are mainly intuitive as they are in writing textbooks. Jacobs (1962) pointed out that to construct a good program of this kind, one needs to know the common errors that are made at each choice point, the source of these errors, and the remedial material that will be most effective for each one.

Adjunctive Programing

Pressey and others who believe that self-instruction should be an adjunct to teaching rather than the main medium take a very different view of programing from those described above. According to Pressey's (1963) point of view, the *initial* presentation of most types of instructional material should not be in bits and pieces but in a larger, meaningful whole. Most often this would be by textbook, but it might be, for example, by field trip, demonstration, or experiment. After the first presentation has given the learner a chance to "move about freely in the material" and to grasp its larger structure, self-instruction might very well be used to enhance the clarity and stability of the subject matter. Used in this way, a self-instructional program "will deal only with issues which need further clarification or emphasis. Such adjunct autoelucidation will *not* cover everything, may jump from one point to another or even back and forth."

Selecting items for such an adjunctive program would involve a determination of those points in any subject matter that cause the most difficulty for learners. The order of presentation of the items would not be particularly important, for the structure of the subject matter is presented in other ways. The initial error rate is of no particular importance either, for the student is expected to correct his own mistakes. In Pressey's opinion, the items usually should be presented as multiple-choice questions with one notably clear right answer and "only such wrong alternatives as express common misunderstandings."

Although Pressey offered no specific techniques for constructing items, Stephens (1960) investigated several special arrangements of multiple-choice alternatives. With a standard inside-alternates procedure, where each of the wrong alternatives for each item appears as a right choice for another item, no increase in learning was found. A special grouping in which each right alternative appeared as a wrong alternative for the next three items improved practice performance but did not affect recall. However, a paired-inside-alternates arrangement (putting two Russian words at the beginning and end of each line and their English equivalents between) did improve performance on the recall test. Stephens' study shows that it is possible to investigate multiple-choice items objectively in order to improve them.

THEORETICAL CONSIDERATIONS

In Chapter 6 we noted that the early literature on audiovisual techniques was concerned almost entirely with practical and applied aspects and that the theoretical problems were a secondary consideration. Quite the reverse has been true of the field of self-instruction, where theory has been a central concern throughout the past decade. The literature on teaching machines and programed learning is marked by claims and counterclaims, arguments and counterarguments, often supported by only the most tenuous assumptions.

The Operant Conditioning Model

No one in the self-instruction field has applied theoretical constructs to the design of devices and programs as persistently and as confidently as have Skinner and those who share his views. The operant conditioning principles and methods that appear to work so successfully in training animals are assumed to apply to human learning as well. The assurance with which the Skinnerian theorists apply their animal training techniques to the complexities of human behavior is illustrated by this passage from Holland (1960):

> When developing a complex performance in a pigeon, we may first reinforce simply the behavior of approaching the food tray when it is presented with a loud click. Later the pigeon learns to peck a key which produces the click and the food tray. Still later, he may learn to peck this key only when it is lit, the peck being followed by the loud click and approach to the food tray. In the next step, he may learn to raise his head or hop from one foot to another, or walk a figure-8, in order to produce the lighted key which he then pecks; the click follows; and he approaches the food tray. This principle of gradual progression runs through many of the teaching machine techniques. Both human and avian scholars deserve the same careful tutorage.

The Skinnerian approach exemplified by this passage proposes to revolutionize education by leading the learners through a carefully arranged series of small steps from ignorance to mastery while they seldom if ever encounter failure. Let us ignore for a moment the ghost of Rasputin (or is it George Orwell) and try to judge Skinner's concepts on their psychological merits. First of all, there are some obvious things to be said about the pigeon analogy. People are not pigeons. They do not behave like pigeons and probably do not—except under certain restricted circumstances—learn like pigeons. Further, the complex sequence described above that was taught the laboratory pigeon has no inherent structure and organization except in the thinking of the experimenter and thus has no meaning to pigeons in general. In fact, the learned behavior has no meaning and serves no adaptive function for the pigeon that learned it except under the arbitrary and artificial arrangements of the operant conditioning laboratory. In contrast, the sort of behavior taught to human students in schools is meaningful to people in general, serves adaptive purposes in a variety of situations in school and out, and is subject to confirmation or correction by the way it falls into place within the larger area of human knowledge and experience. No one would disagree seriously with these comments except at one point: psychologists do disagree as to whether learning is one constant biological function that applies to all species at all times. Can principles of learning that describe the behavior of animals in laboratories be transposed without modification to meaningful human behavior?

Limitations of the Operant Model

The attempt to reduce all learning to the operant conditioning model has found many in disagreement. Hilgard (1956) concluded, "There are probably a number of different kinds of learning which have emerged at different evolutionary periods, . . . It is quite probable that these different kinds of learning follow different laws." Significantly, the differences in learning patterns have been most apparent and most impressive to people whose primary concern is with meaningful human learning in education and training, while the enthusiasm for applying conditioning principles to these human situations has been generated originally by animal psychologists.

For our present purposes, we shall skirt the general issues of learning theory and confine ourselves to several questions about the use of the conditioning model to describe programed learning. In the first place, although the concept of reinforcement is of prime importance in Skinner's analysis, it is not without ambiguity. In operant conditioning, reinforcement is an external

event brought about by a response which increases the probability that the response will reoccur. In self-instruction or programed learning as in other operant learning, the reinforcement presumably must be made *precisely contingent* upon the behavior that is being taught (Porter, 1958). However, when we examine the behavior of the learner more carefully, we cannot be completely sure what constitutes the reinforcement. Is it the manipulation involved in operating a device? Skinner (1954) himself said, "The sheer control of nature is itself reinforcing," but an individual can control a simple Skinner teaching box or programed book whether his answer is right or wrong. If manipulative control is an important reinforcer, then we should stick to teaching machines that progress to the next question only after a correct response has been made. Inasmuch as Skinner abandoned that type of controlled progression, we must assume that he depends on reinforcements other than "the sheer control of nature."

Is confirmation of correctness the reinforcement? Carr (1959) objected that confirming the correctness of a learner's responses may be expected to be reinforcing only if the learner's motivation is intrinsic to the task being learned. In other words, confirmation in and of itself is not enough; the learner must be otherwise motivated to perform. Further, evidence is accumulating that shows confirmation of correctness not to be an essential feature of self-instruction. Skinner and Holland (1960) reported that students using their teaching disks showed a tendency to put down any answer in a hurry in order to move ahead and see the correct check answer. And seeing the answer was not "precisely contingent" upon making the correct response, for it sometimes followed an incorrect response. In this case, was it just *any* response that was being reinforced? Again, Homme and Glaser (1960) reported instances in their experimental work on programed materials when the correct answers were omitted inadvertently from the cards used by the learners. To their surprise, the learners sometimes insisted that the omission made no difference: "Oh, it didn't bother me, I knew my answers were right anyway." To these learners, *extrinsic* confirmation of correctness was not always necessary and no external reinforcement was "precisely contingent" upon their responses, yet they learned the material.

We are left with the feeling that no one has pinned down the exact nature of the reinforcement in self-instruction and that learners sometimes learn even without specific reinforcements. Human students often are too impatient to wait around to have their behavior shaped bit by bit, especially if the new material is meaningful and fits well into their present knowledge. In our opinion, meaningful learning is controlled more by the organization of the subject matter, the way it conforms to prior knowledge, and the adaptive functions it serves than by discrete rewards.

Another question raised by Skinner's approach to programed learning is whether the elimination of errors in education and training is necessary or even desirable. The bit-by-bit linear programs are designed on the assumptions that errors are aversive and should be minimized, that many reinforcements of correct responses are desirable, and that complex behavior is learned by follow-

ing a series of small steps from simple to complex. According to Amsel (1960), there is no body of experimental evidence to support Skinner's assumption that errors should always be minimized, and he suggested two circumstances when it might be desirable to evoke errors. If a learner starts instruction with relatively strong incorrect response tendencies, these incorrect responses should be elicited so that they can be nonrewarded and thus weakened. Amsel's second circumstance concerns the consequences of making an error. To the extent that an incorrect response might have serious or dangerous consequences, to that extent should it be elicited so that it can be weakened.

Amsel's argument is that incorrect responses in some circumstances are desirable from the point of view of efficient learning. Pressey made somewhat the same point with respect to selecting the alternatives for multiple choice questions. He suggested that only those alternatives should be used which represent common misconceptions. A more commonly expressed argument is that errors serve a useful purpose in informing the teacher where further instruction is necessary. As Crowder said, errors indicate when the communication process has failed and when another or a different approach is needed.

In spite of all arguments to the contrary, however, Skinnerians are firm in their belief that errors should be minimized or eliminated in learning. On this basis they reject multiple-choice questions because of the possibilities for incorrect response and they reject Crowder's type of branching programs because they are designed on the assumption that errors will occur. (The only type of branching acceptable to Skinnerians is to skip over a certain number of items.) Even if this arbitrary restriction of the learner's performance to *correct* responses is conducive to efficient learning of those particular responses that appear in the program—and this point has not been proved—we wonder what effect it might have on related behavior outside the learning situation. Is a learner who never is permitted errors equipped to deal with the realities of human living?

Inflexibility of Linear Programs

If we were to attempt a summary evaluation of linear programs, it would be that they are too inflexible to do justice to human capabilities in learning and creative thought. The concepts of linear programing tend naturally toward an educational regimentation that does not make adequate allowance for the differences that exist among learners, among their teachers, and among the subjects to be taught. Nor does a linear program take advantage of the many avenues of communication that can be used in teaching or the many types of experiences that promote fuller understanding of a subject matter.

As we have pointed out previously, a linear program dictates the same sequence of responses for all learners. Yet human individuals bring to the learning situation wide differences in ability and present knowledge. A program that serves the needs of a relatively dull or relatively uninformed individual serves as a drag on one who is better equipped. Linear programers have made much of what they call the self-pacing feature of self-instruction, but in reality the business of writing out many discrete an-

swers makes it impossible for bright students to move ahead at a rate commensurate with their ability.

Skinner's notion that linear bit-by-bit programs permit all learners to achieve mastery of a subject matter also has been questioned. Kendler (1959), for example, reminded us that "mastery" of a program may reflect quite different levels of learning in different individuals. Because of differences in ability, in prior learning, in their symbolic processes, and so forth, learners will show differences in the kind and amount of transfer from a mastered program or course to other areas.

Linear programs not only fail to make allowance for individual differences among students, but they also provide a very poor medium for expressing individual differences of opinion among teachers or experts. The whole concept of linear programing is based on a right-wrong, black-white view of the material to be taught. The programer becomes the voice of authority and shapes the behavior of the learner along prescribed correct pathways. This may be an acceptable method of teaching that $2 + 2 = 4$, but we believe that it is a very poor way to approach the fluid, controversial subject matters that make up such an important part of higher level instruction. Because of what has been called a linear program's natural tendency to infallibility, it would be very difficult, if not impossible, to use one to make a balanced presentation of conflicting opinions. Linear programs are particularly inappropriate for political, ethical, or artistic subject matter (Resnick, 1963).

Programed self-instruction often is called the tutorial or Socratic method of teaching because it involves continuous give-and-take between the student and his mechanical tutor. Jordan (1963) recently objected to this misuse of the term *Socratic teaching*, pointing out that ordinary programs by no means teach by the method of inquiry but are completely authoritative.

One of the most serious deficiencies of linear programs is the restricted nature of the material they present. Linear programers make almost no use of nonverbal visual displays and other supplementary materials. In contrast, adjunctive programers, looking on a self-instructional program as just one technique among many, are free to use well illustrated textbooks, audiovisual materials, live interaction in the classroom, field trips, experiments, demonstrations—the whole repertoire of instructional techniques that are available in modern schools. It is significant that one of Skinner's earliest associates in programing research suggested recently that programs should be considered as just one type of teaching tool to be used within the context of the teacher-student relationship (Markle and Bossone, 1963).

It is our belief that teaching a course by linear program is deliberately limiting the media of communication, the experiences of the student, and thus the range of understanding that he achieves. We believe that the most promising approach to education is to provide the student with a broad context of experience by resorting to all of the activities and all of the communicative media at our disposal. We would include both verbal and nonverbal material, and would assume that the student will learn by responding to the perceptual organization of his environment. We should

not fear a certain number of errors if there is opportunity for him to explore the consequences of these errors and to correct them. We should expect him to learn some problem-solving skills that can be generalized to future problems and to gain some appreciation for those areas where there are no absolutely certain answers but only a set of possible alternatives to be judged according to their apparent merits.

In Defense of Reading

The very real values inherent in self-instructional methods (Hilgard, 1961) are in danger of being obscured by the extreme positions taken by some adherents of Skinner's principles. Programed learning is put forward as the instructional method par excellence. Said Homme and Glaser (1960), "we are convinced that if psychologists were armed with complete course programs, they could bring about some startling events in the world." But these startling events presumably are precisely contingent on the use of linear, bit-by-bit, constructed-response programs. Holland (1960) referred to other techniques as, "The ill-advised efforts of some of our friends who automatize their courses without adopting the new technology. . . ."

The "new technology" of operant conditioning is held to be superior not only to other programing techniques but also to textbook learning as well, and Glaser *et al.* (1960) have even said that, "it is possible that present-style textbooks will become outmoded as teaching aids." Lumsdaine (1963) echoed this opinion, predicting that within a decade or so the textbook as we know it may decline (or die) in favor of the combination of sequenced programs and reference handbooks or source books. It is here that many educators and psychologists are beginning to take a stand in defense of a technique that has served man well for thousands of years. In Pressey's (1963) words:

> . . . for skimming for main ideas, for review—for any use except that initial go-through—the programed book is almost impossible and the teaching-machine roll entirely so. Mostly, even for the first go-through, they are unsatisfactory, because most important matter to be learned has structure, which the programing destroys except the serial order, and most important learning is integrative and judgmental, so requires a looking about in what is being studied; for all such purposes a teaching machine seems about as hampering as a scanning device which required that one look at a picture only 1 square inch at a time, in a set order. . . .
>
> . . . For a learner with reading-study skills, conventional textual matter orders and structures its contents in paragraphs and sections and chapters, exhibits that structure in headings and table of contents, makes all readily available in index with page headings and numbers. The learner thus has multiple aids to the development and structuring of his understanding. If need be he can, with a flick of the finger, move about in the material; he can skip that already known, turn back as a result of a later felt need, review selectively. As a way to present matter to be learned, the average textbook may not be best. But thousands of frames on a teaching-machine roll or strung through a programed book would seem close to the worst.

Working through a program does not teach the basic skills of reading as they are needed in modern education and modern life. Reading is a highly dynamic activity. Its speed and efficiency depend not only on print size and legibility, but also upon the orderly arrangement of words, sentences, and paragraphs on consecutive pages. Linear programs would be of little or no help in teaching readers how to grasp the meaning of printed verbal material at high speeds. In spite of the convictions and predictions of programing enthusiasts, we believe that reading is still the key to success in school just as books are still the indispensable tools of educated man.

Establishing Cybernetic Control

Our own ideas about behavior organization and learning suggest some procedures and interpretations of programing that differ basically from those of Skinner. In general terms, we describe learning as the establishment of specialized patterns of feedback control over behavior in relation to the physical and social environment. The control patterns may involve unaided responses, they may involve tool or machine skills, and they may involve symbolic manipulations or abstract knowledge. In the chapters on training, we outlined some definite principles relative to the learning of overt perceptual-motor skills, and in our opinion these same fundamental principles apply to symbolic learning as well. Behavior involves dynamic generation of activity, continuous feedback control and error correction based on spatial differentiation of stimuli, and the integration of different movement components in the total response pattern. The effectiveness of any trainer, learning aid, or teaching machine depends on how well it fulfills the requirements of cybernetic design for the particular type or level of feedback control which is being established—direct, instrumental, symbolic, or abstract.

For many centuries, man has been educated in the audio-visual-social context of the classroom, using verbal-nonverbal techniques and relying heavily on the verbal-graphic patterns of textbooks. We do not believe that the design of these teaching techniques and devices has developed haphazardly. Rather, we believe that most of them have stood the test of time because they have been effective in establishing feedback control of knowledge and skills.

One of the most obvious differences between the conventional teaching situation and programed self-instruction is in the variety of perceptual-motor activity generated in the learner. A Skinnerian program makes no provision for manipulating the material in flexible ways to discover unusual relationships and varied meanings. When linear, small-step programs are used, the learner's performance may take on the characteristics of a vigilance task, in which restrictive sensomotor conditions prevent effective feedback control. Such programs reduce the possibilities for individualized control over the learning situation by rigidly restricting the activity of the learner to a series of discrete responses. Such monotonous design can be justified only for practice in discrete unitary items, such as spelling words, and then not for too long a period.

One of our primary principles is that behavior is basically space-organized, and that consequently a temporal sequence is in a sense artificial and can be learned most efficiently if it is integrated into some spatially referenced pattern of response. That is, the discrete responses of a temporal series should be supported and cued by a more general response pattern that has spatial reference.

There are many sources of spatial organization in school learning, not the least of which are the design features of ordinary textbooks. The subject matter in a book is arranged in paragraphs, sections, and chapters, set off by headings of various qualities. These organizational features generally outline the logical structure of the specialized subject matter of the book and gives the student a framework within which more detailed facts can be arranged and remembered. In addition, most textbooks are embellished with tables, graphs, and illustrations that supply additional spatial patterns to enhance the learning and retention of detail. We believe that a very important feature of internalized systems of knowledge are such spatially organized frameworks which—though they have been transformed and reduced —may have had their original source in visual design features of the learning situation.

Inasmuch as linear programs are thought by Skinnerians to be analogous to an operant conditioning sequence, no thought is given to their spatial reference systems. The questions and answers compose a temporal series of discrete units, and few if any organized perceptual displays are given the student to help him understand the over-all organization of the subject matter. Thus for material that has inherent logical structure, a linear program is a poor teacher. Audiovisual teaching machines have some advantages over restricted verbal programs in that they can display graphs and illustrations to give spatial reference to the verbal material.

Another one of our principles, that

behavior involves a multidimensional integration of different response components, implies that the focal discrete responses in a learned pattern are just a part of the pattern. For example, there are certain general meanings portrayed by prose passages that are not conveyed by limited phrases and sentences. The presentation may vary in terms of the emotional values or attitudes expressed, the concreteness of the ideas, the dynamic rate and facility of expression, and the articulation of the material in terms of the amount of detail. Linear programing tends to focus its attention only on this last aspect and in so doing establishes no general context or style. There is no general body of knowledge that does not lose some of its meaning and significance if presented mechanically as a series of discrete steps. It would appear to be almost impossible for a linear program to teach the broader aspects and meanings of a subject.

Our belief that symbolic learning involves systematic feedback transformations from more direct sensory patterns implies that graphic material supplies important supportive meanings to purely verbal presentations. Programing tends to emphasize the juggling of verbal units rather than integrating verbal presentations with graphic displays, demonstrations, and direct experience. We believe that graphic materials not only support verbal meanings but convey new ideas, and that this is as true in the sciences and the humanities as in more practical areas such as industrial training, advertising, and marketing. A student introduced to a new subject can establish a higher level of control over its concepts if he can deal with it both verbally and nonverbally in an integrated way.

Another reason for presenting subject matter in diverse ways is that this flexibility contributes to a greater transfer potential of the learned behavior. In discussing skill training, we emphasized the necessity of simulating the performance situation but noted that any significant variations that might occur in that situation should be represented in training. In school learning, the behavior that is learned should be very general—that is, very transferable—for it must be used under many diverse conditions. The best way to insure generality is to vary the learning conditions. Linear programers attempt to do this by including general rules and many examples and by varying the wording in program frames, but their presentations still are very limited when compared with the many different aural and visual, verbal and nonverbal techniques of the classroom.

The main limitation of the Skinnerian type of teaching box and programed book is that their discrete confirmations do not provide immediate, clear-cut feedback effects that are tied in dynamically with the student's response. Confirmations that are obained by fumbling with a crank or by turning a page apparently satisfy the theoretical requirements for discrete, extrinsic reinforcements, but they do not satisfy the requirements of good cybernetic design. All kinds of learning situations benefit from immediate and dynamic feedback information and from the opportunity for the learner to maintain continuous control. Better feedback effects result from reading a well designed book than from a Skinnerian program, especially if the book incorporates graphic displays that generate exploratory activity, provide perceptual variations in the material, organize novel details in spatial patterns, and provide many prompts that enhance the meaning of the words. Immediate dynamic confirmation of specific response is provided by automated teaching machines such as Pressey's or even by Chemo Cards and punchboards but not by the verbal write-in models.

Our principles of cybernetic design support Pressey's general position that small-step programs are not a good way to introduce new subject matter in schools. We believe that teaching machines and question-and-answer programs do have a valid and important role in educational design, but no one teaching machine or type of program is appropriate for all learning situations (Briggs, 1959). Small-step constructed-response programs apparently are very useful in teaching unambiguous material such as spelling and arithmetic, especially when automated devices are used, but it should be noted that even these materials have been introduced in broader, more organized contexts by the child's previous reading and other experiences. Extended practice in the detail of spelling and arithmetic to the point of overlearning helps to make the responses autonomous in the same sense that overlearned skills become autonomous. For more complicated subject matter, we believe that multiple-response teaching machines provide better design features than write-in answer programs for drill and review in specific details. We would incorporate graphic materials along with verbal materials and aural along with visual as much as possible.

Complete course programs are undoubtedly valuable and justified for certain specialized purposes, such as instruction in the home, in hospitals and institutions, in schools for retarded children, in centers for the unemployed, in industry, and in the Armed Forces. For example, mechanized complete course programs might be used to fulfill the urgent training needs of large numbers of military personnel. Self-instruction can be used economically in industry for special training purposes, and it also is useful in prisons, where the special needs of inmates can be met by choosing different types of programs (Gotkin and Goldstein, 1963). In public schools, programs can be used to provide academically talented children with individual opportunities for advanced courses (Feldhusen, 1963a) or to teach specialized subjects in small remote schools.

For general educational needs, mechanized and automated self-instruction serves as an important and valuable adjunct but rarely can perform the entire teaching job as effectively as a more varied and personalized approach. This opinion agrees with the general evaluation of programed learning given by Minnesota public school principals in a 1963 survey ("Is Programed Learning Effective?").

SUMMARY

1. Linear programs present material in an unvarying sequence of small units, each followed by confirmation or correction. They usually require constructed responses and make no provision for individual differences except in their self-pacing feature. Small steps are used to keep errors to a minimum.

2. Branching programs provide alternative sequences of items depending on the learner's responses. Correct answers

to key questions may permit the learner to skip over a number of items, or an error may initiate a corrective or remedial sequence.

3. The opinion of Skinnerians that constructed responses are superior to multiple-choice answers is not shared by all programers. Both response modes are used and sometimes both in the same program.

4. Repetition of items is usually provided by the design of linear programs. Both repetition and drop-out can be incorporated as features of teaching machines.

5. Most programs insure a high level of accuracy by providing in the early stages many cues and prompts which are gradually withdrawn. Although performance in self-instruction usually is self-paced, there are some devices that pace the learner to increase speed in skill learning.

6. Immediate knowledge feedback to the learner is considered desirable in self-instruction but sometimes is delayed in branching programs. Opportunity for correction is not always provided in linear programs inasmuch as they are designed to minimize errors.

7. A programer's task involves defining the terminal behavior required, describing the nature of the student and what knowledge or skill he should possess at the start of a program, and constructing an effective series of program items. The effectiveness should be tested and improved by tryout and revision.

8. Linear programers have provided many specific suggestions for constructing and ordering program items, stressing small steps, prompts, repetition, and the effective sequencing of general concepts and examples.

9. The repetitious nature, easy stages, and artificiality of linear programs often lead to boredom and disinterest in the learner, especially at higher levels of learning and in older students.

10. Branching programing is not as concerned with small items and error rate, for the material is usually presented in expository style and errors are used to control the sequence of items.

11. Adjunctive programing involves integrating self-instructional material into a total learning situation which includes many other materials and techniques. Inasmuch as an adjunctive program does not do the entire teaching job, its sequencing is not considered of vital importance.

12. The principles of linear programing are derived from the operant conditioning techniques developed in animal laboratories. The strength and stability of learned responses are held to depend on the occurrence of reinforcements following the responses.

13. The nature of the reinforcement in self-instruction has never been defined precisely, and learning often seems to occur without specific reinforcement. Further, the elimination of errors in human learning has not been shown to be necessary or even desirable.

14. Linear programs are too inflexible to make adequate allowance for individual differences among learners or differences of opinion among teachers and experts in controversial areas. Further, their restricted nature limits the range of understanding of the learner unless other and more varied material and experiences are provided.

15. Reading and books are still essential for human education, and linear

programs do not teach a high level of reading skill.

16. Feedback theory evaluates techniques of self-instruction according to how well they conform to principles of cybernetic design. In order to optimize feedback control of symbolic knowledge and skills, original presentations should be more varied and flexible than is permitted by most teaching machines and programs. Spatially organized systems of reference are especially important. However, self-instruction is useful for drill and review in specific details.

17. Although complete-course programs are useful for some subjects and for some special teaching and training needs, adjunctive programs appear to be more appropriate for general school needs.

CHAPTER
12

Research on Programed Instruction

Commenting on the fast growing experimental literature on self-instructional programing, Gilbert (1960b) judged that comparing the efficacy of constructed responses and multiple-choice alternatives in a teaching program was:

> ... the most popular experiment current in education. However, since I know what the experimental results are, I shall describe them, hoping to save others time.
>
> Briefly, the experiments comparing multiple-choice selection with answer construction will demonstrate considerable individual differences on whatever criteria are used. Some investigators will, with statistical equivocation, conclude in favor of the construction method; some in favor of multiple choice; some will fail to conclude anything; and some will qualify their findings with reports of statistical interactions.

This wry prediction was to prove all too true not only with respect to response-mode comparisons but for many other aspects of programing research.

A careful survey in 1961 (Silberman, 1962) concluded that the most consistent finding was that no significant difference was found among treatment comparisons and, when significant differences were obtained, they seldom agreed with other findings on the same problem. With this state of affairs, it is obvious that our summary of research will produce no final concise answers on how to construct programs or how to use them to best advantage in teaching and training. The most we can hope for from this body of literature is to glean some hints about principles of meaningful human learning.

ATTITUDE STUDIES

The initial reaction of learners to programed self-instruction at all levels of schooling and in adult training situations has been generally favorable. This is especially true with school children, who usually welcome the opportunity to work with teaching machines. One exception has been noted by Stolurow

(1961) in teaching arithmetic to retarded children by means of fill-in machines. These students were initially apprehensive and anxious but by the end of the semester they were engrossed in the machine work and most of them said they preferred it.

In High School

Students in high school generally take balanced attitudes about the desirability of using self-instructional programs as an alternative to conventional teaching. In Roanoke, Virginia, where approximately 900 students participated in a field study evaluation of programed materials in mathematics, few of the students rejected programed courses outright but equally few would have cared to have all of their course programed ("First Reports on Roanoke Math Materials," 1961). Most of the students welcomed live teaching occasionally to supplement their programed work.

Eigen (1963) administered an attitude scale to seventy-two high school boys who had worked through a program in modern mathematics either by Skinner-type machine or programed book for an hour a day (in two half-hour sessions) for five days a week. The average time needed to complete the program was approximately five hours, with the machine group taking significantly longer than the book group. The attitude scale contained eight positive and eight negative statements about programed instruction, each of which was to be marked on a five-point scale. Although there was great variability in expressed attitudes, the mean total attitude score was positive. With forty-eight representing a neutral score, the machine

group had a mean score of 53.5 ± 23.5 and the programed text group, 58.2 ± 22.2. This difference in favor of the programed text was significant.

In College

Engelmann's (1963) study compared the use and acceptance of programed materials in biology with other materials and techniques—lectures, laboratory materials, texts, and so forth. A total of 167 students were asked to evaluate the effectiveness of the various methods in preparing them for examinations. With respect to the programed materials, twenty-eight percent of the students thought they were "absolutely essential"; thirty-six percent thought they were "helpful ninety percent of the time"; twenty-one percent considered them effective half of the time; while fourteen percent thought programed materials were helpful occasionally or not at all.

This same general pattern of moderately enthusiastic acceptance was shown in a study by N. H. Smith (1962) on teaching elementary statistics to cadets at the Air Force Academy by means of a scrambled book. Almost four-fifths of the students using the book said they enjoyed the programed course but fewer than three-fifths preferred it over conventional teaching and thought they learned with less effort from the program.

A whole series of studies carried out on student attitudes toward Holland and Skinner's programed material eventually published as a book, *The Analysis of Behavior*, gives a clearer idea of long-term acceptance of programed instruction in a college level area of knowledge. Attitude measurements obtained from stu-

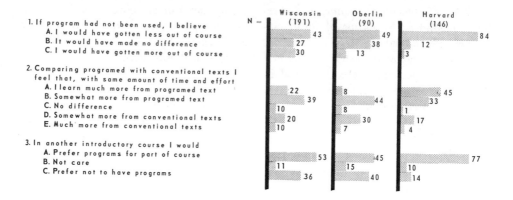

Figure 12.1.   Percentages of students at three institutions who expressed favorable, neutral, and unfavorable attitudes about Holland and Skinner's book, *The Analysis of Behavior*. (Data from Banta. Attitudes toward a programed text: "The analysis of behavior" compared with "A textbook of psychology." *Aud.-vis. Commun. Rev.*, 1963, **11**, 227–240.)

dents at Harvard University, the State University Teachers College at Geneseo, New York, and Central Washington State College were strongly positive toward this program (Naumann, 1962; Skinner and Holland, 1960; Van Atta, 1961), whereas measures obtained from students at Oberlin College and the University of Wisconsin were somewhat less favorable (Banta, 1963; Van Atta, 1961). Banta's (1963) summary of responses of Harvard, Oberlin, and Wisconsin students to the same favorable-unfavorable attitude items is represented as a bar graph in Figure 12.1. The Harvard data were reliably different from both the Wisconsin and the Oberlin data but Oberlin's and Wisconsin's distributions were not reliably different from each other. Inasmuch as Holland and Skinner developed their teaching program at Harvard, it appears that these data point up one difficulty encountered in interpreting studies of this sort. Students may have a tendency to reflect

their teachers' enthusiasms and to react in the expected manner.

Banta collected further attitude data on the Holland-Skinner text by asking the students to rate it on a series of semantic differential scales seven times during the ten-week period while the book was being used. During the last part of the course, a conventional text then in use was rated twice on the same scales. The graphs in Figure 12.2 show these nine ratings. All ratings of the programed text changed toward neutral during the ten weeks, with most of the change occurring within the first three weeks. When the conventional text was introduced, its first ratings were reliably different from the last ratings of the programed text in all cases but one. The new text was rated more Interesting and Good, as might be expected with new material, but also more Tense and more Slow. This indicates that the expressed attitudes were not entirely a function of the novelty effect of chang-

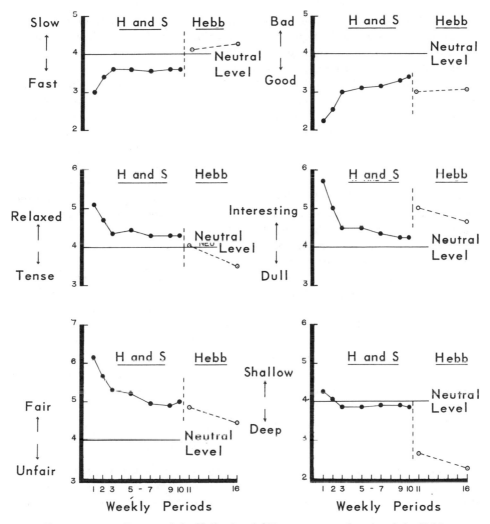

Figure 12.2.   Ratings of the Holland and Skinner programed text and the Hebb conventional text as a function of data collection periods during a semester course. (From Banta. Attitudes toward a programed text: "The analysis of behavior" compared with "A textbook of psychology." *Aud.-vis. Commun. Rev.*, 1963, **11**, 227–240.)

ing. The marked differences on the Shallow-Deep scale reflect a rated lack of depth in the programed text. Bright students rated Hebb relatively much more Good than did average and below average students.

Another study of attitude changes to-

ward Holland and Skinner's programed text was reported by Roth (1963). Of twenty-four undergraduate students who liked the text at the beginning, only two liked it at the end, although seven of the twenty-two who disliked it thought that they had learned something. Most of these students would not have finished the programed course without prodding. Of twenty-six graduate students who worked through the program, all liked it at the beginning but only five still liked it at the end. Stated objections were that the program was tedious, repetitious, mechanized, nonthought-provoking, and anti-insightful.

In Industry

A number of studies of industrial training courses have included attitude data indicating favorable attitudes toward programed instruction. At IBM, a comparison was made between conventional classroom instruction and self-instruction with programed books for training computer service men on the IBM 7070 Data Processing System (Hughes and McNamara, 1961). Of the seventy men trained by means of programed materials for approximately eleven hours training time, eighty-seven percent liked it better than conventional teaching, eighty-three percent favored using programs in the future, and ninety-three percent thought that learning from programs was less difficult than from conventional instruction. Specific positive features of the program named by the trainees were its instructional effectiveness, its repetition of important points, its gradual and logical sequence, the way it maintained concentration, and its flexibility in allowing the learner to proceed at his own rate.

Attitudes and Learning

Several studies have reported specific data indicating that general acceptance attitudes toward programed instruction have no predictive value in assessing the teaching effectiveness of the programs.

In Eigen's (1963) study of programed learning in high school boys, he found that the correlation between total attitude scores and achievement test scores was only 0.018. In college students, Roe *et al.* (1960) found that "liking" ratings of various methods of programed instruction did not correlate with either aptitudes or performance on criterion tests, and Hough and Revsin (1963) reported that there was no significant difference between high and low achievers in their attitudes toward programed instruction.

These results are not surprising in view of similar findings in many areas of human behavior research (Brayfield and Crockett, 1955). For example, in Chapter 6 we reported that liking for or interest in audiovisual materials bears little relation to their teaching effectiveness. The apparent fact is that *general* attitude measurements predict neither learning nor performance in a particular situation.

TEACHING EFFECTIVENESS OF PROGRAMS

There are dozens of demonstrations and controlled experiments showing that self-instruction techniques promote learning and other dozens of studies, more or less carefully controlled, comparing programed instruction with conventional teaching procedures. A sampling of some of these research efforts will give some idea of their significance.

Learning from Self-instructional Programs

One of the first controlled studies of machine teaching of grade school children was reported by Keislar (1959), who developed a program to teach understanding of area of rectangles to fifth and sixth graders. His fourteen experimental subjects and fourteen controls were matched individually on the basis of intelligence, sex, reading ability, and pretest scores. The experimental group spent one-and-a-half to two hours working through the program and the control group were given no instruction. All except one of the experimental subjects showed a higher posttest score than did their matched controls.

A somewhat different type of study from military research shows that a self-instruction device can promote learning even when used voluntarily as a *game* without any special motivation. Hatch (1959) used a Navy Automatic Rater to present cards with selected multiple-choice items concerning instrument flying. Out of a total of 320 items, one-fourth were not used in the machine, one-fourth were used on one card each, one-fourth on two cards each, and one-fourth on three cards. In this way, the frequency of item presentation could be varied and tested for its effect on learning. The entire pool of items was used to make up three equivalent test forms which were used for a pretest, a posttest, and a delayed test six to twelve months later. The two groups of pilots used as subjects were located at different Air Force bases but were equated in terms of flying duties, type of aircraft flown, and other relevant factors. After the pretest, the self-tutoring device was left for two months in the crew lounge of the experimental group. The men were not told of the experiment. Posttests at the end of the two months showed significant improvement in the experimental group over the control group in machine items, related directly to the frequency of item exposure, but no significant difference in the nonmachine items.

A special use of teaching machines that has attracted particular attention is to teach foreign languages in a hurry. Rocklyn and Moren (1962) used a tape-recorder device to teach five American soldiers enough basic Russian to give commands and obtain tactical information in Russian and to translate the information back into English. After about twenty-three days of study, they not only performed creditably on a test but were able to interrogate native Russians and obtain most of the information given.

Programed versus Conventional Instruction

Silberman (1962) reported that of fifteen field-study comparisons of programed and conventional instruction, nine favored the programs with respect to criterion scores and six showed no significant difference. All fifteen comparisons showed that programed instruction took less time. This general pattern of results can be found in more recent research as well, although the results of some few studies have favored conventional instruction.

In interpreting these comparative data, there are several points to keep in mind. First, many of the comparisons are between small groups who are instructed in limited subject matter for relatively short periods of time. Second, the novelty effect undoubtedly operates in many cases to favor the new techniques. Third, there are important uncontrolled factors in most of these comparative studies, particularly the time factor. When the total amount of time spent on study and instruction is equated for experimental and control groups, we expect more reliable results. We shall describe a few recent studies to illustrate some of these points.

Working with third graders, Edgerton and Twombly (1962) used a simple teaching machine to teach spelling to a pilot group of twenty-four and an experimental group of sixty children, while sixty-six were in a control group taught by conventional methods. At the end of the year, the machine groups had gained significantly more in grade-equivalent scores than had the control group and had spent less time in doing it. Although the novelty factor is not entirely ruled out, this study confirms a number of others that have indicated the effectiveness of machines in teaching spelling to elementary pupils.

Stolurow (1963) reported that programs can be used to teach retarded children reading—teaching both vocabulary and comprehension. Although programs were significantly better than conventional class instruction, it was concluded that the best method was to alternate class and program. Many educators, including Pressey, have made this point: that integrating different techniques is usually more effective than using only one.

In the Roanoke field study ("First Reports on Roanoke Math Materials," 1961) classes were conducted in three ways. The conventional class was taught as usual except that the students were told that they would be part of the experiment. In the second, the programed material was used with no help from the teacher except to discuss examination results. In the third, the programed material was used with help from the teacher. The experimental

classes had no homework but the conventional classes used homework as usual. Thus the time factor was not controlled in this study.

The percentage of failures in geometry, algebra, and trigonometry classes in three Roanoke high schools are shown in Table 12.1. The data are not entirely consistent but these first results seem to favor the experimental classes using programs. No definite conclusions can be drawn inasmuch as the study had a number of uncontrolled variables (for example, one teacher who failed thirty percent of the program group was described as hostile), and the criterion used here for comparative purposes is admittedly rough. Among those students who took standardized tests in geometry and algebra, twelve percent of those who had been taught conventionally fell below the eighth percentile but only five percent of those taught by machine.

Another large scale scale field study carried out by Lumsdaine and Klaus in Pittsburgh high schools compared the effectiveness of programs and conventional lectures in a somewhat different way (Klaus, 1961b). Of fifteen physics classes which were receiving regular instruction, watching daily televised lectures, using a textbook, and carrying out laboratory exercises, some were given in addition self-instructional programs in physics for six weeks. Although the use of these programed materials was not required, the classes in which they were available showed a substantial increment in test scores when compared with the classes without programs. Ten physics classes which did not receive the televised lectures were all given the programed materials and some of these had live classroom lectures in ad-

TABLE 12.1   PERCENTAGE OF FAILURES IN ROANOKE MATH
              CLASSES[a]

	High School		
	A	B	C
Geometry			
Program and help	6	7	6
Program, no help	8	0	0
Conventional	15	8	0
Algebra			
Program and help	21	25	4
Program, no help	20	29	3
Conventional	23	9*	11
Trigonometry			
Program and help	10	0	—
Program, no help	4	0	—
Conventional	18	7	—

[a] First reports on Roanoke math materials. *Aud.-vis. Instruction*, 1961, 6, 150–151.
* Only case in which percent of failures did not correspond to available test scores on the national standardized examination.

dition. There was no significant difference in achievement related to the use of lectures.

The apparent superiority of self-instructional programs can not always be demonstrated, however, in more carefully controlled experimental comparisons. In a study by Dessart (1962), eighty superior eighth graders with a mean IQ of 121 were instructed for one week in certain features of the limit concept. Two types of program were prepared, one linear and the other branching, and two experimental study procedures were used in which the supervising teacher either did or did not answer questions. The experimental groups were compared with a control group taught in a conventional way by a teacher. In addition, the time factor was controlled by having some of the experimental groups restudy the materials until they had spent the same amount of time as the conventional group. Although eight combinations of the three experimental variables (the programing, teacher-help, and time variables) are possible, the experimenter actually used, in addition to the controls, only six experimental groups: three with the linear program and three with the branching; three with and three without teacher help; and three who studied the program once and three who studied as long as the controls.

This fairly complicated experimental design produced few significant differences among groups. The control group exceeded the experimental groups once, but when time was equated, there were no significant differences. Very little help was given by the teachers so that this variable had questionable effects on the results. The conventionally taught group performed significantly better than the combined branching groups but did not exceed the combined linear groups. The difference between the branching groups and linear groups itself was not significant.

One thing should be noted about this type of experiment. The novelty effect of using new materials probably is less relevant when the control group as well as the experimental groups are participating in special work separate from their regular curriculum. This is one possible explanation for the relatively poorer showing of the programed learning groups in this study as compared with some of the field studies.

An experimental comparison by Hough (1962) of teaching-machine and lecture-discussion instruction at the college level involved forty-one students taking a course in Secondary Education. When an unannounced quiz was given after the first week, the machine-instructed group scored significantly higher than the controls, but no significant differences were found between the groups on a quiz and final test that were announced. This effect was interpreted as being due to the extra study time spent on lecture notes by the control group in preparation for announced tests. The machine group used no home study and spent a mean instructional time of 305 minutes on the program whereas the control group spent a mean total time in class and home study of 578 minutes.

The general finding that programs for teaching limited subject matter save time with no decrement in achievement has been reported a number of times for college-level and adult learners. N. H. Smith (1962) reported that 128 cadets at the Air Force Academy learned statistics faster with a scrambled book than in a conventional class. Hosmer and Nolan (1962) reported similar time-saving in three military courses. Wendt and Rust (1962) taught beginning students to use a college library by means of illustrated lectures or by automated machine presentation of the slides and instructions. A forward branching procedure in the program which eliminated unneeded material for the more knowledgeable students permitted some of them to finish in one-fourth the ordinary instruction time. Three students taught stenotype keying in the IBM experimental computer-controlled teaching system covered material in fifty hours which might have taken 200 to 300 hours of conventional instruction (Uttal, 1962).

Several studies of industrial training have shown programed instruction to be as effective as or better than conventional instruction. At Eastman Kodak, supervisors taking a course in human motivation by means of programs retained twice as much as those who attended lecture-discussion classes (Lysaught, 1962). Further, a questionnaire administered after the course indicated that the programed-learning students showed a greater tendency to act on and apply the course material than the conventionally taught students. The questions asked and the percentage of each group of students answering Yes are shown in Table 12.2.

At IBM, programed texts reduced instruction time for a 7070 training course from fifteen hours to eleven hours while increasing mean test scores from 86.2 to 95.1 (Hughes and McNamara, 1961). A programed training course developed at Spiegel, Incorporated trained package-billing clerks in one-third less time

Teaching Effectiveness of Programs309

TABLE 12.2 RESULTS ON ACTION QUESTIONNAIRE ADMINISTERED
TO SUPERVISORS AFTER COURSE IN HUMAN MOTIVA-
TION*

	Percent Answering YES	
	Control	Programed
Have you given any thought to this material?	73	100
Have you discussed it with anyone?	60	78
Have you tried to explain it to anyone?	34	57
Have you made any effort to apply some of its ideas?	41	100

* Lysaught, J. P. Programed learning and teaching machines in industrial training. In S. Margulies and L. D. Eigen (eds.), *Applied programed instruction.* New York: Wiley, 1962, pp. 23–43.

than previously, although the reorganization of the course probably would have increased the efficiency of classroom instruction as well (Hickey, 1962). An interesting study carried out at Schering Corporation compared conventional training of new representatives at a training center with training by programed material sent through the mail (Hain and Holder, 1962). The control group was given a brochure and background information, trained for four and three-fourths hours by lectures combined with audiovisual materials, then told to study for an examination. The experimental group were sent programed material by mail and told that they would be tested after they arrived at the training center. Mean test scores were 60.1 for the control group and 91.9 for the experimental. The difference was highly significant.

These industrial studies indicate that self-instructional programs may make it possible to reduce costs and save time while maintaining a satisfactory level of standardized industrial training. Indeed programed instruction may prove

invaluable for many special teaching and training purposes. But for the day-in, day-out, year-in, year-out needs of our schools and colleges, the role of self-instruction is not yet clear. Many of these early global-comparison results sound promising indeed, but as Pressey (1959) has noted: "It is a commonplace of educational research that first trials even of bad ideas usually come out well, because only teachers interested in them first try them, and pupils like the novelty and the special attention. Almost any reasonable method involving pupil activity and adjustment to individual differences will show gains." The effects of novelty and special attention on performance are known in industrial research as well, ever since some studies on employees in an electrical assembly plant more than 30 years ago spelled out what has come to be known as the Hawthorne Effect (Roethlisberger and Dickson, 1939).

Although the literature on self-instruction is liberally sprinkled with cautious references to the Hawthorne Effect, it rarely can be either measured or con-

trolled but remains to dampen our enthusiasm for reports such as the following (Goldberg, 1963). In a Michigan
public school, thirteen children with a
median IQ of 104 but considerably below grade level in reading and spelling
performance were chosen as subjects for
a study of programed spelling instruction. After several months of preliminary
programing tryouts, the parents of the
children were induced to construct thirteen teaching machines for a fullscale
test. By the time these children reached
third grade, it was reported that half of
them scored higher on a standardized
spelling test than "could have been predicted from their school history," and
that these same children had advanced
to the top reading group. The subjects
were reported to have developed a pro-
education orientation, to have assumed
leadership roles, to be working better,
and to be asking better questions. After
all the special attention from the experimenter, teacher, and parents, we would
say, "small wonder!"

PROGRAMING VARIABLES

In the first few years of programing
activity, many *a priori* judgments were
pronounced about how best to present
material in a self-instructional program,
but experimental evaluations of programing variables lend scant support to
some of the early assumptions. Silberman's (1962) summary of eight comparative studies yielded the data represented in Figure 12.3. No clear pattern
emerges from these comparisons. Often
achievement criteria favored one mode
while time criteria favored another.
More often than not, there were no
significant differences in achievement
due to programing treatment. Accord-

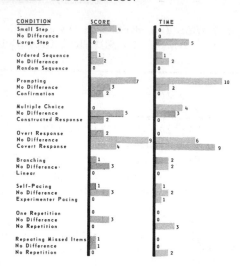

Figure 12.3.   Number of experimental comparisons prior to 1962 favoring different programing variables and showing no significant
difference according to achievement and time
criteria. (Data from Silberman. Characteristics
of some recent studies of instructional methods. In J. E. Coulson (ed.), *Programmed learning and computer-based instruction.* New
York: Wiley, 1962, pp. 13–24.)

ing to Silberman, many of these studies
involved short instructional programs
worked in an hour or so by small samples of highly motivated subjects who
then were tested by means of hastily
improvised quizzes. Often wide individual differences completely masked out
treatment effects even when the criterion
measures were sensitive enough to detect them. However, a number of more
recent analyses of programing variables
and their interactions may help to clarify some of the problems and warrant
some tentative conclusions.

Manner of Presentation

Widespread enthusiasm for the teaching machine technique as an intrinsically
superior learning mode has been tem-

pered considerably by research facts. Although machines and programs may prove useful, economically feasible, and adequate for many purposes, they are not necessarily the best way to present subject matter.

Device versus Programed Book

The first aspect of self-instruction to prove unnecessary was the machine itself. Pressey and his students early substituted simple punchboards and Chemo Cards for the more complicated devices, and Skinner advanced from device to programed book. These changes may have been brought about partly by practical matters related to ease of use and distribution, but they are vindicated by research comparisons of different ways of presenting programs.

Goldstein and Gotkin (1962) reviewed eight experimental comparisons between teaching machines and programed books. The studies involved linear programs including from sixty-five to more than 3000 frames in mathematics, English, physics, and psychology administered either by Skinner-type machines or programed texts and requiring from twenty-seven minutes to fifty-one hours to complete. Subjects included elementary school, junior high, high school, and college students and technical trainees. Posttest scores, time scores, and attitudes were reported. Over all, there were no significant differences between the two presentation modes, although four studies reported that significantly less time was required to use the programed text. In two recent comparisons between machines and programed texts, it has been reported that students expressed some preferences for machines (Hough and Revsin, 1963),

and that students expressed more positive attitudes toward texts (Eigen, 1963). On the basis of the research evidence, then, the choice between teaching machines and programed texts would have to be based on such practical matters as cost, preference of instructor, administrative convenience, and adaptability to subject matter.

Small Step versus Large Step

Most linear programers have agreed that each step in a program should be *small* enough to insure correct response. Step size usually is defined in terms of difficulty rather than in terms of the amount of informational material given in a frame. Thus research on step size usually varies the size by increasing or decreasing the number of frames used to cover a given unit of material. A small step is easily taken while a large step is more difficult because some of the intermediate steps have been eliminated.

Research on step size defined as step difficulty usually has favored small steps over large in terms of posttest criteria, although large-step programs take less time (see Figure 12.3). In a recent experiment of Smith and Moore (1962), however, in which step size and pictorial cues were varied in a spelling program, no difference was found in learning achievement related to step size and the large step method saved time. The authors reported that very small steps and over-cueing may produce disinterest.

Since it would seem that less intelligent students might need smaller steps than bright students, Shay (1961) attempted to study the relationship of intelligence to step size in programing. His statistical analysis revealed no such relationship, and his data suggested that small steps produced more learning at all ability levels.

Although Shay felt that his results lent support to Skinner's position that it is not necessary to provide more than one program to make allowance for different initial ability, we do not find in this one study a conclusive answer to the problem of step size. In the broader problems posed by linear programing techniques, size of step is but a secondary consideration. First we must determine whether it is necessary or even desirable to break up subject matter into small bits to be presented in successive frames. Second, we need to know how important it is to require frequent specific responses throughout the learning sequence. If we adopt other methods of presenting information than a sequence of programed items, then the problem of step size becomes irrelevant.

Ordered versus Random Sequence

Another problem of limited significance concerns the order of frames in an instructional program. The Skinnerian approach to programing is to prepare a carefully ordered sequence of items leading from ignorance to mastery of a subject matter, and Pressey's early teaching-machine materials have been criticized because they presented items in no particular order. However, when the principle of orderly sequencing is put to an experimental test, it does not always prove valid. Silberman's summary listed three comparisons of ordered and random sequences. One favored the ordered sequence in both posttest scores and time but the other two showed no significant differences. Feldhusen (1963b) concluded that for short sequences program

frames can be scrambled with no decrement in learning.

Here again the relevance of the problem depends on other programing variables, the characteristics of the subject matter, and the role assigned to self-instruction in the total teaching situation. If the initial presentation of a subject is made by means of textbook or lecture, presumably an attempt will be made to present the material logically. Then if a self-instruction program is used for adjunctive purposes, the sequence of items will not be of critical importance. The research results on ordered versus random sequence indicate that even in a complete-course program, the absolute order of items may not be as important as some linear programers have assumed.

Linear versus Branching

The differences between linear and branching programs have been assigned more theoretical importance than research results seem to warrant. In an early comparison of a linear and a forward-branching program, Coulson and Silberman (1960) found no significant differences in criterion test scores between the linear and branching group, but they did find a significant saving in time with branching. Thus the amount learned per unit time was greater for the branching than for the nonbranching procedures. A later experiment by Silberman et al. (1961) again failed to show a significant difference in achievement relative to the presentation modes, but Coulson et al. (1962) demonstrated that branching was superior when it was based on self-evaluation items as well as errors. Roe (1962) compared a number of procedures including linear, forward branching, and backward branching for remedial items. Both the linear and the forward branching procedures were significantly faster than backward branching but none of them produced significantly higher test scores.

Individual versus Group

There is some research evidence to indicate that programed instructional materials can be presented to groups rather than individuals with no decrement in learning. Keislar and McNeil (1962) described two studies in which group procedures were compared with individual self-instruction. The first involved 300 children in the primary grades who were given a three-week program in science. The children who were taught individually by videosonic teaching machine learned more than those who were taught in groups of twelve to fifteen by means of audiofilm strips. In another comparison, however, children in groups of eight to ten who saw slides projected from a single teaching machine, each using his own response panel, learned just as much as children taught individually by teaching machine. Feldhusen and Birt (1962) compared several methods of presenting programed material to individuals and groups and found no significant differences among them. It appears that under some circumstances, at least, the self-pacing permitted individuals working alone offers no special advantage.

Program versus Conventional Text

Inasmuch as no method of presenting programed material appears to be clearly superior to other methods, we begin to wonder wherein lie the advan-

tages of the programs. Why not rewrite the items from an instructional program in the familiar paragraph style of our conventional textbooks and test their teaching effectiveness? Several research workers have done just that with results generally favoring the texts, or at least showing no differences between programs and texts. And McNeil and Keislar (1962) showed that there is no difference in children's learning from program items written in the form of questions and those written as statements. Reviewing all relevant studies, Alter and Silberman (1962) concluded that under a variety of experimental conditions, it has not been demonstrated that a programed format requiring specific responses of the learner is superior to a textual format requiring reading.

Although this conclusion seems to bring us back to where we started, in the preteaching-machine era, we must remember that it necessarily is based on a limited number of studies involving limited numbers of subjects under restricted conditions. We are not yet ready to decide that the whole teaching-machine self-instructional concept is illusory. Before making any further judgments, we must consider another research area dealing with the manner and the role of student response in self-instruction.

Response Mode

A distinguishing feature of self-instructional methods specified by both Pressey and Skinner is the elicitation of specific responses from the learner, but the form that these responses should take has generated a certain amount of theoretical controversy and considerable research activity.

Multiple-Choice versus Constructed Response

As indicated in Figure 12.3, some of the experimental comparisons of multiple-choice and constructed responses have favored constructed responses on the basis of achievement criteria, but most have shown no significant differences. More often than not, multiple-choice responses have saved time. In a given amount of time, the most efficient learning might be achieved by some combination of multiple-choice and constructed responses in order to provide extra practice on items that are causing some difficulty. Hough (1962) compared constructed responses, multiple-choice responses and a combination of the two and found no significant differences, but time was not controlled in this experiment and no opportunity was given for review. A study by Briggs *et al.* (1962), described in the next section, throws further light on the relative advantages of constructed and multiple-choice responses.

Overt versus Covert Response

The experimental comparisons of the relative advantages of overt and covert responses in programed instruction have been reviewed by Lumsdaine (1961), Silberman (1962), and Feldhusen (1963b). Lumsdaine's general conclusion, which was based on studies of instructional films (see Chap. 6) as well as of self-instructional techniques, was that covert responses are as effective as overt in most situations tested and on some occasions may be more advantageous. Silberman's listing in Figure 12.3 shows two comparisons favoring overt response, four favoring covert, and nine showing no difference in terms of post-test criteria. In terms of time, nine comparisons favored covert responses and six showed no difference. Feldhusen's 1963 conclusions were that students can learn just as well when responding covertly as when responding overtly to program items, and that they usually can learn just as well from reading the items with the blanks filled in to make statements. The conclusion we reached with respect to audiovisual materials can be repeated with respect to self-instruction. It is desirable to insure student participation in the instructional situation, but covert participation often is just as effective as overt.

The important problem with respect to student response mode is to determine when it is advantageous to require overt responses and when it is not. What are the variables that interact with response mode to affect learning achievement?

A study by Krumboltz and Weisman (1962b) produced suggestive evidence that overt response might be better than covert for long-term retention even though no differences were apparent in immediate test scores. Their college-level subjects responded overtly, responded covertly, or simply read the program with the blanks filled in. The immediate posttest showed no significant differences among groups, but after two weeks the overt-response group scored higher than either the covert or the reading group. However, several other studies comparing immediate with delayed retention have found contradictory results. In one study a reading group was found superior to an overt response group immediately and when tested in ten weeks (Briggs *et al.*, 1962), while in two other studies, no significant differences were found between overt and covert responses after one week (Evans *et al.*, 1962) and after one year (Wittrock, 1963).

Another phase of research having to do with the interaction between response mode and response difficulty has led Evans *et al.* (1962) to hypothesize that the relevance of such variables as response mode is inversely related to the probability of correct responding in the course of learning. Thus anything that increases the probability of correct response, according to these authors, might reduce the importance of the form of the response. If this were true, one would expect to find no significant differences among response modes for programs easy for all learners but differences between overt and covert responses as programs became more difficult. Research results indicate that the relationship is not that simple. Wittrock (1963), for example, found that school children with mental ages above the median learned more from a science program with covert than with overt responses, while those children with mental ages below the median, who presumably found the program more difficult, learned more by responding overtly. The interaction was no longer apparent in retention test scores one year later.

A series of studies carried out at the American Institute for Research by Briggs, Goldbeck, and their associates have produced results showing that the relative advantages of overt, covert, and reading responses vary with a number of factors, including level of difficulty (Briggs *et al.*, 1962; Goldbeck and Campbell, 1962). In one study, low-difficulty items were learned best by the

reading group and covert responders whereas items of intermediate difficulty were learned best by the overt responders. For a high-difficulty program there was little difference among groups. However when test scores were divided by learning time to obtain *learning efficiency* scores, it was found that reading was most efficient and overt responses least efficient at all levels of difficulty. In another study in which only one program was used, the reading group again was fastest and did significantly better in a retention test after ten weeks. In this delayed test, the overt-response group was slightly superior only in those test items which contained stimulus and response terms that were identical or highly similar to those used in the learning program. This indicates that requiring the subjects to construct specific responses may actually have interfered with their learning of other relevant material. The authors of this report speculated that constructing a response and then seeing the confirmation may have created a *closure* effect which was absent for members of the reading group.

In an effort to equate the time factor for groups using different response modes, Briggs *et al.* (1962) compared four groups, all of whom studied for two hours. One group had eight pages of mimeographed text and the second had an overview of the topics followed by the text, with each page of text followed by a summary outline page. The third and fourth groups had Skinner-type programs; one group responded with the first letter of each word while the last group wrote complete responses. As each subject finished his assigned material he was given multiple-choice review questions on chemical paper to confirm the correct responses, but one-third of the original material, varying by subject, was not covered by review. It was found that learning without review did not vary for the different groups, but learning with review favored the text-plus-review group. Again the overt-response groups were superior only in answering those test questions which were the same as program items. Many of the errors made by these groups resulted from applying responses learned in the constructed-response programs to the wrong test questions.

Among the most significant results of this study were findings testifying to the value of the multiple-choice review questions. It was found that these questions produced highly significant increases in scores on test items having answers that were the same as the correct answers in the response portion of the multiple-choice question. Furthermore, the amount of increased learning due to review ranked perfectly among groups with the amount of time available to each group for review. Review also enhanced learning of information which appeared in the stimulus portion of the multiple-choice questions as well as in the response choices. In contrast, results indicated that information to be taught by constructed-response program frames must be assigned to the response portion of the frame.

This last study is particularly interesting in that it provides a direct experimental test of the relative validity of Pressey's and Skinner's views on self-instruction. The study by Briggs *et al.* (1962) not only confirms what other experiments have shown, that is, that a bit-by-bit linear program is a slow and inefficient way to present a subject, but

it also shows that in a given amount of time more can be learned by textbook reading and selective review than with a linear program. Further, the results indicate that learning from the constructed-response program was more specific to the actual responses made than learning promoted by the multiple-choice questions. More general information was learned from the review questions than from the constructed-response items. This study appears to vindicate Pressey's position concerning the form a self-instructional program should take as well as its adjunctive role in teaching.

Error Rate

The easy bit-by-bit progression characteristic of most linear programs has been dictated by an assumption not easily put to a direct experimental test—Skinner's assumption that errors are aversive and do not belong in an effective learning program. A number of early studies of programed learning, including those reported by Meyer (1960) and Keislar (1959), offered as presumptive evidence for the low-error hypothesis the fact that the error score during learning was inversely related to learning achievement, that is, the more errors a sudent made while working a program, the poorer his achievement score was at the end. A more obvious explanation of this finding is that students of lower ability or poorer preparation make more errors and learn less than brighter or more knowledgeable students.

The low-error hypothesis came to have practical overtones after Skinner-type fill-in teaching machines had been put into commercial production. These simple boxes made no provision for

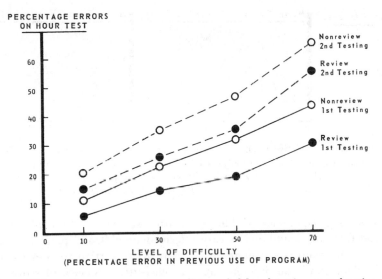

Figure 12.4.   Percent errors in immediate and delayed testing as a function of level of difficulty for Review and Nonreview Groups. (Redrawn from Holland and Porter. The influence of repetition of incorrectly answered items in a teaching-machine program. *J. exp. Anal. Behav.*, 1961, 4, 305–307.)

immediate correction of errors or review of missed items. However, when Holland and Porter (1961) tested the effect of repeating incorrectly answered items, they were admittedly surprised to find that such review raised the level of learning significantly. This was true at all levels of item difficulty, as determined from error rates in previous use of the program, and in both the immediate posttest and in a delayed retention test given unannounced six months later. These results are summarized in Figure 12.4, which shows the percentage of error on the criterion tests as a function of item difficulty. The review group maintained its superiority throughout, and after six months did almost as well as the nonreview group did on the immediate test.

Inasmuch as the loss in retention from first to second testing was relatively less for low-difficulty items, Holland and Porter concluded somewhat arbitrarily that programs should be designed so that every item is of low difficulty to insure better retention. They failed to observe that the same effect can be achieved more efficiently (and probably more surely) by the simple expedient of reviewing error responses. The importance of immediate correction of errors and review has been confirmed by many investigators including Stephens (1960), who found that students learned more from a self-instructional program if they were required to correct errors before proceeding to the next item.

The inverse relationship between errors and learning achievement that was reported in some of these early studies has not always been found. Gagné and Dick (1962), for example, reported very low correlations between learning errors and test performance in seventh graders who were given a teaching machine pro-

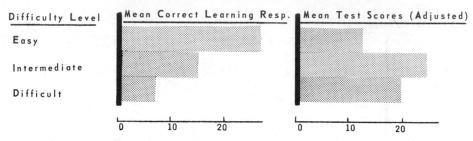

Figure 12.5.   Relative accuracy of learning and test responses at three levels of difficulty. The test scores were adjusted by the California Reading Maturity Test. (Data from Goldbeck and Campbell. The effects of response mode and response difficulty on programed learning. *J. educ. Psychol.*, 1962, **53**, 110–118.)

gram in solving equations. Goldbeck and Campbell (1962) found that an easy program taught overt responders less effectively than either an intermediate or a difficult program. The bar graph in Figure 12.5 compares the relative accuracy of learning responses for their three programs with the relative achievement scores in the posttest. The authors hypothesized that the learners performed in quite a perfunctory manner with the highly cued *easy* program. They made few errors in learning but, on the other hand, they did not really learn very much. In contrast, the intermediate difficulty program stimulated more active participation and resulted in much better achievement scores.

Goldbeck and Campbell analyzed their results further to determine the relative accuracy of test responses that had been preceded by correct and incorrect learning responses. Each program item had a corresponding test item, and these pairs for all subjects were classified according to whether the program item had been answered correctly or incorrectly during learning. The bar graph in Figure 12.6

Figure 12.6.   Percentage of test responses correct that had been preceded by correct and incorrect learning responses. (Data from Goldbeck and Campbell. The effects of response mode and response difficulty on programed learning. *J. educ. Psychol.*, 1962, **53**, 110–118.)

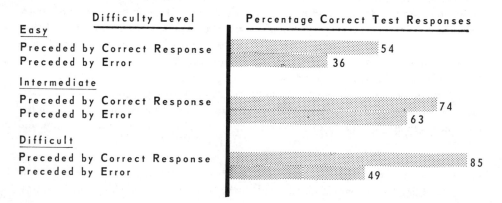

shows the percentage of each of these categories that was answered correctly in the test. At each level of difficulty, the learning errors were followed by relatively fewer correct test responses than those items that had originally been answered correctly. This is not surprising, for the correctly answered items probably included some that were known to the subjects beforehand as well as some relatively easy items. The interesting thing about these data is that error responses in the intermediate difficulty program were followed by higher learning achievement (sixty-three percent correct in the posttest) than the correct responses in the easy program (fifty-four percent correct in the posttest). In other words, it is not always the easy program with its low error rate that produces the most learning but the program that for one reason or another stimulates the most active participation on the part of the learner.

In another experiment, Goldbeck and Campbell compared the overt-, covert-, and reading-response procedures with an option procedure in which the learner could write his response if he were sure it was correct or leave the blank empty, if unsure, and proceed to the check answer. It was thought that this option response mode would reduce the number of errors made and thus mitigate any adverse effect of error responses. Results showed no significant differences among groups in posttest scores.

A somewhat different approach to the problem of errors was devised by Melaragno (1960). In a program of fifty frames, he inserted five deliberately ambiguous frames and called all answers to them wrong, assuming that these frames would provide "negative reinforcement." If these five error frames were inserted consecutively in the middle of the program, the students scored less on the posttest, particularly on the material which appeared just before and just after these frames. When the five frames were distributed evenly throughout the program, learning was not disrupted significantly although these subjects learned somewhat less than the group who received only "positive reinforcement." From these results it has been concluded that errors occurring consecutively have a deleterious effect and should be avoided by reducing the over-all probability of errors.

To our mind, these results suggest another interpretation—that of the importance of promoting understanding of the subject matter. Ambiguous frames not only produce errors, they also produce confusion and lack of assurance about the material being learned. They reduce knowledge of accuracy. Errors as such may not be detrimental to learning if they are corrected immediately and if the student understands why one answer was wrong and another answer right. It has been observed by a number of investigators that informing a student that an answer is *wrong* is not effective unless the reason becomes self-evident. With complex material it is important to provide an explanation. Bryan and Rigney (1956) tested the relative advantages of explanations and no explanations with groups of NROTC students. The group who were given explanations of their choices learned significantly more than groups who received no explanations. Bryan and Schuster's (1959) study found that explanations were particularly valuable in training students to follow optimal sequences of steps in electronic troubleshooting.

Coulson *et al.* (1962) found that remedial branching techniques may not prove superior to linear programs unless some allowance is made for student understanding of the material. Branching based entirely on errors proved no more effective than a linear program, but when branching was based on errors plus the student's evaluation of his own understanding, posttest scores were significantly higher for the branching group than for a fixed-sequence group.

Over all, the experimental studies of programed self-instruction leave one wondering what all the excitement has been about. These automated self-instructional techniques that were heralded as revolutionary developments in education—are they really as irrelevant as many of the research findings indicate? It appears that the form of presentation is of little importance and that the response mode need not be specified precisely. About the only conclusions we can draw from the facts presented so far are that the learner should participate actively (even if implicitly) in the learning situation and that he should be helped to understand the subject matter beyond simple confirmations or corrections. These ideas are not new in the field of self-instruction but have long been known in education. What, then, is new? It is neither the exact form of stimulus presentation or the exact form of the response but the specific participation and the knowledge feedback process explicitly provided for in all the various forms of teaching-machine learning and programed self-instruction.

Reinforcement or Feedback?

The Skinnerian view of self-instruction appears to interpret the confirmation process as the positive reinforcer postulated by the operant conditioning model. Many psychologists and educators have objected to the use of this model in describing programed learning. Snygg (1962) observed that reinforcement theory is relatively useless as a guide to teaching for two reasons. First, the basic question of how to get the student to perform the desired act for the first time is neither asked nor answered. Second, this theory offers no guides for predicting what will be reinforcing to learners.

Wohlwill (1962) objected that programed learning is not analogous to the gradual shaping of an animal's responses according to operant techniques, in which an animal's behavior is rewarded when it makes a response that approximates the one desired in outward appearance, spatial location, or directional characteristics. The kind of symbolic knowledge taught in program frames is not related in such obvious ways but rather by semantic and syntactic characteristics. Fitzgerald (1962) said, "A word rarely has the semantic specificity of reference and effect to persons that a grain of corn or a flashing light has to laboratory animals."

Lumsdaine (1962b) has shown sustained interest in programed self-instruction for many years, but he feels that it does not conform to the reinforcement learning model. He voiced his objections in these words:

I question very seriously whether theories placing primacy on the manipulation of reinforcement provide an adequate or even a very useful theoretical model for the development of programs. . . . Manipulation of reinforcement contingencies does not seem to be what even the most ardently Skinnerian programmers actually *do* when they start writing the frames of a program . . . what preoccupies the programmer's attention . . . is the manipulation of prompting cues, not the manipulation of reward schedules.

Several lines of research evidence throw doubt on the reinforcement interpretation. In the first place, a number of studies have shown that explicit confirmations are not always necessary in programed learning. As an example, we shall describe a study that attempted to carry the operant conditioning analogy to the point of setting up schedules of partial reinforcement in programed learning. In typical operant conditioning of animals, the stimulus and the response and the reinforcement remain the same whereas in programed learning these features change constantly. Nevertheless, Krumboltz and Weisman (1962a) attempted to determine the differential effects of various reinforcement schedules on performance and learning in programed self-instruction. Using both fixed-ratio and variable-ratio schedules of sixty-seven percent and thirty-three percent confirmation, as well as continuous confirmation and no confirmation, they found that the consistency of confirmation affected errors made during learning but had no effect at all on posttest achievement scores.

A second line of evidence throwing doubt on the reinforcement interpretation consists of reports that linear programs, if prolonged, induce boredom (Feldhusen *et al.*, 1962; Reed and Hayman, 1962; Rigney and Fry, 1961). Yet Skinner proposed linear programs as a sure source of *positive* reinforcement in contrast to the *negative* reinforcement of the conventional classroom. It appears to us that if programs become boring, they are not offering positive reinforcement. On the other hand, students can learn even when they are bored, and we do not believe that the process is contingent on reinforcement, either positive or negative.

Skinner's theoretical concepts were defined by experimental procedures in which the experimenter waits for an animal to emit the desired response and then rewards it. The situation is very different in human teaching and training, where we can instruct the learner in the responses we wish him to make. Even in skill learning where the response pattern to be learned cannot be called out at will, we use verbal instructions and nonverbal demonstrations to help the learner organize his responses, and verbal knowledge commonly is taught with as complete and as well organized a set of cues as we can devise.

A number of studies have compared the relative advantages of prompting and confirmation in promoting learning. Using paired associates, Cook and Spitzer (1960) and Cook (1961) found that prompting in three out of four trials was more effective than no prompting, and that the effectiveness did not depend on the learner's making an overt response. Angell and Lumsdaine (1961) studied the effects of mixing prompting and confirmation trials. Their results were not entirely clear but indicated that a training sequence will be more effective if it includes some unprompted trials along with the prompted ones. These results support the standard programing practice of using and then withdrawing prompts.

Summarizing some of the research studies on the Subject-Matter Trainer, Briggs (1961) has concluded that the best training sequence probably is one in which prompting trials are used first followed by confirmation trials. The exact procedure followed probably should be tailored to fit the subject matter and the learner's ability, stage of mastery, and so on.

In our opinion, the distinction between prompting and confirmation is somewhat arbitrary when made in relation to symbolic learning. A stimulus cue or prompt presented to a learner may be in itself a discrete event, but it sets up in the learner a whole series of responses which through the processes of sensory feedback serve as further prompts (or stimuli) to further action. Much of this activity is implicit and thus hidden from the observer, but it is no less real to the learner. The confirmation in a learning sequence is not that alone but serves also to prompt further responses, while a so-called prompt functions as well to confirm the learner's perceptions and understanding of the material. As learning progresses, the learner needs fewer external cues with which to monitor his symbolic behavior patterns, but the optimal sequence for providing and withdrawing external prompts and confirmations undoubtedly varies with different types of learning and different individuals.

Just as the novice tracking operator must learn to follow target movements with a high degree of precision, the task of the student in school is to establish patterns of knowledge and skill that conform to the patterns presented to him. This process is facilitated by continuous and accurate feedback which compares the responses of the learner to the patterns to be learned. Feedback is not confined to an occasional confirmation or correction after an overt response but is a part of all of the perceptual-motor participative patterns that occur during learning. Herein lies the value of reading well organized textual material in contrast to a series of deliberately simplified program frames. A textbook or lecture or other diversified presentation helps to establish a frame of reference against which all new facts are checked and which itself can be checked against the learner's prior knowledge. What the programers eliminate from frames as *extraneous* material often should be left in to provide as rich a feedback context as possible.

The use of self-instructional materials within an integrated teaching program is valuable not because it provides the *only* feedback to the learner about his responses, but because it provides precise feedback on important specific points and possibly a diagnostic check on his progress. As we have seen, it matters little whether he chooses or constructs an answer or whether he makes errors as long as he corrects his errors and understands why he was right or wrong. He does not need a *reward* for performing correctly; he needs differential feedback to show him how closely he is approaching the prescribed pattern. Furthermore, he needs immediate feedback for optimal effectiveness—an idea that was confirmed many years ago by Pressey (1950). An extensive study involving more than 400 students, which was designed to assess the use of punchboard practice tests, found that the groups receiving immediate feedback from the punchboard scored higher on all types of examination questions than either the groups using practice tests without immediate confirming feedback or control groups who used no practice tests.

GENERAL PROBLEMS

Our present assessment of the significance of teaching-machine instruction and programed learning corresponds neither with the optimism of some of the first Skinnerian programers who saw in their operant techniques the educational wave of the future nor with the pessimism of Feldhusen (1963b), in a summary which was entitled, "Taps for Teaching Machines." Our own judgment of the practical values of programed instruction lies somewhere between these two extremes. However, with respect to the need or desirability of complete-course programs in our schools, we are inclined to agree with Pressey (1960), who wrote:

> At this comparatively early and conceivably sometimes overenthusiastic stage of attempts at automation, might this "null hypothesis" be desirable: that students and teachers can (on the task in question) do at least as well without the special device or programming as with it! Only if results have warranted the rejection of this hypothesis, can development of special devices or programmings, or comparisons of short versus longer steps or objective versus write-in answers, continue without risk of being found fatuous.

Any final assessment of programed learning must be based on more than global comparisons and the research results on programing variables. Two general questions that must be considered are how well self-instruction meets the needs of different individuals and how well programed learning transfers to problems outside the classroom.

Adapting to Individual Differences

We can make no final statements about the relative advantages of self-instruction for students of different ages and different levels of ability. There are some indications that the techniques are more successful with school children than with college students, but this may be because the subject matter taught young children is more often standardized and unambiguous.

Programs have been used to teach individuals of all ability levels, from retarded children to superior students, but only incidental information is available concerning the relative advantages at different levels. Little (1934) reported that the feedback methods appeared to be of more benefit to poorer students but Briggs (1947) reported later that the techniques were especially suitable to superior students. Reed and Hayman (1962) reported that at the tenth grade level high achievers did better with a programed text while low achievers learned more with conventional teaching, but Stolurow (1963) found that retarded children learned more from a program than from conventional teaching. Freeman (1959) reported that poor students benefited more from machine training than did the better students, while Keislar and McNeil (1961) found evidence that machine teaching was more effective for children of superior reading and study habits. Obviously the relative advantages of teaching programs for different ability levels depend on other factors, such as type of subject matter and type and difficulty of programs.

Another problem, which has implications for Skinnerian theory of programed instruction, is whether students of all ability levels can attain comparable levels of mastery by working at their own rate through a self-instructional program. One of the most careful analyses of this problem was made by Stolurow (1961) with retarded children. Two versions of a program to teach fractions were prepared, varying in *degree of change* between frames. Groups using the two versions were given an immediate posttest and, two weeks later, a delayed test of retention and transfer. No significant differences were found in posttest and transfer scores, but the retention scores favored the group using the *less change* version. Correlation coefficients then were computed between individual scores and different types of ability and intelligence scores. The posttest scores from the group using the *less change* version correlated significantly with certain special ability scores, such as Reading Comprehension and Arithmetic Fundamentals, but not with general IQ scores or total language scores. That is, the *less change* programs produced learning scores that did not correlate with general intelligence. In contrast, scores from the group using the *more change* version correlated significantly with full scale IQ and total language scores. Stolurow concluded from these and other relevant findings that within limits it is possible to compensate for intellectual differences by designing optimal teaching programs.

The phrase to note here is *within limits*. If we are striving to teach limited criterion behavior, within the capabilities of all the learners in a group, then a carefully sequenced linear program self-paced by each individual learner may do the job. On the other hand, if we are interested in stimulating each learner to realize his fullest potential, such a program for the better students would be only a first step and possibly a boring first step. Even so, we would expect the bright students to learn more than the dull whether or not differences appeared in achievement scores. Along with the assertions that appear in the literature to the effect that good programs "permit the quick and the slow to attain fairly comparable levels of mastery" (Blyth, 1963) are other observations that the real learning achievement of bright and dull students is not always measured adequately by the posttests used in programing research. Although self-instruction may mask certain differences among learners, it does not actually eliminate the differences.

Transfer from Programed Learning

Very little experimental evidence applies directly to the problem of transfer from programed learning. Gagné and Dick (1962) used a teaching machine program to teach seventh graders how to solve equations. Although reasonably good scores were obtained in verbal and performance posttests based on the programed materials, scores on a transfer test involving new equations of the same general type were very low indeed. Such evidence confirms what is known generally, that learning often is very specific to the materials used.

There is some evidence to indicate

that a Skinner-type teaching program—that is, a fixed-sequence, constructed-response, arbitrarily simplified, bit-by-bit, easy sequence of frames—is a poor self-instructional technique when judged according to its possible transfer value. As we related in an earlier section, Briggs *et al.* (1962) found that multiple-choice questions used for review purposes taught more general knowledge than constructed-response frames in a linear program. Cartwright used systematic and unsystematic sequences of frames to teach fractions to mentally retarded adolescents (Stolurow, 1963). The groups using the systematic sequence remembered more of the specific facts taught, but the group using the unsystematic sequence transferred more of their knowledge to other problems. Krumboltz and Bonawitz (1962) tested the effect of presenting confirming responses in a program as complete thoughts, usually by repeating the relevant parts of frames with the desired responses inserted, instead of as isolated words or phrases. Their groups showed no difference in knowledge of terminology, but the *context* group excelled in ability to apply principles. Finally, Nunn (1961) compared the use of a linearly programed text in English grammar with a self-directing workbook of a more conventional type. The group using the linear program scored higher than the workbook group on the commercial tests furnished with the texts, but scored lower on a somewhat more complex test prepared by the teacher. The conclusion was that the linear program was so gradual and easy that it required a minimum of thinking on the part of the students.

Evidence such as this suggests that carefully limited linear programs teach equally limited knowledge. If we wish to teach a rigidly prescribed system of specific responses, then a linear program may do the job, but education in the broader sense needs a variety of materials, a variable approach, and flexible responses on the part of the learner. A variable, flexible interaction between the learner and the learning environment will provide many types and patterns of feedback related to many different aspects of that environment. In this way we can vary the learner's point of view and help him transfer his learned responses from the specific to the general.

Training Teachers to Program

In the long run, decisions about when, where, and how to use self-instructional programs are made best by teachers and administrators. Briggs (1962) has said:

> One goal is to avoid a strained effort to make something work where it doesn't fit. Flexibility is to be sought, both as to choice of teaching machine and method of programing, and as to the decision when or whether to use automation at all.

Assigning the responsibility of making such decisions to the teacher reflects Senders' (1962) belief, "that the only true teaching machine is an adaptive (learning) device; such a device is a teacher, rather than merely a communicative channel for a teacher."

The best way to train teachers in integrating self-instructional techniques into their total teaching effort is to train them in these techniques. They should be taught not only the theoretical significance of programing research but also how to program materials for classroom use. Komoski (1961) listed several reasons why it is desirable to have teachers prepare teaching programs instead of relying entirely on commercial programers. One reason is that there are advantages to having a diversity of activity in a new field. Another is that there is important interaction between the program and the curriculum so that the program must be designed to fit the neeeds of the curriculum. The most important reason is that in learning how to program, teachers and teachers-in-training learn a great deal about how to teach and about the nature of meaningful learning. Programed instruction not only supplies the student with informational feedback but also provides the teacher with a continuous check on the quality of the teaching effort.

Possibilities for training teachers and exploring teaching methods with the new devices and programs are nearly unlimited. These techniques permit empirical control and reproduction of the variables involved in formal instruction to a degree never before possible. Teaching devices, particularly the audiovisual machines, simulate the teaching situation in much the same way that a complicated skill trainer simulates the perceptual-motor machine relationships of the skill. With such objective simulation techniques we can train student teachers to prepare and control instructional material and can evaluate their ability to do so.

Perhaps the greatest significance of teaching machine and programing technology is that it provides a new objective approach to the study of meaningful learning while at the same time providing new insights into how such learning occurs. Although the first few years of programing research have had generally negative and inconclusive results, these studies nevertheless have made some important contributions. First, programing research has focused attention on the inadequacies of reinforcement learning theory as a model of meaningful human learning and thereby has opened the field to new theoretical and experimental approaches. Second, it has been made clear that research carried out with hastily written programs and poorly designed devices produces few significant results. More variability of research design and flexibility of machine factors are needed to achieve any real understanding of optimal instructional techniques.

There are many indications that far more significant phases of programing research are under way. Research emphasis is shifting toward explorations of the significant interactions in entire teaching systems, made up of teachers, devices, subject matter, and students. Systems study will not confine its efforts to evaluating specific machines or techniques but will broaden its interests to include all types of classroom techniques and materials—including textbooks. Textbook design has been too long neglected by educational researchers. In the next chapter, we are going to explore some of the factors of book design in relation to what we have learned about instructional programing.

SUMMARY

1. Research on programed learning has turned up few conclusive results but has implications for theory of meaningful learning.

2. Students of all ages in schools, colleges, and industry generally react favorably toward teaching machines and pro-

grams. Over a period of time, however, the novelty effect wears off and routine programs become boring.

3. General attitude surveys have no predictive value in relation to learning achievement.

4. It has been demonstrated repeatedly that self-instruction techniques effectively promote learning.

5. Comparisons between programed and conventional instruction often favor the programs, especially in terms of time scores. These results are not entirely conclusive because of uncontrolled variables such as the novelty effect, time spent on the different methods, and the personalities involved. There are reasons to believe that integrating different techniques is preferable to using only one.

6. Programs have been used effectively for special industrial training needs and offer a promising method of reducing time and costs for standardized training.

7. Simple teaching machines and programed books appear to be equally effective methods of presenting programs.

8. Most but not all of the research on step size favors small steps over large. Such research is more relevant if discrete-step programs are to be used for initial presentation of subject matter.

9. For short program sequences, the order of frames can be randomized without affecting learning seriously.

10. Experimental comparisons of linear and branching programs have shown few significant differences. Remedial branching was shown to be superior when it was based on self-evaluation as well as on error responses.

11. Programs often can be presented to groups as effectively as to individuals especially if each learner has a response-feedback device.

12. Conventional textual material has been shown to be as effective as or more effective than discrete program frames in promoting learning.

13. Few significant differences have been demonstrated between constructed and multiple-choice responses relative to their advantages in learning achievement. Multiple-choice answers usually save time and may promote more transferable knowledge than constructed responses.

14. Covert responses and reading often are just as effective as overt responses if the learner is participating attentively. The relative advantages of different types of response depend in part on program difficulty, probably because it affects the level of participation.

15. With study time equated, reading plus adjunctive multiple-choice review questions were more effective than linear programs.

16. There is no conclusive evidence that errors as such are detrimental to learning if they are corrected immediately and if the learner understands why he was wrong. The easy programs do not always promote the highest achievement scores.

17. The reinforcement interpretation of learning from programs does not explain why explicit confirmations are not always needed or why boring programs can still promote learning. Research has shown that specific prompts are more valuable in a learning sequence than specific confirmations.

18. Sensory feedback is a more useful concept in understanding learning than either confirmation or reinforcement for it describes the differential process by

means of which the individual compares his performance with a prescribed pattern.

19. Although self-instruction may mask individual differences, it does not eliminate them. Care must be taken to avoid bringing brighter students down to the level of programs which can be mastered by the slower students.

20. There is evidence that arbitrarily limited teaching programs do not pro-vide a varied enough feedback context to assure adequate generalization and transfer.

21. Teachers should be trained in programing techniques so that they can prepare their materials to fit their specific needs. Such training is generally useful in that it provides insights into good teaching procedures and the nature of meaningful learning.

CHAPTER
13

Textbook Design

In the last eight chapters, we have surveyed the design and use of contemporary teaching devices and techniques which supplement live instruction and books in our schools and training centers. At the early stages of development of some of these modern techniques, it was believed by some that they would decrease the use of books as teaching devices, but no such effect has occurred or is likely to occur. Rather than displacing books, each new teaching medium has increased their use. But in emphasizing our need for books as generalized teaching tools, the new techniques also have emphasized the importance of design in determining a book's effectiveness.

The unhappy fact is that the design of man's oldest and most universal educational device has received little attention from behavior science. We do not know in objective terms the advantages and disadvantages of conventional books or how they can be improved. However, we can make some informed guesses. We suspect that the universality and durability of books as learning media can be attributed to the intrinsically organized verbal and nonverbal sensory-feedback processes of reading and creative writing. Book learning is more widely generalized and transferred than learning from more specialized devices. But to integrate verbal and nonverbal knowledge effectively, books must be as contemporary in their design as the knowledge they attempt to portray. In order to keep pace with the advancing front of human knowledge, books as well as other teaching media must be designed to communicate the significant features and interactions of the human condition.

VERBAL-NONVERBAL DESIGN

From our general knowledge of teaching media and meaningful learning, we derive these tentative principles about how to design books to promote effective learning. We believe that nonverbal illustrative content should be integrated with the verbal content to enhance the realism of concrete situations and to structure the pattern of learning; to promote active student participation in the instructional situation; to reveal organizational features of the subject matter and to provide stable visual patterns as a background for the articulated verbal material. Patterns of verbal-nonverbal materials in books provide differential feedback patterns which structure the student's reactions and determine the course and content of learning. What we are striving for is a broad understanding of the subject matter—meaningful knowledge that is general, transferable, and adaptable. If we are successful, the student's reaction patterns will not be limited to those explicitly structured by the author of the book but will be flexible enough to apply to many diverse situations. In this way we hope not only to provide the student with factual knowledge but also to stimulate him to processes of inventive activity and original thinking.

Learning from Illustrations

The research literature relating directly to the problems of book design as here formulated is extremely limited. The earliest work, according to a review by Spaulding (1955), was concerned mainly with children's preferences in pictorial illustrations. It has been observed that children like pictures with color and action. Ferguson (1957) reported that pictures of animals or objects in action elicited roughly twice as many free responses from children as nonaction pictures. Children like pictures of animals and pictures that tell a story. Most importantly, they want realism; children prefer monochromatic illustrations that are realistic to illustrations that are colored but unrealistic (Rudisill, 1952). As we have seen, however, students' preferences are not predictive of the teaching effectiveness of different educational materials.

Most of the studies comparing the relative effectiveness of illustrated and nonillustrated verbal presentations in promoting learning were hampered by the fact that achievement was measured by verbal tests. As we saw in relation to studies of learning from films, verbal tests do not measure adequately what is learned from nonverbal materials. In view of this fact, any measurable increase in verbal learning from the use of nonverbal illustrations may reflect a more significant increment in achievement than is revealed by the data.

A 1944 study of Halbert, described by Spaulding (1955), compared the effectiveness of reading a booklet with and without pictures and looking at the pictures without the text. Children reported more information after reading the illustrated text than after seeing the text or pictures alone. However, a similar study of second graders by Weintraub, reported by Wendt and Butts (1962), found that comprehension tests significantly favored the method of presenting stories without pictures rather than with pictures.

Several studies on older children also found that illustrations did not increase learning. Burdick reported that passages in high school science textbooks were not improved in teaching effectiveness by illustrating them with cross-sectional drawings or perspective cutaways (Wendt and Butts, 1962). Vernon (1953b, 1953c, 1954) tested the effectiveness of many different kinds of illustrations, including photographs, pictorial charts, diagrams, and graphs for all ages of learners from school children to adults and found no significant increases in learning that could be attributed to the use of illustrations. It must be remembered that the criteria of learning in all of these studies were verbal.

Another line of evidence drawn from research on multichannel presentations by means of various audiovisual media suggests that the addition of pictorial material to verbal presentations does indeed produce an increment in learning. Hartman (1961b) reviewed all studies which compared presentations of related pictorial-verbal material with verbal alone. In some cases the verbal material was presented aurally, by recording or sound track, and in some cases visually by means of printed text. Experimental comparisons almost invariably favored the combined pictorial-verbal presentations over either visual or aural verbal material in spite of the fact that most of the tests of learning were verbal. Hartman concluded that the research evidence at that time strongly indicated an advantage for combining presentation channels.

A recent analysis of how pictures contribute to verbal learning from recorded sound narration was carried out by Ketcham and Heath (1962). The authors were interested in determining whether the presentation of pictures relevant to the verbal material would increase learning of verbal facts not actually embodied in the pictures. They prepared a recorded narrative account of a fictional holdup-murder-trial episode which referred to and identified relevant pictures (for example, pictures of the judge or the jail) and then went on to recount additional facts that could not be obtained directly from the pictures. Four groups of graduate student subjects listened to the narration under four different conditions: (a) sound alone; (b) sound plus relevant pictures;

(c) sound plus abstract illustrations of geometric forms; and (d) sound plus unrelated pictures of landscapes. Figure 13.1 shows the scores made by each group on a posttest based on facts given in the narration but not in the pictures. A significant variation was produced in learning scores by varying the type of visual presentation. The use of relevant pictures resulted in a learning increment, but abstract and unrelated pictures apparently served as a distracting influence and produced a learning decrement.

These findings support what we have suspected, that the use of visual displays does more for the teaching situation than simply increasing the amount of information presented. Pictures and other illustrations provide a stable, spatially organized visual framework or background for the more highly articulated and more temporally organized verbal presentation. A visual display provides a pattern which helps to establish the interrelationships among more discrete facts. It serves as a memory device to facilitate recall of significant features.

Figure 13.1.   Learning from recorded narration presented alone or with pictures not embodying the criterion test material. The variation in scores was significant at 0.01. (Data from Ketcham and Heath. Teaching effectiveness of sound with pictures that do not embody the material being taught. *Aud.-vis. Commun. Rev.*, 1962, **10**, 89–93.)

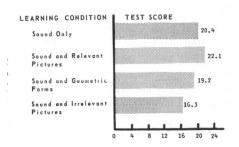

It serves both to prompt and to confirm responses of the learner. In brief, it facilitates learning by helping to organize the material to be learned.

Analyzing Specific Factors

A critical issue in using illustrative material is how to use it most effectively. What factors in illustrations interact with what factors in the text and in the learner to determine what is learned?

One of the most interesting analyses bearing on this general problem was carried out by Spaulding (1956) in connection with a project set up to publish and distribute reading materials to newly literate adults in Latin America. For a pilot study, eleven illustrated booklets were prepared on such useful subjects as farming practices, with each left-hand page carrying a pictorial illustration plus its caption and each right-hand page, the related text. For comparative purposes, the same textual material was presented in another set of nonillustrated booklets. A total of 102 adults in Costa Rica and Mexico were given the two types of booklets and then were tested by means of recall and association tests. For eight of the booklets, sixty-six percent more information was recalled after reading the illustrated versions, but for the other three booklets, twenty-six percent more was remembered after reading the nonillustrated versions. The experimenter suggested two reasons for this apparently detrimental effect of pictures in three booklets. Two of them were illustrated with pictures in a woodcut style that violated perspective and did not give clear-cut realistic presentations. The third of these three booklets dealt with complex information that was not clarified by the pictures.

In a further study in Costa Rica and Mexico, an attempt was made to define more clearly the illustrative factors that contribute to learning. A total of 252 pictures, including realistic line drawings, woodcuts, and stylized drawings, were presented to ninety-eight adults who were asked to tell what they saw in the pictures. An analysis of their reports showed that the interpretations of the viewers were structured by past experience and were extremely literal. For the type of reader studied here, Spaulding concluded that very realistic pictures were necessary and that color should not be used unless it was realistic. The amount of detail and action in a picture should be limited to the important points to be illustrated to avoid confusing or misleading the viewer with too much extraneous material.

Similar findings were reported by Fonseca and Kearl (1960) from a study carried out in rural Brazil. Several hundred members of a farm youth organization, ten to eighteen years old, were tested for their ability to recognize pictorial symbols which had different degrees of fidelity to objects (for example, ant, pig, church), arbitrary symbols (for example, question mark, dollar sign), and picture stories (for example, drink boiled water, how to kill ants with insecticide). The authors concluded that the ability to interpret many symbols is a learned skill and thus varies with age, experience, and education. For maximum teaching effectiveness, pictorial symbols and picture stories should be as realistic as possible but should not have excessive detail. Formal education increased the understanding of abstract symbols, picture series, and symbols not related to the viewer's daily life.

Difficulties in interpreting abstract symbols and drawings are not limited to children and the poorly educated but are found in students at all educational levels as well as in adults. After a series of studies on the use of cross-section drawings, diagrammatic symbols, and process-diagrams in American schools, Malter (1948) concluded that children need adult help to enable them to read diagrams. An extensive series of observations carried out on grade school and high school students and airmen in England led Vernon (1953b) to the conclusion that considerable intelligence and training are needed to understand diagrams, charts, and graphs. In general she found that numerical figures were understood about as well when presented in tables as in diagrams or charts, although the drawings may stimulate more interest in the material. As a rule diagrams needed verbal explanations to make them clear.

One of Vernon's conclusions was that different types of data require different types of diagrams. A few objective comparisons of different kinds of diagrams or graphs provide some specific suggestions about what particular form will be most effective for certain purposes. Investigating eight different graphical representations of the relative size of parts of a whole, Peterson and Schramm (1954) found that a circle graph was read most accurately and multiple area columns least accurately. A single segmented bar was slightly more effective than a disc, multiple bars, multiple cylinders, multiple square columns, or a partial cosmograph. Culbertson and Powers (1959) found that bar graphs were better than line graphs for evaluating and comparing specific quantities.

Vertical bars were slightly more effective than horizontal bars, but horizontal bars had the advantage of providing more space for labels and quantities. These authors found correlation coefficients of 0.551 to 0.557 for graph reading ability and numerical, verbal, and abstract reasoning aptitude scores, and a coefficient of 0.427 for graph reading ability and a general IQ score. Feliciano et al. (1963) found that bar graphs were more effective than tables in presenting statistical information.

One feature of verbal-nonverbal programing that deserves careful study is the relative density of nonverbal display in a presentation or the rate at which visual illustrations are introduced during a continuous verbal discourse. There are few objective data assessing the visual density factor in book design, although one of the earliest research efforts estimated that perhaps one-half of the space in children's books should be given over to illustrations (Spaulding, 1955). Relative to this problem, we have made some controlled observations on the behavior of people listening to audiovisumatic lectures while the presentation rate of visual illustrative slides was varied. High school students, college students, and adult groups were observed. The relative effectiveness of different visual densities was judged according to the number of persons in the audience maintaining their orientation to the projection screen.

We observed first of all that recorded lectures presented with no coordinated visual material did not hold the attention of a class very well. With nothing to stabilize or direct visual orientation, both students and adults after ten or fifteen minutes began to look around, shift position, chew their finger nails, read, and talk. However, the addition of almost any kind of visual slides served to sustain the attention of the audience at what appeared to be an acceptable level. Our general observation was that the consistency of orientation toward the visual presentation varied with the rate of changing slides up to a rate of about two slides per minute. Although these observations cannot be applied directly to visual density in book design, they suggest that optimal verbal-nonverbal patterns might be established.

The most specific conclusion we can draw from the studies reported here is that care must be taken in using abstract and graphical materials, especially in books prepared for lower educational levels. In spite of the tentative nature of our knowledge about illustrations and learning, however, a few years ago it was proposed seriously that a manual should be prepared and distributed by publishers telling authors how to illustrate their textbooks (Miller *et al.*, 1957). Unfortunately, it may be some time before such a manual could be written that would make sense to the publishers and authors as well as to learning theorists and audiovisual educators. Meanwhile any author interested in the relation of book design to learning is relatively free to formulate his own hypotheses.

AN EXAMPLE OF TEXTBOOK DESIGN

In the absence of a definitive body of experimental literature on book design, we are going to illustrate our concepts further by describing some specific techniques that we used in preparing a textbook and workbook in introductory psychology (Smith and Smith, 1958; Smith,

et al., 1958). Most of the techniques have been used elsewhere in books, periodicals, manuals, advertising brochures, and so on, but our purpose here is to describe them in terms of principles of verbal-nonverbal programing. Inasmuch as we were writing for the college level, we assumed that our readers would have had some experience with different types of artistic and graphic expression.

Promoting Participation

The activity known in general terms as *reading a book* includes a variety of perceptual and symbolic reactions carried out at various levels of attention, concentration, and participation. Different phases of this dynamic observational behavior can be described as alerting reactions, perceptual orientation reactions, and articulated responses to sequences and patterns of symbolic stimuli. A primary purpose of visual illustrations is to regulate orientation and to maintain a high level of concentration on the symbolic response patterns.

The use of lavish illustrations to attract and hold attention is a common technique, particularly in advertising and merchandising displays. This sort of perceptual control of behavior often is described as *perceptual motivation* in recognition of the fact that the motivation to react to a diversified perceptual environment is implicit in the activity itself. Whereas a nonillustrated textbook must maintain the reader's participation by verbal symbolism alone, the use of illustrations makes the participative activity more certain by providing a continually varying visual space. This diversification is known to be important in children's books, and we believe it to be important for advanced students as well.

Part of the tedium induced by linear programs probably is due to their routine and unvarying visual design.

On the other hand, perceptually motivated behavior is of little use in the learning situation unless it advances the reader's learning or understanding of the subject matter. Thus visual material must be selected to direct and regulate the ongoing participation of the reader in such a way as to promote effective learning. Using illustrations in this way might be called *nonverbal prompting,* and it is especially valuable in difficult or complex material where pictorial displays keep the reader oriented toward the important points and help to structure his understanding of the subject matter. New concepts are better understood if they are defined by nonverbal as well as verbal patterns. To insure effective integration of verbal and nonverbal materials, the illustrations of the textbook we are describing were planned while the text was being written.

The workbook prepared for use with the text used conventional question-and-answer techniques but its over-all design was based on the same principles of verbal-nonverbal programing. The objectives were to insure overt participation of the student in the subject matter, to use visual material to provide cues for and to help confirm the overt responses, and to stimulate the student to apply his knowledge to new projects and the solution of new problems. Many of the drawings were similar to textbook illustrations to give the student a feeling of familiarity but not identical to them. Captions were eliminated and certain details changed so that the student responded to somewhat different patterns than had appeared in the text. Thus he

not only was given the opportunity for review but also was helped to generalize his learning to somewhat different situations.

Except for a self-quiz in each chapter, for which the answer keys were given in the back of the book, the student was kept working throughout the workbook with related visual and verbal material, that is, identifying graphically displayed phenomena, comparing objects and interactions, and finding solutions to partially portrayed problems. Some visually structured projects were given to be carried out by individuals or by groups and some of these required the construction of graphs from data obtained by the student himself. Thus, in some ways, the workbook simulated a laboratory situation.

Simulating Reality

An obvious function of book illustrations is to enhance the reality of the material for the reader. However, the best way to simulate reality is not necessarily to use artistic realism. Photographs and realistic paintings and drawings often are useful but in many cases they are less effective than other types of graphic or artistic representation. Even in trainer design, as we saw in Chapter 7, the best simulation may not be the most realistically complete but the one which integrates the most significant features of the skill in an effective temporal and spatial pattern.

In textbook art, the type of graphic or artistic technique used should depend on the function it is to serve as well as the educational level of the reader. We used photographs and drawings of laboratories, experimental techniques, and other relevant situations to induce a feeling of familiarity with the methods, techniques, and phenomena of the science of psychology. Further, pictures of real people carrying out ordinary—or extraordinary—activities were used to remind the student that psychological events occur not just in laboratories but in behavior everywhere.

To provide an organized backdrop for the beginning student emphasizing the variety of the subject matter, many different kinds of persons were portrayed in relation to the verbal accounts of psychological research and psychological concepts. The two drawings in Figure 13.2 show how the artist used *graphic diversification* to illustrate a study on executive behavior and ability and to provide a theme drawing for the chapter on individual differences. One comment made about this book, meant to be derogatory, was that one never could see such a collection of characters except on a New York subway. In a sense this was what the authors and the designer had in mind.

Techniques of *graphic segregation* were used to identify important points or to isolate details or parts which the student should learn to discriminate. For such purposes, a drawing that emphasizes or exaggerates the significant details is more useful than a realistic picture. An experiment we described earlier lends support to this idea. Ryan and Schwartz (1956) found that to pro-

Figure 13.2. Two uses of graphic diversification to illustrate different types of individuals. (From Smith and Smith. *The behavior of man: introduction to psychology.* New York: Holt, Rinehart and Winston, 1958.)

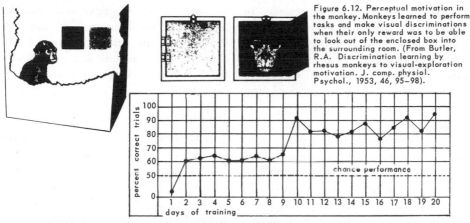

Figure 6.12. Perceptual motivation in the monkey. Monkeys learned to perform tasks and make visual discriminations when their only reward was to be able to look out of the enclosed box into the surrounding room. (From Butler, R.A. Discrimination learning by rhesus monkeys to visual-exploration motivation. J. comp. physiol. Psychol., 1953, 46, 95–98).

Figure 13.3.   Combining pictorial displays and graphs to provide two levels of abstraction and help establish the meaning of the graphs. (From Smith and Smith. *The behavior of man: introduction to psychology.* New York: Holt, Rinehart and Winston, 1958.)

mote learning of the details in a picture, a cartoon-type drawing was more effective than either a photograph or a realistic drawing. We sometimes used diagrams to segregate or isolate important points that could not be represented pictorially. Color was used to isolate or emphasize specific parts of drawings and a number of full-color illustrations gave realism to the discussion of color vision.

Generalizing from research on the value of color in training films and educational television (May and Lumsdaine, 1958; Rosenstein and Kanner, 1961), we would not expect the lavish use of color, except when needed to aid identification or discrimination, to add greatly to a book's teaching effectiveness. However this point can be established only by objective study. It is possible that full-color illustrations are significantly more effective than black-and-white for some purposes, for example, for teaching young children. Certainly there are many types of subject matter that benefit from graphic displays in several colors

—biological and medical drawings and maps come immediately to mind. In view of the expense involved in color reproductions, however, it would seem worthwhile to make a systematic analysis of their value in textbooks.

An important function of illustrations is to promote generalization and transfer by techniques of *graphic integration* wherein the design illustrates the generality of a concept rather than its specific manifestations. Abstract drawings and graphs are themselves abstracted or generalized concepts and thus can be used to represent a class of events rather than single instances. In some cases, a nonverbal abstraction helps establish the meaning of a concept or interaction that is difficult to express verbally.

Many processes and interactions in nature can be represented most precisely by quantitative graphic functions, but as we have seen in the research literature, the meaning of graphs is not always immediately apparent, especially to beginning students or those with little background in mathematics or science. In some cases, we combined pictorial displays and graphs in order to provide additional prompts and to add more specific meaning to the generalized process or interaction being represented. An example is shown in Figure 13.3.

Inasmuch as the subject matter of the book we are describing was psychology, many discussions concerned internalized patterns of behavior—emotion, thought, and so on—which are experienced subjectively but are marked by little overt activity. We found that even these subjective patterns often could be illustrated effectively by the techniques of expressionistic art, that is, getting from the artist graphic patterns that expressed

his own inner, subjective reactions. As an example, the drawing in Figure 13.4 shows how the artist represented the hallucinatory reactions of a subject who took part in an experiment on sensory restriction.

Providing Nonverbal Organization

It is recognized generally that meaningful, organized subject matter is learned more readily and retained more effectively than material with little or no intrinsic organization. Accordingly, it is easier to learn and to remember a fact that can be integrated into an established pattern than some incidental item that seems to stand alone.

Organization and patterning are so

Figure 13.4.   Expressionistic representation of hallucinatory reactions. (From Smith and Smith. *The behavior of man: introduction to psychology.* New York: Holt, Rinehart and Winston, 1958.)

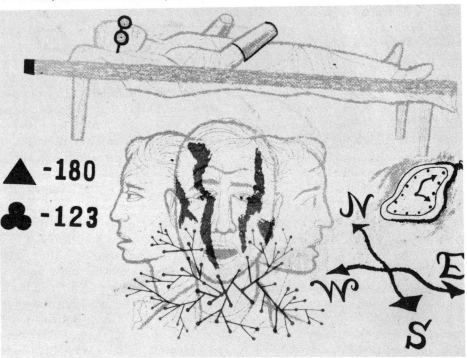

important in learning that we often establish arbitrary patterns to help us organize, learn, and retain loosely organized material. One interesting but little understood facet of human behavior is the development by some individuals of *memory forms* which provide a spatially organized framework for number systems, dates, days of the week, and so on. For example, a person known to the authors who has an internalized pattern of this sort for the days of the week automatically thinks of the seven days arranged consecutively around an oval pattern. It seems quite certain that implicit perceptual patterns of this sort, even when arbitrary in their organization, facilitate learning and memory of discrete facts that can be "located" on the pattern.

Spatial patterns and other organizational features are just as important in textbook learning. Purely verbal material is organized temporally for the most part and may be difficult to grasp as an organized whole. With a nonillustrated book, a reader must organize and project himself into the described events and situations on the basis of verbal symbols alone, supported by his own limited experience with the situations. Illustrations quicken this organization and give more immediate meaning to the words. In this process, pictorial and graphic displays act as patterned, meaningful reference systems against which the sensory-feedback effects of reading can be continually checked. As shown in the study by Ketcham and Heath (1962), relevant pictures helped the students learn and remember even those details that did not appear in the pictures. Illustrations provide sustained perceptual backgrounds

for the temporally sequenced verbal articulations.

One organizational feature of verbal exposition is that of sequencing the presentation of topics according to their meaningful interrelations. A general statement of a concept usually is given first followed by more detailed descriptions of more specific phenomena or principles that can be subsumed within the general category. The verbal design of a textbook indicates graduated levels or categories by means of chapter divisions and within-chapter headings of different value.

It is possible to sequence visual displays according to these same organizational principles. In our textbook, each chapter was headed by a theme drawing or display designed to suggest the overall nature of the subject. Within the body of chapters, general displays were used first to familiarize the student with new concepts and new experimental areas and the like. These were followed by more detailed presentations including quantitative diagrams and graphs. Still another organizational technique was to use sequential displays to represent stages in a process going on in time.

Dimensions of Meaning

The primary purpose of verbal-nonverbal programing is to facilitate and enlarge the student's understanding of the subject matter, that is, to make the material meaningful to him. The nature of *understanding* is related to the nature of *meaning*, but neither of these important concepts can be defined precisely in objective terms. We can say a lot about them, but we cannot tie them down to any specific behavioral phenomena.

Our difficulty in defining and dealing with understanding and meaning is due in part to their fluid nature. Meanings are not absolutely fixed from person to person or even within the same person but change with experience and with circumstances. The behavioral correlates of meaning involve not just overt behavioral and symbolic processes but emotional and physiological variables as well. Thus the meaning of a word cannot be specified exactly in terms of related verbal symbols because of its important nonverbal and subjective components.

One approach to the analysis of meaning (Osgood, 1952; Osgood and Suci, 1955) is in terms of *semantic differential* scales. (For use of such scales in attitude measurement, see Figure 12.2.) Their procedure was to have subjects rate the meaning of a word in terms of fifty pairs of adjective opposites such as bad-good, rough-smooth, and so on. Each rating was made on a seven-point scale representing the continuum from one adjective to its opposite. Thus a word such as *polite* might be rated entirely *good*, approximately midway on the *rough-smooth* and *cold-hot* scales, more *strong* than *weak*, more *fresh* than *stale*, and so on. When the semantic differential profiles of many words were analyzed statistically, it was found that they varied principally in terms of three factors, which were identified as *evaluation*, *potency*, and *activity*. Although these factors themselves do not mean the same thing to everyone, they do indicate that in order to convey language meanings in full it is necessary to provide reference meanings related to intensity of belief, evaluation or comparative values, and activity.

The major types of activity which might give meaning to words and concepts are diagramed in Figure 13.5. This drawing suggests that there are a number of behavioral reference systems which define meanings—in this case the meaning of *snake*. These activity categories include direct perceptual-motor actions triggered by the presence of real snakes, emotional-motivational reactions, various types of nonverbal symbolic actions such as gestures and expressive movements, artistic representations by means of graphic or plastic techniques or observing these representations, and verbal reactions including the use of the word *snake* in all sorts of descriptive, definitive, comparative, and evaluative contexts. In the diagram, the action categories are arranged roughly according to their level of symbolic abstraction. The symbolic actions not only occur as specific behavior patterns in their own right but also come to represent the more direct behaviors and to mediate their meaningful effects. Pictorial displays are a particularly effective medium for symbolic representation because of their flexibility and variety. Thus we believe that illustrative material in books serves as one source of sensory data from which language meanings are derived.

Word meanings represent a dual level of abstraction, that is, the level related to direct perceptual-motor and emotional behavior and the level related to symbolic actions which themselves are abstract representations of direct action. Because nonverbal symbols, including pictorial and graphic representations, are themselves partly abstract, the meanings derived from them are often more generalized than those based on direct environmental interactions. Thus pic-

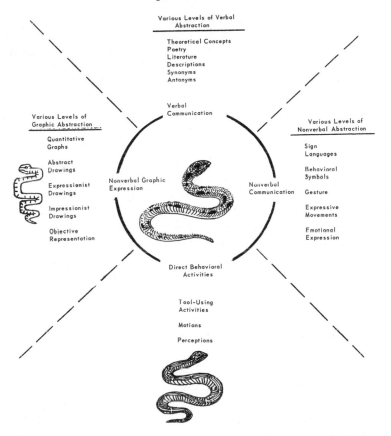

Figure 13.5.   Word meanings are derived from different behavior reference systems, including direct perceptual-motor reactions, emotional-motivational reactions, nonverbal communicative movements, expressive movements, graphic or plastic representations, and verbal responses. The components of meaning vary in level of abstraction.

torial art and graphic displays can interact in various ways with verbal symbols to provide general meanings for and understanding of the environment and its space, time, and kinetic properties.

Promoting Different Forms of Thought

The learning promoted by reading is mainly cognitive and may involve different forms or patterns of thought—for example, imagination or dreaming, concrete thought, logical thought, emotional thought, evaluative thought, and creative thought. It cannot be said that any one type of thinking is generally better or more successful than another, for the usefulness of a pattern of thinking can be judged only in terms of the function to be served. In teaching formal knowledge, we sometimes wish to promote concrete or logical thinking and at other times imaginative or creative thinking. Students should learn to deal with ambiguous and controversial subject matters in different ways than they deal with rigidly defined, generally accepted facts. In human affairs there are even areas where emotional or evaluative thinking is not out of place.

One of our ideas about book design was that different forms of artistic expression and graphic display could be used to promote different patterns of thinking to serve different functions. Photographs and concrete, realistic drawings are related to accurate detail and standardized repetitive experience. In contrast, impressionistic and expressionistic displays are related to analytic patterns of thinking. Impressionistic drawings emphasize observational accuracy and can be used to depict analytically the specialized variables and properties of human perception—color, form, movement, and so on. Expressionistic art provides the artist's analytic portrayal of emotion and feeling in projected perceptual terms. Abstract art represents general ideas as opposed to specific events. Abstract designs as well as quantitative graphs can be used to represent temporal and spatial interactions and to suggest functional interrelationships that are difficult to describe verbally.

The different forms of artistic expression can be used most significantly to adjust the level of nonverbal expression to that of the verbal discussion of the subject matter. In this way the visual art of the book is correlated with the mode and level of treatment of specific subjects. In our textbook, general human situations often were depicted with photographs. Experiments demonstrating successive changes in behavior over a period of time were illustrated by realistic drawings showing the sequential

stages. For the discussion of various social phenomena, the artist observed the scenes from above, suggesting the vantage point of a scientific social observer. In certain areas of conjecture and theory, an attempt was made to convey by means of illustrations as well as words the tentative or controversial nature of the subject matter.

In our opinion an important function of artistic and graphic material in textbooks is to arouse the curiosity and imagination of the reader in the hope of promoting creativity in thought. In most fields of knowledge, creativity is as dependent on nonverbal manipulation as on verbal. Modern science and tech-

Figure 13.6.   A representation of Freudian theory intended to provoke critical examination of the concepts. (From Smith and Smith. *The behavior of man: introduction to psychology.* New York: Holt, Rinehart and Winston, 1958.)

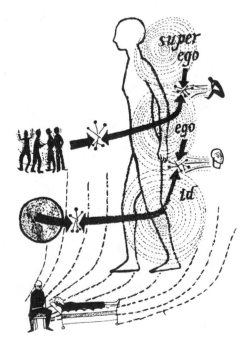

nology particularly incorporate nonverbal concepts about machine design, graphic representation, and systems interaction without which the verbal constructs are relatively meaningless.

How much creative thinking we actually promoted with our illustrative techniques is, of course, a matter of conjecture, but we shall describe here several specific illustrations that were intended to be more provocative than

definitive. The drawing in Figure 13.6 is a visualization of Freudian theory of the nature of personality and some of its important interactions. It was intended to be controversial and to make students feel uneasy about the somewhat fuzzy concepts of psychoanalysis and theories of unconscious motivation. According to observational evidence, these effects were achieved.

The drawing in Figure 13.7 might be

Figure 13.7.   An exploratory display, in which a number of aspects of an interesting subject are represented graphically but not described in detail verbally, either in the text or in the caption. The student must work out some of the implications of the drawing for himself. (From Smith and Smith, 1958.)

called an *exploratory display*. It is intended to force the student to explore the significance and the implications of the drawing and thus to enhance the meanings of the subject matter. This drawing combines a series of objects, situations, and events and indicates some of their interactions but does not identify them specifically either in the caption or in the related text. The student must establish some of the meanings and search out some of the relationships for himself.

We believe that the use of correlated abstract, impressionistic, and expressionistic forms of graphic art invests the verbal information in the text with immediate and potent nonverbal impressions and meanings in an interaction within the reader that may very well be the key to a whole new line of thought. In areas of complex interactions and human relationships, such art forms may convey meanings that cannot be communicated by formal language. The ability to visualize abstract interactions and dynamic phenomena related to power, energy, operations, development, motivation, conflict, and human values may make the difference between routine learning and creativity.

We think that it is particularly important to bring to the study of human behavior and the social sciences a recognition of human values. People must be observed not as rats in a maze or pigeons in a box but as individuals with emotions and sensibilities and a life to live in society. Expressionistic drawings such as the one shown in Figure 13.8 often can do more than many pages of text to give the reader some measure of understanding of a human problem.

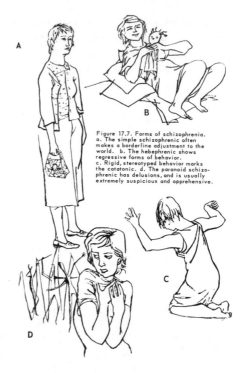

Figure 17.7. Forms of schizophrenia. a. The simple schizophrenic often makes a borderline adjustment to the world. b. The hebephrenic shows regressive forms of behavior. c. Rigid, stereotyped behavior marks the catatonic. d. The paranoid schizophrenic has delusions, and is usually extremely suspicious and apprehensive.

Figure 13.8.   An expressionistic representation of different forms of schizophrenia. A drawing of this sort portrays human values in a way not possible either with words or photographs. (From Smith and Smith, 1958.)

Publishing ventures of the sort we are describing, for which professional artists executed several hundred illustrations, are expensive and can be justified economically only in areas where the demand for books promises extensive sales. However, we are convinced that the principles of verbal-nonverbal programing should lead to more effective textbooks even when illustrations are used on a much more limited scale. Authors are deterred from applying these principles for at least two major reasons. One is that actual techniques of verbal-nonverbal integration have not yet been assessed adequately by objective analyses. The other reason reflects the comment that Pressey (1960) made about teaching machines; for busy teachers, using the machines was often just too much trouble! So it is with authors. They write their books and insert a few pictures and graphs and then turn their attention to other pressing interests.

Student Attitudes toward Illustrated Text

A limited amount of evaluative data concerning our highly illustrated textbook is available in the form of attitude ratings collected from students who used the book in regular courses. One survey asked the students to rate several general aspects of the book and another obtained ratings comparing this text with another more conventional text and a book of readings.

Arrangements were made to use the personnel and procedures of an annually scheduled student survey of college courses to obtain attitude data on the illustrated textbook from students who had used it in a course in general psychology. Planned and carried out by a student organization on the university campus, the survey sampled student reactions to lectures and quiz sections as well as to the textbook. The main items concerning the textbook were that the text: 1. is well organized; 2. provides too much detail; 3. provides too little detail; 4. is relevant to the course; 5. presents an impartial view of the subject; 6. is an asset to the course; 7. presents material at the level of the course; 8. with the workbook, provides sufficient texts for the course. Student workers distributed and collected the survey materials. Of the

250 students in the class, 202 participated in the survey, marking the survey sheets anonymously. The materials and results were sent to the professor in charge of the course (*not* an author of the book) after final grades had been recorded.

The bar graphs in Figure 13.9 summarize responses of the entire group to six of the survey items dealing with the general nature of the illustrated book and its relation to the course. They show generally favorable student attitudes toward the text in spite of the fact that their attitudes toward the course were not consistently positive. This same class expressed a high level of disapproval of quiz-section instructors.

Figure 13.9.   Student attitudes toward a highly illustrated textbook. (Data furnished by Prof. H. Leibowitz.)

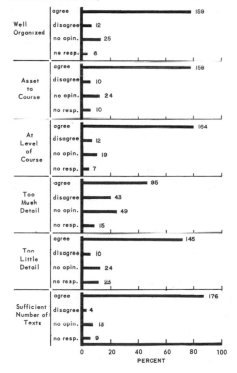

When attitude data were broken down according to college class, grade-point level, type of major, and sex, no differences were found related to grade-point level. Psychology majors more often judged the text as relevant to the course and nonmajors more often judged it as well organized. More fe- · males than males expressed positive attitudes but the differences were not reliable. Seniors showed lower positive attitude frequencies on all items than the other three classes.

On another college campus, a comparative survey was made of student attitudes toward three books used in a course in introductory psychology: the highly illustrated text, a conventionally designed textbook on human behavior written by an author whose prose style is recognized as excellent and who took a rigorously logical, theoretically oriented approach to the subject matter, and a collection of contemporary readings drawn from psychological research literature. *Agree, disagree,* and *no opinion* responses were obtained on three items:

1. the book was well organized
2. the book was interesting
3. the book was too difficult

Figure 13.10 summarizes the percentage of responses in each category for the first item relating to opinions about the organization of the three books— the attitudinal variable in which we are most interested. It can be seen that the illustrated texbook was judged to be *well organized* far more often than the conventional text. Positive judgments about the book on contemporary readings were at an intermediate level. Although comparative attitude data of this sort have only limited significance, they

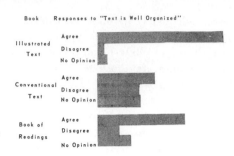

Figure 13.10.   Percentage "agree," "disagree," and "no-opinion" responses to "Text is well organized" item in survey comparing student attitudes toward three textbooks. (Data furnished by Prof. A. H. Hastorf.)

suggest that the verbal-nonverbal integration of the illustrated text may have contributed to the students' understanding of the subject matter and their judgments that the book was well organized.

An interesting finding in this survey was that nearly half of the class could not make up their minds whether or not the illustrated text was too difficult. We would like to believe that this uncertainty resulted from the fact that difficult material had been made to appear less difficult by the manner of presentation, but we are aware of the possibility of less favorable interpretations.

THEORIES OF GRAPHIC COMMUNICATION

Our ideas about verbal-nonverbal integration in book design can be clarified by comparing and contrasting them with two thoughtful analyses of the nature and significance of graphic communication—one from a psychologist and one from an emeritus curator of prints in the Metropolitan Museum of Art. The ideas drawn from these two diverse sources support, in certain important ways, our own concepts.

Gibson's Theory
of Pictorial Perception

J. J. Gibson (1954) launched his analysis of the significance of pictorial communication in behavior organization by defining *surrogates* as those artificial stimuli that are used to convey meaning. A surrogate is artificial in that it conveys information at second hand. It might be any symbol such as a spoken or written word, a picture, a model, a gesture, and so on used to communicate meaning about objects or events not immediately present.

Surrogate making serves not only a communicative function but a self-stimulatory function as well. A person who speaks stimulates himself as well as his listener and in so doing may set up a pattern of thought. Thinking is not limited to verbal surrogates however. Pictures too can be used to mediate thought as well as to convey information from one person to another. Thus persons learn to think in terms of pictorial as well as verbal surrogates.

The communicative function of surrogates, in Gibson's analysis, varies with their degree of conventionality or nonconventionality. Pictures and graphic symbols vary from extremely realistic nonconventional representations of particular objects, places, or events to conventional, arbitrary symbols such as words that stand for abstract or general things or ideas. The more arbitrary a surrogate is, the more free it is to represent general rather than specific concepts, but its general meaning which is accepted in a culture must be learned. Most pictorial and graphic designs are neither completely realistic nor completely abstract but lie somewhere between these two extremes. Such mixed surrogates, especially pictures executed by hand, can signify some measure of concreteness and some measure of generality. They achieve their abstract quality by distorting the fidelity of their representation of specific things.

According to Gibson, the design of pictorial surrogates for instructional purposes can be based on the assumption that the perceiver does not need all of the properties of an absent object in order to know how to deal with it— only those that are relevant or significant for his purposes. Inasmuch as it is a waste of effort to simulate the object with complete realism, pictures and other mixed surrogates should follow the principle of selective emphasis to focus attention on the most important parts, properties, or relationships. The danger we encounter in reducing the fidelity of a picture is that its meaning may become vague or too nonspecific.

Gibson summed up his analysis of the functions of graphic surrogates by saying that realism provides a substitute for first hand experience and thus teaches concrete things, whereas arbitrary and conventional surrogates stimulate the imagination and help to teach abstractions and general rules. They communicate information about properties, variables, groups, classes, and universals.

Ivins' Theory of Visual
Communication

Ivins' (1953) provocative account of the part played by exactly repeatable pictorial statements in the history of human thought and action in his own words, "grew out of a long endeavour to find a pattern of significance in the story of prints." For Ivins, this story took on significance not as a relatively minor chapter in the history of art but as a major contribution to the development of science, technology, and general knowledge. For not until men learned to print pictures were they able to repeat exactly a pictorial statement in the same sense that they had been able to repeat verbal statements for thousands of years.

Two of man's most important media of communication are words and pictures, but these differ, as Gibson and many others have said, in their degrees of abstractness or concreteness. Once a word is adopted by a culture, it can be spoken or written with many variations of vocal sound or graphic design and still represent the same word or symbol. Thus words are exactly repeatable even though their visual or auditory forms vary somewhat. On the other hand, a picture that is copied by hand is not exactly repeated; it is now a different picture. Not until the fifteenth century did Western man learn how to reproduce pictures mechanically, so to speak, thus making it possible to repeat his pictorial statements exactly.

What is the significance of this relatively late development of pictorial repetition? To Ivins, the most characteristic ideas, skills, and technologies of our modern civilization have depended on man's ability to communicate his pictorial and graphic knowledge from person to person and from place to place in as invariant a form as he communicates his verbal knowledge. One or two men cannot develop a science or technology; they must communicate what they have thought and what they have

done to others lest it be lost. But in order for their knowledge to be preserved so as to contribute to a growing accumulation of knowledge, it must be repeatable. Insofar as our modern sciences and technologies involve nonverbal pictorial or graphic knowledge, they depend on prints to communicate that knowledge.

The ancient Greeks, whose systems of thought are still revered today, could repeat their verbal statements by hand copying but had no technology for exactly repeating pictorial statements. Consequently their intellectual activity was structured mainly along verbal lines. According to Ivins (1953), "The Greeks were full of all sorts of ideas about all sorts of things, but they rarely checked their thought by experiment. . . ." Lacking concrete reference systems, they sought reality in the abstractions represented by words. "Plato's ideas and Aristotle's forms, essences, and definitions, are specimens of this transference of reality from the object to the exactly repeatable and therefore seemingly permanent verbal formula." The only sciences in which the Greeks made significant advances were geometry and astronomy; for the first, words and repeatable line drawings serve to store and communicate meanings, and for the second, the stars on a clear night serve as repeatable visual patterns for every one. Other natural sciences were not advanced by the Greeks; certain botanists wrote descriptions of plants and illustrated them with realistic drawings, but the drawings suffered so at the hands of copyists that the Greeks finally gave up even trying to describe the plants and simply listed all the various names by which each plant was known in different localities and told what ailments it was good for.

The development of methods of printing pictures in the fifteenth century heralded the downfall of the tyranny of words in man's systems of knowledge. Modern science and technology gradually took shape as their indispensable pictorial components were cut or engraved or etched on printing surfaces for widespread dissemination. But not until after the development of photographic techniques did pictorial representation attain such precision that it became a *source* of knowledge as well as a means of distributing it. In Ivins' words:

> The complete revolution that has taken place in the basic assumptions of physics during the last fifty years could never have been accomplished without the data provided by the photographic emulsion.

For example, photographs of an eclipse in 1919 verified Einstein's hypothesis about the action of gravitation on light, and photographs taken in Cavendish Laboratory of vapor condensations in cloud chambers were accepted as evidence of the complexity of the atom. Thus photographs sometimes reveal things that man cannot see directly; the permanence and repeatability of pictorial statements provide a basis for challenging old ideas and formulating new ones; and their duplication makes it possible to communicate and instruct in nonverbal media as well as verbal.

The import of this analysis is that purely verbal structures are apt to get out of hand and lose contact with reality unless they can be checked and corrected against observable specific events. It occurs to us that the dangers of verbal

abstraction are still with us, for example, in behavioral and social theory. Consider the concept of *reinforcement* in learning. Although it is accepted as a necessary component of the learning model by many theorists, it is difficult to pin it to specific events. An event that is *reinforcing* at one time may not be at a later time. Or one man's reinforcer may be another man's poison. Perhaps the reality lies only in the word!

Behavioral Basis of Graphic Communication

These two analyses of graphic communication have a number of interesting points in common and differ principally in matters of emphasis. Both indicated that graphic symbols can be thought of as lying on a continuum from concreteness to abstractness, with most of them lying somewhere in between. Thus Gibson emphasized "mixed surrogates," and Ivins compared different types of prints in terms of their degrees of specificity or generality. Although he spoke of the usefulness of exact representation in photographs, he also described how conventionalized drawings can be used to represent classes of objects or events when the artist selects or emphasizes features that distinguish one class from all others.

Our principal objection to these two analyses is that neither makes explicit allowance for the dimensionality of meaning and its behavioral base. We do not think of word symbols as complete abstractions, as Ivins implies, because to a given individual a word may have rather specific meanings derived from different behavioral reference systems. Nor do we assume, as Gibson seems to do, that an abstract symbol to be useful in communication must have exactly the same conventional meaning for the individuals using it. Because of the subjective components of meaning, we believe that symbols can have only roughly equivalent connotations for several individuals. Thus we would not expect to be able to specify exactly how individuals will react either to verbal or to pictorial symbols, but we do believe that authors can make their meanings clearer by supporting verbal presentations with nonverbal adjuncts, and vice versa. Finally we would emphasize more strongly Gibson's brief reference to the ability of arbitrary symbols to stimulate the imagination. Insofar as graphic symbols have different meanings for each individual and can be combined in new patterns, to that extent can we hope to generate creative thought.

One point made by Ivins is particularly applicable to our general theory of behavior organization. He suggested that the linear time order in which words must be used leads naturally to a verbal breaking down of real things into their definable qualities which have only conceptual existence. In words reminiscent of a gestaltist analysis, he said that a real object is a unity that cannot be broken down into separate qualities without becoming merely a collection of abstractions. What interests us here is Ivins' suggestion that a linear time-order analysis of an environmental object or situation is artificial and does not reflect the observer's direct perceptions. Putting this into behavioral terms, we say that the behaving system or individual is organized in such a way as to respond to the environment primarily according to spatial patterns and only

secondarily in a temporally organized series of reactions. At any given time, the individual's responses are structured according to spatial differences in stimulus intensities at sensory sources, but each response modifies these spatial patterns and through the mechanisms of sensory feedback structures the next response. Thus we believe that the temporal organization of responses is mediated by intervening spatial regulatory patterns.

To our mind this distinction between temporal and spatial organization is of critical importance in psychology. The conventional verbal models of behavior and learning are temporally sequenced models, in which successive stimulus-response-reinforcement units are linked together in time. We believe that these are arbitrary descriptions of what actually occurs—as Ivins has said, they are time-ordered collections of abstractions that have only conceptual existence. We believe that to understand the realities of behavior, we must analyze its spatial organization and that to understand learning, we must analyze how spatial patterns become reorganized in relation to the cumulative effects of experience. We address ourselves to these problems in the chapters to follow.

SUMMARY

1. Principles of verbal-nonverbal design are that books should integrate verbal and nonverbal material to simulate reality, to promote participation of the reader, and to provide stable patterns to help organize the subject matter.

2. Illustrations cannot always be shown to increase learning from verbal textual material when learning is as-

sessed by means of verbal tests. However, some experimental comparisons have favored pictures plus text over text alone even when tested by verbal tests.

3. Studies have shown that the communicative potential of pictures and symbols varies with age, education, and experience. For children and relatively uneducated adults, pictures should be realistic to be most effective. Considerable intelligence and training are needed to understand diagrams, charts, and graphs.

4. Specific techniques of verbal-nonverbal book design are based as much on assumptions as on facts. A primary consideration is to use illustrations to motivate the student to read the book attentively.

5. Participation can be guided and structured by using illustrations as nonverbal prompts, especially in relation to overt participation with workbook materials.

6. Illustrations can be used to simulate reality, but the most effective simulation may involve selective emphasis or abstraction as well as pictorial realism. Specific techniques are graphic diversification, graphic segregation, and graphic integration. Expressionistic art can be used to simulate subjective reactions.

7. Illustrative material can help to organize the subject matter for the reader by pointing out important topics, sequencing them logically, and providing stable visual patterns as backgrounds for temporally sequenced verbal material.

8. Promoting understanding or establishing the meaning of subject matter is complicated by the fact that meanings cannot be specified exactly but vary among individuals along several behavioral dimensions.

9. Osgood and Suci's semantic differential analysis indicated three primary factors in word meanings which they identified as *evaluation, potency,* and *activity.*

10. Meanings develop from various types of activity, including direct reactions, emotional and physiological reactions, and various types of verbal and nonverbal symbolic reactions. Inasmuch as symbolic reactions are more or less abstract, the meanings derived from them are more generalized than those based on direct responses to the environment.

11. Different artistic techniques can be used to stimulate different forms of thought. Realistic art is related to standardized concrete experiences; impressionistic and expressionistic art represent analytic portrayals of qualities of perception and emotion; and abstract designs suggest scientific generalizations and functional interactions.

12. It is believed that various forms of artistic expression can be used to arouse curiosity, stimulate the imagination, and promote creative thinking.

13. Attitude data indicate that verbal-nonverbal integration in books may enhance the reader's conception of subject matter organization.

14. Gibson and Ivins both indicated that the communicative function of graphic symbols depends on their degree of concreteness or abstractness. Ivins suggested that the development of modern science and technology hinged on man's ability to print pictures—that is, to make exactly repeatable pic-

torial statements with which to check the meaning of verbal statements.

15. An important difference between verbal and pictorial patterns is that the former are temporally organized and the latter are spatially organized. It is be-lieved that behavior is organized primarily according to spatial patterns and that each successive phase in a temporal sequence reflects a changed spatial pattern.

CHAPTER

14

Experimental Behavioral Cybernetics

The past two decades have seen a gradually growing recognition in human factors studies of a new kind of experimental science oriented toward the investigation of feedback control in living systems. We use the term experimental behavioral cybernetics to refer to this research approach to understanding the feedback mechanisms involved in performance and learning. This new approach conceptualizes behavior not in terms of discrete units of response but as the continuous activity of a self-governing system. A basic assumption is that the efficiency of performance and the nature of learning are aspects of the level and complexity of closed-loop feedback control that the individual can maintain over the various facets of his own behavior. Thus the guiding principle of cybernetic research design is to investigate parameters of feedback control—that is, to analyze how variations in different properties of feedback stimuli affect the efficiency of performance and the course of learning.

In experimental cybernetics, a fundamental distinction is made between closed-loop and open-loop operating systems. Closed-loop systems readjust themselves continuously by means of their inherent capacity to detect directional differences. They are self-regulating or feedback-regulating systems. Open-loop systems would be those with no internal feedback regulatory mechanisms whose reactions in all cases would be direct functions of external stimulating conditions.

Closed-loop regulation is analyzed experimentally in terms of direct functional relationships between stimulus and response or motor and sensory action, whereas open-loop operations can be analyzed and described in statistical or probabilistic terms. By virtue of their dependence on self-generated sensory signals, closed-loop systems operate primarily in terms of *intrinsic* relationships between responses and sensory processes. Thus, closed-loop cybernetic analyses are quite different from conventional learning studies, which presumably deal only with *extrinsic* factors or open-loop contingencies.

We are not trying to imply that open-loop studies have no place in behavior science. It is obvious that much of our psychological knowledge has been derived from just such probabilistic analyses of the relationships between extrinsic variables and response variation. In many cases, an open-loop analysis is the only practicable way to approach a problem, particularly when one wishes to study the effects of discrete extrinsic events over which the organism has no immediate control. On the other hand, we believe that the interpretation of open-loop analyses always should be qualified by recognition of the closed-loop nature of the behaving system.

CYBERNETIC CONCEPTS OF BEHAVIOR ORGANIZATION

Our basic hypotheses are that the behaving organism possesses the control properties of a cybernetic system but, as a living system, exhibits flexibility and change in patterns of control. The basic properties of behaving cybernetic systems are:

1. they generate their own sensitizing and directionally oriented movements

2. they detect differences between such self-generated actions and certain targets or standards

3. dynamic regulation and redirection is achieved by feedback control

4. integration of receptor systems and of the multidimensional components of response also is achieved by dynamic feedback control

5. control patterns are specialized in terms of temporal, spatial, kinetic, sampling, and transformational characteristics of sensory feedback

Nature of Reflex Action

The conventional reflex concept implies an invariant stimulus-response unit —a discrete response of an effector released by the stimulation of a specific receptor. As psychologists have known for many years, it is impossible to demonstrate such invariant behavior in a normally functioning organism. Even such relatively automatic sensorimotor relationships as the regulation of posture, breath control, and locomotion are far from being invariant, while the more articulated patterns of behavior exhibit almost infinite variability.

The cybernetic view of behavior starts not with an invariant reflex unit but with a reflexive sensorimotor process characterized throughout by dynamic variation. It is in the nature of the behaving system to adjust its output according to its receptor input, but the nature of the sensory input is determined not just by stimulus events external to the organism but by genetically determined closed-loop movement mechanisms intrinsic to the behaving system.

Receptor action is determined by a number of different kinds of self-regulating control systems. For example, tremor and flick movements of specific receptors maintain *sensitivity* by preventing adaptation. Feedback mechanisms such as the pupil of the eye and the tympanum and ossicle system of the middle ear adjust input signal *intensity* and *quality*. Receptor-efferent neurons from the brain to the retina, cochlea, and skin act as input facilitators and inhibitors and thus

modulate the *patterning* of the afferent process. Neurohormonal mechanisms act directly on the receptors and on the brain to maintain afferent neural organization and thus to sustain integrated perceptual activity. The many intrinsic motor mechanisms not only maintain receptor sensitivity, but achieve differential perceptual activities in alerting reactions, orientation, and vigilance.

Differential Neural Action

A cybernetic system regulates its own activity by detecting differences between some output condition and a target or standard. In the case of the behaving individual, the nervous system itself is viewed as such a differential detection mechanism. Instead of conceptualizing nerve cells as linear conduction agents which relay impulses from one ending or synapse to another, as indicated in Figure 14.1a, we assume that individual neurons act as *differential* conductors that are sensitive to differences in stimulation between two points, as shown in Figure 14.1b. Each neuron is thought of as being related to two sources of stimulation at its dendrite endings, and an impulse is assumed to be generated only when a difference in stimulation exists between the two points.

This view rejects the traditional synaptic theory which postulates that neural integration is achieved by the passing or blocking of impulses at the synapse—the blank space between neurons. In our opinion, there is no evidence that changes in synaptic threshold excitability can occur rapidly enough to account for the speed and precision characteristic of ordinary behavior patterning. Further, an in-line conductor such as a synapse offers no basis for dif-

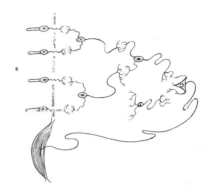

Figure 14.1.   Synaptic and neuronic interpretations of neural action. *a*. The traditional synaptic concept. The nervous system is considered an in-line conduction network in which the synapse can inhibit or facilitate transmission of impulses. *b*. The neuronic interpretation. Neural action is thought to be initiated by stimulus differences at dendrite points.

ferential cybernetic control. We believe that the only way to account for the feedback regulation of behavior is to postulate differential neural action by the neuron itself. This is a neuronic interpretation of neural integration as opposed to the traditional synaptic interpretation. Supporting evidence comes from studies indicating the existence of direction-specific internuncial neurons (that is, neurons which respond to movement in one direction) in the visual centers of guinea pigs (Smith and Bridgman, 1943) and neurons which respond to differences in direction of stimulation in the retina of rabbits (Barlow and Hill, 1963) and in the visual system of frogs (Lettvin *et al.*, 1959) and cats (Hubel and Wiesel, 1962).

Simultaneous Multidimensional Control

A behaving system not only can move in any dimension, but it also can move different parts of the body simultaneously in endless patterns of integrated motion. To account for response multidimensionality, the cybernetic interpretation assumes that different levels of feedback control are involved in performance and learning. We postulate separate feedback mechanisms for postural, transport, and manipulative control and other mechanisms which integrate the separate components into patterned behavior. In this view, any response involves integration of cybernetic receptor regulation with the different component movement systems to determine a unified pattern of action.

In general terms, we think of the brain as a spatial detector system which controls the direction of movements and effects simultaneous control of the different movement components. As shown in Figure 14.2, we assume that this simultaneous regulation depends on detection of spatial differences in stimulation by particular central nervous system neurons. A number of such directional detector neurons are represented in the drawing as detecting changes in stimulation related to head movements, to relative movements of the two eyes, and to movement of a single eye.

In our opinion, different neural centers contain neurons for different stimulus-response interrelationships. First of all, there is a general differentiation of brain function related to the three main movement systems. The postural mecha-

Figure 14.2.   Representation of differential control mechanisms. Different neural centers are assumed to regulate different movement systems and to integrate component movements into organized patterns. (From Smith. The geometry of human motion and its neural foundations: II. Neurogeometric theory and its experimental basis. *Amer. J. phys. Med.*, 1961, **40**, 109–129.)

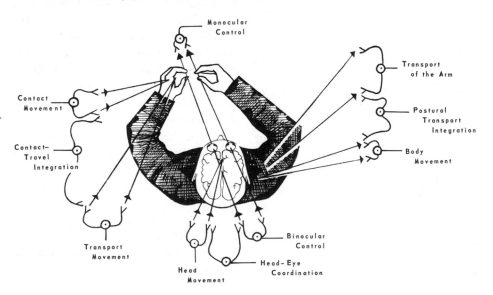

nism dominates phylogenetically older levels of the brain stem and matures first in the individual. The transport systems are represented in newer levels of the brain stem, in the cerebellum, and in limited regions of the cortex. Most of the cortex, which developed last in phylogeny and matures last in ontogeny, is given over to mechanisms that regulate the fine movements of the hands, feet, eyes, and mouth. Thus the precise manipulations and verbal articulations that characterize human behavior depend on a highly differentiated human cortex whose individual detector neurons are related to specific spatial points on the sensory surfaces and other neurons. In addition to the primary regulatory centers for the different movement systems, the brain contains other systems that interrelate the main centers and integrate the different movement components in over-all behavior patterning.

These assumptions that the brain is made up of specific cybernetic neuron systems which control sensitivity of the receptors, detect directional patterns of stimulation, and regulate particular articulated movements of both receptors and the skeletal system are supported by research on the neural control of posture (Dusser de Barenne, 1934) and locomotion (Ruch, 1951) and studies on the neurophysiology of learning (Culler and Mettler, 1934; Lashley, 1944; Marquis and Hilgard, 1937; Morgan, 1951; Smith, 1951; Wing and Smith, 1942).

Spatial versus Temporal Control

The cybernetic theory assumes that both receptor regulation and control of body movements are dependent on the ability of individual neurons to detect spatial differences in stimulation. Instead of assuming that one response automatically triggers another, as in conventional learning theory, we believe that each response changes the pattern of stimuli on the sensory surfaces and that succeeding responses are regulated according to those spatial patterns. Thus a temporal sequence of responses is mediated by response-generated spatial patterns. In such a view, behavior never becomes an automatic, temporally organized chain of responses but always retains its spatial reference.

We also believe that the components of a multidimensional behavior pattern are integrated spatially rather than temporally. The assumption is that detector neurons exist which detect spatial relationships between responding members. Transport movements are integrated with postural movements in terms of relative positions, and manipulative movements are integrated with transport movements in the same way. In such a skill as throwing a ball, the fingers release the ball at a certain spatial position in the motion pattern and not according to a temporal interval or sequence.

As we indicated in Chapter 8, we believe that the postural and transport movement systems not only support the body and move its members, but also provide a two-dimensional reference system within which finer movements are organized. The postural movement system, being regulated principally with reference to gravity, is a vertically oriented system of reference, while the bilaterally organized transport movement system provides orientation in the right-left dimension. These intrinsic *direction-*

finders provide a frame of reference for the more highly articulated focal movements.

Flexibility and Change

The patterns of control in a behaving system are never fixed absolutely but change in reversible and irreversible ways throughout life. The important irreversible changes are those associated with maturation, learning, and aging. Through the processes of maturation, the individual first gains postural-movement control then transport control and finally manipulative control. From the start, behavior is organized and controlled by spatial differences in stimulation. This is true even of the first mass movements elicited in an unborn fetus, although in these first responses only the grossest spatial differentiations can be observed. For example, a stimulus on one side of the body will produce a different reaction from a stimulus on the other side. After birth, the course of development is marked by progressive refinement of the spatial patterning of behavior and the gradually increasing importance of learning as a factor in that refinement. However, the course of learned change depends always on the nature of the feedback-control mechanisms that have developed prior to the learning situation.

It is obvious to everyone that each species starts life with somewhat different behavior capabilities, but learning psychologists tend to think of these innate differences in terms of artificially separated sensory and motor capacities. Thorndike set the pattern for this dichotomy by suggesting that any response of which a person is capable can be associated with any stimulus to which he

is sensitive. This idea that stimuli and responses can be isolated and manipulated separately never has been questioned seriously by learning psychologists; nor have they felt it necessary for learning research to question closely the nature of the original reflexes, for they have felt that the course of learning is defined by events external to the organism.

Because of this emphasis on extrinsic experiential factors, learning theory has never dealt adequately with primary factors of selectivity in behavior—the factors that determine more or less specifically what an individual will do in a given situation regardless of his learning background. Suppose, for example, you place a year-old infant on the floor and roll a small ball toward him. More likely than not, the child will grasp the ball when it comes within reach. Now do the same with a kitten or a puppy. The kitten likely will bat the ball with a paw and the puppy will seize it in its mouth. Differences such as these are so obvious that their importance tends to be overlooked. They reflect differences in the genetically defined behavior organization of different species. They not only are manifested in the behavior of the maturing infant but also define and delimit the nature of his learned activity throughout life. Thus, learning is not imposed on a completely undefined activity base, as is implied by concepts of *random* activity or *emitted* response, but on well-organized, species-defined, sensorimotor patterns of control.

A striking demonstration of how genetic differences even within a species can lead to differences in learning has been reported by Jones and Fennell (1965). These investigators obtained rats from two different strains—the Long-Evans strain used by Tolman and his associates in California and a strain of black-hooded rats used by Spence and his colleagues in Iowa. When rats from both strains were tested in a simple U-maze, highly significant differences in performance and learning were noted. The Long-Evans rats spent long periods of time in the maze, exploring, sniffing, and often retracing their steps. Their initial performance times were more than twice as long as those of the Spence rats, which traversed the maze from start to goal in a systematic fashion, seemingly almost oblivious of their environment. The significance of these observations lies in the fact that these two strains of rats provided raw data for the most prominent schools of thought about the nature of learning. For thirty years or more, the dispute continued between the California Tolman school and the Iowa Hull-Spence school—the dispute as to whether learning involves perceptual and cognitive organization of environmental patterns or mechanical associations between stimuli and responses. It now appears that the great debate of learning psychology arose from differences in genetic make-up of two strains of rats which determined the initial behaviors brought to the learning situations.

The cybernetic view takes cognizance of the fact that early maturation establishes receptor-feedback systems which regulate afferent sensitivity as well as various orientative reaction patterns. These control mechanisms define the perceptual sets which constitute the initial behavior in a learning situation. Early development also establishes patterns of postural and transport action which provide a context within which all finer movements, including speech, must be learned. We assume that these postural and transport mechanisms constitute a built-in coordinate reference system used for the feedback guidance of all movements in space. From infancy on, the individual brings to a learning situation these guidance mechanisms for closed-loop control along with cybernetic receptor activities. Learning is conceptualized as a process of refining and extending the patterns of closed-loop regulation of response and physiological interaction that were established in early maturational development.

In cybernetic theory, learning involves changes in the detector neurons and systems of receptor and sensorimotor control. To become functional early in life, such neurons must be activated. To retain their precision of control, they must be reactivated repeatedly. We believe that aging involves deterioration of neuronic control which proceeds more rapidly if the cybernetic control systems are not used. Coordinate changes in control which persist as learning changes or memory are believed to involve biochemical changes in the neurons themselves rather than the synapses.

The implication of these ideas is that a learning experiment never starts at behavior zero or with a state of equilibrium; it does not even start with random activity. It starts with organized patterns of stimulus-controlled, feedback-regulated responses that can change with practice, can become further differentiated or further generalized, can shift in the nature of their movement-component integration or of their mode of sensory control, or can be transformed in size or in degree of overtness. Most learning involves a specialization of the finer manipulative movements within the larger transport and postural context. To understand the determining conditions of learning change, we need to know something about the feedback integration process itself and how feedback-control patterns have become specialized in a particular species.

The most general implication of these ideas is that learning is not the principal cause of behavior organization, as has been assumed by conventional learning psychology, but represents modifications and refinements of the primary control patterns along lines that conform to the nature of the cybernetic system. That is, we attribute the integrative pattern in human behavior to dynamic feedback relationships in behavioral and instrumental design that define how man's sensory and motor systems can interact in performance.

Cybernetic concepts shed new light on some of the perennial problems of learning that are not handled well by conventional learning theories. For example, no theory of behavior organization or learning currently in vogue can tell us why an animal turns right when a light appears in its right visual field, or turns left when a bell is sounded to the left. Yet such orientation responses or states of alertness or postural sets or what you will are known to affect subsequent learning. Cybernetic theory assumes that such sets involve integrated postural-transport motion patterns for which genetically defined mechanisms are available. An animal or individual orients toward a specific stimulus because it has direction-specific neurons that react to spatial differences in stimulation. Such

directional behavior patterns set the stage for the focal activities involved in learning and provide a spatial reference system within which discrete responses and manipulative patterns are established.

Another problem concerns the nature of equivalence in learning and memory. Whenever we try to define conditions of generalization, differentiation, transfer, or interference, we are caught up short by problems of stimulus and response similarity and equivalence. In Chapter 16, we shall describe attempts to analyze similarity and equivalence not in terms of stimulus factors or response factors alone but in terms of feedback relationships that characterize stimulus-response interactions.

A third problem is to explain the positional effects that are noted in serial learning. As we indicated in Chapter 2, we think that the serial position curve can be interpreted more meaningfully in terms of spatial patterns and boundaries than in terms of conventional temporal association concepts. We believe that these and other problems of learning will be clarified by an understanding of the sensory-feedback mechanisms of patterned response.

RESEARCH METHODOLOGY

Experimental cybernetics deals with four related areas of research:

1. receptor cybernetics, dealing with the mechanisms that regulate receptor action
2. studies of the integration of sensorimotor-feedback systems by varying the space and time properties of feedback signals
3. studies of psychophysiological-

feedback interactions between internal and somatic systems

4. analyses of transformations of feedback control as involved in the use of instruments, symbolic rules, and social mechanisms

This last area provides a new approach to the study of cognitive behavior.

In cybernetic research, we try to break into a sensory-feedback loop by means of which the individual is controlling a pattern of behavior in order to produce systematic variations in some property of the feedback signal. In this way, we establish quantitative relationships between patterns of response and characteristics of the controlling feedback process. The efficiency of performance as well as the rate and upper limit of learning are studied in relation to different parameters of feedback control. Thus, we do not study learning by manipulating the temporal relationships of external stimuli or the contingencies of reinforcement as in conventional learning experiments but by varying properties of the feedback patterns generated by performance.

The types of feedback variation that have been studied most extensively are spatial displacement and temporal delay. The simplified diagram in Figure 14.3 illustrates the principle involved with relation to visually controlled behavior. The subject performs some task, such as tracing a pattern, with a displacing or delaying device inserted between his movements and his eyes. The top diagram indicates how a prism can be used to invert the visual feedback pattern while the lower diagram indicates the use of a delay system to insert a temporal interval between the subject's

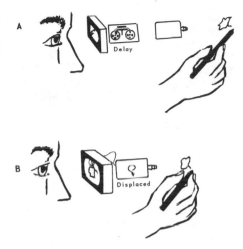

Figure 14.3. Basic methodology of feedback research. *a.* Delaying visual feedback by a delay system. *b.* Spatial displacement of visual feedback by an inverting prism as used by Rhule and Smith (1959b). (From Smith. Sensory feedback analysis in medical research: I. Delayed sensory feedback in behavior and neural function. *Amer. J. phys. Med.*, 1963, 42, 228–262.)

movements and his perception of those movements.

Optical methods of displacing the visual field have been in use since Stratton (1896, 1897, 1899) carried out his studies almost seventy years ago. Different types of experimental spectacles and prism arrangements have been designed to invert, reverse, or rotate the visual field or to displace the line of sight. Mirrors have been used to displace the locus of vision and to displace the visual field in various ways.

The first controlled experiments (Lee, 1950a, 1950b, 1951) on feedback delay used the experimental technique shown in Figure 14.4. To delay the auditory feedback of speech, the individual is fitted with special headphones which ex-

Figure 14.4.   Standard method of delaying the auditory feedback of speech. The speech pattern is recorded on audio-tape and played back to the subject's ears after a controlled delay interval. (From Smith. Sensory feedback analysis in medical research: I. Delayed sensory feedback in behavior and neural function. *Amer. J. phys. Med.*, 1963, **42**, 228–262.)

clude almost all air-borne sounds except those that are transmitted via the phones. The subject then speaks into the microphone of a magnetic tape recorder which stores the recorded speech pattern for a specified delay interval, typically a fraction of a second. After the delay, the recorded sounds are played back to the subject's ears as delayed auditory feedback. The intensity usually is raised somewhat above that of normal speech in order to mask bone-conducted sound which, of course, is not delayed. Similar audio-tape techniques are used to delay the auditory feedback from other sound producing movements, such as tapping and playing musical instruments.

Closed-Circuit Television Techniques

The photograph in Figure 1.5 illustrates one of our experimental closed-circuit television set-ups which have been used in many experiments to displace the visual feedback of handwriting, alignment reactions, positioning reactions, tracing, and the like (Smith and

Smith, 1962). This method permits precise control of the amount and dimensions of displacement and thus provides comparative data concerning the differential effects of different spatial variations.

Our basic technique is to use closed-circuit television chains, as illustrated, to provide the individual wih a substitute visual feedback of his own performance. In this procedure, the subject cannot see his performance directly but must guide his motions by watching them in a television monitor. The feedback image is provided by a television camera and can be altered experimentally in various ways by changing the position of the camera, the lenses used on it, or its electronic circuits. The image can be inverted, reversed, rotated angularly to any desired degree, or distorted in size. The locus of vision can be displaced by moving the camera to any position desired, much as if the eyes were removed from the head and located, still functioning, at some new position relative to the body.

We also have adapted television methodology to analyses of temporal characteristics of the feedback process in experiments on delayed visual feedback. Experimental manipulation of the intrinsic temporal relationships of response was achieved first with the audio-tape recording method described above, used to delay the auditory feedback of speech and other sound-producing motions. We have used a comparable method to study delayed visual feedback. A televised image of the subject's performance is recorded on video-tape and then presented to him on the television monitor after a controllable delay interval.

Computer Methods
in Experimental Cybernetics

High-speed digital computers can be used in specially designed closed-loop cybernetic systems to control many different properties of sensory feedback from diverse response patterns (Smith, Ansell *et al.*, 1964; Smith, Mysziewski *et al.*, 1963). For such purposes, we program the computer to manipulate electronic signals related to feedback variables. Figure 14.5 shows the steps involved in studying the effects of per-

Figure 14.5.   Diagram of the components in a computer-controlled system for feedback research. The sounds made by the piano are converted to digital form, manipulated by the computer, and reconverted to sound waves at the ears of the performer, who thus plays the instrument while hearing experimentally perturbed auditory feedback.

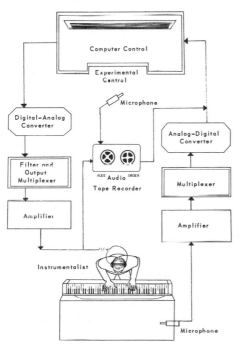

turbing the auditory feedback of piano playing. In this set-up, the sounds produced by the piano are picked up by a microphone located nearby and transduced to electronic signals which then are converted to digital signals. The computer accepts these signals and perturbs them according to its programed instructions. For example, the signals can be time-sampled, samples can be inverted, or the form of the sound signal can be transformed. After the computer operations, the signals are transmitted to a digital-analog converter to be reconverted into continuous form, after which the electrical signal is put into usable auditory form at the ear of the subject. As indicated on the diagram, a tape recorder can be used to obtain a permanent record and to insert extrinsic auditory effects into the feedback loop if desired.

Figure 14.6 gives a diagrammatic interpretation of how analog-to-digital and digital-to-analog conversions are achieved in the case of closed-loop control of auditory speech feedback. The block diagram atttached to the microphone indicates how the continuous electrical signal of the sound is received by the converter and scanned at a sampling rate of around eight thousand samples per second. Each of the lines interrupting the continuous sine wave represents a voltage measurement made by the converter. Each of these samples is transmitted to the computer as a discrete electrical signal. Reconverting the digital signals after they have been varied by the computer is a reverse process. In this case, the digital-analog converter sums electrical values to equal a given digital signal coming from the computer. A sequence of voltage values then is

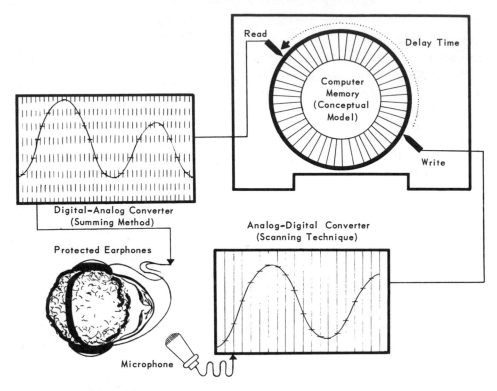

Figure 14.6. Some of the conversion processes used in computer-controlled feedback research. The analog-digital converter represents a continuous wave in terms of sampled voltage values, while the digital-analog converter sums these values to produce a continuous signal. The converter can delay a feedback signal by reading out at a point spatially separated from the write-in point.

smoothed into a continuous wave form that can be amplified and sent to the headphones.

Figure 14.6 also represents diagrammatically how the computer itself can be used to delay a feedback signal. If we consider the memory system of the computer as a series of magnetic points into which we can write in and read out information, we can think of the process of delaying a computer signal as one of reading out a signal at some point removed in space from the point at which it was written into the computer core. This is represented in the diagram in the form of a circular disk at the center of the computer. A short delay would involve reading out a signal at a point only a short distance removed from the write-in point, while a long delay would involve a greater distance.

Computer methods provide a revolutionary approach to feedback research because of their nearly unlimited possibilities in controlling the cybernetic process. Figure 14.7 suggests some of the different types of feedback perturbation that can be programed through the computer for feedback analysis of such skills as handwriting, drawing, and trac-

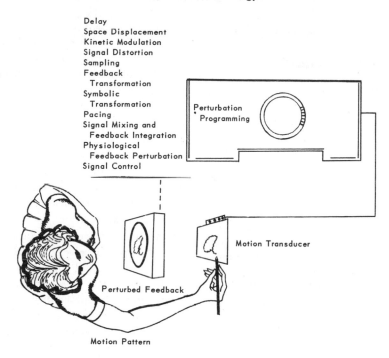

Delay
Space Displacement
Kinetic Modulation
Signal Distortion
Sampling
Feedback
 Transformation
Symbolic
 Transformation
Pacing
Signal Mixing and
 Feedback Integration
Physiological
 Feedback Perturbation
Signal Control

Perturbation
Programming

Motion Transducer

Perturbed Feedback

Motion Pattern

Figure 14.7.   Different parameters of feedback perturbation that can be studied in a computer-controlled system.

ing. Furthermore, the computer system can be used not only to produce these different types of feedback variation but also to make accurate comparisons between these different forms of perturbation and their effects on the patterns of performance. In addition, the computer can be programed to monitor, regulate and calibrate a series of experimental trials at the same time that it is controlling the feedback process.

Figure 14.8 reproduces the first three and the last three records of a series of forty trials in which a subject was trying to maintain a steady alignment of a needle cursor with a line indicator by means of visual feedback that was delayed 0.8 second. The top line of each series shows the computer-controlled oscillograph display which the subject used as a visual-feedback source. Also shown on this line are solid black signals which the computer generated as warning signals. The bottom line in each record is the input signal from a stick control which is identical with the top record except for the warning signals. The middle record of high frequency waves is the differentiation of the hand motion record and indicates the velocity of all the movements made. It can be seen that each trial is preceded by four warning signals. The first two warn the subject that the computer is going to run a calibration on the zero setting of the system and that he should keep his hands off the control stick. After the calibration is run, the third and fourth

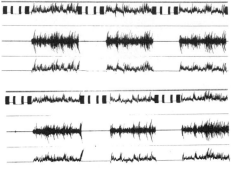

Figure 14.8. Records of manual alignment motion with a visual feedback delay of 0.8 second. The top line of each record, which provided the feedback display, shows computer-generated signals which indicated a calibration and the beginning of a trial. The middle line represents movement velocity and the bottom line is the movement input.

signals warn the subject that a trial is about to begin. After ten trials, the machine prints out a longer signal that the experimental run is at an end.

Physiological Perturbations of Somatic Control

Among the various kinds of computer-controlled perturbations indicated in Figure 14.7, we wish to call particular attention to *physiological feedback perturbation*, for this technique provides a new way of analyzing the effects of internal physiological states, including emotional states, on overt behavior.

By physiological perturbation, we mean the variations introduced into somatic movements by actions of the inner organic systems. These internal actions may produce excessive tremor, a quavery voice, or even movements that keep time with the pulse rate. For example, when a person crosses one leg over the other while sitting still, the foot may bob with the heart beat. In ordinary skilled behavior, the individual compensates for these disturbances to some extent in his control patterns.

With sensitive recording techniques, we can demonstrate that hand movements, head movements, and breath control are being perturbed continuously by the heart pulse and breathing rhythm. In order to analyze control of breath pressure, we give the subject a visual feedback display indicating the pressure he is exerting on a pneumatic recording tambour held between the lips. He attempts to maintain a constant pressure by watching a needle cursor that moves around a constant indicator line. In some cases, the heart pulse is seen clearly in the breath-control record, as it may be in records of hand alignment or other bodily movements. Also, breathing movements often produce discernible variations in other movement systems which may show up in tremor records such as those in Figure 14.8.

Inasmuch as the direct effects of heart and breathing action are not consistently clear in visual-feedback displays of movement, we use the computer to enhance the visible effects. That is, we can record the heart pulse and breathing movements of a performing subject and admix a visual indication of these internal actions with the visual-feedback indication of breath control, hand alignment, or other movement. We then can analyze the subject's ability to compensate for these perturbations in controlling his movements.

The ultimate objective of such experiments on physiological perturbation is to investigate how emotional reactions and other internal events may be involved in feedback regulation of somatic response. We believe that both neural and mechanical interactions between internal and external activities are involved. The possibility also exists that various feedback effects of somatic behavior can modify the actions of the internal organs and musculature. Some such effects are assumed to provide the basis of psychosomatic disorders. Computer techniques of feedback research provide a distinctive new experimental approach to the study of organic-somatic interactions and may in time produce new ideas about how the internal effects of emotion and stress can be controlled by performance and learning.

DELAYED SENSORY FEEDBACK

The experiments to be described in the rest of the chapter support our point of view that perceptual-motor behavior is organized, learned, and retained according to spatial patterns rather than in temporal sequences. Two types of evidence will be presented. In this section, we shall show that the intrinsic temporal relationships of stimulus and response are very rigidly defined so that organized behavior breaks down if the feedback interval is delayed artificially. This indicates that behavior flexibility and learning do not depend on various temporal arrangements or rearrangements of stimuli and responses, for the intrinsic temporal factors are relatively fixed for every type of movement and permit little or no variation. In the next section, we shall show that performance variability and the course of learning are related directly to spatial relationships between the individual and his sensory-feedback patterns.

The effects of delayed sensory feedback on behavior integration were observed first not under controlled experimental conditions but in relation to certain human engineering problems in World War II, as described in Chapter 7. The nature of the problem was not defined clearly at that time, but experimental analyses of tracking carried out after the war confirmed the idea that any kind of feedback delay is detrimental to performance (K. U. Smith, 1962).

Controlled experimental analyses of delayed feedback include research on delayed auditory feedback of speech and other sound-producing motion, studies of delayed visual feedback of the graphic trace of handwriting, our own research on delayed pictorial feedback by means of closed-circuit television and video-recording techniques, and more recent studies of computer-controlled delay of both visual and auditory feedback. In all of these cases, the results of an artificial delay in the feedback process were strikingly similar. Under such conditions, the organization of behavior breaks down and the individual finds it difficult or impossible to carry out ordinary performances.

Experimental Techniques

In most of our television studies of delayed feedback (K. U. Smith, 1962), we used one video-tape recorder to record the image of a task and then, by switching the recorder to playback, to transmit the delayed image to the subject's monitor after the task has been completed. This procedure is not directly comparable to the audio-tape techniques of studying delayed auditory feedback, where an audio recording head and a playback head are used simultaneously to delay a speech pattern for a fraction of a second and then to present it to the subject's ears while he continues to speak.

A limited series of observations was carried out with two video recorders, as diagramed in Figure 1.6 (W. M. Smith et al., 1960). The subject carried out various writing and drawing tasks on a handwriting motion analyzer while watching a feedback image which was delayed by a constant interval of approximately a half second. These were the first observations made of performance proceeding concurrently with delayed *pictorial* feedback of motion.

We devised one further television technique to study some of the effects of delayed pictorial feedback—in this case a technique of simulating a feedback image. We arranged a dual closed-circuit television system in which a trained observer reproduced the subject's manual movements for televised presentation after various delay intervals. The subject was not informed about the actual procedure but was told that he would see in his monitor an image of his own movements delayed electronically. Wearing a white glove and black arm cover, ostensibly to provide good visual contrast, he began to trace a paper-and-pencil maze on his easel. An image of the maze could be seen in his television monitor and, after a specified delay interval, a white-gloved hand and black arm appeared there reproducing the movements that the subject had just made. The observer-reproducer who actually was making the movements watched by the subject did so by watching a televised image of the subject's performance. He started his feedback reproduction either after a short delay of one to two seconds, which was as soon

as he could react accurately to the subject's movements, after the subject had completed half the maze, or after the subject had concluded his performance.

Other controlled experiments on delayed visual feedback have been carried out by van Bergeijk and David (1959) and Kalmus et al. (1960) with devices that permitted delay of the graphic trace of handwriting or drawing. In these experiments the subjects saw not their own hands performing writing tasks, but a delayed graphic trace of the letters or symbols that they were forming with a stylus.

General Effects of Delayed Feedback

The most general result of experimentally delayed sensory feedback is a serious disturbance of behavior patterning amounting in some cases to a complete breakdown of performance. In addition, increased tension and emotional disturbances usually are observed.

When the auditory feedback of speech is delayed, the speech pattern slows down, increases in intensity and pitch, and shows serious disturbances in articulation described as an artificial stutter (Black, 1951, 1954; Chase, Harvey et al., 1961; Chase et al., 1959; Fairbanks, 1955; Lee, 1950a, 1950b; Rawnsley and Harris, 1954). Many errors occur, including additions, omissions, and substitution of words and syllables (Fairbanks and Guttman, 1958). Analogous disturbances have been produced by delaying the auditory feedback of other sound-producing movement patterns, such as whistling, playing musical instruments, tapping wireless signals, and handicapping (Chase, Harvey et al.,

1961; Chase, Rapin *et al.*, 1961; Kalmus *et al.*, 1955; Lee, 1950b).

Delaying the graphic feedback of handwriting and drawing produces effects very similar to those observed with delayed speech (Kalmus *et al.*, 1960; van Bergeijk and David, 1959). Performance slows down and becomes disorganized, and errors are introduced.

Our own observations on the effects of delayed pictorial feedback concurrent with performance were carried out on two subjects, each of whom performed nine writing tasks including writing the letters of the alphabet, two nonsense syllable tasks, two word tasks, star tracing, drawing simple geometric forms, tracing a paper maze, and dotting circles. Introducing the delay seriously disturbed all tasks and made some of them next to impossible to perform. Localizing movements had but poor success, while tracing movements that normally are fast, smooth, and highly precise became erratic and jerky regardless of all attempts to control them. Handwriting of either novel or familiar material was severely degraded and in some cases completely illegible but in general suffered far less than the tracing or localizing performances. The difference here was between tasks that required the subject to conform to visual patterns and tasks in which the patterns could be controlled by learned symbolic patterns. In drawing familiar forms and writing letters and syllables, it is very likely that the subjects mitigated the effects of the visual delay by shifting to some extent to tactual and kinesthetic control.

Figure 14.9 plots the relative durations of contact and travel movements in the different tasks under the three viewing conditions. The values represented by the bars were calculated by letting the movement times with normal direct feedback equal one, and expressing the movement times with nondelayed televised feedback and delayed televised feedback as ratios of the base value. Whereas the time needed to draw simple forms was affected very little by the delay and the time needed to form letters, syllables and words was only about doubled or tripled, the time required for tracing and dot location increased fivefold with delayed feedback over nondelayed televised feedback. That is, movements which required either continuous visual control or precise location were affected far more by the delay than tasks that can be carried out with a minimum of visual guidance. Travel movements were retarded far less than the contact movements.

Analysis of movement times for different letters of the alphabet revealed a relationship between the effects of delay and spatial complexity. In general, those letters that take longest to write normally were slowed down relatively more by delayed feedback. That is, the increment in movement time showed a reliable tendency to be proportional rather than constant. This relationship supports our contention that a skill such as handwriting is regulated continuously by sensory-feedback patterns. When the timing of the regulatory stimuli was interrupted, the magnitude of the resulting disturbance varied with the spatial complexity of the response. The general concept of temporal association of unit responses would predict no such relationship.

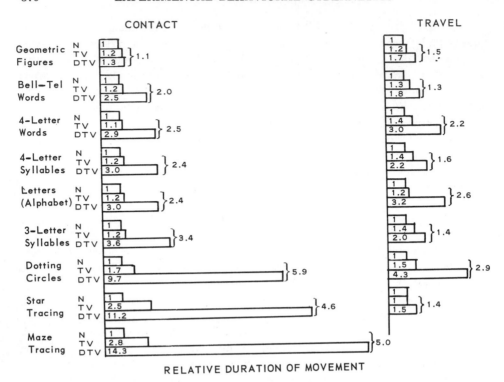

Figure 14.9.   Relative durations of writing, drawing, dotting, and tracing movements with normal vision, nondelayed televised feedback, and delayed televised feedback. The ratios between measures for delayed and nondelayed televised feedback are indicated at the end of the bars. (From Smith. *Delayed sensory feedback and behavior.* Philadelphia: Saunders, 1962.)

Quantitative Functions of Delay Magnitude

Considerably more quantitative data are available on the effects of delayed auditory feedback than delayed visual feedback. Fairbanks (1955) analyzed a number of different characteristics of speech as functions of delay magnitude, using intervals of 0.1, 0.2, 0.4, and 0.8 second. He found that speech duration and number of speech errors both increased with delayed feedback, while words per second and correct words per second decreased. The greatest disturbance was found with delays of 0.2 sec-

ond. The intensity and pitch of speech also increased as a result of feedback delay but changed little as the magnitude of delay was varied. Chase *et al.* (1959) also found a maximum disturbance in correct word rate with a delay interval of somewhat more than 0.2 second. Their data are compared with Fairbanks' data in Figure 14.10. We obtained a similar function for disturbance in playing a musical instrument with various delay intervals programed through a digital computer.

As yet no peaking functions have been reported for delayed visual feedback. Van Bergeijk and David (1959) re-

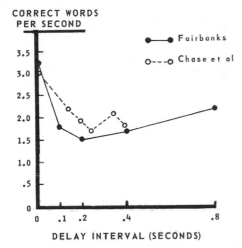

Figure 14.10.   Correct words per second as a function of magnitude of feedback delay. (Redrawn from Fairbanks. Selective vocal effects of delayed auditory feedback. *J. speech hear. Dis.*, 1955, **20**, 333–346; and from Chase et al. *Sensory feedback influences on motor performance.* Communications Lab., Columbia Univ. and Dep. Biometrics Res., State of N.Y., Res. Report, 1959.)

ported increases in duration and errors of writing and decreases in neatness with increases in delay magnitude up to 0.52 second, but no peak effects were found within that range. Our study of computer-delayed visual feedback of a manual alignment task, illustrated by the records in Figure 14.8, indicated that performance became generally more inaccurate as delay intervals were increased. Some subjects exhibited almost complete loss of control with delays exceeding two seconds.

We found some effects related to delay magnitude in the experiment on simulated delayed feedback in which the task was to trace a path through a paper-and-pencil maze. The maze pattern was blocked off into a series of areas and each trial was scored by counting the

number of areas entered. Four subjects performed at each of the delay intervals —short, half-task, or full-task. Each subject completed five trials in each of three practice periods two days apart.

The tracings indicated that little improvement in control resulted from practice. Subjects who performed with concurrent delayed feedback (that is, after a short delay) showed a jerky, erratic pattern of motion whereas the subjects who performed *blind* during half or all of the task in general executed a smoother but less accurate pattern. The concurrent delayed feedback provided a rough means of controlling accuracy that was not available with the longer delays. A subject performing with a short delay interval would make a jerky movement and then wait for the televised image to catch up before he moved ahead.

The accuracy of performance as a function of delay interval is indicated by the graphs in Figure 14.11. The subjects performing with a short delay were

Figure 14.11.   Tracing precision as a function if delay magnitude. (From Smith. *Delayed sensory feedback and behavior.* Philadelphia: Saunders, 1962.)

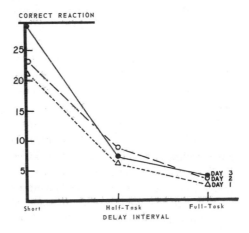

able to follow the maze with far greater precision than the groups given a longer delay. Also the subjects performing with half-task delay were able to perform more accurately than those with full-task delay. The feedback image appearing halfway through the task enabled the subjects to make some gross adjustments in their orientation that bettered their scores somewhat.

In our computer-controlled study of a manual alignment task, we obtained records of motion with a number of different magnitudes of feedback delay. These findings confirmed our prediction that the spatial pattern and integration of a response will change as delay magnitudes are varied.

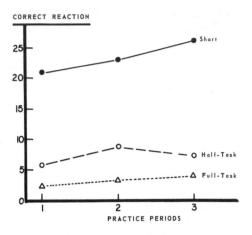

Figure 14.12.   Tracing precision as a function of days of practice. (From Smith. *Delayed sensory feedback and behavior.* Philadelphia: Saunders, 1962.)

Adaptation to Delayed Feedback

Available evidence indicates that little or no learning occurs under conditions of delayed feedback except in some simple tasks. When adaptation does occur, it is in the nature of a movement reorganization, for the individual is unable to pattern his behavior in the same way with delayed feedback as with normal feedback timing.

The experiment on simulated feedback described above provides some evidence for this general conclusion. The accuracy of performance in the three successive practice periods is shown in Figure 14.12. Statistical analysis showed that variance related to days of practice was not significant.

Further evidence comes from a series of studies carried out on blind performance followed by consecutive delayed feedback. The technique here, as described earlier, is to use one video-tape recorder to record a televised image of a performance and then to play it back

to the subject's television monitor after the task has been completed. The subject does not get a concurrent delayed feedback image during the period of actual performance; he performs a task blind and sees a delayed picture of his movements only after he has stopped performing. Results of studies on maze-tracing and star-tracing indicated only the most haphazard performance and little, if any, learning. That is, even though the subject was given complete pictorial knowledge of results of what he had done less than a minute before, he was unable to use that knowledge to improve future performance beyond the most limited change.

Computer studies of delayed visual feedback of alignment movements suggest that individuals made some adaptation to delay in this simple task. However, performance with delay was not as stable as with normal vision.

The literature on delayed auditory feedback includes a number of studies of adaptation to speech delay, either during a single exposure period or throughout a series of exposures. The results of these studies are variable and inconsistent, but provide no evidence that an individual can relearn his normal speech coordinations using the delayed auditory signals. However, subjects who speak or read during repeated exposures to delayed feedback usually make a limited adjustment, shown both by decreased reading time and by increased accuracy. Goldiamond *et al.* (1962) reported that subjects sometimes "solve the problem of delayed feedback" by lowering their voices, "spitting out" the words, or reading without normal inflection. It seems clear from available evidence that individuals never truly adapt to delayed speech, although they may learn to ignore it and get along without air-borne feedback.

Studies completed in our laboratory indicate that the learning and retention of the *content* of verbal material are affected adversely by auditory-feedback delays of 0.15 to 0.3 second. That is, subjects neither can learn to use the delayed signals to control their performance nor can they learn new material efficiently when practicing it under delayed feedback conditions.

Theoretical Significance of Delayed-Feedback Research

Although the effects of delayed sensory feedback have been known for nearly two decades, their full theoretical significance still is not universally appreciated. These findings are of greatest import for learning theory: (1) the temporal S-R relationship in particular responses cannot be varied in a flexible way and still serve to maintain the or-

ganization of the movements; (2) the over-all spatial patterning of movement changes with the magnitude of the delay; (3) any adaptation to delay conditions that occurs involves integrative changes in response patterning and control.

There is nothing in reinforcement learning theory that would predict these facts. As we noted in Chapter 8, studies of the time relationships between responses and reinforcers have shown that the effectiveness of a reinforcement is greatest when it appears immediately and thereafter begins to fall off. However, the decline in effectiveness is not a function of a few milliseconds but has been plotted over many minutes, whereas feedback delays shorter even than reaction time have disastrous effects on performance and learning.

SPATIALLY DISPLACED SENSORY FEEDBACK

When Stratton (1896, 1897) donned experimental spectacles to spend a few days of his life in an inverted world, he hoped to provide definite proof or disproof of Helmholtz's hypothesis that space perception is learned—that the world appears to be upright because we learn that it is upright. His results were equivocal. In many ways he adapted to the displaced visual feedback, but his adaptation was variable and incomplete, as was the adaptation of subjects in later experiments by Ewert (1930), Peterson and Peterson (1938), Snyder and Pronko (1952), and Kohler (1955). All of these experimenters, along with Wooster (1923), Brown (1928), Cox (1928), and Siipola (1935), reported convincing evidence that individuals can learn to perform specific tasks under widely varying visual displacements. Further, the specific coordinations learned under unusual spatial conditions of visual feedback were retained almost perfectly without further practice for months and even years (Peterson and Peterson, 1938; Snyder and Snyder, 1957). However, the observed adaptation to displaced vision was not an all-or-none effect but a process that varied in rate and final level according to the nature of the displacement and the nature of the performance.

Although these earlier studies of displaced vision accumulated a large body of data, few final conclusions could be drawn from them because of variations in devices and procedures. In this respect our closed-circuit television techniques offered definite advantages. We were able to displace the visual feedback of performance in any desired dimension independently of other aspects of the performance situation. We could invert, reverse, both invert and reverse, rotate the field of vision, or displace the locus of vision in any plane. Thus direct comparisons could be made of performance and learning under different feedback conditions, and learning functions could be determined relative to controlled variations in geometric displacement.

In extending Stratton's experiment, we not only refined the experimental technique but also revised the theoretical base. Whereas Stratton was trying to determine whether or not space perception is learned, our interest is in defining how performance and learning vary with variations in the geometric relationships between movements and their dynamic sensory feedback (Smith and Smith, 1962).

Inverted and Reversed Vision

One group of experiments were designed to determine the relative effects of inversion, reversal, and combined inversion and reversal of visual feedback. Certain prior assumptions were based on our general theory of movement organization which postulates two built-in reference mechanisms for the sensory-feedback regulation of behavior, one related to the postural system and the other related to the bilateral mechanisms of dynamic transport movement. We believed that disturbing the more primitive postural mechanism—the up-down reference system—would have more detrimental effects than disturbing the right-left transport mechanisms. Consequently we predicted that visual inversion would produce a greater initial disturbance than visual reversal and that the final level of learning would be less with inversion than with reversal. We predicted that the combined inversion-reversal condition would be somewhat less disturbing than inversion alone, inasmuch as the field relationships would be the same as in normal vision but rotated 180 degrees.

In order to carry out controlled studies on the effects of these various displacement conditions, we modified the electronic circuits of a television camera so that the televised image can be reversed or inverted instantaneously by throwing an appropriate switch. Throwing both switches together gives combined inversion-reversal. Figure 14.13 indicates the nature of the feedback variations in an experimental situation. The subject here is shown writing a word while the television camera is giv-

Figure 14.13.   Televised visual feedback displaced in four dimensions. The solid lines in the monitor represent an inversion of the word *cat*. The dashed-line words illustrate normal, reversed, and inverted-reversed feedback conditions.

ing her an inverted feedback image. The dotted lines indicate how the same word would appear with normal feedback (upper left in the monitor), reversed feedback (upper right), and inverted-reversed feedback (lower right).

Learning under these four different feedback conditions was studied in an experiment on tracing a four-pointed grooved star with numerous *culs-de-sac* along its pathways to prevent tactual guidance. Time and errors of performance were recorded by an electronic behavior-recorder attached to the star.

Four groups of eight subjects each traced the star twenty-four times per day for four days, each group with a different feedback condition.

Learning curves showing the differential effects of the different visual displacements are shown in Figure 14.14. Each point represents the mean score for eight consecutive trials. The data show that the course of learning varied systematically with displacement conditions and confirm our predictions concerning the relative difficulty caused by the different experimental displacements.

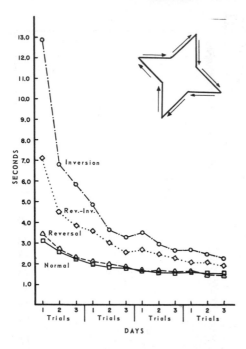

Figure 14.14.   Learning curves for tracing a four-pointed star with four different conditions of visual feedback. (From Smith and Smith. *Perception and motion: an analysis of space-structured behavior.* Philadelphia: Saunders, 1962.)

In this star-tracing task, subjects performed and learned equally well with reversed feedback as with normally oriented televised feedback. Statistical analyses confirmed that the improvement due to practice was significant for all conditions, with the greatest number of significant changes occurring in the inversion curve and the next greatest in the inversion-reversal curve.

Our original assumptions were that effectiveness of performance and learning with displaced feedback would depend on the nature of the task as well as on the nature of the displacement. Specifically, we predicted that motions of greater spatial complexity and precision

would be disturbed more and learned less effectively in an unusual visual field than less complex or less precise motions. This prediction has been confirmed in a number of studies.

A major question raised by all studies of displaced vision but never answered conclusively is whether adaptation is ever complete. Our assumption was that the final level of performance reached in learning to respond to different displacement conditions would depend both on the displacement and the performance being studied. The curves in Figure 14.15 show movement times for handwriting tasks during extended training in an inverted visual field. Even after twenty days, the contact movement times in the more complex tasks had not reached the normal level. There was still a definite spread among the different tasks that showed no signs of disappearing. On the twentieth day, variation in contact times related to different tasks was statistically significant. These results are in keeping with the findings of prior studies which indicated that only the simplest tasks can be learned to normal levels of efficiency in an inverted visual field.

Angularly Displaced Feedback

There are many ways in which visual feedback can be displaced spatially other than inversion or reversal. The entire frontal field can be rotated to any angle, the line of sight can be displaced angularly by means of prisms, or the locus of vision can be shifted by means of mirrors or a television camera. This last condition achieves the effect of locating the eyes somewhere in space away from their normal position. Prior studies of angular displacements other than inver-

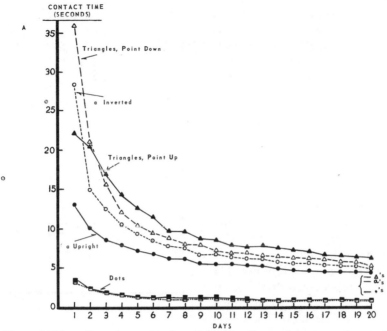

Figure 14.15.   Learning curves for writing, drawing, and dotting tasks practiced for 20 days in an inverted visual field. *a*. Contact times, with normal means shown at right. *b*. Travel times, with normal means shown at left. (From Smith. The geometry of human motion and its neural foundations: II. Neurogeometric theory and its experimental basis. *Amer. J. phys. Med.*, 1961, 40, 109–129.)

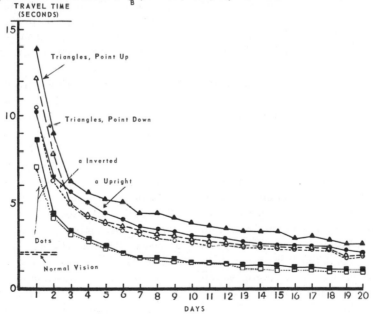

sion and reversal indicated over all that subjects may show little or no disturbance with minor angular displacements but may be completely unable to adapt to major angular displacements or odd combinations of different types of displacements. With our television techniques, we were able to obtain more precise data on some of these effects by carrying out systematic observations on performance and learning with controlled variations in the locus of vision in both horizontal and vertical planes. We predicted that for any given response pattern we would find a range of angular displacement which would have no effect on the response and its learning, but that a limit of this normal displacement range would be found beyond which organization and learning of the movement would be disturbed. Within the breakdown range, we predicted that the degree of disorganization and the rate and amount of learning would vary as functions of the magnitude of the displacement angle.

The insert drawing in Figure 14.16 shows the general method of displacing the locus of vision (Smith, Wargo *et al.*, 1963). The subject is given a manual task to perform while watching his movements on a television monitor. The experimental variable is the position of the television camera, which is shifted to different positions relative to the performance field. The curves in this figure represent the learning progress of three groups of ten subjects who performed a target-tapping task with the three camera placements indicated. Each group showed a well-defined learning curve, and performance times were significantly different for the different camera placements. A similar study of a pin-

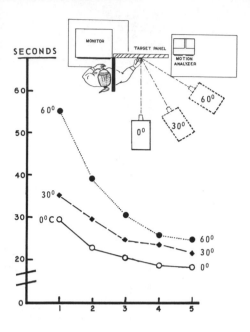

Figure 14.16. Learning curves for target-location task under three different magnitudes of angular displacement of visual feedback. (From Smith *et al.* Delayed and space-displaced sensory feedback and learning. *Percept. mot. Skills*, 1963, **16**, 781–796.)

assembly task showed that subjects could perform this less precise task at nearly normal efficiency with fairly large displacement angles. However, their performance deteriorated when the television camera was displaced by 120 and 180 degrees.

In another experiment, learning functions were determined for two tasks. One required that the performance pattern conform to a visual pattern, and the other task was executed according to symbolic instructions in the absence of a visual pattern (Gould and Smith, 1962). The two tasks were (1) to trace a pencil maze, consisting of fifty-one gates in irregular positions and varying orientations that had to be traversed in

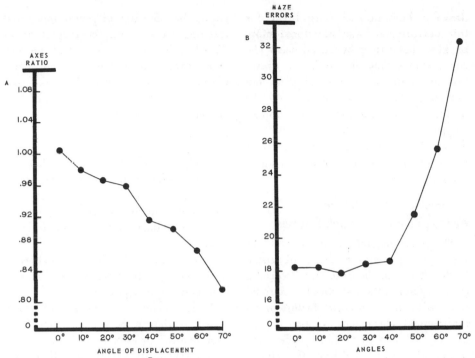

Figure 14.17.   Quantitative functions of performance at varying displacements.
a. Circle-drawing accuracy tested on the tenth day of practice. As the displacement
angle increased, the circles were drawn progressively more elliptical. *b.* Maze-
tracing accuracy tested on the tenth day of practice. Performance remained stable
from 0 through 40 degrees, after which it became progressively worse as the displacement angle increased. (From Smith and Smith. *Perception and motion: an
analysis of space-structured behavior.* Philadelphia: Saunders, 1962.)

a prescribed order and (2) to draw a
perfect circle on a blank sheet of paper.
Twenty-four subjects practiced both
tasks for nine days with visual-displace-
ment conditions of 0 degrees, 20 degrees, 40 degrees, and 60 degrees. On
the tenth day, all subjects were tested in
both tasks with eight camera positions
from 0 to 70 degrees. Performance criteria were the number of errors made
in the maze and, for the circle drawing,
a ratio of the two axes of the circles
that indicates how nearly the drawings
approached a true circle. The functions
shown in Figure 14.17 were obtained.

Accuracy in maze tracing held at a constant level with displacements from 0
degrees through 40 degrees, but thereafter a sharp increase in performance
errors occurred. This is a graphic demonstration of what we mean by normal
and breakdown ranges of geometric displacement; for this particular maze-
tracing task, subjects maintained equivalent performance while their visual feedback was varied through a forty-degree
angle, but after this breakdown angle
had been reached, the efficiency of performance varied with the magnitude of
displacement. The function for circle

drawing shows no such sharp break, for this performance was monitored more by kinesthetic than by visual cues. The curve shows that the circles as drawn became more and more elliptical but the effect was a gradual one. As the feedback angle increased, the subjects compensated more and more for the distorted feedback images seen in their television monitor even while trying to draw true circles.

Theoretical Significance of Displaced Feedback Studies

The most general significance of our research on spatially displaced visual feedback is that the differential learning effects found in these studies had nothing to do with time contiguity factors or reinforcement contingencies. The experimental variables that defined differences in rate of learning and level of performance for any given task were variations in the geometric relationships between performance and visual feedback of that performance. While other environmental factors were kept constant, the varying spatial characteristics of the response-feedback interaction defined highly significant variations in rate and degree of learning.

More specifically, the space displacement experiments showed that performance and learning vary with the nature and magnitude of feedback displacement and with the motion pattern, its precision, and its spatial complexity. Visual inversion was more detrimental than visual reversal but less disturbing than some extreme nonsystematic displacements. For any given task, a normal range of angular displacement could be found within which performance was not disturbed; but beyond the breakdown angle, the efficiency of performance and learning varied with the magnitude of the displacement. The extent of the normal range, within which performance remained stable, depended on the precision and spatial complexity of the movements involved.

SUMMARY

1. Cybernetic theory holds that the primary determinants of learning are to be found in the intrinsic sensorimotor integrating factors; extrinsic factors exert a secondary influence on what is learned.

2. Experimental behavioral cybernetics investigates the parameters of closed-loop control of behavior.

3. The cybernetic concept of reflex action is that it is a continuous feedback-control process that maintains receptor sensitivity and defines the nature of sensory signals.

4. It is thought that cybernetic control is achieved by differential neural action. The neuronic interpretation that neurons react to stimulus differences between input points differs from the traditional synaptic interpretation of in-line neural conductive action.

5. Simultaneous multidimensional control of behavior is attributed to specialized brain centers which can control different movement components simultaneously and integrate them into continuous behavior patterns.

6. Cybernetic theory assumes that behavior is organized primarily according to spatial patterns and spatial differences in stimulation, and that temporal sequences are mediated by movement-generated changes in spatial patterning.

7. A living cybernetic system is marked by flexibility and change in its

patterns of control. Maturation and learning involve progressive integrative changes and refinements in the spatial patterning of behavior.

8. Behavior that precedes learning is not random but selective, reflecting the genetically defined patterns of perceptual-motor response in a species.

9. Learning is the process of reorganizing feedback-regulated activity patterns in relation to new environmental patterns.

10. Two basic methods of perturbing the properties of sensory feedback are spatial displacement and temporal delay. Displaced vision first was studied by optical methods and later by means of closed-circuit television. Feedback delay is achieved by electronic recording of auditory or visual (televised) feedback, or by means of computers.

11. Feedback delayed by small fractions of a second is seriously detrimental to performance. The degree of degradation is related to precision and spatial complexity of the motion involved and to the magnitude of the delay interval.

12. No effective learning occurs under conditions of delayed feedback. The adaptation that does occur results from movement reorganization or shift in sensory control.

13. Comparisons of inverted, reversed, and inverted-reversed vision showed that inversion was more detrimental to performance and learning than reversal, and combined inversion-reversal, somewhat less so than inversion. This is explained by assuming that inversion disturbs the primitive up-down reference system related to posture while reversal disturbs the bilateral transport system.

14. The magnitude of disturbance was directly related to the complexity and precision of motion. After prolonged practice in an inverted visual field, different types of movements stabilized at different levels but, except for the simplest movements, did not equal performance in normal visual fields.

15. Normal performance remains stable with slight angular displacements of the line of sight or the locus of vision. Experimental angular displacements of the locus of vision revealed that the magnitude of the breakdown angle varied with movement precision and complexity, and that in the breakdown range the magnitude of disturbance varied with the magnitude of the displacement.

16. The studies of performance in displaced visual fields produced systematic learning functions, usually highly significant. The differential learning effects were related to dimensions and magnitudes of displacement and to the nature of the task, not to temporal contiguity or reinforcement factors.

CHAPTER
15

Analysis of Educational Skills

The cybernetic view of behavior provides a new approach to the study and understanding of educational skills. These skills of speaking, tool using, drawing, writing, reading, singing, musical instrumentation, numerical manipulation, and controlled observation are closed-loop activities characterized by cybernetic features—that is, generation of productive activity, intrinsic patterns of receptor and sensorimotor organization, feedback control, integration of multidimensional response, and instrumental and symbolic transformations of feedback control. Educational skills do not yield readily to open-loop analysis, nor are they readily explained in terms of conventional association concepts of learning.

In this chapter, we shall describe a series of studies, our own and others', on the sensory-feedback control of writing, drawing, reading, and speech. A number of new research techniques have yielded supporting evidence for our view that the learning of these behavior patterns is guided and delimited by intrinsic

stimulus-response interactions and have identified features of cybernetic control which relate the educational skills to other adaptive behaviors and to the fundamental response systems of the body.

INSTRUMENTAL BASIS OF EDUCATIONAL SKILLS

Three of man's most important educational skills—writing, drawing, and reading—are instrumental behavior patterns requiring the use of man-made devices for their execution. In the far reaches of antiquity, these skills were far more rugged tool-using behaviors than they are today, demanding the use of such tools as chisels and hammers. But with all the refinements through the ages, reading, writing, and drawing continue to be instrumental behavior patterns whose learning is tied to special tools and devices.

A first step in understanding educational skills, therefore, is to investigate the general characteristics of tool-using behavior. The experiments to be described here were designed to test certain general assumptions of cybernetic theory in relation to tool using.

Differential Feedback Effects in Instrumental Skills

The only scientific area dealing specifically with tool-using behavior is the field of human engineering, where many studies have been done on man-machine relationships. Of necessity, most of these studies have focused on the analysis and design of specialized machine systems rather than on more basic questions concerning the properties of instrumental behavior and their differential effects on learning.

In the cybernetic view, tools and machines involve different levels of feedback regulation of activity inasmuch as the use of a tool in a motion pattern multiplies the possible sources of sensory feedback and varies the geometrical relationships of the different feedback patterns. We distinguish three main sources of feedback in tool-using operations: feedback from the actual movements of the hand or arm; feedback from the physical motions of the tool or machine; feedback from the action of the tool or machine on environmental materials or objects. We refer to these three different kinds of response-generating stimulation, respectively, as *reactive, instrumental,* and *operational* feedback.

The different feedback patterns can vary from each other in many ways, depending on the type of motion, the tool being used, and the objects or material being altered by the operation. In some simple instrumental tasks, all three patterns may be congruent. For example, as one writes with a pencil, the spatial pattern executed by the hand conforms very closely to the movement of the pencil point and the resulting graphite trace on the paper. However, if the same words are typed, there is very little similarity among the reactive, instrumental, and operational feedback patterns. Thus we say that feedback patterns can be congruent or noncongruent. They can vary in size, as, for example, when a tool magnifies or reduces the actual movements of the operator. The patterns can resemble each other directly or in a compensatory way, as when a downward movement at one end of a lever produces an upward movement of the other end. The effectiveness of a particular tool or machine for human use and an individual's efficiency in learning to use it are affected by the relationships among the varying feedback patterns. Some transformations from reactive to instrumental to operational feedback are readily learned whereas others never may be mastered.

In some of our first studies dealing specifically with tool-using feedback, we used television techniques to isolate patterns of reactive, instrumental, and operational visual feedback and to test their differential effects on learning. One technique is pictured in Figure 15.1, showing how a closed-circuit television system was used to give the subject a substitute image of all three types of feedback or of one kind alone, isolated by special illumination effects. The subject's task was to use a marking tool to trace a prescribed pattern in the circular field. Under normal lighting, reactive, instrumental, and operational feedback all appeared on the monitor screen as shown at the upper left. By using special lighting, an arm and hand cover, and darkened paper and tool it was pos-

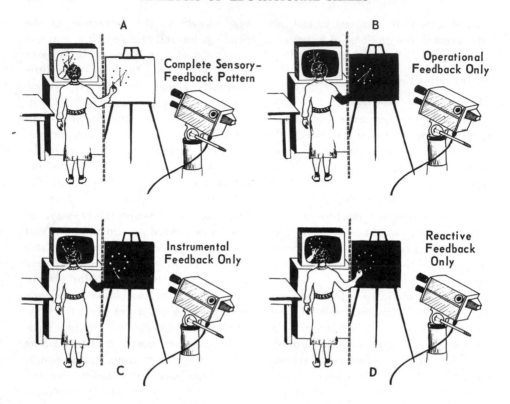

Figure 15.1. Using television for controlled presentations of reactive, instrumental, and operational feedback of tracing motions. *a.* All three sources of feedback combined. *b.* Operational feedback only. *c.* Instrumental feedback only. *d.* Reactive feedback only.

sible to hide the path traced, the pencil, or the hand in the televised image and thus to display reactive, instrumental, or operational effects singly.

A series of observations carried out with this experimental technique showed that no one type of feedback presented alone was as effective in controlling performance as combined instrumental and operational feedback effects. Performance was maximally efficient when the operational effect and its relation to the instrumental action were displayed. A further study investigated the effects of different amounts and different loci of instrumental visual feedback from the action of a tracing tool. The hypothesis was that as the locus of available sensory data was shifted away from the focal point of operational action of the tool, the level of organization of the behavior would decline.

The task of the subject in this study was to trace through the white gates of the path with a special pencil, guiding his movements by watching the television monitor. Four different tracing pencils were prepared by painting them in different patterns of black and white, as shown in Figure 15.2. Only the white

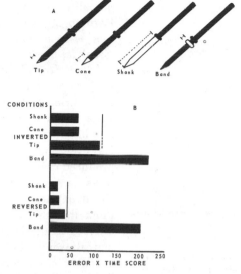

Figure 15.2.   Differential effects of different amounts and loci of instrumental feedback on tracing motions. *a*. The four experimental pencils showing the visible white sections. *b*. Time-error scores for the different feedback conditions.

areas showed up in the television monitor, so that the subject guided his movements by watching the tip, the cone, the shank, or the band of a pencil, depending on the one being used. The white gate markings of the path also were visible. The results of this study showed that performance with the band-marked pencil was very much poorer than performance with all other pencil markings. That is, moving the effective feedback locus nearly three inches from the focal point of operation of the tool was highly detrimental to performance efficiency.

Dynamic versus Static Feedback

In another study of feedback factors in tool using, we tested the assumption that the learning and performance of an instrumental response pattern would be more efficient with dynamic movement feedback than with static knowledge of

results. In order to provide a subject with a truly static pattern showing the results of his movements, it was necessary to delay presentation of the visual image until the response had been completed. Consequently we used delayed televised feedback techniques, as described in Chapter 14, to compare the effects of static and dynamic patterns.

The task in this study was to use a heavy felt marking pen to dot twelve small circles arranged in two concentric rings in the order shown in Figure 15.3. The subjects who received dynamic feedback saw a delayed image of their hand dotting with the marking pen, while those receiving static feedback saw only the pattern of dots left at the end of their performance. The graph in Figure 15.3 shows that dynamic feedback produced significantly more accurate performance throughout five days than did static knowledge of results.

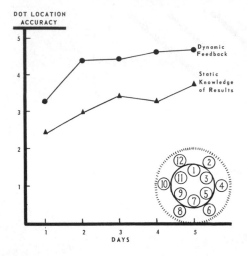

Figure 15.3.   Median dot-location accuracy during learning with delayed dynamic visual feedback and delayed static knowledge of results. The insert shows the pattern that was dotted in the order indicated by the numbers.

The implication of these results is that one can learn an instrumental task more efficiently when provided with dynamic feedback of the motion pattern than with a static presentation of the effects of motion. This was true even when the feedback was delayed—a condition which in itself is unfavorable to learning. Interesting comparisons can be made between this experiment and one described in Chapter 8 in which Annett (1959) attempted to differentiate between *action* feedback and *learning* feedback. It will be recalled that subjects were instructed to learn the *feel* of exerting a specific pressure on a plunger. Those subjects who were given dynamic visual feedback of a pressure gauge performed accurately but did not learn kinesthetic control, whereas those who were given static knowledge of results at the end of performance gradually learned kinesthetic control. We noted that it was

unrealistic to expect the first group to learn to use kinesthetic feedback when they were provided with more efficient visual feedback.

In our experiment described above, all subjects were deprived of visual feedback during performance and all learned some measure of kinesthetic control on the basis of delayed visual feedback. However, the dynamic pattern that reproduced the appearance of the subject's own movements was more effective than static knowledge of results. We think that this conclusion can be generalized to the learning of handwriting and drawing skills, inasmuch as the coordinations involved are very similar. Dynamic feedback of motion is far more effective in organizing such closed-loop performances than static aftereffects.

HANDWRITING RESEARCH

Prior studies of handwriting have been almost entirely task oriented, relating to practical problems of teaching and evaluating writing skill. The central problem is one of legibility—what constitutes legible writing and how it can best be taught.

Some of the oldest studies of handwriting within the area of educational research have been attempts to apply psychometric procedures to the development of legibility scales. The first of these in America, according to Herrick and Erlebacher (1963), was developed by Thorndike in 1910 and was followed within a few years by Ayres' and Freeman's scales for judging handwriting. Thereafter no important contributions to legibility measurement were made for more than forty years. Recently Herrick and Erlebacher described rating procedures for developing legibility scales that take into account characteristics of slant and size of letters.

Present teaching procedures in the United States, according to a survey by Herrick and Okada (1963), emphasize correctness of letter formation, neatness, uniformity, spacing, size, and alignment, in that order. Teaching handwriting is usually a matter of providing samples, pointing out their desirable characteristics, and requiring repeated practice in imitating them. Some attention is paid to the position of the body, arm, wrist, fingers, writing instrument, and paper; but apparently these positional factors are stressed less now than in the past, when penmanship was assigned relatively greater importance among educational skills than it is today. Current teaching procedures emphasize body position and paper orientation more than other positional factors and pay little attention to the dynamics of movement organization. Writing is not always an easy task and many individuals never master a relaxed, cursive style. It has been suggested by Callewaert (1963) that children should be put through a preapprenticeship training in making cursive and inscriptive movements without an instrument and then in drawing lines and loops with a soft pencil on glossy paper.

Callewaert's analysis and similar treatments are based principally on remedial work, for very little basic research has been carried out on the nature of movement control in handwriting. One series of studies has been reported by Harris and Rarick (1963), who investigated legibility in relation to sex, intelligence, speed, point pressure, and such physiological measurements as galvanic skin response and muscular tension. The results showed certain trends but were not entirely clear-cut. In general, increased legibility was associated with more stable motor control of writing. Brighter children showed a greater stability in psychophysiological activity and in legibility than did the slow learners, and girls showed generally more stability and smoother integration in handwriting than did boys. In general, slow writing rates were associated with better legibility, but this relationship was not consistent.

Theoretical Approaches

Conventional reinforcement learning doctrine has been applied by Mowrer (1963) to handwriting. Mowrer assumes:

> . . . that the best way to get children to *like* to write is to have the teacher's samples or models followed by pleasant rewarding experiences. . . . The first concrete use which children are likely to find for writing is in connection with note passing, which, paradoxically, is commonly disapproved and punished . . . why not give school children extensive opportunity to communicate in precisely this way, by note-passing?

The crux of Mowrer's theory of how verbal skills are acquired lies in his concept of imitation. An oral or written response occurs in the first place because of the individual's ability to imitate a stimulus pattern. Then it must be rewarded or reinforced positively in order for it to be repeated and stabilized. Mowrer fails to explain how an individual is able to imitate—why some children make legible copy and others do not, although the teacher stands ready and eager to reward all slight successes.

A second theoretical approach to handwriting research is our own sensory-feedback concept of space-structured behavior, emphasizing not the reward but the mechanisms of production and feedback control of the imitative response. We believe that the movement patterns of handwriting are determined cybernetically. The individual not only must produce and control symbols by means of the different reactive, instrumental, and operational patterns of feedback but also must do this according to certain rules of educational and symbolic design.

Every written language has its distinct letter forms, its grammatic and syntactic design, and its rules for manipulating and communicating information. The child must learn to integrate movements and receptor activities to conform to conventionalized phonetic, syntactic, and grammatic design. He also must learn conventional rules which define the context and the specific meanings of words and phrases. Writing may be used to record, to store information, to communicate, and to manipulate symbolic information. The rules of information manipulation define special meanings for each different operation such as classifying, identifying, transposing, simplifying, reducing, amplifying, comparing, translating, differentiating, and integrating information. Writing extends instrumental and operational control to the manipulation and handling of all kinds of information. To learn to use written patterns means integrating the multidimensional movement and receptor activities involved in writing, reading, and speech according to conventional rules of symbolic design. °

Feedback Analyses of Writing

Our principal techniques for handwriting research are those described in the previous chapter—to delay and displace the visual feedback of motion and to measure the differential effects on performance and learning.

Using handwriting analyzers to measure component movements, we have established a number of basic facts about the primary coordinations and interactions in writing (Smith and Murphy, 1963). First, it has been demonstrated in a number of ways that the contact and travel movements of writing are independently variable response components that interact in certain ways in learning, transfer, fatigue, and stress. The level of correlation between contact and travel durations in different writing tasks generally is much higher than that found for simpler sequential movements. That is, variation in the spatial complexity of written characters typically produces marked variation in the duration of travel movements between characters, even though the distance of travel remains constant. Second, our studies have shown that individuals differ markedly in their manipulative-travel coordinations. Some individuals show consistent positive correlations between the durations of these two components in different writing tasks, while others show negative or chance correlation.

When subjects were instructed to double and then quadruple the size of their writing movements, the duration of the writing movements increased about twenty percent. However, no such time increase occurred when the size of the televised feedback pattern was enlarged while the writing motions themselves remained of constant magnitude. Decreasing the size of the actual movements to about one-fourth of normal also slowed writing motion, but comparable reduction in the size of visual feedback produced no marked effect on movement time. Performing very large or very small writing for long periods of time was a very frustrating and tiring task and could not be sustained by unpracticed subjects. The size of *normal* writing varied somewhat with the precision of the writing point; with a finer point, the size of the writing tended to decrease.

To obtain measures of legibility, we used a Q-sort technique in which samples of writing were ordered by judges into rating levels within a predefined distribution of such ratings. The legibility of three separate samples of writing of 100 college students was so rated by five judges and from these Q-sort ratings were obtained mean legibility scores which were correlated with the measured durations of contact and travel movements. The results of this extensive experiment indicate that contact movement time is more closely related to legibility than is travel movement time although even the contact time-legibility correlations were very low. The times for writing words generally correlated more highly with legibility scores than did the times for writing single characters.

The general methods and effects of delaying sensory feedback were reviewed in the previous chapter, where it was pointed out that even the slightest delay of a small fraction of a second greatly disturbs an organized pattern of movement. Van Bergeijk and David (1959)

delayed the visual feedback of handwriting by using a telewriter to convert the pattern of writing into electrical signals and then to transmit it to an electronic viewing tube where it was reconverted to a visual pattern. A delay circuit inserted between the performance and its feedback enabled them to separate the two by controlled delay intervals up to about a half second.

When subjects were told that their performance would be scored for speed, neatness, and errors, the results graphed in Figure 15.4 were obtained. As the delay intervals were increased from 0.04 to 0.52 second, neatness decreased (the neatness rating was an inverted score) and errors increased. The time per letter increased although the subjects were attempting to maintain their speed. There is no indication in these results of whether or not a maximum disturbance had been reached. When subjects were instructed to write "the best you can," it was found that they could eliminate errors in writing by slowing down markedly, but the legibility of their writing

Figure 15.4. Neatness, error, and time scores as a function of magnitude of feedback interval. (Data from van Bergeijk and David, 1959; from Smith. *Delayed sensory feedback and behavior.* Philadelphia: Saunders, 1962.)

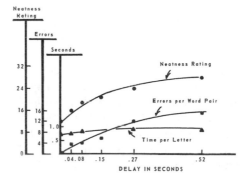

still was degraded severely by delayed feedback.

Observations comparable to these were reported by Kalmus *et al.* (1960) after experimentally delaying the action of a telescriber in transmitting the movements of a stylus to an ink-writing pen. Subjects watching a delayed graphic feedback wrote more slowly, became disorganized in their movements, and made many spelling and writing errors. When they tried to trace graphic patterns, performance time and errors both appeared to increase with increased magnitude of the delay. These authors noted that the only adaptation observed under the delay condition was a matter of changing the mode of response.

Our own observations on delaying the televised feedback of handwriting, described in Chapter 14, also showed that the execution of organized patterns of legible handwriting requires normally synchronous visual feedback. Writing is a continuous series of differential responses based on precise sensory discriminations, and the timing of successive responses and feedback stimuli cannot be tampered with without degrading the entire performance.

Spatially Displaced Handwriting Feedback

We carried out a series of displaced-feedback studies to test our assumption that writing involves production of directional movements which are controlled by the coordinate feedback reference systems of postural and transport movements. We assumed that feedback inversion would disturb handwriting efficiency and legibility more than right-left reversal because the postural (up-down) reference system is a more generalized

and primitive system of motion control than the bilateral transport mechanisms. We also assumed that combined inversion and reversal of feedback would have less effect on writing performance than inversion alone, because the latter distorts the normal field relationships involving integrations between the two reference systems in addition to disturbing the postural reference system.

Figure 15.5 illustrates how an electronic handwriting analyzer is combined with a closed-circuit television system to

Figure 15.5.   Integration of television and electronic motion analysis instrumentation for systematic studies of sensory-feedback control of handwriting. (From Smith and Greene. A critical period in maturation of performance with space-displaced vision. *Percept. mot. Skills*, 1963, **17**, 627–639.)

invert and reverse the visual feedback of writing movements. The top figure shows the subject's hand screened from direct vision while he watches his performance on the monitor screen. The figure below shows the subject's hand on the writing surface of the analyzer directly underneath the television camera. The camera is modified to permit rapid change of the feedback condition—normal, inverted, reversed, or inverted-reversed.

The bar graphs in Figure 15.6 show mean contact and travel times of twenty-four subjects who wrote a's, drew triangles, and made dots repetitively with the four feedback conditions. While all abnormal displacements significantly increased performance time, it can be seen

Figure 15.6. Durations of contact and travel movements of handwriting and drawing tasks with normal, reversed, inverted, and inverted-reversed feedback. (From Smith and Smith. *Perception and motion: an analysis of space-structured behavior.* Philadelphia: Saunders, 1962.)

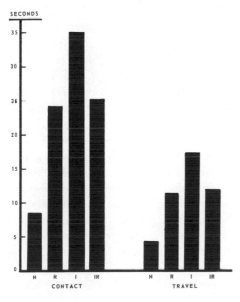

that the effects of inversion were most severe and of reversal, the least severe. The inverted-reversed condition slowed performance only slightly more than did reversal. Both contact and travel movements were affected by the experimental displacement in the same relative order.

When the movement time data were broken down according to the nature of the task, the simple task of making dots showed only slight differences relative to the experimental displacements and most of the differences were not significant. Movement times for writing a's and drawing triangles varied in the same way as the combined tasks in Figure 15.8. Normal times were always significantly fastest and movement times with inversion were always significantly slower than with reversal. The inverted-reversed condition usually was significantly different from inversion but not from reversal. The different displacement conditions had the same relative effects on legibility as on writing speed.

We presented results in Chapter 14 showing that the differential effects of spatial feedback factors are relatively permanent and are not equalized by practice. Twelve subjects who practiced writing a's, drawing triangles, and making dots in an inverted visual field for one-half hour per day for twenty days never completely adapted to the altered feedback relationships. Half of these subjects wrote normally so that their symbols appeared inverted and half performed in a compensatory way, that is, they inverted their movements so that the a's appeared upright in the inverted field and the triangles appeared point up. The learning effects in this long-term experiment were given in Figure 14.15. After twenty days, movement

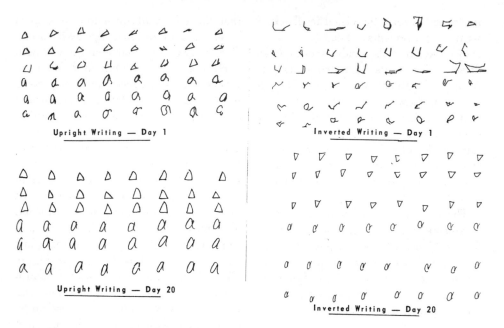

Figure 15.7. Samples of writing and drawing from two subjects on first and twentieth days of practice in an inverted visual field. (From Smith and Smith. *Perception and motion: an analysis of space-structured behavior.* Philadelphia: Saunders, 1962.)

times had leveled off but in most cases remained elevated above the normal means (which were established by subjects who practiced only ten days). The curves for the direct and compensatory modes of response still differed slightly, but stood in different order for contact times than for travel times.

Improvements in legibility during these twenty days of practice are illustrated in Figure 15.7 for two subjects, one of whom performed direct responses (upright) and one of whom wrote and drew in a compensatory way. Although considerable improvement occurred from the first day to the twentieth day, the letters and symbols still were somewhat irregular and distorted. Our conclusion is that the sensory-feedback relationships involved in movement integration are intrinsically organized and not completely flexible even though marked learning changes can occur with space-displaced vision. The efficiency with which a motion can be performed with displaced feedback depends on the dimension of displacement, the nature of the movement, and the criterion of performance efficiency. Simple tasks can be relearned to acceptable levels if they need not be too precise, especially with reversed feedback. We assume that very complex tasks requiring a high degree of precision might never be performed adequately in an inverted field. We also have reason to believe that performance in abnormally displaced fields would deteriorate more under conditions of stress than normally controlled performance.

The second main hypothesis which we

tested experimentally is that the focal movements of forming letters and of arranging them on a straight line are controlled by differential feedback signals relative to the angular relationships between the movements and their reference patterns. According to the cybernetic concepts outlined in Chapter 14, we assume that a given task can be performed effectively within a measurable normal range of angular displacement but deteriorates with more extreme angular displacements that define the breakdown range. The angle at which performance begins to deteriorate is known as the breakdown angle, and its value changes according to the precision and spatial complexity of the movement pattern.

In one of our first experiments, subjects were tested when the television camera was displaced in a horizontal plane 30 degrees, 90 degrees, and 180 degrees from the normal locus of vision (W. M. Smith et al., 1956). Legibility was poorest with the ninety-degree displacement.

In a more extensive study, we analyzed learning functions for both direct and compensatory writing motions in angularly displaced visual fields. One group of right-handed subjects performed with normal direct vision, one with televised feedback positioned at 0 degrees, and two groups with each of the angular displacement conditions—90 degrees, 180 degrees, and 270 degrees to the left. At each of these experimental displacements, one group of subjects performed with direct reactions and the other group with compensatory reactions, making symbols that looked normally oriented in the displaced fields.

The method and the learning data of this experiment are shown in Figure 15.8. All groups showed improvement with practice, as indicated by performance time. The groups showing the greatest disturbance were those attempting to write symbols in a compensatory manner with displacements of 90 and 180 degrees. Although these groups improved greatly, they did not achieve the speed of the other groups in the nine days. It should be noted that displacing feedback 270 degrees, or 90 degrees to the right, was far less disturbing than displacing it 90 degrees to the left, at least for these right-handed subjects. Further, the subjects who made compensatory responses at the two-hundred-and-seventy-degree displacement condition performed better than any other displacement group throughout most of the experiment. With the locus of vision moved 90 degrees to the right, it apparently was easier to make symbols that were oriented to appear upright in that field than to make symbols in the normal manner. If we had tested left-handed subjects, the results might have been different.

Results such as these indicate that the differential effects of using direct or compensatory reactions in displaced fields are not easily predictable, for they depend on the type and magnitude of displacement, the nature of the movement pattern, probably the handedness of the subject, and other variables. If visual displacement caused only a perceptual disturbance, one would expect the compensatory movements to aid in readjustment. However, this is not usually the case. When we displace visual feedback we disturb the entire perceptual-motor integrative process, and each movement pattern is disturbed and can be relearned according to its own

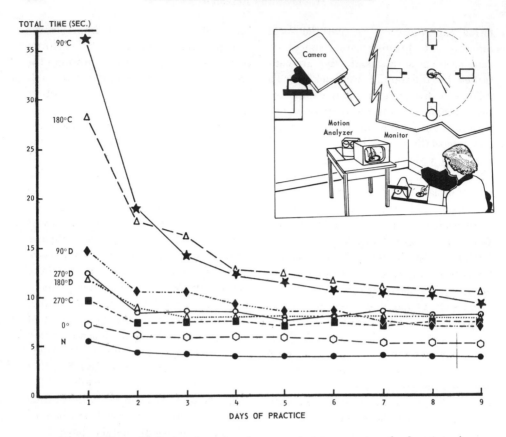

Figure 15.8.   Method and results of an experiment comparing the learning of direct (D) and compensatory (C) writing responses with different magnitudes of angularly displaced vision. The 90-degree condition indicates displacement to the left and the 270-degree condition is equivalent to 90 degrees toward the right. With 180-degree displacement, the handwriting trace appears inverted and reversed. (From Smith and Smith. *Perception and motion: an analysis of space-structured behavior.* Philadelphia: Saunders, 1962.)

characteristic organization. Well-defined learning functions such as those plotted in Figure 15.8 show this very clearly and emphasize once again the fact that learning is determined by specific spatial organizational features of the whole perceptual-motor interaction.

The results of a number of investigations of writing in angularly displaced fields indicate that there is practically no disturbance of the movements with horizontal camera displacements between zero and 20 to 30 degrees. Beyond this angular value, however, legibility deteriorates and is at its worst between 80 and 120 degrees. As the one-hundred-and-eighty-degree condition is approached, an axial position where the handwriting trace appears inverted and reversed, legibility improves slightly. When subjects practice writing or drawing with different feedback displacements within the breakdown range, their performance improves but rarely equals performance in the normal displacement range.

The results of these studies on angular displacement combined with those on axial displacement of visual feedback conform generally to our cybernetic notions of coordinate spatial feedback control of movements. Handwriting is both perceptual and motor, an integrated activity with receptor and sensorimotor feedback control. Its basic orientation is related to the axial reference systems provided by the postural and bilateral transport mechanisms. Thus learning the general orientation of writing patterns involves these reference systems. Focal control of the writing act depends on receiving exteroceptive feedback within the normal range of angular displacement.

Handwriting Training

The results of our research on handwriting have certain implications for applied problems of handwriting training in both normal and remedial situations. The main pedagogical implication is that handwriting in the growing child cannot be considered an isolated activity that is unrelated to other movement factors. Handwriting and drawing are functionally interrelated in terms of their sensory-feedback mechanisms and the tools used, and both develop in a context of space-organized sensory-feedback control. It is our belief that training in writing begins the day that the child holds a stick or pencil in his hand and moves it about on a smooth surface.

We assume that the cybernetic mechanisms regulating handwriting are space-organized detection systems. We also as-

sume that they involve bilaterally differentiated transport movement systems and thus are closely tied in with general dominance factors. We expect that discoordinations related to handedness will affect movement control of writing. Consequently, we believe that an effort should be made to identify children with disturbed dominance relationships in order to provide them with special training in all kinds of movement integrations.

We believe that training children in postural and dynamic transport movement control would benefit the development of all educational skills, including writing. Training should start in infancy, with emphasis on local control of body movements. Writing, drawing, and other fine manipulations very likely depend for their full development on ability to recognize and regulate different foci of local movement as well as precise control of the operational form of the movement pattern. In addition to training in control of postural and transport movements that provide the built-in inertial reference systems of motion, we believe that children would benefit from specialized training in displaced sensory fields. The advantages of establishing flexible patterns of sensory control would not be confined to specific skills such as handwriting and drawing but, we believe, would be reflected in increased versatility in all related verbal and symbolic processes.

Many cases of deficient writing are related to disturbed dominance. Even strongly left-dominant individuals often cannot adjust easily to writing patterns that have been standardized for right-handed writers. Permitting a left-hander to use his left hand is not a complete solution, for the form processes are not equivalent when shifted from the right to the left hand unless the left-hander produces mirror-writing. Children who show tendencies toward left handedness or ambidexterity very likely should be trained extensively in writing with both hands while they are quite young. If a child seems truly ambidexterous, dominance training should be given to establish normal bilateral patterns as much as possible.

Finally, we believe that the learning of handwriting could be facilitated by improvements in the writing tool. Human factors research on pencils should come up with an instrument that is better suited to the operations of handwriting than the standard lead pencil. Present training emphasis on the way that the pencil is held is probably less important in promoting legible handwriting than improving the instrumental design.

DIMENSIONAL ANALYSIS OF READING

Prior psychological studies of reading generally have been concerned either with such static concepts as attention, recognition, and memory storage or with a description of eye movements in reading. This latter type of research is one of the oldest areas of scientific motion analysis. Javal (1878) first noted that the eyes in reading do not follow the line of print smoothly but progress by little jumps. By the end of the nineteenth century and the early years of the twentieth, several psychologists had attempted various techniques for recording eye movements, but the first adequate method was devised by Dodge (1903), who reflected a beam of light from the cornea to ex-

pose a steadily moving film. This early photographic method and later electrical recording techniques have provided a wealth of descriptive information about overt reading movements and have been adapted to many applied and clinical problems.

Reading involves the cybernetic sensitizing, directional, and vigilance activities of the eyes in relation to the symbolic designs of handwriting, printing, and spoken speech. Reading exemplifies what we mean by the cybernetic generation of receptor activity essential to the manipulation of specific symbolic information. The reader's eyes explore a field of conventional marks and differentiate successive patterns of letters and words which are identified as phrases and sentences with meaning.

In order to study the dimensional characteristics of reading activity, we carried out some exploratory experiments under conditions of displaced visual feedback (Smith, Cambria, and Steffan, 1964). The first of these experiments, which investigated the effects of inverting and reversing reading material, showed that inverted and reversed reading were learned with equal efficiency.

Rotational Breakdown Thresholds of Reading

A further experiment on reading dimensionality tested reading efficiency while the reading matter was being rotated to determine the angle at which breakdown of normal reading rate would occur. Angular breakdown thresholds were determined for rotation to the right and to the left for both right-handed and left-handed subjects. The reading rotator shown in Figure 15.9 was used.

The task of the subject in this situation was to read aloud while the disk and reading pacer slowly rotated at a rate of approximately 180 degrees per minute. The subject viewed the material without turning his head. When the point was reached where the subject fell behind his normal pace, the rotation was stopped and the angle was recorded.

The graph in Figure 15.10 shows the mean breakdown angles in successive trials for right-handed and left-handed subjects and for rotation to the right and to the left. Although there are some inconsistencies in these data, some differential effects appear to be reliable. Over all, the subjects tolerated significantly larger displacements to the left than to the right. This difference may be related to the fact that most individuals displace their writing paper toward the left and thus become accustomed to reading their own writing while it is rotated to the left. These results also show a marked difference between right-handers

Figure 15.9.   The reading rotator for determining angular breakdown thresholds for reading behavior. (From Smith *et al.* Sensory-feedback analysis of reading. *J. appl. Psychol.*, 1964, **48**, 275–286.)

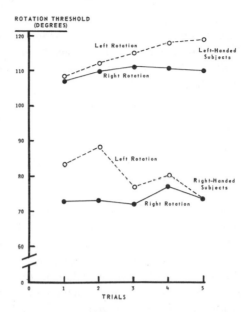

Figure 15.10.   Rotational breakdown thresholds of reading for right- and left-handed subjects in successive trials. Solid lines are for rotation to the right and broken lines for rotation to the left.

and left-handers, with the left-handers showing more flexibility in being able to read normally with very large displacement angles. One further difference between the right- and left-handed subjects was that the left-handers showed more marked individual differences. Some of them tolerated larger rotational displacements to the right than to the left, although the over-all difference between left- and right-rotation thresholds was statistically significant. We have no explanation of why the curve for right-handers dropped in successive tests of the left breakdown angle while the other curves rose, except that the performance criteria used in this exploratory study were rough. More careful measurements and controls would be needed to determine exact functions.

In spite of the tentative nature of these results, they are interesting in suggesting a definite relationship between handedness and the form perception involved in reading.

BEHAVIORAL ANALYSIS OF SPEECH

Underlying the symbolic processes of writing and reading is the most basic and most primitive verbal behavior system of all—that of oral speech. The patterns of speech, like other perceptual-motor behaviors, are multidimensional integrations of postural, transport, and manipulative or articulative movements. Vocal coordinations in the infant incorporate unlearned breath control movements, undifferentiated sounds, and articulated babblings. The learning of a specific verbal language involves progressive modification of these coordinations to conform to the sounds, inflections, and phrasings used by other people.

Speech is more than just movements and sound production, because it is organized according to specific symbolic rules of language. The semantic and grammatic rules are much like tools or instruments. They have a definite design which determines how syllables are to be vocalized, articulated, and grouped to function as language and communication. Once the rules of controlling speech according to language design are learned, speech can be used as we indicated that writing can be used—to manipulate information in many different ways. Speech involves the closed-loop feedback control of postural, syllable-pulsing, vocalizing, and articulative movements—a mutidimensional pattern which must be controlled according to definite features of language design and information manipulation.

Meaning and organization in speech emerge from its distinctive features of symbolic design and regulation, as well as from its operational functions and behavioral feedback control. All of these human factors are combined in a given communication or thought situation to generate speech in a varied and creative way, rather than in a repetitive and mechanical way. But no matter whether the speaking is applied to language communication or to information manipulation, the basic control processes of speech production are related to the multidimensional feedback regulation of movements which form and group the syllables.

Speech Intelligibility

Traditionally there has been more experimental interest in the acoustic patterns of speech than in the movement patterns. This emphasis is due in part to the very practical problems encountered by the communications industry in their efforts to devise equipment to transmit intelligible speech efficiently and economically. Consequently there have been many precise measurements of the acoustic characteristics of speech and many experimental evaluations of intelligibility requirements in the acoustic pattern.

After summarizing this extensive research field, Licklider and Miller (1951) concluded that "vocal communication is highly resistant to distortion." Verbal messages can be understood when the upper half of the speech frequency spectrum is eliminated and also when the lower half is eliminated. The wave form can be distorted in many ways or even turned off half of the time without destroying intelligibility. Listeners "get the message" in spite of great variations in power, the introduction of masking noises, or increases in speaking rate. Intelligibility does not depend on amplitude, frequency, or time alone but on the over-all patterning of the speech sounds.

Although research on the acoustic flexibility of intelligible speech has enabled telephone and radio engineers to devise more efficient communications systems, it has not provided a clear understanding of how speech is produced or controlled behaviorally. For this we need an analysis of the response mechanisms themselves.

Movement Components of Speech

The relatively limited number of careful studies of speech movements date from Rosapelly's (1897) and Rousselot's (1897) recording efforts, but no other analysis can compare with that of Stetson (1951) in providing a clear definition of the response patterning of verbal behavior.

Stetson was one of the most outstanding laboratory instrumentalists in the history of psychology. He was developing and using direct current amplifiers and multichannel oscillographic methods of recording for psychophysiological analysis a decade before these techniques were known in the popular streams of psychology. Starting out with refined kymographic techniques to record movements of the abdomen, chest, neck, jaw, tongue, and lips in speech, he later worked with a series of outstanding students to develop remarkable electronic methods of relating these recorded movements with myographic recordings. His graphic correlational analyses of the

overt movements, the sound spectrum, and the action potentials of the muscle systems of speech are outstanding examples of behavior analysis (Figure 15.11).

Stetson's description of the integrated movements of speech, which was summarized in Chapter 4, can be translated very readily into the terms we have used to describe the multidimensional make-up of human motions. We identify Stetson's breath group movements—as he did—as the large postural component of speech. The pulsing movements of the chest which generate the syllables are dynamic transport movements. Stetson described syllable pulses as ballistic movements, and as such they are comparable to movements of the legs in walking or of the arms in moving the hands quickly from one position to another. The articulatory movements which change the shape, size, and closure of the upper vocal canal and thus give the syllables their consonantal and vowel qualities are manipulative movements comparable to the refined manipulations of the hands in arresting and modulating the dynamic transport movements of the arms.

Feedback Control of Speech

A critical turning point in the science of verbal behavior came when Lee (1950a, 1950b, 1951) first demonstrated the effects on oral speech of delaying the auditory feedback process. We related in Chapter 14 how Lee and later workers used audio-tape to store the airborne sounds made by a speaker and to play these sounds back through headphones as delayed auditory feedback. We also described some of the definite qualitative and quantitative aspects of the loss of control resulting from feed-

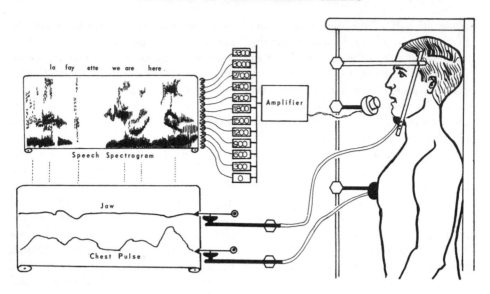

Figure 15.11.   Stetson's (1951) recording techniques used for correlational analysis of the movements and sounds of speech. (From Smith and Smith. *Perception and motion: an analysis of space-structured behavior.* Philadelphia: Saunders, 1962.)

back delay. The effects of delayed speech feedback include slowing of speech rate, increased loudness of speaking, elevation of pitch of the voice, and a blocking of the normal flow of words that results in *artificial stutter.* Many errors of articulation appear, including omissions, additions, and substitutions of syllables or words. Whereas the disturbances in speech rate and articulation reach a maximum with a feedback delay of about 0.2 seconds and fall off thereafter, increases in speech intensity and pitch show little or no such peaking effect (Fairbanks, 1955).

It is possible that the occurrence of a maximal disturbance in speech patterning with delays of about 0.2 second may be related to the fact that the normal rate of uttering syllables is approximately four to five per second. That is, the maximal disturbance might occur

when the delayed sound of a syllable comes at just the time when the next syllable should be uttered. This interpretation would explain why other types of behavior which do not involve regularly repetitive movements do not show points of maximal disturbance such as are found with speech. This interpretation is speculative at this time.

Our computer-controlled research facility described in Chapter 14 has made it possible to compare the effects of delayed auditory feedback of speech and other distortions of the feedback signal within the same controlled experimental situation (Smith, Ansell *et al.,* 1964). Using a system similar to that diagramed in Figure 14.8 we can delay the auditory feedback signal from near zero to about 2.5 seconds and can produce other types of distortions of the speech sounds as well. Selected time samples of the auditory data can be inverted so that syllables are heard reversed. Artificial doubling or *computer stutter* can be introduced. The voice quality pattern can be altered according to mathematically defined manipulations. Such distortions can be introduced singly or in combination with feedback delay.

A main objective of one of our first studies with this computer speech system was to determine the relative severity of disturbance produced in speech by feedback delay and by other types of distortion of the speech signal. Observations on some ten subjects showed that computer-delayed feedback produced the same slowing, blocking and disorganizing effects that have been reported with audio-tape methods. We observed marked slowing of reading, slurring of many syllables, additions, repetitions, difficulty of voice control, and increased effort on the part of the subjects in their attempts to maintain continuous speech. In contrast, other types of distortions such as sound inversions and doublings produced relatively minor effects. Thus, changes which presumably affected the informational content of the speech sounds were less detrimental than feedback delays.

We have noted a wide range of individual differences in the effects produced in speech by delayed auditory feedback. Some individuals show terribly disrupted speech patterns similar to those related to neurological injuries, whereas others are affected only in limited ways. Marked reactions occur much more frequently to multisyllable words. Some persons block and slow down on compound words but show no effects on single syllables. There is evidence that once a person starts stuttering and slowing his speech in the delay situation, he will not recover his control, so that individuals who initially show limited disturbance may eventually lose control if they continue to speak or read. One study indicated that the subjects who make few actual errors under the delay condition may be under greater emotional stress than reactors, injecting a crying or sobbing quality into their speech. They may not recognize or remember what they read. Another study indicated that reactors retain the content of the verbal material better than non-reactors.

Our studies have confirmed the finding reported in Chapter 14 that individuals do not learn to use the delayed signals to control their own speech. When adaptation does occur, it apparently is related to a shift in the pattern of control. For example, subjects may change from a smooth pattern to a series of ejaculations. Those who are able to ignore the delayed sounds can speak relatively fluently by using alternative sources of feedback—possibly kinesthetic, or bone-conducted sound. We have interpreted this failure of subjects to learn to use delayed signals as evidence of the closed-loop nature of the speaking process. When the feedback signals that are used to regulate the ongoing pattern are delayed, the nature of the response integrations necessarily changes. One response does not automatically trigger the next by means of direct in-line association; rather, the sequence of responses is regulated by means of response-generated changes in the pattern of stimuli on the sensory surfaces.

Delayed Auditory Feedback and Stuttering

As pointed out by Yates (1963) in a recent discussion of the relevant literature, the experimental methodology and findings of the delayed feedback studies may herald a breakthrough in the understanding and control of stuttering. The so-called artificial stutter induced by delayed feedback has been recognized as a typical effect ever since Lee's first report, but few attempts have been made to determine whether the delayed feedback stutter is related to real-life stutter in terms of common origins.

Stuttering has been interpreted a number of times as a habit pattern that is learned and maintained according to the familiar drive-reduction model (Sheehan, 1958). Discoordinations appear normally in the speech of young children, and the assumption is that overconcerned parents call attention to the errors and try to eliminate them. This is supposed to arouse anxiety in the child related to the act of speaking. It is not clear how the anxiety is reduced by learning to stutter—possibly stuttering is reinforced by its power to gain parental attention.

Yates has proposed an alternative interpretation that stuttering may be due to some asynchrony in the feedback signals of the stutterer comparable to the experimental asynchrony induced in the delayed feedback experiments. This possibility had been discussed previously by Cherry and Sayers (1956), who carried out a series of experiments both on stutterers and on the effects of delayed auditory feedback. They were the first to introduce delayed speech feedback to the

speaker's ears by means of a bone-conduction pathway—an effect achieved by transmitting the delayed signals to vibrators placed on the temporal bone instead of to headphones. Delayed bone-conducted feedback proved to be far more disturbing than delayed air-conducted feedback. These results appeared to be related significantly to other results showing that stuttering can be eliminated if stutterers are prevented from hearing the low-frequency components of their own speech—components which are mainly bone-conducted. Cherry and Sayers argued that stuttering might be due to a genetic defect which interfered with the bone-conducted feedback loop.

Yates has initiated investigations of the effects of delayed feedback on the speech of stutterers, trying different delay times and different intensities. In some cases, stuttering can be suppressed by the experimental manipulation and in other cases not, but only extended study will reveal whether stuttering actually can be attributed to false or conflicting feedback signals. This appears to be a very promising line of research which may in time provide new insight into all kinds of deficiencies in the control of speech. Another possibility is that disturbances in the motor control of speech might reflect some deficiency in the transport movement system involved in the generation of syllable pulses. The transport movements of speech seem to lack the sort of bilaterality that characterizes movements of the limbs, and we do not yet know how or whether lateral dominance is expressed in the speech movement systems. Our expectation is, however, that if speech disorders prove to be related to specific cybernetic defects, then specific corrective procedures can be devised.

Speech Development and Learning

The experiments on delayed auditory feedback suggest that the auditory signals ordinarily play an important role in the regulation of speech but that fairly good control can be established on the basis of proprioceptive signals under certain circumstances. The integration of the different types of speech movements—breath control, syllable pulsing, and articulation—into an organized pattern must depend on a precise integration of multiple feedback inputs. As a multidimensional response, speech undoubtedly derives some of its characteristic integrations from genetically defined relationships among the movement components.

The course of development of vocalization and speech in infants and children indicates that both maturation and learning contribute to the progressive refinement of this multidimensional feedback-controlled behavior. The first vocalizations of the child in crying can be interpreted as generalized postural movements as yet undifferentiated by transport and articulatory action. In the later babbling stage, the infant generates syllables repeatedly and modulates them in limited ways but does not yet attach them to specific objects. This is undoubtedly a critical stage for establishing patterns of auditory-feedback control, as evidenced by the repetitive nature of the babblings. As different syllables become attached to specific objects, they are learned within the generalized context of postural and transport movements in much the same way as fine manual movements are differentiated out of larger actions of the arm and hand.

It often is said that a child learns to speak by imitating the speech sounds made by others. We believe that the child's ability to imitate is based on his ability to generate and explore different articulative combinations in a feedback-controlled, self-regulated activity. The child can imitate words spoken by others because he already has developed the ability to imitate himself—that is, to control his verbalizations according to the feedback signals from prior verbalizations. The first words of infancy and childhood are not exact imitations of adult words but represent patterns similar to adult words over which the child already has achieved feedback control. The progressive refinement of his speech reflects increasingly accurate differential feedback control and thus increasingly accurate imitative abilities. We believe that this developmental process comes about through maturation as well as through learning.

This sensory-feedback concept of speech does not depreciate the importance of learning as a factor in vocal integration; it emphasizes that the primary integrative factors are intrinsic and related to the interactions among the postural, transport, and manipulative movement systems. The refined articulative system provides for nearly unlimited variations in syllables that can be learned with respect to specific reactions to stimuli and objects. It is these highly refined movements that are most subject to learned modifications, but whatever their symbolic meanings, their integration within the total speech context follows intrinsically determined patterns of control.

SUMMARY

1. A cybernetic approach to educational skills emphasizes the closed-loop nature of drawing, writing, reading, and speech, and analyzes them as multidimensional motions controlled by intrinsic stimulus-response relationships as well as feedback from special tools or devices.

2. Writing, drawing, and reading are instrumental behaviors that have features in common with other tool-using activities.

3. The three sources of feedback in tool using are reactive, from bodily movements; instrumental, from movements of the tool; and operational, from the effect of the tool on the environment. The various feedback patterns can be congruent or can vary in many ways, all of which affect the tool user's effectiveness.

4. When the three sources of feedback were isolated by television techniques, it was found that performance was most efficient when the relation of the operational effect to the instrumental action could be seen. Changing the amount and locus of instrumental feedback affected performance efficiency.

5. Dynamic movement feedback was more effective than static knowledge of results in promoting learning of an instrumental task when both were delayed for the same interval.

6. Most handwriting research has been concerned with handwriting scales, teaching methods, and positional factors in the movement pattern. It has been difficult to obtain clear-cut correlations between legibility and psychological or physiological measurements.

7. Reinforcement learning theory maintains that reinforcement contingencies are the most important determining factors in handwriting learning. Sensory-feedback theory holds that the primary determining factors are to be found in the intrinsic regulatory mechanisms that control motion.

8. Contact and travel movements of handwriting vary independently under different conditions of performance. Contact time correlates more highly with legibility than does travel time.

9. Experiments on delayed handwriting feedback have shown that the execution of smooth, legible writing requires normally synchronous feedback.

10. Visual inversion degrades handwriting performance more than reversal, but it is less disturbing than some extreme nonsystematic displacements.

11. Handwriting learning should benefit from generalized training in drawing skills, in postural and transport movement control, in dominance, and in performance in displaced fields for dimensional control.

12. Preliminary experiments on the sensory-feedback control of reading have shown that subjects can learn inverted and reversed reading with about equal facility and can read at normal rates with very large angular displacements of the reading material.

13. Intelligible speech is highly resistant to distortions of frequency, rate, or intensity patterns.

14. Stetson's analysis of the movements of speech revealed a multidimensional motion pattern made up of large postural movements of the trunk, dynamic syllable-pulsing movements of muscles between the ribs, and articula-

tive modulations of the upper vocal canal.

15. Experiments on delayed auditory feedback opened a new chapter in speech research by emphasizing the closed-loop nature of the process and its dependence on normally synchronous feedback signals.

16. The severe disturbances produced by computer-delayed speech feedback were not found with other kinds of acoustic distortion that affected the informational content. Adaptation in the delay situation appeared to involve changes in movement integration or in pattern of control.

17. It is possible that stuttering and other speech disorders arise from defects or asynchronies in feedback-control loops and that discoordinations can be relieved or eliminated by experimental adjustments in the feedback signals.

18. Speech development in infancy proceeds from generalized postural control to successively more refined transport and articulative control in which the child's ability to imitate others is related to his ability to generate and control many different articulative combinations. Verbal learning is more concerned with the articulative patterns, but these are always learned within the larger transport and postural context.

CHAPTER
16

The Problem of Transfer

The success or failure of any educational program must be judged in the long run not only by how well it succeeds in the laboratory or even in the classroom but also according to how well it prepares the individual for some organized life situation. The acquisition of skill and knowledge will be of limited significance unless the learned behaviors can be adapted to some longer-term life process than the learning situation itself. The problem is to understand what determines learning generalization so as to predict the transfer effects in specific situations.

For well over fifty years, it has been a well documented laboratory fact that learned reactions interact to affect subsequent performance. The research of Müller and Pilzecker (1900) is a milestone in the study of interaction effects in human memory. These workers reported that learned material is recalled less well in a subsequent memory test if new learning activity is interpolated between the original learning and the test. This is a classic example of one aspect of response interaction—that of interference between two types of ac-

tivities. Transfer phenomena—another aspect of interaction—usually are described and demonstrated in another way: in terms of the degree of facilitation in a second learning task attributable to practice in a first task. Here too the influence may be negative, so that we distinguish between positive and negative transfer.

The purpose of this chapter is to explore some of the phenomena of transfer from a cybernetic point of view. We shall attempt to explain similarity in transfer situations not in terms of stimuli alone or of responses alone but in terms of common factors in feedback control, recognizing that self-generative movement systems can interfere with each other in learning. Thus we shall attempt to interpret both transfer and interference in cybernetic terms.

PHENOMENA OF LEARNING TRANSFER

Phenomena of transfer have been studied in many different ways in psychology and education in efforts to understand the effects of prior learning on the acquisition of present responses.

Traditionally the analysis of this problem has been dealt with in terms of identical elements or of stimulus and response similarity, but no criteria of equivalence or similarity ever formulated have been satisfactory in all situations.

Cross Education

One of the most straightforward manifestations of learning transfer, which is often referred to as cross education, is the bilateral transfer of specific learned motion patterns from one side of the body to the other side. Bray (1928) demonstrated that skill in aiming at a target seen in a mirror transferred not only from hand to hand but from hand to foot. Cook (1934) tested this intermember transfer further by training subjects to trace an irregular stylus maze while blindfolded. He found that transfer was greatest between symmetrical members—from hand to hand or from foot to foot—and next greatest between a hand and foot on the same side of the body, and least between a hand and foot on opposite sides.

A special kind of bilateral transfer was reported by Volkmann (1858), who noted that subjects being tested for their two-point tactual discrimination threshold became more sensitive in the practiced area, in some adjacent areas, and also in the area corresponding to the practiced area on the other side of the body. These effects lasted only for a few days and never have been explained satisfactorily beyond the suggestion that subjects learn the difference in *feel* between two points and one. However, this does not explain the area limitations of the effects.

Bilateral transfer of learned skills usually is explained in part in terms of general learning of methods, techniques, or principles and of reduction of initial anxiety; these general factors do not explain why there is more transfer between hand and foot on the same side of the body than on opposite sides. We believe that the phenomena of bilateral transfer exemplify the operation of organized bilateral cybernetic mechanisms for right-left directional control of movement.

Transfer of Formal Discipline

Among the early studies of transfer are experiments by James (1890) and Thorndike (1924), which destroyed rather conclusively certain prescientific notions about the existence of general faculties of learning and memory that can be trained by "formal discipline" in the classical areas of education. Thorndike was so successful in exploding some of the myths about "training the mind" that the whole idea of transfer lost status in learning psychology to its detriment. The fact is that the symbolical learning of the classroom rarely is used directly but must be transferred from abstract formulations to concrete situations in order to be used at all. But the process that assumes the highest significance in human learning receives only the most desultory attention in learning psychology.

James measured the time it took him to learn 158 lines of Hugo's *Satyr* as a pretest of memory and then spent a month memorizing Milton's *Paradise Lost.* He then memorized another 158 lines of the first poem and found that it actually took longer than the first effort. This study still stands as a convincing demonstration that memory is not an independent faculty that can be trained in and of itself. Thorndike's systematic study assessed the transfer potential of different high school subjects to performance in a general test of "selective and relational thinking." The test results showed only small effects attributable to the different subjects, with no marked advantage accruing from any particular course. These findings, which have been confirmed by other investigations, emphasize James's conclusion that practice in verbal learning does not improve a general learning ability and show that formal discipline in education cannot be depended on to produce a general increment in mental ability.

On the other hand, it has been demonstrated that general improvement in learning can occur following systematic training in good learning methods or general principles. Woodrow (1927) compared two groups of subjects with a control group in memory tests. One experimental group had practiced memorizing poetry and nonsense syllables while the other group spent the same amount of time receiving instruction in memorizing techniques and applying them in exercises. This latter group showed marked improvement over both the control group and the drill group. Judd (1908) had two groups of boys practice shooting targets underwater, but one group was first taught the principles of light refraction. Both groups learned to shoot at the initial target about equally well but the instructed group transferred much more readily to a target located at a different depth. Similar results were reported by Katona (1940) relative to teaching principles of doing geometric puzzles and other tricks. It generally is concluded from studies of

this sort that abstract and symbolic knowledge can facilitate the learning of new specific skills. Thorndike's research may have punctured the pretensions of formal discipline adherents, but it did not negate the fact that general symbolic learning and knowledge of its rules transfer regularly to specific cases.

Similarity Factors

In experiments on learning transfer, it is not always possible to predict in advance whether positive or negative effects will occur. For example, in studies of transfer in skill learning, Webb (1917) found that performance in learning a maze was greatly improved in subjects who had had prior experience in learning a maze. However, Cook (1941) found that mirror tracing in one position resulted in marked negative transfer to mirror tracing in another position. In other cases there are small or negligible interactions between learned skills.

One of the first attempts to analyze the conditions determining transfer was a study reported by Thorndike and Woodworth (1901), who tested perceptual transfer in learning to estimate areas, lengths, and weights. Their general finding was that improvement due to transfer was undependable and usually slight. Later Thorndike (1913–1914) crystallized his interpretations of learning transfer by proposing that, "A change in one function alters any other only in so far as the two functions have as factors identical elements." This theory of identical elements does not, however, predict whether the influence will be positive or negative. Although it implies that identical elements will promote positive transfer in some types of situations, there are other situations described in the psychological literature in which, "the greater the similarity, the greater the interference." Obviously a more careful analysis is needed to predict transfer effects.

Many of the difficulties posed in this area seem to have been resolved by distinguishing between stimulus similarity and response similarity in the different learning tasks. Wylie (1919) stated that transfer will be positive if an old response is associated with a new stimulus but negative if a new response must be associated with an old stimulus. Although this generalization is still accepted as a limited statement of the case, it has been followed by many efforts to clarify what happens when stimuli and responses are varied independently or simultaneously.

There are a number of studies showing that the amount of transfer or the degree of recall varies directly with the degree of stimulus similarity. For example, Yum (1931) had subjects respond with four-letter words to hyphenated nonsense syllables and then introduced stimulus variations by changing one or more letters in the nonsense syllables. These changed syllables were then classified by raters according to their degree of similarity to the original syllables. Similar procedures were followed with visual figures. When a series of stimuli ranging from identity through different degrees of similarity was used to test recall, a progressive decrease in the percentage of responses recalled was found, as shown in Figure 16.1. Similar findings have been reported by Gibson (1939) for tactual vibratory stimuli.

When stimuli are kept constant and responses varied, the effects are not as

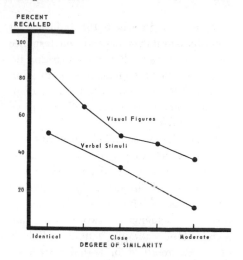

Figure 16.1.   Degree of recall as influenced by stimulus similarity. (Data from Yum. An experimental test of the law of assimilation. *J. exp. Psychol.*, 1931, 14, 68–82.)

clear-cut. In general, changing the responses produces an interference or negative transfer effect, but in some cases facilitation has been observed in the form of reduced learning time for the test material (Underwood, 1945). This has been attributed to general *practice effects* in the particular type of learning being tested. There is general agreement, however, that with identical stimuli and changed responses, one can expect negative transfer that becomes greater as the responses become less similar.

Even more complicated relationships are obtained when both stimuli and responses are varied. Gibson (1941) showed that the amount of positive transfer decreased with increasingly similar stimuli if the responses were different, and other data indicate that the amount of transfer increases (or negative transfer decreases) as the responses become more similar. Thus, in this type of analysis, the transfer function is a complex one in which the influence of stimulus similarity depends on response variation. Inasmuch as most learning interactions involve changes in both stimulus and response conditions, it is readily apparent why transfer effects are so unpredictable.

In studies of so-called similarity factors, there is no general agreement as to what constitutes similarity. The many empirical definitions include physical dimensions of change, the number of identical elements in two sets of materials (for example, letters, syllables, or words retained in verbal material), variations in meaning, variations in spelling, degree of association value, and similarity of task and operation. Many of these variables would have to be assessed separately for each new situation and consequently do not lend themselves to general formulations. Even when a measurable dimension is chosen to define similarity, it may lead to ambiguous results and misinterpretations of data. The extensive literature on stimulus generalization will illustrate this last point.

Stimulus Generalization

Pavlov (1927) himself made the first observations on stimulus generalization in conditioned response learning, noting that dogs trained to salivate to a tactual stimulus at a certain point on the skin gave decreasing amplitudes of response as the distance increased between the original point and the test point. Similar generalization effects have been observed in responses conditioned to tones and tested with tones of different pitch (Hovland, 1937a) and loudness (Hovland, 1937b). Analogous generalization effects also occur in discrimination learning

and have been demonstrated for visual and other stimuli. The form of the generalization gradient is not definite, as it has been reported in various studies to accelerate negatively, to accelerate positively, and to follow a linear course. Yet these studies have seemed to indicate that generalization is a definable function along some measurable stimulus dimension and as such can be used to predict transfer effects in learning.

There are some phenomena of learning transfer, however, that are not handled at all well by the generalization hypothesis. For one thing, the many examples of negative transfer are not effectively covered, nor is the occurrence of cross-modal generalization explained. It has been shown that animals trained to respond to a visual stimulus sometimes generalize their response to an auditory stimulus, both in discrimination learning situations (Smith, 1936) and in conditioning (Wing and Smith, 1942). Inasmuch as sights and sounds cannot be placed on an ordinary stimulus similarity continuum, we must assume that these transfer effects are based on other aspects of behavior organization. Further, although animals often will generalize a learned visual response to an auditory stimulus, they rarely will generalize from auditory to visual. There are more factors to be considered in transfer than limited features of the stimulus or the response.

Another area that is handled poorly by the similarity analysis is the type of research known as transposition experiments. Learning theorists in the Pavlovian tradition have argued that learned responses are associated with absolute characteristics of the stimulus (Spence, 1936), although demonstrations of transposition seem to show that discrimination learning involves responding to the relation between stimuli. For example, Köhler (1918) demonstrated that hens trained to peck for grain on the darker of two gray papers usually would choose the darker of any new pair even when the original positive choice was paired with a still darker paper. Similarly, Klüver (1933) demonstrated that monkeys would transpose choices of a heavier box or a larger box to new stimulus pairs, although the relative judgment sometimes gave way to what appeared to be an absolute judgment. The breakdown of transposition behavior under certain circumstances has led to a long theoretical controversy in which the absolutist position represented by Spence (1937) has been that the combination of generalized excitation and generalized inhibition induced by discrimination learning could lead to what appears to be relational transfer. This interpretation never has been accepted by the relational or gestalt theorists, and indeed there is evidence that transposition behavior does not break down in human individuals old enough to symbolize the relationship verbally (Kuenne, 1946).

Aside from indicating that learning transfer sometimes may be based on response to relationships rather than absolute stimulus qualities, the transposition experiments have done little to solve the transfer enigma; while another type of animal discrimination study has led to even greater ambiguity. A long series of studies of form discrimination presumably demonstrated a high order of perceptual abstraction and transfer in infrahuman animals. It has been concluded that rats can develop form "concepts" (Fields, 1932), and that monkeys show "abstractive performance" (Révész, 1925). Lashley (1938) reported results that throw doubt on this type of interpretation. He found that rats trained to jump to a square paired with a diamond would transfer to a stimulus pair showing the lower halves of the original figures but not to a pair showing the upper halves. Also rats which learned to discriminate an upright from an inverted triangle when the two were presented as solid white figures on a black ground transferred to white line figures on black but did not transfer to black figures on white.

The true limitations of animals in transferring learning on the basis of perceptual abstractions were demonstrated by Gentry et al. (1954, 1956), who trained monkeys, children and adults on two series of stimulus pairs. One set of paired forms was haphazardly arranged so that the positive and negative choices of each pair had to be learned independently. The other set constituted an equivalent series which always presented a triangular form of some sort as the correct choice. Different groups of subjects were trained in the two different series in order to determine whether the conceptual similarity in the equivalent series would make it easier to learn than the haphazard series.

The learning data from this experiment for two groups of monkeys and two groups of human adults are plotted in Figure 16.2. The monkeys showed absolutely no evidence of stimulus generalization or transfer based on the concept of triangularity. The human adults using the equivalent series quickly detected

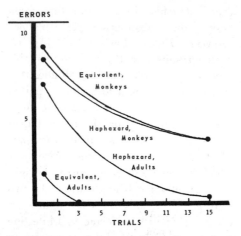

Figure 16.2. Learning curves for monkeys and human adults showing correct discriminations of haphazard stimulus pairs and "equivalent" pairs, in which the correct choice always was a triangle. The monkeys showed no ability to transfer learning based on the abstract geometric concept which permitted the adults to learn a series in two trials. (Based on Gentry *et al. Studies in abstractive generalization: comparison between performance of the macaque and the human adult on the same problem.* USAF Sch. aviat. Med., Rep. No. 12, 1954.)

the correctness of triangles and achieved perfect discrimination scores in a matter of two or three trials. Four- and six-year-old children performed no better than the monkeys with the haphazard series but showed some transfer effect in the equivalent series. Twelve-year-olds performed about as well as adults.

The meaning of these results for a general understanding of transfer phenomena is that *similarity* and *equivalence* may not mean the same thing for two different organisms. As a rule, characteristics of the stimulus and the response cannot be considered separately, for neither exists separately in behavior. We also must remember that in multidimensional response patterns transfer

effects can occur at different levels of movement specialization. An animal that learns to respond to a light may show a generalization gradient to lights of different intensities, but it also may transfer its learned response at full strength to the sound of a buzzer. Demonstrations of cross-modal transfer indicate that stimuli to which an animal responds readily may be integrated readily into a situational habit pattern once it is learned.

The main result of these generalization studies is to reveal the general inadequacy of the similarity concept in transfer situations. To understand generalization or transfer, we need a more sophisticated understanding of stimulus-response commonality than has been offered heretofore under the similarity label. Such an understanding must involve an analysis of both receptor cybernetics and of sensory-feedback control of multidimensional behavior. A learned response involves more than one type of movement and thus is regulated by more than one type of stimulus. Defining similarity in terms of one stimulus dimension or in terms of one aspect of the total response pattern is useful only when other contributing factors can be kept relatively constant—a situation that is difficult to achieve even under experimental conditions. When a major change is made in the performance situation, transfer is determined by similarities and differences in the control patterns that are used in the two situations.

CYBERNETIC ANALYSIS OF TRANSFER

The cybernetic view of behavior organization suggests a new basis for understanding similarity between two learning situations. If behavior is a continuous, closed-loop control process, the stimuli and responses involved should not be abstracted from the process and considered as independent entities but should be recognized as interrelated events in the feedback loop. Similarity between activities and thus the degree and kind of interaction between them depends not on isolated stimuli or isolated motor responses alone, but on relationships between over-all patterns of control.

We assume that transfer can take place when the learning and generalization situations incorporate some common feature of cybernetic control, either in the specialized activities related to the control of receptor input or in those involved in the motion patterns used in the two situations. For example, the different sensitizing, orientative, and vigilance activities involved in feedback regulation of receptor input define what have been called perceptual attitudes or learning sets. Similarities in the specialized perceptual activities used in different learning situations help define transfer effects. Transfer effects also depend on similarities in response patterns specialized in terms of their component make-up and the way their movement components are integrated into over-all control patterns. Response similarities cannot be defined in terms of one feature of a total motion pattern. Writing one's name on a horizontal surface is a different response from writing it on a vertical surface. Writing it while seated with the arm supported is a different response from writing it while standing with no arm support. Each of these responses is controlled by its own specialized feedback patterns, and the similarity

of one to another depends not just on focal stimuli or responses but on the spatial organization of the multidimensional control processes. Other features of feedback control, such as physiological perturbation, also play a part in response specialization and thus help define transfer.

In order to understand transfer, we must understand something of what is involved in response specialization, of the different kinds of interactions that can occur between components of a motion pattern, and of the differential learning and transfer effects that can occur in multidimensional skills. In this section, we shall describe several different kinds of experiment that bear on these problems. However, we want to point out at the outset that, in our opinion, predicting transfer effects in specific situations always will present difficulties because of the complexities involved in multidimensional cybernetic control and man's flexibility in shifting and modifying his patterns of control as a result of practice or of changed conditions. Further, predicting specific transfer effects is hampered by wide individual differences that exist in the control patterns used in certain tasks.

Component Movement Specialization

Developmental studies indicate that component movements used in both receptor control and bodily motion become specialized to some extent during the course of maturation. Further, studies of motion organization show that the different movement mechanisms interact in characteristic ways in performance. Posture provides a relatively stable context of action within which more dynamic and detailed movements are organized. Transport movements are directly dependent on the postural base for their direction, force, and timing. Conversely, the performance of a dynamic travel movement instigates shifts in posture so that the gravitational balance of the body is maintained. Analogous reciprocal relationships hold between transport and manipulative movements. While the manipulative movements may be more detailed and refined, their execution usually depends on preparatory transport action while the whole pattern is supported by the postural base. Thus the performance of a precise skill involves not only the fine manipulation itself, but its smooth coordination with transport and postural actions of the arms and body.

The intrinsically organized control patterns of movement components not only define and delimit the course of learning but also determine how a learned specialization will transfer to a new situation. In patterned behavior, postural and transport movements are relatively generalized actions which are not greatly altered by practice. It is in the manipulative movements that the greatest degree of learning change and specialization occurs. Thus in a new response configuration, the manipulative component, being the most specialized, is the least likely to generalize or transfer.

Studies have shown that manipulation and travel components of different tasks may show markedly different learning and transfer functions. Differential learning effects are relatively more pronounced for simple sequentially organized patterns of behavior than for complex motion patterns in which vari-

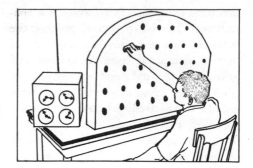

Figure 16.3.   A panel-control motion analyzer used to study movement components and response interaction in learning and transfer.

ous types of interaction occur between different components.

The motion analyzer shown in Figure 16.3 was used to analyze the movement components of a panel-control task in which the subjects manipulated various switches in specified patterns. In a first study, the learning curves shown in Figure 16.4 were obtained for a simple angular motion pattern. The travel movement showed almost no learning change but the manipulative movement

Figure 16.4.   Learning differential for the components of a simple sequential panel-control task.

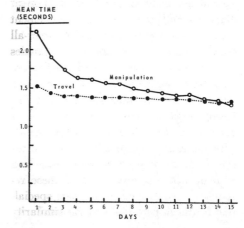

MEAN TIME
(SECONDS)

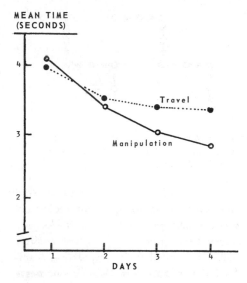

Figure 16.5.   Learning differential for the
manipulation and travel components of a dial-
setting task. (Based on Hecker *et al.* Dimensional analysis of motion: X. Experimental
evaluation of a time-study problem. *J. appl.
Psychol.*, 1956, 40, 220–227.)

changed significantly and continuously
throughout the fifteen days of practice.

With more complex or more precise
tasks, the discrepancy between manipulation and travel curves was less marked
(Hecker *et al.*, 1956). Figure 16.5 shows
the practice curves of twenty-four subjects who learned a dial-setting task in
which they were required to make successive precision settings on eight dials.
The curves represent average scores for
three trials per day on four successive
days. Although the learning curves for
component movement time are significantly different, they are much more
similar than the curves in Figure 16.4.
By increasing the spatial precision of
the manipulative movement, we structured a situation where the travel movement too became subject to marked
learning change.

Other studies have produced similar
results showing that an increase in the
spatial complexity of a motion pattern
generally increases the degree of movement interaction within it and thus reduces the learning differential between
components. For example, in a simple
pin-assembly task where a motion analyzer was used to time the separate
grasp, loaded transport, position, and
empty travel movements of the assembly
cycle, the grasp component showed a
marked learning effect with practice
whereas the position and travel components showed little or no learning
change (Smader and Smith, 1953). Im-
posing a discrimination on the assembly
cycle, however, increased the amount of
learning differentially in different components depending on the location of the
discrimination (Simon, 1956). When the
discrimination was within the position
component, more learning occurred in
the grasp and position components.
When the cue was in the loaded travel
component, both of the travel movements and the grasp movement showed
more learning change. In general, increasing the reactive complexity of the
assembly task or increasing the precision of movement required to position
may cause all components to display
significant learning changes.

The manipulation and travel components of sequential response patterns
show not only learning differentials but
also marked differences in transfer effects. In a study of transfer differentials, four different panel-control tasks
were used which differed only in the
pattern of their travel movements, as
diagramed in Figure 16.6 (Von Trebra,
1951). In each case, nine switches were
to be turned in the order indicated. Each

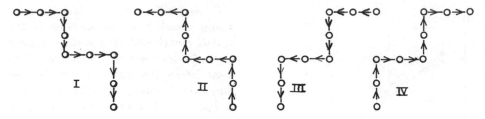

Figure 16.6.   The panel-control task patterns used to study transfer differentials.
(From Von Trebra and Smith. The dimensional analysis of motion: IV. Transfer
effects and direction of movement. *J. appl. Psychol.*, 1952, **36**, 348–353.)

group of subjects practiced one task pattern for eight days and then was tested
on the other three patterns. Transfer
indexes, as indicated in Figure 16.7,

Figure 16.7.   Indexes of negative and positive transfer for manipulation and travel
movements between tasks differing in their
pattern of travel movements. Each training
group was tested for transfer on the three
other patterns of motion. (Based on Von
Trebra. *Learning and transfer effects in human manual motion in relation to direction of
movement.* Unpublished master's thesis. University of Wisconsin, 1951.)

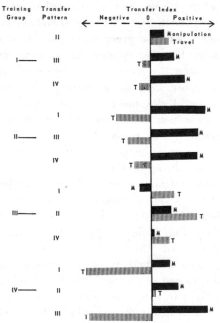

showed seemingly irrational variability.
Inasmuch as the manipulation movement
was not changed in the four tasks, one
might have expected consistent positive
values for all of the manipulation transfer indexes. However, there is one negative index and one approximating zero.
The travel movements showed even more
variable transfer effects.

A partial explanation of the variability
of these results comes from an examination of the learning data. Travel movements for patterns I and III were fastest
throughout learning but manipulation
movements for patterns II and IV were
fastest and showed the greatest decrease
during training. In other words, the performance patterns with the slowest travel
movements had the fastest manipulation
movements. These reciprocal relationships complicate what might otherwise
appear to be a fairly simple training-
transfer situation and undoubtedly contribute to the variability of the results.

A study such as this emphasizes the
importance of intrinsic characteristics of
motion coordinations in determining
performance, learning, and transfer. It
appears that the different movement patterns used in this experiment were not
equivalent for the performing individual
and as a result we got learning and transfer differentials. An interesting sidelight

of this experiment points up the influence of intrinsic organizational factors even more strongly. The four groups of subjects were given transfer tests for both left-handed and right-handed performance. The right-hand scores were used to compute the transfer indexes described above but further comparisons were made between right-hand and left-hand performance on the test patterns. More often than not, performance was better on a transfer pattern with the left hand than with the right. That is, training with the right hand on a given pattern produced faster left-hand performance than right-hand performance on the other patterns. Although we cannot offer a complete explanation of this effect, we assume that it involves psychophysiological factors in the bilateral motion systems of the body.

Correlating Component Movements

An important aspect of the transfer interaction is that two different movements can affect each other in different ways. They can correlate with one another, complement one another, compensate for one another, or oppose one another. In these interplays, the different reaction components may possess different relative generality in new situations, so that the transfer effect is not uniform.

One way to explore the relationships among movement patterns and movement components is by means of correlational procedures. In applying this method, we have measured the durations of component movements in many different reaction patterns and then have determined how different kinds of movements correlate with one another and how the level of correlation is affected

by the nature of the reaction pattern, the progress of learning, and other variables.

In general, these studies have shown extremely low correlations between manipulation times and travel times—correlations which tend to decrease with practice. There was evidence that the interrelation between the two types of movements increased with the complexity of the task. However, in some cases the correlations were negative, indicating a compensatory relationship between travel times and manipulation times. Higher correlation values usually were obtained between similar components in different tasks than between different components of the same task.

In a correlational study of handwriting movements, large individual differences were noted. High positive correlations between movement components were found for some individuals and negative or chance correlations for others.

The movement correlation studies indicate that movement components interact in different ways in different situations and in different individuals. This greatly increases the complexity of transfer effects, for the influence of one response on another varies with many different factors of motion organization. We have reason to believe that the level of interaction between the components of a motion pattern increases with increased complexity, but this relationship may be obscured by individual differences in the pattern of integration. Some individuals show a direct or positive relationship whereas other individuals show a negative or compensatory relationship. It may be true that movements are more highly integrated in complex tasks, but the pattern of integration varies. Thus, the transfer potentialities of some learning situations are defined not only by apparent similarities between stimuli and responses but also by the way component movements are coordinated within particular individuals.

Experiments such as we have described in this section and many other observations on psychomotor skills have led to the formulation of some definite ideas about different ways in which components from a learned reaction pattern can interact with different kinds of components in a transfer task. The individual brings to a new task certain integrations related to over-all patterning and timing by means of which he has maintained control over similar tasks in the past. In order to establish control over the new task, he may adjust transferred movements (for example, travel components) to the demands of the new movements (for example, manipulative components) in several different ways; or he may experience interference. The principle ways in which *old* and *new* components can interact, as illustrated in Figure 16.8, are these: (1) direct correlation; (2) complementary interaction, in which one movement supports, follows, or has a dependent relation to another; (3) compensatory interaction, in which one component corrects for or negates some weakness or limitation of another; and (4) opposition, in which one response directly opposes or interferes with the newly learned response.

Our correlational data show that various patterns of coordination are established in psychomotor tasks and that they vary with the complexity of the task as well as the level of learning. The level of correlation between the com-

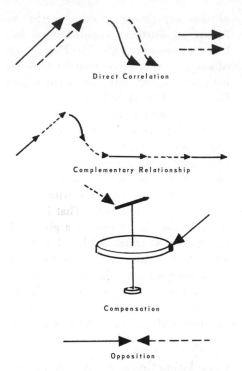

Figure 16.8.   Dynamic patterns of response interaction in learning, transfer, and memory. Dotted arrows represent previously learned movements and solid arrows, newly learned movements in: direct correlation; complementary relationship, where the transferred response supplements or fills in for some limitation of the newly learned movement; compensation, where the transferred response operationally corrects for some feature of the newly learned movement; opposition, where the transferred response directly opposes or interferes with the newly learned response.

ponents of very simple sequential response patterns is very low at the outset and tends to decrease with learning. However, correlations between movements of the same kind in different tasks tend to increase with practice. This indicates an intertask commonality among similar components—a parallelism between travel components in similar tasks and between manipulative components.

One would expect from these effects to find positive transfer effects between tasks with the same over-all space patterning, even if the manipulations are changed considerably.

Specialization of Feedback Control

One of the most significant assumptions of a cybernetic analysis of transfer is that responses become specialized in terms of spatial properties of their feedback-control patterns. This assumption applies to unaided movements as well as to more complex instrumental and symbolic reactions which involve transformations of feedback properties.

An experiment described in part in Chapter 14 provides striking evidence of the relation of movement specialization in learned performance to spatial variations in the feedback pattern. Four groups of subjects traced the star maze shown in Figure 14.14 under four different displaced feedback conditions. An electronic motion analyzer recorded time of performance in the eight different directions of movement defined by the segments of the star. Each subject performed twenty-four trials per day for four days, half clockwise and half counterclockwise. The starting point was varied systematically by subject. Thus, the differences in speed in the different star segments could be attributed to the varying spatial relationships of the movements and their visual feedback.

For each displacement condition, there were eight separate time scores representing mean performance times for the eight directions of movement. The various conditions are represented in Figure 16.9, where the arrows show movement directions. Bars under the arrows indicate that the specific movement

conditions underlined were not significantly different from one another. Any two arrows not underlined by a common bar represent movements that differed significantly in duration at or below the 0.05 level. It can be seen that the different movement segments were least differentiated with normal feedback, somewhat more variant with reversed feedback, and most differentiated when the feedback was inverted or inverted-reversed.

This experiment shows how simple movements of constant length are learned differentially according to their varying spatial relationships with the body and the visual feedback of performance. Eight variations in movement direction and four different feedback conditions produced dozens of differential effects in the time needed to trace a maze segment of constant length. Further, the differences became more significant during the course of learning. When we realize that more than eighty significantly different performances were induced by thirty-two combinations of visual orientation and movement direction, we begin to appreciate the countless possibilities for specific space-structured sensory-feedback interactions that might exist under ordinary conditions of behavior. The nearly limitless spatial relationships that might occur seem to provide an adequate basis for the equally unlimited distinct responses that can be learned and retained independently.

Another type of evidence for spatial specificity of learned responses comes from studies of displaced vision. In two studies of human adaptation to visual inversion and reversal produced by experimental spectacles, some of the specific performances learned during the

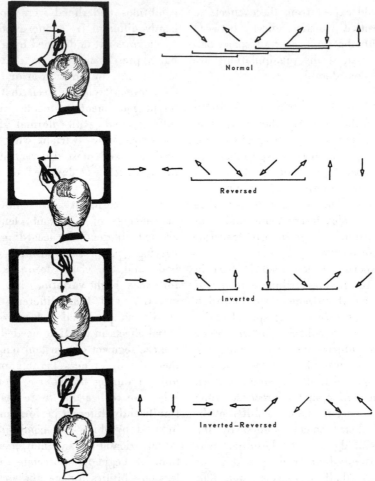

Figure 16.9.   Range test diagram indicating significant differences in mean performance time for movements in different directions under conditions of normal, reversed, inverted, and inverted-reversed visual feedback. Arrows not underlined by a common line indicate movements that differed significantly in duration.

period when the spectacles were worn were tested long afterward, eight months in one instance (Peterson and Peterson, 1938) and two years in the other instance (Snyder and Snyder, 1957). It was found that the subjects retained their specific performances learned with inverted vision almost perfectly, even though no practice with the experimental displacement condition was given during the intervening months. This evidence contradicted the assumption that had guided the design of most of the displaced vision experiments, namely, that subjects should wear the experimental optical devices continuously to avoid interfering with their adaptation to displacement by periods of normal vision.

We made a direct test of this assumption by comparing adaptation to optically produced inversion with continuous and intermittent exposure (Smith and Smith, 1962). One group of subjects practiced handwriting in an inverted visual field for short intervals on twenty different days, while another group practiced the same total amount of time all on one day, during which time no normal vision was allowed. Except for transitory initial differences, movement times for these two groups were nearly identical. Shifting back and forth daily between inverted and normal vision did not interfere with adaptation to inverted feedback.

In a similar study, a control group of five subjects traced the grooved star maze with inverted-reversed feedback for one-half hour per day for twenty days while an experimental group performed the same task for fifteen minutes each day and spent the other fifteen minutes practicing with normally oriented feedback. Performance of the experimental group was somewhat superior to that of the control group, indicating that alternating the feedback conditions did not interfere with each specific learning task.

A further study tested the extent to which specialized reading training in an inverted visual field would facilitate subsequent learning of writing tasks in the inverted field (Rhule and Smith, 1959a). Twelve subjects received pretraining in inverted reading for five days while twelve others received no pretraining. When tested on handwriting tasks in an inverted visual field, the groups showed no significant differences in performance. These results support the view that learning carried out under experimental visual displacements is specific to the motions and feedback conditions involved.

The implication of all of these experiments is that responses become specialized and thus achieve an independent status in the behavior repertoire in terms of their spatial properties and feedback organization. However, because behavior is multidimensional, the spatial properties of one component are never independent of the other components. Because behavior is continuous, its spatial properties at one moment are never independent of its preceding spatial organization. Thus to understand how a response is organized and to predict its transfer potential to a new situation we must analyze the patterning of all components and their interactions in the complete motion pattern. We say that responses become specialized during learning, but this specialization involves sensory-feedback interactions that control each component in relation to the others. A specific manipulation, for example, does not become an independent response entity but achieves its identity in a larger transport and postural context. In a different movement context, the manipulation has a different identity deriving from its sensory-feedback interactions in the motion pattern.

Neuronic Interpretation of Interference

Any theory of response specialization and generalization inevitably must cope with the phenomena of response interference. The interference effect sometimes has been known as inhibition, but inasmuch as no satisfactory account of the inhibitory process has been proposed, putting this label on interference phenomena has not served to clarify

them. No learning theory ever has explained how a learned reaction can interact at some later time with responses
which must be made in a transfer situation.

In our opinion, these temporal interactions are due to the spatial relationships between the feedback patterns
involved in the two situations. We interpret response interaction in spatial
terms and conceptualize both excitation
and inhibition in performance, learning,
and memory as being due to neuronic
rather than synaptic integrative processes.

In Chapter 8, we discussed briefly our
general ideas about the nature of inhibitory phenomena as manifested in
differential sensitivity and relative response strength. We pointed out that
phenomena of relative sensitivity usually
are thought to involve neural inhibition
which reduces the sensitivity of certain
sensory sources relative to others. The
same type of explanation usually is offered for *temporal inhibition*, in which
the effects of a given auditory, tactual,
or visual stimulus are reduced if it is
preceded by another stimulus that pre-
empts the sensory mechanism. Another
effect ascribed to inhibition is the relative dominance of one movement over
another in compound motion patterns.
For example, in bilateral manual operations, the action of one hand blocks or
inhibits action of the other unless it is
used in a subordinate way.

One of the advantages of our neuronic
concept of neural function is that it can
be extended to a meaningful interpretation of inhibition and response interference. Our basic idea is that the nervous system if it is to function as a
closed-loop control system must have

built-in mechanisms by means of which
it can block some afferent input channels
relative to others. Yet we assume that individual neurons are permissive detection mechanisms that respond if a stimulus differential exists at their dendrite
points. However, such a neuron could
be rendered inactive—that is, inhibited
—even when a stimulus differential exists if a new stimulus were introduced
to equalize the two stimulus sources.

In our opinion, this equalizing or in-
hibitive function is carried out by special internuncial collateral cell mechanisms that operate to match the effects
of stimulation on other neurons. Collateral cells are known to exist in the
retina and in other receptor systems,
and we assume that they exist in all
neural centers to inhibit or interfere
with some neural pathways in favor of
others in close spatial proximity. This
concept of neuronic inhibition is diagramed in Figure 16.10. In these drawings, active neurons or receptor cells
are indicated by speckled cell bodies,
and inactive cells are indicated by black
cell bodies. The arrows at the left indicate sources of stimulation. In 16.10a,
the primary internuncial neuron in the
center responds because it is stimulated
at one point while the other point receives no stimulation. In 16.10b, the
internuncial neuron · at the bottom responds in this same way while the one
at the top is rendered inactive by stimulation from a collateral cell. The collateral cell is activated differentially by
the same source that stimulates the primary internuncial neuron. It then in
turn stimulates the adjacent neuron,
rendering it inactive by equalizing its
two sources of stimulus input. If a number of such primary detector cells of an

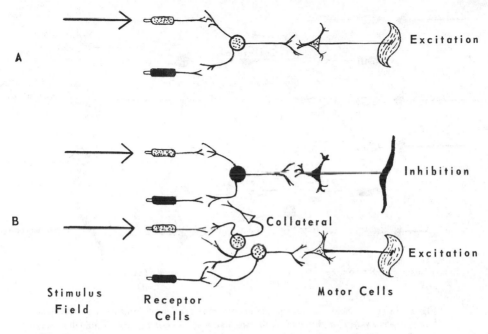

Figure 16.10.   Neuronic interpretation of excitation and inhibition of primary internuncial neurons. *a.* Excitation resulting from a stimulus at one of the dendrite endings of a primary cell. *b.* Excitation of one cell and inhibition of an adjacent cell by means of collateral cell activity. The external input of the neuron at the top is matched by input from the collateral neuron so that no excitation occurs.

afferent ganglion were inactivated in this way, partial or graded inhibition could occur.

In our opinion, similar mechanisms exist throughout the brain to achieve spatial or neurogeometric inhibition of internuncial cells. We postulate that collateral cells which are excited by a dominant input source inhibit secondary sources of stimulation by matching that level of stimulation. This mode of operation is illustrated in Figure 16.11. In Figure 16.11*a*, two equal sources of stimulation result in two active pathways. In Figure 16.11*b*, one of the sources is stronger than the other, causing unequal states of excitation in the central nervous system. A collateral cell related to both of these pathways is ex-

cited because of the stimulus inequality at its dendrite endings and inhibits the less dominant pathway by providing an input that equals that of the external source.

Receptor-efferent collateral cells have been found throughout the main receptor systems of the body—in the skin, the eyes, and the ears—and very likely occur in the other receptor systems as well. There also is convincing evidence that types of collateral efferent-afferent connections are found in the higher levels of the nervous system, for stimulation of efferent pathways has been shown to produce effects in afferent centers (Jabbur and Towe, 1960; Magni *et al.*, 1959). Our neuronic interpretation of brain function regards these efferent-

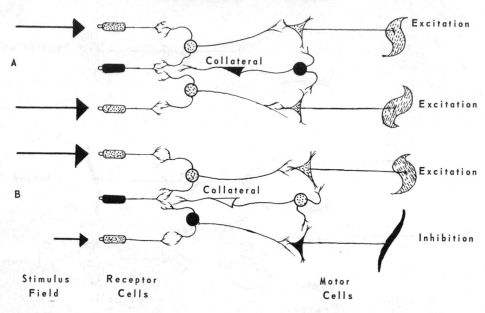

Figure 16.11.   Neuronic interpretation of efferent-afferent inhibition in the central nervous system. *a.* Excitation in two pathways resulting from equivalent external sources. The collateral fails to respond because it receives two equal inputs. *b.* Inhibition of a pathway stimulated by the weaker of two external sources. The collateral cell responds because it detects a difference in level of excitation and matches the weaker input of the neuron at the bottom.

afferent collateral connections as specific feedback regulators which monitor different levels of the afferent pathways and serve as spatial inhibitors governed both by the state of stimulation and by response.

The theory of spatial inhibition just described provides a meaningful interpretation of response interference in learning and transfer as well as phenomena of graded perceptual sensitivity. In this view, the interaction between a learned response and a reaction in a later transfer situation is defined in spatial terms. Thus, negative transfer effects might occur as a result of overlapping of the feedback patterns of the two activities. With identical feedback patterns, there would be facilitation, but

with partial overlapping, there would be interference or inhibition. On the other hand, two specific reactions which do not overlap would not interfere with each other. Transfer studies provide evidence that close similarity of stimulus-response patterns may result in negative transfer or lower degrees of positive transfer than less close similarity.

This cybernetic or neuronic theory of interference or inhibition assumes that *similarity* and *equivalence* in a transfer situation must be defined in terms of the feedback mechanisms regulating sensory processes and motion patterns. However, cybernetic theory implies further that the individual as a self-controlled system regulates to some degree the specific spatial patterns used in any situation and thus exerts a determining influence on what will be perceived focally and peripherally and what movements will be used in the control pattern. Thus it is assumed that interference can be minimized by shifts in the regulatory pattern of motion. It follows that the more a situation can be brought under closed-loop control, the less the possibility of negative transfer. Conversely, the more behavior is a product of open-loop or external stimulus control, the greater the possibility of inhibitory interaction or interference between different learned reactions. These ideas provide a cybernetic interpretation of the establishment of *learning sets*. They also suggest an explanation of the elusive nature of the *interference* effect in transfer research (Bilodeau and Bilodeau, 1961).

ASYMMETRICAL TRANSFER

One aspect of transfer of considerable interest in applied training psychology is the asymmetry that sometimes is found in transfer between two tasks. That is, the level of transfer from one task to a second may be higher than the level of transfer from the second to the first. The problem is to discover what variable or variables are responsible for this inequality. Any valid generalization about the factors that determine relative effectiveness of transfer in one direction or another would be useful in designing training situations. That is, should a training task be easier than a performance task or more difficult? Should it include all the parts or only some? Should it be simpler or more complicated? Answers to questions such as these are of great practical importance for training design.

The Difficulty Variable

The results of a number of transfer studies have suggested that asymmetrical transfer between tasks of varying difficulty favors the difficult-to-easy order of training. Given two related tasks, subjects who are trained on the difficult task are likely to transfer more to the easy task than subjects who follow the easy-to-difficult order. For example, in the study of direct and compensatory writing illustrated in Figure 15.8, transfer tests showed that relatively greater degrees of transfer occurred from compensatory to direct reactions with ninety-degree and one hundred and eighty-degree displacements but from direct to compensatory with 270 degrees (Smith and Smith, 1962). That is, the most effective training order for each displacement condition was the difficult-to-easy order.

A careful survey of transfer studies, however, such as has been made recently by Holding (1962), shows that the relative effects of difficulty are inconsistent. Although some studies favor the difficult-to-easy order of training, others have produced results favoring easy-to-difficult. In Holding's words:

> . . . the use of the concept of difficulty must give way to far more detailed analysis of the appropriate skill, if asymmetrical transfer is to be successfully predicted.

The Inclusion Principle

One explanation of the difficulty effect, where it applies, has been that a more difficult task contains more than an easy task and in some sense includes within it elements or components of the easy task. This idea harks back to Thorndike's theory of *identical elements,* although current interpretations do not require that the included elements be physically identical.

The principle of inclusion can be applied to many different instances of learning transfer: when the teaching of general principles transfers to specific instances (Judd, 1908; Katona, 1940); when greater transfer is obtained from multiple tasks than from single tasks (Duncan, 1958); when training in a whole task is shown to be superior for transfer to training in parts or training in a simplified whole (Briggs and Naylor, 1962). On the other hand, there are many clearcut instances of transfer which seem superficially to have little to do with inclusion or identical elements, including ordinary demonstrations of stimulus generalization.

If we are to apply either the concept of inclusion or the concept of similarity to transfer phenomena, we must define them not in terms of discrete stimulus and response characteristics of behavior but in terms of more dynamic features of response organization. The feature in a training situation that is included in a transfer task may be not a particular response unit but a cybernetic configuration. Or the similarity between training stimulus and transfer stimulus may have nothing to do with their physical characteristics but may depend upon their function in the feedback-control loop. Thus a learned response elicited originally by a visual stimulus may transfer to an auditory stimulus which is presented at the proper point in the learned context.

The Precision Variable

Many of the experiments that show greater transfer from easy to difficult tasks are studies of tracking, where level of performance is measured in terms of an accuracy or precision score rather than in terms of performance time, as in the experiment on direct and compensatory writing described previously. Often the *easy* tracking task as measured by precision transfers better to the *difficult* than vice versa. This has been demonstrated by Holding (1962) for tracking courses of different amplitudes and by other experimenters for different target speeds, although the latter results are inconsistent and ambiguous. Holding has suggested that there may be a tendency to carry over mean error size in transferring from one task to another. This would result in better transfer from easy courses with small errors than from difficult courses with relatively larger errors. However, as Holding pointed out, this effect depends on the capacity of the subjects to track to the same degree of accuracy in both training and transfer tasks.

Some data comparing transfer effects among direct, aided, and velocity tracking are applicable here. As described in Chapter 7, direct tracking is the most precise of the three tasks and also might be called the *easiest* inasmuch as it produces the best scores. Lincoln (1952) trained subjects in the three types of tracking and then tested transfer effects among all pairs of tasks. He found that transfer was better from direct to aided and from direct to velocity than from either aided or velocity to direct. Also, transfer was greater from aided to velocity than from velocity to aided. In each case, the more precise task transferred to a higher degree to the less precise task than vice versa. However, we are unwilling to attribute this effect to precision alone, for there are also differences in motion organization among the three types of tracking. In direct tracking, the subjects must control the larger motion of the cursor as well as make constant small corrections to stay on course. In aided and velocity tracking, the motor output by controlling the rate function reduces the complexity of the subject's motion pattern. His performance is less precise, but it also is less complicated in terms of its movement integrations.

The Complexity Variable

It is possible that both the *difficulty* effect and the *precision* effect in asymmetrical transfer can be included in a *complexity* variable. We hypothesize that, in general, when two tasks differ in the spatial complexity of their motion patterns, the complex-to-less-complex order of training will be superior.

Our analyses of motion components have shown that as the complexity of a motion pattern is increased, its component parts become more highly interrelated. We expect less transfer between complex patterns than between simpler motion patterns because of the higher degree of specialization in intratask integration in complex motions.

On the other hand, we expect greater transfer from a complex to a simple task than from a simple to a complex task. The reason for this asymmetry can be rationalized in several ways. For one thing, a complex task involves more components and more interactions among components than a simpler task, so that there is a greater probability that a learned specialization from the complex pattern will facilitate the simple pattern than vice versa. This is essentially a statement of the principle of inclusion. The relationship also can be understood in terms of the spatial requirements of motion patterns of different levels of complexity. The complex pattern is integrated more precisely and thus involves a greater precision in feedback control than the simpler pattern. This difference is manifested in a number of ways, including the measured differences in normal range of angular displacement. As described in Chapter 14, it can be shown experimentally that complex motions break down at a smaller feedback displacement angle than do simpler motions. When we consider the transfer potential between the complex and simple tasks, we assume that the motion that is learned and performed in a more precise spatial pattern will benefit the simpler pattern more than the less precise simpler pattern will benefit the complex.

Possibly related to this general complexity principle is the idea that transfer will be superior when training involves more active participation of all the motion systems of the body, assuming an efficient integration of the components. As an example, Gerall and Green (1958) studied the effects of changing the force required to operate the controls of a two-hand tracking task. When the training torque of two pounds was changed to fourteen pounds, a large and persistent performance decrement resulted; changing from heavy to light produced only a small and transient decrement. Training with the heavier torque requirement may have been superior because it involved more complete participation of the individual in the task. Possibly the same sort of explanation could be applied to Ammons and Ammons' (1951) finding that bilateral transfer of a rotary pursuit skill was greater from the left hand to the right than from the right hand to the left. Right-dominant individuals might become more totally involved in training the left hand than in training the right.

Feedback Transformations

The complexity of motion patterns to which we have referred repeatedly is not easily defined but undoubtedly is determined in part by the kinds and degrees of feedback transformation which may be involved. Transformation effects are particularly important in determining learning specialization and transfer in tracking, tool using, and complex machine operation. The feedback of a control movement such as might be used to steer a car or to operate a lathe can be transformed in various ways by the machine. It may be delayed, displaced spatially in different directions and different dimensions, or distorted in some other way. Some transformations, as in aided tracking, involve changes in the manner of integrating movement components. The indeterminate nature of tracking transfer undoubtedly is due to the complexities introduced by feedback transformation and the resulting changes in movement integrations.

The degree of specialization of machine operations is related to the nature of feedback transformations introduced by the machine. The transformed feedback of a movement may be more complex or simpler than the movement pattern itself, or it may represent some mathematical transformation of the movement pattern as in optical tracking devices. Control movements with similar mathematically or spatially defined feedback transformations very likely will transfer positively to each other.

The processes known as thinking are based on the human capacity to make the symbolic transformations required in the use of language and other symbol systems. Instead of reacting directly to objects or people or machines or other particular situations on the basis of immediate sensory cues, the thinking individual transforms the available cues into symbolic terms and reacts according to this transformed information. Such symbolic information also can be communicated from person to person to facilitate individual learning and to enhance coordinate social control of the environment.

Once an individual has learned to use verbal and nonverbal symbol systems, he can make further integrative transformations of these symbols and thereby greatly enhance his ability to learn and accumulate knowledge. He can use his knowledge to describe and communicate, to define and classify, to search out special properties of situations and analyze them, to solve problems about the situations, and to create new forms of knowledge about the world. These different ways of manipulating symbols representing the temporal, spatial, kinetic, and qualitative sensory properties of nature constitute the different forms of thinking and reasoning.

Because certain kinds of symbol systems, such as language, number systems, mathematics, and musical notation, are built on systematic rules representing the properties of nature and of human experience, the symbolic transformations of the information in these systems are performed according to the rules that govern their use. For example, the various systematic transformations performed with numbers include expanding, reducing, transposing, substituting, converting, classifying, or patterning numbers in different ways by addition and subtraction and multiplication and other numerical manipulations. These are formal logical modes of transforming symbolic information or the informational feedback of symbolic patterns of behavior.

The primary and formal modes of symbolical transformation influence learning and transfer in many different ways. We can think of symbolic transformations of feedback as built-in cybernetic tools which can be manipulated variously to speed up, facilitate, telescope, and broaden the individual's resources in learning. Inasmuch as symbol systems represent the accumulation of man's tested experience with nature, they can be used to solve problems that cannot be handled in individual experience. The general utility of symbol systems and modes of transformation of symbols rests on the speed and facility with which these tools can be manipulated, the ease with which the individual can carry them with him from one situation to another, and their systematic rules and structure which enable him to apply tested human knowledge to specific situations in life. These properties define the generality of thinking and its wide transferability in the ongoing organization of human behavior.

SUMMARY

1. Training and education imply the ability of the individual to transfer or generalize learning from one situation to another. The study of transfer is the study of how one performance influences another in either a positive or negative way.

2. Cross education refers to the bilateral transfer of skills from one side of the body to the other or between hands and feet.

3. Although studies by James, Thorndike, and others have shown that practice in verbal learning or formal school studies does not result in general learning improvement, other studies show that training in general principles will facilitate learning of particular activities to which the principles apply.

4. An early attempt by Thorndike to analyze the factors responsible for learning transfer led to his theory of *identical elements* as the basis of response interaction. A later analysis of stimulus and response factors offered the interpretation that positive transfer results from associating an old response with a new stimulus and that negative transfer results from associating a new response with an old stimulus.

5. Many studies indicate that the amount of positive transfer is a direct function of stimulus similarity, and it is generally agreed that negative transfer increases as responses become less similar. When stimuli and responses are both varied, the results are complicated and hard to predict.

6. Many of the facts of stimulus generalization seem to follow the similarity analysis, but transposition experiments and many studies of form discrimination

in animals indicate that generalization is not necessarily based on absolute stimulus properties or on physical similarity.

7. Analyses of stimulus and response similarity cannot handle the complexities of behavior organization and its cybernetic nature.

8. Travel and manipulation movements are learned at different rates and to different degrees. Travel movements change little during learning of simple motion patterns but show a greater learning change in complex motions.

9. Transfer differentials can be demonstrated between travel and manipulation components. Changing the direction of a travel pattern usually produced negative transfer in the travel component although the manipulative component showed positive transfer. The transfer effects were complicated by reciprocal time relationships that developed between the two types of movements.

10. One way of identifying commonality in response is by correlational procedures. Correlations between the same type of components in related tasks tend to be higher than intratask correlations of travel and manipulation movements. Many individual differences occur.

11. Negative correlations indicate compensatory interactions between movements. Movements also may show direct correlation, complementary interactions, and opposed relationships. These possible types of response interaction and individual differences in response integration make it difficult to understand and predict transfer in complex behavior.

12. Many studies of motion organiza-tion indicate that responses are specialized in terms of their spatial organization. Spatial variations in movements and in their feedback relationships give rise to specific responses that are learned differentially and retained independently.

13. A neuronic interpretation of response interference or inhibition postulates that collateral nerve cell systems inactivate some pathways by providing a second stimulus input that equals a primary input. In this view, specialized responses are those that do not overlap in the nervous system and thus do not interfere with each other.

14. Asymmetrical transfer sometimes is demonstrated between related tasks. The optimal direction of transfer cannot be predicted in terms of relative difficulty but possibly is related to the spatial complexity of the tasks. In general, more transfer occurs from complex patterns to simple than vice versa. Asymmetrical transfer is sometimes accounted for in terms of the inclusion principle.

15. In general, complex tasks have more highly interrelated components and thus are more specialized and transfer less to other complex tasks than do simple to simple. However, we expect greater transfer from complex to simple than vice versa.

16. Tool using and machine operation involve spatial, temporal, and kinetic transformations of the feedback properties which help define the nature of the learning function and the kind and degree of transfer.

17. Symbolic transformations of direct sensory feedback mediate the various forms of human thought and facilitate learning and transfer of general knowledge.

CHAPTER
17

Human Specialization of Learning

The cybernetic view of behavior provides many new insights into the most significant and most specialized area of human learning: the processes of communication, thinking, and reasoning. In this area, conventional learning theories have been so seriously limited that many psychologists and educators have turned instead to the conceptions of psychoanalysis and related clinical practices. Our own approach turns in another direction—to the analysis of both thinking and communication as cybernetic control processes involving manipulation of symbolic information.

At the close of Chapter 16, we outlined briefly our ideas of how the sensory-feedback mechanisms of response have been extended in man to the symbolic level, thereby increasing the generality of learning. This view can be called a feedback transformational theory of thinking. Thought is achieved in the use of tools, in graphic behavior, and in speech and reading by systematic symbolic transformation of patterns of closed-loop feedback control. It extends the scope of organized regulation of behavior by manipulating symbolic information in many specialized ways. Thus, we believe that thinking is dependent not only on the movements and educational skills which constitute symbolic response but also upon the factors of instrumental and symbolic design which govern the different operations involved in manipulating symbolic information.

In this chapter, we shall consider the experimental study of thinking from a cybernetic point of view. This approach to cognition is of interest for a number of reasons. It suggests for the first time how thinking can be productive in generating information according to certain rules and symbolic operations. It provides a meaningful account of the way in which the basic movement components of symbolic behavior are related to the various modes and operational functions of thinking. It deals with concepts of symbolic design as evolution-determined rules and procedures of forming symbolic patterns and of using them to manipulate information either on an individual or group basis.

COMMUNICATION THEORY

Every psychological tradition—mentalistic, introspective, physiological, behavioral, and their various offshoots and amalgamations—has had its own interpretation of cognitive processes, but the different interpretations often have dealt with different aspects of the phenomena in question. Thought has been described and investigated as conscious processes, as rational introspections, as memory, as higher brain processes, as implicit muscle responses, as a higher form of learning, as symbolic behavior, as problem solving, and more recently as decision making analogous or comparable to computer operations. The learning interpretation was expounded first by Mach (1905), who discussed thinking in terms of knowledge and error and described its procedures as "thought experiments." Ebbinghaus's (1913) emphasis was on memory, and his lasting contribution to psychology was the development of experimental methods for studying memory. In his efforts to give a complete introspective account of thought, Titchener (1909) called attention to its possible sensory and motor counterparts. James (1890) gave a first good account of the dynamic nature of the continuous stream of conscious activity, and this dynamism was given new direction by Freud (1938), who related various levels of thought to developmental phases of unconscious motivation. Later learning theorists, including Thorndike (1927), Watson (1924), Hull (1943), Skinner (1953), and others, typically used concepts of conditioning and reinforcement or effect to account for both learning and thinking.

That the entire human educational effort and symbolic knowledge structure should depend on such tenuous assumptions as the law of effect or the postulate of reinforcement is unacceptable to many and ridiculous to some. The experimental base of reinforcement theory involves mainly studies of animal behavior in relation to motivational effects that are periodic or reversible or both. However, human symbolic behavior involves usable and efficient knowledge related to the detail and structure of the environment. Cognitive behavior in man is neither periodic nor reversible; it is cumulative, systematized in relation to the sensory properties of adaptive situations, systematized in terms of larger organized patterns of symbolic information, and integrated into dynamic manipulations of symbolic activities in relation to the behavioral environment. The most general feature of cognition is that it has some coherence with nature as man has come into contact with it.

Considerations such as these have led other psychologists—Tolman (1932), Lewin (1936), Leeper (1951), Festinger (1957), and Snygg (1962), among others—to emphasize the cognitive features of human behavior and learning. However, by not providing a sensorineuromotor interpretation for the processes they describe, cognitive theorists tend to divorce their area of interest from the more objectively defined manifestations of behavior.

Many recent efforts have been made to formulate the problems of cognition in new terms. Within the fields of mass communication and audiovisual education, the aspect of cognitive behavior of most immediate concern is its communicative function, by means of which knowledge or information is transmitted from speaker to audience or from teacher to student either directly or by device. The general framework within which recent communication theories have been developed is that of cybernetics. We have adopted this term to refer specifically to behavioral cybernetics, or the study of properties of self-regulation in behaving systems. Although we emphasize the feedback concept, there are other cybernetic concepts of mathematical-engineering origins which are influential in a number of sectors of behavior science.

Cybernetic Origins

The development of the science and technology of control systems revealed some interesting parallels between electromechanical controlling devices and living organisms. Shortly before and during World War II, it became increasingly apparent to a number of mathematicians, engineers, physiologists, and behavior scientists that explorations of control problems in devices held significance for the field of neurophysiology and vice versa. One of the first publications outlining this new interdisciplinary field of theory and research was Wiener's book, *Cybernetics,* which appeared in 1948. The ideas expressed there reflected a variety of sources, including training psychology and human engineering of the war years where many of the problems of man-machine control systems first were formulated.

The name cybernetics was coined from the Greek word for *steersman* and

thus calls to mind a first important cybernetic concept—that of feedback. As we have indicated earlier, a control device with feedback—that is, a servomechanism—is one which automatically adjusts its output according to feedback signals that supply information about how closely the controlled action is approximating the desired condition. (The steering engines of ships were among the first well-developed feedback mechanisms.) The essential characteristic of such a system is that it transmits a message by means of which the response of the system is controlled. Thus the application of power in a servosystem is controlled or directed by means of a signal or message which in itself contains only a minimal amount of power.

The problems connected with transmitting messages or information in control engineering are some of the same that are dealt with by engineers in the communications industries—problems concerned not only with the technical aspects of transmission but also with a mathematical and theoretical understanding of information itself. Many messages (for example, verbal) involve sequences of symbols which are dependent on each other to varying degrees and have unequal probabilities of occurring at various points within a sequence. Thus to measure the amount of information transmitted over a communication channel requires a statistical analysis of the symbols used and their probabilities of occurring in a message. The more probable it is that a given symbol will occur, the less information it conveys, for if it is certain to occur, it conveys no new information.

Contemporary   information   theory

originated mainly in the work of Shannon (1948), who reported the derivation of a mathematical measure defining the amount of information available in a source in terms of its statistical structure. He referred to this measure as *entropy* because the same mathematical expression with the opposite sign is called entropy in thermodynamics. Others refer to the measure as negative entropy, and still others feel that this designation is unfortunate. Analyzing the informational possibilities of communication sources according to Shannon's hypotheses, it is possible to compare the efficiency of a normal speaker with artificial sources. For example, it has been estimated that human speakers communicate less than 0.1 percent as many bits of information in a given time as could be transmitted by a source that generated random auditory frequencies (white noise) of the same bandwidth as speech (Licklider and Miller, 1951).

Once a message has been selected by a source, it is *encoded* by a transmitter, sent over a communications channel, and then *decoded* by a receiver at the destination. The rate at which information can be sent depends on both the information available at the source and the physical characteristics of the channel. How much of the information can be retrieved at the destination also depends on whether the channel carries *noise*—that is, signals from some other source that may interfere with the message under consideration. Thus the efficiency of a communication system as a whole is defined in part by the probability that noise will change the information content of the message.

Communication Models

In addition to founding a mathematical theory of communication, Shannon's work focused attention on the nature of the communication process in general. Among mass communication and audiovisual specialists, there have been a number of attempts to formulate communication models to conceptualize the significant aspects and interactions in communication transactions that typically involve both physical and physiological systems. The simplest communication model specifies only a communicator, a message about an object or an event, and a communicatee. Although this might describe face-to-face communication adequately, the use of artificial channels complicates the interactions and has inspired further model-building efforts.

Lasswell (1948) proposed that communication theory and research are concerned with, *"Who* says *what* through *what channels* to *whom* with *what effect."* Gerbner's (1956) verbal model was somewhat more detailed. He identified ten basic aspects of communication in the following terms: "(1) Someone (2) perceives an event (3) and reacts (4) in a situation (5) through some means (6) to make available materials (7) in some form (8) and context (9) conveying content (10) of some consequence." For each of these ten aspects, Gerbner identified specialized areas of study and research. For example, communicator and audience research relates particularly to the first aspect ("Someone"), perception research to the second, investigation of channels, media, and facilities to the fifth, content analysis and study of meaning to the ninth, and so on.

Gerbner went on to construct graphic models to represent different types of communication. His basic generalized model, shown in Figure 17.1a, introduces the principal components of communication and the dimensions of interaction. M represents man or machine, either the source or receiver of a message. An event (E) is perceived by M as E'. The message is a statement (S) about the event (E). Symbolized in this way,

Figure 17.1.   Gerbner's communication models. a. Generalized communication model. b. Model of a telephone communication from M_1 to M_4 about E. (Based on Gerbner. Toward a general model of communication. Aud.-vis. Commun. Rev., 1956, 4, 171–199.)

a telephoned message could be diagramed as in Figure 17.1b, where the speaker (M_1) makes a statement about an event (SE) which is encoded (SE') by the transmitter (M_2) and transmitted as a signal about a statement about an event (SSE). At the other end of the line, the receiver (M_3) decodes SSE' and gives the final message (SSSE) to M_4, who perceives it (SSSE') and may act to modify the event (E_c) according to instructions. In Figure 17.2, Gerbner used his own symbols to represent the communication process as diagramed by Shannon.

Gerbner represented communication essentially as an open-ended system in contrast to closed-loop servosystems with feedback. In another analysis of communication, Westley and MacLean (1955) emphasized the fact that feedback can occur in mass communication, although it may be minimized or delayed. These authors identified three roles in communication: A is the com-

Figure 17.2.   Shannon's diagram of a general communication system (top) compared with the progress of a signal in the same system as illustrated on Gerbner's graphic model. (Based on Gerbner. Toward a general model of communication. Aud.-vis. Commun. Rev., 1956, 4, 171–199.)

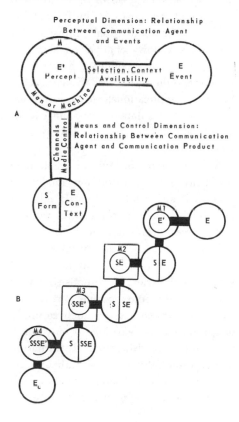

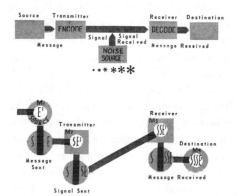

municator, B is the receiver or audience, and C is the passive channel or means of relaying the message. The message is transmitted from A through C to B, and feedback can occur from C to A, from B to A, and from B to C. The occurrence of feedback assures the systems character of the communication loop, according to these authors.

Further observations about the dynamic systems characteristics of communication have been made by Hoban (Stanford University Institute for Communication Research, 1960), who also specified that feedback is an aspect of communication systems. Hoban distinguished between the characteristics of information that are controlled primarily at the source (rate, reliability, redundance, ambiguity, time-phasing, quantity, and discriminability of information) and those that are controlled primarily by the receiver (exposure, selectivity, capacity, receptivity, and durability of information) and suggested that matching the source-controlled and receiver-controlled operations is the art of communication.

Information, Communication, and Behavior

Although information theory arose in a communication context, its applications in behavior science have by no means been confined to problems traditionally classified as communication. In fact, those theorists concerned with the broader aspects of communication in education and other areas of social interchange may pay their respects to Shannon's mathematical formulations without attempting to put them to any direct use. The general cybernetic concept of feed-back is more useful in communication models than the more rigorous measures of information or entropy. The communication models themselves are interesting descriptive accounts of certain types of social behavioral interactions. However, they provide little insight into the nature of communicative behavior in the individual or into the relation of such symbolic reactions to other types of response.

Originally, information theory was applied to situations involving a source, a channel, and a receiver—which might be two persons and a physical communication system—but in most psychological applications, the mathematical formalism is used to deal with the statistical relationship between a series of stimuli and a series of responses in individual behavior. The individual himself "is treated as a noisy channel causing less than perfect correspondence between the stimuli and the responses" (Luce, 1960). In these applications, an information analysis of the data is used instead of other statistical procedures such as analysis of variance.

Although some behavioral events may conform to the information model, in general it appears to be poorly adapted to behavior analysis for several reasons that have been indicated by Luce (1960). Information theory takes cognizance of sequential relations in series of stimuli and series of responses, but it does not take into account any cumulative changes in a series such as might be produced by learning or any other progressive modification. Information theory essentially treats stimuli and responses as static, discrete events which occur in a certain sequence but are not assumed to interact in any other way. Shannon's theory was a bivariate analysis, and it has very limited success when generalized to multivariate interactions. Further, a system reacting according to information theory accepts *bits* of information, all of the same value, but ignores the spatial or temporal patterning of these bits although responses are sometimes based on the patterning of discrete stimuli as well as on the nature of the individual stimuli. An obvious example occurs in vocal communication: the phrasing and inflections of a series of syllables may convey more meaning than the absolute auditory stimuli making up the series. Licklider and Miller (1951), who were among the first psychologists to become interested in the applications of information theory, showed clearly in their analysis of speech perception that patterning is more important than absolute stimulus qualities in conveying meaning. Finally, it has been observed that information theory cannot identify constant errors, and it does not assign values to errors but treats them equally.

Unfortunately, the pros and cons of information theory are not confined to a technical argument about which kind of statistics to use in behavior analysis but have a much broader significance in behavior theory. The whole cybernetic analogy, including the information model, has influenced thinking in the life sciences to an important degree. Something of the extent of this influence can be gained by noting the number of articles in general scientific publications on the relation between computer processes and human cognitive processes. This is a fascinating field, but, we believe, it can represent a fruitless trend

in behavior theorizing unless the limits of information theory in experimental behavior analysis are clearly understood.

THE THINKING MACHINES

High-speed digital computers are a boon to all areas of scientific research because of their possibilities for data processing and systems simulation, but they also represent a trap to the unwary. Computers can carry out many procedures analogous to human cognitive processes, but we should be misled if we were to believe that the symbolic operations of a computer are carried out *in the same way* as are human cognitive reactions. A digital computer system can simulate many aspects of behavior, but it is not for that reason a valid model of a behaving system.

Computers as Models

The cybernetic analogy relating computers to the nervous system which was outlined by Wiener in 1948 has developed into a very special field of interest concerning computer models of thinking, logical processes, symbolic creativity in a number of fields, and even learning. The main features of this analogy are simple. The brain—like a digital computer—is a logical machine. It accepts information signals from its input stations (sensory end-organs) on a binary basis much like the computer's yes-no decision making, for the neurons of the brain in reacting on an all-or-none basis have only two alternatives of action. They are likened to relays with two states of activity—firing and repose. The brain, like a computer, has both short-term and long-term memory. It is thought (in the analogy) that impulses travel in a closed neural circuit much like a short-term repeater circuit until needed to complete a current process. Long-term memory involves permanent changes in the synaptic thresholds of the brain or of the memory recording system of the computer. Unlike the computer, however, the brain never can be completely cleared of its past records for a new run, so that a behavior lifetime is analogous to a single run of the computer. After the computations or logical decisions have been made, the brain or computer transmits information to the output system or effector organs. Neither the brain nor the computer puts out energy; each transmits information. Wiener (1948) carried his analogy to the point of suggesting that the mechanical brain might learn just as the living brain does: "there is nothing in the nature of the computing machine which forbids it to show conditioned reflexes."

In the years since Wiener's words appeared in print, computers have been programed to solve intricate problems, to prove mathematical theorems, to play checkers and chess, to translate foreign languages, to compose music, and to perform many other marvels of comparing, analyzing, and decision making. They have been programed to *learn*, that is, to make present decisions according to a consideration of what tactics worked best in the past. For example, a checker-playing machine with enough *experience* stored in its memory circuits can in time defeat its programer. In addition to these procedures that are analogous to thinking and learning, machines are being designed which display rudimentary perceiving functions—they can to some extent recognize the spoken word or visual patterns.

Many of these computer functions are enormously useful. All of them are intriguing. All of them depend on the ingenuity of the programer who provides the machine with its memory and instructs it in the procedures to follow, yet there has crept into many discussions of computer functions an almost mystical feeling that here is something that transcends not only the speed and accuracy limitations of its programer but perhaps even his intelligence. Wiener (1960) himself came uncomfortably close to ascribing magical and therefore dangerous properties to the thinking machines when he recalled the story of the sorcerer's apprentice and warned that a computer operates at such a pace that, "we may not know, until too late, when to turn it off." His feeling was that programing techniques that make a computer learn, "remove from the mind of the designer and operator an effective understanding of many of the stages by which the machine comes to its conclusions and of what the real tactical intentions of many of its operations may be." This statement was disputed vigorously by Samuel (1960), who maintained: "Since the machine does not have a mind of its own, the 'conclusions' are not 'its.' The so-called 'conclusions' are only the logical consequences of the input program and input data. . . . The 'intentions' which the machine seems to manifest are the intentions of the human programmer, as specified in advance, or they are subsidiary intentions derived from these, following rules specified by the programmer."

Those who escape the influence of computer magic—hopefully, this includes most of us—may, however, fall into an even more insidious fallacy about the significance of these machines: the fallacy of model building. Far too many have accepted the cybernetic analogy of the thinking machine without inquiring too closely into its scientific validity. But is it really true that if we construct a machine that simulates thinking, this mechanical model enhances our understanding of the behavioral processes of thought? Is it true that if we construct a machine that simulates learning, this mechanical model enhances our understanding of the learning changes in behavior? If we construct a *neural-net* type of machine that simulates purposeful activity affected by *rewards* and *punishments*, does this mean that the living individual learns according to the effects of reinforcement? If we design a machine that simulates pattern recognition on the basis of a series of binary decisions, does this mean that behavioral perception is based on a series of discrete events? The danger in cybernetic model building lies in the tendency to answer these questions affirmatively in the face of convincing evidence to the contrary.

The basic fallacy in a computer model of a responding system is the assumption that the nervous system is digital in character. This assumption, which has been accepted at least tentatively by many behavior scientists as well as mathematicians and engineers, has also been rejected by theorists in many disciplines. An engineer, Jones (1963), recently stated:

> The frequently drawn comparison of the brain to a telephone switchboard or a digital computer is probably as misleading an analogy as can be imagined. On the basis of present neurological evidence, one cannot accept the statement that neurons act as relays or binary elements.

And again:

> Present evidence forces one to conclude that although the transmission of information is discrete, the actual operations performed upon the information are carried out by means of continuous variables.

Computers as Tools

Rejection of the computer model of behavior does not imply rejection of computer simulation techniques in behavior analysis, for the digital computer is one of the most versatile research tools of our time. Whether the computer is looked upon as a model or as a tool depends to a large extent upon one's preconceived ideas about how behavior is organized and controlled. As it happened, Wiener's cybernetic analogy fit very neatly into the kind of psychological theorizing that describes behavior as a sequence of discrete stimulus-response events. The computer model is essentially a static open-ended system which accepts input and delivers output by making appropriate central decisions. It corresponds rather well to orthodox stimulus-response psychology, but it does not correspond at all to our concepts of space-structured multidimensional response constantly monitored by feedback interactions. The variables that we have found to be of primary importance in patterning behavior and defining the course of learning—that is, spatial, temporal, and kinetic perturbations of the feedback relationships—have no analogs in computer models, where all functions are represented as a sequential series of discrete events.

However, if we accept computers for what they are and do not try to read into them any behavioral significance, they make superb instruments for analyzing characteristics of behavior. Figure 17.3 diagrams three types of activity that we have studied with our computer-controlled system—speech, eye movements, and the physiological activity pattern known as brain waves. The sounds of speech are converted to electrical signals by a microphone, and the pattern of eye movements, by a photoelectric recorder. Brain waves are, of course, known only as an electrical pattern. In each case, the electrical impulse is a continuously varying pattern, which is converted to digital form to make it acceptable to the computer. After the experimental perturbation by the computer—delay, displacement, kinetic modulation, or other transformation—the signals are reconverted into a sensory-feedback pattern. The sounds of speech are presented to the subject as an auditory pattern through earphones. The signal from eye movements (in one experiment) appeared as a spot of light on an

Figure 17.3.   Diagram of a closed-loop computer system designed for sensory-feedback analysis of behavior. Three types of activity patterns are indicated—speech, eye movements, and the electroencephalogram—along with appropriate input and output equipment. In each case, the activity pattern is transduced into an electric signal which can be sampled and converted into digital bits acceptable by the computer. After these signals are varied experimentally according to programed instructions, they are reconverted to a feedback pattern that can be perceived by the subject. A closed-loop system investigates parameters of self-regulation of response in contrast to the study of external variables.

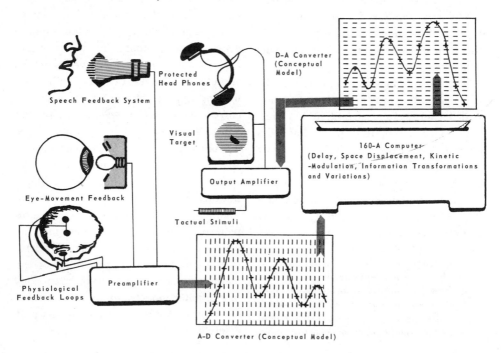

Speech Feedback System

Protected Head Phones

D-A Converter (Conceptual Model)

Visual Target

160-A Computer (Delay, Space Displacement, Kinetic -Modulation, Information Transformations and Variations)

Eye-Movement Feedback

Output Amplifier

Tactual Stimuli

Physiological Feedback Loops

Preamplifier

A-D Converter (Conceptual Model)

oscilloscope so that the subject attempts to fixate a visual signal controlled in space by his own movements. In some exploratory studies of brain waves, the wave frequency was presented to the subject as a flashing or flickering light synchronized with the rate of oscillation of the electroencephalogram.

Although no systematic presentation of our research findings will be attempted at this time, the results on speech analysis mentioned in Chapter 15 should be recalled here in relation to the application of Shannon's information theory to psychological problems. Our findings appear to offer evidence that the feedback control of speech does not conform to the information model. Various perturbations of the feedback signals that could be interpreted as *informational,* such as introducing *noise,* deleting parts of the sequence, rearranging the order of signals, distorting their quality, or producing repetitions, had only minor effects on the speech output, whereas even a very slight delay of the feedback signal seriously disturbed the behavior. To us this means that the self-regulation of behavior is a dynamic integrative process requiring continuous immediate feedback control—a process that cannot be represented as a static sequence of discrete events.

TRANSFORMATIONAL THEORY OF COGNITIVE BEHAVIOR

Our main purpose in this chapter is to develop a systematic point of view about the human specializations of behavior and learning known as cognitive and to suggest possible experimental approaches to research in this area. Neither current learning theories nor formulations based on information theory

specify how the movement patterns involved in thinking are generated or how different forms of thinking are specialized. These views lack concepts of symbolic design, which are needed to account for the gradual evolution and development of specialized cognitive forms of behavior. Although information theory indicates certain rules for the manipulation of information, it contains no suggestions as to how such rules can be organized as transformations of control of actual behavior.

Symbolic Transformation of Sensory Feedback

The theory that we are proposing assumes that the distinctive form processes of cognitive behavior are based on systematic transformations of sensorimotor feedback relationships, as in speech, gesture, graphic representation, and mathematical notation. By means of these transformations, information from primary sensory sources is symbolized in abstract terms, but the behavior processes do not lose their stimulus-response character. Thus we interpret cognition and thinking as peripheral or sensorimotor events controlled by the dynamic spatial, sequential, temporal, and kinetic properties of feedback. Thinking is action—in fact, it can be hard work—but it is not an open-ended sequence of subvocal speech as might be indicated by Watson's (1924) theory. Rather, it is response controlled. It demands precise integration of many intrinsic sources of sensory stimulation; it requires, except in reverie and fantasy, a high degree of vigilance in monitoring the different spatial, sequential, temporal, and kinetic variations in the feedback pattern. It differs from overt work or performance in that it is controlled by symbolic or abstract representations of objects, rules, and events rather than by their concrete sensory properties.

The understanding of cognition is a central problem of educational design because all significant human behavior is integrated in part by symbolic mechanisms. The higher the form of skill, talent, or creative activity, the more complex its symbolic pattern. In this complexity of symbolic integration we see the true nature of human adaptation to the environment. Everything in the man-made world—clothing, the tools and machines of technology, the structures of the environment, the objects of art, the layout of towns and cities, and the form of speech and writing—symbolize the propensities, the needs, and the features of man in action. The form processes of symbolism are defined not so much by the degree to which they resolve unconscious tensions or lead to vegetative rewards as they are by the accuracy with which they represent and control human action in relation to specific and general properties of the environment. Man is a thinking and creative species because he is able to make symbolic transformations of sensory information to relate his body and its functions to the physical and social properties of the environment.

Symbolic transformations of sensory information vary in complexity and in their degree of abstraction or generality. We have such different forms of nonverbal symbolism as gesture; pictorial description; graphic representation; musical, numerical, and mathematical notation; the various patterns of verbal representations in speech, writing, and reading. A given problem or series of

events can be dealt with at different levels of feedback control, involving both direct and transformed information. Figure 17.4 illustrates three levels of feedback control in building a house: the direct use of tools to build it, the use of marking tools to draw up and check graphic plans for its design, and the use of verbal symbolism to prepare specifications for what is to be done or to describe what has been done. All three levels of response involve thinking and knowledge, but the generality of the knowledge differs. The knowledge and skills related to specific tools used in building have relatively limited transfer to other areas of activity, whereas the

Figure 17.4.   Three levels of feedback control in human situations: overt control, nonverbal symbolic control, and verbal symbolic control. The activities of building a house require cognitive integration of all three levels.

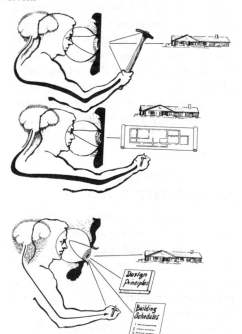

symbolic activities are more generally applicable. However, all three types of behavior help control the building activity. The nonverbal activity of drawing up plans defines the spatial organization of the situation at a more general and organized level than the actual tool using, whereas the verbal descriptions and specifications represent a still more general level of knowledge and communication. Words can be used to integrate nonverbal symbolism with the actual work activity of building. They can be used to record the processes used and to check logically all of the related details of these processes against prior knowledge and experience.

Cybernetic Mechanisms of Thinking

The processes of thinking and cognition vary in generality from those used to control specific response situations to very general verbal and mathematical symbolisms. We can distinguish among concrete behavior, concrete symbolism, and abstract symbolism. Concrete symbols designate specific objects and events whereas abstract symbols denote such general properties as geometric relationships and principles, temporal relationships, force and energy requirements, and the values involved in the situation. Individual behavior is regulated by such abstract feedback transformations in much the same way as it is by the feedback from concrete symbols and specific objects; but the knowledge used to recognize and manipulate the geometric, temporal, kinetic, and other abstract properties of the situation is far more generalized than that related to concrete events. The degree of control that an individual can level over his environ-

ment increases with the generality of his symbolic understanding. Further, the evolution of knowledge in human culture has seen a gradual expansion of symbolic control from primitive spatial representations of the environment to the advanced historical, geometric, kinetic, economic, artistic, and scientific concepts of modern man.

It is our view that both communication and the verbal and nonverbal symbolic transformations used in thinking may involve many different kinds of operations. The different processes known as memory, reasoning, problem solving, and creativity are distinctive ways of using verbal and nonverbal symbols to control adaptive perceptual-motor behavior. Some of the specific reactive operations which are used to manipulate different forms of symbolism are: (1) free recall; (2) controlled recall, as in answering multiple choice questions; (3) translation, as in language translation; (4) representation, as in simulation or description; (5) reduction, or bringing order into a lot of specific information by combining it in various ways; (6) differentiation, or distinguishing among different events on the basis of specific properties; (7) integration, or interrelating different materials or information; (8) elaboration, or creative production of new forms or ideas. Problem solving may involve any one or a combination of these patterns of symbolic manipulation, for a problem may vary in complexity from trying to recall a specific symbol to trying to create a new design or plan.

Whatever the level of the symbolic manipulation, we believe that it is reactive and dynamic and that it involves signs and symbols derived from primary sensorimotor relationships and their feedback properties. Both the artist and the mathematician think in terms of symbolic processes, but their thoughts always bear some relation to the world of real objects as perceived and experienced by the thinker. Cognitive behavior can have emotional or motivational components, but its most general feature is that it has some coherence with nature in real time and space and thus can be used to define the spatial, temporal, and kinetic relationships of events. Even fantasy and dreaming reflect some coherence or integration between symbols and direct reactions to the environment.

This description of the way that symbolic behavior is used to control the make-up and perceptual properties of human situations contrasts sharply with orthodox association and reinforcement interpretations of thinking. To say that cognitive learning is defined only by contiguity and/or reinforcement fails to explain the logical relationships that characterize thought and hence meaning and understanding. The thinker does not reach correct conclusions that can be checked against actual events because of chance association or because his ideas lead to vegetative or emotional reinforcements; he reaches them because symbolic meanings and relationships are derived primarily from the sensory-feedback effects of direct experience. Thus even at its most abstract level, thinking is organized reactively similarly to overt behavior. The significant difference between them is that cognition extends the scope of human control far beyond particular concrete events in the here and now.

Memory and Forgetting

One aspect of cognitive behavior that has received a great deal of experimental and theoretical attention in psychology is that of memory and its converse, forgetting. The problem of memory also has attracted the attention of mathematical theorists interested in computer simulation because of the nearly infinite capacity of the individual to store information.

We consider memory a central problem of human thinking because it reflects the high degree of specialization of behavior which can be achieved through meaningful symbolic and educational design. Most of the remembered information that individuals possess represents not direct psychomotor responses but symbolic responses which they have had to manipulate in the past. It is our view that memory reflects the generative and productive features of response which we have emphasized as the basis of cognition. We do not look upon memory as a storehouse of reactions but as a main aspect of dynamic production and control of behavior. Except in rare instances, reproduction of learned material is somewhat different from reactions learned or reproduced in the past. This is especially true for symbolic memory.

The general evidence about memory conforms broadly to the central assumptions of cybernetic control of both psychomotor and symbolic response. The most general characteristics of human memory revealed by experiments as well as by observations are that it is productive rather than repetitive and that it is accumulative and cannot be erased by the withdrawal of rewards. Further, memory does not wax and wane with motivation. Many if not most of man's learned responses can be repeated again and again over long periods of time without the support of extraneous reinforcements. Memory is an organized, integrative process combining both perceptual and motor activities. Even when a response is not performed it is not necessarily forgotten, for it may be recalled in an appropriate context. The remote memories demonstrated during hypnosis bear witness to the relative permanence of learning change. Psychomotor skills appear never to be completely forgotten, and perceptual experience accumulates as a storehouse of impressions that can be drawn upon throughout life for discussion and stories.

An important characteristic of memory demonstrated by Müller and Pilzecker (1900) is that learned reactions are not retained as static independent units but are subject to change due to interactions with subsequent behavior. Whether these interaction effects appear as retroactive inhibition, proactive inhibition, negative or positive transfer, they reflect an organizational feature of learning and performance that is conceptualized as poorly by standard theories of forgetting as it is by conventional theories of learning.

The simplest explanation of the forgetting process is that learned associations decay in time through *disuse*. This explanation obviously does not account for response interaction effects in memory. The more widely accepted *interference* theory postulates that new learning interferes with prior memories, but it does not explain why some interac-

tions produce interference while others produce facilitation. The Freudian theory that explains forgetting in terms of motivated *repression* of experiences that caused anxiety, shame, or guilt is far too limited to account for the differential interactions that define retention. Only the gestalt theory of *leveling* describes memory in terms of dynamic change rather than purely negative decay, inhibition, or suppression. The gestaltists believe that memory traces are subject to the same dynamic forces that organize perception. Thus a remembered perceptual figure becomes a *better* figure as time goes on. It becomes more unified and symmetrical and loses some of its incidental detail. Such a leveling process can be demonstrated in perceptual memory but fails to account for many specific instances of interference and facilitation in retention.

The cybernetic view assumes that the more highly organized the control processes of a response pattern, the less likely it will be interfered with by other learned reactions and the less likely it will be forgotten. An outstanding fact about learning, memory, and cognition is that organized materials are remembered better than less organized—meaningful materials are remembered better than nonmeaningful. Memory does not constitute a series of discrete, sequential reactions but a body of specialized and integrated responses which can be drawn upon according to rules of symbolic design and applied to communication and information manipulation.

We attribute the organization and specialization of both learned skills and symbolic knowledge to the establishment of spatially differentiated patterns of feedback control, either direct sensory feedback or transformed symbolic feedback. Symbolic knowledge is built on basic meanings derived from the feedback-controlled organization of overt action, and verbal knowledge derives its meanings from overt action, nonverbal pictorial and graphic symbolism, and the culturally determined rules of symbolic design. The nearly unlimited differentiation of knowledge that can be learned and remembered by an individual does not depend entirely on direct relations between overt behavior and word symbols; it also depends upon systematic organization of verbal symbols in relation to graphic designs, pictorial representations, and many other forms of nonverbal symbolization in gesture, mathematics, music, and so on. The cumulative effects of learning lead to the acquisition of more and more detailed patterns of response—direct and symbolic—in increasingly larger complexes of organized behavior and knowledge.

We believe that the accumulation of symbolic knowledge is mediated by the same sort of sensori-neuromotor processes that account for the organization and differentiation of specific movements in development and learning. Each specialized pattern of response requires some geometric differentiation of nerve cells by means of which the movements are controlled relative to variations in sensory feedback. Detailed reactions are integrated into larger patterns as spatially defined units. The more words, pictures, symbols, and their reference situations can be bounded and integrated into readily identifiable patterns, the more easily they are detected, learned, and remembered as distinctive experiences.

The concepts of receptor cybernetic control lead us to believe that memories are organized and specialized in terms of specific sensory channels. Several different kinds of research results point to the perceptual specificity of memory effects. As a recent example, Sperling (1960) has shown that the rate of decay of immediate memory for visual material is different from that for auditory material. Conrad and Hille (1958) have shown further that visual and auditory immediate memory interact in complex ways so that it may be possible to predict visual memory better from certain auditory information than from the visual learning data.

More often than not, memory reflects the spatial structuring of behavior. Past events are recalled in terms of where they occurred, or at least in terms of the spatial arrangement of the significant components. Many people recall facts read in books by visualizing them in their proper spatial location on a page or in relation to an illustration. As we have noted before, one of the great advantages of illustrations is that they provide a spatial pattern that helps to organize learned detail. Most people are not aware of the extent to which remembered symbolic knowledge is organized spatially, even their own, but some individuals recognize this aspect of memory and even take advantage of it. Memory forms are spatial patterns which organize systems of symbolic knowledge with no inherent space quality. For example, the days of the week, the months of the year, the sequence of arithmetic numbers, or the course of historic time may be represented cognitively by an individual in a spatial pattern upon which specific days, months, numbers, or dates can be located and thus manipulated and remembered more easily. Typically, individuals with memory forms develop them early in life with no awareness of the process. In fact, a person may never be aware that he utilizes such symbolic structures unless the possibility is called to his attention. Expert memorizers, however, make a point of reducing detail to systematic patterns for easier learning and better retention.

The position effects found in serial learning can be analyzed meaningfully in spatial terms. The beginning and ending of a sequence of responses form spatial boundaries where units can be discriminated more readily than in the middle of the series. The nearer a unit is to a boundary, the sharper it becomes.

Comparing the organization of overt skills with the organization of cognitive behavior helps us to understand the nature of forgetting as well as the nature of memory. Forgetting is defined mainly by the organized structure of the responses in question, including the degree of detailed differentiation of reactions within larger patterns. We expect little or no forgetting within response patterns that are marked by highly distinctive movement integrations, as in particular instrumental or psychomotor skills. The details of verbal knowledge are more likely to be forgotten because the responses involved are more general, are used in many contexts, and thus are subject to less highly differentiated feedback control.

On the other hand, both overt and symbolic learned responses can be elicited more readily in the proper context —that is, if the whole pattern can be reconstructed rather than just isolated parts. A person asked to demonstrate a skill usually needs to execute an integrated pattern of motion in order to perform the detailed movements within it correctly. A bowler, for example, would have trouble in demonstrating just what his movement integrations are at the moment he releases the ball. He needs to start the pattern from the beginning in order to have the detailed coordinations fall into place in their normal temporal and spatial patterning. Similarly, an individual can remember detailed symbolic knowledge more efficiently in the normal behavior context. An acquaintance's name which is "forgotten" in unusual circumstances may be retrieved readily if the person is seen in his accustomed surroundings. The different methods of studying memory—recognition, reconstruction, anticipation, and recall—vary in the degree to which the original learning context is reproduced by the experimenter and the amount retained by the subject, as demonstrated by his responses, is a function of this over-all structuring of the situation.

The organization principle is all-important in human education, for what the educated individual acquires is a set of interlocking systems of knowledge rather than a multitude of independent facts. A student of history may forget the exact date of the battle of Waterloo, but he does not forget its approximate location in historical time or the general meaning of the event in human affairs. Furthermore, the educated person knows how to determine the date if he needs it—he knows whom to ask or what book to consult to establish the answer to this specific question. Thus a part of his education is learning to understand systems of knowledge in general and how they are recorded in books, encyclopedias, newspapers, journals, and so on.

Response Interaction in Cognitive Behavior

We have pointed out similarities between psychomotor skills and symbolic responses because we believe that their stimulus-response organization is basically similar and that the feedback mechanisms of symbolic behavior are derived from the primary feedback mechanisms controlling direct response to the perceptual environment. It is fully as important, however, to understand the differences between direct and symbolic behavior and learning. From the point of view of movement organization, perhaps the most significant difference between psychomotor skills and symbolic knowledge lies in their degree of specialization. As we have said, symbolic responses are far more general or less highly differentiated than overt skills.

The general or abstract nature of symbolism leads to marked interaction among learned symbolic responses. On some occasions, the interaction may appear to be detrimental, as when one verbal pattern interferes with the learning or retention of another verbal pattern. More significantly, however, we see in symbolic interactions the processes of facilitative transfer and generalization that characterize human thought. Inductive or deductive reasoning is the application of general procedures of information manipulation to particular situations, utilizing the rules of grammar, syntax, and semantics. Thus cognitive learning can proceed more rapidly than skill learning because of the generality and transferability of

its response components. Detailed facts may be lost or forgotten, but a pattern of knowledge remains.

The speed and flexibility of symbolic interactions make cognition and thought highly efficient forms of behavior, but this efficiency would be negated were cognitive responses not firmly based on perceptual knowledge of the real world of objects and events as related to bodily movements. Whatever their level of abstraction, the symbolic transformations that control cognitive responses were derived originally from the spatial, temporal, kinetic, and informational properties of the environment. A set of symbolic rules and techniques reflects general knowledge of environmental relationships, sequences, and interactions that can be applied generally in many different situations. This is true in all kinds of organized human effort—in crafts, in technology, in science, and in the arts. Cognitive behavior is efficient because it can be checked against behavioral reality and can be used to control people and events.

ANALYZING COGNITIVE TRANSFORMATIONS

Our thesis in this chapter is that the essential characteristic of human cognitive behavior is that it involves systematic transformations of direct sensory information about the environment and one's relationship to it into symbolic forms. Most psychological studies of thinking, as in concept formation, problem solving, and other forms of information handling, have described the processes involved in only the most general terms. However, in recent years there have been a number of attempts to apply cybernetic concepts to cognitive research in order to achieve a more precise description of the significant events and possibly to identify predictive variables.

Information Analysis of Cognition

In a provocative series of experiments, Posner (1962) has applied concepts drawn from statistical information theory to studies of information handling, concept formation, and similarity scaling. The basis of these studies was the idea that many cognitive processes, such as data summarization and concept formation, are characterized by information reduction between stimulus input and performance output. That is, the individual's response contains less information in a statistical sense than the sensory data which he processes to get the response. While not committed to information theory as the best system of describing behavior, Posner adopted the statistical information measure as a means of identifying systematic relationships in the transformational processes of thought.

In one series of experiments, subjects performed a variety of operations on series of numbers presented in sequence. Tasks included recording the numbers as heard, adding them in different patterns, and classifying them according to schemes of varying difficulty. Each task was classified according to the amount of information reduction involved. The simple recording task conserved all information, but the other tasks reduced the input information by a measurable number of "bits." Performances were measured objectively and the tasks also were rated by subjects according to their judged difficulty. In all studies, the greater the information re-

duction, the greater the difficulty of the task, whether measured objectively or rated subjectively. The relationship appeared to be linear.

A second group of experiments dealt with subjects' ability to discriminate and generalize perceptual patterns from an original learning series to test series which were distorted to various degrees from the original. The stimuli were sets of dot patterns, each of which contained an original and five distortions, as shown in Figure 17.5. Each distortion was constructed according to definite rules and differed from the original according to a specified degree of statistical uncertainty.

Using materials of this sort, in which

Figure 17.5. Sample set of dot patterns used to study the effect of perceptual uncertainty on generalization and discrimination. (From Posner. *An informational approach to thinking.* Dept. of Psychology, Univer. of Michigan, tech. Rep. AFOSR–2635, 1962.)

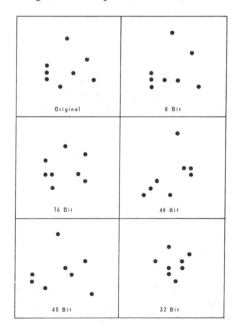

the similarity variable was statistically defined, Posner was able to show that the difficulty of the learning tasks was linearly related to the degree of uncertainty of the patterns, as was the perceived similarity of the patterns, the time of recognition, and the degree of transfer from one series to another.

As Posner himself pointed out, his informational analysis of the organization of input and output of cognitive problems made no assumptions about the actual procedures followed by the subjects in performing the tasks. Moreover, an informational analysis is of necessity limited to variables that can be expressed in informational terms. Further insights into cognitive processes can be gained by analyzing other types of transformation that occur in specialized behavior, particularly dynamic variations of the spatial, temporal, and kinetic feedback relationships that regulate the patterning of response.

Computer Simulation of Thinking

If cognition involves transformation of sensory-feedback control of basic movements in manipulating information, as we believe that it does, experimental study of the parameters of control should be advanced greatly by a tool which permits precise simulation of many types of dynamic variation of perceptual and feedback patterns. Digital computers constitute such a tool, although up to this time they have been used mainly for numerical data processing and for static simulations such as those described in Chapters 9 and 10. Inasmuch as most cognitive problems of manipulating information are closed-loop problems, the real promise of computers is in applying them to cybernetic control in thinking.

One application of computers which promises to provide insight into some of the procedures of creative thinking is in the field of musical composition. Mathews (1963) recently has given a careful explanation of how digital computers can be used not only to generate musical sounds according to detailed programed instructions specified by a composer but also to generate musical scores with varying degrees of human control over the actual pattern of the composition. Computer music can range from quite random arrangements of notes generated according to a set of general rules about its acoustic pattern to completely specified compositions programed by the human composer. According to Mathews, a computer could be used by serious composers to avoid much of the repetitious work involved in composing and trying out musical ideas. A musical theme could be fed into a computer with instructions to repeat it, to transpose it to another pitch range, to play it on another instrument, to change its tempo or loudness, or to harmonize it according to simple rules.

These transformations of musical themes suggested by Mathews plus many other possible dynamic perturbations that can be produced by a computer simulate, we believe, some of the important form processes of musical creativity. What a composer does is not just to arrange notes in a series; he takes a given sequence of notes—a theme—and presents it in many variations. These variations are produced by just the sort of dynamic transformations that Mathews spoke of and that we have been describing in this chapter.

In order to investigate the transformational processes in musical creativity, we have designed an experimental computer system, as shown in Figure 17.6, to transmit musical sounds with considerable fidelity and to perturb the acoustic patterns in many different ways. The musician or composer selects a musical theme, puts it on tape, plays it repetitively through the converting and programing circuits of the computer system, and introduces dynamic transformations by operating a set of switches on a control panel. He can vary the order of notes, the kinetic character of the theme, the relative timing of different parts, and so on. The resulting sound pattern is fed back to him by the loudspeaker and recorded on a second recorder.

The critical aspect of this procedure is that the composer controls the dynamic parameters of perturbation and variation of the music rather than its substantive content. For example, chosen samples of the theme can be delayed, an amplitude distribution of its frequency content can be produced and played out as a background sound pattern, the sound can be looped through the system with a delayed reverberating effect, time samples of the music can be repeated, and reversals of time samples of the theme can be introduced to produce inverted themes. Computer programs of the same or of other themes can be manipulated to enrich the primary theme. As the composer introduces his computer variations, he gets an immediate auditory feedback of what he has done, and a permanent tape record also is available for later use. Such a

Figure 17.6.   Experimental computer system for the analysis and control of the dynamic properties of creative musical composition.

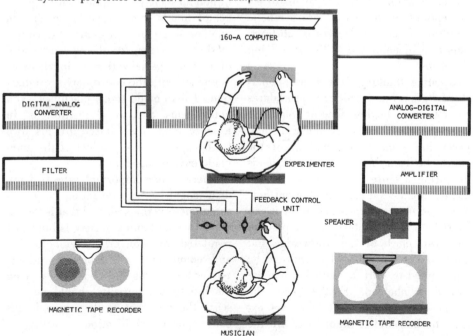

system should prove to be a valuable aid to musicians in understanding the dynamic nature of their creative efforts as well as advancing our psychological understanding of some aspects of creativity.

The idea that a composer might create music by a deliberate, knowledgeable manipulation of the dynamic physical properties of its acoustic pattern illustrates what we believe to be the most important characteristic of cognitive creativity: its problem-solving and problem-controlling nature. Creative thinking, far from being a happy accident, is the work of an individual who can bring to bear on the problem at hand a wealth of systematized observations represented in different forms and at various levels of symbolism. William James (1890) said that genius is a matter of perceiving in an unhabitual way. We would extend that idea to say that creativity is based on man's ability to transform his direct perceptions of the world into symbolic patterns of varying degrees of abstractness and of unlimited utility in solving problems.

Creative thinking is not well-understood because its significant procedures cannot always be described or communicated by the thinker. A musical composer has some understanding of the effects he is trying to create. If he is preparing a score for combined instruments, he knows a great deal about how each instrument sounds and what it can contribute to the total musical pattern. However, much of this knowledge and understanding is nonverbal and can be represented to only a limited extent by formal symbolism. Furthermore, the composer's understanding does not extend to a complete knowledge of the

physical characteristics of the acoustic pattern with which he is working. Therefore his creative work involves an element of trial and error: a certain degree of randomness that reduces the systematic nature of his procedures.

Computer simulation techniques call attention to the fact that man's creative talents are specialized in relation to the tools, machines, and symbol systems that have been developed in human society. For example, in the computer simulation system described above, the computer acts as a specialized instrument by means of which the composer can extend not only his understanding and his control of musical patterns but his ability to symbolize their dynamic properties. That is, a higher level of cognitive behavior is achieved by using a specialized instrument to extend primary human abilities.

The specialized tools and instruments of human society are in one sense a product of man's cognitive behavior but in another sense they structure the course of that behavior, for the upward spiral of human specialization is inextricably bound up with the coordinate specialization of man-made tools, machines, symbol systems, and social institutions. In a sense man lifts himself by his own bootstraps: he is a product of the man-made environment.

There is one important aspect of human cognitive specialization which is sometimes overlooked, and that is the extent to which human society is built and regulated by nonverbal symbolization and communication. Man's traditional reliance on words and books to carry on his intellectual pursuits should not obscure the fact that modern man in his contemporary civilization controls his activities with mathematical language, graphical language, computer language, and other nonverbal symbolizations. It is especially important that man's interdependence with his machine systems and nonverbal symbol systems be recognized in the educational domain, for society is pressing the limits of the use of words to describe its actions and its systems. Verbal language is notably inadequate in conveying the technical concepts that regulate our social and industrial world. Thus educators cannot afford to turn their backs on contemporary technology. The intellectual or cognitive development of modern man and his tremendous resources in memorizing information are dependent to a significant degree on the response specialization promoted and sustained by man-made instrumental and symbolic design.

Several kinds of evidence suggest that individuals learn to think, or develop their cognitive abilities, over a considerable period of time (Lehman, 1954; Piaget, 1928; Vinacke, 1951); but once they acquire the techniques of cognitive manipulation, their capabilities in dealing with the environment are almost unlimited. The course of human development in cognitive behavior is a specialized aspect of the more general study of human specialization in learning and performance skills. In the next chapter we shall examine some of the high points of this story and explore some of its implications for educational design.

SUMMARY

1. Human learning achieves its highest degree of specialization in cognitive behavior, which deals with the physical and social environment by means of symbolic rather than direct responses.

2. A new approach to cognitive behavior that interests many in psychology as well as those in communication and audiovisual fields is cybernetics, generally known as the comparative study of living organisms in relation to electromechanical control and communication systems.

3. Cybernetics was outlined first by Wiener and was extended by Shannon's mathematical formulations, known as information theory, which defined measures of information in communication systems in statistical terms.

4. A number of general communication models draw on information theory concepts but utilize the mathematical measures of information less than the cybernetic concept of feedback—the essential characteristic of a closed-loop system.

5. Information theory is being applied widely in psychology to describe the statistical relationships between series of stimuli and series of responses. Inasmuch as it applies to static sequences of discrete events, it is not applicable when cumulative changes occur in behavior or when dynamic patterning of stimuli define response.

6. A related trend is to conceptualize human behavior, especially cognitive behavior, as a cybernetic series of events analogous to the digital operations of computers. The danger in such computer model building is that it misrepresents the most significant characteristics of behavior and neural action. Behavior is not defined by sequences of discrete bits of information but by dynamically interacting variables that operate in a closed-loop system.

7. Computers can be used to help analyze behavior and cognition but they should be recognized as tools, not models. Inserted in the feedback-control loop of a behaving system, they can be used to vary many dynamic properties of perceptual feedback to study the effects on performance and learning.

8. Dynamic feedback analysis is important in the study of cognition and thought, for we believe that these forms of behavior involve symbolic transformations of the primary sensory properties of feedback but retain the basic reactive organization of overt behavior.

9. Symbolic behavior and direct behavior vary in complexity and generality, but both relate systematically to the properties of the environment and are used to control it. Nonverbal symbolism is more general than direct manipulation, and verbal symbolism is more general than nonverbal. These general symbolic forms of behavior permit a higher degree of environmental control.

10. Different cognitive operations which can be used in solving problems include free recall, controlled recall, translation, representation, reduction, differentiation, integration, and elaboration; all of these types of reaction bear some relation to the individual's direct perceptual-motor responses.

11. Human memory is accumulative, is affected by dynamic interactions among responses, and is better for organized materials than for nonorganized. Specific details are forgotten more readily than the larger patterns of knowledge.

12. Cognitive reactions as well as psychomotor skills are specialized in learning and memory by their feedback control mechanisms. Memories thus reflect a perceptual specialization and organization derived from their sensorimotor regulation.

13. Many observations indicate the spatial organization of memory in both animals and human individuals. Utilizing arbitrary patterns or *memory forms* facilitates remembering and cognitive manipulation of facts.

14. Although the stimulus-response organization of psychomotor skills and cognitive responses is basically similar, the latter are far more general or less highly differentiated and facilitate the rapid generalizations characteristic of thought.

15. Among the few stimulus-response analyses of cognitive processes are studies by Posner that apply the concepts of information theory to thought processes. The greater the information reduction involved in his cognitive tasks, the greater its difficulty.

16. Computers can be used to simulate or aid creative thinking by providing a means of perturbing dynamic spatial, temporal, and kinetic properties of feedback patterns, as in musical themes.

17. Creativity and cognitive problem solving reflect the level of man's technology and specialized tools, machines, and symbol systems as much as the level of his human abilities. For human specialization is both a source and a product of the technological specialization of society.

CHAPTER
18

Human Design and Educational Design

A cybernetic approach to educational design assumes at the outset that education is the applied science of human development as well as the applied science of human learning. It recognizes that learning proceeds in a developmental context wherein its course is defined not only by the general features of human design but also by the developmental progress of the particular individual. Further, so-called normal development is dependent on appropriate sensory experiences, often at critical stages. Thus valid principles of educational design must encompass some understanding of the development-learning interaction.

In this book we have developed the point of view that the individual learner can be thought of as a control system whose performance is regulated by feedback mechanisms which not only structure immediate response but also are the means by which genetic endowment defines progressive changes in behavior. We view learning as a refinement of the developmental process by means of which self-regulated activities become adapted to special environmental conditions. This means that the changes introduced by learning are not imposed on some common relatively undifferentiated behavior base but serve to modify already specialized response patterns that reflect the genotype of the particular individual.

As we conceptualize the course of development, all of the transitional phases involve specialized patterns of closed-loop control of response. In early maturation, the responding individual has but limited control over his environment and thus over the feedback effects of environmental stimulation. As a result, the effects of early stimulation on behavior organization are general in nature and are not marked by the sort of differential change known as learning. Only when the individual matures to the point where his specific responses can be used to control the sensory effects of movement can his behavior development be articulated by true learning.

EARLY DEVELOPMENT

Although the terms development and maturation sometimes are used interchangeably in psychology and education, maturation usually refers more specifically to the uniformities of species development in relation to age. We shall use the term development to represent the over-all elaboration of the individual and his behavior resulting from the interactions between genetic endowment and environmental conditions.

For many years, the interrelation between maturation and learning in development was obscured by the idea that the two processes were controlled more or less independently by intrinsic, genetic factors and extrinsic environmental factors. This nature-nurture dichotomy is being corrected by fundamental research on developmental interactions in prenatal and infant behavior.

The most provocative idea that has emerged from developmental research in the last dozen or so years is that there are critical periods in development for the establishment of environmentally organized behavior patterns. Thus certain types of responses that are in one sense learned depend explicitly on the availability of appropriate sensory stimulation at certain stages of maturational development. In such cases, the old distinction between learned and unlearned behavior breaks down as does the separation between environmental and genetic factors.

One of the clearest examples of a learning-maturation interaction at a critical period occurs in imprinting, a term originally used to describe the establishment of following behavior in newly hatched geese and other ground-nesting birds. Although the concept of critical periods was introduced in this fairly limited context, it undoubtedly has wide applicability in behavior—how wide we are only beginning to appreciate. Many established notions of mental development and educational design may have to be changed as we learn more about the critical aspects of human development.

Dimensions of Development

Patterns of behavior in a normal human individual are subject throughout life to change and differentiation defined by both intrinsic and extrinsic factors. We can categorize these changes roughly as gross bodily growth, finer neural differentiation or maturation characteristic of the species, and specific learning changes. These different aspects of development follow different schedules so that their relative importance in defining behavior differentiation varies during the individual's lifetime.

Figure 18.1 represents the different aspects of development as processes that originate early in life and influence behavior differentiation until they level off at different stages. Bodily growth goes on through adolescence and during that time continues to effect changes in behavior patterning. Although growth changes influence the patterning of many overt performances and skills, they have a relatively slight influence on higher psychological capacities. Finer neural maturation characteristic of the species probably contributes to behavior differentiation through early adulthood or until middle maturity, when human symbolic abilities and creativity appear to reach their peak. Specific learning changes—including reactive, instrumen-

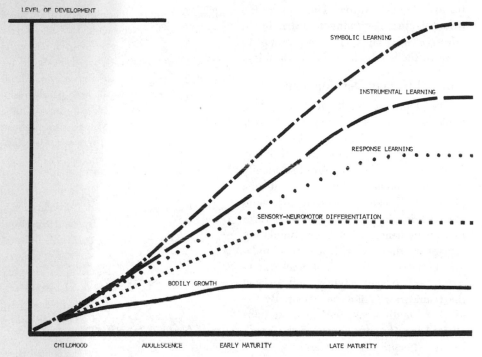

Figure 18.1.   Dimensions of development. Different aspects of development reach their peak level at different times of life.

tal, and symbolic learning—continue to extend the differentiation of behavior throughout life. These so-called types of learning vary in their relative importance at different periods and contribute to different levels of behavior organization.

The different developmental processes originate early in life and all are dependent on environmental stimulation. In fetal and neonatal life, the influence of the environment is mainly supportive and general, but even in early infancy it is believed that behavior differentiation is influenced by specific sensory-feedback factors. Maturational elaboration requires articulated sensory experience lest it be retarded or distorted by sensory deprivation.

The course of behavior development is affected very little by specific learning changes until late in the first year of life. Specific learning becomes a significant aspect of development only when the child can begin to control his environment with articulated responses. Then the maturing feedback-regulated behavior patterns become specialized by specific learned environmental control.

A significant aspect of human design is that instrumental and symbolic learning originate at about the same time in life as the simpler learning that we have called *reactive*. Learned specialized activities begin to appear to a significant degree when the infant is almost a year old, at about the same time that his babblings are being specialized into culturally defined words. Thus when the infant is just beginning to learn in an effective way he also is beginning to acquire the symbolic tools for thinking.

Normal Human Development

The definitive work on human fetal behavior was carried out by Hooker (1944), who made many observations on the response organization of living fetuses that had been removed surgically from the mother. The results of one phase of Hooker's research are summarized in Figure 18.2, which pictures motion sequences elicited by stimulating fetuses on the face with a hair stimulator. Fetuses of about eight weeks menstrual age turned slightly and twisted the trunk in a C-like movement. By the ninth to tenth week, the same stimulus elicited specific movements of the head; by the twelfth to fourteenth week, a fetus made highly specific movements of facial muscle groups. At this time the nature of the reaction varied with the locus of the stimulus.

Responses to stimulation at other loci than the head region—for example, on the palm, foot, or trunk—developed somewhat later but otherwise were in line with those described for stimulation of the face. The pattern of behavior development was from general to specific, from large to small movements—a process of differentiating finer movements from more generalized patterns.

Hooker's observations showed that almost all of the fundamental forms of segmentally integrated reflex response appear during the period of rapid development from eight to fourteen weeks fetal age. After this early prenatal motor sequence, few other reactions develop before birth, but the sensory control of

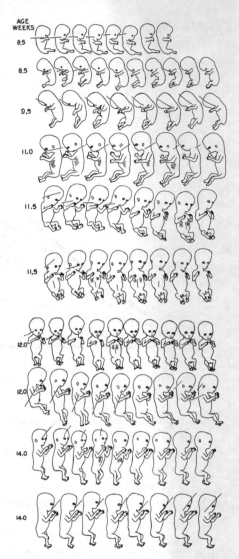

Figure 18.2.   Differentiation of response to tactual stimulation of the face in human fetuses of eight to fourteen weeks menstrual age. (Adapted from Hooker. *The origins of overt behavior.* Ann Arbor: University of Michigan Press, 1944.)

existing reflex systems expands and various receptor input systems are integrated at the midbrain level to establish arousal-type reactions to stimulation. Movements similar to breathing can be elicited within the fifth month of fetal age and it appears that all of the main receptors except the eyes are functional by the seventh month. McGinnis (1930) observed optic-following reactions to a moving striated pattern in an infant born one month prematurely.

The results of many studies of post-natal development indicate that during approximately the first two years infant behavior follows another sequence of sensorimotor development, which also is described as general to specific. Postural movements appear first, followed by dynamic transport coordinations and finally articulated manipulative movements. This postnatal motor sequence is not a continuation of the fetal developmental pattern but constitutes a new sequence in which distinctive space-structured patterns of movement regulated in relation to exteroceptive stimulation are established. Development proceeds roughly from head to foot and from proximal to distal loci.

We interpret the generalized movements of the neonatal period (the first month) as the beginnings of postural control which gradually enables the infant to hold up his head, roll over, and sit up. The repetitive, inaccurate reachings, kickings, twistings, and babblings of the early months are the first phases of regulation of dynamic transport movements. Although a few specific reactions, such as breathing, sucking, and crying, are present at birth and a few others appear within two to four months after birth, controlled movements of the head and limbs develop somewhat later. The refined articulated movements that begin to appear in the second half of the first year represent the manipulative sector

of behavior with its greater spatial precision. Many refined manipulations—apposition of thumb and fingers, specific vocalizations, and articulated foot movements in walking—have developed by about twelve months. Behavior maturation involves integration of the three movement systems as well as the development of the sensory-feedback mechanisms of each.

The cybernetic interpretation of development assumes that maturation of behavior patterns requires sensory stimulation at all stages. The process is not one of separate differentiation of sensory and motor functions but an elaboration of integrated sensorimotor activities wherein the component movements are controlled with respect to specific sources of environmental stimulation. The developing postural system establishes a gravitational feedback mechanism which provides the infant not only with postural control but also with a built-in vertical reference system for directional regulation of transport and manipulative movements. The transport systems of movement establish a right-left directional reference system and provide the mechanisms of lateral dominance. The development of the postural and transport systems during the first year of life makes the behaving infant an orientation system for the most part. Only later, when the manipulative component becomes more prominent, do learning and symbolic control begin to dominate the developmental picture.

A number of experiments on learning in human fetuses, neonates, and infants indicate that specific learning is extremely limited before the age of about one year and that the pattern and level of learning depend on the stage of maturational integration of response components. It has been found virtually impossible in controlled studies to set up stable, consistent conditioned responses either in fetuses (Spelt, 1948) or neonates (Wenger, 1936; Wickens and Wickens, 1940). We interpret all of these research findings as evidence that learning plays little or no role in defining the response patterns that appear in the infant during the first few months of life.

From about six months of age onward, the maturation of various kinds of refined movements sharply increases the number of responses that can be specialized by experience and practice. The infant at this stage may begin to grasp specific objects, to make specific responses to parents, and to make other specific situational reactions that are retained and repeated. A few months later he begins to isolate vocalizations that are accepted as words by others and to use them in specific situations. Larger movement integrations are for the most part maturationally defined, but refined manipulative movements are specialized through learning to control specific objects and events in the environment.

By two years of age, the infant has refined his manipulative and articulated speech movements sufficiently to learn specific reactions independently of more generalized orientation response patterns. Within a few months he will be capable of performing delayed reactions and somewhat later of learning double alternation habits (Hunter and Bartlett, 1948). It has been suggested that the ability to perform these responses is closely associated with a certain level of

verbal learning and the ability to learn independently articulated manual movements.

Perceptual-Motor Integration and Control

Many of the developmental refinements of infancy involve specific space-structured perceptual control patterns. McGinnis (1930) found that optic-following reactions are present in the neonate at birth. These reactions are optokinetic responses that can be elicited by movement of compound striated patterns but not by single lines or objects. They were found even in a premature baby one month prior to full term. During the first weeks of life, the optokinetic responses persist and become integrated some four to six weeks after birth with specific pursuit movements elicited by moving single objects or light sources. Fantz (1963) also described optokinetic movements in newborn infants.

Developmental research on infant animals has revealed that highly organized patterns of response, integrating receptor processes with sensorimotor control of movements and orientation, appear in the normal course of maturation. For example, visual-placing reactions of the forelimbs in kittens appear abruptly at just the time, some twenty-six days after birth, when maximal visual acuity has developed (Warkentin and Smith, 1937).

A remarkable demonstration of unlearned spatial control of behavior has been carried out by Gibson and Walk (1960), who tested human infants and several species of animals on what they called the visual cliff. As shown in Figure 18.3, subjects were placed on a plate glass surface that extended from a solid opaque area across a chasm to another

Figure 18.3.   The "visual cliff" as used by Gibson and Walk (1960) to test perceptions of depth in infancy.

solid area. Both human and animal babies tested in this situation systematically avoided moving across the visual cliff and were distressed when placed on the glass over the visual depth. Such observations show that fear of falling is not entirely learned but incorporates maturational patterns of integrated visuomotor behavior involving three-dimensional vision.

As Piaget (1928) was the first to emphasize, the year-old baby not only has developed organized space perception but uses space-organized behavior in manipulative activities such as grasping, pulling, pushing, turning, and so on. These basic manipulations and their integration into the larger postural-transport contexts are a part of the infant's human endowment as are further refinements of perceptual-motor behavior that will develop later, but a further aspect of development is that these manipulative patterns can become specialized through learning in order to deal more effectively with the particular characteristics of the infant's own environment.

We think of the baby as a control system whose organized patterns of motion from birth are self-regulated insofar as is made possible by the maturing feedback regulatory mechanisms. As development goes on, the baby not only controls his body and movements in relation to environmental factors, but comes to exercise control over certain features of the environment. By his actions he can change the arrangement of objects in space, summon parents, get food and drink, and so on. It is in developing this control that learning begins to assume a significant role as an organizing factor, for the infant learns to make specific responses to specific objects, people, and situations. During the first three years of life, the child progresses from almost complete inability to control his environment to a condition of highly effective manual, verbal, and locomotor regulation of his stimulus surround.

In a series of experiments on infants, we analyzed the development of different patterns of transport and manipulative movements to control environmental stimulus patterns (Smith and Smith, 1962). We assumed that control by means of orientative transport movements would precede manipulative control by some months. We also compared visual, auditory, and tactual aspects of cybernetic control. The general method in some preliminary observations was to test whether the infants would use simple manual contact movements to activate various stimulus devices. These included a television monitor with various kinds of images and a tape recorder that played music, a parent's voice, a baby's crying, or other sounds. We also tested whether infants would use a soft blanket in order to avoid sitting or lying on a rough surface.

Our conclusions from these preliminary observations were that babies from the age of a few months to two years will orient toward auditory and visual stimulus devices but usually are not able to learn the trick of controlling them by making a specific manipulative response. Further clarification of the course of development was sought in two controlled experiments which measured specific responses of infants at different ages. The two situations used are diagramed in Figure 18.4. One set-up used a revolving playpen which was activated by vocalizations of the infant by means of a voice relay. Any fairly audible sound made by the child would start the playpen revolving slowly for one complete revolution. When the number of vocalizations during this experimental condition was compared with the number during a control period of continuous revolution of the playpen, a significant increase was found for infants from twelve to eighteen months and from eighteen to thirty-six months of age. Infants younger than one year gave almost no vocalizations under either condition.

The second set-up diagramed in Figure 18.4 located a television monitor close to a continuously rotating playpen. Children ranging in age from ten to thirty-eight months were tested in the playpen to determine how many seconds out of a minute they would maintain their orientation toward the monitor when it displayed the image of their mother or a strange woman either reading a book or performing a number of common playful activities while speaking informally to the child. The graph in Figure 18.5 plots the mean number of seconds spent orienting toward the monitor—this involved continuous corrective movements in the rotating playpen—for

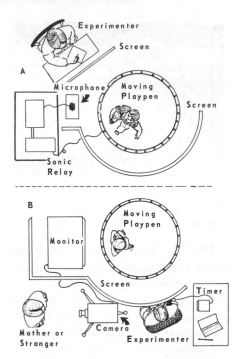

Figure 18.4.   Two experimental set-ups used to test infant control of the environment. *a.* Sound-activated playpen. Vocalizations and other sounds made by the child cause the playpen to revolve slowly. *b.* Watching television from a moving platform. Placed in a continuously moving playpen, the child can watch the television screen only by changing position constantly. (From Smith and Smith. *Perception and motion: an analysis of space-structured behavior.* Philadelphia: Saunders, 1962.)

the four different types of images as a function of age. The most pronounced changes occurred at about twenty to twenty-two months. It also was discovered in this whole series of observations that infants at about this same critical age of twenty-two months were more inclined to cry when their environment was disturbed than infants of other ages.

Although our conclusions from these studies are tentative and await confirma-

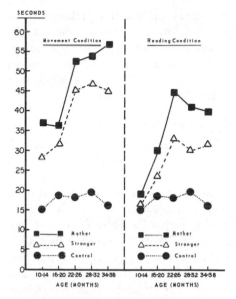

Figure 18.5.   Mean time spent watching the television monitor from the revolving playpen as a function of age. The four types of experimental images were of the mother or of a strange woman either active or reading a book. The control image was of a blank wall and window. (From Smith and Smith. *Perception and motion: an analysis of space-structured behavior.* Philadelphia: Saunders, 1962.)

tion or revision by further research, they do fit in with our general ideas of the infant's developing abilities to control the perceptual environment. The type of control that develops during the first two years is principally in the nature of directional orientation toward or away from foci of stimulation. As the child learns to creep or to walk, he can approach favored stimuli such as parents, avoid obstacles, and the like. During this time he also is developing many manipulative abilities, but the evidence is that he is not yet able to adapt fine manipulations to any great extent to effect precise environmental control. Objects that are encountered will be manip-

ulated, but only incidentally within the larger behavior context.

During this early stage, the domination of behavior by gross postural-transport directional activity is reflected in related motivational and emotional effects. The loss of a focal stimulus, such as the disappearance of the mother, may cause marked distress in the infant of about twenty to twenty-two months. An infant of this age also may appear overly destructive because he often treats toys and other objects as things to push aside or to smash with large transport movements.

Many changes in behavior organization occur when the child becomes capable of exerting manipulative control of environmental patterns, typically from about the age of two years. Experimentally it has been shown that children between two and three years of age are able to make delayed reactions and somewhat later can learn double alternation tasks (Hunter and Bartlett, 1948). These symbolic capabilities appear at about the time that the child learns to organize his vocalizations into grammatical forms rather than uttering words as independent units.

Maturational changes wrought in behavior patterning and learning are by no means complete in infancy or in the preschool years but continue to occur for many years. However, the course of perceptual-motor development is poorly charted for children of school age although there may be maturational changes of utmost significance to the child who is attempting to learn the basic educational skills.

The existence of a critical period of space-organized feedback control late in childhood was revealed by a developmental study of response to different conditions of visual displacement (Smith and Greene, 1963).

A number of boys ranging in age from nine-and-a-half to thirteen-and-a-half years were asked to perform writing tasks with televised feedback, as described in Chapters 14 and 15, when the televised image was either normally oriented, reversed, inverted, or both reversed and inverted. The subjects were asked to write in a compensatory fashion so that the characters always appeared upright in the monitor whatever the displacement condition.

The results of this study showed a very definite age differential in ability to perform the experimental tasks. Of fifteen boys aged nine through eleven, only one was able to perform under all feedback displacement conditions. In contrast, half of the boys aged twelve and thirteen performed successfully under all conditions and half of those who failed were able to perform under all but the inversion condition. The difference between the age groups was statistically significant.

These findings suggest that some maturational change occurs around twelve years of age affecting the spatial integrations of the sensorimotor systems so as to permit the child to perform compensatory movements in displaced fields. This critical period comes at about the same time as other significant changes in behavior development, including the stabilization of handedness and transport movement coordinations. This is roughly the age at which symbolic thinking develops, according to Piaget (1928), and at which concepts of social relationships are formed, according to Vinacke (1951). The possibility that maturation

of certain spatial integrations of the perceptual-motor system is related to the developing ability of the child to organize and use symbolic and abstract knowledge is of the highest importance in psychology and education.

Environmental Factors

Many studies dealing with the effects of sensory restriction and special stimulation in infancy support the assumption of cybernetic theory that early phases of behavior maturation require specific activation of receptor and sensorimotor control processes for their normal development. The earliest sensory restriction studies were of amphibia (Carmichael, 1926; Harrison, 1904; Matthews and Detwiler, 1926). They provided excellent evidence of the genetic determination of swimming patterns without revealing any detrimental effects of restriction. Later studies indicated, however, that response deficiencies might result if infant animals were raised in the dark (Goodman, 1932; Mowrer, 1936) or were restricted in their movements for too long a period in infancy (Dennis, 1941).

The classic study of sensory deprivation is that of Riesen (1950), who subjected infant chimpanzees to varying degrees of visual deprivation for periods up to sixteen months. His work showed that complete deprivation of visual stimulation or deprivation of pattern vision by fitting the animals with translucent goggles impaired development of the chimpanzees' visual coordinations and produced deficiencies that lasted at least for some months. One animal that was permitted normal vision for one-and-a-half hours each day suffered no ill effects. Analogous results were found by

Nissen *et al.* (1951) in a study in which they enclosed the hands of infant chimpanzees in restricting containers for a period of time. Serious deficiencies in manipulative coordinations resulted. The inescapable conclusion is that normal space-organized perceptual-motor behavior is necessary for the functional maturation of the response systems.

The results of the sensory deprivation studies complement in various ways clinical observations of children whose vision has been impaired from infancy by cataracts and restored later by surgery. Such children show deficiencies in visuomotor coordinations which take some time to overcome (Senden, 1932).

The method of sensory deprivation in infancy has been extended to studies of social isolation in puppies (Thompson and Melzack, 1956), monkeys (Harlow and Harlow, 1962; Harlow and Zimmerman, 1959; Mason, 1960), and other animals. Results of the various studies of infant animals lead to the general conclusion that early sensorimotor deprivation not only may arrest development of particular sensorimotor mechanisms but also may change and disturb adult motivation, emotional organization, and social behavior. It appears that an appropriate level of stimulation is necessary not only to provide opportunities for learning but also to maintain normal maturational development. An infant whose development is retarded in both its maturational and learning aspects may never catch up with the normal level.

The question remains as to whether these conclusions that are based primarily on animal research can be applied directly to human infantile development. Some relevant information comes from observations of infants in foundling homes and hospitals. The studies of Fischer (1952), Spitz (1945, 1946, 1951), and Spitz and Wolf (1946, 1949) revealed definite patterns of depression in infants separated from their mothers and placed in the socially deficient environments of homes and hospitals. Although the full significance of these isolation effects is not as yet clearly established (Pinneau, 1955), it seems likely that the observed emotional and motivational effects persist in these infants.

A physiological interpretation of the results of early deprivation turns on the specificity of the restrictive conditions and of their subsequent effects. The likelihood is that no one psychophysiological effect is responsible for the various kinds of deficiencies noted. Whereas specific sensorimotor restriction such as visual deprivation may retard the maturational growth and integration of specific sensori-neuromotor mechanisms, general social isolation may lead to an over-all condition very like our concept of stress. Heretofore, stress has been spoken of in psychology primarily in relation to conflict frustration and physiological deprivation, but it is possible that general sensory deprivation and social isolation also can produce stress reactions. Prolonged stress may impose developmental anomalies on animal and human infants as well as inducing emotional and motivational alterations in both infants and adults (Solomon, 1961).

Many studies have been carried out to determine the effects of special conditions of sensory experience in infancy.

The effect known as imprinting is the clearest result that has been induced experimentally. Newly hatched ducks, chicks, and other ground-nesting birds show a strong tendency to follow the first large moving object they see during the critical early period and continue to follow this same object as if it were the mother (Jaynes, 1956, 1957).

According to a summary by Denenberg (1962), a number of studies have shown that such extrinsic stimulation of infant rodents as shocking or handling reduces the emotionality scores of these animals when they are tested later in the open field, and it increases their aggressiveness with their peers. A moderate amount of extrinsic stimulation during infancy improved learning performance in later tests.

All of these studies of the effects of special stimulation on infant laboratory animals should be interpreted cautiously, for the animals usually are special inbred strains that are housed regularly in very restricted environments. That is, the "normal" life of a caged laboratory rat actually is a very restricted life, far removed from the living conditions of its wild cousins. Administering special forms of stimulation or permitting special kinds of activity may produce measurable effects because they help to alleviate the negative effects of the laboratory regime; in this sense, the studies are not directly applicable to animals and human babies developing in their normal habitat.

There is no clear evidence that special conditions of nursing, handling and other stimulation in human infancy alter later psychological make-up in any decisive way independently of intervening conditions. Human sensorimotor mecha-nisms mature so slowly that it is unlikely that specific movement integrations would be affected by special handling or stimulation, at least during the first year of life. Whether changes in general motivational and emotional make-up can be induced by special handling of human infants has not been determined. However, the evidence from the restriction studies indicates that human developmental needs are served best by conditions of diversified stimulation, much human contact, and varied activity for the developing infant and child.

CYBERNETIC CONCEPTS OF TEACHING AND TRAINING

A cybernetic interpretation of the developmental literature, taking into account the closed-loop nature of behavior and its self-regulating characteristics, suggests some definite ideas about teaching and training. We emphasize the idea that behavior is specialized and integrated in different ways at different periods of development and during the different phases of adaptive and meaningful learning.

We propose two broad training principles: that the individual at all ages should be aided in gaining control over his own actions in relation to the environment and over features of the environment as well, and that the teaching of specific skills or knowledge must be adjusted to the phase of development of the feedback-control mechanisms. Teaching and training design should be adjusted to the level of control already achieved and also should be sensitive to the potential changes in response organization that may come in due time through maturation.

Human Engineering
of Educational Design

Human engineering as an area of study grew out of the need to adjust technological design to human design for effective man-machine control. In the area of education, the problem is one of adjusting educational design to teaching needs. By educational design, we refer to the effectiveness of teaching tools, symbol design, and the rules of language as organizing devices for feedback control; we refer to the operational procedures of manipulating information and symbols in the schooling process. Educational design reflects the effectiveness of current teaching technology and language usage in the classroom.

Good educational design should be based on an understanding of the human individual as a feedback-regulated control system whose activities relating perceived stimulus patterns with patterns of motion have definite spatial, temporal, and kinetic properties. If an instrument or symbolic device or rule is to be incorporated into the control loop, its properties should be adjusted to human capabilities for greatest efficiency. Inasmuch as human design changes radically from infancy to adulthood, educational design must be adjusted to changing human needs.

Until the child is almost two, his instrumental actions are almost entirely transport in nature. He pushes, pulls, pounds, and throws before he can fit things together or balance a column of blocks. Because the finer control movements that will develop must be supported and directed by larger movements, it is important that the child have ample opportunity during this early period to develop postural and transport control in three-dimensional space. The first toys should be designed to enhance directional control but not to require fine manipulation.

One of the most significant aspects of early development is the emergence of thinking behavior along with related overt perceptual-motor coordinations. Almost as soon as he is able to learn anything, the child starts to acquire the symbolic tools of thought in the form of words, numbers, expressive movements, and graphic representation. In order to facilitate this cognitive development, we believe that children should be taught rules of grammar and syntax and how to manipulate information with symbols as soon as possible in their school experience. New visual techniques very likely are needed for this purpose.

Features of bilateral coordination and lateral dominance become established typically during the first few years of schooling, when the child is learning to read, to write, and to use numbers. The development of bilateral coordination in feedback control is basic to the use of many common tools, toys, and instruments, including marking tools, pencils, cutting and forming tools, and mechanical devices of various sorts such as steering toys. Such instruments can be used with limited efficiency early in this developmental phase; as handedness becomes stabilized, the control movements become more refined. In time more complex machines involving transformations in sensory feedback can be operated.

During this critical period of early education, the instruments used by children should be designed both for reactive and operational efficiency. That is, they should *fit* the child's hand or body and movement patterns as well as being suitable for the particular cutting, forming, marking, or other operation to be performed. In culturally standardized activities, such as writing, the design factors often are overlooked.

There is strong suggestive evidence that the early development of many symbolic skills, including mathematical operations, is related to the emergence of lateral dominance and patterns of bilateral coordination during childhood. Thinking involves many specialized forms of symbolic control, both verbal and nonverbal, that begin to appear during the period when bilateral control in psychomotor activities is developing. In our opinion, this correspondence reflects a common origin of symbolic control and complex psychomotor control in the development of the basic movement systems and their integration through both maturation and learning. Symbolic responses are differentiated out of direct responses; implicit symbolism is a refinement of overt symbolism. Thinking represents no radically new form of behavior organization or control but is differentiated gradually from other kinds of response.

There is evidence from developmental studies, particularly those of Piaget (1928, 1950, 1957), that patterns of symbolism and thought are not entirely the products of learning but depend as well on maturation. There is further evidence that symbolic learning may depend upon satisfactory development of the basic movement mechanisms of the body (Delay, 1963). A set of procedures worked out by Delacato (1963) and Doman in a rehabilitation center are based on this idea. These workers treat such problem cases as slow readers, stutterers, and brain-injured children by training them in the normal patterns of motor development in order: crawling, creeping, walking, and so on. Striking results have been reported on severely disabled and retarded children who gradually began to show normal psychomotor and symbolic behavior after having been trained painstakingly to creep, walk, and develop other bodily coordinations in their normal order of appearance. A significant procedure used by these therapists is dominance training: establishing lateral dominance of eye, hand, and foot by specific training practices. It has been reported that these rehabilitative practices—crawling, creeping, and dominance training—not only help children with obvious disorders but also improve academic aptitudes in normal school children. If confirmed, this finding would offer strong support to our idea of the dependence of symbolic abilities on firmly established psychomotor control.

Response Control with Feedback Perturbation

The increasing control that an individual develops over his own responses through maturation and learning is essentially a matter of establishing some stability of performance under widely varying conditions of sensory feedback. A response never is performed twice under exactly the same conditions. It is carried out under varied conditions of posture, with varied sensory conditions, with different movement systems, and with different instruments. Furthermore —and this is most important—a response must be performed under varying physiological conditions including tension and stress. The main function of practice and learning in behavior organization is to establish some response constancy in this diversity: to achieve control of performance with many kinds of feedback perturbation.

A basic principle of training is to perturb the feedback properties of response systematically in order to provide the learner with opportunities to extend his understanding and control of his own actions in relation to the environment. Common skills such as writing and drawing should be carried out with different instruments and using different parts of the body. These larger action patterns will extend his understanding and control of the letter forms and will facilitate the fine manipulative control which must be learned later in writing. Teaching writing, drawing, speaking, and reading with different conditions of space- and time-perturbed feedback very likely will enhance the child's ability to carry out the space- and time-patterned symbolic manipulations of arithmetic, mathematics, science, art, and engineering.

In addition to the sensorimotor variations and instrumental and symbolic transformations that provide a source of feedback perturbation, there is a less obvious source in the psychophysiological perturbation produced by reciprocal tremor of muscle groups and the rhythmic actions of the heart, respiratory system, digestive system and other internal organs. All of these variations disturb movement integrations and affect response control. Before the child gains explicit control over psychomotor tasks, he must learn to compensate for the rhythmic perturbations of sensory feedback produced by his own internal actions.

A major aspect of learning, which should be recognized in educational design, is achieving both general bodily and compensatory control over the perturbing effects of the emotional, respiratory, and heart actions on somatic motion. Many performances, in particular those involving machine operation, should be trained under conditions of stress as well as under more normal conditions to enable the individual to improve emergency control. The performing arts, especially musical performances which are dependent on breath control, need special training to perfect response patterns under many changes in physiological status. Competitive games, skill practice under competitive conditions, and other exercises that involve excitement and strain provide training in psychomotor control under conditions of physiological perturbation.

Diversity in Education

When it comes to general education—to the teaching of basic knowledge and skills that are to be used adaptively by the individual in countless different situations throughout life—there can be no simulation training as such. The best we can do for the learner is to provide him with a diversity of sensory experience and to encourage him to react in diverse ways. Supporting evidence for this point of view comes from the developmental literature. In view of the clearly detrimental effects of restricted sensory and social environments, we cannot afford to give a child anything less than broad opportunity for reacting variously to many different kinds of stimulation.

Our theoretical reason for encouraging diversity in educational techniques and opportunities is related to specialization of feedback control. An individual extends his knowledge, understanding, and control of the environment by responding to it under many varieties of perturbed feedback. In this way he establishes an ever-expanding accumulation of adaptive response patterns and stable symbolic meanings. In this way he transfers a learned response from one situation to another and recalls in one context a response learned in another.

In teaching children, it is important to provide diverse social contexts as well as to vary the sensorimotor response patterning. If symbolic behavior such as speech is learned principally with one or two persons, it tends to become specialized in relation to those persons and to have somewhat limited transfer value. Children should learn their educational skills in varying group structures as well as in varying sensorimotor contexts and under conditions of stress.

The implication of these ideas for educational design is that there is no one educational technique that is superior to a number of techniques used in an integrated fashion. A good teacher knows this intuitively, and varies the materials used and the procedures followed from day to day and from hour to hour. Textbooks, audiovisual aids, lectures, discussions, field trips, laboratory sessions, self-instruction programs, tests—all are used because all enhance the learner's control of knowledge and skill. A fact presented in many contexts becomes a response controlled under many patterns of feedback. It is learned more effectively because it can be manipulated in relation to many other facts and can be retrieved in many situations.

It is possible to marshal some evidence from educational research in support of this point of view. Some experiments designed to compare two techniques have found that the combination of the two produced the best learning. As one example, Vernon (1946) compared the value of films and film strips in teaching British seamen and found that even for specialized knowledge by far the most learning resulted when the two techniques were used in combination. Helliwell (1953) reported the same general result after a study comparing filmstrips and field trips as methods of teaching secondary school pupils knowledge of dairy and newspaper establishments. The combined techniques produced the best learning.

Other studies have indicated that the use of multiple textbooks promotes better reading and study skills and understanding of subject matter than a single textbook, although the advantage may not show up in specialized tests of learning. This result has been found in controlled investigations of learning in elementary schools (Causey, 1958; Schneider, 1958) where single textbooks often are customary. Most teachers of more advanced students would not question the value of multiple textbooks.

The need for diversity in educational materials and techniques is one that has not been met by machine teaching and self-instructional programs and constitutes perhaps their most serious limitation.

HUMAN MOTIVATION

Our main concern in this book has been the *how* of behavior—how it works —but there is still the question of *why?* Why does the individual respond? What moves him, energizes him, motivates him? The ramifications of these questions define another whole area of psychological study beyond the scope of our present discussion, but some brief statement should be made to clarify our general point of view about the nature of human motivation.

There are two aspects of behavior that must be considered in any discussion of motivation. First, organized behavior usually is oriented toward certain objects or features of the environment: it has directional characteristics. Second, behavior occurs at different levels of energy expenditure: responses vary in speed, rate, and intensity and with varying patterns of physiological involvement.

Homeostasis or Homeokinesis?

Psychological discussions of the nature of motivation often start with a description of the physiological concept of homeostasis and with good reason, for modern behavior theory is imbued with the doctrine of the steady state—the presumed tendency of the organism to return to equilibrium. Whatever homeostasis means in physiology, in psychology it means nothing at all. The living, responding organism is designed to respond, to be active rather than inactive, to be dynamic rather than static, to behave constantly until it achieves the pseudoequilibrium of death. Thus we have proposed a new term to characterize behavior: it is *homeokinetic* rather than homeostatic, for its organization depends on constant motion generated by the motion systems themselves.

Homeostatic thinking is reflected in some of the most basic concepts of orthodox psychology and has left its mark on theories of motivation as well

as on the standard theories of learning. Hull's (1943) drive-reduction theory serves to illustrate the prevailing point of view. The individual is motivated to respond by needs that contribute to a drive state and continues until he achieves drive-reduction by an appropriate response.

In our own theory of behavior organization, we do not, of course, deny the existence of physiological needs but we do deny their primary status as activating agents. The normal condition of the behaving individual is activity, and we need postulate no poorly defined drives or motives to account for it. The constant activity of the organism includes more than breathing, heart action, and other internal actions; it includes uninterrupted responses of the skeletal muscles as well. Reciprocal tremor movements of opposing muscle groups constantly perturb the sensory-feedback patterns registered by the receptors and thus generate the sensory data by means of which behavior patterns are regulated. These primary response patterns are activated not by generalized drive states but by conditions intrinsic to the response mechanism.

Given an individual in a normal state of feedback-regulated activity, we assume that his directional patterns and levels of energy expenditure can be defined in part by such extrinsic factors as tissue needs, chemical and hormonal agents, disease, and so on. However, these are not the only factors that define motivation nor are they necessarily the most important ones. For as behavior develops from infancy through adulthood, its directional patterns—that is, the goals around which it is organized—are derived in large part from the perceptual-motor activities themselves. Thus we believe that the most significant features of human motivation are defined by the developing patterns of perceptual-motor response.

Perceptual-Motor Origins of Motivation

The established notion that patterns of motivation are derived originally from physiological drives has hindered our understanding of these patterns in human individuals. The orientation of human behavior often seems to bear no relation to vegetative needs or satisfactions, yet traditional theories assume that such motivational patterns are secondary or learned or derived but in any case stem originally from biological need.

In recent years, there have been attempts to modify this physiological description of motivation. It no longer can be overlooked that many animals including man are normally active or playful and exhibit many responses organized with respect to the perceptual environment that appear to serve no biological purpose. Further it has been demonstrated experimentally that animals will learn new responses when their only reward is perceptual-motor activity. Results of this sort posed a problem, for standard learning theory assumes that behavior reorganization is defined by a need that is satisfied or a drive that is reduced. Consequently, the concepts of drive and motivation have been extended to include perceptual motivation and activity motivation.

We would modify these ideas still further for it is our belief that the perceptual-motor aspects of motivated behavior are not separate drives but rather

are definitive components of all motivational patterns. Even behavior that directly or indirectly satisfies a biological need derives its specific organization from the perceptual-motor patterns that develop through maturation and learning. In the human adult, goals, aspirations, and the relative effort expended in different activities reflect the course of behavior development in that individual and for the most part are but remotely related to tissue needs.

The motivational aspect of perceptual-motor behavior originates in the directional patterns of response that serve to orient the infant toward certain stimulus features of his environment. His developing visuomotor system orients his eyes toward lights, faces, and objects. Later he can direct his whole body toward environmental features and move toward them or away from them. He can grasp an object with his hand or kick it with his foot. A child seems to become attached to his parents and siblings, but only because they are there in his sensory environment consistently enough for him to specialize his responses toward them. The human infant's orienting behavior is not as rigidly defined as that of the newly hatched duckling which is imprinted upon the first large moving object that appears, but the organizational principle is the same in both cases. Directional patterns are a function of the developing response systems and need not be attributed to physiological drive states.

Some of the people and objects toward which the infant orients serve to satisfy his biological needs, and this relationship helps to establish the goal-seeking nature of his responses. However, we believe that it is a mistake to assume that the drive-goal situation is the primary factor organizing the response. The integration of response patterns with more or less specific physiological conditions such as hunger and thirst does not explain how a response originally developed but only how it is used on occasion. For example, if a cracker is offered to an infant for the first time, he will grasp it and very likely bring it to his mouth. He would do the same with any small object. The fact that the cracker tastes good and disintegrates in his mouth helps to specialize his responses to this type of small object and also helps to establish it as a goal or an incentive when he is hungry, but this is a secondary effect. The baby originally grasps the cracker and brings it to his mouth because this is the way his movement systems have developed. The drive-reduction or reinforcing state of affairs that results from tasting or eating the cracker does not organize the response to the cracker, although it may have something to do with when and how often it is performed.

As the child develops, his motivational patterns continue to be structured more by his own movement systems and by the social and physical design of his environment than by the physiological needs of his body. Most of the significant events in an individual's life after infancy are related either to the use of tools, instruments, and devices or to specific social interactions. This social and cultural context defines goals and aspirations, sets performance standards, and establishes patterns of work and living.

Within a particular culture or social context, certain types of behavior are used by adults and are taught to the young either directly or indirectly because of their intrinsic utility—that is, because they are useful to the individual in adapting to the organization of his society. The significant patterns of response used by human individuals throughout their lifetime are selected not because they lead directly to vegetative rewards but because they enable the individual to fulfill his roles within the family, place of work, recreational groupings, and so on. Thus the utility of a response pattern is defined by the tools and equipment, symbol systems, institutional structures, and materials of consumption of contemporary society.

The child in school no less than the adult at work experiences utility only in some context of behavior that is intrinsically organized or specialized by the tools, materials, and symbolic processes of his culture. Meaning emerges for him as he establishes feedback control in specific situations related to the larger aspects of complex human systems, and his appreciation of the utility of his knowledge expands as he extends his organized feedback control to encompass more complicated space and time concepts and more specialized techniques of simplifying, reducing, transposing, reordering, and creating information. For the human learner in school, utility and satisfaction emerge not from extraneous rewards but from the intrinsic coherence of logical knowledge and skilled activities—from the correctness of solutions, from the validity of concepts, or from the esthetic balance of artistic efforts.

Interesting support for these ideas comes from a series of experiments by Smedslund (1961) in which children were taught logical concepts about the conservation of substance and weight.

He described the process of cognitive development as one of gradual formation of self-reinforcing structures that are not dependent on external reinforcement of large numbers of separate responses. Smedslund tested the children to see whether their learned concepts would extinguish as an operant conditioned response does when the reinforcement is withheld. He "cheated" the children by carrying out deceptive demonstrations purporting to show that the conservation of substance does not always hold true. However, instead of rejecting the logically consistent concept that they had learned, the children looked for a way out so that they would not have to believe the false demonstrations. In other words, their cognitive structure, once it was established, did not yield easily to an illogical demonstration.

Because the utility and meaning of human behavior are defined by the organizational context, the utility of any mode of response changes as a result of developmental changes in tools, symbol systems, and social structures. As new human systems develop, new modes of response become useful and certain older behavior patterns decline in utility. Currently we are entering an age when computing devices are being used ever more widely to integrate numerical and verbal communication. These machines and the technological systems they control make certain newly evolving patterns of behavior—for example, the use of computer language—enormously useful because they fit the design of the systems; at the same time, many older patterns of response are becoming obsolete just as surely as the Stone-Age skill of flaking arrowheads became obsolete. Thus the utility of behavior is not a random effect but is a selective process defined by the evolutionary differentiation, specialization, and integration of human systems.

The most general trend in human motivational patterns, however, is defined neither by biological satisfactions nor by biosocial utility but by man's nearly universal drive to exercise control over his environment and over his own behavior in relation to that environment. Theories of learning based on physiological drives and extrinsic rewards never have been able to account for motivated acts of creation, of discovery, of seeking, and of volition in individual behavior. Sensory-feedback theory sees their genesis in the young child's persisting efforts to exercise direct control over his own sources of stimulation. Obstinate behavior in the two-year-old may achieve neither utility nor extrinsic reward, but it gives the child a certain measure of control. Often he is more interested in doing things in his own way—that is, as he can control them—than he is in attaining social approval or extrinsic reward offered for some other mode of response.

The drive to control the environment is not confined to human individuals but has been described in animals as well. According to Kavanau (1964), wild rodents subjected to the artificial restrictions of laboratory regimes will for a time seize almost any means of controlling their environment that does not lead to great stress. If they have switches to manipulate or levers to press, they will manipulate and press even though the resulting effects are not particularly desirable to rodents. Given a switch that operates an activity wheel, a rat will turn it on when the experimenter turns it off and turn it off when the experimenter turns it on. If the experimenter turns a light on, the animal will turn it off; if the experimenter turns it off, the animal will turn it on even though it is a nocturnal species and presumably prefers the dark. These observations offer an explanation for certain paradoxical results in animal experiments which have seemed to indicate that stimuli that are rewarding under some circumstances are punishing under others. When the animal's primary motivation is to exercise control, the extrinsic effects often are of secondary importance.

The importance to a human individual of exercising feedback control should be recognized in all training and teaching situations. With too little guidance, a learner may lose interest by not being able to establish any significant degree of control over a task. On the other hand, too much guidance also deprives him of personal control. The goal is to enable the learner to establish his own patterns of control over tasks, skills, and knowledge that have social utility lest he turn his attention to less desirable activities.

The degree to which the individual can gain definitive control over the many different static and dynamic sources of stimulus feedback in his physical and social environment varies, of course, with his behavioral and symbolic capacities. As development proceeds, the intelligent child achieves more and more control not only over specific stimulus sources but over the pattern of his own behavior in relation to physical and social environmental demands. In other words, he develops motivated self-control, and this process of achieving self-discipline is one of extending pri-

mary forms of sensory-feedback control to the regulation of his own activity by symbolic means. Treating the individual as a control system implies that at all levels of learning he is also a self-governing system. When we understand in more detail the space and time organization of feedback control of response, we shall begin to understand how the individual functions as a self-governing system that to some degree controls its own destiny.

EVOLUTION OF EDUCATIONAL DESIGN

As we pointed out early in the book, there are a number of interesting parallels between the ontogenetic development of the human individual and the evolutionary development of the human species. The over-all pattern in both cases is one of increasing control of the environment, proceeding from gross patterns of control involving dynamic transport and tool-using movements to finer and finer patterns involving manipulative control and symbol systems. The symbolic tools of thought emerge in roughly the same order in the child and in the human race. Spatial concepts of position, size, and shape precede temporal concepts. The young child is limited as was his prehistoric ancestor in having no real sense of time or of temporal order of events and thus no real appreciation of history or of causative sequences. The developing understanding of temporal organization is followed by complicated machine skills and abstract concepts of relationships and interactions.

In the development of the species as in the development of the individual, it is impossible to differentiate between the effects of genetic and environmental factors. Just as the individual at any time is a product of the maturation-learning interaction, the status of the species at any point in history or prehistory reflects both the level of genetic evolution and the cultural and technological context in which the young develop and are educated. Whether man today is genetically superior to his ancestors of 10,000 years ago or 5000 years ago or 2000 years ago is an academic question unlikely to be resolved to every one's satisfaction. But it is unquestionably true that man's culture and intelligence and ability to learn are organized at more complex levels as time goes on. This upward spiral involves interacting changes in social organization, technological development, and human design. Advances in one sphere are both causes and effects of advances in other spheres.

As a result of these reciprocal relationships, human design is a function of educational design, and human learning is understood best in its educational setting. This is the theme with which we introduced the book: that the significant patterns of human learning are determined by the level of development of educational skills and by the design of human symbol systems. The theoretical basis for this idea is the sensory-feedback concept of behavior organization, which provides an objective interpretation of biosocial development of educational design and the evolution of man's intelligent behavior.

In contrast to this cybernetic concept of learning, conventional association theories have but limited relevance to human education because they incorporate no generally valid concepts of educational design. The designs for learning

which have originated in learning laboratories have yielded many so-called categories of learning—classical conditioning, operant conditioning, rote-verbal learning, psychomotor learning, problem solving, and more—but they have provided no systematic understanding of the sensorimotor factors which define behavioral control in an educational setting. Cybernetic theory postulates that all of these various learning categories represent different conditions and transformations of feedback control, and that human education can be designed according to the same general cybernetic principles that govern other instances of learning change.

The failure of conventional learning theories to generate successful concepts of educational design stems from their signal lack of success in accounting for efficiency and precision in behavioral control processes. According to these theories, we are supposed to believe that the high degree of precision and efficiency achieved in speech, in writing, in reading, in mathematics, in technology, and in artistic production are learned on the basis of vaguely defined temporal contiguities or rewards and punishments which by chance are associated with particular response systems. In contrast, cybernetic theory postulates that precision and efficiency of biological and behavioral control can be attributed to the objectively defined and infinitely variable sensory-feedback patterns in terms of which behavior is regulated. Furthermore, cybernetic theory postulates that precision of response control has increased in human evolution as an aspect of evolving educational design. Man has increased the accuracy, delicacy, and effectiveness of his control systems through the evolution of tools and symbols which systematically enhance his potentialities for closed-loop regulation of adaptive response.

A fundamental cybernetic concept is that human evolution and history have produced progressive instrumental and symbolic transformations of feedback control of behavior which determine educational design and result in related increases in human intelligence. The progress of man from a hominoid using an eolithic tool through the phases of hand-ax culture, early tool making, the handicraft tradition, the development of language, the emergence of civilized order, the development of writing, and the discovery of history and of temporal causation can be considered in terms of these progressive elaborations of the feedback control of behavior. Each of these broad changes and traditions can be thought of as representing another level of transformation of sensory-feedback control of the behavioral environment. Each phase demanded a somewhat different pattern of behavioral control and of learning, but at the same time each extended the learner's ability to control the environment and his relation to it in time and in space. Civilization developed when the first glimmerings of a time-extended process of man's destiny were represented geometrically in the cities of temples and tombs that marked the life and after-life sojourn of the king-gods who owned all the land and all the people. The accumulation of written information gradually modified this space-ordered concept of the world and of the hereafter to an appreciation of history and temporal causation, thus establishing the basis of scientific reasoning and discovery.

In this human factors account, human evolution is seen as involving the progressive establishment of specialized patterns of instrumental and symbolic behavior, each of which transforms in some distinctive way the primary sensory-feedback effects of overt behavior. Tool using not only changed man's body form, but it also developed new patterns of overt reaction in controlling the environment. The tool-making tradition did more than create technology; it altered man's mechanisms of learning by changing the modes of reaction and the patterns of stimulation in both primary sensorimotor activities and in complex motivated patterns of behavior. Besides producing diverse tools, the handicraft tradition also involved the development of cave drawing, tool marking, and the use of spoken tribal languages. The temple-tomb traditions created the beginnings of civilization and in this process laid the foundations for written symbolization, the concepts of the calendar and of time, and the first notions of time-ordered historical destiny of man. This expansion of feedback control is still going on. In our contemporary technological culture, complex machines and symbol systems provide new means of environmental control and at the same time enhance human understanding of relationships and interactions among environmental events.

The advancing forefront of human knowledge and conceptual ability means that each succeeding generation must cover more ground in order to be educated. Secondary school pupils today handle concepts and symbol systems that top scientists a few generations ago had not even dreamed of. To do its job effectively, our educational system needs more than teachers and books. It needs all the technological and symbolic machinery that mediates the new knowledge. It needs all the avenues of verbal and nonverbal communication that have been developed. For the machines and techniques of society are more than the fruits of man's knowledge; they are the means of communicating specialized knowledge and skills and the tools for generating new knowledge, skills, techniques, and machines.

Current changes going on in the educational domain sometimes are referred to as a *revolution* in education. Actually, it is not a revolution at all but an inevitable evolution of educational design generated by reciprocal feedback relationships with human, technological, and social development. The school and the educational process are not isolated events in the elaboration of man's organized system; they are essential parts of every sector of this development. The elementary school cannot limit itself to the three R's any more than advanced study can be designed completely around a set of great books. Each level of education must adjust to organizational changes and developments in every facet of human society. Education must reflect technological as well as communicative changes and social as well as human behavioral changes if it is to play its role in the progressive evolution of human culture.

The main challenge in the science of human learning is to understand the requirements of educational design at all levels—that is, in providing feedback control to initiate learning, in designing tools and symbolic processes to integrate individual development with social-cultural evolution, and in simulating human organization to provide specialized pragmatic experience. The challenge of education is to maintain its role as the mediator of human progress. Education must keep pace with intellectual and technological change for it is the means of conserving and consolidating such change. Only by passing on his educational skills can man escape the space-ordered world of his sensory environment into the abstractions of scientific and creative thought.

SUMMARY

1. Educational design must be adjusted to all aspects of developmental change in the individual and not just learning change.

2. The earlier idea that genetic and environmental influences in behavior could be separated is no longer acceptable; both maturation and learning are functions of genetic-environmental interactions.

3. There are critical periods in development for the emergence of certain types of behavior patterns if appropriate environmental conditions obtain at that time.

4. Behavior differentiation throughout life is influenced by different aspects of development—growth, maturation, reactive learning, instrumental learning, and symbolic learning—each of which exerts its major influence and levels off at a different time of life.

5. Fetal behavior follows a course from general to more specific response patterns. After birth, the infant displays another sequence of development from general postural movements, through large transport movements, to finer manipulative movements, all of which

are organized with respect to exteroceptive stimulation.

6. Learning does not begin to play a significant role in human development until toward the end of the first year of life, when the infant begins to control his environment with specific responses.

7. Primary space-organized perceptual-motor coordinations are defined by maturation, not learning. A demonstration of unlearned spatial control of behavior is the response of human and animal infants to the *visual cliff*.

8. Young infants control their perceptual environment by their ability to use postural and transport movements for directional orientation and motion. As a rule, they do not develop refined manipulative control until late in the second year. Somewhat later they are able to use symbolic control in delayed reactions and similar tasks.

9. During the early years of schooling, children develop bimanual control and stabilize their lateral dominance. Along with these abilities come more complicated spatial integrations and the ability to formulate and use abstract concepts.

10. Both specific sensory deprivation and more general social isolation in infancy are detrimental to normal development.

11. Two broad educational principles are to help the learner gain control over his own actions in relation to the environment, and to adjust educational designs and schedules to the learner's pattern of development.

12. Educational design should follow human engineering principles of adapting the operational situation to the design of the human learner as it changes in development.

13. Through maturational and learning changes, the individual gains increasing control over his own responses. This is mainly a matter of establishing stability of responses under many conditions of feedback perturbation.

14. General knowledge and skills should be taught under a wide variety of feedback conditions with many materials and techniques to help the learner achieve broad understanding and control, and stable learned patterns.

15. Feedback theory of behavior organization rejects homeostatic concepts of motivation in favor of homeokinetic —that is, conforming to the idea that activity is the normal state of the behaving individual. This interpretation does not attribute all motivation to extrinsic drive states, for it is believed that energizing processes are intrinsic to the behavior patterns themselves.

16. The most significant aspects of human motivation derive from perceptual-motor behavior as seen originally in the directional responses of infants. Directional patterns can be specialized by learning both with respect to biological needs and to biosocial utility. The latter changes with the evolution of new tools, machines, symbols, and human systems and thus is defined by the social context.

17. Children in school are motivated by the biosocial utility of response patterns just as adults are. But perhaps the most general characteristic of human motivation is the drive to exercise control over the environment, which may take precedence over other rewards and satisfactions even in animals. As the individual develops feedback control of spatial relationships, progressing to control of temporal, kinetic, symbolic, and

abstract relationships, he becomes in effect a self-governing system.

18. The human species evolved along with human technology, symbol systems, and social institutions, with advances in one sphere benefiting from and contributing to advances in other spheres.

19. Human learning is understood best in its educational setting, where human design interacts with the accumulated cultural and technological knowledge and skills of the race to generate new levels of knowledge and skill and of technological and social progress.

References and Author Index

Abbott Laboratories. Flickering television and epilepsy. *What's new,* 1961, No. 225, 10–11. [162]

Adams, J. A. Motor skills. *Ann. Rev. Psychol.,* 1964, **15,** 181–202. [209]

Adamson, R. E. Functional fixedness as related to problem solving: a repetition of three experiments. *J. exp. Psychol.,* 1952, **44,** 288–291. [43]

AERA-APA-DAVI Joint Committee on Programed Instruction and Teaching Machines. Teaching machine guidelines: a joint statement. *Aud.-vis. Instruction,* 1961, **6,** 358–359. [275]

AERA-APA-DAVI Joint Committee on Programed Instruction and Teaching Machines. Criteria for assessing programed instructional materials. *Aud.-vis. Instruction,* 1963, **8,** 84–89. [275]

Agricola, G. *De re metallica.* (Trans. by H. C. Hoover and L. H. Hoover.) London: Mining Magazine, 1912. [76, 105]

Allen, M. J., P. M. Fitts, and A. J. Slivinske. *A moving target optical projector for use in air traffic control research.* USAF Wright Air Dev. Cent. tech. Rep. 53–417, 1954. [186]

Allen, W. H. Research on film use: class preparation. *Aud.-vis. Commun. Rev.,* 1955, **3,** 183–196. [147]

Allen, W. H. Research on film use: student participation. *Aud.-vis. Commun. Rev.,* 1957, **5,** 423–450. [146]

Almstead, F. E. Television can serve education. *N.Y. State Educ.,* 1957, **45,** 18–21; 70. [150]

Alter, M., and R. E. Silverman. The response in programed instruction. *J. progr. Instruction,* 1962, **1**(1), 55–78. [313]

Ammons, C. H., and R. B. Ammons. Bilateral transfer of rotary pursuit skill. *Amer. Psychologist,* 1951, **6,** 294. [428]

Ammons, R. B. Effects of knowledge of performance: a survey and tentative theoretical formulation. *J. gen. Psychol.,* 1956, **54,** 279–299. [204, 206]

Ammons, R. B. See also Ammons, C. H., 1951.

Amsel, A. Error responses and reinforcement schedules in self-instructional devices. In A. A. Lumsdaine and R. Glaser (eds.), *Teaching machines and programmed learning: a source book.* Washington, D.C.: National Education Association, 1960, pp. 506–516. [291]

Angell, D., and A. A. Lumsdaine. Prompted and unprompted trials versus prompted trials only in paired-associate learning. In A. A. Lumsdaine (ed.), *Student response in programmed instruction.* Washington, D.C.: National Academy of Sciences, National Research Council, 1961, pp. 389–398. [321]

Angell, G. W., and M. E. Troyer. A new self-scoring test device for improving instruction. *Sch. and Soc.,* 1948, **67,** 84–85. [248]

Annett, J. Learning a pressure under conditions of immediate and delayed knowledge of results. *Quart. J. exp. Psychol.,* 1959, **11,** 3–15. [206, 386]

Annett, J., and H. Kay. Knowledge of results and skilled performance.

Occup. Psychol., 1957, **31,** 69–79. [206]

Ansell, S. D. *See* Smith, K. U., 1964.

Arbuckle, D. A., and T. Gordon. *Industrial counseling.* Boston: Bellman, 1949. [238]

Arnheim, R. What do the eyes contribute? *Aud.-vis. Commun. Rev.*, 1962, **10**(5), 10–21. [165]

Aronson, A. E. *See* Irwin, J. V., 1958.

Ash, P., and N. Jaspen. *The effects and interactions of rate of development, repetition, participation and room illumination on learning from a rear-projected film.* USN Spec. Dev. Cent. tech. Rep. 269-7-39, 1953. [146]

Atkinson, C. J. *See* Goldiamond, I., 1962.

Bain, A. *The senses and the intellect.* (3d ed.) New York: Appleton, 1879. [43]

Bales, R. F. How people interact in conferences. *Sci. Amer.*, 1955, **192**(3), 31–35. [229]

Banta, T. J. Attitudes toward a programed text: "The analysis of behavior" compared with "A textbook of psychology." *Aud.-vis. Commun. Rev.*, 1963, **11,** 227–240. [302, 303]

Barlow, H. B., and R. M. Hill. Selective sensitivity to direction of movement in ganglion cells of the rabbit retina. *Science,* 1963, **139,** 412–414. [355]

Barron, F. *Some test correlates of response to psychotherapy.* Berkeley, Calif.: Institute of Personality Assessment and Research, 1956. [237]

Barrow, L. C., Jr. *See* Westley, B. H., 1959.

Bartlett, S. C. *See* Hunter, W. S., 1948.

Basic Systems, Incorporated. Present and emerging needs for job training. In S. Margulies and L. D. Eigen (eds.), *Applied programed instruc-*

tion. New York: Wiley, 1962, pp. 161–188. [223]

Bavelas, A. A mathematical model for group structures. *Appl. Anthropol.*, 1948, **7,** 16–30. [229]

Bavelas, A. Communication patterns in task-oriented groups. *J. acoust. Soc. Amer.*, 1950, **22,** 725–730. [229]

Beals, A. *See* Cline, V. B., 1956.

Beck, J. On some methods of programming. In E. Galanter (ed.), *Automatic teaching: the state of the art.* New York: Wiley, 1959, pp. 55–62. [286]

Beckmann, J. *A history of inventions, discoveries, and origins.* (4th ed.) (Trans. by W. Johnston; rev. and enlarged by W. Francis and J. W. Griffith.) London: Bohn, 1846, 2 vols. [73, 75, 97, 106]

Beer, M., R. M. Jayson, V. E. Carter, and F. H. Kresse. *Survey of escape training in the air force.* USAF Wright Air Dev. Div. tech. Rep. 60-792, 1961. [183]

Berlyne, D. E. *Conflict, arousal, and curiosity.* New York: McGraw-Hill, 1960. [46, 215]

Besnard, G. G., L. J. Briggs, and E. S. Walker. *The improved Subject-Matter Trainer.* USAF Armament Sys. Personnel Res. Lab. tech. Memo. 55-11, 1955. [250]

Bilger, R. C. *See* Goldiamond, I., 1962.

Bilodeau, E. A., and I. McD. Bilodeau. Motor-skills learning. *Ann. Rev. Psychol.*, 1961, **12,** 243–280. [206, 425]

Bilodeau, I. McD. *See* Bilodeau, E. A., 1961.

Birt, A. T. *See* Feldhusen, J. F., 1962, 1962.

Black, B. J. The protected workshop. In M. Greenblatt and B. Simon (eds.), *Rehabilitation of the mentally ill.*

Washington, D.C.: AAAS, 1959, pp. 199–211. [242]

Black, J. W. The effect of delayed side-tone upon vocal rate and intensity. *J. speech hear. Dis.*, 1951, **16**, 56–60. [368]

Black, J. W. Systematic research in experimental phonetics: II. Signal reception: intelligibility and side-tone. *J. speech hear. Dis.*, 1954, **19**, 140–146. [368]

Bloom, R. *See* Smith, K. U., 1956.

Blyth, J. W. Programs: an aid to balanced instruction. *Aud.-vis. Instruction*, 1963, **8**, 76–79. [324]

Bobren, H. M., and S. L. Siegel. Student attitudes towards closed-circuit instructional television. *Aud.-vis. Commun. Rev.*, 1960, **8**, 124–128. [149]

Bonawitz, B. *See* Krumboltz, J. D., 1962.

Borgatta, E. F. *See* Meyer, H. J., 1959.

Boring, E. G. *A history of experimental psychology.* New York: Appleton, 1929. [27]

Bossone, R. M. *See* Markle, S. M., 1963.

Bouman, H. D. *See* Stetson, R. H., 1933.

Brandon, J. R. The relative effectiveness of lecture, interview and discussion methods of presenting factual information on television. Unpublished doctoral dissertation, Univ. of Wisconsin, 1955. [140]

Bray, C. W. Transfer of learning. *J. exp. Psychol.*, 1928, **11**, 443–467. [407]

Brayfield, A. H., and W. H. Crockett. Employee attitudes and employee performance. *Psychol. Bull.*, 1955, **52**, 396–424. [304]

Bridgman, M. *See* Smith, K. U., 1943.

Briggs, G. E., and J. C. Naylor. The relative efficiency of several training methods as a function of transfer task complexity. *J. exp. Psychol.*, 1962, **64**, 505–512. [426]

Briggs, G. E. *See also* Naylor, J. C., 1963.

Briggs, L. J. Intensive classes for superior students. *J. educ. Psychol.*, 1947, **38**, 207–215. [248, 323]

Briggs, L. J. *A trouble-shooting trainer for the E-4 fire control system.* USAF Personnel Train. Res. Cent. dev. Rep. TN 56-94, 1956. [245, 250, 260]

Briggs, L. J. Two self-instructional devices. *Psychol. Rep.*, 1958, **4**, 671–676. [245, 250, 260, 279]

Briggs, L. J. Teaching machines for training of military personnel in maintenance of electronic equipment. In E. Galanter (ed.), *Automatic teaching: the state of the art.* New York: Wiley, 1959, pp. 131–145. [297]

Briggs, L. J. Prompting and confirmation conditions for three learning tasks employing the Subject-Matter Trainer. In A. A. Lumsdaine (ed.), *Student response in programmed instruction.* Washington, D.C.: National Academy of Sciences, National Research Council, 1961, pp. 375–387. [322]

Briggs, L. J. The probable role of teaching machines in classroom practice. *Theor. Pract.*, 1962, **1**, 47–56. [325]

Briggs, L. J., R. A. Goldbeck, V. N. Campbell, and D. G. Nichols. Experimental results regarding form of response, size of step, and individual differences in automated programs. In J. E. Coulson (ed.), *Programmed learning and computer-based instruction.* New York: Wiley, 1962, pp. 86–98. [314, 315, 316, 325]

Briggs, L. J. *See also* Besnard, G. G., 1955; Irion, A. L., 1957.

Brogden, W. J. Sensory pre-conditioning. *J. exp. Psychol.*, 1939, **25**, 323–332. [34]

Brooks, G. W. *See* Chittick, R. A., 1961.

Brown, G. G. Perception of depth with disoriented vision. *Brit. J. Psychol.*, 1928, **19**, 117–146. [373]

Brown, J. S. *See* Cantor, J. H., 1956.

Bryan, G. L., and J. W. Rigney. *An evaluation of a method for shipboard training in operations knowledge.* USN Off. Naval Res., Psychol. Sci. Div., Personnel Train. Br., tech. Rep. 18, 1956. [319]

Bryan, G. L., and D. H. Schuster. *An experimental comparison of troubleshooting training techniques.* USN Off. Naval Res., Psychol. Sci. Div., Personnel Train. Br., tech. Rep. 30, 1959. [319]

Bryan, W. L., and N. Harter. Studies on the telegraphic language. The acquisition of a hierarchy of habits. *Psychol. Rev.*, 1899, **6**, 345–375. [41]

Buckhout, R. *See* Hood, P. D., 1960.

Buel, J. The linear maze. I. "Choice-point expectancy," "correctness," and the goal gradient. *J. comp. Psychol.*, 1934, **17**, 185–199. [24]

Bugelski, B. R. *The psychology of learning.* New York: Holt, Rinehart and Winston, 1956. [45]

Butterworth, B. (ed.) *The growth of industrial art.* Washington, D.C.: U.S. Government Printing Office, 1892. [68, 72, 73, 78, 96]

Butts, G. K. *See* Wendt, P. R., 1962.

Cahill, H. E. *See* Gustafson, H. W., 1960.

Callewaert, H. For easy and legible handwriting. In V. E. Herrick (ed.), *New horizons for research in handwriting.* Madison: Univ. of Wisconsin Press, 1963, pp. 39–52. [387]

Cambria, R. *See* Smith, K. U., 1964.

Campbell, V. N. *See* Briggs, L. J., 1962; Goldbeck, R. A., 1962.

Cantor, J. H., and J. S. Brown. *An evaluation of the Trainer-Tester and Punchboard-Tutor as electronics troubleshooting training aids.* USN Spec. Dev. Cent. tech. Rep. NTDC-1257-2-1, 1956. [249]

Carmichael, L. The development of behavior in vertebrates experimentally removed from the influence of external stimulation. *Psychol. Rev.*, 1926, **33**, 51–58. [464]

Carpenter, C. R., L. P. Greenhill *et al. An investigation of closed-circuit television for teaching university courses. Report No. 1.* University Park, Pa.: Pennsylvania State Univ., 1955. [148]

Carpenter, C. R., L. P. Greenhill *et al. An investigation of closed-circuit television for teaching university courses. Report No. 2.* University Park, Pa.: Pennsylvania State Univ., 1958. [148]

Carr, W. J. *Self-instructional devices: a review of current concepts.* USAF Wright Air Dev. Cent. tech. Rep. 59–503, 1959. [278, 286, 290]

Carroll, J. E. Final report and recommendations concerning 1957 experiments with television conducted at USAES. Unpublished report, Fort Belvoir, Va., 1957. [154]

Carter, R. F. *The perceived appeals of television program content.* Univ. of Wis. Telev. Lab. res. Bull. 8, 1957. [162]

Carter, R. F. *See also* Stanley, R. J., 1955.

Carter, T. F. *The invention of printing in China and its spread westward.* (Rev. ed.) New York: Columbia Univ. Press, 1931. [96, 100, 101, 102]

Carter, V. E. *See* Beer, M., 1961.

Causey, M. E. A comparative study of reading growth: enriched versus a limited program of instruction. *Dissertation Abstr.*, 1958, **18,** 956. (Abstract) [470]

Cave, R. T. *See* Hood, P. D., 1960.

Chall, J. S., and H. E. Dial. Predicting listener understanding and interest in newscasts. *Educ. Res. Bull.*, 1948, **27,** 141–153; 168. [140]

Chamberlain, P. L. *Whither educational broadcasting?* Syracuse, N.Y.: General Electric Company, 1959. [159]

Chard, R. D., and B. D. Schwartz. A new modified concept formation test. *Amer. Psychologist*, 1947, **2,** 274–275. [44]

Chase, R. A., S. Harvey, S. Standfast, I. Rapin, and S. Sutton. Studies on sensory feedback: I. Effect of delayed auditory feedback on speech and keytapping. *Quart. J. exp. Psychol.*, 1961, **13,** 141–152. [368]

Chase, R. A., I. Rapin, L. Gilden, S. Sutton, and G. Guilfoyle. Studies on sensory feedback: II. Sensory feedback influences on keytapping motor tasks. *Quart. J. exp. Psychol.*, 1961, **13,** 153–167. [369]

Chase, R. A., S. Sutton, I. Rapin, S. Standfast, and S. Harvey. *Sensory feedback influences on motor performance.* Communications Lab., Columbia Univ. and Dep. Biometrics Res., State of N.Y., res. Rep., 1959. [368, 370, 371]

Cherry, C., and B. McA. Sayers. Experiments upon the total inhibition of stammering by external control and some clinical results. *J. psychosom. Res.*, 1956, **1,** 233–246. [402]

Chittick, R. A., G. W. Brooks, F. S. Irons, and W. N. Deane. *The Vermont story: rehabilitation of chronic schizophrenic patients.* Burlington, Vt.: Queen City Printers, 1961. [241]

Chow, K. L. *See* Nissen, H. W., 1951.

Cline, V. B., A. Beals, and D. Seidman. *Evaluation of four-week and eight-week basic training for men of various intelligence levels.* Hum. Resources Res. Off., George Washington Univ., tech. Rep. 32, 1956. [151]

Coch, L., and J. R. P. French, Jr. Overcoming resistance to change. *Hum. Relat.*, 1948, **1,** 512–532. [229]

Cohen, J. S. Employer attitudes toward hiring mentally retarded individuals. *Amer. J. ment. Deficiency*, 1963, **67,** 705–713. [242]

Cohen, M. *La grande invention de l'écriture et son évolution.* Paris: Imprimerie Nationale, 1958. [87, 91, 94]

Conrad, R., and B. A. Hille. A decay theory of immediate memory and paced stimuli. *Canad. J. Psychol.*, 1958, **12,** 1–6. [446]

Cook, J. O. From audience participation to paired-associate learning. (and) Response analysis in paired-associate learning experiments. In A. A. Lumsdaine (ed.), *Student response in programmed instruction.* Washington, D.C.: National Academy of Sciences, National Research Council, 1961, pp. 351–373. [321]

Cook, J. O., and M. E. Spitzer. Supplementary report: prompting versus confirmation in paired-associate learning. *J. exp. Psychol.*, 1960, **59,** 257–276. [321]

Cook, S. W. (ed.) *Army air forces aviation psychology program research report no. 12: psychological research on radar observer training.* Washington, D.C.: U.S. Government Printing Office, 1947. [172]

Cook, T. W. Studies in cross education.

III. Kinaesthetic learning of an irregular pattern. *J. exp. Psychol.*, 1934, **17,** 749–762.   [407]

Cook, T. W. Mirror position and negative transfer. *J. exp. Psychol.*, 1941, **29,** 155–160.   [408]

Cornsweet, J. C. *See* Riggs, L. A., 1953.

Cornsweet, T. N. *See* Riggs, L. A., 1953.

Cotterman, T. E. *See* Hood, P. D., 1960.

Coulson, J. E., D. P. Estavan, R. J. Melaragno, and H. F. Silberman. Effects of branching in a computer controlled autoinstructional device. *J. appl. Psychol.*, 1962, **46,** 389–392.   [312, 320]

Coulson, J. E., and H. F. Silberman. Effects of three variables in a teaching machine. *J. educ. Psychol.*, 1960, **51,** 135–143.   [312]

Coulson, J. E., and H. F. Silberman. Automated teaching and individual differences. *Aud.-vis. Commun. Rev.*, 1961, **9,** 5–15.   [266]

Coulson, J. E. *See also* Silberman, H. F., 1961.

Cox, C. M. Comparative behavior in solving a series of maze problems of varying difficulty. *J. exp. Psychol.*, 1928, **11,** 202–218.   [373]

Cram, D. *Explaining "teaching machines" and programming.* San Francisco: Fearon, 1961.   [261]

Critchley, M. Evolution of man's capacity for language. In S. Tax (ed.), *Evolution after Darwin. Vol. 2.* Chicago: Univ. of Chicago Press, 1960. [84]

Crockett, W. H. *See* Brayfield, A. H., 1955.

Crowder, N. A. Automatic tutoring by means of intrinsic programming. In E. Galanter (ed.), *Automatic teaching: the state of the art.* New York: Wiley, 1959, pp. 109–116.   (260, 277, 287]

Crowder, N. A. Automatic tutoring by intrinsic programming. In A. A. Lumsdaine and R. Glaser (eds.), *Teaching machines and programmed learning: a source book.* Washington, D.C.: National Education Association, 1960, pp. 286–298.   [260, 277, 278, 287]

Culbertson, H. M., and R. D. Powers. A study of graph comprehension difficulties. *Aud.-vis. Commun. Rev.*, 1959, **7,** 97–110.   [333]

Culler, E., and F. A. Mettler. Conditioned behavior in the decorticate dog. *J. comp. Psychol.*, 1934, **18,** 291–303.   [357]

Curtiss-Wright Corporation, Electronics Division. *Study program for simulator component interconnections.* USAF Aeronaut. Sys. Div. tech. Rep. 61–71, 1961.   [182]

Dahlstrom, W. G. *See* Welsh, G. S., 1956.

Dailey, J. T. (ed.) *Army air forces aviation psychology program research report no. 13: psychological research on flight engineer training.* Washington, D.C.: U.S. Government Printing Office, 1947.   [172]

Damrin, D. E. *See* Glaser, R., 1954.

Darwin, C. *The descent of man.* London: Murray, 1871, 2 vols.   [84]

David, E. E., Jr. *See* van Bergeijk, W. A., 1959.

Davis, K. Mental hygiene and class structure. *Psychiat.*, 1938, **2,** 55–65. [239]

Davis, R. A. *Psychology of learning.* New York: McGraw-Hill, 1935. [42]

Davis, R. C., The domain of homeostasis. *Psychol. Rev.*, 1958, **65,** 8–13. [36]

Davy, E. *See* Wilcoxon, H. C., 1954.

Deane, W. N. *See* Chittick, R. A., 1961.

Deese, J. Comment and summary: a mine of possible applications. *Aud.-vis. Commun. Rev.*, 1961, **9**(5), 79–87. [131, 132]

Deese, J. Skilled performance and conditions of stress. In R. Glaser (ed.), *Training research and education.* Pittsburgh: Univ. of Pittsburgh Press, 1962, pp. 199–222. [185]

Delacato, C. H. *The diagnosis and treatment of speech and reading problems.* Springfield, Ill.: Thomas, 1963. [236, 468]

De Laguna, G. A. *Speech, its function and development.* New Haven, Conn.: Yale Univ. Press, 1927. [85]

Delay, J. Maverick methods give help to brain-injured children: return to babyhood. *Life*, 1963, **55**(8), 31–38. [468]

Demaree, R. G. *Development of training equipment planning information.* USAF Aeronaut. Sys. Div. tech. Rep. 61–533, 1961. [191, 192, 193, 195]

Denenberg, V. H. The effects of early experience. In E. S. E. Hafez (ed.), *The behaviour of domestic animals.* London: Baillière, Tindall, and Cox, 1962, pp. 109–138. [466]

Denes, P. *See* Kalmus, H., 1955, 1960.

Dennis, W. Spalding's experiment on the flight of birds repeated with another species. *J. comp. Psychol.*, 1941, **31**, 337–348. [464]

Desiderato, O. L., J. H. Kanner, and R. P. Runyon. Procedures for improving television instruction. *Aud.-vis. Commun. Rev.*, 1956, **4**, 57–63. [151]

Desiderato, O. L. *See also* Kanner, J. H., 1954, 1955; Runyon, R. P., 1955.

de Solla Price, D. J. An ancient Greek computer. *Sci. Amer.*, 1959, **200**(6), 60–67. [72]

Dessart, D. J. A study in programed learning. *Sch. Sci. Math.*, 1962, **62**, 513–520. [307]

Detwiler, S. *See* Matthews, S., 1926.

Dial, H. E. *See* Chall, J. S., 1948.

Diamond, A. S. *The history and origin of language.* London: Methuen, 1959. [85]

Dick, W. *See* Gagné, R. M., 1962.

Dickson, W. J. *See* Roethlisberger, F. J., 1939.

Dittberner, V. F. *See* Stanley, R. J., 1955.

Dodge, R. Five types of eye movement in the horizontal meridian plane of the field of regard. *Amer. J. Physiol.*, 1903, **8**, 307–329. [171, 202, 396]

Dowell, E. C. *An evaluation of Trainer-Testers.* USAF Tech. Train. Air Force Rep. 54–28, 1955. [249]

Downs, J. E. *See* Parker, J. F., 1961.

Draper, J. W. The Arabs in Spain. *Harper's new mon. Mag.*, 1860, **20**, 370–377. [103]

Dubois, P. H. *See* Vasilas, J. N., 1953.

Duncan, C. P. Transfer after training with single versus multiple tasks. *J. exp. Psychol.*, 1958, **55**, 63–72. [426]

Dusser de Barenne, J. G. The labyrinthine and postural mechanisms. In C. Murchison (ed.), *A handbook of general experimental psychology.* Worcester, Mass.: Clark Univ. Press, 1934, pp. 204–246. [357]

Dworkin, S., and A. Holden. An experimental evaluation of sound filmstrips vs. classroom lectures. *J. Soc. Motion Pict. TV Engr.*, 1959, **68**, 383–385. [141]

Dyson-Hudson, R. Men, women and work in a pastoral society. *Nat. Hist.*, 1960, **69**(10), 42–57. [71]

Ebbinghaus, H. *Memory: a contribution to experimental psychology.* (Trans. by H. A. Ruger and C. E. Bussenius.)

New York: Teachers Coll., Columbia Univ., 1913. [21, 38, 432]

Eckdahl, M. *See* Olshansky, S., 1960.

Edgerton, A. K., and R. M. Twombly. A programmed course in spelling. *Elem. Sch. J.*, 1962, **62**, 380–386. [306]

Eigen, L. D. High-school student reactions to programed instruction. *Phi Delta Kappan*, 1963, **44**, 282–285. [301, 304, 311]

Electronic flight visulator. *Mech. Engng*, 1959, **81**(3), 82–83. [123]

Engelmann, M. D. Construction and evaluation of programmed materials in biology classroom use. *Amer. Biol. Teacher*, 1963, **25**, 212–214. [301]

Ericksen, S. C. Variability of attack in massed and distributed practice. *J. exp. Psychol.*, 1942, **31**, 339–345. [38]

Erlebacher, A. *See* Herrick, V. E., 1963.

Estavan, D. P. *See* Coulson, J. E., 1962; Silberman, H. F., 1961.

ETV channels going begging. *Chicago Sch. J.*, 1964, **45**, 189. [159]

Evans, J. L., R. Glaser, and L. E. Homme. An investigation of "teaching machine" variables using learning programs in symbolic logic. *J. educ. Res.*, 1962, **55**, 433–452. [315]

Evans, J. L., L. E. Homme, and R. Glaser. *The ruleg (rule-example) system for the construction of learning programs.* Pittsburgh: Univ. of Pittsburgh, 1960. [285]

Evans, J. L. *See also* Glaser, R., 1960.

Ewert, P. H. A study of the effect of inverted retinal stimulation upon spatially coordinated behavior. *Genet. Psychol. Monogr.*, 1930, **7**, 177–363. [373]

Fairbanks, G. Selective vocal effects of delayed auditory feedback. *J. speech hear. Dis.*, 1955, **20**, 333–346. [368, 370, 371, 400]

Fairbanks, G., and N. Guttman. Effects of delayed auditory feedback upon articulation. *J. speech hear. Res.*, 1958, **1**, 12–22. [368]

Fantz, R. L. Pattern vision in newborn infants. *Science*, 1963, **140**, 296–297. [460]

Fearing, F. Human communication. *Aud-vis. Commun. Rev.*, 1962, **10**(5), 78–108. [165]

Feldhusen, J. Programing and the talented pupil. *Clearing House*, 1963a, **38**, 151–154. [297]

Feldhusen, J. F. Taps for teaching machines. *Phi Delta Kappan*, 1963b, **44**, 265–267. [312, 314, 323]

Feldhusen, J. F., and A. Birt. A study of nine methods of presentation of programmed learning material. *J. educ. Res.*, 1962, **55**, 461–466. [313]

Feldhusen, J. F., H. Ramharter, and A. T. Birt. The teacher vs programed learning. *Wis. J. Educ.*, 1962, **95**(3), 8–10. [321]

Feliciano, G. D., R. D. Powers, and B. E. Kearl. The presentation of statistical information. *Aud.-vis. Commun. Rev.*, 1963, **11**, 32–39. [333]

Fennell, R. S., III. *See* Jones, M. B., 1965.

Ferguson, M. N. A comparison of the chain associations of nursery school and kindergarten children to action-picture stimuli. *Speech Monogr.*, 1957, **24**, 56–64. [330]

Festinger, L. *A theory of cognitive dissonance.* Evanston, Ill.: Row, Peterson, 1957. [432]

Fields, P. E. Studies in concept formation: I. The development of the concept of triangularity by the white rat. *Comp. Psychol. Monogr.*, 1932, **9**, No. 2. [411]

Filep, R. T. Teaching machines and programed instruction. *Aud.-vis. Com-*

mun. Rev., 1963, **11**, 145–148. [276]

Finn, J. D., and D. G. Perrin. *Teaching machines and programed learning: a survey of the industry, 1962.* Washington, D.C.: U.S. Government Printing Office, 1962. [275]

First reports on Roanoke math materials. *Aud.-vis. Instruction*, 1961, **6**, 150–151. [301, 306, 307]

Fischer, L. K. Hospitalism in six-month-old infants. *Amer. J. Orthopsychiat.*, 1952, **22**, 522–533. [465]

Fitch, F. B. *See* Hull, C. L., 1940.

Fitts, P. M. Factors in complex skill training. In R. Glaser (ed.), *Training research and education.* Pittsburgh: Univ. of Pittsburgh Press, 1962. Pp. 177–197. [186, 198, 201]

Fitts, P. M. *See also* Allen, M. J., 1954.

Fitzgerald, H. T. Teaching machines: a demurrer. *Sch. Rev.*, 1962, **70**, 247–256. [320]

Fitzpatrick, R. *See* Vasilas, J. N., 1953.

Flanagan, J. C. (ed.) *Army air forces aviation psychology program research report No. 1: the aviation psychology program in the army air forces.* Washington, D.C.: U.S. Government Printing Office, 1948. [172]

Fleishman, E. A. *A summary of psychomotor test development research accomplished in the skill components research laboratory.* USAF Personnel Train. Res. Cent. lab. Note SCRL 55-1, 1955. [197]

Fleishman, E. A. The description and prediction of perceptual-motor skill learning. In R. Glaser (ed.), *Training research and education.* Pittsburgh: Univ. of Pittsburgh Press, 1962, pp. 137–175. [197]

Fleishman, E. A., and W. E. Hempel. Factorial analysis of complex psychomotor performance and related skills.

J. appl. Psychol., 1956, **40**, 96–104. [197]

Fleishman, E. A. *See also* Hempel, W. E., 1955.

Follettie, J. F. *Effects of training response mode, test form, and measure on acquisition of semi-ordered factual materials.* Hum. Resources Res. Off. res. Bull. 24, 1961. [141]

Fonseca, L., and B. Kearl. *Comprehension of pictorial symbols: an experiment in rural Brazil.* Madison: Dep. of Agricultural Journalism, Univ. of Wisconsin, 1960. [332]

Franks, P. E. *See* Hansen, O. K., 1959.

Freeman, J. T. The effects of reinforced practice on conventional multiple-choice tests. *Automated Teachg Bull.*, 1959, **1**, 19–20. [323]

French, J. R. P., Jr. *See* Coch, L., 1948.

French, R. S., and L. B. Martin. *A flight-line trouble-shooting trainer for a complex electronic system: the "MAC II Trainer."* USAF Personnel Train. Res. Cent. develpm. Rep. TN–57–106, 1957. [188]

Freud, S. *The basic writings of Sigmund Freud.* (Ed. and trans. by A. A. Brill.) New York: Modern Library, 1938. [432]

Fritz, M. *Survey of television utilization in army training.* USN· Spec. Dev. Cent. hum. engng Rep. 530–01–1, 1952. [151].

Fry, D. B. *See* Kalmus, H., 1955, 1960.

Fry, E. B. Programming trends. *Aud.-vis. Instruction*, 1961, **6**, 142–143. [275]

Fry, E. B. *See also* Rigney, J. W., 1961.

Gagné, R. M. Military training and principles of learning. *Amer. Psychologist*, 1962a, **17**, 83–91. [172]

Gagné, R. M. Simulators. In R. Glaser (ed.), *Training research and educa-*

tion. Pittsburgh: Univ. of Pittsburgh Press, 1962b, pp. 223–246. [183]

Gagné, R. M., and W. Dick. Learning measures in a self-instructional program in solving equations. *Psychol. Rep.,* 1962, **10,** 131–146. [317, 324]

Galanter, E. The ideal teacher. In E. Galanter (ed.), *Automatic teaching: the state of the art.* New York: Wiley, 1959, pp. 1–11. [276, 286]

Gardner, F. M. *See* Glaser, R., 1954.

General Electric Research Laboratory. *Thermoplastic recording.* Schenectady, N.Y.: General Electric Research Information Services, 1960. [117]

Gentry, G., S. J. Kaplan, and I. Iscoe. *Studies in abstractive generalization: comparison between performance of the macaque and the human adult on the same problem.* USAF Sch. Aviat. Med. Rep. 12, 1954. [411, 412]

Gentry, G., S. J. Kaplan, and I. Iscoe. *Studies in abstractive generalization: comparisons between various human age groups and monkeys on similar learning tasks.* USAF Sch. Aviat. Med. Rep. 55–83, 1956. [411]

Gerall, A. A., and R. F. Green. Effect of torque changes upon a two-hand coordination task. *Percept. mot. Skills,* 1958, **8,** 287–290. [427]

Gerbner, G. Toward a general model of communication. *Aud.-vis. Commun. Rev.,* 1956, **4,** 171–199. [434, 435]

Gibson, E. J. Sensory generalization with voluntary reactions. *J. exp. Psychol.,* 1939, **24,** 237–253. [409]

Gibson, E. J. Retroactive inhibition as a function of degree of generalization between tasks. *J. exp. Psychol.,* 1941, **28,** 93–115. [409]

Gibson, E. J., and R. D. Walk. The "visual cliff." *Sci. Amer.,* 1960, **202** (4), 64–71. [460, 461]

Gibson, J. J. A theory of pictorial perception. *Aud.-vis. Commun. Rev.,* 1954, **2,** 3–23. [347]

Gilbert, T. F. An early approximation to principles of programming continuous discourse, self-instructional materials. In A. A. Lumsdaine and R. Glaser (eds.), *Teaching machines and programmed learning: a source book.* Washington, D.C.: National Education Association, 1960a, pp. 630–634. (Abstract) [286]

Gilbert, T. F. On the relevance of laboratory investigation of learning to self-instructional programming. In A. A. Lumsdaine and R. Glaser (eds.), *Teaching machines and programmed learning: a source book.* Washington, D.C.: National Education Association, 1960b, pp. 475–485. [300]

Gilbreth, F. B., and L. M. Gilbreth. *Applied motion study.* New York: Sturgis and Walton, 1917. [171, 176]

Gilbreth, L. M. *See* Gilbreth, F. B., 1917.

Gilden, L. *See* Chase, R. A., 1961.

Gillen, F. J. *See* Spencer, B., 1912.

Glanzer, M. Curiosity, exploratory drive, and stimulus satiation. *Psychol. Bull.,* 1958, **55,** 302–315. [25, 215)

Glanzer, M. Experimental study of team training and team functioning. In R. Glaser (ed.), *Training research and education.* Pittsburgh: Univ. of Pittsburgh Press, 1962, pp. 379–407. [209, 227, 231, 233]

Glanzer, M., and R. Glaser. Techniques for the study of group structure and behavior: II. Empirical studies of the effects of structure in small groups. *Psychol. Bull.,* 1961, **58,** 1–27. [230]

Glaser, R. Christmas past, present, and future. *Contemp. Psychol.,* 1960, **5,** 24–28. [275]

Glaser, R. Learning and the technology of instruction. *Aud.-vis. Commun. Rev.*, 1961, **9**(5), 42–55. [132]

Glaser, R. Psychology and instructional technology. In R. Glaser (ed.), *Training research and education.* Pittsburgh: Univ. of Pittsburgh Press, 1962, pp. 1–30. [195]

Glaser, R., D. E. Damrin, and F. M. Gardner. The Tab Item: a technique for the measurement of proficiency in diagnostic problem solving tasks. *Educ. psychol. Measmt*, 1954, **14**, 283–293. [249]

Glaser, R., L. E. Homme, and J. L. Evans. An evaluation of textbooks in terms of learning principles. In A. A. Lumsdaine and R. Glaser (eds.), *Teaching machines and programmed learning: a source book.* Washington, D.C.: National Education Association, 1960, pp. 437–445. [293]

Glaser, R. *See also* Evans, J. L., 1960, 1962; Glanzer, M., 1961; Homme, L. E., 1960.

Goldbeck, R. A., and V. N. Campbell. The effects of response mode and response difficulty on programed learning. *J. educ. Psychol.*, 1962, **53**, 110–118. [315, 318]

Goldbeck, R. A. *See also* Briggs, L. J., 1962.

Goldberg, A. L. Programed spelling: a case study. *Aud-vis. Instruction*, 1963, **8**, 94–96. [310]

Goldiamond, I., C. J. Atkinson, and R. C. Bilger. Stabilization of behavior and prolonged exposure to delayed auditory feedback. *Science*, 1962, **135**, 437–438. [373]

Goldsmith, P. B. *See* Kanner, J. H., 1958a, 1958b.

Goldstein, L. S., and L. G. Gotkin. A review of research: teaching machines vs. programed textbooks as presentation modes. *J. progr. Instruction*, 1962, **1**(1), 29–36. [311]

Goldstein, L. S. *See also* Gotkin, L. G., 1963.

Goodman, L. Effect of total absence of function on the optic system of rabbits. *Amer. J. Physiol.*, 1932, **100**, 46–63. [464]

Gordon, T. *See* Arbuckle, D. A., 1949.

Gotkin, L. G., and L. S. Goldstein. Programed instruction in the schools: innovation and the innovator. *Aud.-vis. Commun. Rev.*, 1963, **11**, 277–287. [297]

Gotkin, L. G. *See also* Goldstein, L. S., 1962.

Gould, J., and K. U. Smith. Angular displacement of the visual feedback of motion. *Science,* 1962, **137**, 619–620. [378]

Green, R. F. *See* Gerall, A. A., 1958.

Greenblatt, M. The rehabilitation spectrum. In M. Greenblatt and B. Simon (eds.), *Rehabilitation of the mentally ill.* Washington, D.C.: AAAS, 1959, pp. 13–23. [239]

Greene, D. *See* Hecker, D., 1956.

Greene, P. *See* Smith, K. U., 1963.

Greenhill, L. P. Research on televised instruction at the Pennsylvania State University. In J. C. Adams, C. R. Carpenter, and D. R. Smith (eds.), *College teaching by television.* Washington, D.C.: American Council on Education, 1958, pp. 74–83. [148]

Greenhill, L. P. *See also* Carpenter, C. R., 1955, 1958.

Greenway, J. Conversations with the Stone Age. *Sat. Rev.*, 1964, **47**(7), 21–23. [13]

Grob, S. *See* Olshansky, S., 1960.

Gropper, G. L. Why *is* a picture worth a thousand words? *Aud.-vis. Commun. Rev.*, 1963, **11**, 75–95. [165]

Grosslight, J. H. Conditions of learning

in a closed-circuit television system. In J. C. Adams, C. R. Carpenter, and D. R. Smith (eds.), *College teaching by television.* Washington, D.C.: American Council on Education, 1958, pp. 42–48. [149]

Grosslight, J. H. *See also* Kale, S. V., 1955.

Grubb, R. E., and L. D. Selfridge. *The computer tutoring of statistics: a preliminary report.* IBM Corp. Thomas J. Watson Res. Cent. res. Rep. RC–724, 1962. [267]

Guilfoyle, G. *See* Chase, R. A., 1961.

Gustafson, H. W., and H. E. Cahill. The role of task analysis in deriving training and training equipment requirements for the AN/ULD–1 system. In *Uses of task analysis in deriving training and training equipment requirements.* USAF Wright Air Dev. Div. tech. Rep. 60–593, 1960. [193, 194]

Gustafson, H. W., W. D. Honsberger, and S. Michelson. Determination of task analysis content. In *Uses of task analysis in deriving training and training equipment requirements.* USAF Wright Air Dev. Div. tech. Rep. 60–593, 1960. [192]

Guthrie, E. R. *The psychology of learning.* (Rev. ed.) New York: Harper & Row, 1952. [33]

Guttman, N. *See* Fairbanks, G., 1958.

Hain, K. H., and E. J. Holder. A case study in programed instruction. In S. Margulies and L. D. Eigen (eds.), *Applied programed instruction.* New York: Wiley, 1962, pp. 294–297. [309]

Hale, W. H. A legacy from the Model T to the age of ETV. *Reporter,* 1957, **16**(11), 10–15. [154]

Hall, M. *See* Hull, C. L., 1940.

Hall, R. L. Group performance under feedback that confounds responses of group members. *Sociometry,* 1957, **20,** 297–305. [232]

Hall, R. L. *See also* Rosenberg, S., 1958.

Hansche, J. *See* Smith, K. U., 1958.

Hansen, O. K., P. E. Franks, and J. A. Modrick. *Nature and use of the MAC-2 (malfunction and circuitry) trainer.* USAF Wright Air Dev. Cent. tech. Note 59–140, 1959. [188]

Hanson, L. F. Schools using programed materials. *Aud.-vis. Instruction,* 1963, **8,** 101–103. [275]

Harley, W. *See* Smith, W. M., 1956.

Harlow, H. F., and M. K. Harlow. Social deprivation in monkeys. *Sci. Amer.,* 1962, **207**(5), 136–146. [465]

Harlow, H. F., and R. R. Zimmerman. Affectional responses in the infant monkey. *Science,* 1959, **130,** 421–432. [465]

Harlow, M. K. *See* Harlow, H. F., 1962.

Harris, J. D. *See* Rawnsley, A. I., 1954.

Harris, T. L., and G. L. Rarick. Physiological and motor correlates of handwriting legibility. In V. E. Herrick (ed.), *New horizons for research in handwriting.* Madison: Univ. of Wisconsin Press, 1963, pp. 55–88. [387]

Harrison, R. G. An experimental study of the relation of the nervous system to the developing musculature in the embryo of the frog. *Amer. J. Anat.,* 1904, **3,** 197–220. [464]

Harter, N. *See* Bryan, W. L., 1899.

Hartman, F. R. Recognition learning under multiple channel presentation and testing conditions. *Aud.-vis. Commun. Rev.,* 1961a, **9,** 24–43. [142]

Hartman, F. R. Single and multiple channel communication: a review of research and a proposed model. *Aud.-*

vis. *Commun. Rev.*, 1961b, **9**, 235–262. [141, 331]

Harvey, S. *See* Chase, R. A., 1959, 1961.

Hatch, R. S. *An evaluation of the effectiveness of a self-tutoring approach applied to pilot training.* USAF Wright Air Dev. Cent. tech. Rep. 59–320, 1959. [305]

Hayman, J. L., Jr., and J. T. Johnson, Jr. Exact vs varied repetition in educational television. *Aud.-vis. Commun. Rev.*, 1963, **11**, 96–103. [166]

Hayman, J. L., Jr. *See also* Reed, J. E., 1962.

Heath, R. W. *See* Ketcham, C. H., 1962.

Hecker, D., D. Greene, and K. U. Smith. Dimensional analysis of motion: X. Experimental evaluation of a time-study problem. *J. appl. Psychol.*, 1956, **40**, 220–227. [415]

Heidbreder, E. An experimental study of thinking. *Arch. Psychol., N.Y.*, 1924. **11**, No. 73. [43]

Heidbreder, E. The attainment of concepts. *J. gen. Psychol.*, 1946, **35**, 173–189; 191–223. [44]

Helliwell, S. An investigation into the values of the film-strip and the educational visit as methods of instruction to secondary modern school pupils of 14–15 years. *Brit. J. educ. Psychol.*, 1953, **23**, 129–131. [470]

Helmholtz, H. L. F. von. *Handbuch der physiologischen Optik.* Hamburg and Leipzig: Voss, 1856–1866, 3 vols. [21]

Hempel, W. E., and E. A. Fleishman. Factor analysis of physical proficiency and manipulative skill. *J. appl. Psychol.*, 1955, **39**, 12–16. [197]

Hempel, W. E. *See also* Fleishman, E. A., 1956.

Herbert, E. Programmed learning. *Int.*

Sci. *Technology*, 1963, No. 16, 54–64. [264]

Herrick, V. E., and A. Erlebacher. The evaluation of legibility in handwriting. In V. E. Herrick (ed.), *New horizons for research in handwriting.* Madison: Univ. of Wisconsin Press, 1963, pp. 207–231. [386]

Herrick, V. E., and N. Okada. The present scene: practices in the teaching of handwriting in the United States—1960. In V. E. Herrick (ed.), *New horizons for research in handwriting.* Madison: Univ. of Wisconsin Press, 1963, pp. 17–32. [387]

Herron, L. W. *See* Plattner, J. W., 1962.

Hickey, A. E. Programed instruction in business and industry. In S. Margulies and L. D. Eigen (eds.), *Applied programed instruction.* New York: Wiley, 1962, pp. 282–293. [309]

Hilgard, E. R. *Theories of learning.* (2nd ed.) New York: Appleton, 1956. [36, 290]

Hilgard, E. R. What support from the psychology of learning? *NEA J.*, 1961, **50**(8), 20–21. [293]

Hilgard, E. R. *See also* Marquis, D. G., 1937.

Hill, R. M. *See* Barlow, H. B., 1963.

Hille, B. A. *See* Conrad, R., 1958.

Hoban, C. F., Jr., and E. B. Van Ormer. *Instructional film research, 1918–1950.* USN Spec. Dev. Cent. tech. Rep. 269-7-19, 1950. [139]

Hochberg, J. The psychophysics of pictorial perception. *Aud.-vis. Commun. Rev.*, 1962, **10**(5), 22–54. [165]

Holden, A. *See* Dworkin, S., 1959.

Holder, E. J. *See* Hain, K. H., 1962.

Holding, D. H. Transfer between difficult and easy tasks. *Brit. J. Psychol.*, 1962, **53**, 397–407. [425, 426]

Holland, J. G. A teaching machine program in psychology. In E. Galanter (ed.), *Automatic teaching: the state of the art.* New York: Wiley, 1959, pp. 69–82. [254, 282]

Holland, J. G. Teaching machines: an application of principles from the laboratory. In A. A. Lumsdaine and R. Glaser (eds.), *Teaching machines and programmed learning: a source book.* Washington, D.C.: National Education Association, 1960, pp. 215–228. [289, 293]

Holland, J. G. Evaluating teaching machines and programs. *Teachers Coll. Rec.,* 1961, **63,** 56–65. [277, 287]

Holland, J. G., and D. Porter. The influence of repetition of incorrectly answered items in a teaching-machine program. *J. exp. Anal. Behav.,* 1961, **4,** 305–307. [317]

Holland, J. G., and B. F. Skinner. *The analysis of behavior.* New York: McGraw-Hill, 1961. [258, 279, 282, 286]

Holland, J. G. *See also* Skinner, B. F., 1960.

Hollingshead, A. B., and F. C. Redlich. *Social class and mental illness.* New York: Wiley, 1958. [239]

Homme, L. E., and R. Glaser. Problems in programming verbal learning sequences. In A. A. Lumsdaine and R. Glaser (eds.), *Teaching machines and programmed learning: a source book.* Washington, D.C.: National Education Association, 1960, pp. 486–496. [284, 291, 293]

Homme, L. E. *See also* Evans, J. L., 1960, 1962; Glaser, R., 1960.

Honig, J. M. *See* Seibert, W. F., 1960.

Honsberger, W. D. *See* Gustafson, H. W., 1960.

Hood, P. D., R. L. Krumm, F. J. O'Sul-livan, R. Buckhout, R. T. Cave, T. E. Cotterman, and M. R. Rockway. *Conference on integrated aircrew training.* USAF Wright Air Dev. Div. tech. Rep. 60–320, 1960. [182]

Hooker, D. *The origins of overt behavior.* Ann Arbor: Univ. of Michigan Press, 1944. [458]

Hosmer, C. L., and J. A. Nolan. Time saved by a tryout of automatic tutoring. In S. Margulies and L. D. Eigen (eds.), *Applied programed instruction.* New York: Wiley, 1962, pp. 70–72. [308]

Hough, J. B. An analysis of the efficiency and effectiveness of selected aspects of machine instruction. *J. educ. Res.,* 1962, **55,** 467–471. [308, 314]

Hough, J. B., and B. Revsin. Programed instruction at the college level: a study of several factors influencing learning. *Phi Delta Kappan,* 1963, **44,** 286–291. [304, 311]

Hovland, C. I. The generalization of conditioned responses: I. The sensory generalization of conditioned responses with varying frequencies of tone. *J. gen. Psychol.,* 1937a, **17,** 125–148. [410]

Hovland, C. I. The generalization of conditioned responses: II. The sensory generalization of conditioned responses with varying intensities of tone. *J. genet. Psychol.,* 1937b, **51,** 279–291. [410]

Hovland, C. I. Human learning and retention. In S. S. Stevens (ed.), *Handbook of experimental psychology.* New York: Wiley, 1951, pp. 613–689. [38]

Hovland, C. I., A. A. Lumsdaine, and F. D. Sheffield. *Experiments on mass communication.* Princeton, N.J.:

Princeton Univ. Press, 1949. [139, 145]

Hovland, C. I., and W. Weiss. The influence of source credibility on communication effectiveness. *Publ. Opin. Quart.*, 1951–1952, **15**, 635–650. [140]

Hovland, C. I. *See also* Hull, C. L., 1940; Kurtz, K. H., 1953.

Hubel, D. H., and T. N. Wiesel. Receptive fields, binocular interaction, and functional architecture in the cat's visual cortex. *J. Physiol.*, 1962, **160**, 106–154. [355]

Hughes, J. L., and W. J. McNamara. A comparative study of programed and conventional instruction in industry. *J. appl. Psychol.*, 1961, **45**, 225–231. [304, 308]

Hull, C. L. *Principles of behavior.* New York: Appleton, 1943. [29, 35, 432, 471]

Hull, C. L., C. I. Hovland, R. T. Ross, M. Hall, D. T. Perkins, and F. B. Fitch. *Mathematico-deductive theory of rote learning.* New Haven, Conn.: Yale Univ. Press, 1940. [41]

Hull, R. B. A note on the history behind ETV. In L. Asheim *et al.*, *Educational television: the next ten years.* Stanford, Calif.: The Institute for Communication Research, Stanford Univ., 1962, pp. 334–345. [112]

Hunter, W. S., and S. C. Bartlett. Double alternation behavior in young children. *J. exp. Psychol.*, 1948, **38**, 558–567. [460, 463]

Irion, A. L. Rote learning. In S. Koch (ed.), *Psychology: a study of a science. Vol. 2.* New York: McGraw-Hill, 1959, pp. 538–560. [41]

Irion, A. L., and L. J. Briggs. *Learning task and mode of operation variables in use of the Subject Matter Trainer.*

USAF Personnel Train. Res. Cent. tech. Rep. 57–8, 1957. [250]

Irons, F. S. *See* Chittick, R. A., 1961.

Irwin, J. V., and A. E. Aronson. *Television teaching: conventional lecture versus highly visualized film presentation.* Univ. of Wis. Telev. Lab. res. Bull. 11, 1958. [143]

Is programed learning effective? *Minn. J. Educ.*, 1963, **44**(1), 32. [297]

Iscoe, I. *See* Gentry, G., 1954, 1956.

Ivins, W. M., Jr. *Prints and visual communication.* London: Routledge and Kegan Paul, 1953. [67, 347, 348]

Jabbur, S. J., and A. L. Towe. Effect of pyramidal tract activity on dorsal column nuclei. *Science*, 1960, **132**, 547–548. [423]

Jacobs, P. I. *Some implications of testing procedures for auto-instructional programming.* USAF Med. Res. Lab. tech. doc. Rep. 62–67, 1962. [286, 288]

Jacobsen, E. Electrophysiology of mental activities. *Amer. J. Psychol.*, 1932, **44**, 677–694. [42]

James, W. *Principles of psychology.* New York: Holt, 1890, 2 vols. [40, 407, 432, 452]

Jaspen, N. *Effects on training of experimental film variables, Study I: Verbalization, rate of development, nomenclature, errors, "how-it-works," repetition.* USN Spec. Dev. Cent. tech. Rep. 269-7 17, 1950a. [146, 147]

Jaspen, N. *Effects on training of experimental film variables, Study II: Verbalization, "how-it-works," nomenclature, audience participation, and succinct treatment.* USN Spec. Dev. Cent. tech. Rep. 269–7–11, 1950b. [147]

Jaspen, N. *See also* Ash, P., 1953.

Javal, L. E. Essai sur la physiologie de

la lecture. *Ann. Oculistique,* 1878, **82,** 242–253. [396]

Jaynes, J. Imprinting: the interaction of learned and innate behavior: I. Development and generalization. *J. comp. physiol. Psychol.,* 1956, **49,** 201–206. [466]

Jaynes, J. Imprinting: the interaction of learned and innate behavior: II. The critical period. *J. comp. physiol. Psychol.,* 1957, **50,** 6–10. [466]

Jayson, R. M. *See* Beer, M., 1961.

Jenkinson, N. L. *See* May, M. A., 1953.

Jensen, B. T. An independent-study laboratory using self-scoring tests. *J. educ. Res.,* 1949, **43,** 134–137. [248]

Jespersen, O. *Language: its nature, development and origin.* New York: Holt, Rinehart and Winston, 1922. [85]

Johnson, A. P., and J. L. Milton. An experimental comparison of the accuracy of sighting and triggering with three types of gun-sight hand-grip controls. In P. M. Fitts (ed.), *Psychological research on equipment design.* Washington, D.C.: U.S. Government Printing Office, 1947. [175]

Johnson, J. T., Jr. *See* Hayman, J. L., Jr., 1963.

Jones, D. B. Quantitative analysis of motion picture content. *Publ. Opin. Quart.,* 1942, **6,** 411–428. [162]

Jones, H. E. Psychological studies of motion pictures: II. Observation and recall as a function of age. *Univ. Calif. Publ. Psychol.,* 1928, **3,** 225–243. [140]

Jones, H. L., and M. O. Sawyer. A new evaluation instrument. *J. educ. Res.,* 1949, **42,** 381–385. [248]

Jones, M. B., and R. S. Fennell, III. Performance in a U-maze by black-hooded Spence and Long-Evans rats.

Unpublished manuscript, Psychiatry Dep., Univ. of Florida, 1965. [358]

Jones, R. *See* Smith, K. U., 1963.

Jones, R. W. An engineer looks at physiology. *Science,* 1963, **140,** 461–464. [439]

Jordan, J. A. Socratic teaching? *Harv. educ. Rev.,* 1963, **33,** 96–104. [293]

Jorgensen, E. S. The relative effectiveness of three methods of television newscasting. Unpublished doctoral dissertation, Univ. of Wisconsin, 1955. [140]

Judd, C. H. Practice without knowledge of results. *Psychol. Rev. Monogr. Suppl.,* 1905–1906, **7,** 185–198. [204]

Judd, C. H. The relation of special training to general intelligence. *Educ. Rev.,* 1908, **36,** 28–42. [408, 426]

Kale, S. V., J. H. Grosslight, and C. J. McIntyre. *Exploratory studies in the use of pictures and sound for teaching foreign language vocabulary.* USN Spec. Dev. Cent. tech. Rep. 269–7–53, 1955. [146]

Kallegian, V. *See* Tannenbaum, R., 1954.

Kalmus, H., P. Denes, and D. B. Fry. Effect of delayed acoustic feed-back on some non-vocal activities. *Nature,* 1955, **175,** 1078. [369]

Kalmus, H., D. B. Fry, and P. Denes. Effects of delayed visual control on writing, drawing, and tracing. *Language and Speech,* 1960, **3,** 96–108. [368, 369, 390]

Kanner, J. H. Future trends in television teaching and research. *Aud.-vis. Commun. Rev.,* 1957, **5,** 513–527. [151, 152]

Kanner, J. H. Teaching by television in the army—an overview. *Aud.-vis.*

Commun. Rev., 1958, **6**, 172–188. [151]

Kanner, J. H., S. Katz, and P. B. Goldsmith. *Television in army training: evaluation of "intensive" television for teaching basic electricity.* Washington, D.C.: Dep. of the Army, Off. of the Chief Signal Officer, 1958a. [151]

Kanner, J. H., S. Katz, W. Mindak, and P. Goldsmith. Television in army training. *Aud.-vis. Commun. Rev.*, 1958b, **6**, 255–291. [151]

Kanner, J. H., and W. P. Marshall. Television in basic training: the improvement of training by television. *Aud.-vis. Commun. Rev.*, 1963, **11**, 191–199. [151, 153]

Kanner, J. H., W. Mindak, and S. Katz. *Television in army training: the application of television and kinescope recordings to reduce instructor and student training time and training costs.* Washington, D.C.: Dep. of the Army, Off. of the Chief Signal Officer, 1958c. [151]

Kanner, J. H., R. P. Runyon, and O. L. Desiderato. *Television in army training: evaluation of television in army basic training.* Hum. Resources Res. Off., George Washington Univ., tech. Rep. 14, 1954. [151]

Kanner, J. H., R. P. Runyon, and O. Desiderato. Television as a training and educational medium. *Aud.-vis. Commun. Rev.*, 1955, **3**, 163–172. [151]

Kanner, J. H. *See also* Desiderato, O. L., 1956; Rosenstein, A. J., 1961; Runyon, R. P., 1955, 1956.

Kaplan, S. J. *See* Gentry, G., 1954, 1956.

Karpinski, L. C. *The history of arithmetic.* Chicago: Rand McNally, 1925. [104]

Karsten, A. Psychische Sättigung. *Psychol. Forsch.*, 1928, **10**, 142–254. [213]

Katona, G. *Organizing and memorizing.* New York: Columbia Univ. Press, 1940. [408, 426]

Katz, S. Some of Johnny's best teachers are machines. *Maclean's,* 1962, **75**(6), 9–11; 32–36. [262]

Katz, S. *See* Kanner, J. H., 1958a, 1958b, 1958c.

Kavanau, J. L. Behavior: confinement, adaptation, and compulsory regimes in laboratory studies. *Science,* 1964, **143**, 490. [474]

Kay, H. *See* Annett, J., 1957.

Kearl, B. E. *See* Feliciano, G. D., 1963; Fonseca, L., 1960.

Keislar, E. R. The development of understanding in arithmetic by a teaching machine. *J. educ. Psychol.,* 1959, **50**, 247–253. [288, 304, 316]

Keislar, E. R., and J. D. McNeil. Teaching scientific theory to first grade pupils by auto-instructional device. *Harv. educ. Rev.,* 1961, **31**, 73–83. [323]

Keislar, E. R., and J. D. McNeil. Teaching science and mathematics by auto-instruction in the primary grades: an experimental strategy in curriculum development. In J. E. Coulson (ed.), *Programmed learning and computer-based instruction.* New York: Wiley, 1962, pp. 99–112. [313]

Keislar, E. R. *See also* McNeil, J. D., 1962.

Kendler, H. H. Teaching machines and psychological theory. In E. Galanter (ed.), *Automatic teaching: the state of the art.* New York: Wiley, 1959, pp. 177–185. [292]

Kendler, H. H. Stimulus-response psychology and audiovisual education.

Aud.-vis. Commun. Rev., 1961, **9**(5), 33–41. [131, 135]

Kersh, B. Y. The motivating effect of learning by directed discovery. *J. educ. Psychol.*, 1962, **53**, 65–71. [46]

Ketcham, C. H., and R. W. Heath. Teaching effectiveness of sound with pictures that do not embody the material being taught. *Aud.-vis. Commun. Rev.*, 1962, **10**, 89–93. [331, 339]

Kight, S. S. *See* Smith, E. E., 1959.

Kilbourn, R. W. Midwest airborne television and the technology of education. *Aud.-vis. Commun. Rev.*, 1961, **9**, 201–205. [120]

King, D. M. The operator as a self-regulating system (a factory experiment). *Ergonomics*, 1962, **5**, 467–470. [224, 225]

Kinkade, R. G. *A differential influence of augmented feedback on learning and on performance.* USAF Wright Air Dev. Cent. tech. docum. Rep. 63–12, 1963. [207]

Klaus, D. J. The art of auto-instructional programming *Aud.-vis. Commun. Rev.*, 1961a, **9**, 130–142. [282, 286]

Klaus, D. J. Programming: a re-emphasis on the tutorial approach. *Aud.-vis. Instruction*, 1961b, **6**, 130–132; 148. [306]

Klüver, H. *Behavior mechanisms in monkeys.* Chicago: Univ. of Chicago Press, 1933. [27, 411]

Knight, C. (ed.) *The arts and industry of all nations.* London: Dutton, 1860, 2 vols. [73, 96, 99]

Koehler, J. *See* Smith, K. U., 1963, 1964.

Koffka, K. *Principles of gestalt psychology.* New York: Harcourt, 1935. [37]

Kohler, I. Experiments with prolonged optical distortion. *Acta Psychol.*, 1955, **11**, 176–178. [373]

Köhler, W. Aus der Anthropoidenstation auf Teneriffa. IV. Nachweis einfacher Strukturfunktionen beim Schimpansen und beim Haushuhn: über eine neue Methode zur Untersuchung des bunten Farbensystems. *Abh. Preuss. Akad. Wiss., Berlin.* 1918, pp. 1–101. [411]

Köhler, W. *Gestalt psychology.* New York: Liveright, 1929. [37]

Komoski, P. K. What are the schools doing? *NEA J.*, 1961, **50**(8), 28–30. [326]

Kopstein, F. F., and I. J. Shillestad. *A survey of auto-instructional devices.* USAF Aeronaut. Sys. Div. tech. Rep. 61–414, 1961. [188, 246, 247, 250, 252, 253, 255, 256, 257, 259, 261, 262]

Kresse, F. H. *See* Beer, M., 1961.

Krueger, D. B. *See* Pasamanick, B., 1959.

Krumboltz, J. D., and B. Bonawitz. The effect of receiving the confirming response in context in programmed material. *J. educ. Res.*, 1962, **55**, 472–475. [325]

Krumboltz, J. D., and R. G. Weisman. The effect of intermittent confirmation in programed instruction. *J. educ. Psychol.*, 1962a, **53**, 250–253. [321]

Krumboltz, J. D., and R. G. Weisman. The effect of overt versus covert responding to programed instruction on immediate and delayed retention. *J. educ. Psychol.*, 1962b, **53**, 89–92. [314]

Krumm, R. L. *See* Hood, P. D., 1960.

Kuenne, M. R. Experimental investigation of the relation of language to transposition behavior in young children. *J. exp. Psychol.*, 1946, **36**, 471–490. [411]

Kühn, H. *On the track of prehistoric man.* (Trans. by A. H. Brodrick.) New York: Random House, 1955. [61]

Kurtz, K. H., and C. I. Hovland. The effect of verbalization during observation of stimulus objects upon accuracy of recognition and recall. *J. exp. Psychol.*, 1953, **45**, 157–164. [143]

Lacy, J. R. Psychophysiological approaches to the evaluation of psychotherapeutic process and outcome. In E. A. Rubinstein and M. B. Parloff (eds.), *Research in psychotherapy.* Washington, D.C.: American Psychological Association, 1959. [237]

Landy, D., and H. Raulet. The hospital work program. In M. Greenblatt and B. Simon (eds.), *Rehabilitation of the mentally ill.* Washington, D.C.: AAAS, 1959, pp. 71–87. [241]

Lantos, T. P. A professor converts to the electronic age. *Reporter*, 1957, **16**(11), 15–17. [163]

Lashley, K. S. *Brain mechanisms and intelligence.* Chicago: Univ. of Chicago Press, 1929. [26]

Lashley, K. S. The mechanism of vision. I. A method for rapid analysis of pattern vision in the rat. *J. genet. Psychol.*, 1930, **37**, 453–460. [26]

Lashley, K. S. Learning: III. Nervous mechanisms in learning. In C. Murchison (ed.), *A handbook of general experimental psychology.* Worcester, Mass.: Clark Univ. Press, 1934, pp. 456–496. [26]

Lashley, K. S. The mechanism of vision. XV. Preliminary studies of the rat's capacity for detail vision. *J. gen. Psychol.*, 1938, **18**, 123–193. [27, 411]

Lashley, K. S. Studies of cerebral function in learning: XIII. Apparent absence of transcortical association in maze learning. *J. comp. Neurol.*, 1944, **80**, 257–281. [26, 357]

Lashley, K. S., and J. B. Watson. *A psychological study of motion pictures in relation to venereal disease campaigns.* Washington, D.C.: U.S. Interdepartmental Social Hygiene Board, 1922. [138]

Lasswell, H. D. The structure and function of communication in society. In L. Bryson (ed.), *The communication of ideas.* New York: Harper & Row, 1948. [434]

Lawrence, E. The school-masters of the Middle Ages. *Harper's new mon. Mag.*, 1871, **43**, 559–566. [103]

Lawrence, L. C., and P. C. Smith. Group decision and employee participation. *J. appl. Psychol.*, 1955, **39**, 334–337. [229]

Leavitt, H. J. Some effects of certain communication patterns on group performance. *J. abnorm. soc. Psychol.*, 1951, **46**, 38–50. [229, 230]

Lee, B. S. Effects of delayed speech feedback. *J. acoust. Soc. Amer.*, 1950a, **22**, 824–826. [361, 368, 399]

Lee, B. S. Some effects of side-tone delay. *J. acoust. Soc. Amer.*, 1950b, **22**, 639–640. [361, 368, 369, 399]

Lee, B. S. Artificial stutter. *J. speech hear. Dis.*, 1951, **16**, 53–55. [361, 399]

Leeds, D. *See* Roe, A., 1960.

Leeper, R. Cognitive processes. In S. S. Stevens (ed.), *Handbook of experimental psychology.* New York: Wiley, 1951, pp. 730–757. [432]

Lefkowith, E. F. *The validity of pictorial tests and their interaction with audio-visual teaching methods.* USN

Spec. Dev. Cent. tech. Rep. 269–7–49, 1955. [143]

Lehman, H. C. Men's creative production rate at different ages and in different countries. *Sci. Mon.*, 1954, **78,** 321–326. [453]

Lemkau, P. W. *See* Pasamanick, B., 1959.

Leonardo da Vinci. New York: Reynal, 1956. [104]

Lettvin, J. Y., H. R. Maturana, W. S. McCulloch, and W. H. Pitts. What the frog's eye tells the frog's brain. *Proc. Inst. Rad. Engr.*, 1959, **47,** 1940–1951. [355]

Lewin, K. *Principles of topological psychology.* New York: McGraw-Hill, 1936. [432]

Lewin, K. The dynamics of group action. *Educ. Leadership*, 1944, **1,** 195–200. [232]

Lewin, K., R. Lippitt, and R. K. White. Patterns of aggressive behavior in experimentally created social climates. *J. soc. Psychol.*, 1939, **10,** 271–299. [228]

Lhote, H. Saharan rock art. *Nat. Hist.*, 1960, **44**(6), 28–43. [61]

Licklider, J. C. R., and G. A. Miller. The perception of speech. In S. S. Stevens (ed.), *Handbook of experimental psychology.* New York: Wiley, 1951, pp. 1040–1074. [398, 434, 437]

Lincoln, R. S. Instrumental dimensions of motion in relation to training effects in visual pursuit tracking. Unpublished doctoral dissertation, Univ. of Wisconsin, 1952. [426]

Lincoln, R. S., and K. U. Smith. Systematic analysis of factors determining accuracy in visual tracking. *Science*, 1952, **116,** 183–187. [175, 180]

Lippitt, R., and R. K. White. An experimental study of leadership and group life. In G. E. Swanson *et al.* (eds.), *Readings in social psychology.* (Rev. ed.) New York: Holt, Rinehart and Winston, 1952, pp. 340–355. [228]

Lippitt, R. *See also* Lewin, K., 1939.

Little, J. K. Results of use of machines for testing and for drill upon learning in educational psychology. *J. exp. Educ.*, 1934, **3,** 45–49. [247, 323]

Luce, R. D. The theory of selective information and some of its behavioral applications. In R. D. Luce (ed.), *Developments in mathematical psychology.* New York: The Free Press, 1960, pp. 1–119. [436]

Luchins, A. S. Mechanization in problem solving—the effect of *Einstellung. Psychol. Monogr.*, 1942, **54,** No. 6. [43]

Luchins, A. S. Implications of gestalt psychology for AV learning. *Aud.-vis. Commun. Rev.*, 1961, **9**(5), 7–31. [133]

Lumsdaine, A. A. Teaching machines and self-instructional materials. *Aud.-vis. Commun. Rev.*, 1959, **7,** 163–181. [262]

Lumsdaine, A. A. Some issues concerning devices and programs for automated learning. In A. A. Lumsdaine and R. Glaser (eds.), *Teaching machines and programmed learning: a source book.* Washington, D.C.: National Education Association, 1960, pp. 517–539. [280]

Lumsdaine, A. A. (ed.) *Student response in programmed instruction.* Washington, D.C.: National Academy of Sciences, National Research Council, 1961. [38, 144, 145, 146, 314]

Lumsdaine, A. A. Experimental research on instructional devices and materials. In R. Glaser (ed.), *Training research and education.* Pittsburgh: Univ. of Pittsburgh Press, 1962a, pp. 247–294. [209]

Lumsdaine, A. A. Some theoretical and practical problems in programmed instruction. In J. E. Coulson (ed.), *Programmed learning and computer-based instruction.* New York: Wiley, 1962b, pp. 134–151. [320]

Lumsdaine, A. A. Instruments and media of instruction. In N. L. Gage (ed.), *Handbook of research on teaching.* Chicago: Rand McNally, 1963, pp. 583–682. [158, 293]

Lumsdaine, A. A. *See also* Angell, D., 1961; Hovland, C. I., 1949; May, M. A., 1958.

Lyle, J. *See* Schramm, W., 1961.

Lysaught, J. P. Programed learning and teaching machines in industrial training. In S. Margulies and L. D. Eigen (eds.), *Applied programed instruction.* New York: Wiley, 1962, pp. 23–43. [308, 309]

McAtee, O. B. The industrial mental hygiene service. *Amer. J. Psychiat.,* 1951, **107,** 623–627. [238]

McBride, J. *See* Meierhenry, W., 1962.

McClusky, F. D. *Audio-visual teaching techniques.* (2nd ed.) Dubuque, Iowa: W. C. Brown, 1949. [139]

McCrary, J. W. *See* Smith, W. M., 1960.

McCulloch, W. S. *See* Lettvin, J. Y., 1959.

McDill, J. A. *See* Stetson, R. H., 1923.

McDonald, F. J. Motivation and the communication processes. *Aud.-vis. Commun. Rev.,* 1961, **9**(5), 57–67. [131]

McGinnis, J. M. Eye-movements and optic nystagmus in early infancy. *Genet. Psychol. Monogr.,* 1930, **8,** 321–430. [459, 460]

Mach, E. *Erkenntnis und Irrtum.* Leipzig: Barth, 1905. [43, 432]

McIntyre, C. J. *See* Kale, S. V., 1955.

MacLean, M. S., Jr. *See* Stanley, R. J., 1955; Toch, H., 1962; Westley, B. H., 1955.

McNamara, W. J. *See* Hughes, J. L., 1961.

McNeil, J. D., and E. R. Keislar. Questions *versus* statements as stimuli to children's learning. *Aud.-vis. Commun. Rev.,* 1962, **10,** 85–88. [313]

McNeil, J. D. *See also* Keislar, E. R., 1961, 1962.

Magni, F., R. Melzack, G. Moruzzi, and C. J. Smith. Direct pyramidal influences on the dorsal-column nuclei. *Arch. Ital. Biol.,* 1959, **97,** 357–377. [423]

Mahl, G. F. Disturbances and silences in the patient's speech in psychotherapy. *J. abnorm. soc. Psychol.,* 1956, **53,** 1–15. [237]

Maier, N. R. F. Reasoning in humans: II. The solution of a problem and its appearance in consciousness. *J. comp. Psychol.,* 1931, **12,** 181–194. [43]

Malter, M. S. Children's ability to read diagrammatic materials. *Elem. Sch. J.,* 1948, **49,** 98–102. [333]

Markle, S. M., and R. M. Bossone. Programed materials: a teaching aid. *Clearing House,* 1963, **38,** 148–151. [293]

Marquis, D. G., and E. R. Hilgard. Conditioned responses to light in monkeys after removal of the occipital lobes. *Brain,* 1937, **60,** 1–12. [357]

Marshall, W. P. *See* Kanner, J. H., 1963.

Martin, G. L., and C. H. R. Over. Therapy by television. *Aud.-vis. Commun. Rev.,* 1956, **4,** 119–130. [163]

Martin, L. B. *See* French, R. S., 1957.

Mason, W. A. The effects of social restriction on the behavior of rhesus monkeys: I. Free social behavior. *J.*

comp. physiol. Psychol., 1960, **53,** 582–589. [465]

Massey, M. See Roe, A., 1960.

Mathews, M. V. The digital computer as a musical instrument. Science, 1963, **142,** 553–557. [450]

Matthews, S., and S. Detwiler. The reactions of Amblystoma embryos following prolonged treatment with chloretone. J. exp. Zool., 1926, **45,** 279–292. [464]

Maturana, H. R. See Lettvin, J. Y., 1959.

Max, L. W. An experimental study of the motor theory of consciousness: III. Action current responses in deafmutes during sleep, sensory stimulation, and dreams. J. comp. Psychol., 1935, **19,** 469–486. [42]

Max, L. W. An experimental study of the motor theory of consciousness: IV. Action current responses in the deaf during awakening, kinesthetic imagery, and abstract thinking. J. comp. Psychol., 1937, **24,** 301–344. [42]

May, M. A., and N. L. Jenkinson. Developing interest in reading with film. Aud.-vis. Commun. Rev., 1953, **1,** 159–166. [139]

May, M. A., and A. A. Lumsdaine. (eds.) Learning from films. New Haven, Conn.: Yale Univ. Press, 1958. [139, 145, 147, 337]

Meierhenry, W. C. (ed.) Learning theory and AV utilization. Aud.-vis. Commun. Rev., 1961, **9**(5). [130, 131]

Meierhenry, W., and J. McBride. Exchange of instructional television materials: report of the Nebraska survey. In L. Asheim et al., Educational television: the next ten years. Stanford, Calif.: The Institute for Communication Research, Stanford Univ., 1962, pp. 266–285. [124, 125]

Melaragno, R. J. Effects of negative reinforcement in an automated teaching setting. Psychol. Rep., 1960, **7,** 381–384. [319]

Melaragno, R. J. See also Coulson, J. E., 1962; Silberman, H. F., 1961.

Melton, A. W. (ed.) Categories of learning. New York: Academic Press, 1964. [219]

Melzack, R. See Magni, F., 1959; Thompson, W. R., 1956.

Mengle, L. I. 3 dimensional TV system. Radio TV News, 1958, **60**(4), 45; 128. [115]

Mergen, M. See Smith, K. U., 1963.

Merrill, I. R. Attitude films and attitude change. Aud.-vis. Commun. Rev., 1962, **10,** 3–13. [139]

Mettler, F. A. See Culler, E., 1934.

Meyer, H. J., and E. F. Borgatta. An experiment in mental patient rehabilitation. New York: Russell Sage Foundation, 1959. [242]

Meyer, S. R. A program in elementary arithmetic: present and future. In E. Galanter (ed.), Automatic teaching: the state of the art. New York: Wiley, 1959, pp. 83–84. [254, 281]

Meyer, S. R. Report on the initial test of a junior high-school vocabulary program. In A. A. Lumsdaine and R. Glaser (eds.), Teaching machines and programmed learning: a source book. Washington, D.C.: National Education Association, 1960, pp. 229–246. [316]

Meyers, J. K., and L. Shaffer. Social stratification and psychiatric practice: a study of an outpatient clinic. Amer. sociol. Rev., 1945, **19,** 307–310. [239]

Michelson, S. See Gustafson, H. W., 1960.

Miller, G. A. *See* Licklider, J. C. R., 1951.

Miller, N. E., *et al.* Graphic communication and the crisis in education. *Aud.-vis. Commun. Rev.*, 1957, **5**(3). [130, 133, 334]

Miller, R. B. Analysis and specification of behavior for training. In R. Glaser (ed.), *Training research and education.* Pittsburgh: Univ. of Pittsburgh Press, 1962, pp. 31–62. [193]

Milton, J. L. *See* Johnson, A. P., 1947.

Mindak, W. *See* Kanner, J. H., 1958b, 1958c.

Mobius, J. B. *See* Westley, B. H., 1960.

Modrick, J. A. *See* Hansen, O. K., 1959.

Moore, J. W. *See* Smith, W., 1962.

Moren, R. I. *See* Rocklyn, E. H., 1962.

Morgan, C. L. *Animal behaviour.* London: E. Arnold, 1900. [23]

Morgan, C. T. The psychophysiology of learning. In S. S. Stevens (ed.), *Handbook of experimental psychology.* New York: Wiley, 1951, pp. 758–788. [357]

Moruzzi, G. *See* Magni, F., 1959.

Mowrer, O. H. "Maturation" vs. "learning" in the development of vestibular and optokinetic nystagmus. *J. genet. Psychol.*, 1936, **48**, 393–404. [464]

Mowrer, O. H. Two-factor learning theory: summary and comment. *Psychol. Rev.*, 1951, **58**, 350–354. [35]

Mowrer, O. H. *Learning theory and the symbolic processes.* New York: Wiley, 1960. [35]

Mowrer, O. H. Learning theory and pedagogical practice. In V. E. Herrick (ed.), *New Horizons for research in handwriting.* Madison: Univ. of Wisconsin Press, 1963, pp. 95–110. [387]

Müller, G. E., and A. Pilzecker. Experimentelle Beiträge zur Lehre vom Gedächtniss. *Z. Psychol.*, 1900, Ergbd. **1**, 1–288. [406, 445]

Münsterberg, H. *Psychology and industrial efficiency.* Boston: Houghton Mifflin, 1913. [183]

Murphy, R. E. Effects of threat of shock, distraction and task design on performance. *J. exp. Psychol.*, 1959, **58**, 134–141. [186]

Murphy, T. J. *See* Smith, K. U., 1963.

Muybridge, E. *Animal locomotion.* Philadelphia: Lippincott, 1887. [67]

Mysziewski, M. *See* Smith, K. U., 1963.

Nagle, B. F. Productivity, employee attitude and supervisor sensitivity. *Personnel Psychol.*, 1954, **7**, 219–233. [227]

Naumann, T. F. A laboratory experience in programed learning for students in educational psychology. *J. progr. Instruction*, 1962, **1**(1), 9–18. [302]

Naylor, J. C., and G. E. Briggs. Effects of task complexity and task organization on the relative efficiency of part and whole training methods. *J. exp. Psychol.*, 1963, **65**, 217–224. [145]

Naylor, J. C. *See also* Briggs, G. E., 1962.

Nelson, H. D., and A. W. VanderMeer. *The relative effectiveness of differing commentaries in an animated film on elementary meteorology.* USN Spec. Dev. Cent. tech. Rep. 269–7–43, 1955. [143]

Nelson, L. M. The financing of educational television. In L. Asheim *et al.*, *Educational television: the next ten years.* Stanford, Calif.: The Institute for Communication Research, Stanford Univ., 1962, pp. 166–190. [158]

Newsom, C. V. Radio and television. *Sci. Mon.*, 1954, **79**, 248–252. [151]

Newton, J. M. *Training effectiveness as*

a function of simulator complexity. USN Train. Dev. Cent. tech. Rep. 458–1, 1959. [183]

Nichols, D. G. *See* Briggs, L. J., 1962.

Nissen, H. W. The nature of the drive as innate determinant of behavioral organization. In M. R. Jones (ed.), *Current theory and research in motivation: a symposium. Vol. 2.* Lincoln: Univ. of Nebraska Press, 1954, pp. 281–321. [42, 214]

Nissen, H. W., K. L. Chow, and J. Semmes. Effects of restricted opportunity for tactual, kinesthetic, and manipulative experience on the behavior of a chimpanzee. *Amer. J. Psychol.,* 1951, **64,** 485–507. [465]

Noiré, L. *The origin and philosophy of language.* (2nd ed.) La Salle, Ill.: Open Court Publishing Company, 1917. [85]

Nolan, J. A. *See* Hosmer, C. L., 1962.

Nunn, G. An English teacher looks at programed learning. *Aud.-vis. Instruction,* 1961, **6,** 141–142. [325]

Okada, N. *See* Herrick, V. E., 1963.

Olshansky, S. Employer receptivity. In M. Greenblatt and B. Simon (eds.), *Rehabilitation of the mentally ill.* Washington, D.C.: AAAS, 1959, pp. 213–221. [242]

Olshansky, S., S. Grob, and M. Eckdahl. Survey of employment experiences of patients discharged from three state mental hospitals during period 1951–1953. *Ment. Hyg.,* 1960, **44,** 510–521. [241]

Osgood, C. E. The nature and measurement of meaning. *Psychol. Bull.,* 1952, **49,** 197–237. [340]

Osgood, C. E., and G. J. Suci. Factor analysis of meaning. *J. exp. Psychol.,* 1955, **50,** 325–338. [340]

O'Sullivan, F. J. *See* Hood, P. D., 1960.

Over, C. H. R. *See* Martin, G. L., 1956.

Paget, R. A. S. *Human speech.* New York: Harcourt, 1930. [85]

Parker, E. B. *See* Schramm, W., 1961.

Parker, J. F., and J. E. Downs. *Selection of training media.* USAF Aeronaut. Sys. Div. tech. Rep. 61–473, 1961. [182, 183, 184, 193, 195]

Parloff, M. B. *See* Rubinstein, E. A., 1959.

Partington, J. R. Evolution of the chemical laboratory. *Endeavour,* 1942, **1,** 145–150. [76]

Pasamanick, B., D. W. Roberts, P. W. Lemkau, and D. B. Krueger. A survey of mental disease in an urban population: prevalence by race and income. In B. Pasamanick (ed.), *Epidemiology of mental disorder.* Washington, D.C.: AAAS, 1959. [239]

Pask, G. Electronic keyboard teaching machines. *Educ. and Commerce,* 1958, **24,** 16–26. [280]

Patrick, D. Retardees in a work adjustment program. *Amer. J. occup. Ther.,* 1960, **14,** 297–300. [236]

Pavlov, I. P. *Conditioned reflexes.* (Trans. and ed. by G. V. Anrep.) London: Oxford Univ. Press, 1927. [27, 28, 410]

Pearl, B. E., J. R. Simon, and K. U. Smith. Visual tracking: IV. Interrelations of target speed and aided-tracking ratio in defining tracking accuracy. *J. appl. Psychol.,* 1955, **39,** 209–214. [175]

Perkins, D. T. *See* Hull, C. L., 1940.

Perrin, D. G. *See* Finn, J. D., 1962.

Peterson, J., and J. K. Peterson. Does practice with inverting lenses make vision normal? *Psychol. Monogr.,* 1938, **50,** No. 5, pp. 12–37. [373, 374, 420]

Peterson, J. C. A new device for teaching, testing, and research in learning.

Trans. Kansas Acad. Sci., 1930, **33**, 41–47. [247]

Peterson, J. C. The value of guidance in reading for information. *Trans. Kansas Acad. Sci.*, 1931, **34**, 291–296. [247]

Peterson, J. K. *See* Peterson, J., 1938.

Peterson, L. V., and W. Schramm. How accurately are different kinds of graphs read? *Aud.-vis. Commun. Rev.*, 1954, **2**, 178–189. [333]

Piaget, J. *Judgment and reasoning in the child.* (Trans. by M. Worden.) New York: Harcourt, 1928. [44, 453, 461, 464, 468]

Piaget, J. *The psychology of intelligence.* (Trans. by M. Piercy and D. E. Berlyne.) London: Routledge and Kegan Paul, 1950. [468]

Piaget, J. The child and modern physics. *Sci. Amer.*, 1957, **196**(3), 46–51. [44, 468]

Pilzecker, A. *See* Müller, G. E., 1900.

Pinneau, S. R. The infantile disorders of hospitalism and anaclitic depression. *Psychol. Bull.*, 1955, **52**, 429–452. [465]

Pitts, W. H. *See* Lettvin, J. Y., 1959.

Plattner, J. W., and L. W. Herron. *Simulation: its use in employee selection and training.* Amer. Mgmt Ass. Bull. 20, 1962. [227]

Poortenaar, J. *The art of the book and its illustration.* London: Harrap, 1935. [65]

Popham, W. J. Tape recorded lectures in the college classroom. *Aud.-vis. Commun. Rev.*, 1961, **9**, 109–118. [141]

Popham, W. J. Tape recorded lectures in the college classroom—II. *Aud.-vis. Commun. Rev.*, 1962, **10**, 94–101. [141]

Porter, D. Teaching machines. *Harv.*

Grad. Sch. Educ. Ass. Bull., 1958, **3**, 1–5. [257, 290]

Porter, D. Some effects of year long teaching machine instruction. In E. Galanter (ed.), *Automatic teaching: the state of the art.* New York: Wiley, 1959, pp. 85–90. [254]

Porter, D. *See also* Holland, J. G., 1961.

Posner, M. I. *An informational approach to thinking.* Dep. Psychol., Univ. of Michigan, tech. Rep. AFOSR–2635, 1962. [449]

Postman, L. Human learning and audiovisual education. *Aud.-vis. Commun. Rev.*, 1961, **9**(5), 68–78. [132, 134]

Powers, R. D. *See* Culbertson, H. M., 1959; Feliciano, G. D., 1963.

Pressey, S. L. A simple apparatus which gives tests and scores—and teaches. *Sch. and Soc.*, 1926, **23**, 373–376. [46, 245, 246]

Pressey, S. L. A machine for automatic teaching of drill material. *Sch. and Soc.*, 1927, **25**, 549–552. [46, 245, 246]

Pressey, S. L. A third and fourth contribution toward the coming "industrial revolution" in education. *Sch. and Soc.*, 1932, **36**, 668–672. [46, 245, 246]

Pressey, S. L. Development and appraisal of devices providing immediate automatic scoring of objective tests and concomitant self-instruction. *J. Psychol.*, 1950, **29**, 417–447. [245, 247, 248, 322]

Pressey, S. L. Certain major psycho-educational issues appearing in the conference on teaching machines. In E. Galanter (ed.), *Automatic teaching: the state of the art.* New York: Wiley, 1959, pp. 187–198. [245, 249, 309]

Pressey, S. L. Some perspectives and major problems regarding teaching machines. In A. A. Lumsdaine and R. Glaser (eds.), *Teaching machines and programmed learning: a source book.* Washington, D.C.: National Education Association, 1960, pp. 497–505. [245, 249, 323, 345]

Pressey, S. L. Teaching machine (and learning theory) crisis. *J. appl. Psychol.*, 1963, **47,** 1–6. [245, 249, 288, 294]

Pronko, N. H. *See* Snyder, F. W., 1952.

Quinn, A. K. How to program (in 10 difficult lessions). *Aud.-vis. Instruction*, 1963, **8,** 80–83. [281, 287]

Radlow, R. *The relation of some measures of ability to measures of learning from sound motion pictures.* USN Spec. Dev. Cent. tech. Rep. 269-7-58, 1955. [143]

Ramharter, H. *See* Feldhusen, J. F., 1962.

Rapin, I. *See* Chase, R. A., 1959, 1961, 1961.

Rarick, G. L. *See* Harris, T. L., 1963.

Ratliff, F. *See* Riggs, L. A., 1953.

Raulet, H. *See* Landy, D., 1959.

Rawnsley, A. I., and J. D. Harris. *Comparative analysis of normal speech and speech with delayed side-tone by means of sound spectrograms.* USN Med. Res. Lab. Rep. 248, 1954. [368]

Redlich, F. C. *See* Hollingshead, A. B., 1958.

Reed, J. E., and J. L. Hayman, Jr. An experiment involving use of English 2600, an automated instruction text. *J. educ. Res.*, 1962, **55,** 476–484. [321, 323]

Reisel, J. *See* Weschler, I. R., 1958.

Resnick, L. B. Programmed instruction and the teaching of complex intellectual skills; problems and prospects. *Harv. educ. Rev.*, 1963, **33,** 439–471. [292]

Révész, G. Experimental study of abstraction in monkeys. *J. comp. Psychol.*, 1925, **5,** 293–343. [411]

Révész, G. *The origins and prehistory of language.* (Trans. by J. Butler.) London: Longmans, 1956. [85]

Revsin, B. *See* Hough, J. B., 1963.

Rhule, W., and K. U. Smith. Effect of visual pretraining in inverted reading on perceptual-motor performance in inverted visual fields. *Percept. mot. Skills*, 1959a, **9,** 327–331. [421]

Rhule, W., and K. U. Smith. Effects of inversion of the visual field on human motions. *J. exp. Psychol.*, 1959b, **57,** 338–343. [361]

Riesen, A. H. Arrested vision. *Sci. Amer.*, 1950, **183**(1), 16–19. [464]

Riggs, L. A., F. Ratliff, J. C. Cornsweet, and T. N. Cornsweet. The disappearance of steadily fixated visual test objects. *J. opt. Soc. Amer.*, 1953, **43,** 495–501. [37, 211]

Rigney, J. W., and E. B. Fry. Current teaching-machine programs and programming techniques. *Aud.-vis. Commun. Rev.*, 1961, **9**(3). [277, 286, 321]

Rigney, J. W. *See also* Bryan, G. L., 1956.

Roback, A. A. *Destiny and motivation in language.* Cambridge, Mass.: Science-Art Publishers, 1954. [85]

Roberts, D. W. *See* Pasamanick, B., 1959.

Robertson, E. G. Photogenic epilepsy: self-precipitated attacks. *Brain*, 1954, **77,** 233. [162]

Rocklyn, E. H., and R. I. Moren. A special machine-taught oral-aural Russian language course: a feasibility study. *Aud.-vis. Commun. Rev.*, 1962, **10,** 132–136. [305]

Rockway, M. R. *See* Hood, P. D., 1960.

Roe, A. A comparison of branching

methods for programmed learning. *J. educ. Res.*, 1962, **55**, 407–416. [312]

Roe, A., M. Massey, G. Weltman, and D. Leeds. *Automated teaching methods using linear programs.* Univ. Calif., L.A., Dep. Engng, Rep. 60–105, 1960. [304]

Roethlisberger, F. J., and W. J. Dickson. *Management and the worker.* Cambridge, Mass.: Harvard Univ. Press, 1939. [226, 309]

Rogers, C. R. A tentative scale for the measurement of process in psychotherapy. In E. A. Rubinstein and M. B. Parloff (eds.), *Research in psychotherapy.* Washington, D.C.: American Psychological Association, 1959. [237]

Rosapelly, M. Apparatus for larynx movements. In P. J. Rousselot, *Principes de phonétique expérimentale. Vol. 1.* Paris: Welter, 1897, p. 98. [399]

Rose, R. The 21-inch classroom. *Reporter*, 1957, **16**(11), 17–20. [154]

Rosenberg, S., and R. L. Hall. The efects of different social feedback conditions upon performance in dyadic teams. *J. abnorm. soc. Psychol.*, 1958, **57**, 271–277. [232]

Rosenstein, A. J., and J. H. Kanner. Television and army training: color vs black and white. II. *Aud.-vis. Commun. Rev.*, 1961, **9**, 44–49. [337]

Ross, R. T. *See* Hull, C. L., 1940.

Roth, R. H. Student reactions to programed learning. *Phi Delta Kappan*, 1963, **44**, 278–281. [303]

Rothkopf, E. Z. Some research problems in the design of materials and devices for automated teaching. In A. A. Lumsdaine and R. Glaser (eds.), *Teaching machines and programmed learning: a source book.* Washington,

D.C.: National Education Association, 1960, pp. 318–328. [279]

Rousselot, P. J. *Principes de phonétique expérimentale. Vol. 1.* Paris: Welter, 1897. [399]

Rubinstein, E. A., and M. B. Parloff. (eds.) *Research in psychotherapy.* Washington, D.C.: American Psychological Association, 1959. [237]

Ruch, T. C. Motor systems. In S. S. Stevens (ed.), *Handbook of experimental psychology.* New York: Wiley, 1951, pp. 154–208. [357]

Rudisill, M. Children's preferences for color versus other qualities in illustrations. *Elem. Sch. J.*, 1952, **52**, 444–451. [330]

Ruger, H. A. The psychology of efficiency: an experimental study of the processes involved in the solution of mechanical puzzles and in the acquisition of skill in their manipulation. *Arch. Psychol., N.Y.*, 1910, **2**, No. 15. [43]

Runyon, R. P., O. L. Desiderato, and J. H. Kanner. Factors leading to effective television instruction. *Aud.-vis. Commun. Rev.*, 1955, **3**, 264–273. [151, 152]

Runyon, R. P., and J. H. Kanner. Present status of signal corps television research. *Aud.-vis. Commun. Rev.*, 1956, **4**, 83–91. [151]

Runyon, R. P. *See also* Desiderato, O. L., 1956; Kanner, J. H., 1954, 1955.

Rust, G. *See* Wendt, P. R., 1962.

Ryan, T. A., and C. B. Schwartz. Speed of perception as a function of mode of representation. *Amer. J. Psychol.*, 1956, **69**, 60–69. [147, 336]

Sainsbury, P. Gestural movement during psychiatric interview. *Psychosom. Med.*, 1955, **17**, 458–469. [237]

Samuel, A. L. Some moral and technical consequences of automation—a refutation. *Science*, 1960, **132**, 741–742. [438]

Sawyer, M. O. *See* Jones, H. L., 1949.

Sayers, B. McA. *See* Cherry, C., 1956.

Schlosberg, H. *See* Woodworth, R. S., 1954.

Schmid, L. Teaching art on television. *Educ. Dig.*, 1963, **29**(4), 30–31. [158]

Schmuller, A. M. *See* Thorpe, L. P., 1954.

Schneider, F. W. An experimental study comparing the effects of the multiple textbook approach and the single textbook approach to elementary school social studies. *Dissertation Abstr.*, 1958, **19**, 97–98. (Abstract) [470]

Schramm, W. What we know about learning from instructional television. In L. Asheim *et al.*, *Educational television: the next ten years*. Stanford, Calif.: The Institute for Communication Research, Stanford Univ., 1962, pp. 52–76. [148, 156, 157]

Schramm, W., J. Lyle, and E. B. Parker. *Television in the lives of our children*. Stanford, Calif.: Stanford Univ. Press, 1961. [161]

Schramm, W. *See also* Peterson, L. V., 1954.

Schuster, D. H. *See* Bryan, G. L., 1959.

Schwartz, B. D. *See* Chard, R. D., 1947.

Schwartz, C. B. *See* Ryan, T. A., 1956.

Scott, W. A. Research definitions of mental health and mental illness. *Psychol. Bull.*, 1958, **55**, 29–45. [239]

Seale, L. M. Purposes of task analysis; methods of obtaining task analysis information; time phasing. In *Uses of task analysis in deriving training and training equipment requirements*. USAF Wright Air Dev. Div. tech. Rep. 60–593, 1960. [192]

Seibert, W. F., and J. M. Honig. A brief study of televised laboratory instruction. *Aud.-vis. Commun. Rev.*, 1960, **8**, 115–123. [150]

Seidman, D. *See* Cline, V. B., 1956.

Selfridge, L. D. *See* Grubb, R. E., 1962.

Semmes, J. *See* Nissen, H. W., 1951.

Senden, M. von. *Raum- und Gestaltauffassung bei operierten Blindgeborenen vor und nach der Operation*. Leipzig: Barth, 1932. [465]

Senders, J. Adaptive teaching machines. In J. E. Coulson (ed.), *Programmed learning and computer-based instruction*. New York: Wiley, 1962, pp. 129–133. [325]

Servos, G. H. *See* Smith, K. U., 1964.

Severin, D. G. Appraisal of special tests and procedures used with self-scoring instructional testing devices. In A. A. Lumsdaine and R. Glaser (eds.), *Teaching machines and programmed learning: a source book*. Washington, D.C.: National Education Association, 1960, pp. 678–680. (Abstract) [249]

Shaffer, L. *See* Meyers, J. K., 1945.

Shannon, C. E. A mathematical theory of communication. *Bell Syst. tech. J.*, 1948, **27**, 379–343; 623–656. [434]

Shay, C. B. Relationship of intelligence to step size on a teaching machine program. *J. educ. Psychol.*, 1961, **52**, 98–103. [311]

Sheehan, J. G. Conflict theory of stuttering. In *Stuttering: a symposium*. New York: Harper & Row, 1958. [402]

Sheffield, F. D. *See* Hovland, C. I., 1949.

Shillestad, I. J. *See* Kopstein, F. F., 1961.

Siegel, S. L. *See* Bobren, H. M., 1960.

Siipola, E. M. Studies in mirror drawing. *Psychol. Monogr.*, 1935, **46**, No. 6, pp. 66–77. [373]

Silberman, H. F. Characteristics of some

recent studies of instructional methods. In J. E. Coulson (ed.), *Programmed learning and computer-based instruction.* New York: Wiley, 1962, pp. 13–24. [300, 305, 310, 314]

Silberman, H. F., R. J. Melaragno, J. E. Coulson, and D. Estavan. Fixed sequence versus branching auto-instructional methods. *J. educ. Psychol.,* 1961, **52,** 166–172. [312]

Silberman, H. F. *See also* Coulson, J. E., 1960, 1961, 1962.

Silverman, R. E., The comparative effectiveness of animated and static transparencies. *Aud.-vis. Commun. Rev.,* 1958, **6,** 238–239. (Abstract) [147]

Silverman, R. E. *See also* Alter, M., 1962.

Simon, J. R. The duration of movement components in a repetitive task as a function of the locus of a perceptual cue. *J. appl. Psychol.,* 1956, **40,** 295–301. [415]

Simon, J. R., and K. U. Smith. Theory and analysis of component errors in aided pursuit tracking in relation to target speed and aided-tracking time constant. *J. appl. Psychol.,* 1956, **40,** 367–370. [175]

Simon, J. R. *See also* Pearl, B. E., 1955.

Skinner, B. F. *The behavior of organisms: an experimental analysis.* New York: Appleton, 1938. [30, 35]

Skinner, B. F. "Superstition" in the pigeon. *J. exp. Psychol.,* 1948, **38,** 168–172. [30]

Skinner, B. F. *Science and human behavior.* New York: Macmillan, 1953. [32, 46, 432]

Skinner, B. F. The science of learning and the art of teaching. *Harv. educ. Rev.,* 1954, **24,** 86–97. [11, 245, 251, 290]

Skinner, B. F. *Verbal behavior.* New York: Appleton, 1957. [212]

Skinner, B. F. Reinforcement today. *Amer. Psychologist,* 1958a, **13,** 94–99. [245, 251]

Skinner, B. F. Teaching machines. *Science,* 1958b, **128,** 969–977. [245, 251, 253, 284]

Skinner, B. F. Teaching machines. *Sci. Amer.,* 1961a, **205**(5), 90–102. [245, 251, 280]

Skinner, B. F. Why we need teaching machines. *Harv. educ. Rev.,* 1961b, **31,** 377–398. [32, 46, 245, 251]

Skinner, B. F., and J. G. Holland. The use of teaching machines in college instruction. In A. A. Lumsdaine and R. Glaser (eds.), *Teaching machines and programmed learning: a source book.* Washington, D.C.: National Education Association, 1960, pp. 159–172. [278, 282, 290, 302]

Skinner, B. F. *See also* Holland, J. G., 1961.

Skornia, H. J. Educational radio: its past and its future. In L. Asheim *et al., Educational television: the next ten years.* Stanford, Calif.: The Institute for Communication Research, Stanford Univ., 1962, pp. 354–375. [111]

Slivinske, A. J. *See* Allen, M. J., 1954.

Smader, R., and K. U. Smith. Dimensional analysis of motion: VI. The component movements of assembly motions. *J. appl. Psychol.,* 1953, **37,** 308–314. [415]

Small, W. S. An experimental study of the mental processes of the rat. *Amer. J. Psychol.,* 1900, **11,** 133–165. [24]

Smedslund, J. The acquisition of conservation of substance and weight in children: III. Extinction of conservation of weight acquired "normally" and by means of empirical controls on a balance; V. Practice in conflict situations without external reinforcement; VI. Practice on continuous v. discontinuous material in problem situations without external reinforcement. *Scand. J. Psychol.*, 1961, **2**, 85–87; 156–160; 203–210. [473]

Smith, C. J. *See* Magni, F., 1959.

Smith, D. E. P. Speculations: characteristics of successful programs and programmers. In E. Galanter (ed.), *Automatic teaching: the state of the art.* New York: Wiley, 1959, pp. 91–102. [283, 286, 287]

Smith, E. E., and S. S. Kight. Effects of feedback on insight and problem solving efficiency in training groups. *J. appl. Psychol.*, 1959, **43**, 209–211. [227]

Smith, K. U. Visual discrimination in the cat: III. The relative effect of paired and unpaired stimuli in the discriminative behavior of the cat. *J. genet. Psychol.*, 1936, **48**, 29–57. [410]

Smith, K. U. Learning and the associative pathways of the human cerebral cortex. *Science*, 1951, **114**, 117–120. [357]

Smith, K. U. Audiovisumatic teaching: a new dimension in education and research. *Aud.-vis. Commun. Rev.*, 1960, **8**, 85–103. [263]

Smith, K. U. The geometry of human motion and its neural foundations: II. Neurogeometric theory and its experimental basis. *Amer. J. phys. Med.*, 1961, **40**, 109–129. [356, 377]

Smith, K. U. *Delayed sensory feedback and behavior.* Philadelphia: Saunders, 1962. [17, 180, 206, 367, 370, 371, 372, 389]

Smith, K. U. Sensory feedback analysis in medical research: I. Delayed sensory feedback in behavior and neural function. *Amer. J. phys. Med.*, 1963, **42**, 228–262. [361, 362]

Smith, K. U., S. D. Ansell, J. Koehler, and G. H. Servos. Digital computer system for dynamic analysis of speech and sound feedback mechanisms. *J. Ass. Computg Machinery*, 1964, **11**, 240–251. [363, 400]

Smith, K. U., and R. Bloom. The electronic handwriting analyzer and motion study of writing. *J. appl. Psychol.*, 1956, **40**, 302–306. [176]

Smith, K. U., and M. Bridgman. The neural mechanisms of movement vision and optic nystagmus. *J. exp. Psychol.*, 1943, **33**, 165–187. [355]

Smith, K. U., R. Cambria, and J. Steffan. Sensory-feedback analysis of reading. *J. appl. Psychol.*, 1964, **48**, 275–286. [396, 397]

Smith, K. U., and P. Greene. A critical period in maturation of performance with space-displaced vision. *Percept. mot. Skills*, 1963, **17**, 627–639. [390, 464]

Smith, K. U., and T. J. Murphy. Sensory feedback mechanisms of handwriting motions and their neurogeometric bases. In V. E. Herrick (ed.), *New horizons for research in handwriting.* Madison: Univ. of Wisconsin Press, 1963, pp. 111–153. [388]

Smith, K. U., M. Mysziewski, M. Mergen, and J. Koehler. Computer systems control of delayed auditory feedback. *Percept. mot. Skills*, 1963, **17**, 343–354. [363]

Smith, K. U., and W. M. Smith. *The behavior of man: introduction to psychology.* New York: Holt, Rinehart and Winston, 1958. [44, 334, 336, 337, 338, 342, 343, 344]

Smith, K. U., and W. M. Smith. *Perception and motion: an analysis of space-structured behavior.* Philadelphia: Saunders, 1962. [16, 175, 362, 374, 376, 379, 391, 392, 394, 400, 421, 425, 461, 462, 463]

Smith, K. U., W. M. Smith, and J. Hansche. *Workbook for the behavior of man.* New York: Holt, Rinehart and Winston, 1958. [334]

Smith, K. U., L. Wargo, R. Jones, and W. M. Smith. Delayed and space-displaced sensory feedback and learning. *Percept. mot. Skills,* 1963, **16,** 781–796. [378]

Smith, K. U., and R. Wehrkamp. A universal motion analyzer applied to psychomotor performance. *Science,* 1951, **113,** 242–244. [176]

Smith, K. U. *See also* Gould, J., 1962; Hecker, D., 1956; Lincoln, R. S., 1952; Pearl, B. E., 1955; Rhule, W., 1959a, 1959b; Simon, J. R., 1956; Smader, R., 1953; Smith, W. M., 1956, 1960; Von Trebra, P., 1952; Warkentin, J., 1937; Wehrkamp, R., 1952; Wing, K. G., 1942.

Smith, N. H. The teaching of elementary statistics by the conventional classroom method versus the method of programmed instruction. *J. educ. Res.,* 1962, **55,** 417–420. [301, 308]

Smith, P. C. *See* Lawrence, L. C., 1955.

Smith, W., and J. W. Moore. Size-of-step and achievement in programmed spelling. *Psychol. Rep.,* 1962, **10,** 287–294. [311]

Smith, W. M., J. W. McCrary, and K. U. Smith. Delayed visual feedback and behavior. *Science,* 1960, **132,** 1013–1014. [368]

Smith, W. M., K. U. Smith, R. Stanley, and W. Harley. Analysis of performance in televised visual fields: preliminary report. *Percept. mot. Skills,* 1956, **6,** 195–198. [393]

Smith, W. M. *See also* Smith, K. U., 1958, 1958, 1962, 1963.

Smythe, D. W. Reality as presented by television. *Publ. Opin. Quart.,* 1954, **18,** 143–156. [162]

Snyder, C. W. *See* Snyder, F. W., 1957.

Snyder, F. W., and N. H. Pronko. *Vision with spatial inversion.* Wichita, Kan.: Univ. of Wichita Press, 1952. [373]

Snyder, F. W., and C. W. Snyder. Vision with spatial inversion: a follow-up study. *Psychol. Rec.,* 1957, **17,** 20–31. [374, 420]

Snyder, W. U. Some investigations of relationships in psychotherapy. In E. A. Rubinstein and M. B. Parloff (eds.), *Research in psychotherapy.* Washington, D.C.: American Psychological Association, 1959. [237]

Snygg, D. The tortuous path of learning theory. *Aud.-vis. Instruction,* 1962, **7,** 8–12. [320, 432]

Solomon, P. *Sensory deprivation.* Cambridge, Mass.: Harvard Univ. Press, 1961. [465]

Spaulding, S. Research on pictorial illustration. *Aud.-vis. Commun. Rev.,* 1955, **3,** 33–45. [330, 333]

Spaulding, S. Communication potential of pictorial illustrations. *Aud.-vis. Commun. Rev.,* 1956, **4,** 31–46. [332]

Spelt, D. K. The conditioning of the human fetus *in utero. J. exp. Psychol.,* 1948, **38,** 338–346. [460]

Spence, K. W. The nature of discrimination learning in animals. *Psychol. Rev.,* 1936, **43,** 427–449. [410]

Spence, K. W. The differential response in animals to stimuli varying within a single dimension. *Psychol. Rev.,* 1937, **44,** 430–444. [411]

Spence, K. W. Theoretical interpretations of learning. In S. S. Stevens (ed.), *Handbook of experimental psychology.* New York: Wiley, 1951, pp. 690–729. [34]

Spencer, B., and F. J. Gillen. *Across Australia.* London: Macmillan, 1912, 2 vols. [58, 61, 70]

Sperling, G. The information available in brief visual presentations. *Psychol. Monogr.,* 1960, **74,** No. 11. [446]

Spitz, R. A. Hospitalism: an inquiry into the genesis of psychiatric conditions in early childhood. *Psychoanal. Stud. Child,* **1,** 53–74. New York: International Universities Press, 1945. [465]

Spitz, R. A. Hospitalism: a follow-up report. *Psychoanal. Stud. Child,* **2,** 113–117. New York: International Universities Press, 1946. [465]

Spitz, R. A. The psychogenic diseases in infancy: an attempt at their etiologic classification. *Psychonal. Stud. Child,* **6,** 255–275. New York: International Universities Press, 1951. [465]

Spitz, R. A., and K. M. Wolf. Anaclitic depression: an inquiry into the genesis of psychiatric conditions in early childhood, II. *Psychoanal. Stud. Child,* **2,** 313–342. New York: International Universities Press, 1946. [465]

Spitz, R. A., and K. M. Wolf. Autoerotism: some empirical findings and hypotheses on three of its manifestations in the first year of life. *Psychoanal. Stud. Child,* **3/4,** 85–120. New York: International Universities Press, 1949. [465]

Spitzer, M. E. *See* Cook, J. O., 1960.

Standfast, S. *See* Chase, R. A., 1959, 1961.

Stanford University Institute for Communication Research. *New teaching aids for the American classroom.* Stanford, Calif.: Institute for Communication Research, Stanford Univ., 1960. [436]

Stanley, R. J., M. S. MacLean, Jr., R. F. Carter, and V. F. Dittberner. *Content preferences in television.* Univ. of Wis. Telev. Lab. res. Bull. 4, 1955. [162]

Stanley, R. J. *See also* Smith, W. M., 1956.

Stave, A. M. *Human factors in design of automatic programming and recording for trainers (AN/ASG–15–TI fire control system trainer).* USAF Wright Air Dev. Div. tech. Rep. 60–558, 1960. [182]

Steffan, J. *See* Smith, K. U., 1964.

Stenius, A. C. Auditory and visual education. *Rev. educ. Res.,* 1945, **15,** 243–255. [139]

Stephens, A. L. Certain special factors involved in the law of effect. In A. A. Lumsdaine and R. Glaser (eds.), *Teaching machines and programmed learning: a source book.* Washington, D.C.: National Education Association, 1960, pp. 89–93. [248, 288, 317]

Stetson, R. H. *Motor phonetics: a study of speech movements in action.* Amsterdam: North Holland Publishing Company, 1951. [83, 171, 399, 400]

Stetson, R. H., and H. D. Bouman. The action current as measure of muscle contraction. *Science,* 1933, **77,** 219–221. [171, 174]

Stetson, R. H., and J. A. McDill. Mechanism of the different types of movement. *Psychol. Monogr.,* 1923, **32,** No. 3, 18–40. [171, 202]

Stolurow, L. M. *Teaching with machines.* Urbana, Ill.: Psychology Dep., Univ. of Illinois, 1961. (Mimeo.) [300, 324]

Stolurow, L. M. Programed instruction

for the mentally retarded. *Rev. educ. Res.*, 1963, **33**, 126–136. [306, 323, 325]

Stratton, G. M. Some preliminary experiments in vision without inversion of the retinal image. *Psychol. Rev.*, 1896, **3**, 611–617. [16, 361, 373]

Stratton, G. M. Vision without inversion of the retinal image. *Psychol. Rev.*, 1897, **4**, 341–360; 463–481. [16, 361, 373]

Stratton, G. M. The spatial harmony of touch and sight. *Mind*, 1899, **8**, 492–505. [16, 361]

Suchman, R. J. Inquiry training: building skills for autonomous discovery. *Merrill-Palmer Quart.*, 1961, **7**, 147–170. [46]

Suci, G. J. See Osgood, C. E., 1955.

Sutton, S. See Chase, R. A., 1959, 1961, 1961.

Tannenbaum, R., V. Kallegian, and I. R. Weschler. *Training managers for leadership.* Inst. Ind. Relat., UCLA, Reprint 35, 1954. [226]

Taylor, F. W. *The principles of scientific management.* New York: Harper & Row, 1911. [171]

Teaching by television. New York: Ford Foundation and Fund for the Advancement of Education, 1959. [118, 120, 124]

Teaching by television (2nd ed.) New York: Ford Foundation and Fund for the Advancement of Education, 1961. [148, 151, 154, 155, 156]

Thompson, W. R., and R. Melzack. Early environment: *Sci. Amer.*, 1956, **194**(1), 38–42. [465]

Thorndike, E. L. Animal intelligence: an experimental study of the associative processes in animals. *Psychol. Monogr.*, 1898, **2**, No. 8. [23, 34]

Thorndike, E. L. *Educational psychology.* New York: Teachers Coll., Co-

lumbia Univ., 1913–1914, 3 vols. [23, 34, 408]

Thorndike, E. L. Mental discipline in high school studies. *J. educ. Psychol.*, 1924, **15**, 1–22; 83–98. [407]

Thorndike, E. L. The law of effect. *Amer. J. Psychol.*, 1927, **39**, 212–222. [432]

Thorndike, E. L. *The fundamentals of learning.* New York: Teachers Coll., Columbia Univ., 1932. [23, 35]

Thorndike, E. L., and R. S. Woodworth. The influence of improvement in one mental function upon the efficiency of other functions. *Psychol. Rev.*, 1901, **8**, 247–261; 384–395; 553–564. [408]

Thorndike, R. L. *The human factor in accidents, with special reference to aircraft accidents.* USAF Sch. Aviat. Med. Proj. 21–30–001, Rep. 1, 1951. [183]

Thorpe, L. P., and A. M. Schmuller. *Contemporary theories of learning.* New York: Ronald, 1954. [45]

Titchener, E. B. *Lectures on the experimental psychology of the thought-processes.* New York: Macmillan, 1909. [432]

Toch, H., and M. S. MacLean, Jr. Perception, communication and educational research: a transactional view. *Aud.-vis. Commun. Rev.*, 1962, **10**(5), 55–77. [165]

Tolman, E. C. *Purposive behavior in animals and men.* New York: Appleton, 1932. [25, 37, 432]

Towe, A. L. See Jabbur, S. J., 1960.

Troyer, M. E. See Angell, G. W., 1948.

Twombly, R. W. See Edgerton, A. K., 1962.

Underwood, B. J. The effect of successive interpolations on retroactive and proactive inhibition. *Psychol. Monogr.*, 1945, **59**, No. 3. [409]

Uttal, W. R. *On conversational interaction.* IBM Corp. Thomas J. Watson Res. Cent. res. Rep. RC–532, 1961. [268]

Uttal, W. R. *My teacher has three arms!!!* IBM Corp. Thomas J. Watson Res. Cent. res. Paper RC–788, 1962. [269, 271, 308]

Van Atta, L. Behavior in small steps. *Contemp. Psychol.*, 1961, **6**, 378–381. [302]

van Bergeijk, W. A., and E. E. David, Jr. Delayed handwriting. *Percept. mot. Skills*, 1959, **9**, 347–357. [368, 369, 370, 389]

VanderMeer, A. W. Color vs. black and white in instructional films. *Aud.-vis. Commun. Rev.*, 1954, **2**, 121–134. [140, 147]

VanderMeer, A. W. *See also* Nelson, H. D., 1955.

Van Ormer, E. B. *See* Hoban, C. F., Jr., 1950.

Vasilas, J. N., R. Fitzpatrick, P. H. Dubois, and R. P. Youtz. *Human factors in near accidents.* USAF Sch. Aviat. Med. Proj. 21–1207–0001, Rep. 1, 1953. [183]

Vernon, M. D. Perception and understanding of instructional television programmes. *Brit. J. Psychol.*, 1953a, **44**, 116–126. [140]

Vernon, M. D. Presenting information in diagrams. *Aud.-vis. Commun. Rev.*, 1953b, **1**, 147–158. [330, 333]

Vernon, M. D. The value of pictorial illustrations. *Brit. J. educ. Psychol.*, 1953c, **23**, 180–187. [330]

Vernon, M. D. The instruction of children by pictorial illustration. *Brit. J. educ. Psychol.*, 1954, **24**, 171–179. [330]

Vernon, P. E. An experiment on the value of the film and film-strip in the instruction of adults. *Brit. J. Psychol.*, 1946, **16**, 149–162. [470]

Vinacke, W. E. The investigation of concept formation. *Psychol. Bull.*, 1951, **48**, 1–31. [44, 453, 464]

Volkmann, A. W. Über den Einfluss der Übung auf das Erkennen raumlicher Distanzen. *Sächs. Akad. Wiss. Ber. Leipzig*, 1858, **10**, 38–69. [407]

Von Trebra, P. J. Learning and transfer effects in human manual motion in relation to direction of movement. Unpublished master's thesis, Univ. of Wisconsin, 1951. [415, 416]

Von Trebra, P., and K. U. Smith. The dimensional analysis of motion: IV. Transfer effects and direction of movement. *J. appl. Psychol.*, 1952, **36**, 348–353. [416]

Walk, R. D. *See* Gibson, E. J., 1960.

Walker, E. S. *See* Besnard, G. G., 1955.

Warden, C. J. The relative economy of various modes of attack in the mastery of a stylus maze. *J. exp. Psychol.*, 1924, **7**, 243–275. [24]

Wargo, L. *See* Smith, K. U., 1963.

Warkentin, J., and K. U. Smith. The development of visual acuity in the cat. *J. genet. Psychol.*, 1937, **50**, 371–399. [460]

Watson, J. B. *Psychology from the standpoint of a behaviorist.* (2nd ed.) Philadelphia: Lippincott, 1924. [29, 432, 441]

Watson, J. B. *See also* Lashley, K. S., 1922.

Webb, L. W. Transfer of training and retroaction. *Psychol. Monogr.*, 1917, **24**, No. 3. [408]

Wehrkamp, R., and K. U. Smith. Dimensional analysis of motion: II. Travel-distance effects. *J. appl. Psychol.*, 1952, **36**, 201–206. [175]

Wehrkamp, R. *See also* Smith, K. U., 1951.

Weider, A. A mental hygiene program in industry—a clinical psychological contribution. *J. clin. Psychol.*, 1947, **3**, 309–320. [238]

Weisman, R. G. *See* Krumboltz, J. D., 1962a, 1962b.

Weiss, W. *See* Hovland, C. I., 1951–1952.

Welsh, G. S., and W. G. Dahlstrom. (eds.) *Basic readings on the MMPI in psychology and medicine.* Minneapolis: Univ. of Minnesota Press, 1956. [237]

Weltman, G. *See* Roe, A., 1960.

Wendt, P. R., and G. K. Butts. Audiovisual materials. *Rev. educ. Res.*, 1962, **32**, 141–155. [139, 140, 148, 330]

Wendt, P. R., and G. Rust. Pictorial and performance frames in branching programmed instruction. *J. educ. Res.*, 1962, **55**, 430–432. [308]

Wenger, M. A. An investigation of conditioned responses in human infants. *Univ. Iowa Stud. Child Welfare*, 1936, **12**, No. 1, 7–90. [460]

Wertheimer, M. *Productive thinking.* New York: Harper & Row, 1945. [43]

Weschler, I. R., and J. Reisel. *Inside a sensitivity training group.* Los Angeles: Institute of Industrial Relations, UCLA, 1958. [226]

Weschler, I. R. *See also* Tannenbaum, R., 1954.

Westley, B. H., and L. C. Barrow, Jr. *Exploring the news: a comparative study of the teaching effectiveness of radio and television.* Univ. of Wis. Telev. Lab. res. Bull. 12, 1959. [143]

Westley, B. H., and M. MacLean, Jr. A conceptual model for communications research. *Aud.-vis. Commun. Rev.*, 1955, **3**, 3–12. [435]

Westley, B. H., and J. B. Mobius. *The effects of "eye-contact" in televised instruction.* Univ. of Wis. Telev. Lab. res. Bull. 14, 1960. [162]

White, R. K. *See* Lewin, K., 1939; Lippitt, R., 1952.

Wickens, C. *See* Wickens, D. D., 1940.

Wickens, D. D., and C. Wickens. A study of conditioning in the neonate. *J. exp. Psychol.*, 1940, **26**, 94–102. [460]

Wiener, N. *Cybernetics.* New York: Wiley, 1948. [202, 433, 438]

Wiener, N. Some moral and technical consequences of automation. *Science*, 1960, **131**, 1355–1358. [438]

Wiesel, T. N. *See* Hubel, D. H., 1962.

Wilcoxon, H. C., and E. Davy. *Fidelity of stimulation in operational flight trainers: I. Effectiveness of rough air simulation.* USN Spec. Dev. Cent. tech. Rep. 999–2–3a, 1954. [183]

Wilson, C. L. On-the-job and operational criteria. In R. Glaser (ed.), *Training research and education.* Pittsburgh: Univ. of Pittsburgh Press, 1962, pp. 347–377. [183]

Wing, K. G., and K. U. Smith. The role of the optic cortex in the dog in the determination of the functional properties of conditioned reactions to light. *J. exp. Psychol.*, 1942, **31**, 478–496. [357, 410]

Wittrock, M. C. Response mode in the programing of kinetic molecular theory concepts. *J. educ. Psychol.*, 1963, **54**, 89–93. [315]

Witty, P. Surveys of TV—1949–62. *Sch. and Soc.*, 1963, **91**, 334–336. [161]

Wohlwill, J. F. The teaching machine: psychology's new hobbyhorse. *Teachers Coll. Rec.*, 1962, **64**, 139–150. [320]

Wolf, K. M. *See* Spitz, R. A., 1946, 1949.

Wolf, W. *Die Welt der Ägypter*. Stuttgart: Kilpper, 1954. [64, 90, 102]

Wolfe, H. E. A survey of vocational rehabilitation at Longview State Hospital for 1959. *Ment. Hyg.*, 1961, 45, 167–170. [241]

Wolfe, J. B. The effect of delayed reward upon learning in the white rat. *J. comp. Psychol.*, 1934, 17, 1–21. [212]

Wolfle, D. Training. In S. S. Stevens (ed.), *Handbook of experimental psychology*. New York: Wiley, 1951, pp. 1267–1286. [209]

Woodrow, H. The effect of type of training upon transference. *J. educ. Psychol.*, 1927, 18, 159–172. [408]

Woodworth, R. S. Reinforcement of perception. *Amer. J. Psychol.*, 1947, 60, 119–124. [35]

Woodworth, R. S., and H. Schlosberg. *Experimental psychology*. (Rev. ed.) New York: Holt, Rinehart and Winston, 1954. [40, 41]

Woodworth, R. S. *See also* Thorndike, E. L., 1901.

Wooster, M. Certain factors in the development of a new spatial co-ordination. *Psychol. Monogr.*, 1923, 32, No. 4. [373]

Wylie, H. H. An experimental study of transfer of response in the white rat. *Behav. Monogr.*, 1919, 3, No. 16. [409]

Yates, A. J. Recent empirical and theoretical approaches to the experimental manipulation of speech in normal subjects and in stammerers. *Behav. Res. Ther.*, 1963, 1, 95–119. [402]

Yates, P. W. Training of labour for skilled work. *Manager*, 1959, 27, 177–180. [223]

Yerkes, R. M. *The dancing mouse*. New York: Macmillan, 1907. [25]

Youtz, R. P. *See* Vasilas, J. N., 1953.

Yum, K. S. An experimental test of the law of assimilation. *J. exp. Psychol.*, 1931, 14, 68–82. [409]

Zajonc, R. B. The effects of feedback and probability of group success on individual and group performance. *Hum. Relat.*, 1962, 15, 149–161. [232]

Zimmerman, R. R. *See* Harlow, H. F., 1959.

Zorbaugh, H. A perspective of televised instruction—panel discussion. In J. C. Adams, C. R. Carpenter, and D. R. Smith (eds.), *College teaching by television*. Washington, D.C.: American Council on Education, 1958, pp. 23–27. [149]

General Index